Music of Three More Seasons
1977–1980

MUSIC OF THREE MORE SEASONS 1977–1980

Andrew Porter

Alfred A. Knopf   NEW YORK   1981

Library of Congress Cataloging in Publication Data

Porter, Andrew, [date]
Music of three more seasons, 1977–1980.
Collected from the author's Musical events column
in The New Yorker.
Includes index.
1. Music—Addresses, essays, lectures.   2. Music—New York
(N.Y.)   I. New Yorker (New York: 1925)   II. Title.
ML60.P894   780′.9747′1   81-47504
ISBN 0-394-51813-6   AACR2

Contents

PART I

1977–1978

A Composer for Our Time

Sir Michael Tippett's fourth opera, *The Ice Break*, an important and beautiful piece, had its first performances, at Covent Garden, in July. It is brief—the three acts last about twenty-two, twenty-five, and twenty-eight minutes—but substantial: a drama in which large events pass in review, and a score so rich in emotional and intellectual resonances that the attentive listener needs the breathing space of the intermissions. Each of Tippett's operas has its starting point in a sudden vision or inspiration—an "idea" for a music-drama around which there then gather related images, musical, dramatic, and literary, from which the work is built. Each of the operas makes the impression of being a "necessary" composition, one that demanded to be written. There was no question of casting around for a suitable new subject: these subjects forced themselves upon the composer, and drove him to find words and music for their expression.

Tippett's first opera, *The Midsummer Marriage* (1955), is the lyrical, exuberant, elaborated setting down of an actual vision: in the composer's words, "I *saw* a stage picture . . . of a wooded hilltop with a temple, where a warm and soft young man was being rebuffed by a cold and hard young woman . . . to such a degree that the collective, magical archetypes take charge." *King Priam* (1962) grew from contemplation of Homer's great scene in which Priam visits Achilles in his tent. In *The Knot Garden* (1970), seven characters tread an emotional maze, and a series of encounters leads to self-discovery and self-understanding; the last act of *Figaro*, Virginia Woolf's *Between the Acts*, and, most evidently, the encounters on Prospero's enchanted isle underlie the action. Allusiveness is an essential part of Tippett's technique. It is both literary (Aristotle, Stefan George, and Yeats jostle in a key passage, the "messenger's speech," of *King Priam;* Shakespeare, Jung, and Paul Valéry join a parallel passage of *The Ice Break*) and musical (Beethoven's Ninth Symphony is prominently quoted in Tippett's Third; a Schubert song has an important part in *The Knot Garden*). Other great minds play upon his. He brings things together. He has written of "the feeling a creative artist has when he knows he has become the instrument of some collective experience—or, as Wagner puts it, that a Myth

3

is coming once more to life," and of his belief that "somewhere or other, in books, in pictures, in dreams, in real situations, everything is sooner or later to be found which *belongs* for all details of the work."

The Ice Break, which Tippett began to compose in 1973, had its start in reflection on two different kinds of violence—the imprisonment of free thought in Russia and the brutality of race riots. Two musical images began to sound in his mind, and he describes them in the preface to the libretto:

> In the music there are two archetypal sounds; one related to the frightening but exhilarating sound of the ice breaking on the great northern rivers in the spring; the other related to the exciting or terrifying sound of the slogan-shouting crowds, which can lift you on their shoulders in triumph or stamp you to death.

A scene took shape: an American airport at which there are arriving, by the same flight, as-it-were Solzhenitsyn (in the opera Lev, whose name means "lion") and as-it-were Muhammad Ali (in the opera Olympion, "a black champion"). The plot is schematic and shapely. There are three couples: Lev and his wife, Nadia ("hope"), who emigrated to America twenty years earlier, with their infant son, when Lev went to a prison camp; Yuri, that son, who has grown up sullen, rebellious, and difficult, and his shallow, high-spirited white girlfriend, Gayle, "around for kicks"; Olympion, who mouths simple slogans like "I'm beautiful: I'm black . . . I am the greatest," and his girlfriend, Hannah ("grace"), a black nurse, the heroine of the piece, in whose kindly hands, generous soul, and instinctive compassion for all kinds of suffering the composer discerns a limited chance for healing some of the world's divisions. The divisions shown in the opera are threefold: between political systems, between generations, and between races of different colors. A seventh character, Luke ("the beloved physician"), a young doctor, remains shadowy both as a person and as a symbol; perhaps he represents the technical means man has for making whole what has not been smashed beyond repair.

There are three crowd scenes, contrasted in tone, unified in their condemnation of mindless, stereotyped mass emotion: in Act I a chorus of welcome for Olympion, during which Gayle throws herself at him ("I make amends. . . . Come kiss me now, black beauty") and is contemptuously spurned; in Act II a white-against-black confrontation in which Olympion and Gayle are killed and Yuri is gravely injured; in Act III a group "trip," which is Tippett's ironical presentation of any attempt to answer life's difficult questions by recourse to drugs. But these crowd scenes can shift in the course of a measure to intimate dialogues between the principals, in intimate surroundings, and then shift back again. One moment, the listener is in the thick of mob activity; the next, within walls and within the minds of those reflecting on the world outside. Tippett asks much of his interpreters; at Covent Garden, by Sam Wanamaker's direction, Ralph Koltai's décor, Walter Raines's choreography, and David Hersey's lighting he was faithfully and imaginatively served. It was one of the most brilliant presentations of a difficult new opera I have seen. The stage images were found to match the swift contrasts and sudden simultaneities of the music.

At the start of Act III, Nadia is dying. At her bedside, Lev is reading the last chapter of *Wilhelm Meisters Wanderjahre*—the passage about a youth hurtling toward destruction. He asks bitterly, "Why did I leave that other country? What have I come here for? To watch my wife's death and my son's hatred?" Hannah seeks to console him, and reflects, "Struggle is always, Is here, Ev'rywhere in this vast world of ghettos." Nadia dies, recalling her Russian childhood and the excitement of the spring ice break; but hope does not die with her. At the end, the plaster encasing Yuri's shattered limbs is broken, and he steps out "reborn." There is an echo of the Prodigal Son in a simple, musically eloquent exchange of "Father!" "Son!" The three survivors—Hannah, Yuri, Lev, one from each couple—are reconciled. Lev, who is naturally given to quotation (in the prison camp, "poetry upheld me"), repeats, as the final lines of the opera, Wilhelm Meister's joyful exclamation over that other threatened youth, whom he snatched from death, and in whom he recognized his lost son: "Yet you will always be brought forth again, glorious image of God, and likewise be maimed, wounded afresh, from within or without." It is not quite the confident affirmation toward the close of Tippett's early oratorio *A Child of Our Time* (1944): "Here is no final grieving, but an abiding hope. The moving waters renew the earth. It is spring." His thought and his music have grown darker, but there remains at least "the momentary vision of a possibility." "Deep within me," he said a few years ago, "I know that part of the artist's job is to renew our sense of the comely and the beautiful. To create a dream." That was in a television talk (later reprinted), "Poets in a Barren Age." He also said:

> I have been writing music for forty years. During those years there have been huge and world-shattering events in which I have inevitably been caught up. Whether society has felt music valuable or needful I have gone on writing because I must. And I know that my true function within a society that embraces all of us is to continue an age-old tradition . . . to create images from the depths of the imagination and to give them form. . . . Images of the past, shapes of the future. Images of vigor for a decadent period, images of calm for one too violent. Images of reconciliation for worlds torn by division. And, in an age of mediocrity and shattered dreams, images of abounding, generous, exuberant beauty.

The Midsummer Marriage was done in London in August—at a concert performance, during the Proms. (It was the Welsh National Opera production, which has been played to enthusiastic audiences up and down Britain, and it came to the Proms in a joyfully secure, youthfully accomplished performance.) That opera holds Tippett's richest store of abundant, generous, exuberant imagery. The vocal lines leap and sing, the rhythms dance, and the orchestra is filled with fresh colors. The music seems at once new-minted—pouring forth in a shining stream of spontaneous invention—and inevitable, as if it had existed, waiting to be sounded, since the earth saw its first spring, nature's renewing round first began, and a boy and girl first fell in love. It is a masterly score. Tippett is not only a poet and visionary but a craftsman. Like a romantic boy, he has retained that power whose loss Wordsworth lamented—of being able to relate experiences so that nothing felt, seen, read, heard, or dreamed need remain absolute. As a mature man, he learned how to harness this power—to command his lines, harmonies, timbres, and forms. There were years of hard wrestling with his medium before he attained to eloquence. Sosostris, the visionary soothsayer in *The Midsummer Marriage*, like Wagner's Erda, rises from rich dark dreams to the day and—in music of memorable power and beauty—voices a creator's agony and passion ("O bitterness, O bitterness of a Pythia's fate") before proceeding to the clear relation of a vision ("Truth shall shine through me. . . . I speak as a seer"). Her successors—each of Tippett's operas has a "messenger"—are less confident. In the penultimate scene of *King Priam*, Hermes comes forward with the warning "Do not imagine that all the secrets of life can be known from a story. O but feel the pity and the terror as Priam dies." Mangus, who, Prospero-like, manipulates much of the action in *The Knot Garden*, is driven at last to the rueful admission that "Prospero's a fake." And Astron, the "psychedelic messenger" of *The Ice Break*, pronounces just two sayings, of obscure significance: "Dear friends, Take care for the Earth. God will take care of himself" (from a Jung letter), and "Spring comes to you at the farthest, In the very end of harvest" (a couplet from the masque in *The Tempest*, agriculturally unsound, pointful only when we recall that *The Tempest* was played for the winter betrothal of Princess Elizabeth, James I's daughter, and the Prince Palatine). Hailed by the euphoric, drugged crowd as "Our Saviour Hero," Astron chirpily replies, "Saviour?! Hero?! Me!! You must be joking."

It is a joy to revisit the fresh, enchanted world of *The Midsummer Marriage*, where hope is more than a gleam of what might be, where dreams come true. (The stage action shifts between reality and dream; none of the three British productions of the piece has done visual justice to its visions.) It is painful in *The Ice Break* to listen to the confident hymn (to a Methodist tune that the Ku Klux Klan adopted):

> *A band of pure Caucasians,*
> *the noblest of the klan,*
> *we stand in rank together,*
> *white woman with white;*

to hear Blue Mountain fiddling, square dance, and clarinet jazz breaks perverted into symbols of race hatred; to watch three of the young people, Gayle and Yuri and then Olympion, don tribal hoods and merge with mobs.

Hannah stays apart: in a long aria, the lyrical center of the opera, she searches within herself to find some sense amid the violence ("I scrabble for unformed letters That might make a word"). Elsewhere in the city, Lev is doing the same, while searching, too, down long corridors of past human suffering that poets have limned. Not for these two—and not for Tippett—the simple shouted slogans or the escapist answers of an Astron. It is inspiring in *The Ice Break* to hear the musical images of calm, reconciliation, and beauty that, in spite of everything, the composer has been able to find. The "ice break" noise itself—fiercely grinding sonorities on lower winds and strings—is violent and terrible but not evil; it holds the promise of spring. The lyrical passages, where the score thins down and lines from a solo instrument may accompany individual reflections, are deeply affecting: they tell of a quest for stillness, for understanding, and for an order not that of crude regimentation. The music is not expansive, except in Hannah's aria. There are few repetitions. The melodies, timbres, and harmonies act directly on a responsive listener. The terse, sure, intricate form of the opera makes it seem in retrospect not so much a series of dramatic actions as a single, complicated vision, piercing and poignant.

The Ice Break is dedicated to Colin Davis, who conducted a performance both carefully prepared and passionate. Heather Harper and John Shirley-Quirk, as Nadia and Lev, and Josephine Barstow and Tom McDonnell, as Gayle and Yuri, were admirable—the older couple marvelously "real," convincing and individual in each inflection and gesture, the younger vivid in their (deliberately) more stereotyped roles. Beverly Vaughn, a young mezzo from Columbus, Ohio, made a much acclaimed Covent Garden début as Hannah; she was warm, smooth, and lovable in her tones and in her enactment of the character. The Olympion of Clyde Walker was the only disappointment; he lacked both the physical presence and the sonic panache for the role. The vocal types required could be suggested by an imaginary City Opera cast, drawn from artists who sang there last season: Johanna Meier and Donald Gramm, Gianna Rolandi and David Holloway, Joy Blackett and Benjamin Matthews. (Olympion's role, designated for tenor, is compassable by a high baritone.) Astron's unearthly voice is projected, through loudspeakers, by a combination of mezzo and countertenor, singing mainly in unison but with some touches of heterophony; his presence is indicated by a glittering cluster of laser beams.

Internationally, Tippett's operas have circulated mainly on records. (There are Philips albums of *The Midsummer Marriage* and *The Knot Garden*.) *The Midsummer Marriage* and *King Priam* have had a single German production each; *The Knot Garden* was done by the Northwestern University Opera Theatre in 1974. In America his music is beginning to be played more often. Solti and the Chicago Symphony give the first performances of the Fourth Symphony in October, and bring it to Carnegie Hall a month later [see page 27]. The Minnesota Opera plans to produce *The Knot Garden* in February. Across the country, fourteen performances of *A Child of Our Time* are billed for this season. When *The Ice Break* does reach America, the excursions into American slang are likely to sound off-key and awkward ("What's bugging you man? Cool and jivey once; Now, touchy and tight"). But Tippett's English is frequently off-key and awkward, too. As a poet, he allows himself a verbal recklessness and promiscuity of allusion at odds with the precision of his notes. For example, over Gayle's body Luke exclaims, "Gayle, bonny Gayle, gone out with the wind." The echoes of Ernest Dowson, Margaret Mitchell, and the Skye Boat Song are inappropriate. Tippett's texts have been often attacked, sometimes defended. After *The Ice Break*, the *New Statesman*'s critic wrote of "the familiar drone of the composer's high-flown libretto trying so hard to get down to earth that it crash-lands in flat and flagrant cliché"; but the *Spectator*'s found the libretto "faultless." Tippett himself describes his libretto writing as "an assemblage of metaphors." Over the years, at repeated hearings of his operas, I have come to accept his often infelicitous diction as an apparently inevitable part of his utterance. Although one may flinch at verbal details, the big dramatic metaphors work. And the awkwardness is a small price to pay for music so communicative, so honest, and so stirring.

September 19, 1977

The Ice Break *came to Boston in May 1979; see page* 383.

Festival Fare

There were only two operas at the Edinburgh Festival this year, but both were important productions: the world première of Thea Musgrave's *Mary, Queen of Scots*, done by Scottish Opera (the American première is due in March, from the Virginia Opera [see page 164]), and a *Carmen* in which Teresa Berganza sang the title role for the first time and which Claudio Abbado, also for the first time, conducted. *Carmen* is best heard in a small house, and the King's Theatre in Edinburgh (seating 1,326) is even smaller than the Opéra-Comique, for which *Carmen* was composed. But small houses can seldom afford the kind of casting that Edinburgh has: Berganza, Mirella Freni, Placido Domingo, Abbado, and the London Symphony Orchestra. It was a true festival production, assembled for the occasion. The better seats cost twenty pounds (about thirty-five dollars). Piero Faggioni, whose work on the Covent Garden *Fanciulla del West* was acclaimed earlier this year, directed. Ezio Frigerio, whose décors for the Scala's *Simon Boccanegra* and the Paris

Opera's *Figaro* were acclaimed in Washington last year, designed. It was the most beautiful *Carmen* I have ever seen, and the most beautifully played I have ever heard. Performances on this particular level of fine, detailed achievement are not encountered in New York. For one thing, the repertory system here is likely to make them impossible (every member of the Scottish Opera Chorus and of the urchin choir, recruited from a local school, seemed to have been individually rehearsed); for another, both Lincoln Center houses are too large for tiny, subtle strokes to tell. In most of the Met or of the State Theater, Miss Berganza's Carmen would have been lost.

For that matter, it was only just big enough for the King's Theatre. Miss Berganza's singing of the role—as could be predicted from her Cherubino, Rosina, and Cenerentola—was exquisitely supple, seductive, and intelligent, but her voice lacked the power to give full dramatic value to such fortissimo outbursts as "Jamais Carmen ne cédera! Libre elle est née et libre elle mourra!," in the final scene. Her timbre is not passionate; it is not surprising that for many years she turned down all invitations to essay the role. In an open letter to the festival director, reprinted in the program book, she explained her ideas about Carmen: "My greatest desire at this point is to be able to banish forever from the mind and imagination of the public the distorted idea of Carmen." The English translation of the letter, facing its Spanish original, introduces some distortions of its own. She did not write that hitherto Carmen has "always" been misrepresented, or that "today one could regard Carmen as an ideal"; she did declare that "in modern terms one could say that Carmen represents an ideal type of emancipated woman, i.e., free, the sovereign and mistress of all her decisions." Even that statement, unqualified, seems to me to be going rather too far: I'd not hold Carmen up as an exemplar for any daughter of mine. Mérimée's Carmen steals, lies, harlots, and incites men to murder, and, although Meilhac and Halévy toned down her wickedness, their libretto—as Winton Dean once remarked, and as Miss Berganza evidently agrees—"furnishes an actress of the right temperament with all the materials for creating a character as close to Mérimée's Carmen as is possible on the operatic stage." It is easy to overplay the part—to be too flamboyant, vulgarly sexy. But today there is perhaps a tendency to underplay it; and modern Carmens are sometimes praised for showing "dignity" even at their first entrance, and not swinging their hips. This is how Mérimée's Don José describes Carmen's entry into his life:

> She was wearing a very short red skirt. . . . She had thrown her mantilla back, to show her shoulders, and a great bunch of acacia that was thrust into her chemise. She had another acacia blossom in the corner of her mouth, and she walked along, swaying her hips, like a filly from the Cordova stud farm. In my country [Navarre] anyone who had seen a woman dressed in that fashion would have crossed himself. At Seville every man paid her some bold compliment on her appearance. She had an answer for each and all, with her hand on her hip, as bold as the thorough gypsy she was.

But in Miss Berganza's opinion Carmen is a hard-working, estimable lass led astray, it would seem, through no fault of her own: "She works in a factory to earn her bread and to save up enough money to visit her mother. Later, pursued by judicial authority, she becomes obliged to dedicate herself to smuggling." That hardly squares with Mérimée's or Bizet's account of her. Miss Berganza is right when she describes Carmen's courageous acceptance of death, predicted in the card scene, imminent in the final duet; she is wrong, I think, to say that in most performances of the card scene the Carmen is "agitated, nervous, and extrovert." Bizet's marking of the passage is "simplement et très également," and most Carmens I have heard have sung it accordingly—as Miss Berganza did. Her ideas about the role, the nature of her voice, and perhaps her slightness of physique conspired to create a Carmen on a small scale, but on that scale she was captivating, vivid, and various. She was also a wittier Carmen than most, mistress of mocking inflections that were sometimes alight with mischief and sometimes flicked out like a lash.

Carmen inevitably dominates *Carmen*, but ostensibly the opera, like the book, is the tragedy of Don José, a man brought to ruin by the wiles of an unscrupulous, irresistible woman. Underlining this, Faggioni opened each act with a gratuitous tableau of José in prison, in a pool of ochre light, awaiting execution: the preludes and entr'actes served as accompaniment; the acts themselves became flashbacks—a narrative recounted, as in Mérimée's tale. It sounds an awful idea, the sort of old-fashioned bright notion that a director should get out of his system as a student, but the execution of it was so skillful that it proved surprisingly effective. The ochre light flooded back, and the rest of the stage dimmed, during major recurrences of the "destiny" motif; this was less acceptable. Otherwise, the staging was marvelously musical and sensitive, imaginative without being tiresomely overinventive, sure in its long dramatic line, packed with fine but unfussy detail. Domingo, although not in his best voice the night I attended (he has spent a summer of heavy singing), was an expert and accomplished José. As Micaëla, Mirella Freni was billed for three of the seven performances, Leona Mitchell for the others. I heard the latter—a warm, true lyric soprano, appealing in timbre but perhaps a shade soft in grain for the music. Tom Krause as Escamillo was weak casting. Jean Lainé, from Bordeaux, was a capital Zuniga.

Abbado was the hero of the evening. Anything missed on the stage—passion, dramatic intensity of timbre, or rhythmic verve from the Toreador—was supplied in abundance from the pit. The King's pit is shallow and open—as shallow and open as the pits of most nineteenth-century opera houses were. Abbado made a virtue of it. One heard every detail of Bizet's amazing score, in which, as Dean wrote, "the sharp outline and virility of Berlioz" and "the grace and economy of Mozart" combine—heard it, was stirred by it, yet never felt, as happened when Karajan conducted the opera at Salzburg, that the limelight was being pulled away from the stage drama, where it belongs, onto the conductor and his virtuoso band. The singers were never drowned; the instrumental lines and colors—strings that seemed to surge through the listener's blood, woodwind playing of bewitching eloquence—supported and inspired them. During the run, Deutsche Grammophon began to make a new recording of the opera, which will also star Berganza and Domingo, Abbado and the London Symphony, but will have a different Micaëla and Escamillo—Ileana Cotrubas and Sherrill Milnes. (It will be finished in London later; Miss Berganza, more dedicated than many of her colleagues, prefers not to spend her days making records while engaged on a series of theatre performances.) No doubt the fire, finesse, and tenderness of Abbado's phrasing and the sound of the superlative orchestra will be caught on the discs; but that will only begin to suggest the full excitement of hearing them, in dramatic context, in the King's Theatre.

Ever since the Edinburgh Festival began, in 1947, there has been talk of building a modern opera house to replace the King's, whose stage and backstage are cramped, and which seemed to burst at the seams, acoustically, when at previous festivals works like *Tristan* and *Die Walküre* were played there. But in recent years grumbles about the place have yielded to appreciation of its merits. It is an attractive building, richly decorated. Andrew Carnegie laid the foundation stone in 1906. The Edinburgh Corporation bought it, from private management, in 1969. A few years ago, at the cost of many seats, the pit was expanded and the lighting modernized. And now the city has set aside its plans for a new opera house. All this is in line with developments elsewhere in Britain: the abandonment of grandiose highway schemes that destroy city blocks, and the condemnation of very tall office and apartment buildings—in general, the concern to conserve and, if necessary, adapt what stands and can still be useful. In London, the English National Opera, which once wanted to build a new house on the South Bank, goes from triumph to triumph in the Coliseum, a noble 1904 theatre where Ellen Terry and Sarah Bernhardt appeared. In Glasgow, the Scottish National Orchestra restored an abandoned nineteenth-century city hall and now has a concert room of unrivaled acoustical excellence, and Scottish Opera, which also had plans for a modern theatre, moved instead into the Theatre Royal, an 1895 building that had been largely gutted to serve as a television studio but is now a very successful opera house, seating 1,560. (The orchestras of St. Louis, Pittsburgh, Oakland, and Vancouver have shown similar enterprise; in New York it surely will not be many years before Lincoln Center regrets not having acquired the Harkness Theatre—which went for a mere million, earlier this year—to be a home for Mozart, Handel, Haydn, and intimate plays.) In Edinburgh, the re-equipped King's proved to be an ideal home for *Carmen*. Frigerio could not, of course, design four spectacular settings; there would not have been room for them. He provided a single construction of great beauty, a plaza enclosed by weather-stained white buildings, picturesque and finely proportioned. By small additions and skillful changes of light, this was able to suggest the tavern, the "site pittoresque et sauvage," and the square outside the bullring of the subsequent acts. Goya drawings seemed to be the designer's inspiration. The first impression was of décor in grisaille, delicately tinted with blue for Micaëla's dress, red for Carmen's, and yellow for the military uniforms. Gradually, the eye perceived the richness and variety within the subdued colors. Scottish Opera plans to take over this scenery; it will then possess one of the most distinguished *Carmen* productions ever seen, and one that is practicable in the fairly small theatres, throughout Britain, where it plays.

Abbado's text was based, not uncritically, on Fritz Oeser's edition; some of the newly published music, but not all of it, was included. The dialogue was spoken but had been cut to the bone; several exchanges essential to a full presentation of the characters were omitted.

September 26, 1977

The Deutsche Grammophon recording of Carmen *appeared on DG 2709083.*

Promenade

The eighty-third season of Henry Wood Promenade Concerts—the Proms—ran, in London, from late July to mid-September. There were fifty-five concerts, most of them given in the Royal Albert Hall, some in Westminster Cathedral, in the Church of St. Augustine, Kilburn, and in the Round House, in Chalk Farm. It is easy for Londoners to take the Proms for granted—as an admirable and jolly institution, a hardy annual, a set of informal concerts marked by lighthearted shouting and banter from the audience before the programs proper begin. A visitor to London soon discovers that they also make up what is probably the richest music festival in the world. If all the more important concerts of a full season in Avery Fisher and Carnegie Halls were brought together along with the Philharmonic's Prospective Encounters and the enterprising choral programs in Alice Tully Hall, something like a Prom repertory would result. This year, twenty-four orchestras and sixteen choirs took part. The conductors ranged from Sir Adrian Boult, aged eighty-eight, to Simon Rattle, aged twenty-two, and included Claudio Abbado, Pierre Boulez, Bernard Haitink, and Riccardo Muti. The Proms are presented by the BBC. All the concerts are broadcast nationally, on the night, and most of them internationally; on Sundays, when there is no live concert, television steps in with filmed repeats of selected works. Last year, according to the BBC, there were, over the season, some three hundred thousand Prom attendances and about a hundred million radio listeners. Attendances were up this year. So were the ticket prices, but not by much. The best seats cost three pounds (about five dollars)—raised to three-fifty on nights when Colin Davis or Haitink conducted. Seventy pence bought admission to the arena and sixty pence to the gallery, the places of "promenade," though most nights when I attended there was not much room to stroll in the arena; the young enthusiasts stood packed shoulder to shoulder.

This has been a vintage Prom year. Some idea of it, and of the general musical richness of a London summer, may be suggested by an account, with digressions to cognate events, of some of what I heard on ten consecutive days—from Saturday, August 6, to Monday, August 15. The BBC regularly commissions new pieces for the Proms, and on August 6 John Buller's *Proença*, one of this year's three commissions, had its first performance. *Proença* is a work for mezzo-soprano, electric guitar, and large orchestra, lasting some thirty-five minutes; the BBC Symphony was conducted by Mark Elder and the singer was Sarah Walker—both leading young artists of the English National Opera. (She was the heroine of, and he conducted, *Toussaint*, a new grand opera by David Blake, which I hope to write about next week.) Buller, born in 1927, is a name re-emergent in British music. He made his mark with some youthful works but then, dissatisfied with his achievement, renounced composition—until recently, when he discovered that there was music within him demanding to be set down. *Proença* is at once a celebration of the brilliant, animated Provençal culture of the twelfth and thirteenth centuries, which was destroyed by the Albigensian Crusade, and, more generally, a musician's reflection on spectacles of violence and power moving against what is youthful, beautiful, and independent. On the cover of the study score (which is published by G. Schirmer and was already on sale at the concert) there is a picture of the ruins atop Mont Ségur, where in 1244 many men and women were massacred; however, the setting of the piece is not only medieval Provence but also Lincoln Park, Chicago, at the time of the 1968 Democratic Convention, as described in Norman Mailer's *Miami and the Siege of Chicago*. Buller's text is an anthology of beautiful, sharp-imaged Languedoc poetry, starting with joyful springtime song and gradually darkening toward the lament of Guiraud Riquièr, the "last troubadour": "I should refrain from singing, For songs must spring from joy. . . . I was born too late." In a program note, the composer remarked that " 'song' is, in a way, what this piece is 'about'—verbal, instrumental, and vocal; the joy it can represent; and the violence it can meet." In his music, three real troubadour songs are used as a source of melodic and rhythmic motifs. The electric guitar, a voice of youth, also "sings," crying out a melody for Arnaud Danièl's "Song that no song shall surpass/for freeing the heart of sorrow." Buller's style is eclectic—he seems to have learned from Boulez and from Berio—but the result is personal. Although his subject matter here is enough in itself to provoke responses literary, historical, political, and, indeed—to anyone who knows Provence—visual even before a note has been played, *Proença* is not one of those works whose program note proves more communicative than the music itself. After hearing it, the abundance and intensity of musical feeling, the sure control of colors and forms, and the vividness of sonic imagery that has sprung from passion and been shaped by technical mastery are what one remembers. *Proença* is a work both picturesque and affecting.

Sunday brought the start of another London festival: South Bank Summer Music and Seminar, three weeks of concerts, master classes, and other events, forty of them in all, held afternoon and evening in the Royal Festival Hall, the Queen Elizabeth Hall, and the Purcell Room—that riverside cluster of modern concert halls which together with the National Film Theatre, the three auditoriums of the National Theatre, and the Hayward Gallery makes up "London's Lincoln Center." Salvatore Accardo, Lynn Harrell, Christoph Eschenbach, and the Cleveland Quartet were the "artists in residence," and the Academy of St. Martin-in-the-Fields, conducted by Neville Marriner, was the resident orchestra. Much Beethoven—including all the quartets and a good deal of other chamber music—was billed, in this year that marks the hundred-and-fiftieth anniversary of his death. Alfred Brendel filled the Elizabeth Hall for two four-hour master classes on the piano concertos. The three-hundredth anniversary of Matthew Locke's death was observed, too. (Around this time, the BBC put out a fine pair of Locke programs that could be matter for a separate article.) Most of the orchestral programs combined Handel and Beethoven with British music (Michael Tippett, Alexander Goehr, Nicholas Maw), and at the opening concert Janet Baker gave the London première of *Phaedra*, the cantata that Benjamin Britten wrote for her in 1975. *Phaedra*, inspired by Handel's dramatic cantatas, accompanied by strings, harpsichord, and percussion, consists of a prologue, presto, and adagio divided by recitatives. The text is taken from Robert Lowell's translation of *Phèdre*; the Racinian weight and grandeur lost in the English couplets are restored by Britten's music. Dame Janet may declaim the big speech to Hippolytus with less forceful emphasis than Sarah Bernhardt brought to it (on a famous record), but she is scarcely less moving. The musical style unites the large, direct lyrical gestures of Britten's early Michelangelo settings and the rhythmic refinements of his later works. *Phaedra* is clear, powerful, and grand. A fortnight later, at the opening concert of the Edinburgh Festival, Dame Janet gave an even more impassioned account of it. In July, at "Chichester 902," she ended a noble recital—her voice filling the great cathedral with glorious sound—with the first performance of three new Walter de la Mare settings, small, subtle, and masterly, composed for her by Lennox Berkeley. (In 1075, William the Conqueror gave command for the building of Chichester Cathedral; nine centuries later, the event was commemorated in a series of festival events, "Chichester 900," which proved so popular that it seemed a pity to wait a hundred years for a repeat; hence the progressive title of this attractive annual festival in a beautiful town an easy day excursion from London.) At a later Prom, Kerstin Meyer was the soloist at the London deuxième of *Phaedra*.

On Monday, Glyndebourne visited the Proms with its new production of

Don Giovanni. Presented on a bare raised platform, costumed only in evening dress, it proved scarcely less dramatic than it had in the Sussex theatre. Haitink conducted a skillful, well-matched cast who brought meaning to each turn of the music. Thomas Allen was a brave, confidently seductive Giovanni, Horiana Branisteanu a mettled Anna, Rachel Yakar a vivid Elvira, Richard Van Allan a resourceful Leporello, Adrienne Csengery a rich-toned yet supple Zerlina, Philip Langridge a beautifully weighted Ottavio, and John Rawnsley a substantial Masetto. With the Statue's tremendous "Si!" in the cemetery and in the inexorable summons of the last scene, Pierre Thau set the spine pricking as he had at Glyndebourne. Peter Hall's production, worthy successor to his famous *Figaro* of 1973, gave the piece the immediacy of a brand-new play, and was securely based on recognition that the details of that play are written by Mozart as well as by Da Ponte. Haitink's reading combined freedom with great strength; the timbres of the London Philharmonic were eloquent. Back in John Bury's strong, somber, Goyesque décor, the show then went on to the National Theatre and to the five towns of the Glyndebourne tour.

Glyndebourne's other new productions this year were of Poulenc's *La Voix humaine,* directed and sung by Graziella Sciutti and done as a curtain raiser to a revival of Janáček's *The Cunning Little Vixen,* conducted by Mr. Rattle, and of Richard Strauss's *Die schweigsame Frau,* directed by John Cox. Mr. Cox did not repeat the success of his *Intermezzo, Ariadne,* and *Capriccio* for the company; the fault, however, lay not with him but with Strauss and with the libretto, an overelaborated version of *Don Pasquale.* The music prattles on skillfully and agreeably—and then suddenly catches one up in episodes of ravishing lyricism. Peter Gottlieb was brilliant as the Barber, the Figaro/Malatesta figure. Three Americans—Janet Perry, from the Cologne Opera, in the title part; Jerome Pruett, from the Vienna Volksoper, as Henry; and Richard Cross, from the Frankfurt Opera, in the central part of Sir Morosus—were fairly good in roles that need the utmost charm and accomplishment of voice and manner. Michael Annals's detailed, busy décor was pretty, and Andrew Davis's conducting first-rate. The piece was done in German, not English, but otherwise a good case was made for Strauss's weakest—if still not negligible—comedy. Meanwhile, Covent Garden revived his previous opera, *Arabella,* and Kiri Te Kanawa sang the title role for the first time, with great poise and beauty of tone. The Munich Festival opened with a new production of his *Daphne,* a generally underrated work. It is short on stage actions. Attending only with my ears, by way of a BBC relay, I found movement and drama enough in the score itself, and admired the free, fresh Apollo of Peter Lindroos, the rock-steady Gaea of Ortrun Wenkel, and, from Lilian Sukis, a Daphne with many gentle, supple phrases. Wolfgang Sawallisch conducted. Glyndebourne's other revivals were of *Falstaff,* a horrid production by Jean-Pierre Ponnelle (I skipped it this year), and of *The Rake's Progress,* a trim, fresh, production by Mr. Cox, with décor by David Hockney. *The Rake* had an ideal new Anne, Felicity Lott, and a new

Nick Shadow, Samuel Ramey, who sounded good but left the character—well, shadowy. Superb choral singing; great conducting by Haitink.

At the Prom *Don Giovanni,* an advertisement in the program book told the audience it was missing the first night of the English National Opera season, which began with the first of three *Ring* cycles. As author of the translation used, I must declare an interest in the ENO *Ring,* but I hope this need not debar me from declaring, too, that Reginald Goodall's conducting of the cycle reached new heights of lyricism and grandeur. The work that he began eight years ago, coaching and inspiring British artists and players new to *The Ring,* has come to full flower. On Tuesday, I was at *The Valkyrie,* but a Sunday TV repeat enabled me to catch up with the heart of the Tuesday Prom: Brendel's wonderfully precise and poetic account of Beethoven's Fourth Piano Concerto with the BBC Symphony under Sir ‚Charles Groves, and Peter Maxwell Davies's *St. Thomas Wake: Foxtrot for Orchestra* (1969). This presents transformations, by techniques both medieval and modern, of John Bull's *St. Thomas Wake* pavan into foxtrots-plus-commentary for a small jazz band and a fairly large orchestra. Some of the more outré percussion devices employed derived from the composer's wartime memories of playing foxtrot records on his windup phonograph in an air-raid shelter, while bombs fell outside and houses collapsed. The piece is high-spirited and serious at once; escapism is both enjoyed and judged.

Maxwell Davies (born 1934), Goehr (born 1932), and Harrison Birtwistle (born 1934), students together in Manchester, came forward in the fifties as a "Manchester Group." They have since pursued separate paths—which converged on the Albert Hall in August. The Wednesday Prom began with Goehr's *Pastorals* (1965), played by the Royal Philharmonic under Groves. Like all Goehr's work, it is lucid. Like all his best work, it holds a listener intent on an arresting musical discourse—shapely statement and logical though often unexpected response. Behind the piece lies *Oedipus at Colonus* and Goehr's incidental music for that play: against a "pastoral" background, evoked in a recurrent three-part chord, the actions are often violent, the climaxes fierce.

On Thursday, I was at *Siegfried* while at the Prom Haitink conducted the London Philharmonic in Beethoven, Brahms, and Dvořák. (There were *some* conventional programs.) At the Friday Prom, Richard Rodney Bennett's *Actaeon,* for horn and orchestra, had its first performance. Composed for Barry Tuckwell, it fully explores his technical and expressive virtuosity but, like so much of Bennett's recent work, seems merely fluent and deft, slipping agreeably through the ear and leaving little trace on the mind. Across the way from the Albert Hall, in the Royal College of Art, there is set up at Prom time a well-stocked shop selling scores, books about music, the musical magazines, and records. Here, too, an hour before concerts, composers talk informally about works of theirs to be played. Bennett said that *Actaeon* was planned as the first in a *Metamorphoses* series. With Ovid open beside him, he should easily be able to provide a few dozen companion pieces in similar vein.

At the Saturday Prom, Birtwistle's *Melencolia I* was played by the Scottish National Orchestra under Sir Alexander Gibson. (They gave the first performance, in Glasgow, last year.) The title, spelled thus, is that of a Dürer engraving; like Birtwistle's *The Triumph of Time* (titled after Brueghel), it is a work that moves very slowly but rewards a listener's patience. A clarinet, partnered by a harp, sits center stage; two string orchestras provide the background. Detail by detail, with many near-static episodes of reflection, a confrontation is prepared. It may sound tedious in description; it proves enthralling, tremendous, in performance. In London, I heard two other new works by Birtwistle, both of them "written in rehearsals" by the composer and his performers at once. *Bow Down,* done at the National Theatre in a music-theatre triple bill, along with pieces by Satie and Mauricio Kagel, was worked out jointly by Birtwistle, the poet Tony Harrison, the director Walter Donohue, and a group of actors and musicians, sitting in a circle. The text is many different versions of the ballad "The Two Sisters" (No. 10 in Child's collection), chanted, declaimed, murmured, or mimed in many different ways. For some fifty minutes, the same cruel tale is told over and over again, but ever with changes of dialect, accent, pace, actors, rhythms, and mode; again, something that may sound tedious in description proved enthralling. *Frames/Pulse & Interruptions,* done in the Round House by the Ballet Rambert, was worked out jointly with the choreographer Jaap Flier, the designer Nadine Baylis, nine instrumentalists, and the dancers. I did find this tedious, but was told that after I'd seen and heard it eight times or so, what seemed like mere repetition or confusion would be revealed as purposive order. I felt that life was short, and too rich in other things, and did not persevere.

On otherwise Prom-less Sunday, there was, on television, Purcell's *Hail, bright Cecilia,* repeated from one of the opening Proms devoted to British music. Else the music-hungry could go to the South Bank to hear Brendel, or stay at home, as I did, to embark on the first installment of the BBC's latest Roberto Gerhard cycle and then catch the third installment of another series, presenting all of Messiaen's piano music. On Monday, the last of the central ten days under review, there were two Proms, one after the other. In St. Augustine's, a noble High Victorian church by J. L. Pearson, the BBC Northern Singers' program included Thea Musgrave's *Rorate coeli,* a large setting for unaccompanied chorus of two William Dunbar poems, and one of the richest and most imaginative things she has done. Later, in the Round House, a rotunda built by Robert Stephenson in 1847 as an engine house for locomotives but now a picturesque, informal theatre and concert hall, there was a "three Bs" concert. Bach, Beethoven, and Brahms were all well represented at the Proms. So were Bruckner, Britten, and Boulez (by *Cummings ist der Dichter* and *Rituel*). But the Round House fare was Sándor Balassa's Quartet for Percussion, Jean Barraqué's *Chant après chant,* and Bartók's Sonata for two pianos and percussion, with two young Hungarian prize-winners, Dezsö Ránki and Zoltán Kocsis, who had played a solo concerto each in preceding days, as the pianists.

At an earlier Monday double, I heard in St. Augustine's the Monteverdi

Vespers sung by the Taverner Choir, accompanied by an orchestra of baroque instruments (in August there was also a week-long festival of early
music, on authentic instruments, in the Wigmore Hall), and then in the
Round House the London première of Maxwell Davies's new opera, *The
Martyrdom of St. Magnus*. The changes of venue, ambience, and acoustics are
an attractive feature of the Proms. Twice they moved to Westminster Cathedral, whose numinous Byzantine vastness was set gently sounding by the
Monteverdi Choir, in a program that brought together the serene Requiems
of André Campra and of Fauré, and was a week later antiphonally explored
by the Schütz Choir. When music is heard in a setting both acoustically and
spiritually suited to it, the listeners' enjoyment and understanding grow. The
Albert Hall, scene of so many stirring rallies, was the right place for Hans
Werner Henze's "popular and militant oratorio" *The Raft of the Medusa*, a
huge concert-hall drama laid out in space, which had its London première at
this year's Proms. The intended world première, in Hamburg in 1968, did not
take place, because a West Berlin choir refused to sing under the Red Flag
and a banner of Che Guevara (to whose memory the piece is dedicated);
there was a student scuffle, and steel-helmeted police troopers marched in to
make arrests. At the London performance, all was outwardly peaceful. David
Atherton conducted the BBC Singers and BBC Symphony with mastery,
Phyllis Bryn-Julson sang Death's alluring cantilenas in full, true tones, and
the bust of Sir Henry Wood which presides over the platform was not replaced by one of Che. The Albert Hall was also the right place for Luciano
Berio's *Coro*, a spacious, hour-long, complicated setting of folk texts shot
through with fragments of Neruda. The Cologne Radio forces for whom it
was composed—forty individual singers, forty-four solo players—visited the
Proms to give the first performance of *Coro* in a longer version than that of its
Donaueschingen première, last year. Berio conducted. *Coro* is a puzzling,
complicated work. Berio's vision is huge. He ranges through love songs, nature songs, charms, choral dances from all over the world. Without direct
musical quotation, except of one Yugoslav melody, he brings folk techniques—the hocketing of African wood-trumpet bands, for example—to bear
on his own kinds of musical material. Each singer sits beside a player. Solos
and dialogues emerge. The center of interest shifts about the platform. Language yields to language, style to style, as we roam the world. But lightness,
gaiety, and love yield ever to the bitter Neruda refrain "Come and see the
blood in the streets," massively stated, at first in fragments and at last in full:
"You will ask me why this poem/doesn't speak of dreams, of leaves,/of the
great volcanoes of my native land?/Come and see the blood in the streets."
The necessity of music's social involvement was a recurrent theme of the
Proms. Buller, Maxwell Davies, and Henze treated it; at the penultimate
Prom there was Beethoven's Ninth Symphony; the season ended with Parry's
setting of Blake's "Jerusalem." Of course, there were also dreams and diver-
sions, songs of faith (Messiaen's *Colors of the Celestial City*) and celebrations
of love (his *Turangalîla* Symphony), much romantic self-expression, and

much absolute, or abstract, music. And in *Coro* all these kinds of music were brought together. I felt unsure whether it was a gallimaufry or a masterpiece.

October 17, 1977

Janet Baker has recorded Britten's Phaedra *on London 26527. The score of Musgrave's* Rorate coeli *appears in the W. W. Norton anthology* Choral Music (*ed. Ray Robinson*), *and the piece is recorded by the BBC Northern Singers on Abbey (a British label) LP8 798. Berio's* Coro *is recorded by the Cologne forces on Deutsche Grammophon 2531270.*

The Right Subjects

"A good rule," Gustav Holst once declared, "is—never compose anything unless the not composing of it becomes a positive nuisance to you." That proclaims the concept of the personally "necessary" composition. Yet many operas—and some very good ones—have been composed not to satisfy any inner need but simply to fulfill a commission. At the worst, such operas may be constructed to tried formulas, with subjects chosen and librettos assembled along the lines of subjects and structures that worked well before. They can be capable, "well made" (which is always preferable to badly made), but are apt to seem unnecessary except as fodder to keep performing companies busy. On the other hand, against the principle of the "necessary" work can be set the large number of excellent pieces—and a handful of masterpieces—brought into being by a specific commission and tailored to, even determined by, its requirements. Last month, I wrote about Tippett's operas, personally "necessary" works if any are, and the way their subjects had seemed to find, and force themselves upon, the composer. Since then, I have seen three good operas, all composed to commissions, whose composers sought—and found—existing subjects that would release the kinds of music they had in mind. All three are "well made." All three seem to have fulfilled both a commission and an inner need. One is based on a play, one on a short story, and one on a biography.

The oldest of the three is Marc Blitzstein's *Regina*, which opened on Broadway, after a Boston tryout, in 1949, was taken into the City Opera repertory in 1953 (it last played there in 1959), and has just been revived in Detroit as the first production of the Michigan Opera Theatre's season. The

Koussevitzky Music Foundation had commissioned an opera from Blitzstein; in a note for a Santa Fe production of *Regina*, in 1959, he recalled how he set about choosing a subject:

> I remember certain things I was looking for. I know I wanted to do a strong piece, rather than a predominantly lyrical one. It was to have a big role for a woman. . . . It was to stress some primary human passion, and some aspect of comedy. At the time I was not much caught by the love-jealousy or love-religiosity axes, so often used in libretto-land; nor by the comic possibilities of mistaken identity or the wrong bedroom. I hit upon human greed. . . . And I wanted a sharp climax which might even resolve in a violent death. Then I recalled Lillian Hellman's *The Little Foxes*, a play I admired enormously; and I realized my plan and story had already been done for me.

Kurt Weill's Broadway opera *Street Scene* had appeared in 1947, and his *Love Life* the year after. Reviewing the latter, John Gassner contrasted it on the one hand with *Where's Charley?*—a mere romp with some colorful dances—and on the other with *The Little Foxes*, whose old-fashioned naturalism, he said, although well suited to raise questions of individual responsibility and guilt ("the Henry James perspective"), was an inadequate medium for the exhibition and discussion of contemporary social problems. Social problems had been the stuff of Blitzstein's earlier operas *The Cradle Will Rock* (1936) and *No for an Answer* (1941). They lie beneath *The Little Foxes* and surface when Addie, the black cook, says: "Well, there are people who eat the earth and eat all the people on it like in the Bible with the locusts. Then there are people who stand around and watch them eat it. Sometimes I think it ain't right to stand and watch them do it." And when Ben Hubbard, one of the locusts, says to his sister Regina: "The century's turning, the world is open. Open for people like you and me. Ready for us, waiting for us. . . . There are hundreds of Hubbards sitting in rooms like this throughout the country . . . and they will own this country some day." Alexandra, Regina's daughter, recalls both speeches in the closing confrontation of the play, when she announces her resolve to fight for what is right, not just be one of those who stand around and watch. Miss Hellman is by her own avowal "a moral writer, often too moral a writer," and Blitzstein was a moral composer. In his reworking of the play, he sets Ben's speech prominently, *pomposo;* on Ben's exit, Alexandra launches the finale with her recalling of it and of Addie's remarks; and the final mother-and-daughter exchange is counterpointed by an offstage chorus of black workers—"Is a new day coming? Certainly, Lord"—which rises to a fortissimo affirmation. By a cunning use of set pieces—rag, jazz, blues, waltz song, popular song, Gottschalk pastiche—Blitzstein transcends the "naturalism" of the play. Weak, pathetic, lovable Birdie's nostalgia for the gracious days on the plantation—"Lionnet. Lionnet. . . . Oh, if we could all go back!"—is set to beautiful old-fashioned music that is at once lovable in itself and a comment on the sentiments it expresses. *Regina* is strong, sharp, clean, both funny and touching, and very well composed. Surely it deserves a central position in the American repertory.

The Detroit production was handicapped by a Regina, Joan Diener-Marre, who showed neither the vocal nor the acting resources for the role. She was coarse, awkward, and unconvincing. But there was a perfect Birdie, Barbara Hocher, and a shining young Alexandra, Sarah Rice. George Gaynes's Horace was very well judged, and Joseph Kolinski's Leo was keenly played and sung. Franco Colavecchia's set, which had dangling ropes where walls should be, was modish rather than helpful to the piece.

Thea Musgrave's *The Voice of Ariadne,* a three-act chamber opera first performed by the English Opera Group at the 1974 Aldeburgh Festival, in the tiny Jubilee Hall, has just been given its American première by the New York City Opera. When Musgrave received the commission, she spent "quite a long time . . . hunting around for the right story": one that would be "suitable for opera . . . and not more suitable for a play"; one compassable by a small cast without chorus and by the thirteen-strong English Opera Group instrumental ensemble; and—this was her special requirement—one in which tape-recorded music could be used to provide "a whole other element and a whole other level of experience." And she hit at last on Henry James's "The Last of the Valerii" (first published in *The Atlantic Monthly,* in 1874), which fulfilled all her requirements. This brief tale, spun from threads in Hawthorne's *The Marble Faun,* tells of a young Roman count and his American bride, Martha; the narrator is the girl's godfather. In Marco, described as a magnificently attractive male animal, there runs, beneath his intelligence and courtesy, a darkly pagan, passionate streak seeking a fulfillment the fair young American cannot give. A statue of Juno is discovered in his garden; the Count worships it, sacrifices to it, but returns at last to reason and to his wife in a final scene evoking Penelope at the loom (Martha bent over her embroidery) and homecoming after a perilous voyage.

Michael Swan, introducing the Penguin edition of the story, remarks fairly that "though James here suspends our disbelief almost enough to convince us that he has a particle of truth to offer, though there is a straining towards symbolism, the story is ultimately nothing more than an exquisite ghost story." Britten's *The Turn of the Screw* (1954) and *Owen Wingrave* (1971) gave precedent for turning James stories of personal dramas touched by the supernatural into chamber operas. Musgrave and her librettist, Amalia Elguera, effected major changes in their original. Not Juno but Ariadne. Not a statue but only its pedestal. And a happy ending only when Marco realizes that by abandoning his wife he has transformed her into the abandoned Ariadne whom he seeks—when her voice blends with, and finally replaces, the magic (tape-recorded) voice of the lost statue. The classical parallels do not run quite true. The psychological imagery defies tidy analysis. But the essential feelings come across; they needed music for their expression, and Musgrave has expressed them in eloquent music. Her score is a natural flowering from the new freedoms, the adventurousness, and the lyrical delight in sound and gesture which she showed in previous orchestral pieces. It is also very well written for the singers: the rightness in matching emotional pitch to actual tessitura, the sense of where in the voice to find a particular shade of feeling, the naturalness of the declamation, and the unstrained transitions from conversation to formal set pieces all tell of a born opera composer.

Marco is a baritone, his wife a soprano, and her godfather a bass-baritone. The cast is enlarged to eight by the provision of the Marchesa Bianca Bianchi (mezzo), a rival for the Count's affections; of Mrs. Tracy (contralto), a caricature American lady of imposing size, a cruder Henrietta Stackpole, and her diminutive Italian admirer, Baldovino (tenor); and of a pair of servants (tenor and bass), descendants of the soldiers in Monteverdi's *Poppea.* And there is the eponymous Voice, heard only on tape, heard only by Marco in his imagination, calling to him across the waves and across the ages. The bass, the old gardener Gualtiero, who believes in the old gods, has an important role: at the start of each act he in effect explains the situation. And each act ends with an Ariadne scene: a monologue for Marco against a background of Ariadne's cries; a monologue for the Countess (in the opera she has no name; even at tender moments Marco can call her only "you"), a *lamento d'Arianna,* when by hallucinatory magic she becomes the abandoned heroine, feels herself alone with the seabirds on the rocky cape; and (as in Strauss's Ariadne opera) a final duet, which is Musgrave's tribute to Monteverdi. In her words:

> The parallel I had in mind was the end of *Poppea,* when all the colors die out, at least in Raymond Leppard's version, and you're left with this marvelous soft, slow, tranquil, fulfilled music—one of the great moments of opera. . . . I wanted to try to get that kind of mood . . . after all the storms had passed, to find this tranquility that would sound final and yet, as the words say, suggest that the pair is setting forth on a new exploration, together at last.

The opera is skillfully planned on all levels. Act II, for example, is a kind of symphony: neoclassical first subject for the scheming Bianca, lyrical second subject from Gualtiero; adagio aria for Bianca; scherzo based on Mrs. Tracy and Baldovino, with playful Handel quotations; and the *lamento d'Arianna* as finale. Meanwhile, the harmonic climate moves from clear diatonicism to troubled atonality, the emotions move from clarity to confusion, and the scene moves from a sunny Roman park to a vision of sea-girt Naxos. The work is written in linked numbers, making up a well-balanced formal sequence of solos, duets, and ensembles. Within the small scale, the sonic effects are rich, but the textures are carefully controlled to let the voices come through. The tape music, created in collaboration with Richard Rodney Bennett—a mysterious voice, Joan Davies's, lapped by echo and distance effects and the sounds of wind and wave—is very successful, partly because it is uncomplicated, partly because the interplay of tape with instruments and live singers is so cunningly handled. Niceties of social behavior are not always accurately observed in the libretto, but it did supply the composer with exactly what she wanted. As always in her music, clear intentions, practical good sense, and imagination are combined. *The Voice of Ariadne* provides an evening of cultivated pleasures.

The City Opera production, like Aldeburgh's, was deftly directed by Colin Graham. Carl Toms designed attractive naturalistic scenery. But no more than at Aldeburgh did the two principals look right. There, in Thomas Allen we saw an English squire and in Jill Gomez a dark-eyed Caribbean beauty. Here, David Holloway, as Marco, seemed very American (no attempt at the "dense sculptural crop of curls," the "close, crisp beard," the "complexion . . . of deep, glowing brown" described by James), and Cynthia Clarey, the Countess, was a tall, dark, graceful aristocrat, rather Latin in appearance and demeanor. Both of them sang very well. Richard T. Gill turned the pagan Gualtiero into a New England country sage—and did not sing well. Sandra Walker's Marchesa and Frances Bible's Mrs. Tracy were both first-rate. The Jubilee Hall holds three hundred people, and the State Theater only some two hundred short of three thousand. In its large spaces, the tape-recorded music sounded better than it had at Aldeburgh, but what should be full-throated lyrical climaxes made less effect. By increasing the strings, Miss Musgrave, who conducted her own work, had brought the orchestra up to twenty-eight. Nevertheless, the delicately accomplished chamber opera was somewhat dwarfed by its setting. The Juilliard Theatre would be a better New York home for it.

David Blake's grand opera *Toussaint, or The Aristocracy of the Skin* was given its première by the English National Opera last month. Blake, born in 1936, came to prominence with a long Ezra Pound cantata, *Lumina*, written for the 1970 Leeds Festival. (Last year, his Violin Concerto, a BBC commission, was heard at the Proms.) On the strength of *Lumina*, Lord Harewood, the managing director of the English National Opera, invited him to compose a work for the company. It was a bold commission—Blake's only previous stage piece was a cheerful little school musical, *It's a Small War*—that paid off. *Toussaint* is colorful, animated, and very interesting. I know no other opera quite like it, although there are plenty of precedents for this or that element. *Les Huguenots, Don Carlos, Boris Godunov,* and Prokofiev's *War and Peace* are in its ancestry; Schoenberg, Hindemith, and Hanns Eisler have left their marks on its music; and Brecht dominates its dramaturgy. But the amalgam is new. In a program note, Blake wrote:

> I'd long wanted to set a text which would express some of my political beliefs in a more specific way . . . to come to terms with issues economic, political, and, as it turned out, racial in an intelligent, interesting, and

entertaining way. . . . I . . . wish in the opera house not *only* to be entertained but to be informed, to be intellectually stimulated (i.e., made to think), and, finally, to be made to take up a position.

Blake is in the music department of York University. He approached Anthony Ward, author of the political novel *Our Human Constitution,* who is in the English department, about a libretto. Ward suggested as a possible subject the transformation, under Toussaint L'Ouverture's leadership, of Saint-Domingue, the richest of all the West Indian colonies, into Haiti, the second—and first black—independent republic of the New World. "Ward's idea for a libretto seemed perfect," and the two of them went ahead. The tale is not tidy but one of traitors, trimmers, and turncoats, of ideals perverted by political expediency, and of power corrupting. In the resulting opera, Lord Acton's famous dictum is cited as if it were already in 1801 a well-known saying, and Acton's next sentence ("Great men are almost always bad men") finds illustration. As the curtain falls, a freed Haiti, in 1803, is about to embark on its appalling nineteenth- and twentieth-century history of revolution, assassination, and tyranny and on its decline from fertility to being one of the poorest countries in the world. Ward spoke of his aim to explore "the confusions of style when a state tries to create itself." His and Blake's achievement has been to present a clear picture of those confusions in a rich music-drama that is neither a simplified didactic parable nor a mere decorative entertainment.

The ironies of the situation are reflected in the styles of the music. The proclaimers of *"Liberté! Egalité! Fraternité!"* decide that they cannot afford to grant freedom and equality to black brothers in their profitable colony. In the first scene of Act II, the songs of the Revolution, "Ça ira" and "La Carmagnole," become the themes of an elegant ancien-régime quadrille, played by a scruffy colonial band, danced by a motley, strutting crew of blacks and whites at Toussaint's court. Toussaint advocates tolerance, compromise, and a multiracial society, and is betrayed. His successor, Dessalines, with a simple policy of "Death to the whites!" drives out the French—to become a tyrant himself. Blake's score embraces voodoo chant and voodoo drumming, neoclassical pastiche, Schoenbergian expressivity, Eislerian theatre songs, and Hindemithian scherzo. It begins (sort of) in C minor and ends (sort of) in C major, and it has tunes—though that statement should perhaps also be qualified by a "sort of," since Blake's fondness for using tritone steps in his melodies makes them devilishly hard to remember. He has said, "I am a lyric composer anyway. I've always been thematic, I've never lost tempo. The thought of writing an opera . . . without all the available tempos and types of harmonic motion at my disposal—I just can't imagine it." He has used all his resources to illustrate the paradoxes of the subject—and at the same time, not incidentally, to provide variety of pace and tone throughout a long evening (three acts, with about three hours of music) and to take theatrical advantage of the picturesque, exotic setting.

Most of the action is history. The chief source is C.L.R. James's Marxist biography of Toussaint, *The Black Jacobins*. The opera does entertain, inform, and stimulate thought. It does not, however, enforce any position taking—and that is probably one of its strengths. There is none of the straightline propaganda of Henze's *We Come to the River*. The libretto is introduced by a list of recommended reading—from C.L.R. James, through Eric Williams and Frantz Fanon, to *The Autobiography of Malcolm X*—which suggests the kind of position the authors may have hoped to prepare. But they remain true to history, and in history the ground kept shifting; Wordsworth's simple acclamation of "Toussaint, the most unhappy man of men!" has long been clouded. The only constant in the operatic tale is Suzanne, Toussaint's wife, who was a real person but has here been amplified into a symbolic figure—uncorrupted, honest, natural, good, an idealized embodiment of "the Haitian people," to whom, "in recognition of their vitality and resilience," the opera is dedicated. At the end of Act I, Suzanne reshapes Wordsworth's sonnet as a series of uneasy questions.

The cast is enormous, and the company—led by Neil Howlett's Toussaint and Sarah Walker's wonderfully eloquent Suzanne—was shown at great strength. Mark Elder conducted with mastery. David Pountney's stage direction was very skillful and Maria Björnson's décor at once economical in its means and rich in its effectiveness.

The Met season opened last week with a revival of *Boris Godunov*, a noble, serious, and beautiful production of a great opera—so good that it surely deserves to be brought to life for an American audience by being sung in English. (How many in that audience could follow, line by line, what Pimen—firmly and eloquently sung by Paul Plishka—was saying?) Martti Talvela may lack the grandeur of tone and manner and the subtlety of inflection and timing to fill the title role completely, but in his large, honest way he was impressive. Wieslaw Ochman, a new Dimitri, was ardent, incisive, and a vivid actor. Marius Rintzler was a small but lively and jolly Varlaam. (The inn scene, however, is spoiled by an excess of low comedy.) Robert Sapolsky, a new Fyodor, was splendidly assured and strong. Florence Quivar made her Met début as a Marina so foggy and faint that the Polish act could with advantage have been omitted; Mussorgsky added it only to provide a gleaming female voice amid the preponderantly male music of the rest. The Simpleton requires stronger casting; Andrea Velis's tenor did not have the needed lyric plangency. Otherwise, all was well. Kazimierz Kord's conducting was assured and well paced.

The second performance of the season was a revival of *Pelléas et Mélisande*, a poetic, serious, and beautiful production of a great opera, distinguished especially by the lucid yet passionate conducting of James Levine and by a Golaud, José van Dam, of rare excellence—one who combined warmth and strength of tone, impeccably clear words, and force of dramatic personality. The "aria" in Act II, Scene 3, "Il est vrai que ce château est très vieux et très sombre," was a particularly fine piece of singing. All the singers except Jerome Hines (Arkel) were new to the production. Teresa Stratas's Mélisande and Raymond Gibbs's Pelléas were both carefully studied; she had some touching and effective moments, but he was prosaic of voice and wooden in his acting.

October 24, 1977

Hill Tunes

Harrison Birtwistle's *Silbury Air*, a Koussevitzky Music Foundation commission, first played in March by the London Sinfonietta (which has thirteen Birtwistle pieces in its repertory), was given its first American performances at the opening concerts of the Chamber Music Society of Lincoln Center season. The work takes its title from a romantic place—Silbury Hill, on the edge of Salisbury Plain. By a Victorian antiquary that huge conical mound, manmade, the largest of its kind in Europe, was claimed as a momument to those who fell in Arthur's last battle, but it must be older than that: the Roman road to Bath swerved to skirt it. Avenues of monoliths march across the fields toward the awesome stone circles of Avebury. No one is quite sure why Silbury Hill was raised (except Michael Dames, who in *The Silbury Treasure*, published last year, identified it as the womb of an enormous representation of the Great Goddess). Whatever the original purpose, it is now a place both numinous and beautiful. I have lain on its summit at noon, listening to lark song, an ecstasy to music turned, pour down from near-invisible dots high above, and have dreamed there at midnight while mysterious lights moved through the enchanted sky. Silbury is a name to conjure with, one not to be taken lightly. Birtwistle's title suggests a piece that might keep company with Peter Maxwell Davies's *Stone Litany*, behind which lies the landscape, both actual and associative, of Maeshowe, that great prehistoric barrow in the Orkneys, and with the Ghost-Nocturne in George Crumb's *Makrokosmos II*—marked "dark, fantasmic, subliminal"—behind which lies the landscape of Stonehenge, not far from Silbury Hill. But in a note on his work Birtwistle disclaims any attempt at "a romantic reflection of the hill's enigmatic location" or "a parallel with any of its evident geometry." What, then, did he have in mind? A "compound artificial landscape or imaginary landscape," it seems, created by music, and kin to Silbury only in being the product of careful, "logical" construction.

Birtwistle has written "music of landscape"—his own term for it—before. An orchestral piece of 1971, rugged, romantic, and laid out in clearly defined sonic planes, was titled *An Imaginary Landscape*. *The Triumph of Time* (1972) and *Melencolia I* (1976) are musical landscapes "after," respectively, a Brueghel painting and a Dürer engraving. These works, like *Silbury Air*, are, in their composer's words, made by "presenting musical ideas through the juxtaposition and repetition of 'static blocks' or . . . objects—the objects themselves being subjected to a vigorous invented logic via modes of juxtaposition, modes of repetition, modes of change." They are slow, reflective pieces. *Silbury Air* differs from them in moving fast; it is almost a dance composition. At the start of the score, there is set out a "pulse labyrinth"— four tables of metronome figures, unexplained—which I don't pretend to understand. (Any figure divided by a higher one to left or right of it yields .9375, but the vertical relationships vary.) A listener, however, needs no such guide to enjoy his sonic adventures through the labyrinth of the music itself. Like Birtwistle's *Meridian*, it begins and ends with repetitions of E, defining a horizon above, beneath, or across which the "objects" are set. The pulse moves from one dancing metre to another. The colors change. (The work, which lasts about eighteen minutes, is scored for woodwind quartet, on alternating instruments; trumpet, horn, and trombone; five strings; piano, harp, and percussion.) The textures alter now by imperceptible small stages, now at a swift, drastic stroke. Gay scraps of almost popular melody, sometimes from a solo instrument, sometimes hocketed within the play of the ensemble, come leaping forward. Gerard Schwarz conducted a buoyant, brilliant performance. The Chamber Music Society audience is generally reckoned conservative in its taste, but it greeted *Silbury Air* with the warmest reception for a contemporary work that I have heard in Alice Tully Hall since Elliott Carter's Third String Quartet had its première.

Earlier this month, at the second program of the Chicago Symphony's season, Michael Tippett's Fourth Symphony, commissioned by the orchestra, had its first performances. (It comes to Carnegie Hall next week.) By his seventieth birthday, in 1975, Tippett had written three operas, three symphonies, three concertos, three string quartets, and three piano sonatas, and said he would like to add a fourth of each. He tackled the largest forms first. The fourth opera, *The Ice Break*, appeared earlier this year; the Fourth Symphony is the latest product of what he has called his passion to project into our mean world music which is rich and generous. Tippett's First (1945) and Second (1958) Symphonies are at once "abstract" music and orchestral complements to, respectively, the oratorio *A Child of Our Time* and the opera *The Midsummer Marriage*. In the one, emotionally dramatic and, in the other, "magical" musical ideas are handled within classical forms. Both are abundantly lyrical and colorful compositions. So is the Third Symphony (1972), but in the finale of that work the composer breaks into words: the *Schreckensfanfare* of Beethoven's Ninth is answered by a soprano singing modern blues. The Fourth Symphony is again "pure"—a closely organized one-movement composition, lasting about thirty minutes, which subdivides into introduction, exposition, development, slow movement, episode, scherzo and trio, episode, and recapitulation. The introduction is based on piled-up *Tristan*-esque harmonies for the horns over soft, far-flung string consonances based on A, C, and B-flat. The horn chords, always with new counterfigures, return to punctuate and define the progress of the piece. The first subject of the exposition, a two-part idea, is labeled "power"; the second also has two parts, labeled "vigor" and "lyric grace." The exposition explodes in a climax of loud-hammered chords; these, too, recur as points of reference, screwed each time to a higher pitch. The plan of the work, though far from simple, is clear, satisfying, and aurally apprehensible. The musical ideas are striking and eloquent, and their adventures can be followed. The slow movement includes beautiful singing melodies for flute, cello, oboe, and English horn. The first episode is a craggy, emotionally tense string fugue. The scherzo is for woodwinds, trumpets, and percussion, and its trio section an exuberant virtuoso excursion for six horns. The second episode is an elaborated paraphrase, for full strings, of an Orlando Gibbons three-part fantasy; as in the slow movement of his First Symphony, Tippett re-creates a seventeenth-century form. (In all his works, one has the sense of past achievements playing upon and helping to order his and our present.) Suddenly, the hammered climax cuts the fantasy short, and the recapitulation, gathering up recollections of all that has gone before, begins. A brass chorale punctuates the close; its timbre suggests that here Messiaen may have set the composer's imagination stirring.

Tippett's feeling for instrumental sound and textures has ever been unconventional. Like Berlioz, he used to be accused of clumsiness, even incompetence, until interpreters appeared who could realize the sense of his heterodox writing: in England, Colin Davis and the London Symphony (whose records of the first three symphonies are available); now, in Chicago, Georg Solti and his matchless orchestra. The solos in the chamber-musical passages (especially one for viola), the sequence of string trills marked "radiant," the woodwinds' scherzo fragments marked "light, 'flying,'" the mercurial six-horn passage—they were played as one imagines no other orchestra could play them. The Chicago performance sounded ideal in every respect but one. At the start and, solo, at the very close, Tippett uses a wind machine, or aeoliphone. The device—a wooden roller rotated against a loop of silk—is unmentioned in Sibyl Marcuse's *Musical Instruments: A Comprehensive Dictionary,* and in the words of Grove "cannot properly be called a musical instrument," although Richard Strauss used it in *Don Quixote,* Ravel in *Daphnis et Chloé,* and Vaughan Williams in his Seventh Symphony, the *Antartica.* In the first, the machine, illustrating a comic episode, is acceptable and effective. In *Daphnis,* it adds to the theatrical excitement. But in the *Antartica,* and in Tippett's symphony, it jars. Grove's "objection to it as an element in composition is that it produces by realistic means what music should suggest in its own terms"; mine, that it sounds not like the polar wind, or like the "gentle breathing," in and out, that Tippett calls for, but like nothing more or less than a roller scrubbing against a loop of silk. It cannot simply be omitted, for in the codas of both symphonies it has a structural part. In some performances of the Vaughan Williams, an electronic device has been substituted, to better effect; maybe something of the kind could be found for the Tippett.

When the record of Tippett's Third Symphony was published, in 1974, a reviewer in *High Fidelity* contrasted its composer with those who "have their vision shifted from the large world about them to the small world of academic fashion and foibles," and continued, "It is difficult to imagine anything as vital as this Third Symphony being written in the U.S. today, because there is really no one around to write this kind of music. . . . It's probably not going to be long before we get the word from Princeton that it's no good." To the charge that many composers are out of touch with the public can be added another: that the public is out of touch with many of its best composers. There does seem to me to be in this country a sad rift between educated musical opinion—not only Princeton's—and the public's. Only here, I believe, could a great composer like Roger Sessions, whose vision *is* on the large world about him, be so much admired and so seldom performed. (Neither *Montezuma* nor *When Lilacs Last in the Dooryard Bloom'd* has yet been done in New York.) The music and the musical personalities of, say, Jacob Druckman, William Bolcom, George Perle, Milton Babbitt, and Leon Kirchner are less familiar to the average man in Avery Fisher Hall, I believe, than are those of Peter Maxwell Davies, Birtwistle, Alexander Goehr, Thea Musgrave, and Elisabeth Lutyens to his British counterpart. In my experience, new works by Carter and Crumb alone have attracted in New York the sort of wide public interest and copious public discussion that new works by Tippett, Maxwell Davies, and the rest do among their compatriots. (London critics flew to Chicago so as to be able to tell their readers about Tippett's new symphony. Would a half-hour Carter première in, say, Berlin be attended by the New York press in that way?) American distances make it difficult to keep ears on all that is happening. Fortunately, radio is coming to the rescue more and more. The Chicago performance of Tippett's Fourth will be broadcast by WNCN. On Sunday last week, a New Yorker could without leaving home aurally attend the San Francisco Opera's *Idomeneo* (WNYC), a Philharmonic concert of last season which included Crumb's *Star Child* (WQXR), the Chamber Music Society concert with the Birtwistle (WNCN), and then the first night of the City Opera's new production of *La fanciulla del West* (WNCN). Many music lovers must wish that the stations would now pool their resources to produce a single informative, detailed, comprehensive program guide from which long-range listening could be planned.

Andrew Imbrie, born in New York in 1921, was no more than a name to me before the Philharmonic brought out, as the first new work of its season, his Flute Concerto. (The orchestra has commissioned four concertos for its players. the others are by Michael Colgrass, for percussion quartet; by Vincent Persichetti, for English horn; and by John Corigliano, for clarinet.) But it was a name I heard often, spoken on campuses with admiration and affection, and Imbrie's *Angle of Repose*, done by the San Francisco Opera last year, was praised by many. His biography suggests the very model of an "academic" composer: study under Sessions at Princeton from 1937 to 1942 and at Berkeley from 1946 to 1947; American Prix de Rome; appointment, on graduation, to the Berkeley faculty, where he still is. Campus composers are not necessarily dull ones (Ralph Shapey, who has been at the University of Chicago for thirteen years, is not at all dull; listen to the new CRI recording of his oratorio *Praise*), but Imbrie's Flute Concerto does seem to me the very type of what is called an "academic" composition. That loose term signifies something carefully written (in whatever style), thoroughly respectable, uninspired—music that has little to say and says it well. The sounds of this concerto hurt not but provide nothing so positive as delight. There are three movements—Allegro con fuoco, Andante tranquillo, and Vivace—and the piece lasts about twenty-two minutes. In a program note, Imbrie remarks that "I never compose by scenario but have always allowed the structure of my music to develop gradually, in response to what I perceive as the demands of my initial ideas." The ideas here are drab and the demands they make unexacting. However, the composer shows much skill in meeting the particular requirements of the commission: devising textures in which a single flute can be balanced against the large (triple woodwinds) orchestra, and making much of the large, full tone of Julius Baker, the dedicatee, and soloist at the first performance. Some beautiful passages remain in my mind after two hearings: an episode for the soloist and his three colleagues in the ranks; the tranquil close of the first movement; a meandering horn melody at the start of the Andante, to which the soloist soon adds a romantic countermelody. Mr. Baker played with all his heart, but I suspect that the score as a whole could be more lovingly and more purposively shaped than it was by Erich Leinsdorf. Colors and contrasts apparent on the written page were reduced in performance by a dynamic range held, most of the time, between *ff* and *mf*. The concert will be broadcast by WQXR.

October 31, 1977

Death in Ferrara

Rossini's melodramma eroico *Tancredi* appeared in Venice in February 1813, and his dramma giocoso *L'italiana in Algeri* in May; with them the composer, aged twenty-one, established his supremacy in veins serious and comic. Soon his works dominated the repertory of opera houses the world over. Stendhal's *Vie de Rossini*, published in 1824, began: "Napoleon is dead, but a new conqueror has arisen whose name is on every tongue from Moscow to Naples, from London to Vienna, from Paris to Calcutta. The fame of this man knows no bounds save those of civilization itself—and he is not yet thirty-two." Sooner or later, all empires fall, and little remained of Rossini's when I began operagoing—only *The Barber of Seville*, an occasional revival of *William Tell*, heavily abridged, and some bewitching records by Conchita Supervia of numbers from *L'italiana* and *La Cenerentola*. In the twenties and thirties, Supervia and the conductor Vittorio Gui had for a while given those two comedies new currency. Then, in 1952, when Gui was chief conductor at Glyndebourne, he inaugurated the long series of Rossini comic revivals—*La Cenerentola, Le Comte Ory, L'italiana, La pietra del paragone, Il turco in Italia*—that were instrumental in bringing more than *The Barber* to the stages of the world. The serious pieces had no such regular championship—except *Moïse*, which has been much played since the war. In Italy, I heard Maria Callas sing in *Armida*, Giulietta Simionato in *Tancredi*, Joan Sutherland in *Semiramide*, Virginia Zeani in *Otello*, and Beverly Sills in *Le Siège de Corinthe;* in London there were isolated productions of *Otello* (with Pauline Tinsley), *Elisabetta, La donna del lago* (with Kiri Te Kanawa), and *Tancredi*. But none of those works found a foothold in the modern repertory as the comedies have done.

Tancredi is receiving renewed attention at the moment. There was a production in Rennes last December which also played in Orleans and Angers, came to London in concert form, and has been recorded on the Arion label (published here by Peters International, PLD 017-19). Last month, the Houston Grand Opera opened its season with *Tancredi*. And Eve Queler has announced a Carnegie Hall performance for March [see page 148]. The Houston production is a landmark in Rossini revival: it was given from the critical edition prepared for the Fondazione Rossini by Philip Gossett, and it used the unhappy ending that Rossini composed for the second production of the opera (Ferrara, March 1813). This ending, which failed to please, was dropped from all subsequent productions of the opera—until Houston's.

The libretto of *Tancredi*, by Gaetano Rossi, who also wrote for Meyerbeer, Mercadante, and Donizetti, is drawn from Voltaire's *Tancrède* but recasts the play as an opera seria not very different in temper from those of Handel. Against the martial background of a Saracen threat to Syracuse, a misunderstanding about the intended destination of a compromising letter is prolonged so that it can give rise to a sequence of arias and duets expressing grief, scorn, defiance, etc. Tancredi, the hero (a mezzo-soprano role), and Amenaide, the heroine (soprano), have an aria each in the first act, two arias each in the second, and a duet in each act. Argirio, Amenaide's father (tenor), has an aria in each act. Before each of the scene changes—two in the first act, three in the second—one of the subaltern characters, Tancredi's squire, Roggiero, or Amenaide's confidante, Isaura, is left alone onstage, to comment on the situation in recitative or aria. (Perhaps these soliloquies were meant to be sung before a drop curtain while the set was changed.) The work starts with the familiar nineteenth-century introduzione, an expository chorus enclosing episodes for soloists. Brief choruses punctuate the progress. Act I has an extended finale and Act II (in its original form) a short, almost perfunctory finale, expressing general delight when the epistolary confusion has been cleared up at last. The plot is uninteresting and the characters are cardboard, but the form of the libretto is shapely, and so is the score. *Tancredi*, in Gossett's words, "exhibits the freshness of first maturity, of first formulated principles. . . . Formal procedures in particular, uncertain and tentative in earlier operas, assume the characteristics that were now to dominate Italian opera for several generations." *Tancredi*, to my mind and ears, is a less promising candidate for widespread revival than *Elisabetta*, the first of Rossini's Neapolitan operas, in which the formal procedures are warmed by, in Massimo Mila's happy phrase, "a 'romanticism of the soul' that was subsequently to nourish the operas of Bellini, Donizetti and Verdi." Its successors *Otello* and *La donna del lago* are even more romantic: Rossini in his Neapolitan years became a "reform" composer, breathing new life into opera seria by breaking on occasion the very rules that in *Tancredi* he had helped codify. His Elizabeth (a role Montserrat Caballé has taken up) enters as a radiant, smiling woman, eager to greet the conquering hero she loves; changes to a brilliantly malicious and dangerous tyrant when she learns that her hero has secretly married another; and ends as a grandly magnanimous monarch, declaring that cares of state, not of the heart, will henceforth be her concern. And her music reflects the changes. Rossini's Tancred enters filled with delight at treading his native soil again and at the prospect of seeing Amenaide: "Di tanti palpiti . . . spero mercè." His hopes are soon dashed—and thereafter the emotional situation remains static. For the Ferrara production, Rossini himself transferred the lovers' duet in Act II to their first meeting in Act I, where it fits equally well. Nevertheless, *Tancredi* is worth hearing. The tunes give delight. The score has what Stendhal called "candeur virginale," the freshness and felicity of a young genius enjoying his mastery, the kind of springtime assurance that also marks *Idomeneo* and *Nabucco*. *Tancredi* is not as grand as either of those pieces—it lacks the big sweep and passion of Verdi's score, the marvelous richness and subtlety of Mozart's—but its deftness, high spirits, and charm are captivating. At the start of his career, Rossini often seems to hold hands with Haydn (while at its close, in *Le Comte Ory*, he reaches forward to the Berlioz of the *Troyens* and *Béatrice* nocturnes).

The Houston production, designed by John Stoddart and directed by John Cox, was a little too plain to do full justice to the work. Mr. Stoddart's sets, based largely on arcades taken from fourteenth-century predella panels, were attractive but severe. The stage was stripped almost bare for the final scene, which should represent Rossini's first use of landscape to reflect inner emotions. (The romantic device reaches sublime heights in the finale of *William Tell*, when the clouds roll back, a rainbow shines, an immense prospect of snow-clad peaks is revealed, and one by one the characters raise their voices to greet Switzerland's new-won freedom.) The *Tancredi* libretto prescribes "a mountain chain, precipitous gorges, torrents tumbling down to form the Arethusa; forest covering part of the mountain and of the plain; Etna in the distance; the sun in the west, glowing upon the sea, opposite; some caverns." Picturesque, richly scored music accompanies Tancredi's clambering across the scene and continues between the phrases of his recitative soliloquy: "The streams' fearful clamor, the winds' grim raging 'midst the crags, nature's sad abandon—all increases, all nourishes, in my wretched heart, the gloomy brooding on my betrayed love." But there was nothing in the Houston scene to increase or nourish our sympathy with the hero's plight. Mr. Cox's forte is detailed naturalistic comedy on a small scale—*Intermezzo, Capriccio*, the first part of *Ariadne auf Naxos*. Over opera seria he tends to stumble: a few years ago at Glyndebourne, he made a hash of *Idomeneo;* his handling of *Tancredi* was less clumsy but had little style or energy. Happily, he did not overactivate the long arias, but he did not find the few decisive, imposing moves and the simple, striking dramatic groups by which a director can make his audience forget that nothing happens, except musically, for minutes on end. Such drama as there is in the piece was further dulled by the fact of its being sung in Italian. There is much recitative in *Tancredi* which comes to life only when it serves for direct communication between the actors and their audience. But even the numbers must take their emotional force from words comprehended: Rossini's lively music is often unspecific. Humpty Dumpty–like, he would make one good tune do a lot of work and mean just what he chose it to mean. That jolly crescendo in the romping first-act finale of *The Barber* was first heard in *Elisabetta* to the text "Fatal day! Unforeseen disaster! The sun that rose serene and smiling now sets disturbed, gloomy, spreading a pall of woe!" A lament over Pharaoh's firstborn, struck down by God's thunderbolt, in *Mosè* (Naples, 1818)—"O torments! afflictions! frenzies! Ye rend my heart to shreds!"—reappears in *Moïse* (Paris, 1827) to epithalamic words: "What hear I? O sweet rapture, he is faithful to honor!" Unless an audience follows the words, it cannot know whether to feel sad or merry. And unless the singer knows that her audience is following them, she is merely making sounds at it.

Yet sounds from an accomplished throat, even sounds divorced from verbal sense, can be eloquent. Marilyn Horne, the Houston Tancredi, made wonderful sounds, loud and soft, clarion and dulcet; she was miraculously fleet in passagework and chamois-sure in her leaps from note to note; she brought off feats of vocalism dizzying in their dexterity. (Martin Katz had embellished Rossini's lines with elaborate extra ornamentation of the kind the nineteenth century expected. But he evidently had not written into the singers' scores all the necessary appoggiaturas; "blunt endings" abounded.) Miss Horne did not invest Rossini roulades with the charm, individuality, and expression that Supervia brought to them. She did not make much of the words but tended to blur and soften consonants: lips and tongue sounded lazy in the famous phrase "Mi rivedrai, ti rivedrò"; there were no clear *d*'s to be heard. But there was heroic energy and limitless bravura in her singing. If she was not exactly Tancredi, she was an astonishing, a dazzling virtuosa. Joan Carden's Amenaide had rather more dramatic character. The Australian soprano, making her American début, scored a big success. After an uncertain start, she sang with agility, brilliance, and tenderness. Carolyne James, the Isaura, had lost both her initial solo (in the introduzione) and her aria. Constance Fee, a member of the Houston Opera Studio (a new training ground for young professionals), sang Roggiero's aria pleasingly. Ernesto Palacio, the Argirio, was overtaxed, as almost all tenors except Rockwell Blake are, by Rossini's florid writing. So was Nicola Zaccaria in the small (aria-less) role of Orbazzano, a rival suitor for Amenaide's favor. Nicola Rescigno conducted ably. The harpsichord, a small, weak instrument electrically boosted, sounded horrid. A twenty-five-year-old memory is untrustworthy, but it tells me that Simionato, Teresa Stich-Randall as Amenaide, and Tullio Serafin as conductor made a more living drama of *Tancredi*. But then they were performing in Italian to an Italian audience.

The very first Tancredi, Adelaide Malanotte-Montrésor, had a lover, Luigi Lechi, who was a poet. He wrote the words for the "tragic finale" tried out in Ferrara and now in Houston. In this version, as in Voltaire's play, when Tancredi returns victorious over the Saracens and assured of his Amenaide's innocence, he is also mortally wounded. Instead of a happy reunion, there is a chorus of mourning, recitative, and a dying speech:

> *Amenaide...serbami*
> *Tua fè...quel...cor ch'è mio,*
> *Ti lascio...ah! tu di vivere*
> *Giurami,...sposa...addio.*

(The dots represent not omissions but the broken utterance of the dying hero.) The words of this finale were known, for they are printed in the Ferrara libretto. The music remained unknown until, three years ago, Count Giacomo Lechi produced it from his family archives. Seven pages in Rossini's hand contain the chorus, some accompanied recitative, and the closing quatrain set as very simple, direct declamation, in a chromatic C major, with a shuddering final cadence for tremolando strings. Twenty-five long lines of recitative remain unaccounted for. Rossini often entrusted his secco recitative to other hands, and so with propriety—as well as skill and imagination—Gossett himself has composed the missing lines. (In the *scena ultima* of his edition, eighty-one measures are by Rossini and forty-seven by him.) In Gossett's view, "the tragic conclusion elevates the drama and banishes the insipid happy ending. . . . In this piece, one feels in the presence of the Gluckian ideal, adapted even in this quasi-declamatory music to the beauty of Italian melody and the simplicity of Italian harmony." It is certainly an audacious close to so florid an opera. Whether it is altogether a fitting or effective close I feel unsure. To any experienced reader of eighteenth- and early-nineteenth-century libretti, the artificially sustained tensions of the plot predicate a happy ending; and I find the conventional close satisfying rather than insipid. Rossini's experiment failed in Ferrara; perhaps he was ahead of his time. It was certainly right to try it once again, to put it to the real test of theatre performance.

When Gossett's edition is published, it will, of course, contain *all* the music Rossini composed for *Tancredi* at one time or another. For almost every aria there are one or two alternatives. Giuditta Pasta, a very famous Tancredi, introduced a finale composed for her by Giuseppe Nicolini, to which Rossini himself added ornaments and cadenzas. So this, too, has a certain authenticity, and will appear in the edition. Each cast will be able to assemble the numbers best suited to its talents. The Houston performance followed the Venice original most of the way (except for the substitution of a Milan alternative as the tenor's first aria) and then switched to Ferrara for Tancredi's bravura "Perchè turbar la calma" and the tragic finale. In the editor's words, "later performances of the opera, with a different cast, will be free to make different choices from the authentic material, for there is no uniquely correct version of *Tancredi.*"

In all ways, the event was a happy example of scholars and performers joining forces to bring a composer's work to life. During the run of *Tancredi,* the Central Opera Service held its national conference and the American Musicological Society a regional conference in Houston. (Similarly, next week at Centre College, Danville, Kentucky, the Fifth International Congress of Verdi Studies will coincide with a production of Verdi's *Macbeth*— the original 1847 version—performed from a correct text prepared under the auspices of the American Institute for Verdi Studies by David Lawton.) The importance of the new Rossini scores due from the Fondazione Rossini and the new Verdi scores due from the University of Chicago Press and Casa Ricordi needs no stressing. So far, Alberto Zedda's score of *The Barber,* which appeared in 1968, is, in Gossett's words, "the only edition [in print] of any opera by Rossini, Bellini, Donizetti, or Verdi to get the notes right, not to speak of articulation, dynamics, instrumentation, text, etc."

The Lyric Opera of Chicago opened its season with *L'elisir d'amore* and *Idomeneo.* Both were productions on a high international level. *Elisir* was very prettily designed in a realistic idiom (leaves on the trees) by Ulisse Santicchi; lightly and sensitively directed by Giulio Chazalettes; and expertly conducted by Bruno Bartoletti. The spirit of Donizetti's comedy, tender and witty at once, was ideally represented. Margherita Rinaldi was a sparkling Adina, stylish in her phrasing, charming in her portrayal of the role; an occasional touch of hardness in the timbre was easy to forgive. Angelo Romero, a baritone of merit, was a lively, bonny Belcore, despite his tendency to let strut come to prance. Geraint Evans's Dulcamara had a touch of genius in it; he was a marvelously spontaneous and lovable rogue. Luciano Pavarotti, Nemorino, seemed odd man out—rather heavy and emphatic in a production whose grace and elegance called for someone like José Carreras—and his singing was less sweet and fresh than it used to be. Nevertheless, he was likable. All in all, a delightful evening.

Idomeneo was the Cologne Opera production, designed and staged by Jean-Pierre Ponnelle, which had already been seen in San Francisco. Mr. Ponnelle's set, a single one maintained throughout the opera, was not neoclassical but a gray baroque grotto, its façade a huge mask of Neptune with mouth agape, Bomarzo-style, to provide an entrance, and with movable eyelids that rolled back when the Oracle spoke. His costumes were a mishmash of periods: Idomeneus wore a white soutane, and Electra a black ball dress. Electra perched most unprincesslike on the edge of a table to sing "Idol mio," and Ilia eavesdropped on the aria. Mr. Ponnelle is a great one for eavesdropping—witness his Salzburg *Figaro*—and so there were often characters onstage who had no business there. Ilia's lovely soliloquy to the breezes, "Zeffiretti lusinghieri," had to bear mute contributions from Idomeneus, Idamantes, and Electra; the trio of Act II was staged as a quartet. It all sounds deplorable—and yet the production had a sweep, a grandeur, a dramatic force that are present in Mozart's score but were not captured in any of the nine earlier productions of this increasingly popular opera I had encountered. The cast was strong: Christiane Eda-Pierre (a most musical, if somewhat mature-seeming Ilia), Carol Neblett (a decisive and fiery Electra; not able to take all the technical hurdles quite cleanly, but what Electra does?), Maria Ewing (gauche in demeanor but a vocally very fine Idamantes), Eric Tappy (an able Idomeneus, though he, too, was taxed by Mozart's roulades), Frank Little (who lacked only a trill to be a first-rate Arbaces). There was no affectation in their singing. They declaimed the words strongly. (I am no foe of opera in the original when the words are used as vividly as they were in these two Chicago performances.) They were direct in their eloquence. So was the conductor, John Pritchard, in his.

The New York City Opera has added *La fanciulla del West* to its repertory. I enjoy the first act of the opera; although the situations are absurdly sentimental, it has sustained, well-wrought, and touching music in it. Then the level drops until at last Puccini pulls out a tune again with "Ch'ella mi creda" and caps it with the surefire finale, lilting, cajoling, and irresistible, for his gun-toting heroine. Others rate the whole work high. Earlier this year, London critics seem to have been bowled over by Miss Neblett, Placido Domingo, and Zubin Mehta as conductor in Covent Garden's large, elaborate new production of *La fanciulla,* and to have found merit in Straussian and Debussian passages that to my ear sound like borrowings unassimilated and misapplied. Perhaps, one day, at a performance more luscious and glamorous than the City Opera's, I, too, will succumb.

The New York production, directed by Frank Corsaro and designed by Robert O'Hearn, comes from Miami. It misses the scenic enchantment that David Belasco, the author and director of the play from which the libretto was drawn, and Puccini both counted on. In Act I, there is no view through door and window of "the valley with its wild vegetation of alders, oaks, and dwarf pines all wrapped in sunset glow; in the distance, snowy mountains tinted with gold and purple"; in Act III, no elaborate, realistic representation of dawn in the great California forest. But there *are* horses, and Mr. Corsaro's needless departures from Puccini's careful instructions are confined to dressing up the Indian servant in a bearskin (to make up for the lack of the stuffed bear Puccini asked for?), turning Jake Wallace into a *blind* minstrel (this destroys a touching musical effect when Jake, observing the miners' faces turned in silence toward him, breaks off in mid-phrase, resuming only when they sign to him to continue), and placing a guitar instead of a banjo in Jake's hands (this contradicts Puccini's scoring). Otherwise, he directed a careful, lively production, in which many small parts were taken with accomplishment. Maralin Niska acted Minnie exceedingly well, but her singing was strident at climaxes. Ermanno Mauro was a wooden, unromantic Dick Johnson, redeemed only by some splendidly ringing high notes. (On the first night, Mr. Domingo made the plea for contributions with which City Opera performances begin; one wished that Mr. Mauro had made the speech and Mr. Domingo sung the role.) Charles Long's Jack Rance was lightweight but very sure. Sergiu Comissiona conducted an impassioned yet delicately controlled performance.

November 7, 1977

Enacting the Ineffable

Within a week, three of America's great orchestras—the Philadelphia, the Boston, and the Chicago—visited Carnegie Hall. (Cleveland comes in February.) The Philadelphia Orchestra, under Claudio Abbado, gave the most poetic, most exciting, most beautiful account of a Mahler symphony I have heard in years—since, in fact, Abbado conducted No. 2 with the Philadelphians and No. 6 with the Clevelanders early in 1973. Strange that there should be a hundred Mahler symphony recordings on the market and only one (of No. 2, with the Chicago Symphony) conducted by Abbado. [There are two more now; see below.] He is the most picturesque and most lyrical of Mahler interpreters, and supreme at making the picturesqueness precise, the lyricism lucid. The symphony he did this time was the Fourth. It became a voyage of delights, an adventure of enchanted melodies and sounds, a progress from a pastoral landscape, where the grass still bore prints Haydn and Schubert had left, through scenes of shadow and sadness, dispelled by large shouts of joy, to a vision of untroubled happiness. His use of rubato was bold. He was not afraid to pause for an instant of delicious expectation before launching into some heart-easing melody, to press forward within a phrase toward its climax, to dwell tenderly on a sweet cadence. The Philadelphians played for him like angels. The sensuous beauty of their sound was extraordinary. Every color was clear and full, every line lovingly drawn. And all was in balance. The counterpoints were limpid. There was unusual depth to the sonic picture: some music seemed to come from far, far away, some to spring up under one's feet, and everything conspired to create a world of marvels among which a listener was not lost but led to live an intenser life. Hall, orchestra, conductor, audience disappeared in sound. Although in a performance like this Mahler's music becomes filled again with surprises, fresh as when first encountered, Abbado shapes the forms securely. When we reach at last that E-major heaven where St. Cecilia and her colleagues are court orchestra, and angel voices invite us to mirth, it is clear that the open fifths of the start—B and F-sharp through the merry jingle of sleighbells—have been pointing there all the time, across the smiling G-major meadows and the calm, deep valley of the Adagio. In an age when Mahler has become an everyday composer, played almost as a matter of routine, rarely, rarely in performances of his music come that spirit of delight and that spirit of desolation and despair which make him unique. But Abbado showed that a Mahler symphony—even Mahler's best-known symphony—can still provide a transcendental experience.

At its first New York concert of the season, the Chicago Symphony, with attendant soloist and chorus, did Mahler's Eighth, a work not to be approached lightly by performers or audience, since it is the early twentieth century's great artistic statement of the conflict between faith, humanism, and despair—as Goethe's *Faust* is that of the early nineteenth century. The Eighth, wholly affirmative, is self-sufficient, a complete statement, but nevertheless one that a Mahlerian sets against the doomed close of the Sixth Symphony, the poignant resignation of *Das Lied von der Erde*, the stoic tragedy of the Ninth, and the loving farewell of the Tenth. In the finale of his Fourth Symphony, Mahler used a "Wunderhorn" text—a child's description of Heaven, a naïve intimation of immortality—as symbol for an adult's untroubled joy. The texts of the Eighth Symphony—the "Veni creator spiritus" and the final scene of *Faust*—are symbols, too, "to convey something," Mahler told his wife, "which, whatever form it is given, can never be adequately expressed. . . . Christians call it 'eternal blessedness,' and I cannot do better than employ this beautiful and sufficient mythology—the most complete conception to which at this epoch of humanity it is possible to attain." Similarly, Goethe had told Eckermann that in his final scene he used Christian mythology not as a believer but because "I might very easily have lost my way in vagueness had I not through sharply defined figures and images of the Christian church given my poetic design a beneficently restricted form and substance."

Deryck Cooke, whose numerous fugitive essays on Mahler should be gathered between covers, linked the Eighth Symphony and the third scene of *Faust*, where the philosopher is moved to retranslate the New Testament: In the beginning was . . . the Word? (well, not exactly) . . . the Thought? . . . the Power? . . . the *Deed* (ah, that's the word). The final scene of *Faust*, it has persuasively been argued—by Stuart Atkins—is Faust's last dream in life, a dream of his own salvation. He knows he will not be damned, because "Who ever striving drives himself on, Him we can redeem." Goethe and Mahler both strove to find what Mr. Atkins has called "the supreme and most comprehensive symbol of all those things which men regard as evidence that life is neither Mephistopheles' 'void eternal' nor the romantic's vague aspiring, but is, rather, directed striving with meaning certainly intuitable if not certainly knowable." In *das Ewig-Weibliche*, Faust's knowledge of Gretchen, his dream of Helen, and a vision of Mary, Queen of Heaven, are combined. The scene needs music as fully as do those of the Helen act which specify it. "It will produce a most unusual effect on the stage," Eckermann said of "Helen," "that a piece should begin as a tragedy and end as an opera. But something is required to present the grandeur of these persons and to express the sublime language and verse. . . . If only we could get a good composer." "It should be one," Goethe replied, "who, like Meyerbeer, has lived long in Italy, so that he combines his German nature with the Italian style and manner. However, that will be found somehow or other."

Meyerbeer! If Mozart had lived long, he would have been seventy at the time of that conversation—and, surely, the right composer for *Faust*. Schumann's setting of the final scene is beautiful but not sublime. Mahler's is the adagio, scherzo, and finale of a symphony that has the impetuous "Veni creator" march as its first movement—not music for Goethe's play but a great musical enactment of the "directed striving with meaning certainly intuitable" that is Goethe's theme. In this symphony, as Cooke noted, Word becomes Deed, and Deed Word. It is the text of faith, the "Veni creator," that is set to march music, which (as in Beethoven's Ninth) usually celebrates humanism and the deed, and Goethe's humanistic text that is clad in hymn and chorale, music's symbol of faith.

Sir Georg Solti long ago mastered the technical difficulties of executing Mahler's symphonies. His performance of the Fifth last season showed that he has also begun to respond to their emotional and spiritual content. One looked forward with excitement to the Eighth he was billed to conduct. But he injured himself. Margaret Hillis, director of the Chicago Symphony Chorus, took over. She "saved the show." She beat time efficiently. She held the immense forces together with aplomb. She launched into the first movement with a headlong energy to match Mahler's own when he composed it. But on all other counts it was an unaffecting, earthbound, unworthy performance of a work that should change the world of those who hear it. The soloists made an ill-blended septet in the first movement (Kenneth Riegel's dry tenor hacksawed through the ensemble), and in Part II only Barbara Hendricks, in the brief role of the Mater Gloriosa, sang purely.

As its first Carnegie bill of the season, the Boston Symphony brought two concert performances of Berlioz's *Béatrice et Bénédict*. The piece can be enchanting in the theatre. In concert, its spell is broken when Berlioz's numbers are bridged not by his own brief dialogues but by large chunks of *Much Ado*, and when words spoken and words sung are assigned to different casts. This happened at Carnegie Hall, and things were made worse because in Act I the speakers were largely unintelligible, while in Act II they achieved intelligibility only by delivering Shakespeare's lines at a snail's pace. Frederica von Stade, below form, and Stuart Burrows were acceptable but unremarkable singers of the title roles. Sheila Armstrong gave Hero a spreading tone and an uneven line; Gwendolyn Killebrew was a fuzzy Ursula. Berlioz described his work as "a caprice written with the point of a needle," and one that needs "an extremely delicate performance." Seiji Ozawa's handling of it was lively but neither needle-sharp nor delicate.

Three days after their first *Béatrice*, the orchestra and the admirable Tanglewood Festival Chorus, again under Ozawa, did Brahms's Requiem, in the Church of St. Paul the Apostle, on Columbus Avenue, just south of Lincoln Center. The work had its first performance, in 1868, in Bremen Cathedral. The cathedral-like acoustics of St. Paul's lent impressiveness to the dark, soft tread of the drums and muted strings in the second movement; they caught up and enhanced the voices of the soloists, Judith Blegen and Benjamin Luxon; but they blunted the edge of contrapuntal writing, mushed the fugues on "Der Gerechten Seelen" and "Herr, du bist würdig." The Tanglewood choir adopted an unusual platform disposition, grouped not SATB but with the voices scattered at random. This produced an excellently cohesive choral tone—but at the expense, again, of contrapuntal definition; one did not hear the successive entries strike in from different places. The orchestra, on the other hand, was stratified—all the violins on the left, the double-basses way out on the right, almost in a side aisle. Boston Symphony program books, now edited and largely written by Michael Steinberg, are the best in the country, packed with information and observation, and legibly printed. For this church concert, the orchestra brought along its own publication (whereas in Carnegie the Boston matter gets reset in the small, close type standard for New York programs). Text and translation were included—and then the lights in the church were turned down so that they could not be read.

The St. Paul Chamber Orchestra, billed as the only full-time professional chamber orchestra in the country, came to Alice Tully Hall last month to give three concerts. The programs included a new work, Alvin Brehm's Piano Concerto; two local premières, Hans Werner Henze's *Aria de la Folía Española* and William Schuman's *The Young Dead Soldiers*; and an American première, John Christian Bach's cantata *Cefalo e Procri*, whose autograph is in the Library of Congress. Brehm's concerto was dull. Schuman's piece, a "lamentation" for soprano and horn, accompanied by eight winds and nine strings, looks moving and effective in score. It is a setting of an Archibald MacLeish poem, which the soprano and the horn often "declaim" together, in the same rhythm but to different notes. But the performance fell flat, partly because the vocal line is written so high that the singer, Rosalind Rees, could make nothing of the words. Henze's "aria" is a new set of variations, for small orchestra, on that *folía*, or "Folies d'Espagne," theme that Corelli and other composers have made famous. In Corelli, it is a dignified strain, but Grove notes that the *folía* "was originally a noisy dance accompanied by tambourines and performed by men dressed as women, who behaved so wildly that they appeared to be out of their senses." Henze's piece starts sedately enough but gradually becomes wilder, reaching its climax in an impetuous fandango. It is not one of his major works but an amiable and ingenious stretch of music (about twenty minutes long), including several extended solos for the St. Paul players, for whom it was composed. The J. C. Bach cantata is an elegant trifle, attractively scored: an air for Cephalus, two airs for Procris, an air for Aurora, and a final trio, linked by recitatives. Something could be made of it, but not much was. Angela Bello and Karen Smith sang the title roles in small, clean, pretty voices, without dramatic emphasis; Janis Hardy was a cloudy Dawn. It is mere prejudice, I suppose, to suggest that a scruffy-looking band is unlikely to play *galant* music with aristocratic grace and elegance; if the St. Paul conductor and his players got their hair cut, it might not alter the cut of their musical phrasing. But it can fairly be said that their playing of eighteenth-century music was not exquisite. At the second and third concerts, there was an exquisite soloist, Heinz Holliger, who played Hummel's Adagio and Variations for oboe, Antonín Reicha's Scena for English horn, and Mozart's Oboe Concerto with wit and seductively captivating refinement. At the first concert, Charles Rosen played Beethoven's Second Piano Concerto with magisterial intentions but uneven fingers.

The Chamber Music Society's second program of the season, in Tully Hall, included the first performance of William Bolcom's Piano Quartet, commissioned by the Koussevitzky Foundation. It is a loose-knit four-movement piece, which opens pleasantly by alternating a Chopinesque barcarolle with a section called "Ketjak" (the Ramayana monkey chant; the Balinese original can be heard on the Nonesuch record "Golden Rain"), and drops for its third movement, Intermezzo, into a cocktail-time ditty. James Buswell, the violinist, cued the ensemble by giving a loud sniff before each entry. I felt rather sniffy about the piece, too. On the Society's third bill, Victoria de los Angeles returned to New York after a four-season absence. Before she had sung a note, she won all hearts. She is no exception to the general rule that people look as they sound. She looked adorable. And when she sang—a Vivaldi "motet" (or solo cantata to a sacred text), Falla's *Psyché,* another Vivaldi— the timbre was as limpid, as beautiful, as adorable as ever. She has to husband her voice a little more carefully than before. I doubt whether she could now set Elsa's or Elisabeth's long phrases winging out into the theatre. But the sound of her notes is still a delight, and she is one of the few singers left who unfailingly join notes into a legato line.

The day before, Johanna Meier, in the same hall, gave her first New York recital. The place is not friendly to singers. Its dry, clear acoustics are unflattering. They could not sully the purity of Victoria de los Angeles's tone, but they showed up cruelly Miss Meier's unevenness. She is a puzzling performer. The personality she presents is generous and attractive, and the voice at its best is uncommonly beautiful—a rich, full, shining, warm soprano that evokes comparisons with Leonie Rysanek, even Lotte Lehmann. But Miss Meier has not learned how to keep it at its best; suddenly the focus will blur, the purity go, the tone spread. She sang the first quatrain of Mendelssohn's "Venetianisches Gondellied" magically, and then lost control in what followed. Weber's "Ocean, thou mighty monster" (which, for some reason, she did in a German translation) was in part large, radiant, and steady, as good as can be, and in part unsteady and imprecise. In her first group—Handel, Mozart, Haydn—breaking words into separate syllables and phrases into separate notes, she provided a demonstration of modern nonlegato singing.

November 14, 1977

An Abbado recording of Mahler's Fourth Symphony, with the Vienna Philharmonic and Frederica von Stade as soloist, appeared in 1978, on Deutsche Grammophon 2530 966. An Abbado recording of the Sixth, with the Chicago Symphony, appeared in 1980, on DG 2707 117.

Deryck Cooke's Gustav Mahler: An Introduction to His Music, a BBC booklet of 1960, was republished, with amplifications from some of Cooke's later essays, by the Cambridge University Press in 1980.

What the
Composer Wanted?

The first new production of the Metropolitan season is a *Rigoletto* conducted by James Levine and staged by John Dexter, the company's music director and its director of production. Like much of their earlier work, it suggests that Mr. Levine's talents are ill suited to Italian opera, and Mr. Dexter's to nineteenth-century opera. The production is not careless, but it is undramatic and ineffective; the collaborators' approach seems to be at once innocent, ignorant, and pretentious. Mr. Levine, talking about the show in an intermission of its relay by Channel 13, spoke of "benefiting from all the previous productions we have seen and maybe achieving greater fidelity to what the composer wanted." Mr. Dexter, talking to the *Times*, said, "All I can deal with are practical, technical problems. If something aesthetically interesting arises out of the solution, that's wonderful. But you don't go to a piece with an aesthetic approach—you go with a technical approach." He also said, "Everything I've done is based on economics." The new *Rigoletto* does not look cheap. In fact, it looks as if it cost more to build than four traditional sets of painted canvas and a reversible two-story structure—one side Gilda's house, the other Sparafucile's—would. But I hope it *was* cheap, for then it would have at least economy to recommend it. In this staging, designed by Tanya Moiseiwitsch to Mr. Dexter's prescription, all four scenes of the opera are played on or around a tall, conical, disintegrating tower—part garden pagoda, part Brueghelian Babel—with a walkway around it at second-floor level. Between scenes, it revolves. Mr. Levine suggested that its decrepit condition was intended to reflect the decadence of Mantuan society. (The traditional alternation between the glittering court and "a house of modest appearance" or a low tavern seems to me a more potent symbol of the drama.) If Mr. Levine's and Mr. Dexter's cogitations had produced something fresh and powerful, I would be the first to applaud. But this was not a potent *Rigoletto*, like Walter Felsenstein's, in Hamburg, which departed from nineteenth-century stage techniques to make much of the great dramatic moments patent or implicit in Verdi's score. On the contrary, it missed point after point and seemed almost incompetent in the way it tamed what should be a stirring drama.

As in the Met *Aida*, Mr. Dexter got things wrong from the moment of curtain rise. Verdi began his *Aida* unconventionally, in mid-conversation. "Yes: it is reported that the Ethiopian dares again to defy us" is the first sentence. In Mr. Dexter's production, the high priest makes a big solo entrance toward a Radamès already onstage, and then says "Yes. . . ." Verdi's start to *Rigoletto* is even more unconventional—a transformation of the standard introduzione of Ottocento opera, which consisted of expository choruses enclosing solo utterances. Verdi suppresses the initial chorus. The curtain rises on an empty stage while bright dance music sounds from the background. After sixteen measures, we glimpse dancing in halls that open out of the one before us. At a clearly defined musical moment—the resumption of the opening strain—just two people, the Duke of Mantua and his confidant Matteo Borsa, advance to the foreground and converse over the dance music. The pit orchestra strikes in only to accompany the Duke's ballata, "Questa o quella," which he sings to Borsa (and to the audience), not to an assembled company. A string band onstage takes over (Verdi's indebtedness to the party scene of *Don Giovanni* has often been noted) to accompany a minuet danced in the background while in the foreground the Duke pays court to the Countess Ceprano. At last, Rigoletto makes his sudden, dramatic first appearance with an unaccompanied exclamation, and then the full stage band resumes, *brillante.* Pit orchestra and stage band join forces only when the whole company has mustered; out of the last chord of their ensemble there rings the voice of Monterone, unaccompanied, thundering his monotone denunciation. And so on. The "dramaturgy" of this scene—rightly described by Julian Budden as "a single organism from first note to last" and one without a formal precedent in the whole Italian opera—is set out clearly in the score; and it is all confusion in the Met production.

After this introduzione comes the direction "N.B.—The curtain falls for a moment to allow the scenery to be changed." In Verdi's day, scene changes were generally effected on an open stage. Here he wanted something different. The curtain fall indicates the passing of a day. As the composer said, the party and the abduction of Gilda "could not take place all in one night, because if the party ends toward dawn Triboletto [as Rigoletto was originally called] could not meet the bravo toward *evening,* and moreover it is unlikely that Bianca [Gilda] would have stayed up all night." Therefore, Piave, his librettist, was instructed to write lines making it clear that the courtiers' assignation to gather and take revenge on Rigoletto is for the following evening. But in the Met staging Verdi's "N.B." is ignored. An open-stage scene change is made. Rigoletto does not even leave the set. Crushed by Monterone's curse, he sinks down on the palace floor—and then rises to converse with the street-corner assassin outside the house where he has installed his daughter. On the surface, it may sound like a clever idea. In that *Times* interview, Mr. Dexter described it thus:

> We can't stop the momentum [after the first scene]. What I want is this: After Monterone curses Rigoletto, the jester collapses in a heap on the floor, and the chorus rushes off, leaving him alone. Then this great, decaying Renaissance tower turns slowly, a giant silhouette in the darkness. Suddenly we're in front of Rigoletto's house. As he gets up with the curse still ringing in his ears, he bitterly wipes off his court jester's

makeup, and the stage is set for his sinister meeting with the assassin Sparafucile. It should be very effective—if it works for the audience. You never can know.

It didn't work. And I think you *can* know that this is not the kind of effect that Verdi needs—not when he has specifically prescribed a curtain fall. The curtain not only marks the passage of hours. It gives Rigoletto time for a quick change into mufti: Verdi wrote of a change of costume, and Gilda has no idea what her father's profession is. (At the Met, Rigoletto peels colored patches off his face at the start of the second scene, and he doffs his jester's tunic, bundling it into the gutter, after the first phrase of his monologue "Pari siamo.") It clearly divides Rigoletto's two lives—as a jester, jeering at other fathers' misfortunes, and as a tender, loving father. Mr. Dexter hath rid his prologue like a rough colt; he knows not the stop. All the same, better no punctuation than the once common full-length intermission after the twenty-minute introduction. That *does* stop the momentum.

Miss Moiseiwitsch has taken the trouble to provide, in Act II, the full-length portraits of the Duke and his Duchess, flanking the entrance door, that are called for by the libretto. Monterone should address his bitter "Felice pur anco, o duca, vivrai" to the Duke's portrait, but Mr. Dexter stations him up on the top deck, whence he cannot see it. In Act III, Rigoletto, confronted with a body in a sack, identifies it by the spurs he can feel; but here neither the Duke in his soldier disguise nor Gilda in her riding outfit had been wearing spurs. Those are small points. Another small textual point is that the Duke's Act III order to Sparafucile is "Two things, at once . . . A room and some wine," whereas it later becomes evident that the inn has no rooms. I imagine that Victor Hugo's original line, "Deux choses, sur-le-champ . . . Ta soeur, et mon verre," was simply toned down for Venetian censorship.*
Larger points are the ludicrous handling of Gilda's abduction, which suggests village-hall theatricals, and the tableau at the very end, which dispels concern for Rigoletto amid a melodramatic lighting display.

I attended the second performance. (At the first, the rehearsed Rigoletto, Cornell MacNeil, was ill, and Sherrill Milnes stepped in.) The lighting was absurd. In a bright, full blaze, Rigoletto remarked, during the second scene of Act I, "In such darkness one can see nothing"; in another, during Act III, he called for a light to see by. But the lighting designer, Gil Wechsler, was not responsible. Although this was a performance to a paying audience, it served also as a rehearsal for the television relay, and what Mr. Dexter described as the "soft Giorgionesque light" of his show had been sacrificed to the needs of the cameras. Since Mr. MacNeil had risen from a sickbed to sing, it would be unkind to review his performance (though perhaps not unfair, for it was a public occasion and he had sent no messenger before the curtain to crave our indulgence). As heard over WQXR and seen over Channel 13, three

---

* I imagined rightly. Verdi's sketches and his autobiography read "Tua sorella e del vino"; see Martin Chusid's article in *Verdi Newsletter* 8 (1980).

days later, he was still uneven, and scarcely more interesting than in the past. Once again, there were good notes and evidence of serious thought and study; once again, there were passages—important ones, such as "Ah! veglia, o donna," "Miei signori, perdono," "Piangi, fanciulla," "Non morir"—where the tone became dead and heavy and he failed to be moving. He does not command the timbre of passionate tenderness. It was surprising, however, that so forceful an Amonasro should have brought so little ferocity to the utterance of "Cortigiani, vil razza dannata." Mr. Levine must take some of the blame: no boiling string attacks there but an almost light, rapid, and even accompaniment; and a bland cello line in "Miei signori, perdono."

Placido Domingo, a handsome Duke, sang a fast, stiff "Questa o quella," without the rhythmic and tonal inflections that provide the *eleganza* Verdi asks for. His address to the Countess Ceprano was similarly unwinning. But when he reached "È il sol dell'anima," he and Mr. Levine became different people, adept at the unwritten rubato that gives life to the phrases, and responsive to the written dynamic marks, which range from *ppp* to *ff* and on through a further crescendo up to the climactic B-flat. The Act II aria was also sung with freedom and expression. Mr. Domingo reduced the cabaletta to a single verse, and it went unapplauded. "La donna è mobile" was hard and bright, rather than charming, but it had some bounce, and until the interpolated high B Mr. Domingo's voice stayed purely in focus. Earlier, his tone had sometimes been impure. In a talk transmitted during an intermission of the television performance, he owned to being taxed by both the high tessitura and the high spirits of the Duke, saying that he preferred, when onstage, to be a suffering character. The delicacy he also found difficult; he scamped the little notes—the turns in "È il sol," the passing notes up to "amore" and "tuoi" in the quartet. "La donna è mobile" was not improved by having its second verse sung at Maddalena or by the intrusion of an extra note, almost, consequent on Mr. Domingo's failure to elide "-na" and "è." Verdi's portamento slurs between the third and fourth notes of the famous tune went unobserved, and this also destroyed some of its essential character. (The "è," in fact, gets taken up in the slur when it is properly made.) During the quartet, in the climb to the B-flat on "cons*olar*," just before the reprise of "Bella figlia," Mr. Domingo produced four marvelous notes, generous, open, and free, which shone like the sun.

Ileana Cotrubas's Gilda was delicate, winning, and strong in its portrayal of a girl who, like Juliet, moves from innocence and unthinking obedience to passion, willfulness, and tragedy. She looked enchanting; that piquant face is made for mischief—she is a born Susanna, Adina, Norina—but in distress it can become wonderfully touching. A few years ago, her Tatyana, sitting forlorn in the garden after Onegin's chilly response to the letter, was unforgettable; so were the expression of her Gilda as at the start of Act III she sang "Io l'amo. . . . Ma pur m'adora" and then "Ah, padre mio" and her whole demeanor as she entered the inn to go to her death. Her first dress, described by Miss Moiseiwitsch as "roughly sixteenth-century with strong leanings to the Victorian age," was voluminous and unbecoming; the others were better. She wore all of them well. She sang making much of the words, giving syllables their full value and joining them into eloquent lines. Her voice was limpid and beautiful, and surprisingly large in the climaxes of the "Si, vendetta" duet, the quartet, and the storm trio. It poured out effortlessly. Elsewhere there were some disturbing moments when its steadiness failed, when there was a small but noticeable beat accompanied by a slight flickering of the jaw; then the tone seemed to be pushed out instead of flowing naturally. She must beware of any temptation to force in the huge Met. Her voice is a rare and precious instrument.

Verdi said that Monterone should be entrusted to "the best baritone in the company"—by which he presumably meant the best house baritone, since he designated the role *secondo baritono*. Basses usually sing the part today, and at the Met John Cheek was not imposing enough. (I suppose some ingenious director has already thought of doubling a bass as Monterone and Sparafucile, to be twin manifestations of Rigoletto's nemesis.) Justino Díaz was a smooth and sinister Sparafucile, the more impressive in that he did not bluster. But Mr. Levine held the Sparafucile-Rigoletto duet to so rapid and rigid a pace that it slipped by without making its full effect. (In performances by singers who were coached by Verdi himself, one hears that his metronome marks are only a starting point, not a straitjacket.) Isola Jones was a luscious and almost topless Maddalena—in appearance, not voice. The other roles, Verdi said, scarcely matter; among them, James Atherton's Borsa was animated, lively, and elegant—a Duke in the making, perhaps.

November 21, 1977

Transformations

Castelfranco Veneto is a small town about thirty miles northwest of Venice. Her most famous son is Giorgione, whose *Madonna with Saints Liberalis and Francis* stands in the Duomo. Her next-most-famous son is probably Agostino Steffani (1645–1728), composer, diplomat, and bishop, whose works dominated the German theatres of his day. Accounts of his early life vary, but most of them say he was a singing boy at St. Mark's, Venice, when, at the age of thirteen, he captivated a Bavarian nobleman, who procured his release and took him off to Munich. There he was carefully trained. In 1681, his first opera, *Marco Aurelio*, appeared. In 1689, he moved to Hanover, where the new opera house, described as the most beautiful in all Germany, was inaugurated by his *Henrico Leone*. In 1710, Handel succeeded him as the Hanoverian Kapellmeister. He died in Frankfurt. His life and his music alike provide a bridge between Francesco Cavalli and Handel, between seventeenth-century Venetian opera and international opera of the early eighteenth century. Hugo Riemann, who produced an edition of *Alarico*, one of the two Steffani operas in print, claimed that Alessandro Scarlatti was less intimate, less delicate than Steffani, and that Lully lacked his charm and tenderness of melodic invention.

Castelfranco itself may have played a small part in Steffani's life, but it is playing a large one in the revival of his music. The town's principal theatre, the Teatro Accademico, was designed in the mid-eighteenth century by Francesco Maria Preti (architect of the Duomo, and of the Villa Strà, the most opulent of the villas along the Brenta). It was falling into disrepair when, in 1970, the Commune of Castelfranco acquired it, restored its beauty and usefulness, and re-established it as the center of the town's musical and theatrical life. This exquisite little house—it seats fewer than four hundred—was reopened in 1975 with a performance of Steffani's *Tassilone*, given by the Clarion Opera Group. The following year, Clarion revived *Tassilone* and produced Cavalli's *Giasone*. This year, it did Steffani's *Niobe, regina di Tebe* and Baldassare Galuppi's *Arcadia in Brenta*. In New York, the Clarion Music Society has long been cherished for its productions, in concert form or semi-staged, of unfamiliar works—among them Dittersdorf's *Arcifanfano*, Hasse's *Olimpiade*, Keiser's *Croesus*, Mayr's *Medea in Corinto*, Piccinni's *Didon*. *Tassilone* had its first Clarion performance in Alice Tully Hall in 1973. In Castelfranco, the Music Society becomes an Opera Group, treading the stage, and from its summer base there it ranges through Venetia to provide a three-week Festival of Venetian Music. This year, *Niobe* was also done in the Teatro Olimpico at Vicenza, and *L'Arcadia in Brenta* visited the Teatro Duse in Asolo. The Cavalli Vespers were sung and played in San Zenone degli Ezzelini, in Mogliano Veneto, and in St. Mark's itself. And chamber concerts were given in several of the villas of the region. It is good to hear Venetian music beneath the Venetian skies—church music in the resonant spaces for which it was written and Venetian chamber music in Palladian chambers. Walking to the eighteenth-century Teatro Accademico in the citadel center of Castelfranco—which is walled, and is ringed by a moat and then by enormous plane trees—predisposes a listener to pleasure more surely than walking Broadway to reach Alice Tully Hall. Nevertheless, ambience is not all. The musical pleasures of the Clarion *Niobe* that I heard in Tully Hall this month outweighed those of the Clarion *Arcadia* that I saw and heard in Castelfranco.

The librettist of *Niobe*, Luigi Orlandi, drew his main matter from the sixth book of *Metamorphoses*. Amphion by his song raises the walls of Thebes. The reckless pride of his wife, Niobe, draws down the anger of Diana and Apollo, who slay her children; she turns to stone, a statue with tears of grief trickling down its cheeks. But Orlandi went beyond his source, increased the cast, and, to the Ovidian Argomento that introduces his libretto, added what he called "the following likelihoods": that Creon, a Thessalian prince, came to besiege Thebes (in revenge for the murder by Amphion of Dirce, Creon's aunt by marriage), fell in love with Niobe, and, aided by the arts of Polyphernus, "the chief magician of Attica" and another of Dirce's relations, enjoyed her for a while; that Tiberinus came to Thebes in quest of glory, fell in love with Manto, Tiresias's daughter, and took her back to Latium as his bride; and that Amphion, weary of rule, retired into scholarly seclusion, naming his wife regent and one Cleartes (who was also in love with Niobe) prime minister. Any attempt to relate clearly the elaborate twists of the plot would fail, but in performance one follows it from incident to incident easily enough. And the character drawing of Amphion and Niobe is so vivid that one suspects real life at one of the German courts may even have provided models for the ruler, versed in music, science, and literature, who prefers study to cares of state, and his haughty, ambitious wife, so proud of her position, of her lineage (both granddaughter and daughter-in-law of Jove), of her brilliant children, and of the beauty and intelligence that make distinguished men her slaves. Amphion (a castrato role) and Niobe both seem to be recognizable people. Niobe's relations with her scholarly husband, with her respectful admirer, Cleartes, and with the bold seducer, Creon, who sweeps her off her feet, all seem very real.

After the Argomento, in the original libretto, comes a scenario and then a list of machines. The Munich theatre must have been very well equipped. "From afar, a gigantic monster suddenly appears, moving to the front of the stage. It suddenly changes into many warriors, leaving a small cloud on the ground, in which Creon is discovered sleeping, with Polyphernus standing beside him." At a beautiful air from Amphion, rocks and stones arise, and fall into place as the walls of Thebes. "Creon and Polyphernus ascend from below, astride two monsters." To the strains of a march, Niobe's children advance, on a triumphal car, into the great square at Thebes, thronged with populace; then "in a sudden earthquake one sees buildings fall; clouds darken the stage amid lightning, thunder, and thunderbolts. On high, Latona, Diana, and Apollo appear, with a company of gods, to strike the triumphal car with bolts of lightning, and then depart." Those are a few of the stage directions in a libretto where monsters and clouds provide the principal means of conveyance, and transformation scenes abound. Backstage at Castelfranco, I saw tons of lighting equipment packed for return to the University of California at Irvine, whence it had been borrowed to create, by means of elaborate projections, the setting for *Niobe*. In Tully Hall, things were simpler. Clayton Garrison had reduced his Castelfranco staging to little more than entries and exits; one knew who was present in any scene and who was eavesdropping on whom, and could build the spectacular scenery in imagination while following the libretto that was provided. Since the men of the Clarion cast were very poor actors, I'm not sure that the human drama of *Niobe* was any less well served by this semi-staging.

The drama is created by the music, and Steffani's resources seem to be almost endless. He pulls out one surprise after another. His recitatives have a Venetian suppleness, eloquence, and beauty; one is transported back to the days when opera was young and its utterance united the directness of speech to the affecting power of song. His orchestra includes recorders, "piffari" (oboes were used in this performance), bassoons, and trumpets, and he rings the changes on textures and timbres with subtle mastery. Voice and instruments are often deployed in a kind of concerto grosso technique. His string writing is inventive. His rhythms are unpredictable: a four-measure period may be answered by one of five; in one aria, six-measure and five-measure strains alternate. Sometimes a voice strikes in at the very start of a number; sometimes there is an introductory ritornello; and sometimes the voice cuts into the ritornello before it is done. Steffani is very good at mood music. In the Royal Museum of Thebes, the continuo harpsichord and lutes are silenced, a small string band plays in the distance, recorders and strings play in the pit, and Amphion muses on the harmony of the spheres. In a later scene, strings play a measured tremolo, diminuendo, to represent pangs of grief in Amphion's heart. He and Niobe have the best music. His is largely reflective and reaches its climax in an astounding death scene. The voice part moves by syncopation, large leaps, broken syllables, and sudden triplet sobs. The accompaniment is a poignant network of crisscrossed chromatic lines for strings alternating between a small body and the full ensemble. Niobe joins her dying husband during the reprise of the opening section; her voice then adds cries of grief to his halting melody. He dies in mid-word, and out of key. Niobe's heart is broken; her death scene follows immediately. Again, it is a chromatic lament, but this time one of smooth lines over a simple continuo accompaniment; as she turns to marble, the last word, "morte," dies on her lips after the first syllable, and instruments alone complete the cadence.

Elaine Bonazzi sang Amphion with much feeling for word, phrase, and affect; she was very moving. Niobe's earlier music, as befits her character, is energetic and brilliant; Joy Zornig sang it with considerable bravura and skill, and then made something wonderful of the death scene. Susan Belling was delightful in the simpler, innocent music of Manto. The men had less character, but the smooth, fluent tenor of Hayden Blanchard (Tiberinus) and the well-defined falsetto of Jeffrey Dooley (Cleartes) could be admired. Daniel Collins (Creon), Sidney Johnson (Tiresias), and Raymond Murcell (Polyphernus) completed a confident and well-prepared cast. Newell Jenkins had edited a score from the autograph, which is in Vienna. The work was given with few cuts (the show lasted nearly three and a half hours, with two short intermissions), and even those cuts which had been indicated by Steffani himself could be regretted, since his level of invention is so consistently high. Mr. Jenkins conducted with a sure command of dramatic pace and with great feeling for the variety of moods, the picturesqueness and color of the scoring, and its rhythmic and harmonic points of expression. Where I sat, the two lutes often sounded feeble and faint; some arias seemed to proceed at times over a bare bass line. But otherwise all went well. One looks forward eagerly to *La libertà contenta*, the Steffani opera that Clarion is preparing for performance in Castelfranco next year. [Clarion's New York performance of *La libertà* is reviewed on page 473.]

L'Arcadia in Brenta (which Clarion has not yet presented this side of the Atlantic) is an important work in operatic history—Goldoni's first comic libretto and Galuppi's first great comic success. Within four years of its première, in Venice in 1749, the piece had made the rounds of Italy and Germany. It has an amusing plot—a houseparty in a Brenta villa whose owner lacks the funds to entertain his guests as lavishly as they expect—a witty libretto, lively music, and an extended second-act finale that is a milestone in the history of matching formal musical structure to dramatic incident. But, with the exception of the versatile Miss Bonazzi, the American cast showed small ability to play Italian comedy. Miss Zornig and Miss Belling sang charmingly. The men tended to primp and posture, acting stock fops instead of bringing the characters to life by use of the words. Mr. Jenkins's instrumentalists, from Venice, were less adept than those he had in New York for *Niobe*. With all the Brenta marvels at hand to inspire him, the designer, Richard Triplett, settled for dull, coarse scenery in dark colors. For me, the evening fell rather flat; but I should report that the Castelfrancans evidently enjoyed it.

November 28, 1977

Letters, Numbers, and Notes

Back in the sixteenth century, Josquin des Prez wrote a mass for Ercole, Duke of Ferrara, on a theme whose notes in solmization have the same vowels as *Hercules dux Ferrariae: re ut re ut re fa mi re*. In the seventeenth century, melodic methods of enciphering verbal messages were common. In the early eighteenth century, if the numerologist-musicologists are to be trusted, Bach must have counted, counted, counted while he set notes to paper. If $A = 1$, $B = 2$, etc. (*I* and *J* counting as the same letter), his own name is a mystic network of sevens, woven with a doubled profession of faith (*Credo* = 43, and *Sebastian* = 2×43) and a dedication to God (at the end of his scores he abbreviated *Soli Deo Gloria* to *SDG*, = 29, which is the sum of *JSB*, and half that of *Johann*). *Johann Sebastian Bach* = 158, and $1 + 5 + 8 = 2 \times 7$. *Bach* = $2 \times$

7, or 14, and *J. S. Bach* = 41, its reversal. In one of the latest essays on the subject, Gunno Klingfors's "Number Symbolism in Bach's Cantatas," included in Volume 17 of "Das Kantatenwerk," the recording-in-progress of all Bach's cantatas, the author declares that "it is not unbelievable that Bach looked upon this as a sign that he was 'a born musician.'" He goes on to count numbers of parts, of measures, of notes in the fugue subject, of entries, of notes in the oboe and continuo parts in Cantata No. 50, and to find significance in them.

In the nineteenth century, Schumann devised a musical cipher that enabled him to thread the name of his beloved Clara into composition after composition and, when setting about the composition of a *Hermann und Dorothea* overture, to turn those two names into notes that could provide a starting point for his music. In the twentieth century, Berg used the musical letters in the three names Arnold Schönberg, Anton Webern, and Alban Berg to make themes for his Chamber Concerto—in three movements, the measure counts of which are divisible by three and by forty, Berg's age on the day he completed the piece. For the extramusical determinants of the notes, tempo, and duration of Berg's Lyric Suite, see George Perle's "The Secret Programme of the Lyric Suite," in *The Musical Times* for August, September, and October 1977. In 1969, Olivier Messiaen composed his *Méditations sur le mystère de la Sainte Trinité* by "translating" sentences of St. Thomas Aquinas into music after a system that allots to each letter of the Latin words not only a fixed pitch but also a fixed duration.

These examples of starting points for composition—readers will no doubt think of many others—occurred to me as I read Frank Lewin's remarks on his *Variations of Greek Themes,* a song cycle commissioned by the Chamber Music Society of Lincoln Center, given its first performances last week, and broadcast by WNCN. Lewin's texts are eight of the twelve poems, collected under the same title, that Edwin Arlington Robinson appended to the 1915 edition of his *Captain Craig.* Eleven of them are paraphrases of epigrams by Greek poets, among whom Sappho is the only familiar name. (The twelfth, "With Sappho's Compliments," is a satire by Robinson and was dropped from later editions.) To find music for them, Lewin allowed all sorts of associations—numerological, historical, musicological, ethnic, ancient, popular—to play upon his imagination. Ancient Greece suggests modes. The lines of the first song, "A Happy Man," are set for the most part in the Dorian and Hypolydian modes on A or E (and so the general effect is of a song in A minor, with antique touches). But lines with the word "death" or "dead" in them shift to the Locrian mode on D-sharp or A-sharp—an "unreal" mode, postulated by theorists in the sixteenth century. (Palestrina once wrote the at the time "nonexistent" note D-sharp to give a special strangeness to his setting of the phrase "Timor mortis conturbat me.") The cycle is composed for contralto and an ensemble of flute, viola, harp, and piano. Choirs based on open fifths from harp or piano accompany the first song; a change of instrument marks a change of mode. Between the stanzas, flute and viola play a little refrain, sliding in and out of exact unison or octave in a way that suggests the timbre of folk musicians. Seven-eight is almost the Greek national metre—the classical *epitritos*, the long-short-long-long of popular dances—and the song maintains this gentle, dancing rhythm through its smooth, simple phrases.

The second poem has numbers in it: "The day when Charmus ran with five . . . He came in *seventh*. . . . And with *four* more for company He would have been *eleventh*." They suggested intervals to use. Flute changes to piccolo and evokes a sports-day band. Scurrying figures depict the runners, and canons their successive passages along the same stretch of the course. The third poem deals with twelves—"Eutychides . . . Is going down where he belongs. . . . He is coming with twelve lyres, And with more than twice twelve quires"—and is set in a highly developed twelve-note system. With such a method at his fingertips, Eutychides could obviously pour out his "stuff" by the ream. A crazy piano cadenza touches each note of the keyboard once. Baroque word-painting (like Bach's way of setting the *high* of *high priest* to a high note) is employed to make graphic the bad poet's descent, and mocking laughter. The sound of his name may have suggested some rapid ticking figures. The song is difficult to perform; in fact, it was omitted at the Chamber Music Society première.

Its omission disturbed the shape of this carefully planned cycle. One needed more contrast before the fourth song, which returns to modes and to the methods of the first while using them in a denser, more highly developed way. Next, there is an instrumental dance in 7/8, made from a catchy four-bar "circling" tune—a folk borrowing—repeated, over an open-fifth drone, with simple and then increasingly sophisticated variations. The players imitate the timbres of folk instruments. The tune speeds up to become a spinning accompaniment figure for the fifth song, a dry, rather bitter scherzo. The sixth is a Sapphic epitaph—"This dust was Timas"—which Lewin has set as if it were a Sappho fragment. Only a word or two of each line emerges clearly from a background of humming and vocalizing, of passionate but gentle wailing lament (slides and quarter tones): "Timas . . . almost . . . her bri . . . home . . . Perseph . . ."—the rest is to be imagined, to be deduced from a blurred web of sound in which the falling semitones of grief are prominent and a scrap of a traditional Greek threnody takes shape for a moment. After an epitaph all but lost, one fully preserved: the next poem is a sonnet, a memorial to Doricha, beloved of Sappho's brother. The two quatrains are gravely declaimed, and then the sestet moves into full-throated, affirmative song proclaiming, in effect, that "in eternal lines to time thou growest." The music of the final song, "An Inscription by the Sea," recalls, line by line, the earlier songs, one by one, in reverse order. It is a summation and an envoy. The two principal metres of the cycle are here combined: harp and piano play in 7/8 while voice, viola, and flute move in 2/2. A steady, deep ripple from the piano suggests the ever-moving, cradling sea. In the composer's words, "the opening pedal on A-flat in flute and viola suggests a lonely immensity and the unvarying distant horizon; the harp picks up this note and scatters it through different octaves, providing flecks of brightness." At the line "My fate, O stranger, was to drown" the instruments well up for a moment to engulf the singer. The gap between her voice and the piccolo doubling the chant two octaves higher seems to make manifest distances of time and space.

Music's imagery is formed in many ways. The rumbling of the bass drum in the final scene of *Rigoletto* is simply and directly imitative of thunder, but the sudden streaks from flute and piccolo are a sonic metaphor for lightning. The chromatic humming of the offstage chorus is partly a wind howl imitated but also a regular musical symbol of foreboding. (And the two "derivations" conspire to create a single sense: the moaning of the wind *is* eerie.) Flute and high violins, accompanying Gilda's last utterances on earth, are Verdi's "standard props" for a death scene, and—a more complicated metaphor—he often uses the solo flute to represent a prayer rising to Heaven. High notes to evoke "lassù in cielo" and low notes sounding *de profundis* are satisfactory and self-explanatory symbols. In the patterns of wave and ripple by which composers "depict" ocean and brook, sonic and graphic associations seem to combine. Similarly, when using a long-sustained note to evoke "the unvarying distant horizon," a composer asks a listener's ear to activate his inner eye. Musical imagery of such kinds knows no language boundaries. Aural pictures conjured up by setting one part to pursue another along the same track—in fact, all musical depictions of running, leaping, gliding, spinning, suddenly stopping—can be universally understood. At another pole are what might be called the puns based on the local letter names of notes. A four-note motif on D-E-A-D carries no inherent intimations of mortality. (In transposition, it opens the *William Tell* overture.) If I were asked to compose advertising jingles for brands of *baggage* or varieties of *cabbage*, I would have themes for them ready-made—but they would be in the nature of a private joke, not expressive symbols. Messiaen referred to his musical ciphering of Aquinas as "a game." Nevertheless, letter-note rebuses *can* be expressively used—as by Bach when signing his "name" to the *Art of Fugue* and by Shostakovich when affixing his "monogram" (Д.Ш., in German D, Sch., "spelling out" the notes we call D, E-flat, C, and B) to some of his most personal music. Similarly, number imagery in music can range from the playful (as in Lewin's cycle) to the profound (honoring the Trinity in threefold statements and perfect triads). The philosopher Leibniz, an ornament of the Hanoverian court while Agostino Steffani and Handel were Kapellmeisters there, declared music to be "a secret numeration of the soul." As far as I know, no one has been busily counting notes in Steffani and Handel scores. I rather hope no one does. The results already produced by counting Bach are dizzying—and, disconcertingly, not quite dismissible. The number 144 is prominent in Revelations. Maybe it is not coincidence that Bach's Cantata No. 50, with a text from Revelations, contains 6,138 notes, and that the product of those four digits is 144.

Lewin's *Variations of Greek Themes* is an anthology of widely various ways, direct and indirect, by which a text may determine a tune, a rhythm, a form, a texture. If it were no more than that, it would be a curiosity. It is more. At the start of his notes on the cycle, the composer remarks, "For the listener, no extensive verbal explanations should be needed, since the musical language draws on our familiar vocabulary of expressive music," and at the end of them he says, "It should be emphasized that, though the devices and techniques described above were employed with calculation, the aim at all times was to be expressive, not formalistic." And his songs make their effect directly. His melodies, timbres, harmonies, rhythms, whatever their source, are evocative and affecting in themselves. One need not be able to name, or even recognize, the Greek modes to respond to the sense of antiquity they conjure up. The lilting beat of slow-quick-slow-slow dance patterns courses through a listener's senses whether he has identified the 7/8 metre or not. "Eutychides," I bet, would sound funny in performance whether or not the twelve-note parodies were appreciated. The voice part is beautifully and gratefully written, with a rare command of the weight, speed, and control that make fullest sense of the words. It was eloquently sung by Maureen Forrester, while Judith Mendenhall, flute, Scott Nickrenz, viola, Heidi Lehwalder, harp, and Charles Wadsworth, piano, made up the virtuoso ensemble.

December 5, 1977

Voices in the Wilderness

Early in this century, Edward J. Dent published a book on Alessandro Scarlatti in which eloquent claims were made for the beauty and power—Dent's recurrent words—of his music. Dent was addressing himself to "a generation that has not yet been able to shake off the false sentiment of the romantic movement," one for whom "Schumann, Wagner, and Brahms represent the normal style of musical expression." Scarlatti himself described musical composition as a science, "the daughter of Mathematics." In Dent's words, he belonged to "the severest period of classicism, when beauty and purity of style were still considered as more important than originality and violence of expression"; unlike Monteverdi, Cavalli, Schütz, Purcell, he never produced things that strike a modern listener as "astonishingly modern." He is "entirely devoid of the hysterical romanticism which makes wild experiments in the vague hope of expressing the inexpressible."

Two or three generations have passed since Dent wrote, and the products of romanticism continue to dominate the repertory of our opera houses and orchestras. Moreover, the new attention paid to seventeenth- and early-eighteenth-century music—manifest in editions that make the works available for performance, and in phonograph records that make the performances widely available to listeners—has still to do for Alessandro Scarlatti what it has done for Monteverdi, Schütz, Telemann, Vivaldi, Buxtehude, the Couperins, and Domenico Scarlatti. Slowly, his music is at last coming into print. In the sixties, five of his twenty-three surviving oratorios were published. In 1974, the Harvard University Press embarked on an edition of his operas (he wrote more than a hundred), and four volumes have so far appeared. But performances remain rare. Last week, his oratorio *Agar et Ismaele esiliati* was done in Corpus Christi Church, just north of Columbia University, in its Sunday afternoon Music Before 1800 series. Like all Scarlatti oratorios, cantatas, and operas that I have heard, it proved to be a beautiful and poetic composition.

Hagar and Ishmael Sent into Exile was his first oratorio. The surviving score is dated 1683, and in that year, it seems, Scarlatti was maestro di cappella at S. Girolamo della Carità, Philip Neri's old church and oratory, the birthplace of oratorio. But things had changed since Neri's day. *Hagar* is hardly a devotional piece. Point by point, it conforms to the late-seventeenth-century type of oratorio recommended by the veteran oratorio librettist Archangelo Spagna in his *Oratorii, overo Melodrammi sacri:* three to five characters (*Hagar* has five); a Senecan construction of protasis, epitasis, and catastrophe; rhymed recitatives as well as rhymed arias; no chorus; no narrator (since narrators have much recitative, which becomes dull); an arietta allegra to end with; and, in general, no longer a Biblical narrative but "un perfetto melodramma spirituale." In short, an entertainment scarcely differing from an opera except in its choice of subject matter and in its lack of décor. Scenic descriptions must be worked into the sung text.

This suited Scarlatti, who, as Dent said, "was not by nature a church-composer. . . . In his motets and oratorios he is often picturesque and sometimes quite beautiful; but he is too classical in spirit, too much of a poet, to write such music as is usually considered to be devotional." *Hagar* deals with the emotions of four characters. Part 1 opens with a scene in which Sarah nags, Fricka-like, at her husband, Abraham, until he agrees to send away Hagar, his Egyptian mistress, and Ishmael, the son she has borne him. Hagar and Ishmael have overheard the conversation; as they advance, Sarah departs with a triumphant "Be firm, Abraham." Hagar points out Sarah's avarice ("The more she gets"—after years of barrenness, she has borne Isaac—"the more she wants"); Ishmael offers to let Isaac inherit all. But Abraham *is* firm. The first part ends with a remarkable three-section aria, in three tempos, in which Abraham, Wotan-like, gives vent to grief at the cruel decision he has been forced to make. At the start of Part 2, he tries to shift the blame: "Though false to my son, I am true to God." Sarah remarks that merciful Heaven mingles one person's joy with another's sorrow, and exults in her own good fortune. When Abraham remains sad, she hints that perhaps he is still sighing for Hagar. She is not a likable woman. The scene changes to the burning wilderness, where Ishmael is dying of thirst. There are some poignant and affecting arias for him and his mother. In the nick of time, an angel appears, indicates a refreshing brook, and in an arietta allegra produces a somewhat facile moral: "Foolish, he who thinks his grief eternal: tho' Heaven send darts, it sends also dew. . . . Violets blossom after rime and ice." The final number of an oratorio, Spagna said, should "disperse the audience with universal approval," and I heard the catchy tune of the angel's "È folle chi paventa," which has been sweetly and freshly sung by Jane Bryden, being hummed down Broadway as the Corpus Christi audience dispersed.

The church is small; it holds about three hundred. Built in the thirties, it follows the plan of a late-seventeenth-century city church, with pews and galleried aisles. The walls are paneled in white-painted wood; the ceiling is coffered. The acoustics are ideal—resonant but not boomy, intimate but not cramped. In Scarlatti's day, oratorio performances were sometimes very grand. Handel had twenty-three violins and six double-basses at the première of *La resurrezione* (Rome, 1708, at the Ruspoli palace); G. M. Orlandini had "a great quantity of instruments," including three harpsichords, to accompany his *Il figliuol prodigo* (Florence, 1712, in the Church of S. Jacopo). Louise Basbas, maestra di cappella at Corpus Christi and director of this *Hagar*, had just a baroque string quartet, a dolcian, and a lute or an archlute, while she presided at a small organ. (Most accounts of oratorio performances tell of harpsichords, not an organ; in any case, the instrument used here was almost too gentle to give any decisive lead.) The performance was perfectly scaled to its setting. Young, pure voices filled the church. There was no forcing, yet no feebleness. Energy could be directed to details of expression, and all the performers, singers and players alike, were keen, sensitive musicians and polished, stylish executants. In baroque oratorio, as in baroque opera, transvestism is common: Handel's Magdalen in *La resurrezione* may be a prima donna role, but the Pope reproved Prince Ruspoli for allowing a woman to take it; the Prodigal's mother in Orlandini's oratorio was sung by a male alto. At Corpus Christi, Hagar, an alto role, was taken with exquisite accomplishment by Jeffrey Gall, a countertenor of smooth, firm tones untainted by hoot or shriek, one who ranged high in some apt, well-judged decorations and was led low, into a chest voice that he skillfully matched to the rest, by the written range of the part. Ishmael, a soprano, was brightly, touchingly, and truly sung by Ann Monoyios. Brenda Fairaday was Sarah, another soprano, and Arthur Burrows was Abraham, bass.

As David Poultney, the author of a dissertation on Scarlatti's oratorios, has pointed out, each aria in the *Hagar* libretto is written to a different metre and verse structure. In the music there is nothing quite so patently dramatic as in the later oratorio *Giuditta*—but then Judith is the heroine of a rather more eventful tale. (I once saw *Giuditta* staged—the three-voice version; Scarlatti treated the subject twice—and it worked quite well.) But there is variety of mood as of metre, and there is sharpness in the character drawing. The piece is early Scarlatti: one does not find quite the melodic copiousness of his prime. Many of the arias are built from a ground bass. (One of them,

Hagar's "Qui del sol," has an almost boogie lilt.) None of them is in da capo form. But in all of them, as Dent said of Scarlatti in general, "there is not only a perfect proportion of main divisions, but every bar displays the most subtly ingenious organization of figure." The recitatives are carefully and beautifully composed. The rhythmic periods are flexible. The purity of the melodic outlines is enhanced by vivid coloratura touches of word painting. Voices and instruments are used in delicately balanced dialogue. An Italian-English libretto, distributed free of charge, made the pleasures of the afternoon complete.

Nothing I've heard in the big halls in recent weeks has been as memorable, or worth more than cursory comment. The Philharmonic has put a new piece on just about every other bill—adventurous planning, but so far the works themselves have proved negligible. The second of the season's four concerto commissions for Philharmonic soloists was Michael Colgrass's *Déjà Vu*, for percussion quartet and orchestra. There is technical ingenuity in the way Colgrass uses the main orchestra to enhance percussion sounds: "the way a cook uses herbs—to heighten the subtle flavors of the various percussion instruments and make them more memorable." The result slipped down easily—and was about as nourishing as a stew in which thyme, basil, marjoram, and bay are the main ingredients and meat and veg the seasoning. The third commission, Vincent Persichetti's Concerto for English horn and string orchestra, Op. 137, was dull "well-made" stuff, lit only by the virtuoso playing of Thomas Stacy. Erich Leinsdorf conducted both concerts. At each, there was also a piano concerto. After the Colgrass, Mark Zeltser, an emigrant from the Soviet Union, made his American début as soloist in Prokofiev's Second Concerto, to which he brought huge hands, huge tone, brilliance, energy, and lyricism. He was like a Lazar Berman without the banging. The work doesn't tell one much about a pianist's personality, but it revealed many facets of Mr. Zeltser's formidable technique. Before the Persichetti, Murray Perahia played Mozart's C-major Concerto, K. 467. He is, in my view, an overrated pianist: what some praise as grace and gentleness I hear as a weak and sentimental handling of line. Lyrical phrases are seldom firmly closed but wilt away into coy inaudibility. [In more recent performances, Mr. Perahia's Mozart playing has been firmer.] Jacob Druckman's *Chiaroscuro*, the Cleveland work in the six-orchestra Bicentennial commissions of last season (each piece to be played by each of the orchestras), came to the Philharmonic in a concert conducted by Lorin Maazel. It is made, early-Ligeti fashion, of overlapping washes of sound, dark and dense or simple and shining. The effect was preludial; one waited for something definite and interesting to happen—and was still waiting when, eighteen minutes later, the end arrived. There followed Sibelius's Seventh Symphony, rather lumpily played, and then Shostakovich's Fifth, boldly and bravely done.

The Rotterdam Philharmonic ended its American tour at Carnegie Hall last month with a performance of Mahler's First Symphony, coarsely played, and coarsely conducted by Edo de Waart. Perhaps rigors of touring had upset the players' intonation and rubbed all bloom from their tone. Before the symphony, Jessye Norman sang six Strauss songs. The voice is glorious—warm, supple, and majestic through a very wide range. One beautifully produced note succeeded another: some were soft and floating, some were huge (yet so effortless that one scarcely appreciated their amplitude until one realized that they were sailing easily over an unrestrained full-orchestra swell), and all could be relished. Miss Norman carefully "edited" every note as she went along, and then carefully prepared, placed, and launched the next on its career into the hall. It was noble vocalism that held the promise of tremendous performances once the splendid sounds are joined into a connected sense. The concert opened with Tristan Keuris's Sinfonia, a 1975 piece that, to modest effect, deploys an enormous orchestra with gusto and suddenly fades to a rapt, sentimental close.

At its Carnegie visit last week, the Philadelphia Orchestra was conducted by Riccardo Muti, whose music making was in strong contrast to that of Claudio Abbado, the conductor at its previous visit. Both concerts began with Mozart. Abbado combined the virtues of grace, sensuous beauty, tenderness, and classical integrity; he was "Italian" in the way that Virgil, Dante, Raphael, and Toscanini are Italian. Muti was shallow, showy, and self-seeking. The phrases of his Mozart—the Divertimento in D, K. 334—did not breathe or move naturally. He then introduced to New York Bruno Bettinelli's *Varianti per orchestra* (1970), yet another dull "well-made" piece, and ended the concert with an account of Schumann's Fourth Symphony in which obvious points were stressed in a superficially effective way.

There were greater rewards to be gained by staying at home. One Sunday afternoon, WNCN offered another chance of hearing Michael Tippett's Fourth Symphony played by the Chicago Symphony under Solti. The same day, WQXR broadcast Elliott Carter's Symphony of Three Orchestras, recorded at a Philharmonic concert in February; this, the Philharmonic commission, is the great thing that emerged from that six-orchestra Bicentennial scheme. Another of last season's major events, the Boston Symphony's performance of Roger Sessions's masterpiece *When Lilacs Last in the Dooryard Bloom'd*, became available for repeated hearing on New World Records (NW 296).

December 12, 1977

The Sun's Return

Outside Russia, the operas of Rimsky-Korsakov have still to take the place that should be theirs. Only *The Golden Cockerel*, the last but not the best or most beautiful of them, is played with any frequency. (City Opera revives its production of that piece in the spring.) In nearly a quarter century of assiduous operagoing, I have caught only three other Rimsky operas on the stage: the lovely *Snow Maiden*, which used to be in the Sadler's Wells repertory; *Mozart and Salieri*, a two-man show, and not characteristic; and *Christmas Eve*, which has just been given what was probably its American stage première by the Indiana University Opera Theatre, in Bloomington. But radio and records (in the current record catalogue, Deutsche Grammophon has a *May Night* and Angel a *Tsar's Bride*) have provided chances of hearing most of the rest, and the more I hear of Rimsky's operas the more strongly I feel that received opinion about them needs revision. The commentators pay tribute to his orchestral virtuosity, his long-breathed sinuous melodies, his glittering or lyrical tone pictures, and his buoyant tunefulness in episodes based on or influenced by folk songs. Then they usually spoil things by accusing him of mechanical facility. "There is an inner coldness about his music," say the authors of *The Record Guide*, "which is decorative and ingenious rather than heartfelt." This music, which I find so captivating, is nourished from three rich stores: folk history, legend, and lore; folk song; and the music of composers to whom his response was quick, fresh, and appreciative. His best works live in the seasons and are warmed by the sun. In his autobiography, accounts of composing *The Snow Maiden, Christmas Eve*, and *Sadko* are woven with summer memories of trees, birds, and lakes. Early in his career, he was "enthralled by the poetic side of the cult of sun worship." His second opera, *May Night*, led to "a series of fantastic operas in which the worship of the sun and of sun gods is introduced." In *The Snow Maiden*, folk song, bird song, and ancient chants come together. "The melodies of ancient Orthodox canticles, are they not of ancient pagan origin? . . . The holidays of Easter, Trinity Sunday, etc., are they not Christianity's adaptations of the pagan sun cult?" In the final scenes of *Christmas Eve*, when the sun rises on Christmas Day, not the birth of the Christ Child but the return of the sun gods Kolyada and Ovsen is celebrated. In German, the opera is published as *Sonnwend-nacht*—the night of the solstice.

    Christmas Eve (1895) is the second of Rimsky's two Gogol operas, the other being *May Night* (1880). Both librettos are drawn from the collection of tales *Nights on a Farm near Dikanka* (which also includes *The Fair at Soro-chints*, made into a libretto by Mussorgsky). The Devil, on the last night of his winter reign, before the sun gods put him to flight, decides to play a prank on Vakula the smith. But Vakula succeeds in harnessing *him,* and orders him to change into a fiery steed. In a wild night ride, Vakula flies from the Ukraine to St. Petersburg, through clouds and comets and a swarm of airborne sorcerers, to arrive at Catherine the Great's court. There the Tsaritsa graciously grants his request for a pair of her *cheriviky,* or fine leather boots: Oxana, the haughty village beauty, has demanded a pair as the price of becoming Vakula's bride. The comic characters include the Devil, the deacon, the mayor, and Oxana's father, Chub, all of whom pay Christmas Eve visits to Vakula's mother, Solokha, a merry widow who is also a witch. Each hides in a coal sack when the next inopportunely arrives; and Vakula lugs all the sacks outside, where they are discovered by carolers.

The same tale is the basis of Tchaikovsky's *Vakula the Smith* (1876) and its revision as *Cherevichky* (1887), a bewitching piece and, the composer said, "so far as the music is concerned, almost my best opera." His *Vakula* had won a competition for setting a libretto by Jakov Polonsky. Rimsky, one of the judges, was attracted to the tale but delayed his own handling of it, to his own libretto, until after Tchaikovsky's death. (However, his other Gogol opera had in a way already superseded Tchaikovsky's Gogol opera, in that it was first performed in the *Vakula* décor, vernally repainted to turn Christmas Eve into May Night.) *Cherevichky,* which reached the New Amsterdam Theatre in 1922 and the New York City Opera, as *The Golden Slippers,* in 1955, is indeed a delightful piece, worth a place in the repertory, and a company that does it might as well do *Christmas Eve,* another delightful piece, since the scenic requirements are almost identical. Of Tchaikovsky's eight scenes and Rimsky's nine, six correspond.

Tchaikovsky's *Vakula* and *Snow Maiden* are the scores in which he drew closest to the manner of Glinka and the nationalists, and made most use of folk song: both contain numbers that would not sound out of place in *Christmas Eve* or in Rimsky's *Snow Maiden.* But in an extended comparison differences between the two composers soon become clear. Loving both of them, and all four works, I would keep any comparison uninvidious. It might be suggested that Tchaikovsky's outlines are generally softer, his melodic shapes and his timbres less piquantly national. He often writes what Gerald Abraham has called "that unmistakable kind of cantilena, that species of Bellini-with-a-Russian-accent, to which [he] alone has ever had the real secret." He identifies with young lovers where Rimsky depicts them. Rimsky, as Abraham writes, "more successfully hits off the character of Gogol's coquette. But Tchaikovsky's Oxana is easier to fall in love with." Tchaikovsky appeals directly to the emotions; Rimsky, who did not wear his heart on his sleeve, appeals to the romantic imagination, in a more objective way. One interprets; the other presents. For two acts, *Vakula* and *Christmas Eve* run in parallel. Then Tchaikovsky leads his lovelorn hero to a riverbank, where russalkas sing from beneath the ice and Vakula pours out his grief in a melancholy (and very beautiful) aria. Rimsky, sticking to Gogol, takes him to a wizard's hut, where savory fritters, keeping time to a quaint and cunningly harmonized ostinato, leap from a bowl into the wizard's mouth. One scene is emotional, the other fantastic.

By the time of *Christmas Eve*, Rimsky had worked over Dargomizhsky's *The Stone Guest*, Glinka's two operas, Borodin's *Prince Igor*, Mussorgsky's *Khovanshchina*, and parts of his *Boris Godunov*—scoring, arranging, and editing in various degrees. From all that he touched he learned. Berlioz's *Treatise on Instrumentation* had been his first manual. (The Ride to the Abyss in *La Damnation* is the model for the Ride to St. Petersburg in *Christmas Eve*.) Editing Glinka had been "an unexpected schooling. . . . I had to go through Glinka's style and instrumentation to their last insignificant little note." *The Bartered Bride*, given in St. Petersburg in 1871, left an evident mark on his Gogol operas. The scoring of *The Ring*, given in St. Petersburg in 1889 and closely studied by Rimsky and Glazunov, "began to form a part of our orchestral tricks of the trade." Yet his own manner is entirely personal. It takes its life from a delight in tunes and in presenting them to the best possible advantage, and from a delight in sounds—bright, unusual instrumental timbres and piquant harmonic juxtapositions. The *Christmas Eve* prelude opens with a series of common major chords—on E, C-sharp, A, F-sharp, D, B, G—each differently scored. It might be deemed a mechanical sequence of descending thirds alternately minor and major—yet the effect is fresh and magical. Then a horn melody comes winding out and winging aloft—then violins, then solo clarinet—against a background of slow-shifting harmonies that paint the wide night sky, a background founded on long pedal points and touched with flecks of frosty brilliance from the glockenspiel. One can open the score anywhere to find passages of comparable imagination and beauty.

Rimsky's reading inspired in him a vision of Old Russia: of people living by the seasons, telling their tales, laughing, loving, inventing their songs, and feeling awe at the wonders of the universe. The Russian countryside he viewed with pantheistic eyes: "Every gnarled branch or moss-grown stump appeared to me the Wood Demon or his abode; the forest Volchinyets, the enchanted wood in which Mizgir was lost; the triple echo heard from our balcony, the voices of wood sprites or other supernatural beings." Meanwhile, Berlioz, Glinka, Borodin, and the rest filled his ears with wonderful sounds. A world of captivating stories and another of captivating music lay before him; journeying in both, he set down his adventures with zest, freshness, lyricism, and a natural mastery that, even at its least inspired, I would describe as attractively naïve—so little is it disturbed by self-doubt or straining—rather than heartlessly mechanical.

Loewenberg's *Annals of Opera* (1943) records no performances of *Christmas Eve* outside Russia, but there have been postwar performances in Germany, Switzerland, and Italy. The recent Zurich and Bologna productions were given in décor by Max Röthlisberger, Bloomington's chief designer, and so was the Bloomington production. His village scenes were very attractive. The fritters leaped on cue into the wizard's mouth. The night ride through the sky was a lively, entertaining spectacle managed after the fashion of the Prague puppet theatre. St. Petersburg became visible in the distance and loomed up as a projection filling the front gauze. Catherine's court was a glittering storybook illustration.

Rimsky composed for smooth, flexible, sweetly plangent, superbly trained Russian Imperial singers; the style and the sound need to be studied on records, many of which have now been reissued. (The first Vakula, Ivan Ershov, had just joined the Petersburg troupe; a few years later he made memorable records of Meyerbeer and Wagner arias. Chaliapin, it seems, also played a small part in the première.) Existing English translations of Russian operas often make it hard for singers to preserve the necessary smoothness and suppleness of line, but Richard Strawn and Peteris Silins's most musical new English version of *Christmas Eve*, prepared specially for Bloomington, did much to foster limpid tone and liquid phrasing while making clear dramatic sense. There were two casts, which I heard on successive nights. None of the singing was less than agreeable, and much of it was sweet, true, and accomplished. The outstanding performers were Julia Conwell and Lynelle Frankforter (the two Oxanas, sopranos) Bernard Lowe (Vakula, tenor), and Kevin Langan (a Chub with a smooth, beautiful bass). Students inevitably find it hard to play ripely comic character roles. Ross Allen, who directed, allowed the "heavies" some stock staginess instead of demeanor based on real-life observation, but that—a failing not limited to student stages—was the only weakness in a presentation any professional company might envy. Bryan Balkwill, who conducted, does not favor hard-edged phrasing or gleaming, enameled, unfeeling sound. He stressed the lyricism of the piece, the long romantic unfoldings, the charm. He did not miss the brilliance— what Rimsky conductor could?—but he caught, too, the tenderness and humanity of this lovable, engaging opera.

December 19, 1977

City Pastoral

Rameau's tragédies lyriques and opéras-ballets are so seldom staged in New York that the chance of hearing even a single entrée from one of them becomes something to be grateful for. And when that entrée is the third part, "La Danse," of *Les Fêtes d'Hébé*, expectation runs very high. Readers of Cuthbert Girdlestone's *Jean-Philippe Rameau* will remember his claims that no work of Rameau's "contains more variety or gives so kaleidoscopically complete a view of his range in lyric, tragedy, and pastoral" and that the closing sequence is "one long enchantment"—that "short of bringing the music to the reader, there is no way of expressing its beauty, its peculiar mixture of delight, nostalgic unreality and mystery." Girdlestone tries to express it, with extensive music quotations and in urgent prose:

> The dance that follows, in which the music seems to depict the shepherds, drunk with love, circling blindly round Églé, is certainly more evocative of a mysterious Eastern cult than of rural innocence. It is one of the most impressionistic pieces in eighteenth-century music, and the magic, so often unconvincingly rendered, is here overwhelming. The effect it makes as one turns the page and comes upon it without warning is unforgettable, even when one does not know how it is scored. Musettes and hautboys play in unison, sustained by the thick packing of strings.... This exotic piece gives one the taste which Russian and Spanish music, now so hackneyed, must have given in their novelty to nineteenth-century audiences.

On Monday last week, in Alice Tully Hall, "La Danse" was performed by the Concert Royal Orchestra and the New York Baroque Dance Company, and even though it was a performance on a tiny scale, without décor, it was more than enough to show the greatness of Rameau's music. At the first performance of *Les Fêtes*, in 1739, Rameau had perhaps twenty violins (six first-violin and four second-violin parts survive in the Paris Opera library); James Richman, who directs the Concert Royal, had just five. At the Opéra, there were a chorus of thirty-four and a corps de ballet of sixteen (six nymphs, six shepherds, two fauns, and two sylvans); in Tully Hall there was a chorus of nine and there were just four dancers. Musettes, petites flûtes, the drum that should accompany the entry of Terpsichore and her train, and the optional horns were missing. Since there was only one male dancer, the musette en rondeau of "bergers amoureux d'Églé"—the subject of Girdlestone's paragraph above—had to produce its effect largely in the imagination, and through the ear. But the ear was well served. Georg Muffat, that student of Lullian performance practice, summed up (in 1698) the requirements of playing French dance music:

> *Contactus, plectrum, tempus, mos, atque venustas*
> *Efficient alacrem, dulcisonamque chelyn.*

Which might be rendered: Fingering (and true intonation), bowing, tempo, style, and ornamentation impart vivacity and sweet tone to the instrument. The distich holds good for Rameau, too. The Concert Royal players, who used authentic instruments, played admirably in tune, most of the time. They knew about eighteenth-century bowing. Their tone was sweet. Sparingly but strikingly they obeyed Muffat's instruction to "use with discernment certain ornaments making the pieces much more beautiful and agreeable, lighting them up, as it were, with sparkling precious stones." And because they were playing for dancers they were led to the right tempi. French baroque music, it has been well said, "speaks of the dance in all its guises," and Muffat remarked that the best French fiddlers could find and maintain the right *mouvement* for a piece because they understood the dance so well.

The plot of "La Danse" is slight. Mercury (tenor) has been promised a bride, and Aegle (soprano), a disciple of Terpsichore, a bridegroom. From Eurilas (bass), a swain who believes that by playing it cool he can win Aegle's love, Mercury learns that Aegle's choice has not yet been made. She enters, dancing to the oboe piping of the shepherd Palemon; Mercury adds a vocal descant, and soon she is dancing to *his* tune; Palemon departs in a huff, smashing his pipe. Aegle and Mercury sing a rapturous duet. The shepherds arrive, to dance their amorous rondeau. Aegle, a garland in her hand, joins them in a gavotte—and then presents her garland to Mercury. The scene changes from a woodland to a splendid garden, where, at Mercury's request, Aegle is admitted to Terpsichore's court.

Louis XV's performers were versatile. In a 1747 revival of *Les Fêtes d'Hébé*, Marie Camargo both sang and danced as Aegle. So did Madeleine Guimard in 1770, when M. Dubois, the Palemon, was praised in the *Mercure* for both his oboe playing and his dancing. In the Tully Hall performance, Ann Monoyios, the Aegle, sang sweetly and truly and she also danced with grace. Howard Crook, the Mercury, stood and moved elegantly, and sang sweetly, but should have declaimed the text rather more boldly. His coloratura ariette vive, "L'objet qui règne dans mon âme," was omitted, and this was a pity, for on a recent Nonesuch disc of Purcell airs and duets (H–71343) he shows a pretty command of divisions. Jan Opalach, the Eurilas, sang in soft focus. The choreography was by the directors of the New York Baroque Dance Company, Ann Jacoby and Catherine Turocy, and the latter was a commanding Terpischore. Baroque choreography is a specialist subject; a mere musician can only report that to watch Rameau's music take plastic shape—to see his structures reflected in changing densities of stage pattern (even when the dancers are evidently too few) and hear his phrases and articulations matched to the dance movements of his day—is a revelation.

From similar small beginnings, in London, Lina Lalandi, the director of the English Bach Festival, went on to assemble a company of singers, dancers, and players versed in French baroque style who earlier this year drew a packed house to Covent Garden for their re-creation of Rameau's *La Princesse de Navarre;* the production then visited Versailles (where the piece had had its première, in 1745), Granada, and other cities. For next year, they plan a full-scale *Hippolyte et Aricie.* I hope something similar happens here. The work of the Aston Magna Foundation is helping to produce the right sort of performers. Now they need a real theatre—and, presumably, much more money—to be able to put on complete shows. "La Danse" should follow the comedy of the prologue to *Les Fêtes d'Hébé*, the lyricism of its first entrée, "La Poésie" (with Sappho and Alcaeus), and the tragic scenes of the second, "La Musique" (with Iphise and Lycurgus), for its pastoral enchantments to make their full effect.

In an age when farmers make front-page news riding into Washington by the column on tractors with "giant wheels as high as automobiles," the pastoral convention may seem very remote. But even before Rameau's day it was being questioned. In 1707, in his *Dissertation sur la poésie pastorale,* the Abbé Genest noted, "The pictures one can draw of this innocent and delightful life have no longer anything that chimes with men's feelings or with the objects that the country shows us. The luxury, passions, and anxieties that prevail in cities cause rustic simplicity and occupations to be despised; the state in which we see peasants cannot give us the least desire to resemble such shepherds." Shakespeare's Henry VI, snatching a breather during battle, thinks it a happy life to be no better than a homely swain, and delivers a long speech to that effect. Berlioz's Benvenuto Cellini, given the choice of casting his Perseus within a few hours or being hanged, takes time off to sing a leisurely aria, "Que ne suis-je un simple pasteur." But Rameau's pastoral music carries an undercurrent of melancholy. It is not simply and prettily picturesque; nor is it simply a sigh for an untroubled rural existence—"Ah! what a life were this! how sweet! how lovely!" He is not toying with *bergeries.* His shepherdesses are not modeled in porcelain. In the well-known E-major musette from the 1724 harpsichord collection, which in "La Danse" is reset for orchestra and then for chorus with solo interludes, there is a "cloying heaviness" that is "more than just quiet; it is overpowering," as Girdlestone remarked. "The mood which this very lovely piece embodies can hardly be called pleasant; it is too oppressive for that. . . . If this is the beatitude of the fields and flocks, it is an opiate blessedness and it leaves us unhappy"—as Watteau, to whom Rameau has been likened, can stir us to unhappiness even while we contemplate some of his loveliest pictures. There is more to the third entrée of *Les Fêtes d'Hébé* than an elegant entertainment. For part of each year, I live in the country—in country where peasants earn their living from the land, and in a house that once housed cows, pigs, and peasants, and now has running water and central heating. And, of course, I have the troubled feelings there that anyone who earns a comfortable city living must feel even while he enjoys the beauty around him. Peter Maxwell Davies (in his *St. Thomas Wake* foxtrot), Michael Tippett (in his *Songs for Dov* and passages of the operas *The Knot Garden* and *The Ice Break*), and George Rochberg (in his *Music for the Magic Theatre*) have musically depicted at once various kinds of delectable "escape" from modern life—into well-loved music of the past, into literature, into dreams—and a questioning of them. Rameau, by his harmonies, his scoring, and his constrained melodies, has, more precisely and eloquently than any other composer I know, given musical expression to the emotions of a pastoral delight that is not quite easy.

The Tully Hall program began with Lully: the overture to *Le Bourgeois Gentilhomme,* and the passacaille from *Armide* and the chaconne from *Phaeton* danced in reconstructions of published eighteenth-century choreography. Elizabeth Jacquet de la Guerre's cantata *L'Isle de Délos* was sung with delightful purity by Miss Monoyios, and then Miss Turocy danced that "concerto" for ballerina and orchestra Jean-Ferry Rebel's *Les Caractères de la danse,* choreographed by Shirley Wynne. This is a compendium of different dance moods and movements, made famous by Françoise Prévost and taken up with great success by her pupils Camargo and Marie Sallé (who reworked it as a pas de deux). Mrs. Wynne has treated it in a rather formal way; an early account of Mlle. Prévost's version suggests that she may have "impersonated" different characters—a tremulous maiden, an experienced coquette, etc.—in each of the dances besides giving to each of them a different emotional character.

A well-known portrait of Mlle. Prévost, prefixed to the modern published score of *Les Caractères,* shows her in a freely romantic attitude rather different from any of the courtly positions Miss Turocy used, and wearing a clinging diaphanous dress, with feet bare but for a pair of laced-on sandals; however, that may not have been one of her stage costumes. When Mlle. Sallé (who was the first Terpsichore in *Les Fêtes d'Hébé*) danced in London, "she ventured to appear without skirt, without a dress, in her natural hair, and with no ornament on her head," the *Mercure* reported. "She wore nothing in addition to her bodice and under-petticoat but a simple robe of muslin arranged in drapery after the model of a Greek statue." And people were shocked. All the New York dancers were fully and respectably clad, the women in panniered skirts, the man in a *tonnelet* (that "hooped relic of knightly underwear"). The written accounts of eighteenth-century French dancing suggest not only courtly grandeur but also piquant charm, and a search for bravura which was sometimes denounced as excessive. Miss Turocy had moments of exhilarating brio, but in general there was an air of rather too much carefulness about the dancing. And also about Mr. Richman's direction of the music, from the harpsichord. Muffat said that a listener should "hear" French dance music, so to speak, not only with his ears but in his feet; Mr. Richman's playing and his conducting need more spring.

December 26, 1977

Grand, Small, and Important

Leonard Bernstein's *Songfest,* introduced to New York last month by the Philharmonic, under the composer, is a cycle of twelve pieces—three sextets, a trio, two duets, and six solo songs—for six singers and full orchestra. It lasts forty-five minutes. The text is an anthology of American poetry from Anne

Bradstreet in the mid-seventeenth century to Conrad Aiken, Lawrence Ferlinghetti, Gregory Corso, and June Jordan among the living. Poe, Whitman,
Gertrude Stein, E. E. Cummings, Edna St. Vincent Millay, Langston Hughes,
Julia de Burgos, and Frank O'Hara are the other poets. The work—originally
a Bicentennial commission but not finished in time—was intended, in the
words of the program note, "to draw a comprehensive picture of America's
artistic past, as seen in 1976 . . . through the words of thirteen poets embracing three hundred years of the country's history." Specifically, the poems
were chosen to express "the American artist's experience as it relates to his or
her creativity, loves, marriages, or minority problems (blacks, women, homosexuals, expatriates) within a fundamentally Puritan society," and so the picture is not in fact comprehensive. It includes no celebration of "the varied
and ample land, the South and the North in the light, Ohio's shores and
flashing Missouri"; no "chants of the prairies, chants of the long-running
Mississippi, and down to the Mexican sea, shooting in pulses of fire ceaseless
to vivify all." The only natural images found in it are two conventional similes—Mrs. Bradstreet's "My love is such that Rivers cannot quench" and Miss
Millay's "Thus in the winter stands the lonely tree, Nor knows what birds
have vanished one by one." Most of the poems are intimate and personal.
Bernstein states his purpose when he begins with a setting of O'Hara's "To
the Poem":

> *Let us do something grand*
> *just this once   Something*
>
> *small and important and*
> *unAmerican . . .*
>
> *Not needing a military band.*

The six voices united sing the lines to a hymnlike tune with a Geneva Psalter
purposiveness in its stride, accompanied by an orchestra working the basic
motif in rugged counterpoints. The note of affirmation without bombast is
cunningly caught. There follow three solos. Ferlinghetti's "The Pennycan-
dystore Beyond the El" is set for baritone (John Reardon in this performance). It opens like an improvisation on a memory of "These Foolish Things"
but is also a twelve-note composition: the airy, lilting melody exposes the
basic row twice, its retrograde twice, then the inversion, the retrograde inversion, and so on. Julia de Burgos's "A Julia de Burgos" is a fierce, passionate
poem, fiercely set for soprano (Clamma Dale) in urgent lines impelled by
rhythms of five and seven. The number ends with a sustained high C (which
came ringing out in Miss Dale's performance), but the note is optional, and
the rest can be compassed by a mezzo-soprano. It is a song that would have
suited Conchita Supervia well. It should be published with a glittering piano
reduction, so that singers could adopt it as a pendant to Falla's *Seven Popular
Songs*. Whitman's "To What You Said," unpublished in his lifetime, expresses
with quiet firmness a sentiment outside "the received models of the parlors"
of his day: "I am he who kisses his comrade lightly on the lips . . . I introduce

that new American salute." In Bernstein's setting, a soft pedal C—sustained, gently pulsing, or both at once—sounds throughout, passing from instrument to intrument. During the introduction, a very soft C-minor chord, held by the organ stop of an electric keyboard, emerges as a quiet, contradictory ground swell in the pauses between full-orchestra progressions. (There is a similar effect in Britten's *Peter Grimes*.) A rather sentimental tune steals out on solo cello, and then, while the five other singers pick up and hum this tune, the bass (Donald Gramm) sings Whitman's lines in arioso or recitative, much of the time on a C monotone. The simple dignity of the solo declamation saves the number from becoming cloyingly sweet. The mixture of tenderness and manly plainness matches the poem.

By this point, Bernstein's musical intention has become clear: to find a motif and a manner for each poem and then work it out almost in the manner of a rapid sketch. Eleven of the twelve numbers are based each on a single musical idea. The ideas are well chosen. The sketching is fresh and easy. The invention seems to flow, not to be forced, despite the pretty technical ingenuities that can be discovered. At the center of the work is a group of two duets enclosing a trio, and the first duet is the number built with two ideas. It sets at once Langston Hughes's "I, Too, Sing America," a black boast (for baritone), and, in riposte, June Jordan's "Okay 'Negroes,'" tough, teasing, and sexy (for mezzo, Rosalind Elias). The trio is Anne Bradstreet's "To My Dear and Loving Husband," for the three women's voices. (Nancy Williams sang the alto part.) It is a surprising idea to treat this tender wifely statement as an ensemble, but the result is beautiful. The women's quartet (or trio? Four voices, but two of them sing in unison) from *Peter Grimes* seems to be the inspiration, and one phrase echoes Ellen Orford's "Let her among you without fault." The second duet (for soprano and bass), to Gertrude Stein's "Storyette H.M.," pays apt, elegant tribute to Virgil Thomson's Stein settings.

There follows a second sextet, a rhythmically ingenious handling of Cummings's "if you can't eat you got to"—a disturbing piece, in which despair is understated with an air of deft, deceptively neat nonchalance. Then comes another group of three solos. Aiken's "Music I Heard with You" (mezzo) is set in F-sharp minor with a sudden, surprising twelve-note row sung through twice at its center. Corso's "Zizi's Lament" (tenor, Neil Rosenshein) provides the best song of the group; Bernstein adds an amusing comment on modish Oriental flummery with the ting of finger cymbals and a whining, sinuous tune from a solo viola stopped by a single, slithering finger. Somewhere behind the piece is Ravel's *Shéhérazade*, but the note of bitterness and wry self-mockery is modern. "What Lips My Lips Have Kissed" (alto) seems to me rather mawkish, but not more so than the Millay sonnet it sets. The finale is brilliant—Poe's "Israfel" as a whirling valse sextet, its forced rhyme schemes ringing out in a dance of sounds shot through with sudden bursts of coloratura.

Songfest is a work easy to underrate. *Glib* and *fashionable* are words that the program note brings to mind. *Old-fashioned, thin,* and *pretentious* are words that have been used of the piece. But the very "thinness"—the sense of rapid inspiration, of fleet, sure composition—saves it from pretentiousness. I mustn't *over*rate it. There is more beautiful and more profoundly imaginative music in Berlioz's *Nuits d'été*. Mahler's "Wunderhorn" cycle is richer in musical discourse. *Shéhérazade* is more delicately and carefully scored; *Songfest* seems to have been orchestrated with the same swift, effective, unlabored strokes that mark its composition. But it has more true feeling in it, and less artifice, than *Shéhérazade*. All the same, I don't want to try rating orchestral song cycles in an order of merit. *Songfest* has its own character—urban, just a shade slick, maybe, and a shade sentimental, but very attractive as soon as one decides that it has an honest heart. I was a little surprised that I liked it. Any musician must respond to the sheer technical skill, the felicity, of the facture—but it was more than that. It was rather like meeting someone who's been to charm school—and discovering a genuine, innate charm and warmth beneath the polished formulae.

Four solos from the cycle had their première at the Philharmonic last season. The Bradstreet trio was first sung at the Presidential Inaugural gala a year ago. *Songfest* as a whole had its première in Washington last October, with the same soloists as in the whole Philharmonic performance. (All six were good; Miss Elias was outstanding for the wit of her inflections.) The work is well planned, in a *Bogenform*—the trio as keystone, flanked each side by a duet, then three solos, then a sextet—saved from mechanical symmetry by the "extra" sextet. It does amount to "a real right thing," such as is wished for in the first number.

January 2, 1978

Illusion Regained

The Metropolitan Opera's successful new production of *Tannhäuser*, directed by Otto Schenk, designed by Günther Schneider-Siemssen, and conducted by James Levine, is a twentieth-century landmark in the history of Wagner staging. As far as I know, it represents the first attempt any major company has made in more than a quarter of a century—since Wieland Wagner reopened Bayreuth with his drastic and disastrously influential new versions of his grandfather's works—to do a Wagner opera in the way Wagner asked for it to be done. Wieland was a genius and his work was noble; I count all his Bayreuth productions—those admired with but small reservations and those where the losses seemed larger than what was won by his adventurous approach—among the high operatic events of my life. He seldom worked against the sense of the music, and when he did, it was usually in ways to make understanding of that music more vivid. But he opened paths both to weak imitators and to strong, willful, unmusical men who gave scenic form to their own ideas about Wagner's works rather than to the works themselves. The composer's famous remark "Kinder! macht *Neues! Neues!* und abermals *Neues!*" ("Good people, do something *new, new,* and once more *new,*" in Francis Hueffer's translation) became a parrot cry raised in defense of silly innovations: Rhinemaidens in button boots beside a rusting hydroelectric dam, and a caged Woodbird (Bayreuth, 1976); a Hunding hut whose wall was made of hundreds of dinner jackets on metal hangers, and a Valkyrie rock provided with a kitchen chair and Christmas trees half-hooded in plastic, beneath a light snowfall (Paris, 1976); a Hagen who eavesdrops on the meeting between Waltraute and Brünnhilde (London, 1976). The excesses and absurdities of those three centennial *Ring* productions, evidently very different in temper but at one in their disdain for the composer's own scenic requirements, prompted a public cry of "Hold, enough!" and a general wish to see once again things that the music as well as the stage directions tell of: the beauty and grandeur of nature; human feelings revealed in a glance, a gesture; scenic transformations composed with eye and ear in such close accord that curtain-rise at the wrong moment can destroy the intended effect of a shift in harmony or timbre.

In context, Wagner's "Kinder! macht *Neues!*" provides no warrant for revamping a work of the past. Quite the reverse. It occurs in a letter to Liszt, of September 8, 1852, and is a reproach to Berlioz and Joachim Raff for attempting to "galvanize and resuscitate" works that had failed at first, a condemnation of "artificial remodeling." In the very same letter, Wagner tells Liszt that he has drawn up "tolerably comprehensive instructions for the performance of *Tannhäuser,*" had them printed as a pamphlet, and sent them to theatres that have bought the score. "Über die Aufführung des *Tannhäuser,*" the text of the pamphlet, appears in Volume V of the *Gesammelte Schriften* and in Volume III of the W. Ashton Ellis translation. Mr. Schenk and Mr. Schneider-Siemssen have conceived and executed their Metropolitan production in the spirit, and sometimes according to the letter, of this important essay. About the Act II processional entry, Wagner wrote:

> If the entry of the guests into the Hall of Song be so effected that the choir and supers march upon the stage in double file, draw the favorite serpentine curve around it, and take possession of the wings like two regiments of well-drilled troops, in wait for further operatic business, then I beg the band merely to play some march from *Norma* or *Belisario* and not my music. If, on the contrary, one thinks it as well to retain my music, the entry of the guests must be so ordered as to imitate real life fully, in its noblest, freest forms. Away with that painful regularity of the traditional marching order!

In Wieland Wagner's 1954 production, the guests entered in lockstep, marching, marking time, and sidestepping in a strange forward-then-sideways pattern that suggested an attempt to execute massed knight's moves on the checkerboard pavement of the hall. (The whole production was as formal in action as a game of chess, but the traditional rules were broken when the White Queen rushed forward to protect the threatened Black Knight.) At Covent Garden in 1973, Josef Svoboda had filled the stage with a permanent set based on two narrow, intersecting walkways that spanned the scene like a St. Andrew's cross, and so the guests' moves were limited to diagonal traverses or, by dint of a smart turn at the intersection, V-tracked maneuvers. But at the Metropolitan all proceeds in accord with Wagner's directions: "The more varied and unconstrained are the groups of oncomers, divided into separate knots of friends or relations, the more attractive will be the effect of the whole entry. Each knight and dame must be greeted with friendly dignity, on arrival, by the Landgrave and Elisabeth." Mr. Schenk did "tax the full resources of his art" to achieve during the ensuant song tourney "the easy grouping of its audience and especially the portrayal of their changing and waxing interest in the main action." Many other instances could be given of his intelligent attention to Wagner's production book. The result was not old-fashioned, quaint, or smacking of a musty museum. It was fresh, lively, and faithful to the music; it was dramatic; and it was in itself an answer to those who claim that, while Wagner's music need not be rescored, reharmonized, or otherwise adjusted to modern sensibilities, his stage actions are in sore need of updating. The *Tannhäuser* pamphlet is less dogmatic than the detailed one issued for Verdi's *Otello*, which says:

> It is absolutely necessary that the artists should take full cognition of the staging and conform to it. Likewise, directors and impresarios should allow no alterations of any kind in the costumes; these were accurately studied and copied from pictures of the period, and there is no reason why they should be altered according to the whim of some artist or other.

As if to reassure performers who fear that their individuality may be compromised by strict adherence to the moves, gestures, and "motivations" laid down in this *Otello* production book, Boito, in a preface, quotes Hamlet in words that might be back-translated "Repeat the speech as I said it, but in your own natural voice." Imaginative directors and singers should find it inspiring to perform *Otello*—or *Simon Boccanegra, Don Carlos, Aida*—in their own natural accents yet in accordance with the words, the moves, and even the stage plans that carry the composer's authority. Wagner, like Verdi, sometimes prescribed a move-for-move, measure-by-measure staging. He did so for the Flying Dutchman's opening monologue. His *Tannhäuser* essay contains some straight technical advice to the stage designer, but on the whole it is an appeal to the imagination and understanding of the executants. It is also practical. Wagner describes an ideal representation of his intentions and then discusses the compromises, even cuts, that may have to be made according to the circumstances of particular theatres. Mr. Schenk and Mr. Schneider-Siemssen have shown great sensitivity in using modern stage resources to achieve not anachronistic modern effects but the very effects that Wagner required. Their Venusberg in its gradual disappearance presents just such a picture as the composer asks for, created not by his gradual lowering of "numerous vaporous sheets of painted gauze" and then "a massive, rose-tinted canvas backcloth" but by lanterns and projections more delicate and powerful than were any at his disposal. Gil Wechsler's masterly lighting plays an important part in the production. At the Metropolitan, Venus's grotto is indeed an enchanted and magical place, the scene that the stage directions and the music conjure up in the mind's eye but that Wagnerians had begun to despair of ever seeing in a theatre. At Bayreuth in 1972, in a production by Götz Friedrich, dancers with streamers ran out onto a bare stage and anchored them as if to enclose Tannhäuser within the strings of a giant harp. (Thus did Mr. Friedrich demonstrate his thesis that the Venusberg exists only in the hero's imagination.) At Covent Garden in 1973, Tannhäuser and Venus made love on harsh beds of knapped flints, bathed in candy-stripe projections. At the Metropolitan, a tableau that can easily become ridiculous is taken seriously and is beautiful. Of Norbert Vesak's choreography I could catch only glimpses between the bodies of the latecomers, who were allowed to pour into the house the moment the curtain rose, but those glimpses suggested that he has successfully satisfied the composer's wish for "a wild and yet seductive chaos of movements and groupings, of soft delight, of yearning and burning, carried to the most delirious pitch of frenzied riot."

The transformation from amorous grotto to verdant springtime vale was the best I have ever seen. At Bayreuth, Mr. Friedrich and his designer, Jürgen Rose, turned the vale into an arrangement of duckboards against a gloomy sky, and the gay hunting party into a display of sombre brute force. (Thus did the director demonstrate his curious theses that the pilgrims set out for Rome not valiantly, with hopes high, but already crippled in mind, and suffering, and that the aristocrats are oppressors, who naturally reach for their swords when they later hear what Tannhäuser considers culture.) At the Metropolitan, the thrilling, poetic contrast between the artificial rosy glow and the fair spring landscape beneath a blue sky—with the poet, his position unaltered, central to each—makes its full effect and imposes no single, limiting interpretation. Mr. Schneider-Siemssen's intentions for the second scene are right, but the execution is not quite happy. The foreground trees are built in a mannered, not a realistic style. The background trees, painted and projected, seem much too tall. The wayside shrine of the Madonna bears an unfortunate resemblance to those emergency telephones from which police or fire brigade can be summoned. More leaves are needed: "May is here," sings the shepherd, but spring is evidently late in Thuringia. The sun seems to shine from two places at once. Nevertheless, it is a pleasing scene and one that houses the action well. The set for Act II, based on the real Wartburg, with its rectangular shape modified to suit the actions and help the sound, is splendid. Its basically brown coloring becomes richer and richer as the guests, dressed in quietly glowing costumes by Patricia Zipprodt, assemble. In Act III, the difficulty of superimposing the Venusberg on the valley is very successfully managed. Wagner's essay relates what was wrong at the Dresden première and suggests ways of achieving the tricky visual and sonic perspectives he had in mind. At the Metropolitan, by technical means at once simpler and subtler than those he proposes, his requirements are perfectly fulfilled.

The cast is strong. Leonie Rysanek has sung Elisabeth for many years, in many different kinds of production. Her direct, spontaneous, warm, womanly interpretation, one in which instinctive rightness of expression and profound musicianship are united, is well suited by this uneccentric staging. A little, but only a little, of the old glory has gone from her upper range. There is still power enough to fill the enormous house. The sound of her voice and the use she makes of it are beautiful. Modern singers of Elisabeth have been called upon to do some surprising things. At Bayreuth in 1967, Anja Silja made the long, slow exit after the Prayer backward, holding a complicated pose. At Bayreuth in 1972, Gwyneth Jones caterpillared out on her stomach. In Vienna in Karajan's 1963 production, Gré Brouwenstijn was set far, far back—she seemed to be in the Hotel Sacher—and simply faded from sight. (In that production, the Prayer was accompanied only by the understage winds that Wagner specifies for the later Venusberg music; the effect was rather like that of a phonograph record being played in the distance.) What a pleasure to see Miss Rysanek make the gentle, dignified, poignant exit called for in the score.

Grace Bumbry, the motionless Venus of Wieland's 1961 production (a staging based on the idea of two goddesses, dark Earth Mother and blue-robed Madonna high-enthroned against a golden panel), is by Mr. Schenk allowed to move; she gave a seductive and imposing performance. James McCracken sang his first Tannhäuser with passionate intensity of timbre and of word. He has described the part as "a killer," but he has the stamina for it, and both the intellectual and the vocal resources. On the first night, his Hymn to Venus needed rather more freedom, more bravura. There was lyricism as well as passion in his Rome Narration. Bernd Weikl made his Met début as Wolfram—also his début role at Bayreuth, in 1972. He is warmly forthright, lyrical, romantic and handsome of voice and in appearance, and presented an ideal Wolfram in every respect but one: he missed the smoothness that great Wolframs of the past—Clarence Whitehill and Gerhard Hüsch, to name but two represented in EMI's recorded anthology "Sänger auf dem grünen Hügel"—brought to the phrasing. Like many modern singers, he seems to fear the expressive device of portamento. Even the first two notes of "O du mein holder Abendstern" were separate. John Macurdy was a sonorous Landgrave, but once or twice he seemed to be thinking more about the sound of his voice than the sense of his words. Kathleen Battle was a sweet, pure shepherd; the role was assigned to a soprano, not, as sometimes it is, to a treble. But eight trebles—including the admirable Yniold and Fyodor of the season—formed the corps of pages in Act II. The minor minnesingers were cast at strength, and the chorus was in excellent form.

All season, the Met orchestra has been playing supremely well, with uncommon richness and beauty of tone, and for Mr. Levine they gave of their best. At Cincinnati two years ago, he showed himself to be a remarkably impressive conductor of *Tannhäuser*, and once again his combination of breadth and energy, of lyricism and grandeur, proved irresistible. The musical preparation had clearly been thorough. "The surest sign of the conductor's having completely solved his task in this respect," Wagner said, "would be the ultimate experience, at the production, that his active lead is scarcely noticeable." Met sight lines seem to require the conductor to be jacked up high, and so, at any rate to the eye, Mr. Levine was hardly unnoticeable, but under his baton the music flowed, surged, sank, rose again naturally, convincingly, with unforced urgency. One small point: he must persuade his trombones to play the big tune in the overture more smoothly, to hold the notes for something like their full value.

The Paris version of the score was used, not the common collage of Dresden and Paris versions, and this was one more sign of well-justified confidence in the opera that Wagner composed in the form that he finally gave it. No need to tamper and tinker. Mr. Levine and Mr. Schenk allowed themselves just one small "improvement": they removed Wolfram from the stage during the joyful reunion of Tannhäuser and Elisabeth, and cut his single line of regretful comment ("Thus flees from my life every hopeful gleam") and Tannhäuser's hearty embrace of his friend. I think they did wrong. It is the easy solution to a difficult production point—Wolfram seems to be eavesdropping—but far more serious difficulties were faced and solved on Wagner's own lines. This *Tannhäuser* was never silly or stodgy or outdated. In modernized treatments, the work can seem to be no more than a creaking, long-winded, antiquated text for a dissertation upon varieties of human love, or an artist's social responsibility, or whatever. Here it could be enjoyed in all its richness as an exuberantly romantic grand opera in which a hundred different poetic, picturesque, and political ideas contribute to one lyrical and dramatic adventure.

January 9, 1978

A Promise of
Marvelous Hope

The Juilliard American Opera Center chose *Jenůfa* for its spring production, and was criticized therefor. A less familiar Janáček opera—*Šárka*, *The Beginning of a Romance*, *Destiny*—could have increased our knowledge of the composer. *Kát'a Kabanová* has not yet taken the place it should hold in either the Met's or the City Opera's repertory. But for this *Jenůfa* I feel only grateful. The Center did it well—more movingly than the Met in its 1974 production. The Met production has not been revived. And *Jenůfa* is a work—like *Semele*, *Figaro*, and *Fidelio*—that provides operagoers with sustenance they need to remain emotionally alive. Let me quote a few sentences from the last section of Michael Ewans's sensitive, passionate study *Janáček's Tragic Operas*, published by the Indiana University Press:

> In every opera, Janáček presents men and women who are human beings like us; he does so with the deepest understanding, neither raising metaphysical doubts nor offering a pessimistic view of mankind, but snatching some consolation for mortality even from the jaws of extreme suffering.... Intellect and emotion unite to illuminate a vast range of truth, offering to all who will listen a triumphant demonstration of the worth and dignity of individual man.... Janáček's tragic operas heal our wounds, make sense of our existence: they have within them much of what it is to live.

Jenůfa matters in a way that *Thaïs* and *Adriana Lecouvreur*, *La fanciulla del West* and *The Saint of Bleecker Street* don't.

At the Juilliard, there were alternate casts. The three young principals I heard—Awilda Verdejo as Jenůfa; Fredda Rakusin as the Kostelnička, the sextoness, who is Jenůfa's step- and foster mother; and John West as Laca—had the directness of utterance that Janáček needs. His score is far from simple—the patterning of timbres and rhythms, the long swells and sudden crises of harmony are subtly controlled—but if his interpreters sing with honest feeling and in beautiful tones, and avoid artifice and staginess, the expression can hardly go wrong. Miss Verdejo was warm, tender, and credible. Her portrayal of the hopeful, anxious girl in Act I, the tender mother in Act II, and, finally, the mature, understanding, courageous woman was unaffected and true. She has a full lyric soprano, and at the end of the evening discovered new reserves of shining, ample tone for the great duet. Miss Rakusin's Kostelnička had dignity and force; she was very moving in Act II, where love for Jenůfa drives this strict, upright widow to falsehood, blasphemy, and murder. Her consequent physical collapse was strikingly shown, and so was her newfound, generous grandeur in the penultimate scene. The Kostelnička is a role for a dramatic soprano; Miss Rakusin is a mezzo, and some of the higher notes were strained, but all of her singing was clear, firm, and eloquent. Janáček named his opera *Její Pastorkyňa, Her Stepdaughter*—a title that seems to compound two title roles and suggest that the relationship between Jenůfa and the Kostelnička is at the heart of the opera. In the Juilliard performance, this changing relationship—at the end, the older woman draws strength from the younger—was accurately and beautifully represented. Mr. West does not have much stage presence, but through his singing he told of Laca's fierce, and finally noble, love. His phrasing was fresh, strongly shaped, and smooth. Števa was well done by Tonio DiPaolo, who has added some pure but not yet quite convincing tenor notes to his beautiful baritone. Števa is no conventional villain; Janáček limns his shallow, selfish nature with understanding, even with sympathy. The confrontation with the Kostelnička in Act II—which Mr. Ewans rightly describes as "a study in overreaction," since both she and he are carried away beyond their intentions—was powerfully achieved.

The staging was hampered by Josef Svoboda's clumsy set, based (like the *Tannhäuser* décor he inflicted on Hamburg and Covent Garden) on two narrow diagonal walkways spanning the stage in a St. Andrew's cross. As a result, what should be natural moves across the mill yard of Act I and the room of Acts II and III became stilted progress around an obstacle course. But Gerald Freedman, who directed, minimized the difficulties, and he had inspired all his cast to a true understanding of their roles. Peter Herman Adler's conducting was masterly—alert to every expressive turn of the music, paced to the thought of the characters, quick and keen in its control of color. The Juilliard orchestra was excellent; the violin solos of Dene Olding, accompanying Jenůfa's scena in Act II, were especially eloquent.

Jenůfa is a profoundly moving and at times a terrifying opera. No single person is to blame for the tragedy. A girl becomes pregnant; the young man, her cousin, does not want to be caught in marriage. The drama begins like *Cavalleria rusticana* but continues with a truth and tenderness far removed from Mascagni's melodramatic "verismo." Lola, Alfio, and Mamma Lucia are stock characters; Janáček's numerous secondary characters are vivid and individual in everything they say. Gradually, by small verbal and musical details, the past as well as the present is revealed. Števa Buryja's carefree selfishness has been nurtured by his good looks, his inherited wealth, his upbringing as an orphan by a fond, doting grandmother, head of the Buryja family. In his half brother Laca, who is not a Buryja, an Edmund-like resentment contends with an Edgar-like nobility. The Kostelnička was not always formidable and austere. In youth she married a handsome, worthless Buryja; her severity includes a determination that her beloved foster daughter should not be made unhappy by Števa as she once was by his uncle. These are all real, understandable people. The tragedy develops. Jenůfa bears her child in secret. Števa offers money; Laca offers his hand, but his love falters when he learns of the child. So the Kostelnička tells her lie—"The child died"—and then the stern epitome of village virtues becomes a murderess to make it true. In Act III, the villagers who have arrived to celebrate Jenůfa's marriage to Laca break into horrifying cries of "Stone her!" when the body is discovered. But the Kostelnička, Jenůfa, and Laca rise to greatness—human, not supernatural or mythical, greatness—and achieve it not so much through their own suffering as through their comprehension of others' suffering. All this Janáček has expressed in music that seems to touch directly on the listeners' nerves of understanding and compassion. His methods can be analyzed, his structures plotted, his careful dramaturgy described, and his melodies traced to an origin in the inflections of Moravian speech. But in the theatre one forgets such things in the immediacy of one's response to thoughts, feelings, and character. "The art of dramatic writing," Janáček once said, "is to compose a melodic curve that will, as if by magic, reveal immediately a human being in one definite phase of his existence." And as Rosa Newmarch, an early Janáček champion, wrote long ago, "the disadvantage of the strongly localized accent and lilt need trouble only the unfortunate translator of the text." Whether the first line of the opera is sung in Czech as "Už se večer chýlí, a Števa se nevrací!," in German as "Ach, es wird schon Abend, und Stewa ist nicht zurück!" (which is how I first got to know and love it), or in English as "Soon it will be evening, and Števa has not come back!" (the Juilliard performance, like the Met's, was done in English), the shape of the phrase, the length of the break between the first and the second clause, the repeat of the second with the harmony sharpened and the melodic curve extended to reach higher and sink further, and the placing of the voice as it steals into a void between the tremolando of high violins and that of low cellos—all these conspire to reveal, as if by magic, the anxiety and hope of Jenůfa at one definite stage of her existence. Laca's anger and love are similarly revealed. In Mr. Ewans's chapter on the opera, he makes the interesting observation that in Act I Jenůfa is subconsciously trying to slow the action down, and Laca to advance it. In Janáček's music, both attempts are measured against the recurrent, inexorable clacking of the mill wheel. And at the end of his chapter Mr. Ewans says:

> The wonder of *Jenůfa* is the promise that if sufficiently sensitive and understanding of others, we may by our own experiences attain, as Jenůfa and Laca, a moral maturity which is sufficient in itself, and which does not need—indeed rejects and goes in love beyond—the standards of any given community. A promise of marvelous hope, to Janáček's spectators as they go out into the night.

The promise of *Jenůfa* is repeated at the chilling close of *Kát'a Kabanová*, and throughout *From the House of the Dead*. Those three operas should be central to the twentieth-century repertory.

. . .

Last year, I wrote about a production at Yale which was misleadingly billed as the world première of Debussy's one-act opera *La Chute de la maison Usher*, and suggested that it could more properly be described as a bold student endeavor to give sound and context to an important, extended sketch for that unfinished score. The sketch (it is in the Bibliothèque Nationale, Paris, and was published in facsimile in 1962) is a particella—vocal lines together with the orchestral part indicated in condensed form on two, three, or four staves—of the first two hundred measures or so of the opera. It represents little more than a fifth of the libretto that Debussy devised from the Poe story, and peters out soon after the entry of the principal character, Roderick Usher. Debussy described the work as "a progressive expression of anguish"; here is but the first step of that progress. For the Yale production, it had been transcribed by Carolyn Abbate and orchestrated by Robert Kyr; the rest of Debussy's libretto was then played out as a spoken drama, and rounded off by an orchestration of seven measures that survive on a sheet inscribed "pour la fin de la m[aison] u[sher](?)."

More of *Usher* survives. The particella represents Debussy's attempt in 1915–17, at the end of his life, to resume and complete a work that had obsessed him from 1909 to 1911 and then been set aside. Neither for *Usher* nor for a companion piece based on Poe's "The Devil in the Belfry" could he "find the solution," he wrote in December 1911. "For any single measure that may be free and alive there are twenty that are stifled by tradition." Debussy's stepdaughter still has several pages of *Usher* sketches dating from this earlier attempt, lapping and extending the passages set in the particella. His widow had the generous but regrettable habit of giving away single sheets as souvenirs of her husband; two of these were published in facsimile, two more have since been discovered, and it seems likely that yet more will turn up. The British Library has a sheet for the passage in which Roderick's friend reads to him—in ordinary speech, against music—the story of Sir Ulrich from "notre roman favori." Last December, Frankfurt Radio broadcast a partial reconstruction of Debussy's *Usher* about twice as long as Miss Abbate's, accurately described as "fragments of the lyric drama . . . assembled, transcribed, and orchestrated by Juan Allende-Blin." Mr. Allende-Blin has not confined himself to the particella but has added whatever he could glean of the opera from all stages of its composition. His version, published in vocal score by Jobert, includes, after the long continuous passage represented by the particella, several further stretches of Roderick's monologue, a second strophe of Madeline's song "The Haunted Palace" (there are three strophes in Debussy's 1909 libretto, but only one in his revised 1916 libretto and in the particella), and most of the "Sir Ulrich" reading. But no music has yet been found for the long central dialogue of the opera, and none—apart from those seven measures "pour la fin . . . (?)"—for the dénouement.

The Abbate transcription of the particella was heard in New York last month at a Tully Hall concert given by the Bronx Arts Ensemble. It was described now as "*La Chute de la maison Usher* (reconstructed and edited by Carolyn Abbate)." The Yale score had evidently been revised, and this time no orchestrator was named. In a program note, Miss Abbate wrote "we" in a context to suggest that her collaborator was the Wagner scholar Robert Bailey, her adviser at Yale, and there was a reference to "the Abbate/Bailey edition." The performance, conducted by Johannes Somary, was imprecise and ineffective, but even in a good performance this eighteen-minute fragment, which breaks off just as the drama is about to begin in earnest, could hardly make an effective concert piece. Nevertheless, it is of high interest to Debussyans to hear the composer's preliminary scene setting, his attempt to find motifs, harmonies, and (as revealed by a few indications of scoring) instrumental timbres to suggest the unstable house and the unstable soul of its owner. It should be stressed that the scoring can only be speculative—far more so than, say, Deryck Cooke's scoring of Mahler's Tenth Symphony, made from a particella more precise in its instrumental details than Debussy's. In the Yale stage production, one heard a version for chamber orchestra; a few weeks later, there was a Yale concert performance for an orchestra at full *Pelléas* strength. The Tully forces fell somewhere between the two.

After the Yale performance, I suggested [*Music of Three Seasons* (New York: Farrar, Straus & Giroux, 1978), pp. 532–8] that a reason for Debussy's being unable in 1911 to proceed with *Usher* was, in brief, that he had set himself two impossible tasks: to write an opera on "Usher" which would in no way recall the subject or atmosphere of *Pelléas*, and to write an "Usher" opera to a scenario that utterly destroys the carefully balanced symbolism of Poe's tale. When he took up the sketches again, he was already dying. Debussy's *Usher* cannot in any strict sense be "reconstructed," since it was never fully constructed in the first place. But the fragments that remain, the last, morbid imaginings of a great composer, are fascinating.

January 16, 1978

Grand Opera

The Teatro alla Scala, Milan, which opened on August 3, 1778, with a performance of Antonio Salieri's *L'Europa riconosciuta*, is celebrating its bicentennial in an unusually long season, broken only in August. It opened and will end with *Don Carlos*, and Verdi dominates the bicentennial bill: besides *Don Carlos*, there are *Un ballo in maschera*, *I masnadieri*, *La forza del destino*, *Il trovatore*, and *Simon Boccanegra*—six of the nine grand operas due. The fare is serious: no Rossini, Donizetti, or Bellini, and no verismo but *Madama Butterfly*. *Manon Lescaut* is the only other Puccini. The new opera—like most important European houses, La Scala "creates" an opera each season—is Luciano Berio's *La vera storia*. Luigi Nono's *Al gran sole carico d'amore* is being revived. The main repertory is completed by *Die Entführung, Fidelio* (brought by the Vienna State Opera), *Tristan* (conducted by Carlos Kleiber, staged by Wolfgang Wagner), Monteverdi's *Orfeo, Ulisse,* and *Poppea* (brought by the Zurich Opera), a Ravel double bill, and, in the Piccola Scala, *The Beggar's Opera* in the Britten version. There are also ballets, music-theatre bills, and many orchestral concerts (Abbado, Bernstein, Giulini, Mehta, Mravinsky, and Solti among the conductors) and chamber and solo recitals. Schubert receives extended attention in the year that marks the hundred-and-fiftieth anniversary of his death. The Teatro Lirico and the Palazzo dello Sport are used for shows less aptly housed in the formal, beautiful, neoclassical spaces of La Scala itself; Verdi's Requiem will be sung in the Church of Santa Maria delle Grazie. In the Royal Palace, a huge exhibition is taking shape, devoted not to performers but to the role played in operatic, social, and political history by—in the proud words of the season's brochure—"a theatre that is a model to the world . . . the first to free itself, in 1921, from the yoke of private capital."

La Scala, like Covent Garden, is run on the *stagione* system, which means concentrating on only two or three operas at a time and trying to keep them at performance pitch with stable, fully rehearsed casts. In the first seven weeks of the season, only two operas appear, *Don Carlos* eleven times and *Ballo* seven, both with double casts; all the performances are conducted by Claudio Abbado, the artistic director of the company. *Don Carlos*, staged by Luca Ronconi and designed by Luciano Damiani, was performed from the new Ricordi edition, prepared by Ursula Günther and Luciano Petazzoni—a variorum score that contains nearly all the music Verdi composed for the opera in 1865–67, in 1872, and in 1882–83; i.e., the published Paris, Naples, and Milan versions together with the hitherto unpublished scenes cut before the Paris première (physically cut from Verdi's autograph) which David Rosen and I turned up in the archives of the Paris Opera a few years ago. From this wealth of overlapping material—for all but one of the eight scenes (the auto-da-fé) there are two or three alternatives—a conductor and director must choose what they want to perform, and by that choice they determine in large part the character of a production. The eyes of the world were focused on the Scala's new *Don Carlos*—literally, when one performance went out on *mondovisione* to some twenty countries. James Levine, in New York, was one of the international audience who appeared on the screen during an intermission; he plans a new *Don Carlos* for the Metropolitan next season.

It would be impossible to discuss the Scala production in any detail without first setting out something about the work's nature and some of its complicated history. In the last few decades, it has come to the forefront of the Verdian repertory—in Germany (powerful productions in Hamburg, Munich, and Berlin), Austria (where Karajan has conducted two stagings at the

Salzburg Festival, one directed by Gustaf Gründgens, the other by him), America (where it rejoined the Met repertory in 1950), Britain (where it is in the Royal, English National, and Welsh National repertories), and Italy (where Rome and Milan have paid special attention to it; the new Scala production is the fifth different staging there since the war). *Don Carlos* is the Verdi opera of which I have seen most productions; it would not have been so for a critic in the first half of the century. In the last decade, the work has also come to the forefront of Verdian scholarship: not only extra music but many, many documents (contracts, libretto drafts, copious correspondence relating to every stage of its history, rehearsal schedules, early scene designs, etc.) have been turned up which help to explain why it is the kind—or, in view of the revisions it underwent, the kinds—of opera it is.

Don Carlos is Verdi's most ambitious opera, one that combines his theatrical flair for portraying human beings in extreme plights, rent by conflicting emotional and moral imperatives, with lofty *grand-opéra* pageantry used— more seriously than in the Scribe-Meyerbeer shows—to demonstrate a belief in political and personal freedom. Subaltern characters from Schiller's play—the main source of the libretto—are eliminated, but important crowd scenes are added. Verdi described his piece as an attempt to "transform our theatres," and for nearly twenty years he struggled to give it a shape at once practical, performable without unauthorized cuts, attractive to the general public, and faithful to his vision of an elevated, ennobling drama. The Paris *Don Carlos*, even after the preperformance cuts, was a very long piece—"as long as *Trovatore* and *Traviata* together," the composer said. Philip II of Spain and his son Don Carlos form the common base of three different emotional triangles, whose third points are Elizabeth of Valois (affianced to Carlos, then married to Philip), the Princess of Eboli (Philip's mistress, but in love with Carlos), and Rodrigo, Marquis of Posa (loved and trusted by both Philip and Carlos). If one plots a diagram of passions, joining the five characters by lines of love or desire, two further triangles emerge, on a common base of Elizabeth and Eboli, since both women love Carlos (Eboli's fury as a woman scorned precipitates the catastrophe) and both have shared Philip's bed. In a short *romance* for Carlos, three long duets for Elizabeth and Carlos, three extended solos for Philip, Eboli, and Elizabeth, a duet for Carlos and Posa, and a duet trio for Eboli, Carlos, and then Posa, the relationships are explored; two further duets, for Elizabeth and Eboli (about their love for Carlos) and for Carlos and Philip (about their love for Posa), formed part of the original scheme and were composed but then were cut before the première.

This more-than-Metastasian tangle would be matter enough for an enthralling opera, but, in addition, on the decisions and deeds of the five individuals depend the fates of three nations—France, Flanders, and Spain— and, by extension, of all the people in Philip's vast empire. Posa is the spokesman of liberty; in a duet with Philip he denounces oppression—to "save" Flanders, a country and its people are being destroyed (during performances at the time of the Vietnam war, his words rang out with terrible vividness)—

and urges the King to inspire the world by a model of just government. The Grand Inquisitor is the spokesman of oppression; in a duet with Philip he denounces any tolerance for freedom of thought or action. The librettists, Joseph Méry and Camille du Locle, added this duet to their scheme at Verdi's demand; Verdi himself prescribed that the Inquisitor should be, as in Schiller, "blind and extremely old," and in chilling, powerful music the composer voiced his hatred of Church dominion over men's minds and lives. Emotions and politics are inextricable. In Act I, Elizabeth, in love with Carlos, accepts Philip's hand only to seal a truce between Spain and France and thus end her countrymen's suffering during a cruel war. In the Act IV quartet, three characters sing of personal distress and the fourth comes to a political decision. Posa's principal air, in Act IV, mingles affection for Carlos with an exhortation to him to free Spain and Flanders. In the final duet, Elizabeth bids Carlos "mount Calvary" (Napoleon III's censors added shocked marginal exclamations in the copy of the libretto submitted to them) and save his people. Events come to a public crisis in the second scene of Act III, the auto-da-fé, which Verdi described as the heart of his opera: Carlos, leading a band of Flemish deputies, defies his father. In Acts IV and V, the private consequences of his impetuous, premature defiance are explored. Acts III, IV, and V all end with a bitter affirmation of the Church's unshaken supremacy. A consolatory Voice from Heaven, singing out while heretics are burned alive at the end of Act III, is hardly more than an illusory, almost ironic comment. (Verdi directed that no one onstage should pay any attention to it.) The Inquisitor's voice at the end of Act IV brings an insurgent, rebellious mob to its knees. And at the very end of the opera, when the Emperor Charles V appears, as if rising from the tomb, to rescue Carlos from the hands of the Inquisition, he does so declaring that only in death can a hero discover the peace he longs for. Verdi's view of life was tragic. In *Don Carlos*, both his pessimism and his insistence that a man nevertheless must struggle unceasingly for what he believes to be right were given their fullest expression.

No wonder the work proved unwieldy. Practical considerations also affected the embodiment of the grandiose vision: among them the facts that in mid-composition the role of Eboli was reassigned from a contralto (Rosine Bloch, an Azucena) to a soprano (Pauline Gueymard, a Leonora); that the first Carlos, Morère, was inexperienced (the monologue with which, originally, he was intended to open Act V was rewritten as an air for the prima donna); that the opera had to end in time for spectators to catch the last trains to the suburbs; and that Paris audiences expected an extended ballet (Verdi supplied "La Pérégrina"—not the divertissement that Balanchine has recently made of it but a ballet whose scenario is keyed into the plot). After the first night, Verdi authorized another small cut (the insurrection at the end of Act IV). In 1872, for Naples, whither he went to direct "an accurate execution embodying all the reforms demanded by modern art," he made another small cut and recomposed part of the crucial Philip-Posa duet. In 1882, when *Otello* was already taking shape, he set about a thoroughgoing revision and abridgment, removing the first act (in Fontainebleau) and salvaging from

it only Carlos's *romance*, which he rewrote and added to the new Act I;
dropping the ballet; stripping dialogues and ensembles of "all that is purely
musical, retaining only what is necessary for the dramatic action"; again recomposing the Philip-Posa duet, in a yet more powerful form; and bringing
Acts IV and V—now III and IV—to rapid, abrupt conclusions ("All those
massive choruses weigh on my stomach"). He left the big solos unchanged, as
expansive moments set now in a swift-moving drama whose musical manner
adumbrates that of *Otello*. This four-act *Don Carlos*, translated into Italian,
had its first performance, at La Scala, in 1884. Two years later, in Modena,
there appeared—with the composer's consent and approval, it was said—yet
another version, in which the unrevised Act I preceded the four revised acts.
This was published, in Italian translation only, to form the familiar five-act
score heard in the Solti and Giulini recordings. It was taken up by La Scala in
1960.

Particular interest has always attached to Verdi's "flawed masterpieces"—operas he did not get right at first but valued and later sought to
strengthen: *Macbeth, Simon Boccanegra, La forza del destino,* and *Don
Carlos*. And, as I remarked above, in recent years most interest has attached
to *Don Carlos*, whose various versions record the development of his musical,
his dramatic, and even his political thinking during the quarter century between *La forza* (1862) and *Otello* (1887). The new Scala *Don Carlos* is the latest in a line of important productions each of which has shed new light on the
work. Notable among them were Luchino Visconti's of the "Modena" score
(Covent Garden, 1958); the BBC's studio presentation of the "Paris" score
amplified by the newly discovered ("pre-Paris") passages (1973); Sarah Caldwell's theatrical proving of that very long edition (Boston, 1973); and Karajan's contrary championship (Salzburg, 1975) of the short "Milan" score further abridged by eight large cuts. In addition, Venice (1973), the English
National Opera (1974), and Munich (1975) have essayed mixtures of "pre-
Paris" and "Modena." The next major production due is the Metropolitan's.

Basically, La Scala decided on a five-act "Modena" score lengthened by
two "pre-Paris" scenes: the opening chorus of suffering French peasantry and
the Carlos-Philip duet of mourning over the slain Posa (whose melody Verdi
later reworked as the "Lacrimosa" of his Requiem). But "Paris" was preferred for the final scene (a chorus of inquisitors thundering repeated maledictions, instead of the swift close of the revision, and curtain-fall pianissimo
in A, not fortissimo in B) and also for the start of Act III (a nocturnal fête in
the Queen's gardens, where Elizabeth and Eboli change masks); after it, instead of the "Paris" ballet or the "Milan/Modena" instrumental prelude to
Carlos's entry into the garden, a "pre-Paris" fragment—an ineffective and
rejected partial reprise of the offstage "Mandolines" chorus—had its first
public hearing. Ronconi visualized the opera as one long funeral procession,
proceeding from right to left across the back of a bare stage, against monochrome backcloths made of some translucent plastic material: a solemn Triumph of Death, with dignitaries beneath baldachinos, monks, mourners, regi-
ments of soldiers, victims, oppressors, and elaborate cars bearing images of

the Great Reaper. Nearly three hundred supers were engaged, and eight hundred costumes were made. The processional way was slightly raised; on the front part of the stage, individuals advanced to enact the private dramas. On either side of them, tall wings made of aluminum represented massed tombs, and here the chorus was clustered. Otherwise, there was only the mortuary slab, with recumbent effigy, of Charles V, front-center on the empty stage. It appeared when, at the end of Act I, a shrouding snow-cloth that had represented the forest of Fontainebleau was pulled away, and there it stayed throughout the evening (except in Philip's study, which was represented by two lecterns), serving in subsequent scenes, with faintly ridiculous effect, as a kind of uncomfortable garden bench: there was nothing else for anyone to sit on or lean against. Eboli began the Veil Song balanced on Charles's marble ankles and the garden duet perched beside his head. It may have been Ronconi's idea to suggest the Emperor's stern will still dominating the whole world from his Yuste retreat. As Prescott, whose *History of the Reign of Philip the Second* is a subsidiary source for the libretto, remarked, "Charles was not master of that ignoble philosophy which enabled Diocletian to turn with contentment from the cares of an empire to those of a cabbage-garden. . . . Not only did the emperor continue to show an interest in public affairs, but he took a prominent part, even from the depths of his retreat, in the management of them." After celebrating his own funeral, Charles added a codicil to his will enjoining his son Philip to bring to justice every heretic in his dominions, without favor or mercy to anyone, and to cherish the Holy Inquisition as the best instrument for accomplishing that good work. Such an idea would better match the "Milan" score, which does begin and end at Yuste. But, in any case, Ronconi did not seem to take the Emperor very seriously: from behind his slab, Charles popped up and down on cue, through a trapdoor, like a jack-in-the-box; he was not the awe-inspiring apparition Verdi described, revealed as the bronze gates of the imperial chapel crash open.

Damiani (the scenographer of the Scala *Macbeth* seen in Washington in 1976) is a master designer. His scenes for the Piccolo Teatro's *Galileo* and the famous Salzburg *Entführung* were unforgettable in their Brunelleschian harmony of color and proportion, and the pictures he composed for *Don Carlos*, with richly costumed figures dwarfed by the huge, plain backcloths, were also very beautiful. In the program book, he wrote, "For me, Spain is gray. Thus with the silver of the royal trumpets: metal corroded, tarnished, purulent, a pus that should seem to have oozed from those tombs." But not everything was gray. One backcloth was; others were deep green, canary yellow, intense blue, and sanguine, and they were lit in a way that made them glow. He and Ronconi had created a vision of a rich world cruelly traversed and dominated by tyranny and death, celebrated in lugubrious ceremony. Even the merry masquers of the garden scene were dressed in sinister parodies of auto-da-fé costumes. The long, slow funeral procession was, during the long evening, but once disturbed, when the insurgents ran on in the contrary direction; the arrival of the Inquisitor soon put a stop to that deasil movement. The effect of the whole was not truly Verdian; it was schematic, unvaried, and, after a while, cold. Verdi planned a succession of contrasting stage pictures, set up at different depths not only for practical reasons of swift scene changing but also to provide variety of visual and acoustic density. In the authorized production book for the opera, the stage plan is divided into twelve notional strips, and scenes are indicated which vary in depth from two for the intimacy of Philip's study, through six for the cloister and nine for the prison, to the full twelve—the stage thrown open to its farthest depth—for the coronation scene. One disadvantage of a unit set (the Metropolitan *Prophète* also suffered from it) is a monotony not only of scenery but also of size. Ronconi added monotony of motion; and his idea of physically separating the personal and political actions, by downstage prowling and upstage procession, on different levels, contradicted the essentially Verdian fusion of private emotion with social and moral responsibility. Like many stagings that seek to demonstrate a director's particular thoughts about a work rather than present it as its creator intended, this *Don Carlos* underlined just one—admittedly important—truth about the piece and did so by impoverishing the rich, complicated, unschematic, and, above all, moving drama of human personalities. Ronconi's staging sometimes defeated his own as well as Verdi's ends: it was hard to pay much attention to the details of Posa's denunciation of Philip's policy—in that duet to which the composer attached such importance—when behind the singers an enormous, spectacular barque laden with corpses was being trundled across the stage. Verdi's words and music lost their vividness. And the finale was comical: during the maledictions a posse of monks carrying a big cross chased Carlos and Elizabeth round and round the Emperor's tomb, as if in a children's game. Incidentally, the unit set and bare stage did not represent a bid for economy, as in Bayreuth's first postwar scenes or the Met *Prophète;* the cost of the production was reported as 314 million lire, or about three hundred and sixty thousand dollars.

Verdi cared about the destiny of nations—and also, passionately, about the behavior of individuals. Ronconi is a director who evidently prefers to create explanatory tableaux rather than to work in detail with individual actors. (His staging of *Il trovatore,* which opened the Florence season, and of Gluck's *Orfeo,* which was on show in Bologna, confirmed it.) And, *stagione* system or no, it seems that the soloists of his *Don Carlos* were underrehearsed. The production had a rough critical ride, and the director answered his critics by saying, "I know well the shortcomings of shows like the Scala *Don Carlos,* given that singers continue to perform exactly as they have before. . . . Above all, when it happens that an opera's protagonist arrives in the theatre two days before the show, as happened this time, it is plain that I cannot make good certain shortcomings." Four of the principals were those of Karajan's second Salzburg production: Mirella Freni (Elizabeth), José Carreras (who in 1976 took over the title role there from Placido Domingo), Piero Cappuccilli (Posa), and Nicolai Ghiaurov (Philip). All four are admirable singers and, in a conventional way, reasonably accomplished actors. Karajan has taught them to move through their roles with apt, dignified demeanor, and Ronconi seemed to expect no more of them. In any case, his lighting was seldom bright enough for expressions to be read. Since all four had signed away certain rights in their performances to Karajan, who plans to film his production, a different quartet was engaged for the *mondovisione* evening: Margaret Price, Domingo, Renato Bruson, and Yevgeny Nesterenko. Closeup camerawork unkindly drew attention to the facial blandness of the first three and revealed the passion with which Nesterenko felt his part. But the complete change of cast (the Eboli, the Inquisitor, and the Charles V were also different from those I saw in La Scala) scarcely altered the effect of the whole—which emphasized how thoroughly Ronconi had deindividualized the drama.

Price and Domingo have the fuller, spinto, large-bodied voices needed for much of the music; Freni, a lyric soprano, produced sweeter, more affecting sound in the gentle passages ("très doux" is a repeated marking in Elizabeth's role), and Carreras, a lyric tenor, is a more romantic protagonist. Between the Posas there was little to choose; both have uncommonly beautiful and even baritones, Cappuccilli's being the grander and Bruson's slightly the more varied in color. Ghiaurov (whom I first heard at La Scala, seventeen years ago, as a thunderous Inquisitor to Boris Christoff's King) sings Philip with force and majesty; Nesterenko (a Bolshoy Boris) has a more purely focused bass, with which he drew a supple, precise line. Nadine Denize, my Eboli in the theatre, and Elena Obraztsova, the Eboli on the screen, were both effective, the former being more elegant, the latter more flamboyantly audacious. Nesterenko had been the first-night Inquisitor; in the theatre I heard Bengt Rundgren, who was a shade too plain, and over the air Giovanni Foiani, powerful at the top but weak on the important low notes. (Theatre and television performances cannot be directly compared, of course, but the broadcast sound gave a pretty faithful account of voices that I know well in life.) All the singing, in fact, was on a very high international level, but the production made the soloists seem less important than usual, and there was little dramatic interplay between them (which in this, of all operas, is a grievous fault). The large Scala chorus, clustered against the aluminum wings, sang nobly, but its role in the drama, too, had been subdued; the procession of supers formed the principal crowd. Ronconi was even reported as claiming that today an opera is a show to be seen rather than heard. Abbado can hardly agree. His conducting was magnificent, and so was the playing of the Scala orchestra, a body that seemed to unite the virtues of his two other orchestras—the Vienna Philharmonic's richness and warmth of tone, especially of string tone, and the London Symphony's vigor and precision. His reading was highly colored and very theatrical but not showy. The music gleamed with brighter lights and the contrasts were fiercer than those of Giulini's performance; the phrasing was more natural, less self-consciously exquisite, than Karajan's. And when—as in Posa's "C'est mon jour suprême"—Verdi wrote "pianissimo" and "très doux," the singing *was* very soft and very sweet. The small, correct details printed for the first time in the Günther-Petazzoni score may seem, taken singly, to be minutiae such as make little difference to the run of a whole performance; but I feel sure that their cumulative contribution to the musical excellence of this execution was large.

The performance I attended began at seven-thirty and ended at midnight. There were two intermissions. There were also sections missing from the first and the last duet (which, however, had both been given complete on the first night, I was told). When music that Verdi himself chose to cut is reinstated at the expense of music that he chose to retain, I almost begin to wish that I had left those extra scenes in the Paris Opera library undisturbed. It was thrilling to me to hear Abbado and the Scala orchestra bring to life, so richly, music that had gradually taken shape, line by line, under my eyes as I prized open the stuck-down pages of the 1867 orchestral parts, one after another, and copied them to build up a full score. Nevertheless, the *Don Carlos* performances of recent years have led me to this conclusion: that companies with the resources and time for it should do "Modena" complete; that if, for any reason, abridgment is necessary, it should be Verdi's abridgment—i.e., "Milan" complete rather than "Modena" with cuts; that if, on the other hand, a company still has extra time in hand, it might *consider* beginning with the "pre-Paris" prelude and opening chorus. After hearing that piece in six different productions now, I feel less sure about recommending it than once I did; it makes a dramatic point, but it has weak passages, and there is much to be said for the sudden, striking start that Verdi put in its place. The Carlos-Philip "Lacrimosa" duet, the other "pre-Paris" number included at La Scala, begins magnificently but bursts into the tonic major in a blatant way; and, in any case, Verdi's feeling that after the death of Posa the act should move *"vite, vite, vite"* to its close was surely justified. Neither the Scala's "Paris" addition (the nocturnal fête) nor its "Paris" substitution (the inquisitors' finale) is any improvement on "Milan/Modena." Of course, any music that Verdi wrote in 1866, in full maturity, is worth hearing; a recording, a concert performance, an occasional production (as in Boston) of the very long ur-*Carlos* would be welcome. So would a recording of the "Naples" Philip-Posa duet. It is the mixed versions that have proved unconvincing. The English National essayed one close to La Scala's—mainly "Modena," plus the "pre-Paris" opening chorus and "Lacrimosa" duet and the "Paris" fête and quiet close—but, rightly, abandoned it for something closer to "Modena" when it failed to work well in the theatre. The Scala version reflected Ronconi's ideas in that for every crowd scene (except the insurrection) the most extensive available version was chosen.

The opera was sung in Italian translation, as in Italy it should be. But it was still basically that old translation which, although it passed under the composer's eye, divides the two syllables of *speme* across a breath mark; cannot make up its mind whether the soprano's name is Elisabetta or Isabella; and turns direct statements into fancy ones. In phrase after phrase, Verdi's original rhythms are spoiled [more about this on page 317]. Since the Metropolitan is unlikely to perform *Don Carlos* in English, I hope that it decides to do it in the original.

A final word in praise of the Scala program book, ninety-three pages long (not counting the advertisements, grouped at the back), packed with information, commentary, history, and iconography, and including a libretto and a facsimile of the printed "Modena" production book. The *Radiocorriere*—the program guide to Italian radio and television—for the week of the broadcast also contained the full libretto.

January 23, 1978

Juilliard Enterprise

Peter Heyworth, the music critic of the London *Observer*, was remarking earlier this season that, while indigenous contemporary music figures on programs here as plentifully as it does in most places, New Yorkers seem to show regrettably little interest in discovering what the rest of the world is up to. I am inclined to agree with him. The bill has just reached me of a concert in which the London Sinfonietta this week celebrates its tenth anniversary. It includes five works, from three countries: Harrison Birtwistle's *Carmen Arcadiae Mechanicae Perpetuum*, composed for the occasion, Tippett's *Songs for Dov* (one of more than a hundred pieces of which the Sinfonietta has played the première), two pieces by Luciano Berio, and one by Witold Lutosławski. Birtwistle, Berio, and Lutosławski conduct their own compositions. One seldom encounters a comparable event in New York; the nearest programs are probably those of the Twentieth-Century Music Series at the Juilliard School, conducted by Richard Dufallo, which receive too little public attention. There, amid much new American music, I have been glad to catch up with compositions by, among others, Berio, Stockhausen, Ligeti, Xenakis, Maxwell Davies, and Barry Conyngham.

The latest concern in the series brought the American première of Gilbert Amy's *Seven Sites*, composed in 1975, commissioned by the London Sinfonietta for the concert that Amy conducted with it that year. It is a twenty-minute piece for fourteen players. Amy (born in Paris in 1936), who in 1967 succeeded Boulez as director of the Domaine Musical, has in his compositions also shown himself a follower of Boulez. Everything I have heard of his has been delicate, intelligent, and exquisitely worked out—but not marked by the force of personality that makes Boulez a great composer. *Seven Sites* begins magically. The "sites" seem to be harmonic areas, claimed and successively occupied by different instruments or groups of instruments: celesta;

pairs of violas and cellos, with harp; harp and celesta; solo horn in the distance; celesta and trumpet; flute, clarinet, and trumpet alternating with celesta and strings; strings with vibraphone and harp; strings alone; solo horn in the foreground; etc. The title may also carry a spatial meaning (there was no program note to explain things): the horn plays from four different stations and the clarinet from two, in combinations that give seven different platform dispositions. As I said, the piece begins magically, with captivating sounds stealing out—a clear, silvery trickle, a brief flurry of small, crystalline motifs, a long, bold, highly colored solo melody. I was transported back to the early days of the Royan festival, to a world of refined French sensibility, a landscape of timbres in which sounds from Debussy and Ravel had been filtered, ordered, and regulated by methods devised by the young Boulez of *Le Soleil des eaux, Le Marteau sans maître*, and the first *Improvisations sur Mallarmé*. But as *Seven Sites* continued the magic started to fade. After a while, the piece began to seem merely decorative, a sequence of cunning allurements, not a connected discourse until in the final pages the clarinet embarked on a brilliant, vehement cadenza.

There was more sustenance in the three American works on the program. The Concerto for Horn, by Joel Hoffman (born in 1953), a three-movement piece lasting about seventeen minutes, was given its first performance. It is rich in ideas and rich in sound. Although his "orchestra" consists of but four instruments—clarinet, violin, cello, and piano—the sonorities Hoffman draws from the ensemble are full. The lines are living and active, the thematic arguments arresting, and the points of repose—especially an easygoing, romantic episode in the slow movement which reminded me of Carl Nielsen—well placed. The whole structure is firm. Kazimierz Machala was an eloquent soloist.

Three Poems of Günter Grass, by Ronald C. Perera (born in 1941), given its New York première, struck me as somewhat overcomposed. Grass's verses, laconic and understated, achieve some of their considerable power to chill by leaving things unsaid. Perera, setting them for a soprano accompanied by an apparatus of six players, who also chant from time to time, and stereo tape, amplifies every image and spells out every passing allusion. "Gleisdreieck," the first of the songs, begins with a recording of a train clattering across the hall and clanging to a halt; a reference to a spider spinning the web of steel tracks prompts two extended episodes of busy "spider music." "Klappstühle" is a bittersweet waltz fantasy based on Johann Strauss's "Künstlerleben." "Schlaflos" reaches its climax against a babel of Nazi marching songs and Hitler's voice addressing a rally. Perera's command of communicative harmony, carefully paced metres, and sharp-cut, evocative sounds is impressive. The work is ambitious and never dull. But the final effect is of underlining and self-defeating emphasis. The vocal writing is sometimes happy, sometimes Expressionist, with extravagant leaps that make the words inaudible. Jane Seaman, singing in German, pitched the lines securely but, eyes glued to the score, seemed to have no desire to convey their sense to the audience.

Richard Wernick (born in 1934) was known to me before only as the composer of *A Prayer for Jerusalem,* a poignant, quietly passionate invocation for mezzo-soprano and bell sounds, recorded by Jan DeGaetani and Glen Steele on CRI. His *Introits and Canons,* given its first performance at the Juilliard concert, is a substantial piece (three movements, lasting about twenty minutes in all) of close contrapuntal argument, each paragraph of which is devoted to a clearly stated musical "topic." Most of the topics— perhaps all of them—are related. A string quartet (violin, viola, cello, double-bass) sits on the conductor's left and a wind quartet (flute, clarinet, horn, bassoon) on his right; a row of percussion instruments, commanded by a single player, forms the backdrop. The structure is as schematic as that of Bach's "Goldberg" variations—and the music itself is varied in mood and manner. Logic and lyricism combine in a satisfying composition. More Wernick—his *Moonsongs from the Japanese* and *Haiku of Bashō*—can be heard on another CRI disc, and his *Kaddish-Requiem* and *Songs of Remembrance* are on Nonesuch.

It is rare to encounter four new pieces in a program and find merit in all of them; these four I would eagerly listen to again and would recommend to adventurous program planners. It is almost as rare to hear playing of such unfaltering accomplishment. The Juilliard concerts are free. The players are students there, but the execution is on a high professional level—higher than that heard at some concerts on the common contemporary round. The evening brought forward three horn players—Mr. Machala in the concerto, Paul Taylor with a prominent role in the Amy, and William Parker in the Wernick—of exceptional ability. Kenneth Lieberson played a high, cantabile bassoon solo in the Wernick with beautiful tone. Jean Kopperud shone in the clarinet cadenza of the Amy. Daniel Druckman, Leon Malloy, and Marc Sherman were three sensitive, virtuoso percussionists.

January 30, 1978

Taking Opera Seriously

The Teatro Comunale in Bologna is an opera house rich in history. Box 23 on the second tier is a place of pilgrimage; one night in 1871 Verdi, hoping to remain incognito, slipped into this box to hear *Lohengrin,* his first Wagner opera and the first to be performed in Italy. Four years earlier, under the same conductor, Angelo Mariani, the Comunale had given *Don Carlos* its first Italian performance. (Today, large Art Nouveau bas-reliefs of Wagner and Verdi face one another across the main entrance to the orchestra.) The beautiful theatre, designed by Antonio Galli Bibiena, opened in 1763. Gluck, who was traveling in Italy, composed the inaugural opera, a setting of Metastasio's *Il trionfo di Clelia*, and eight years later Gluck's *Orfeo* was done there—the first Italian production apart from a festal presentation to celebrate an archducal wedding in Parma in 1769. The Comunale revived *Orfeo* only in 1898, with Guerrina Fabbri, and then Gluck's name dropped from its bills until this season. Which is surprising, both because other Italian houses have played his works often and because the Comunale in style and scale is an ideal home for them.

Bologna, a cultivated city that has long provided the world with a model of Communist civic administration, has, in the words of Grove, "always been in the vanguard with its concert programmes and opera seasons, which give proof of an always lively desire for knowledge and culture." Rossini's *Il signor Bruschino*, Verdi's first opera, *Oberto*, Janáček's *From the House of the Dead* (brought by the Prague National Theatre), and Stravinsky's *The Rake's Progress* are on the Comunale bill this season. Haydn's *Il mondo della luna*, Rossini's *La donna del lago*, Rimsky-Korsakov's *Christmas Eve*, Prokofiev's *The Fiery Angel*, and Giacomo Manzoni's *Per Massimiliano Robespierre* (an operatic investigation of Stalinism) have been done in recent years. Productions are toured through the cities of the province. It would have been more adventurous to revive *Il trionfo di Clelia*, but the *Orfeo* did have two points of special interest: it was staged by Luca Ronconi, and it was performed from a "pure" Vienna score—the original, 1762 *Orfeo ed Euridice* (contralto hero, Italian text), not the revised and amplified *Orphée et Euridice* (tenor hero, French text), which Gluck prepared for Paris in 1774, or the mixed version (contralto hero, Italian text partly original, partly translated from the French) that is often adopted.

Last year, after Boston's mixed *Orfeo*, I wrote of my eagerness to hear the strong, concise, swift-moving *Orfeo* of Gluck's original intention. Productions of it are becoming commoner: the Royal Swedish Opera has one; London heard one in concert in 1976, with a countertenor hero; Wolf Siegfried Wagner, the composer's great-grandson, directed another at last year's Wexford Festival, also with a countertenor. The Bologna presentation at last confirmed for me what reading the 1762 score had suggested: that, although with a pang one relinquishes the famous instrumental air with flute solo and Eurydice's lovely "Cet asile," *Orfeo* surpasses *Orphée* in directness and dramatic force. It is short: about a hundred minutes of music. At the Bologna performance, two twenty-minute intermissions divided the three acts, and there was also an unhappily prolonged break in Act II while Hell was dismantled and the Elysian Fields were prepared.

The scenes, designed by Pier Luigi Pizzi, were simple and noble in effect, but the means by which they were achieved was anything but simple. (It apparently required ten monster trucks to transport the décor from Florence, where the production originated last season, to Bologna.) The action unfolded on a stage built about five feet above the regular stage floor. In the basement thus formed, damned souls writhed in firelit torment during the fifteen-minute Hell scene, and otherwise all was dark. The upper stage was enclosed by giant walls of mirror which had within them concealed doors and sliding panels. Under skillful lighting, they reflected sometimes the actors, sometimes elements of the noble Bibiena auditorium, or faded to portray a silvery infinitude. There was also the small grove of cypresses and laurels called for in the libretto, realistically and lovingly modeled, and toward the end some massive architectural décor represented the Temple of Love, which extended forward to embrace the Bibiena proscenium arch. The final chorus was sung from the boxes within it. In his handling of colors, forms, and light, Pizzi seems to me a modern disciple of Adolphe Appia. His *Orfeo* scenery was beautiful, and in large part it was a twentieth-century vision, executed in twentieth-century media, of simplified eighteenth-century décor. The Furies, apparently bare breasted, wore black crinolines and raven fright wigs. Orpheus and Eurydice wore costumes like those seen in early engravings. If Gluck had returned to the Comunale, he would have recognized his opera, though he might have asked why there were iron balconies and a catwalk suspended high above Hell, and why on earth a ladies' orchestra (dressed in Victorian bombazine) should be sitting in the Temple of Love. He would not have recognized the idiom of Geoffrey Cauley's choreography—a brave, intermittently successful attempt to put simple, suitable movement patterns to the music without insisting on either eighteenth-century or classical ballet technique.

Ronconi's staging, as usual with him, sought to subordinate the singers' individual personalities to his "idea" of the piece. In practical terms, there was so little light on Orpheus' face that the actress, Julia Hamari, could not really make direct, immediate communication with her audience; Gluck—and a co-creator of the opera, Gaetano Guadagni, a Garrick pupil, the first Orpheus—would surely not have approved. Neither did I. Miss Hamari's singing was serene, grave, well judged, not passionate. But Ileana Cotrubas, the Eurydice, has so much personality that nothing can subdue it. The performance took on new liveliness during the Orpheus-Eurydice recitative and duet that open Act III; Miss Cotrubas's urgency struck answering sparks from the hero. In Florence, the opera had been conducted by Riccardo Muti; in Bologna, Carl Melles did not get strong enough phrasing from either chorus or orchestra.

The season at the Teatro Comunale in Florence began with *Il trovatore* in a new production, also by Ronconi and Pizzi. In a program note, Ronconi explained that, in effect, Verdi had not understood his opera, since Azucena, torn between maternal affection and filial affection, is not at the heart of it:

Il trovatore should instead be read as a mysterious work. . . . One must find its secret knot: its nocturnal side. . . . At the heart of this knot is

Leonora, the mysterious relationship that binds her to the two brothers, that sees her divide herself between a chaste love (Manrico) and a possessive love (the Count of Luna). Thus the central moment of the opera is the one like a flash of lightning which motivates the trio of Act I: in the dark, Leonora mistakes the Count of Luna for Manrico. Exchange and uncertainty of identity: an authentically romantic motif, with profound roots, too, in German romanticism.

Oh, really! How can a clever man be so silly, and so willfully misread what the composer set down in his score and spelled out in his letters? It is true that two brothers who are engaged in murderous rivalry—whether over divine respect for sacrifices animal and vegetable, over patrimony, or over a woman—have been a recurrent theme of literature. To some extent, Manrico and Luna sound overtones of Abel and Cain, Jacob and Esau, Edgar and Edmund, Karl and Franz Moor, Paolo and Gianciotto Malatesta. Their relationship is important to the plot—but only as it affects Azucena. There is no evidence that Leonora feels any mysterious attraction toward Luna. In the dark, she inadvertently embraces the wrong man, but it would make no difference to the course of events if that "moment like a flash of lightning" did not occur—if she embraced the right man and the other then stepped forward with a challenge.

Ronconi, however, with his new insight, finds that the *Trovatore* libretto "can in its way be more interesting than Boito's for *Otello,* which seeks to reduce a Shakespeare text to a bourgeois play." The poetic mystery, he declares, should therefore be presented in an almost unchanging set, against backcloths hinting at sky, night, fire, and ashes—with fire and, consequently, ashes ever more dominant. On the stage, not objects but only their images or shadows. What this meant in practice was a décor of three tall frames arranged in various dispositions on an almost bare stage cased in mirror walls of dusky gold. Empty, the frames served as portals; filled with gauze, they became screens on which the shadow silhouettes of three identical cypresses were projected to represent the palace garden, and of three identical towers to represent the scene outside Manrico's prison. It was very beautiful scenery, romanticized Appia in idiom, and it did convert *Il trovatore* into a kind of poetic mystery. But it also meant that the actors, reduced to shadows moving through a tenebrous world where only braziers provided points of sparkling light, lost individuality. Ronconi naturally paid special attention to the staging of the encounter before the Act I trio. Leonora's mistake, which in some productions arouses an audience's mirth, seemed easy to make: it was very dark, the brothers were dressed alike, and the action was so arranged that Leonora, hastening toward the Troubadour's voice, would inevitably encounter Luna first. The emphasis on the fraternal motif also led to an unusual intentness in the singing of Manrico's account of his duel with Luna: "The thrust that should have transfixed him already flashed on high when a mysterious impulse stayed my descending hand . . . while a cry from Heaven said to me, 'Do not strike!' " To that "Non ferir!," which Verdi marked "*ppp,* sotto voce," Carlo Cossutta, an able Manrico, brought a strange otherworldly color.

Otherwise, Ronconi seemed content for the principals to give their usual *Trovatore* performances. Fiorenza Cossotto, a veteran Azucena, certainly did. Gilda Cruz-Romo, the Leonora, was sweet and musical but sometimes gentle to the point of feebleness. Her contribution to the "Miserere" was a series of agitated whispered exclamations, which was effective enough. In the preceding aria, at "Lo desta alle memorie" she sounded a quiet descant to a flute solo, and in the duet with Luna there was no flash in her tone for "Vivrà! contende il giubilo." Matteo Manuguerra was the Luna—reliable, solid, a shade lacking in fire. Agostino Ferrin, the Ferrando, delivered the opening narration as if he were really interested in it. (Five of the first six numbers in *Il trovatore* are narratives about the past, and, except at the close of Act III, all the action happens offstage. The singers need to be good at telling stories.) The gypsies were robed in white, as if they had come dressed for *Die Zauberflöte*. Leonora and Manrico sang their Act III duettino divided by a gauze.

Riccardo Muti conducted. The bright, open, translucent acoustics of the Comunale and the conductor's habitual care for orchestral balance combined to produce an unusually clear and vivid account of the score. One could hear each element making up the soft, fully scored chords that open the last scene. Muti's rhythms were alert; his speed changes were precisely judged. In a way, one could hardly hope to hear *Il trovatore* better played. And yet I found much of the result unmoving—exquisite but cold, as Muti's Verdi often is—because his singers were treated as staves of the full score. He never seemed to take sudden inspiration from them but subdued them musically, as Ronconi had subdued them dramatically, to a set idea of the work. There was no living drama of personalities; the dominant presence was the conductor's. The result was not theatre as Verdi understood it. When I got back to New York and heard what heavy going Giuseppe Patanè and his Met cast made of the same music, I felt more appreciative of Muti's lucid textures, springy pulses, and energetic phrasing. But in the Comunale I asked myself why so polished and vigorous a musical execution of this rousing piece should prove so curiously unstirring.

The opera was given complete. Cabaletta reprises were undecorated, and it was claimed as merit that Cossutta added no high C's to "Di quella pira." A final C does produce harmonic clashes, it is true, but the C traditionally thrown in at "Teco almeno" seems to me an admirable enhancement—even a necessary one the second time through when both verses are sung.

Claudio Abbado has become the Verdi conductor who unites all the Verdian virtues. The second opera of the Scala season, after the Ronconi-directed *Don Carlos*, was a revival of Franco Zeffirelli's staging of *Un ballo in maschera*, first done there five years ago with Lou Ann Wyckoff, Placido Domingo, and Piero Cappuccilli in the leading roles and Gianandrea Gavazzeni as conductor, and revived two seasons later with Montserrat Caballé, José Carreras, and Renato Bruson. This season's cast was Shirley Verrett, Luciano Pavarotti, and Cappuccilli, and Abbado conducted. *Ballo* came to the stage three weeks after *Don Carlos* but was described as coming to it unready. (What can Scala rehearsal schedules be like?) The unreadiness showed itself only in some sudden lapses of ensemble between stage and pit. In all other ways, the opera was splendidly executed.

I had seen *Ballo* many times before, but never in the Colonial Boston setting specified in the score—always in the Swedish court of the Scribe libretto from which Antonio Somma's libretto for Verdi was adapted. Renzo Mongiardino had designed handsome scenery in a log-cabin palatial style. Enrico Job's costumes threw Puritans and patricians into picturesque contrast. The program book, ninety pages long, contained not only the libretto but also, in facsimile, the *disposizione scenica*, or production book, published after the opera's first performance, in 1859. Zeffirelli's staging was not always in strictest accord with it, but did not stray unacceptably far from the composer's intentions until, in the final scene, during Riccardo's death all the glittering decorations of the ballroom disappeared, as if by magic—a stagy and inappropriate conceit. Zeffirelli is a master at drawing good acting from his cast, and I have never seen Pavarotti give a more convincing performance of Riccardo—or of any role, for that matter. Moreover, he now seemed so much at ease in the drama that to his newfound vocal force he added the old freshness and freedom, throwing himself into the meaning of the lines, and not just throwing his voice into their notes. Miss Verrett, singing her first Amelia, was moving. A touch of caution, some hints of timidity here and there were not inappropriate to the character. After its recent ups and downs—up to Norma, down to Orpheus—her voice seemed to have settled as a dark soprano, not expansive but intense and affecting in timbre. Cappuccilli sang grandly; Zeffirelli had not quite cured him of some old-fashioned semaphore gestures. Elena Obraztsova was a powerful Ulrica. Daniela Mazzucato, as Oscar, sang charmingly.

Abbado's instrumental reading was bold and very strongly colored. He seized on what are sometimes deemed the crudities of Verdi's orchestration to make them thrilling and eloquent. In a program note, he drew attention to the musical as well as the stage significance of the *disposizione scenica:* "One has only to compare the sequence of stage plans (setting out here soloists, there choral masses, supers) to see how the visual images are always in balance with the musical forces; there is conscious interdependence of these values in the allotment of scenic space." The contrasts of timbre, texture, and density were stressed. The Scala orchestra played superbly. Abbado was forceful but also tender, passionate but also precise. And it was an interpretation that ever took life from, and gave life to, what was happening on the stage.

Back in New York, James Levine and John Dexter's campaign to make the Metropolitan a house that musicians and playgoers take seriously received a setback in the form of a tawdry, unintelligent presentation of Massenet's *Thaïs*, played in a production borrowed from San Francisco. *Thaïs* is a pretty opera, and very skillfully written, but it was a mistake to essay it without a heroine more alluring of voice and more secure on exposed, sustained high notes above the staff than Beverly Sills was. Moreover, Miss Sills was histrionically unconvincing. She seemed too refreshingly sensible and self-aware to have or to inspire any unquestioning belief in her portrayal, and instead invited the audience to enjoy watching her play at playing Thaïs. She brought to her impersonation a twinkling touch of the light, ironical, even critical tone that belongs properly to Anatole France's *Thaïs* and has no place in the heart-on-sleeve, committedly sentimental opera fashioned from it. France's novel is attractive on several counts: its precise, carefully balanced prose and dry, delicate wit; the display of a polished Parisian mind darting over Christian, Stoic, and Skeptic philosophies; the picturesque evocation of fourth-century Alexandrian and Thebaid life; and the depiction of a heroine of extraordinary grace and charm, beautiful in body and in spirit. His source was a play by Hrosvitha, a tenth-century German nun. Hrosvitha's works were staged in Paris, by puppets, in 1888, and France reviewed them favorably. The eleventh Britannica calls them "productions of genius"— which seems to me, who know them only in translation, to rate them too high. In any event, France ranged far beyond the simple moral drama and handled the history in no pious way. At the center of his book is a symposium: Alexandrian philosophers, getting steadily drunker, discuss religion, government, and ethics, and the bold argument is put forward that not as Christ but as Helen of Troy did God's will become incarnate, to suffer all men's violence and wickedness. When the mortal Helen died, her immortal spirit entered new forms; today, mankind's redeemer is Thaïs. Thaïs leaves the party remarking that philosophers are goats, and is a ready prey to the lofty promises held out to her by Paphnuce, the monk who has come to claim her for Christ.

There could be no place for this in an opera. Louis Gallet, Massenet's librettist, omitted the irony, the kaleidoscope of daring speculations, and all the jokes. The tone was quite altered. So was the hero, in more than name. France's Paphnuce is preposterous and unlikable. He spits in Thaïs's face. Only toward the end of the book, when he ceases to regard his sufferings as Heaven-sent and realizes how foolish he had been to reject the glorious gift Thaïs offered him, does the author treat him as anything but ridiculous. Gallet's Athanaël—his name a happy blend of Athanasius, the early Bishop of Alexandria, and Nathanael, the disciple in whom there was no guile—is austere and impressive in his anguish. Both men strive, finally in vain, to repress the promptings of a deeply passionate nature, but Athanaël's torment has dignity. This dignity is denied him in the Met staging, where in the dream sequence of the first scene he starts up, tears open his habit, and lewdly pursues Thaïs. He becomes another goat. The hint of complexity in his motives for seeking the conversion of the courtesan is replaced by comic-strip crudity.

Three years ago, the Baltimore Opera showed how *Thaïs* should be done—with trust in Massenet's stagecraft, in his ability to match musical and visual images for an audience's pleasure. The opera begins with a tranquil white-note melody, picturing the peaceful life of cenobites in the Thebaid, and the curtain rises when, after some mock-modal wanderings, the melody is resumed at its original pitch: "Twelve cenobites and old Palemon are seated around a long rustic table. Palemon, in the center, presides over a frugal, peaceful meal. One place, Athanaël's, is empty." At the Met, the curtain rose on some crudely modeled rocks and cliffs, looking like remnants of a discarded *Ring* set, on which the cenobites stood about as valkyrie-monks awaiting the return of their Brünnhilde-Athanaël. The rocks, variously pushed around, and the flanking cliffs remained onstage for the rest of the evening, while tons of tinselly tat poured down from the flies to deck them as the terrace of Nicias's house in Alexandria ("overlooking the city and the sea, shaded by huge trees") and Thaïs's boudoir. This décor, by Carl Toms, was not merely vulgar and ugly; it was inefficient. The tensions of the boudoir scene disappear when it is played across a space suggesting Grand Central strung with Christmas decorations. The dramatic contrast between Thaïs and Athanaël's passionate dialogue in what should be an oppressively rich, sultry, incense-laden room and their simple, serene duet beneath the palms of the desert oasis is destroyed. On a practical level, Thaïs's gaudy hammock bed, six feet above the ground and accessible only from one of those rocky ramps, seemed a hazardous piece of furniture for a courtesan to have.

Tito Capobianco's staging was similarly vulgar and inefficient. Thaïs began both "Qui te fait si sévère" and "Dis-moi que je suis belle" lying flat on her back—not an easy posture in which to communicate to an audience of thousands. How much more effective if she starts the first advancing toward Athanaël "sweetly and gracefully, and looking at him with a wicked smile"! How cheap to preface the second with an "Ô mon miroir fidèle, rassure-moi" addressed to a full-length ceiling mirror over the bed! Neither piece made much effect; it was as if director and diva had conspired to flatten out numbers that one thought simply couldn't fail to be outstanding. In the straightforward old Paris Opera production, I used to hear singers less beautiful to look at than Miss Sills and no more vocally gifted bring the house down with those passages—because they knew how to present them. Another poor idea of Mr. Capobianco's was to treat the beautiful Méditation as a ballet, danced out in a room of mirrors by Miss Sills and two Doppelgänger. (I think they represented Thaïs in innocent youth and crabbed age, but the lighting was dim and it was hard to be sure.) The violin solo was eloquently played by Raymond Gniewek. "It is precisely in such silken, caressing terms as these," Ernest Newman once wrote, "that a Thaïs would embrace a new faith—she would see the new life opening out before her as promising, for all its renunciations, something of the old sensuous happiness that had been the very breath of her being in the old life." The Méditation, at least, is easily put right: in future performances the Met can drop a curtain, save itself a scene shift, and allow Massenet to depict "those long night hours of lonely musing" in his own way.

Sherrill Milnes sang Athanaël's music strongly but did not declaim the words vividly. Betsy Norden and Isola Jones were a pretty pair of slave girls. As their master, Nicias, Raymond Gibbs quite missed the airy elegance of "Ne t'offense pas," the catchiest tune in all the opera. John Pritchard conducted. He understands the style, and he secured colorful playing from the orchestra. On the first night, director and designer were roundly booed.

February 6, 1978

Renaissance

If I have written seldom about performances of music earlier than that of the seventeenth century, it is not through lack of interest but because most performances I have attended here have struck me as hardly worth writing about—inexpertly executed, or executed by tiny forces in spaces too large for the music to tell. It made better sense to stay at home in the recorded company of the Early Music Consort, Musica Reservata, the Consort of Musicke, and the many other ensembles that have turned medieval and Renaissance music into a household sound. "Early music"—that catch-all term for compositions from about the eighth to the eighteenth century—is big on the contemporary scene. One sign of that is the flourishing of the quarterly magazine *Early Music*, published by the Oxford University Press (from a London house that once belonged to the bishops of Ely), and the second most lavishly produced of all music periodicals. (First place must be given to *About the House*, the magazine of the Friends of Covent Garden.) In the January 1976 issue of *Early Music*, its editor reflected on "When will the early-music bubble burst?"—a question in the air at a time when, in his words, "night after night in London both the Queen Elizabeth Hall and the Purcell Room are thronged with audiences responsive to the larger-scale masterpieces, such as the Monteverdi Vespers, or to the marvelous variety of programmes that unfolds nightly of the less charted regions." The messiah of the movement was David Munrow, the director of the Early Music Consort, a virtuoso player of several wind instruments, and a popular star who opened people's ears and minds to early music in much the way that Isadora once opened people's eyes and minds to dance. He reached wider audiences than had his predecessors in the field—Noah Greenberg, John Beckett. He made many records. The latest to be published in this country, by Angel, is "Renaissance Suite," Munrow's score for the Joël Santoni film about bicycle racing, *La Course en tête*, in which branles from Michael Praetorius's *Terpsichore* (1612) accompany "They're off!" and a basse-danse from Tielman Susato's *Danserye* (1551) represents "On the road." Another Angel record, "Henry VIII and His Six Wives," is the sound track of a BBC production that brought Tudor music on Tudor instruments to many a television loudspeaker. There is, of course, a danger that early music may be debased to medieval Muzak—but Munrow was an educator as well as an entertainer. Although he put communication before authenticity, he knew his styles and had a rare gift for finding treasure in the midden of past centuries. With passionate, infectious enthusiasm, he would lead listeners from some attractive, dancing apéritif to music of solemn grandeur or of intimate spiritual intensity. He gave his last concert— "Monteverdi's Contemporaries," recorded on Angel S-37524—in May 1976. The next day, he killed himself. He was thirty-three.

The early-music bubble has not burst—as a glance at the articles, advertisements, and activity reports in the latest *Early Music* will show. In May last year, there was a conference, chaired by Howard Mayer Brown, Professor of Music at the University of Chicago and editor of Oxford's Early Music Series, on the Future of Early Music in Britain. Performers, publishers, instrument makers, and people from the Arts Council and the BBC (two bodies whose funding makes so many performances possible) assembled to exchange views. Mr. Brown has long urged that the music colleges should set standards as high for their lute, viol, and recorder graduates as for pianists, violinists, and flutists, and should "institute a supporting programme of instruction that will prepare their [early-music] students satisfactorily for a demanding professional life." It will hardly be denied that our conservatories devote most of their technical instruction to a single century of music's long history, or that music of before about 1850—Bach, Mozart, Beethoven, Schubert—is taught mainly on instruments of the Romantic era (except where harpsichordists and organists are concerned). But the number of skillful early-music performers increases. The calendar of their recitals in and around New York (assembled monthly in the *Early Music Newsletter*, published by the New York Recorder Guild) grows long. In and around Boston, early music is even more prominent. (The corresponding Boston calendar is published by the Musical Instruments Collection of the Museum of Fine Arts.) No new Greenberg, no American Munrow has yet emerged—no single popular Pied Piper (under that title Munrow had an afternoon radio show for children which drew a devoted adult following) to set crowds running merrily after the wonderful music with shouting and laughter. But several times this season Alice Tully Hall has been thronged with audiences responsive to a variety of early-music programs.

The hall, with its bleak foyer and (except when the organ is revealed) plain wood-slat auditorium, is not a very jolly place, and it is unresonant, but at recent concerts something has been done to cheer it. When the New York Renaissance Band played there last week, it did so from a kind of bandstand erected on the platform, decked with blue bunting, flanked by palms, fringed by ferns, and brightly lit by more than the usual, vertical light, which leaves performers' eyes in shadow. (But the men all dressed in their customary suits of solemn black, which dulled the effect.) The band, directed by Sally Logemann, had twelve players, who, with instrument changes, formed quartets of shawms, recorders, dulcians, and crumhorns, a cornett-sackbut quartet, a pair of violas da gamba, lute, and percussion. The program was nicely planned: a Susato suite as apéritif; from Italy, a late-fifteenth-century group based on Heinrich Isaac and Josquin des Prez; a Kyrie and set of basse-danses based on the tune "La Spagna." Then, after the intermission, a mixed bag from Italy, with grandeur in the form of a Frescobaldi eight-part canzona and virtuosity from the lutenist, Marc Prensky, in a Francesco da Milano fantasy; and a final group based on cismontane Isaac and Josquin. Much of the fare would have been familiar to record collectors: Josquin's "Scaramella" and Isaac's "Donna, di dentro dalla tua casa" have been at least four times recorded, and that Alonso de Mudarra lute fantasy "imitating the harp as played by Ludovico" at least six times (usually on the guitar). The Top Twenty on the Renaissance hit parade remain pretty constant. But each group makes them sound different.

The most evident difference between otherwise comparable British and American ensembles—the Early Music Consort and the New York Renaissance Band, the Fires of London and Speculum Musicae, the London Symphony and the Chicago Symphony—is that the former *show* their enjoyment in their music making, while the latter tend to treat concerts as solemn, formal occasions. Smiles of pleasure on an American platform—at the sound, at the music, at some neatly turned phrase—are rare. Of the Renaissance Band players, only one of the cornettists and one of the violists really *looked* happy. I'm not sure whether the difference of demeanor makes any difference to the execution, whether it could be heard in a recording, although I suspect it does and could. I am sure that it does make a difference to an audience's response. One would not want all concerts to be "hosted" with the bonny, beaming, chatterbox informality of Charles Wadsworth at those of the Chamber Music Society; but one reason for going to a concert instead of staying at home with records is the sense it provides of shared experience. Moreover, people attend early-music concerts to learn as well as to listen. At this one, there were interesting and useful program notes by Richard Taruskin, and texts and translations of the sung numbers were included. But they were imperfectly reproduced from small, single-spaced typewriting, and the hall lighting was so faint that to follow them needed concentration that should be given to the music itself. Charge a dollar more for entry if necessary (tickets were only six-fifty), and use it to insure that the work of the artists and the music they perform make their full effect.

However, the band did avoid dangers that Mr. Brown has described as "imposing modern standards of showmanship derived at least partly from the demands of the box office" and seeking to "titillate the modern jaded palate with a series of exotic noises from the past." Marchetto Cara's frottola "Non è tempo d'aspettare" sung by Jeffrey Gall, lute-accompanied, became almost a different piece from—less bouncy, less brilliant, but not less attractive than—the one heard on the Early Music Consort's Nonesuch record "The Pleasures of the Royal Courts," where the voice is brightly accompanied by shawm, fiddle, viol, and harpsichord. The lack of violence in the band's playing was most taking, and it did not preclude liveliness, dancing rhythms, or tangy timbres. Balance was unfailingly excellent, within each family of instruments, in dialogues between them, and in broken consorts. They sounded as if they were enjoying themselves. It was a good concert.

Two days earlier, the Concert Royal Orchestra performed J. S. and C. P. E. Bach and early Haydn in the hall, and was joined by the New York Baroque Dance Company in a Georg Muffat dance suite. But the twentieth century beckoned over at the Brooklyn Academy of Music, and I missed them. Earlier that week, the Ensemble for Early Music, directed by Frederick Renz, put on an evening of "Renaissance Revels." The ensemble—two singers and three players—was joined by the New York Cornet and Sacbut Ensemble (its own spelling), the Early Music String Band, two more singers and a percussionist, and the Terpsichore Early Dance Ensemble. As if in emulation of Town Hall, Tully Hall sported a tapestry hung above the platform. It was a lightweight evening of pleasant entertainment, mostly from the early seventeenth century, offered without explanations and without Italian texts. But afterward, in the foyer, Julia Sutton, the director of Terpsichore, invited the audience to learn some of the old steps.

That afternoon, in Corpus Christi Church, a good place in which to hear early music [see page 55], the New York Tudor Consort had offered a modest and pleasing recital. Brenda Fairaday, accompanied by baroque flutes, recorders, and violas da gamba, a harpsichord, and an organetto in varying combinations, sang a group of early-sixteenth-century Italian pieces, a group from the seventeenth century (Monteverdi and Steffani), and then an extended Purcell anthology. Miss Fairaday has a sweet, limpid tone; she is gentle in manner and fluent in divisions. There is no trace of what Mr. Brown once called the "Musica Reservata holler"—that open, uncovered, very direct, almost raw kind of vocal production. I remember eavesdropping while some French students, during the intermission of a Musica Reservata concert in the Sainte-Chapelle, approached Jantina Noorman, the vocalist with the group, to ask her, almost with awe, how she produced the sounds she did. And her reply: "I just open my mouth and scream." She demonstrated. Miss Noorman (who, incidentally, sings this week in the Early Music Series of the Boston Museum of Fine Arts) simplified; it is a cultivated and disciplined kind of "screaming" that she emits. One could do with a touch more hollering in most of the early-music vocalism one hears around New York—less English-choirboy refinement, more of the Montserrat (the monastery, not the diva), or Mediterranean-brat, timbre. And one could do with stronger sounding of the words. There were no texts for Miss Fairaday's recital, and sometimes key words were unintelligible.

February 13, 1978

Playing in Earnest

On Monday last week, Frederic Rzewski played his fifty-five-minute-long piano piece *The People United Will Never Be Defeated!* in Carnegie Recital Hall. Outside, snow was falling. I plowed home through the drifts thinking about Sicily and the sixth Settimana Internazionale in Palermo, where last I encountered Mr. Rzewski and his music. Other things that I planned to write about this week—the Met's revival of *Adriana Lecouvreur*, the Philharmonic's Prospective Encounters concert in the Great Hall of Cooper Union, Harold C. Schonberg's Sunday *Times* article declaring that "Élitism, in the Arts, Is Good"—took shape against a Sicilian background. Snow is still falling, and I am tempted to linger in Sicily for a while.

The sixth Settimana, held during the last five days of 1968, consisted of seven concerts of contemporary music (most of the pieces were receiving their first performances), four bills of music theatre, an art show, and morning and afternoon screenings of "free cinema." Any chinks were filled with lectures and discussions. I also played hooky to attend a decent performance of *Simon Boccanegra* and as much as I could bear—an act and a half—of Giordano's rubbishy *Fedora*, which were on at the Teatro Massimo. The program book—the fullest and most informative I have encountered at an international music festival—opened with a rather coy editorial explaining that the venerable Amici della Musica, Sicily's oldest concert society, had decided to open its portals to, as it were, a young friend in a Marcuse beard:

> Let us hope that during these days we will not often have Poe's tremendous adventure, discovering in the girl's body the features of a painted old hag. Yet even that comes within our scope: to go to exasperating extremes so as to rid the new culture of its inferior elements. All will flee from the ancient house; the maiden will be nude. The Settimana puts things to the practical test.

It began with Luigi Nono's *Contrappunto dialettico alla mente*, a modern madrigal cycle fashioned after Adriano Banchieri's *Festino*, for voices, naturalistic sounds (of the Venice fish market, water lapping in the lagoon, the bells of San Marco), and electronic modifications thereof—all on tape, and assembled by Nono's delicate, precise ear. The work was commissioned as Italian Radio's entry for the Italia prize (awarded for the best radio feature of the year) but then not entered lest, it was said, the finale—a setting of "Uncle Sam wants YOU nigger," from a manifesto of Black Women Enraged and the Harlem Progressive Labor Club—should offend Americans. It is a strong and beautiful composition. I sometimes wonder why orchestras when introducing a difficult score that needs much rehearsal time do not bill on the same program a tape piece—Nono's *La fabbrica illuminata* is another that deserves hearing—which needs no rehearsal time but only a balance test.

The music came to Palermo from all over Europe and from America. Each concert was planned to illustrate a particular aspect of the contemporary scene. No general picture emerged. There was—and is—no general tendency to be discerned in contemporary music. By 1968, the well-defined waves of pointillism, total serialization, huge-orchestra sound structures, and aleatory games had broken, leaving drenched composers to build as best they could amid the debris on the beach. Disciplines clashed. One of the most orderly and seductive compositions heard in Palermo was Morton Feldman's *False Relationships and the Extended Ending*, for violin, cello, trombone, three pianos, and bells. (It is recorded on CRI SD 276.) At the last minute, the conductor who had prepared it, very carefully, was asked not to conduct the performance, since the composer felt his piece might be spoiled if it was given a precise rather than an approximate execution.

One element alone was fairly constant: vociferous, voluble student protest. All over Italy, that season, the opera houses had opened amid student and worker demonstrations; police had been at hand to insure that the bourgeoisie reached the theatres in safety, unmolested except by the flinging of vegetables and insults. In Palermo, the first music-theatre show was held up for an hour, until it was ascertained that the police reinforcements outside the building had been called off. There was no physical violence, none of the steel-helmeted brutality that in Hamburg, earlier in the month, had put an end to the première of Henze's *The Raft of the Medusa*. But in the Sicilian town of Avola, shortly before, two strikers had been killed by the police, and so rallying cries of "Avola!" often rang out. During the rowdy arguments, Baron Francesco Agnello, the festival's organizer, acted as an adroit and sympathetic compere. Curious scene: Imagine holding the Met curtain for an hour on opening night while the management provided a microphone for protesters, defenders, the artists, and any members of the audience who wanted to join in to have their say, and Anthony Bliss delivered sane, conciliatory comment from a box. Of course, things are different here. Although the Met consumes much public money in the form of taxes unpaid on contributions to it, that indirect method of subsidy does not seem to give the public a sense of proprietorship or lead it to question as of right the way its money is being spent.

The questions in Palermo were whether so much money was being justly spent on an avant-garde festival when most Sicilians were poor, and whether publicly subsidized art for the élite could ever be justified in the world today. But protest sometimes shot off at tangents. When Gregory Markopoulos's film *Iliac Passion* was withdrawn from public screening (because Italian censorship disapproved of scenes of homosexual love on public view) and was shown instead to a select audience of critics and consenting adults, the students objected. That evening, Cornelius Cardew's *Two Books of Study for Pi-*

anists was played, by an Italian duo, to an unplanned obbligato of "Film!" and "Markopoulos!" and went largely unheard except by a handful of listeners who clustered round the pianos. The première of Brian Ferneyhough's two-piano sonata was abandoned after a page or two. Only the Danish Wind Quintet, which had come from Copenhagan to introduce some of its compatriots' work, got a hearing: there was plainly no point barracking five youths who did not understand Italian. The more thoughtful students dissociated themselves from the racket over side issues. The main issues were important—and still are—but heated public discussion of them before an audience chiefly impatient to get on with the music generated more sound than sense. Deprived of their film, why should the students deprive themselves—and everyone else—of a concert, too? Because, someone retorted, that was the only way they could make their objections heard. Where were the workers? someone asked. No one asked what workers would make of Nono's or Cardew's music. While Russian musicians were struggling for the right to compose, perform, and hear avant-garde music, Western students were damning music written in an idiom not understood by the people.

It was stimulating to be among people who cared so keenly about music's role in society, salutary to have questions that must lurk in every critic's conscience forced into the open (even if they soon retreated unanswered), and therapeutic to attend, on New Year's Eve, a concert at which the tensions of the preceding days were resolved in mass music making. The work was *Play*, a collective improvisation in which "the rules, the scaffolding, have gradually been stripped away, to be replaced by the more fragile stuff of human trust," and it was put on by MEV, or Musica Elettronica Viva, a Rome-based ensemble of which Rzewski was a founder-member. The concert was given in the Politeama Garibaldi, a pleasantly pretentious building of 1874, crowned by a quadriga by Mario Rutelli, the sculptor of the outsize lyric lion on the steps of the Teatro Massimo. (Its companion the tragic lion is by another hand.) The Politeama has galleries, halls, and homes for learned societies, and at its heart a lofty auditorium designed in a sophisticated expansion of the Pompeian manner. In 1968, it was a little shabby, but when the lights dimmed, the frescoed ceiling and the complicated details of colonnaded galleries became magical. If the ear was bored, the eye could find things to explore. Which is as it should be in a concert hall. *Play* began in dim light with a pretty girl sitting in a translucent, illuminated blow-up chair and clutching a contact microphone to her breast. Through loudspeakers encompassing the hall we heard her breathing; her heartbeat provided the steady pulse of the composition as electronic chitterings and then soft, tentative solos from a handful of instrumentalists around her stole into the sound. A trombonist prowled around the spaces of the hall, adding his improvisations from afar. The texture grew more complicated. It did seem as if a kind of spell were being cast, and people felt an impulse to add musical comments of their own. Since a program note stated that "the intervention of the listener is not treated as an intrusion, but is welcomed," listeners intervened—some gravely, some in jest, some to provide criticism in kind of the increasingly disorderly, loosely linked sound patterns that were now being strung out through the hall. Critics, as it happened, were the first to mount the platform itself, where there were a couple of pianos to spare and the less portable percussion—a selection of thunder sheets, big drums, a wind machine, a rack of tuned wine bottles—remained in place from a previous concert. Children joined them—and a few critics became children again. There is something irresistible about a thunder sheet. Soon everyone was at "play"; the piece had become a high-spirited free-for-all. An exuberant, extended scherzo led to a dying fall and then a pointillist coda as, one by one, the executants acknowledged that playtime was over. We had all been not just listening to but making music—well, music of a kind. And it was an exhilarating experience.

In this month's Carnegie Hall program books, Herbert Kupferberg writes an essay on criticism, and says, "The chiefest of a critic's joys is to serve . . . as a discoverer, a yea-sayer, an enthusiast." Rzewski's *The People United Will Never Be Defeated!* had been discovered before. It was composed in 1975, for Ursula Oppens, and was first played by her at the Kennedy Center early in 1976; later that year she introduced it to New York; it has been recorded by its composer on a Milanese label, Edizioni di Cultura Popolare [and now by Miss Oppens on Vanguard VSD 71248]. But for me it was a discovery at last week's recital, and I am enthusiastic about it. The work is a set of thirty-six variations on a Chilean song, "¡El pueblo unido jamás será vencido!," by Sergio Ortega and the performing group Quilapayún—a song that, according to Rzewski, "is now familiar to millions of people in many countries as a symbol of the Chilean democratic movement" and is "a good example of the New Chilean Song, a form of music that flourished during the years of the Popular Unity Government." The theme, like that little waltz by Diabelli on which fifty composers wrote single variations and Beethoven wrote thirty-three, or the Paganini caprice and Handel theme on which Brahms wrote, respectively, twenty-eight variations and twenty-five variations and a fugue, has a catchy melody, sharp rhythmic outlines, and a firm, simple harmonic structure. And so, like them, it can provide the material for a very long set of variations, held together by more than a tune put through differing paces. The manner of building and of breaking down to build again is that of Beethoven in the Diabelli, the late bagatelles, and the last sonatas. The theme disintegrates into isolated notes scattered across the gamut of the keyboard, solidifies into a sequence of slow "frozen" chords, dissolves into an ecstasy of quiet trills, and is almost silenced during an elliptical episode when the music doesn't quite come through but comes in snatches, dim, then keen, then mute, "like fragments of an absent melody." Sometimes the theme bursts into long tendrils of lyrical cantilena; sometimes it is reduced to a few stern gestures. In some variations, the distinctive march rhythm of the opening, seeming to reiterate "the peo'ple [*rest*] uni'ted," is all that remains of it. There are slow funeral marches with heavy tread, purposeful, springy march sequences that suggest heads held high, dances, meditations, rhapsodies, toccatas, two-part inventions. The thirty-six variations fall into six groups of six, and the last of each group in some way recapitulates ideas from the previous five. The work, its composer says, tells a story that cannot be put into words. In musical terms, it is a story expertly told, which holds a listener's attention securely. The writing is that of a composer-pianist who has mastered late Beethoven through his mind and his fingers at once, and also knows the piano writing and piano thinking of Boulez and Stockhausen. Classical precedent suggests that the work will come to its climax in a fugue; instead, before the last variation Rzewski writes "cadenza," and at his recital he improvised a long, brilliant outburst of music. He is a very fine pianist, with big, strong, clear tone that never became clattery, with velocity, delicacy, an incisive command of rhythm, and a compelling personality. Horowitz and Sviatoslav Richter should look at *The People United.* So should young pianists who, having learned the Diabelli and the Brahms-Paganini, now want an accessible twentieth-century work that puts their stamina and their technique to a comparable test.

Political music takes odd turns. Cardew, who showed one of the most curious and questing minds to be found in British music, has renounced complexity in favor of arranging, very simply, simple ditties, such as the Chinese song "Hatred in my heart sprouts a hundredfold." Henze (in *We Come to the River*) and David Blake (in *Toussaint*) have cast their convictions in grand-opera form. Rzewski's *Coming Together* (1972), on a text by Sam Melville, an Attica inmate, is rebuked in Cardew's polemical volume *Stockhausen Serves Imperialism* ("The error of the piece is that it treats its subject in a subjective way"), but Cardew was the narrator at its London performance in 1976. *Coming Together* and the companion piece *Attica* are recorded by Opus One. Rzewski's declarative style of the early seventies can also be heard in three songs recorded by David Holloway (Folkways FTS 33903): the words carry the weight; the music does little more than give them an extra drive. The third of the songs, "Apolitical Intellectuals," is Ivesian. They are strong and direct, but Rzewski's music is stronger still when he works on a large scale. His big set of piano variations on a song, "No Place to Go But Around" (1974), intended for the Living Theatre production of *The Tower of Money*, is a precursor of *The People United.* (It is recorded by the composer on Finnadar SR 9011.) Late Beethoven, Liszt, and Busoni are the prominent influences.

The People United formed the first part of the Carnegie recital; after the intermission there were new variations on "No Place to Go," improvised *a due* by Rzewski on the piano and Richard Teitelbaum on a Moog synthesizer, and then improvisations *a tre* (Karl Hans Berger, on vibraphone, joined the ensemble) on a tricky little diatonic tune. In the first set, the Moog added background noises, mystic echoes, a voice in descant, a sonic storm. In both sets, Rzewski's collaborators showed themselves to be composers so much less creative than he is that the main interest was in hearing him take up their rather commonplace contributions to make something arresting of them. His skill along those lines I had already discovered at the Palermo *Play* when, from one of the spare pianos, I tossed a sow's ear in C major into the melee and he caught it and, at another piano, spun it into something wonderful.

. . .

The Philharmonic's Prospective Encounters are this season reduced to two and are conducted by Gunther Schuller. His laudable aim is to bring to New Yorkers the work of composers from other parts of the country. His first program consisted of five short pieces: three of them had had their first performances in New England; two were by composers who live in Berkeley; one came from Sweden. Whether by chance or by design, they were all eventful scores, sequences of colorful incidents and striking gestures, not—at any rate, not noticeably—of connected discourse. It was an evening of woodwind virtuosity: Stanley Drucker shone in Olly Wilson's *Echoes*, for clarinet and two-track tape; the flutist Stephanie Jutt was captivating in David Stock's *Scat* and William Thomas McKinley's *Paintings No. 2*. Lynne Webber was the accomplished scat singer. None of the works calls for special comment but none was dull. It was an agreeable evening, and Mr. Schuller, a conductor who can be trusted to convey the spirit of a piece even when the execution of some of its details may be less than meticulous, made listeners feel they had come for enjoyment rather than instruction. Unhappy, and with reason, about the usual form of question time afterward ("Why don't you write tunes?"), he tried a new idea—a gathering of a few composers at the foot of the platform to discuss the works played and "problems in general." His intention, "to create the ambience such as you have in a Parisian café after a concert," was not fulfilled; in the Great Hall it hardly could be. New York concert halls lack cafés where large numbers can congregate to talk. (In passing, let me throw in a lament about Carnegie Hall's once pleasant but now lugubrious café, newly decorated in bordello-parlor taste, with dark-green flock walls, mirrors, gilding, and shrouded lamps. Some benefactor please donate a few gallons of whitewash to the hall.) Perhaps near Cooper Union there is a real café that could be wired for sound so that after a concert an audience could gather and eavesdrop on stimulating conversation; within the Union there was no place to go, nothing to eat, nothing to drink but water (and a long line for that). But there was a table set with nourishing fare for sale in the form of CRI recordings (including Wilson's *Echoes*, on SD 367), and that was good.

Adriana Lecouvreur, in the words of Grove, "is a work of decided charm and accomplishment." It is carefully composed, unexacting, unimportant, and enjoyable when as well sung as in the current Met revival. Essentially, the piece is an opéra comique skillfully expanded to fill a big house: the Prince de Bouillon and the Abbé de Chazeuil are Le Dancaïre and Remendado, from *Carmen*, in new costumes; Frasquita and Mercédès have become actresses at the Comédie-Française. At the Met, Montserrat Caballé made such a meal of the heroine's two arias that they lost any impetus, but otherwise her singing was graceful, touching, and distinguished by many of the ravishing, finely spun, tellingly projected pianissimi for which she is celebrated. José Carreras, as Maurice de Saxe, sang fluently and ardently. He looked unpatrician, and almost unseemly young to be squabbled over to the death by two mature, powerful women: Fiorenza Cossotto was the forceful Princesse de Bouillon. Louis Quilico sang and played Michonnet with apt sentiment. Jesús López-Cobos, conducting, accompanied his cast in glowing orchestral colors.

Jon Vickers has returned to *Otello* in top form, giving what is perhaps his most lyrical, most *sung* performance yet of a role he has always declaimed with uncommon power, intensity, and poetic passion. Katia Ricciarelli was an affecting Desdemona, serious in intention, subtle and musical, not always limpid in timbre yet more satisfying than those who are sweeter in voice but not alert to the shades of Verdi's music. Cornell MacNeil was an impressive Iago. During an intermission quiz on one of Texaco's Saturday-afternoon Met broadcasts, it transpired that the final lines of Iago's Credo—"La morte è il nulla, È vecchia fola il ciel"—were lifted by Boito from the climax of an aria he had written eight years earlier for Alvise in Ponchielli's *La Gioconda;* the aria appears in early, unrevised scores of that piece. The fact, which seems so far to have escaped Verdian scholarship, is an odd one, for the Credo played an important part in persuading Verdi to compose *Otello;* when it reached him, he declared it to be "most powerful and wholly Shakespearean." It was a peace offering from Boito after a disagreement. Boito took a chance: if Verdi had recognized lines already set—very emphatically—by Ponchielli, might he not have thrown them straight back at the poet?

February 20, 1978

Less than Regal

I forget who said that the best French music was too good to be left to the mercy of French performers. Berlioz perhaps; or maybe Boulez during his years of self-willed exile from Parisian musical life. I echoed it while hearing *Les Troyens* cut to shreds at the Paris Opera, and again the week before last, when members of La Grande Écurie et la Chambre du Roy visited the Hunter College Playhouse to play pieces by François Couperin, Rameau, and Joseph Bodin de Boismortier. Under that high-sounding title, Jean-Claude Malgoire, an oboist, has formed an ensemble that seeks to re-create the glories of the Grand Siècle. Louis XIV's musical establishment of some hundred and twenty musicians fell into three divisions: the Musique de la Chambre, the Musique de la Grande Écurie, and the Musique de la Chapelle Royale. The first comprehended the Vingt-Quatre Violons du Roi (who were not all violins; there were six first violins, six players on the bass line, and four each on the three inner parts) and also, from 1656, Lully's expert band of Petits Violons. When wind was needed, it was borrowed from the Écurie, which by the late seventeenth century had five sections: twelve trumpeters; eight players of fife and drum; twelve "players of violin, oboe, sackbut, and cornett"; a varying number of players on crumhorn and marine trumpet; and six players of oboe and musette. The third section was in effect the ten oboists and two bassoonists (masters of other instruments besides) of the Douze Grands Hautbois, who joined the strings of the Chambre to accompany opera performances. Ten oboes to six first violins—that gives some idea of Lullian and Ramellian wind/string balance. The sound of it can be heard, after a fashion, on the Columbia recording of Rameau's *Les Indes galantes,* which is accompanied by Malgoire's group. But its playing on that recording, and on the Columbia recording of Lully's *Alceste,* might be enough to keep musical people away from an Écurie et Chambre concert. However, the words *members of* in the announcement of the concert at Hunter suggested that one might hear the pick of Malgoire's band—musicians who had mastered their instruments sufficiently to play the right notes and play them more or less in tune. What could fairly be expected from the billing? A wind-and-string ensemble twenty strong, adept on authentic instruments? In fact, the Écurie was represented by a single flute and a single oboe, and the Chambre by two violins, a cello, and a harpsichord; and to the out-of-tuneness familiar from the recordings was added wispiness of timbre.

The recital began with Couperin's two-violin sonata *L'Impériale* and some of its attendant set of dances. Flute and oboe joined in, and the second-violin part, when doubled on oboe by Malgoire himself, assumed solo status. Next, there was a suite of numbers culled from Rameau's *Hippolyte et Aricie,* reduced to chamber music, and then true chamber music in the form of a Boismortier sonata. Finally, Boismortier's cantata *L'Hyver* was sung—and enacted—in an incisive and vivid manner by Sophie Boulin. No text sheet was provided, as it should have been, but Mlle. Boulin struck poses to signal the emotions of each passage. The four men of the ensemble wore puce smocks; the three women looked neat and attractive. *L'Hyver* apart, it was a dismal event. The players may well have found the transition from Versailles to the squalor of Hunter College difficult; they seemed disgruntled. The audience was disgruntled, because it had been kept waiting for twenty minutes or so in the cheerless, poky lobby of the playhouse. (Someone announced to the restive crowd that the Hunter stage staff had proved not merely unhelpful to the French visitors but positively obstructive.) Inside, the ventilation system added its own rumbling bourdon to the music. The program sheet did not tally with the program played—which would not have mattered if the works actually done had been identified in more than a graceless mumble. What mattered most was the wretched playing. This New York début of the twentieth-century Écurie et Chambre could well pass unreviewed had not the ensemble won a certain reputation (its numerous recordings have collected six prizes), and were not Rameau and his contemporaries still in need of skillful championship. Even in their own day, their merits were sometimes obscured by inferior execution: in 1762, the *Mercure de France* pointed out that "it is not to our national music but often to the way of playing it that one should attribute the ridicule which foreigners who know it badly or fellow-countrymen who decry it disingenuously wish to shower on it unreflectingly."

If Rameau's shade must have scowled toward New York on the Saturday of this concert, it may have smiled the following Monday and Tuesday. On Monday last week, in Carnegie Recital Hall, Ann Monoyios closed the first half of her program with a pretty account of the early cantata *L'Impatience*. On Tuesday, the Elizabethan Enterprise, which specializes in Tudor music, leaped the Channel, and a century and a half, by inviting a Boston ensemble, Musick for the Generall Peace, to play Rameau's *Pièces de clavecin en concerts*, in St. Stephen's Church on West Sixty-ninth Street. Miss Monoyios's recital began with three Monteverdi songs. It included a song by Frescobaldi, three arias from Bach cantatas, "Bist du bei mir" (of disputed authorship), Purcell's *The Blessed Virgin's Expostulation* (should this be called a cantata?) and his "Music for a while," a Carissimi cantata, and, finally, Clérambault's cantata *La Musette*. In no dryly didactic way—not chronologically but in groups cleverly planned to provide contrasts of emotion and of scale—the program illustrated the development of, on the one hand, the solo lyric scena from early-seventeenth-century *monodia* to *cantate françoise* and, on the other, of sacred song from Monteverdi's "Exulta filia Sion" (which is kin in spirit to the familiar English setting of the text, Handel's "Rejoice greatly") to Bach. The singer was accompanied by harpsichord (James Richman) and gamba (Wendy Gillespie), joined from time to time by flute (Sandra Miller) or oboe (Stephen Hammer); the instruments were baroque—and they were played in tune. Miss Monoyios has a clear, true, and fluent soprano. She is a gentle performer, not vivid in the way Mlle. Boulin was, but not dull, for there was grace in her phrasing and liveliness in her rhythms. I think she could with advantage risk a slightly sharper characterization of some of the various personages—Rameau's and Clérambault's lovelorn shepherds, Purcell's distraught mother, Bach's burdened Soul. To Frescobaldi's defiant swain, an ancestor of the scorned and scornful lovers in Wolf's *Italian Songbook*, she did give the right touch of temper. Her voice had sounded fuller when I heard it in the resonant acoustics of Corpus Christi Church; it had rung out more generously. I think she stood too near the edge of the Carnegie Recital Hall platform to set the place sounding, and wonder whether the large curtains swathing either side of that platform absorbed some of the tone.

Rameau's *L'Impatience* is a tenor cantata; when it is sung by a soprano, an octave up, the pretty crisscrossings of voice and gamba are lost. Clérambault's *La Musette* is a gem. There are several of his organ pieces in the current record catalogues but none of his cantatas, which are described by David Tunley, who wrote an important article about them, as a "repository of neglected masterpieces." *La Musette* certainly suggested that we should hear more of them. A booklet of texts and translations was provided gratis—

and then all the lights in the hall were turned out, so it could not be consulted. Why? Miss Monoyios will not claim that all New Yorkers understand sung Latin, Italian, German, and French with ease, and she is too intelligent an artist not to realize that the effect of her performance is halved if listeners do not know what she is singing about. Someone must have thought the words important, or else they would not have been printed; someone must have thought that words don't matter, or else the lights would not have been turned off. Or did no one think about the lighting at all? It fell upon Miss Monoyios so awkwardly that even when I moved to the front row (where there was just enough light to follow the Clérambault text; I had not been able to memorize it in the intermission) I could not discern the color of her eyes. And everyone knows that comprehensible words and expression in the eyes are among a singer's chief means of communication. [I let my questions stand, although some who *had* given thought to the lighting at this concert answered them and had hard words to say about Carnegie Recital Hall's lighting arrangements. Three years later, they are no better.]

St. Stephen's, a low-ceilinged, friendly church that feels more like a meeting place than a temple, makes a good home for early music and is quite often used for it. The lights were left on during the Rameau, and that was good: it increased the audience's sense of being in one chamber with the performers, and the program—which listed the sixteen titles of the pieces and sought to identify the "persons of taste and skill" who, in the words of the composer's preface, "have done me the honor of giving their names to some of them"—could be used. The five "concerts," which are written for harpsichord "with a violin or flute, and a viol or second violin," can be viewed as a small gallery of friends pictured within, as pure music, and as an exquisite, shapely, and satisfying pattern book of affecting and picturesque devices employed by Rameau in his great operas. The composer declared, not quite truly, that "these pieces lose nothing by being played on the harpsichord alone"; he arranged five of them for harpsichord solo, but not without changes. Robert Hill, the harpsichordist of the Generall Peace, played some episodes of "La Timide" in the harpsichord-solo version, which was interesting to hear beside the trio version, and he boldly introduced the most contrapuntal piece of all, "La Forqueray," as a solo. It made sense that way—and still more sense when, at the repeat, the two other voices were added. To provide variety of timbre, and to demonstrate one of the alternatives allowed on Rameau's title page, David Hart, the flutist of the Elizabethan Enterprise, alternated with and sometimes joined Jean Lamon, the violinist of the Generall Peace. Sometimes the flute is the apter instrument; more often, the violin.

The balance was not quite right. Sarah Cunningham, playing a viola da gamba made in 1741, the year in which the *Pièces* were published, was too reticent. The string players, Rameau said, should distinguish between what is mere accompaniment to the harpsichord and what is thematic, but even when Miss Cunningham had the tune it could hardly be heard. Mr. Hill is a player with very even, fleet, and exact fingers, but one wanted a little more fancy, fire, and fun in the execution. Miss Lamon was the one who suggested that while music making is, of course, a serious business, it often needs a sense of humor as well. Yet on the whole Rameau was well served—played on the right instruments, in a suitable space, by a group of unpretentious but devoted and accomplished young musicians.

February 27, 1978

Pastoral Passions

After *Luisa Miller*, in 1849, Verdi planned to compose a *King Lear*, with Salvatore Cammarano as librettist. It would have to break with "the forms that have been more or less continuously in use up to now," he told Cammarano, and be "treated in an entirely new way, on a large scale, without regard to the *convenienze*" (the standard procedures by which Italian operas were built). Verdi's *King Lear*, like Britten's *King Lear* with Dietrich Fischer-Dieskau in the title role and Peter Pears as the Fool, was oft dreamed about but never composed. (Aribert Reimann's *Lear*, with Fischer-Dieskau in the title role, opens the Munich Festival this summer.) In 1850, Verdi wrote, instead, *Stiffelio*, which has just been given what might be called its American full-scale première by the Opera Company of Boston, in the Orpheum. (The small-scale première was presented, not at all ineffectively, by the New York Grand Opera in the Brooklyn Academy of Music in June 1976.) It was an important production. In the best book so far written about Verdi's music—Julian Budden's *The Operas of Verdi* (Volume III has still to appear)—Budden declares that "with all its imperfections, *Stiffelio* is worthy to stand beside the three masterpieces which it immediately precedes." To range *Stiffelio* beside *Rigoletto*, *Il trovatore*, and *La traviata*, those staples of the international repertory, is to place it high. I place it high, too, if not quite as high as that. The imperfections are dramaturgical. Five letters, written, read, or destroyed unread, and one divorce agreement are too many documents for one opera plot. Two of the scenic directions specify "L'occorrente per iscrivere" (the requisites for writing). The work opens with the bass reading some theological book, perhaps one written by Stiffelius, and ends with Stiffelius reading from the Bible. A copy of Klopstock's *Messias* plays an important part in the action. Yet all this reading and writing propels a taut and interesting dramatic argument, held to the unities of time and place, and concerned with a Protestant pastor's reluctance to practice what he preaches—to forgive a wife who has committed adultery. It was an unconventional choice of subject for a mid-century Italian opera. Marriage laws, public opinion, and personal morality must have been in Verdi's mind at the time: he had recently returned from Paris to live in his native town with a woman not his wife, who had borne—not to him—at least three illegitimate children. Not only in matter but also in manner he broke with the *convenienze*. Instead of a choral introduzione, such as had opened his fourteen previous operas—and was to open most of the later ones—he began with a bass arioso, whose grave scoring, harmonic ambiguity (finally resolved in C major, as is the opera itself), and careful matching of vocal register to rhetoric (the line climbs by steps to a climax on E-flat and *Dio*) promise a work of unusual weight, seriousness, and power. The promise is kept. Stiffelius's two interviews with Lina, before and after her guilt is established, represent something new in Verdi—the first an aria in which each of Lina's interjections moves Stiffelius's music onto a new tack, the second a duet that is almost another tenor aria in the same "dialectical" style until Lina seizes the initiative and, having failed to soften the jealous husband, addresses herself as a penitent to the priest. She does so to a chromatic descending motif over hollow fifths which is derived, whether consciously or not, from the melody in the earlier piece to which Stiffelius owns that forgiveness comes easy only to those who have not themselves been injured. The germ of the phrase has already been heard beneath the arioso at the start of the opera. There are other such unifying motifs. Budden drew attention to sequences of lapped fourths which "it is tempting to regard . . . as a Schenkerian *Grundgestalt* standing for the religious element in the opera." The final, radiant, C-major cadence on *perdonata*, sung by everyone except Lina, seems to be the declarative resolution of the conditional *perdonata*, set to a passing C-minor cadence, that punctuates Lina's preghiera in Act I. On all levels—including that important one of having some very attractive tunes—*Stiffelio* is a remarkable work.

The Boston performance, directed and conducted in masterly fashion by Sarah Caldwell, gave musical and dramatic life to the merits revealed in the printed score, and to past perceptions it added new ones. Miss Caldwell has a genius for discovering the essence of a work. Sometimes—not often—her theatrical exuberance carries her away. Sometimes—not often—her confidence that everything will come together on the night proves misplaced. In her approaches to a work, sound preliminary study and inspired last-minute improvisation are blended; and as a result Boston opera performances are usually among the most exciting to be found today. All the big things and most of the little things about this *Stiffelio*—I saw the third of four performances—were essentially right. Zack Brown's sets—Salzburg castle, cemetery, church—were handsome, apt in style (the painted backcloth of cypresses against a cloudy night sky matched the romantic musical scene-painting that opens Act II), varied in depth, and cunningly planned to create spaciousness and grandeur on a difficult stage. John Lehmeyer's costumes subtly defined the characters and looked good. The orchestra played with a keen, quick sense of Verdi's expressive colors (*Stiffelio* is the most eloquently scored of the pre-*Rigoletto* operas), and the Orpheum's lack of a sunken orchestral pit seemed a positive advantage: the instrumental details told, yet the singers were not drowned.

The title role is one of five—from Zamoro in *Alzira*, in 1845, to Riccardo in *Un ballo in maschera*, in 1859—that Verdi composed for Gaetano Fraschini, his ideal of a tenor; as late as 1871 he wanted him to create Radamès. Fraschini had a ringing, powerful delivery; he was nicknamed the "tenore della maledizione," after the vigor with which as Edgar he used to curse poor Lucy in the second-act finale of Donizetti's opera. Verdi used that maledictory force to great effect in the first-act and (with exposed octave leaps marked "con voce terribile") second-act finales of *Stiffelio*. But the role is far from being all rant. In this most adventurous opera, Verdi also composed passages that represent his closest approach to Bellini—not paradoxically, since Bellini was both the creator of a heroic yet graceful vocal line, charged with fierce emotions yet strictly controlled, and a pioneer in the practice of irregular forms determined by dramatic content. In the accents of Pollio (in *Norma*), over the simplest of Bellinian accompaniments, Stiffelius addresses Lina in Act III. For the title role, Miss Caldwell had found a tenor, Roelof Oostwoud, with a distinct, well-formed delivery of both words and musical phrases. His tones were clean and purely projected, and he was a good actor. He gave an ardent, satisfying account of the most arresting tenor character Verdi composed before Othello. Anna Moffo, Lina at the first two performances, had retired ill; I heard Leigh Munro, who had learned the role in haste yet sang it with complete assurance. Her voice is not large and voluptuous but clear, bright, and true. Lina, like Luisa Miller (the parts were written for the same soprano), needs to be, in Verdi's phrase, "ingenua ed estremamente drammatica." Miss Munro is young, attractive, an excellent actress, and a dramatic interpreter of the music. We will surely be hearing more of her. Count Stankar, Lina's father, was composed for a polished, conventional baritone of the old school, Filippo Colini; for Verdi he had already created Joan of Arc's father. In Donizettian music, Verdi employed Colini's merits and limitations to draw the picture of an old-style aristocrat, but he added an unconventional touch by directing a cabaletta of ferocious, vengeful excitement ("Oh gioia inesprimibile") to be sung "extremely softly throughout, with the exception of the final phrase," a *tutta forza* outburst. Brent Ellis, the Boston Stankar, spoiled the effect by singing the whole movement at a healthy forte. The other characters are subaltern, and were well enough taken.

Stiffelio was done in Italian, not English, and it was presumably to provide a visual gloss to words uncomprehended that Miss Caldwell had Stankar publicly stab Lina's seducer in the back: a thing he would never have done—at any rate, not in front of other people. The plain sense of the words (as well as Verdi's stage direction) was contradicted at the final curtain: "Forgiven, the woman [taken in adultery] rose up"—but Lina remained kneeling. Men wearing hats in church looked odd—though I would not put it past Miss Caldwell to have turned up the hat rules of some nineteenth-century Salzburg sect that did wear them except while actually praying. The church scene sported an enthusiastic organist who mimed away like Virgil Fox in full flight even when the organ was not playing. A bad Caldwell idea: the deliberately static, expectant quality of the music—all are waiting to hear on what text Stiffelius will preach—needs to be matched by a motionless scene. A directorial gloss at the very start—family prayers instead of the solitary reader—can be defended: it removed some of the strangeness from Verdi's opening, but at a stroke it introduced anyone who had not read the libretto to a household anxious, for various reasons, about Stiffelius's return. (It was during his absence on a mission that Lina sinned.) In general, the staging was crisp, intelligent, and very musical. The characterizations of major and minor roles and also of the chorus were sharp, and the complicated ensembles were set out in space so that the right lines came to the fore.

Stiffelio had little success in its day. Verdi valued it but realized that the plot was unacceptable to audiences of the time. The modern setting may not have harmed its chances—although *La traviata*, his only other piece with a nineteenth-century action, was often played in eighteenth-century costumes—but the modern subject matter did. Censorship insisted on drawing its teeth. (It was surprising to hear Miss Munro sing one of the censors' silliest changes: at the climax of the duet, "Rodolfo, ascoltatemi" instead of "Ministro, confessatemi." The point is that Stiffelius as minister is bound to listen to the words that as husband he refused to hear.) In 1856, the composer reworked the opera as *Aroldo*—set in Crusader times, in a castle "near Kent," with a new last act beside Loch Lomond—and threw out from the autograph the pages not taken into the revision. *Stiffelio* could not be performed again until a complete orchestral score was traced. It was, ten years ago, and since then the work has had several productions—generally in editions less full and less faithful than that used in Boston. But it deserves wider recognition still. Budden describes the music of the title role as "designed for a man of authority, of religious zeal and blameless moral life . . . a controlled, less vulnerable forerunner of Othello." The right singer for it exists—one with the power, the passion, and the dramatic intensity, a great Samson (Handel's) and a great Othello. Large opera companies are prepared to mount operas "for" Luciano Pavarotti or Placido Domingo. Which of them is going to have the enterprise to let us hear Jon Vickers in *Stiffelio?*

Verdi's *Macbeth*, composed in 1846–47 and revised in 1864–65, is an even higher achievement than *Stiffelio*, and its merits have been recognized since serious appraisal of Verdi's pre-*Rigoletto* pieces began, in the 1930s. A recent production by the Baltimore Opera, with Ryan Edwards in the title role, Marisa Galvany as the Lady, and Kenneth Schermerhorn as conductor, was enjoyable. *Macbeth* usually is, and Baltimore productions usually are. The Baltimore Symphony, which accompanies the operas, has admirable players. The chorus is enthusiastic and accomplished, and the audience is enthusiastic, too. The Lyric Theatre, modeled on the Leipzig Gewandhaus with a stagehouse added, may be too large for all but the largest operas (it seats twenty-five hundred, more than La Scala) and limited in its scenic resources, but it has a good, friendly feel and excellent acoustics. Nevertheless, I feel I must attack this *Macbeth* as being a demonstration of director's folly. It may be unkind to do so—far worse demonstrations appear on international stages, and are acclaimed—but, as Lady Macbeth says in another connection, "è necessario."

David Hicks, who directed, presumably did not begin by asking himself, "What can I do to make Verdi's music serve my staging, instead of vice versa? How can I convert this hair-raising score into a kind of unnoticed, unemphatic Muzak to accompany stage pictures the composer never intended?" But the result looked as if he might have done so, and as if these were some of the answers he found:

Add to the cast the rump-fed ronyon and her husband, the master o' the Tiger, and set them miming and dancing through the witches' first and second choruses. (From the first, the section "The weird sisters hand in hand . . . thus do go about, about," which Verdi did specify as a round dance, was omitted.) In the Macbeth-Banquo duettino, have Banquo address his asides to the troops. ("The duettino exploits one of the few dramatic advantages that opera possesses over a spoken play—its ability to present simultaneously the emotional content of two consecutive and contrasted speeches, each delivered as a soliloquy"—Budden.) Do not allow Macbeth to conjure up the image of a spectral dagger through vivid acting and singing; project a poster-size painting of a dagger on the front gauze. Later, where Verdi was insistent that the singer of Banquo should also impersonate Banquo's ghost, seated at the banquet, replace him with another front-gauze projection. Make the first-act finale, that depiction of "stupore universale," into the accompaniment to tableaux of actions around a blood-bolter'd Duncan, plonked down center stage. Let Banquo and Fleance sit down comfortably before Banquo sings, "Watch your step, O my son." Masterstroke: Destroy the impact of the sleepwalking scene by placing the doctor and the waiting gentlewoman center stage in a pool of light while Lady Macbeth crouches down in shadows at the side to sing. Get Macbeth to play the scena before his aria "Honor, love, obedience, troops of friends I must not look to have" as a drunk scene, lurching and reeling about.

Such things bewilder me. What is the point of making changes that are not improvements? A conductor does not say, "Let's have that clarinet solo played on a flute; let's reharmonize that passage; let's substitute for those measures these more piquant ones of my own composition." (Well, some conductors have done so, and have been trounced therefor. Mr. Schermerhorn won my admiration for striking out a few conductors' tamperings with Verdi's score—harp additions to the prelude and the sleepwalking scene—which have found their way into the standard Ricordi material; in recent recordings, Claudio Abbado and Riccardo Muti retain them.) Changes *can* be improvements. Sarah Caldwell once added, in spoken dialogue, so felicitous a final twist to the plot of Donizetti's *La Fille du régiment* that it seemed inadvertent of the original librettists not to have included it. But none of Mr. Hicks's additions or changes to *Macbeth* convinced me that he was a better musical dramatist than Verdi.

In 1848, when Naples was planning to mount *Macbeth* with Eugenia Tadolini as the prima donna, Verdi wrote a letter to Cammarano which has often been quoted:

> You know how much I esteem Tadolini, and she herself knows it; but in the general interest I feel I should set some observations before you. Tadolini's qualities are too great for that role! Perhaps that seems to you an absurd thing to say!! Tadolini has a beautiful and benign face, and I want Lady Macbeth to be ugly and evil. Tadolini sings to perfection, and I want a Lady Macbeth who doesn't sing. Tadolini has a marvelous voice, clear, limpid, and strong, and I want the Lady's voice to be harsh, stifled, and hollow. Tadolini's voice has an angelic quality; I want the Lady's voice to have a demonic quality.

How much bad singing has been defended by those words! In the general interest, I feel I should set out two further observations. First, while there is obviously *some* accuracy in his catalogue of vocal vices needed by the Lady, in context the composer's letter reads as an argument *ad feminam*—courteous exaggerations employed as a face-saving way of saying, "For heaven's sake, don't use Tadolini. She'll be no good in the part." Tadolini, though only about forty, was nearing the end of her career; she had made her name in Donizetti; she was still a Neapolitan favorite. Verdi's letter was meant to be shown around; in fact, it continues, "Submit these considerations to the management, to Maestro Mercadante, who will be the first to approve these ideas of mine, to Tadolini herself, and do what in your wisdom you think best." (In the event, Tadolini did sing the role, both that season and the next.) Second, "marvelous" Tadolini voices, clear, limpid, and strong, are not common today, and few sopranos need strive when tackling the Lady's difficult music to achieve harshness and devilish discolorations; they can be left to come of themselves. Montserrat Caballé apart, is there any dramatic soprano—or mezzo—around who *could* sing the role too beautifully?

Miss Galvany let fly too wildly at the top, and she carried chest tone up into the middle range in an overexuberant way. There was a certain coarseness in much of her vocalism which need not have been there, for in the sleepwalking scene she showed that she can be precise and delicate when she chooses. I should like to hear her in a performance in which her first care was to sing the music as truly as possible; given her abundantly dramatic temperament—and the way the role is written—it would be unlikely to be tame. Both she and Mr. Edwards tended to sing out, even to splurge, in passages where they should have concentrated on an almost whispered, very soft yet intense projection of the words. To Felice Varesi, the first Macbeth, Verdi wrote, "I'll never stop telling you to study the words and the dramatic situation; then the music will come right of its own accord." The first duet for the pair is marked to be sung "*sotto voce,* dark and hollow throughout, except for the phrases where 'in full, broad voice' is indicated." The core of the second is marked "*pppp,* with the voice held back." Limpid vocalism à la Tadolini is wrong; so is any crude, loud barking or roaring.

The revised edition of 1865, abridged by several cuts, was used, but Macbeth's final monologue from 1847, "Mal per me," was included. It is better followed by the brief 1847 acclamation of Malcolm than—as in Baltimore—by the 1865 victory hymn. Ara Berberian was the Banquo, rather bumbly in tone. Moises Parker was the Macduff; he has a big voice but no stage presence.

March 6, 1978

Quest

The sorry, broken-backed musical drama that the Metropolitan Opera is billing as "Gaetano Donizetti/*La Favorita*/Opera in three acts/Libretto by Alphonse Royer and Gustave Vaëz" does bear some relation to Donizetti's four-act opera *La Favorite*. But it is a version of that opera docked, cropped, and altered so drastically in words, in plot, and in music that I doubt whether Donizetti, Royer, or Vaëz would care to own the result. If anyone think the doubt unjustified, let him compare the original libretto (it appears in Series III, Volume IV of Scribe's Complete Works) with the libretto on sale at the Met, and compare an early score—or the autograph, of which the Lincoln Center library has a microfilm—with the current Ricordi edition, which the Met is using. To set out the full, tangled tale of *La Favorite* would take many pages, and none of the accounts in print get it quite right; a summary history may help to indicate what is wrong with the work, with this edition of it, and with the dull Met performance.

La Favorite, which was first performed at the Opéra in December 1840, was compiled in haste during the preceding months from three earlier Donizetti scores: the unfinished *Adelaide,* the unfinished *Le Duc d'Albe* (whose libretto was later reworked for Verdi as *Les Vêpres siciliennes*), and the finished but unperformed *L'Ange de Nisida.* Royer and Vaëz were the librettists of *L'Ange de Nisida,* the principal source; Scribe, the librettist of *Le Duc d'Albe,* was evidently called in to supervise the transformation of *L'Ange* into *La Favorite.* He received four thousand francs for his trouble, and half the authors' rights in what became an immensely successful opera in Paris and in the provinces. (The Opéra gave the hundredth performance in 1849, the five-hundredth in 1879.) In Scribe's collected works, authorship "en société avec MM. A. Royer et G. Vaëz" is acknowledged. On the last page of Donizetti's score, Vaëz notes that it was he who wrote the new words into the "cannibalized" pages. Three layers of text, corresponding to *Adelaide*, *L'Ange de Nisida*, and *La Favorite*, can in some numbers still be discerned.

Specifically for *La Favorite*, Donizetti composed connecting passages, the ballet music (probably), and four new arias: Fernand's stirring "Oui, ta voix m'inspire," which ends Act I (it is omitted at the Met), Alphonse's "Léonor, viens" and his "Pour tant d'amour," and Léonor's "Ô mon Fernand." The last three have become celebrated in Italian translation as "Vien, Leonora," "A tanto amor," and "O mio Fernando." Two other well-known arias, Fernand's "Un ange, une femme inconnue/Una vergine, un angel di Dio" and his "Ange si pur/Spirto gentil," are taken from, respectively, *L'Ange de Nisida* and *Le Duc d'Albe*. In addition, during rehearsals Donizetti composed the soprano solo "Fernand! imite la clémence" at the request of the prima donna; she was Rosine Stoltz, the *favorite* of the Opéra director.

La Favorite is thus a musical collage to begin with, but it was skillfully and even scrupulously assembled, and its plot, in which history and fictions are mingled, makes sense. Fernando (to avoid French/Italian complications, I will now use common English forms of the Spanish names), a novice in the cloister of St. James of Compostella, while praying to the angels thought he saw an angel beside him. Offering her holy water, he touched her hand. Now he has lost his vocation: he loves—and is loved by—one who, unknown to him, is Leonora de Guzman, Alphonso XI's mistress. He leaves the monastery, wins glory by repulsing the African invasion of Spain in 1340, and is ennobled by Alphonso and further rewarded by Leonora's hand. (The King thus disposes at once of an unwanted mistress—he has learned of Leonora's new love—and a threat of excommunication if he persists in preferring his favorite to his queen.) Leonora goes to the wedding believing that Fernando knows of her past. He doesn't. When he discovers it, he renounces her and returns to Compostella. She follows him thither, arriving just in time to hear him take his final vows. He sees her, and wishes again to leave the cloister, but she sings, "Be saved from sacrilege, Be saved by my death!" and dies.

In the words of a synopsis appended to the new London recording of the opera (which honestly tells the original story, as opposed to the rubbish sung on the records), "the original French text is openly religious in its theme and constructed to the composer's own ideas and insight into the pilgrimage of the soul." Like Verdi, Donizetti was prepared to stand up to Scribe and see that ideas he cared about found expression. But, again like Verdi, he could not then stand up to Italian censorship and win. "Wretched Italian translation!" he wrote in 1845. "It's a horror, because of the censors." To his Italian publisher he recommended a standard operatic method of not offending Church susceptibilities: call the monks hermits. *La Favorite* reached Italy in two different translations. In one of them, Calisto Bassi's, Alphonso becomes Louis VII and Leonora a Greek maiden, Elda; the action plays in Syria, amid hermits and templars. The other, Francesco Jannetti's is entitled *Leonora di Gusman;* it preserves time and place but laicizes the plot: Balthazar, the prior of Compostella, is turned into the father both of Fernando and of Alphonso's queen. Religion was taboo, but not a spicy near-incestuous touch in Fernando's marrying the woman who has supplanted his own sister in the royal bed. In 1860, at La Scala, the Jannetti version and monastic elements of the original were patched together, leaving many loose ends, and they are still left flapping in the Ricordi score and the Met production. In this version, Balthazar is both a monk *and* the noble father of Fernando and the Queen of Spain. Fernando is both the King's brother-in-law *and* an obscure commoner, a "low-born mountain boy." The ceremony of Fernando's taking his final vows becomes a funeral for the Queen, and the serene, devout melody to which Donizetti set lines meaning

> *I consecrate myself to Thy service, O Lord!*
> *Approach, may Thy grace illumine my heart*

is sung, with absurdly inappropriate effect, to the Italian for

> *May implacable grief upon the guilty woman,*
> *Cause of misfortunes, swiftly descend!*

To the first, Donizetti's Leonora added, "He is lost to this world! Angel, reascend to heaven." At the Met, Leonora sings, "He is crying for vengeance, I am lost!"

In short, the Met is presenting a version of *La Favorite* which in 1978 no serious opera company should consider—a patchwork of what Catholic censorship did in the 1840s, the partial, ineffective repair job of 1860, and the inertia of singers, conductors, and managements content for more than a century to pick up and perpetuate the nearest available score instead of discovering what the composer wrote. The result is an insult to Donizetti. The Met should look to the enterprise of the Houston Grand Opera (which this season performed Rossini's *Tancredi* from a correct score newly edited by Philip Gossett), the Kentucky Opera (which this season performed Verdi's 1847 *Macbeth* from a correct score newly edited by David Lawton), and the Opera Company of Boston (whose returns to what composers really wrote have been numerous). And if America's first house cannot engage a cast able and willing to sing French operas in the original, and therefore chooses to perform them in Italian translation, it should commission new Italian translations, which fit the sense and fit the notes. The standard Italian translation of *La Favorite* (even less acceptable than those of Verdi's *Les Vêpres siciliennes* and *Don Carlos*) is "a horror" not only for what it says but also for what it does to the music by attaching the wrong sentiments to expressive phrases, altering the melodic lines, blunting the rhythms, and plumping out what should be quick and direct. Without music type, it is hard to demonstrate that, but the loss of rhythmic as well as of verbal incisiveness can perhaps be deduced from the difference in syllable count between Donizetti's "Mon Dieu, Fernand, grâce!" and Jannetti's "Oh ciel! Fernando, il tuo perdon io spero." The offense to Donizetti is aggravated by multifarious cutting. In the Ricordi score, there are already omissions; in the Met production, there are many more, ranging from the complete aria already mentioned to a few measures here, a few there. Since *La Favorite* is a *grand opéra* dependent to some extent on large-scale formal repetitions, cuts can make it seem trivial and short-breathed. The positive virtues of repetition were shown when Sherrill Milnes, the Met Alphonso, was allowed both verses of his cabaletta "Léonor, mon amour brave l'univers et Dieu, pour toi." (The bold sentiment is softened in the Jannetti translation.) It is a conventional piece, made from an all-purpose energetic melody that reached *La Favorite* from *Adelaide* via *L'Ange de Nisida.* The melody if sung through once and then dropped would sound perfunctory; with a full repetition, after a bridge passage, it builds into a strikingly effective number.

There were other things wrong with the show. Jesús López-Cobos's conducting was rhythmically slack, and it was apparent from his handling of the overture that he had little feeling for the weight, breadth, and grandeur of the score. The opera is played on a single set, by Ming Cho Lee, borrowed from San Francisco. Balustrades, portals, and arcades are pushed into different patterns to suggest the different places, but all five scenes look much the same and have the same depth, and so monotony results. Patrick Tavernia's stage direction is weak and characterless; better—just—that a production should have no character than the wrong character. The director is positively perverse only when he has Fernando blindfolded at precisely the point where the plot and stage directions require him to take a blindfold off.

On the first night, Shirley Verrett, in the title role, was below form. The electricity that had made her Leonora for Eve Queler (in Carnegie Hall in 1975) so vivid was switched off. The power failed that enabled her to keep the concert audience silent after "Ô mon Fernand" so that aria and cabaletta could be delivered as one thrilling span; at the Met, the tension was dispelled by midway applause. She did offer some seductively smoky and beautiful singing, especially in the last act. It was probably a mistake for the company to attempt to revive *La Favorite* until José Carreras or Alfredo Kraus was available for Fernando, for, while it may not be quite true to say that Luciano Pavarotti, who did the part, brings dramatic death to any scene he appears in (Franco Zeffirelli and Claudio Abbado can still coax a performance from him: witness the Scala *Ballo*), his showing in the Covent Garden *Ballo*, the Chicago *Elisir,* and now the Met *Favorite* suggests that it is almost true. His voice has got bigger and he himself has got a little smaller, but he was no Fernando. He presented the fellow as an amiable booby. In his singing, there was very little of the grace or the ardent, eloquent expression that the music calls for; in his acting, no trace of a spiritual or even an amatory pilgrimage. There was a large, free, flowing tone, admirable as sound, but many phrases were spoiled by a trick of making loud notes louder still until they were cut short by a sort of blurted explosion. As *il favorito* of an uncritical, adoring public, he poured out his voice prodigally; in the London recording, he shows rather more feeling for sense and style. Milnes was nearly an impressive Alphonso: he was "impressive" in a generalized way, and seemed to need stronger musical and dramatic direction to focus his imagination on details that make Alphonso a distinct character, not just another *baritono nobile*. Balthazar, who must thunder anathema through the second-act finale, calls for a stronger, deeper bass than Bonaldo Giaiotti's.

Perhaps the Met should invite Eve Queler to take charge of its *Favorite*, for she certainly knows how to present a work in the best possible light. Whenever I have heard her tackle a score that I previously admired only up to a point (Berlioz's *Lélio*, *La Favorite*, Verdi's *I lombardi*), her advocacy has shifted that point so as to make admiration more nearly complete. Whenever I have heard her tackle a score that I already loved almost without reservations (Smetana's *Dalibor*, Weber's *Oberon*), she has confirmed and deepened the love and lessened the reservations. Her conducting technique may look awkward, but to singers, players, and chorus it plainly conveys a feeling for the right pace, for telling colors, for breathing as if with the composer's own breaths. *Oberon* she conducted in Carnegie Hall, with the Opera Orchestra of New York, two days after the Met's first *Favorite*, and thus tardy recognition was made of the hundred-and-fiftieth anniversary of Weber's death, in 1826—widely commemorated elsewhere but in America almost ignored. (Let us hope that 1986, the bicentenary of his birth, will bring *Der Freischütz*, *Euryanthe*, and *Oberon* back to the New York stage.) *Oberon* is not easy to produce. James Robinson Planché's libretto is a mess, and many have echoed Tovey's regret that Weber should have "poured his last and finest music into this pig-trough." But it is not quite as bad a libretto as people who know it only by report have made out. When Covent Garden, in 1824, commissioned a work from the leading German opera composer of the day, two subjects were proposed, *Faust* and *Oberon*, and Weber chose the latter as being, in his son's words, "so completely congenial to the very essence of his genius." He knew Christoph Martin Wieland, whose *Oberon* (1780) is a long narrative poem of considerable delicacy and charm and some humor—it can still be enjoyed in the very readable translation by William Sotheby (1798), which served as Planché's source—and one apt for operatic conversion.

Sir Huon of Bordeaux has offended Charlemagne, who enjoins him to burst into the Caliph of Baghdad's court at high festival, kill the man on the Caliph's left, and claim the Caliph's daughter with three kisses. On the way to Baghdad, Huon is befriended by Oberon, who gives him a magic horn, and by its help he accomplishes his triple task. (The horn sets all the infidels dancing; Wieland also provided source material for *The Magic Flute*.) But on the way to Rome and marriage Huon and his Reiza "taste ere time the sweet forbidden fruit," and Oberon withdraws his patronage. The lovers are cast on a desert isle and pass three years there in a simple, industrious, penitently chaste life, together with a hermit; there little Huonet is born, painlessly, under fairy anesthetic. About halfway through, Wieland introduces a new character—Titania, who befriends the young unmarried mother—and, rather suddenly, a new theme: that Oberon has forsworn his queen until there can be discovered a pair whose union can "fate's severest stroke sustain" and who "truth prefer mid tort'ring fires to syren pleasure on a profferr'd throne." Pirates take Reiza to Tunis; Oberon's art takes Huon there. Each is offered a throne at the price of infidelity but prefers a pyre. At the last moment, their constancy is rewarded by Oberon's intervention. He is reunited with Titania, and the lovers go off in triumph to Charlemagne.

A good story. Planché, Covent Garden's house librettist and the author of some two hundred stage pieces, changed it. He began with Oberon's "fatal vow," cut Huonet, the hermit, and the island idyll, and altered the motivation so that the lovers' tribulations become trials deliberately set them by Oberon. On the *Entführung* model, Planché contrived a sub-affair between Huon's lusty squire, Sherasmin (an old man in Wieland), and Reiza's merry attendant, Fatima. He rejected the charge brought by Weber's son that the drama is vitiated by the lovers' ability to summon supernatural aid whenever they are in a tight spot. That is true only of Huon's first exploit. Otherwise, their ordeals, more varied and picturesque than Tamino's and Pamina's, are, as Planché indignantly and fairly retorted, "among the severest known to humanity—shipwreck on a desolate island—separation—slavery—temptation in its most alluring forms, and the imminent danger of death in the most fearful manner." And all these when they are "utterly hopeless of fairy aid."

This is also a good story for an opera. The trouble is that Planché told it almost entirely in spoken dialogue—blank verse for the fairies, prose for the mortals—since, as he later explained in his memoirs:

> Ballads, duets, choruses, and glees, provided they occupied no more than the fewest number of minutes possible, were all that the playgoing public of that day would endure. A dramatic situation in music was . . . inevitably received with cries of "Cut it short!" from the gallery.

Weber regretted "the intermixing of so many principal actors who do not sing" and "the omission of the music in the most important moments," but he thoroughly approved the Covent Garden décor and stage machinery (in providing for much scenic transformation, Planché was being true to his subject), and he was compelled to conjure up Wieland's three different worlds—the enchanted, the chivalric, and the Oriental—in tiny space. Into numbers sometimes only a few measures long he packed his memorably vivid, delicate inventions, making every fine touch of harmony and instrumentation tell. *Oberon* is the most concentrated and the most beautiful of his scores. When he was given a chance to expand—in the overture, the chorus and storm, "Ocean, thou mighty monster," and the three act finales—he wrote marvelously gripping dramatic music, but his short pieces are more wonderful still.

There have been many attempts to improve the dramaturgy. For the Met, Artur Bodanzky made a version with sung recitatives which held the stage for three seasons, 1918–21. (Reiza was Rosa Ponselle's second Met role; Martinelli sang Huon.) In 1967, I saw within a few days three different productions of the opera. The Dresden State Opera used an edition by Horst Seeger (at that time Felsenstein's dramaturge), who tidied the plot but disordered the music. Nottingham University added to Weber the melodramas that Mahler composed to underpin the spoken supernatural scenes, and retained enough Planché to expound his whole plot, not just the episodes with music. Cambridge University linked Weber's numbers with dialogue cut to an extent that made the abruptness absurd. After seeing those productions and looking through half a dozen other editions, I became convinced that the way to "save" the opera is not to reshape it but to accept, for better for worse, the original pantomime that Weber turned into poetry. Today, Planché's diction even has a certain period charm. *Oberon* needs only to be superbly well acted, sung, and played, and elaborately staged with every magical trick in the book. I have gone into this detail about it because Miss Queler's concert performance must have whetted many appetites for a full-scale production.

The Opera Orchestra company did just the musical numbers (and did them, for no good reason, in German translation), but listeners were handed a printed libretto containing just enough Planché to provide an immediate context for each item. The straight-through performance of the score, act by act, unbroken by narration or dialogue, focused attention on Weber's leitmotif technique; in ever-changing guises, the call of the magic horn winds through most of the movements. Reiza was sung by Betty Jones, replacing Roberta Knie. She was secure and powerful, a sound musician and a reliable singer. The tone was not exactly beautiful, but the music was all there, clear, definite, and expressively shaped. The role is hard to cast; it needs a Donna Anna who can be as gentle and tender as Agathe in *Der Freischütz*. Sir Huon must be a Max in *Der Freischütz*, a Rienzi, and a Don Ottavio in one; few singers fit that bill as well as Nicolai Gedda. Even if his sustained high notes were hard and screamy, they were well controlled. He gave a brilliant account of the fiendishly difficult rondo "I revel in hope and joy again," which was omitted in the three 1967 productions and is also omitted, by Placido Domingo, in the Deutsche Grammophon recording. Julia Hamari, the Fatima of that set, repeated her supple, attractive, but, except in the "Araby" aria, not quite twinkly enough performance. The loveliest singing of the evening came from Carmen Balthrop as she voiced the mermaid's "witching strain" in smooth, limpid tones. Anne Pinsker, first cello, and Paul Ingraham, first horn, deserve special mention. The singing of the Dessoff Choirs was sure. Miss Queler chose the original, mixed-voice version of the houris' chorus; during rehearsals Weber rearranged the number, more aptly, for female voices. The whole evening was a pageant of enchantments as Miss Queler's baton, like Oberon's wand, transported us by means of Weber's music from flowery bank to foaming river and glittering minarets, to tempest, glorious sunset, and gently lapping waves where mermaids float on the sea and sing in the moonlight—and as, against these backgrounds, the noble pair sang their songs of hope, fear, and steadfast love, and their attendants sang their songs and duet of simple, uncomplicated pleasures. The first-act finale, where Reiza's "O my wild, exulting soul" wings out toward freedom while the music of the Turkish patrol plods and grinds across the stage, is one of the opera's great moments.

The day after *Oberon*, the Juilliard School's opera training department put on a captivating account of Cavalli's *La Calisto*, in the performing edition made by Raymond Leppard for Glyndebourne in 1970. It was described as a workshop production, and the costumes and scenery were assembled from in-house materials, but it was a full performance, lovingly and carefully rehearsed, not a sketch for one. Calvin Morgan's décor boasted an aerial car, a grotto plashy with living waters, and flying devices that enabled Jove and Callisto (as her name is usually spelled) to sing their final duet floating in midair, on their way to the stars. Giovanni Faustini's libretto is a mythological extravaganza. Jove, disguised as his daughter Diana, seduces Diana's favorite nymph, Callisto. Diana is having a secret and tender affair with the shepherd Endymion. Wandering around Arcady, the nymph, the shepherd, Pan (who is in love with Diana), and—indistinguishable—Diana and Jove-as-Diana have plentiful opportunities for mismeeting and mismating. The jealous Juno arrives in a blaze of fury, complaining that Jove gets back to Olympus at night too tired to be of any use to her. A sexy little satyr advances upon Lymphaea, an elderly nymph of Diana's, bored with her virgin state, and is rejected, he claims, only because his little *coda* is still so small and tender. In revenge, he calls his elder brothers, who gather for a scene of gang rape. It is a frankly bawdy libretto—and yet the opera proves extraordinarily poetic and touching. Leppard has added romance in the form of two extra arias for Diana—"Ardo, sospiro, e piango," from Cavalli's *Artemisia*, and "Amara servitù," from his *Mutio Scevola*. Both are pierced by the chromatic stabs of grief that were a Cavalli specialty, and they paint a poignant picture of the virgin goddess racked by love. Yet in *La Calisto* Cavalli was romantic, too. When the little satyr sings of his ancient lineage, the music suddenly becomes proud, grand, and strangely majestic. When Pan's attendants seek to comfort their master for Diana's coldness, it becomes heartbreakingly beautiful. I use the gushy adverb knowing that Leppard himself composed (on Cavalli themes) the melting "Pane, consolati" first-act finale of this version, that he composed (on Cavalli themes) the softly radiant second-act finale, and that he has sentimentalized many of Cavalli's numbers with his singing-strings accompaniments. A glance or two at Cavalli's score is enough to show that, besides adding, Leppard has cut, trimmed, transposed, and shuffled. In time, the Cavalli-Leppard *Calisto* will no doubt be placed beside the Gluck-Wagner *Iphigenia in Aulis* and the Mozart-Strauss *Idomeneo* and be studied only as an example of how one century brought the works of another century to performance. But since, like them, it is an act of restoration undertaken with admiration, love, understanding, and high musical skill—and since, if my memory of the original score is correct, Leppard has not, as in his Monteverdi realizations, destroyed any careful dramatic patterns—I cannot but be grateful for his *Calisto*. It would have been more adventurous of the Juilliard to bring one of Cavalli's unfamiliar operas to the stage (*Eliogabalo* awaits its world première, and there is a score in New York) and to create a performing edition of its own instead of reproducing one devised for the voices and temperaments of Janet Baker (Diana and Jove-as-Diana), Ileana Cotrubas (Callisto), and Hugues Cuénod (Lymphaea), and divided for the two-act evening, interrupted by dinner, that suits Glyndebourne best. But, having chosen *La Calisto*, it did very well by it.

Martin Isepp, the director of the department, conducted (at the Glyndebourne première of the piece he played the harpsichord), and he drew sensitive, stylish phrasing from his singers and players. The outstanding performers in the first of two casts were Gail Dobish, clear, bright, and charming in the title role; Linda Wall, a commanding Juno; and, as Endymion, James Justiss, a pure, even countertenor. David Ostwald, the director, occasionally let his singers fall into boompsadaisy student heartiness, but most of the time he kept them on the tricky stylistic tightrope they must tread if *La Calisto* is to be at once entertaining and profound. The opera was sung in Geoffrey Dunn's neat, witty English translation.

Tovey, in his essay on the *Oberon* overture, tells of three good ideas that Weber discerned in Planché's pantomime and "promptly turned into traits of genius": Oberon's horn, which is "capable of real poetic power" ("When it sounds, we see and hear as if space were annihilated; and everything becomes exquisitely clear and tiny, because its immense remoteness is that of our own inmost soul"); the vision of human love awakening (which brings "the revelation to Sir Huon the Bold of something better in life than boldness"); and—an idea that "even in its crudest manifestations is a sure mark of greatness in the artist who ventures to use it"—"the conviction that 'the light of common day' is not a thing to be blasphemed." *La Calisto* is a set of variations on the expression of a single idea: that love, shattering barriers of caste, creed, and convention, can make men and women break their vows, forget their duty, and tread strange paths of ecstasy, despair, and self-discovery. *La Favorite* as Donizetti composed it was another expression of that idea: set in Spain, and not Arcady; clad in the elaborate trappings of *grand opéra*, and not rendered with seventeenth-century directness and wit. At the Met, that idea is lost in an empty display of costumed vocalism. There are people who do not take opera seriously. The performance of *La Favorite* may show why, but the performances of *Oberon* and *La Calisto* showed that they are wrong.

March 13, 1978

Alphabet of the Stars

"The *Rite of Spring* of our day" and "the best concert of the season" are accolades as imprecise and meaningless as, say, "the best concerto since the *Emperor*" and "the greatest tenor in the world." But if I had to bestow them on a large-scale orchestral work composed since the war and on one concert of the current New York season, they would go unhesitatingly to Pierre Boulez's *Pli selon pli (Portrait de Mallarmé)* and to the Carnegie Hall concert last month at which Arthur Weisberg's Contemporary Chamber Ensemble gave *Pli selon pli* its American première. *Pli* was acclaimed as a towering masterpiece after its first full performances in 1962 and has dominated the contemporary orchestral repertory ever since. But in America none of the great orchestras have played it; nor, for that matter, any of the lesser orchestras. No student orchestras have tackled it. Until last month, we had to make do with the Columbia disc of the piece, recorded in 1969 by the BBC Symphony Orchestra under the composer. But *Pli selon pli* needs to be entered as a living landscape. The printed score is a map of its domain, the disc an account of just one journey through it—a journey recorded in fine, clear detail, it is true, but in two dimensions. At the Carnegie Hall performance, *Pli selon pli* was alive, and it was good to be living with and within it. The poet, Mallarmé said, sets down black on white; "he does not write, luminously, on a dim ground, the alphabet of the stars." But the musician can write in such an alphabet—or so it seems when his black-on-white pages are turned into luminous sound.

Pli selon pli lasts an hour. It has five movements: "Don," "Improvisations sur Mallarmé" I, II, and III, and "Tombeau." The outer movements are for fairly large orchestra (respectively, forty-eight and thirty-seven players); "Don" begins and "Tombeau" ends with an isolated line from a Mallarmé sonnet, sung by a soprano soloist. The central improvisation is for soprano and nine players; I and III are for soprano and, respectively, thirty-five and twenty-six players. In I and II, Mallarmé sonnets are sung; in III, just the first three lines of one. Because of the varied instrumental distributions—seven percussionists in "Don," eight violas in Improvisation I, etc.—fifty-six players are needed in all. The composition extended over some five years. Improvisations I and II ("Le vierge, le vivace et le bel aujourd'hui" and "Une dentelle s'abolit") appeared and were published in 1958; "Le vierge" at that time used just seven players (harp, vibraphone, bells, and four percussion), and "Une dentelle" nine (piano and celesta joined the ensemble). Both pieces were widely performed by adventurous chamber ensembles. "Tombeau" was first done in Donaueschingen in 1959, in memory of Prince Max-Egon zu

Fürstenberg, the founder and patron of the Donaueschingen Festival; it was extended in 1960 and again in 1962, and published in 1971. "Don" was first played by the composer as a piano solo at the 1960 ISCM Festival in Cologne, in an interim performance of a work billed for the first time as *Pli selon pli* (*Portrait de Mallarmé*). But that first version of "Don" disappeared into the chamber piece *Éclat,* later expanded into *Éclat-Multiples,* and a new "Don," for orchestra, using some of the material of the piano solo, appeared in 1961 and was published in 1967. Also in 1961, the first Improvisation was rescored and expanded. (The score has just been published.) Meanwhile, between 1958 and 1960 the sections of Improvisation III ("A la nue accablante tu") had been composed; they remained unpublished.

Fold upon fold, in various performances from 1960 onward, the growing work was revealed. It reached its present form in 1962, at the Holland and Darmstadt Festivals. In 1965, it was heard at the Edinburgh Festival, played by the Hamburg Radio Orchestra. In 1966, a scheduled London première, by the BBC Orchestra under Boulez, was reduced to the first three movements; the players had not been able to master the whole piece to the composer's satisfaction. The BBC gave several performances of the whole work in 1969—in its regular concert series, on a European tour, at a Prom, and in the recording studio. And for his farewell concert as chief conductor of the BBC Symphony, at a 1975 Prom, Boulez chose *Pli selon pli.* That year, the piece was also played by the student orchestra of the Royal College of Music.

"Un coup de dés jamais n'abolira le hasard." A throw of the dice will never do away with chance. Mallarmé's hard saying—set out, with many parentheses and qualifications, as one of his most important poems—was much quoted in those years, about 1955 to 1965, when aleatory music (from *aleator,* a dice player) was a cause to be debated, defended, attacked. In 1957, Boulez published his famous essay "Alea," in which he suggests—to reduce a subtle argument to a crude summary—that an aleatory composer should load his dice so as to keep some control of the chance possibilities among which his performer or performers are allowed to choose. In the first, fourth, and fifth movements of *Pli selon pli,* there are some limited options for the interpreters: antiphonal exchanges at the end of "Don" which may be ordered in any of six different ways; alternative vocal lines in "A la nue accablante tu," and a very intricate network of alternative episodes; and an ad libitum tempo for the coda of "Tombeau." Something, not much, is left to careful choice, and nothing to blind chance. The last line of *Un Coup de dés* proclaims that "toute pensée émet un coup de dés."

In a preface, Mallarmé explains that he has set out his lines of verse (spaced across two pages at a time, in types of differing weight and size) in a fashion that can serve anyone who reads them aloud as a kind of musical score, distinguishing between principal and secondary motifs, suggesting tempi and rhythms, and indicating whether inflections should rise or fall. Not only for its reflections upon chance but in several other ways *Un Coup de dés* provides the best introduction to *Pli selon pli.* The poet (writing in 1897) intimates that he has here reclaimed for letters certain literary devices that music has taken up and developed: placing images or motifs ("prismatic sub-divisions of the Idea") precisely in space and in time; defining the instant of their appearance and their duration "within an exact spiritual mise-en-scène;" making clear "their variable distance, near or far, from the hidden conductor wire" of the text. Syntax and typography conspire to create music's effects of rubato ("d'accélérer tantôt et de ralentir le mouvement"), of *Hauptstimme* and *Nebenstimme*, of counterpoint, of themes recapitulated, extended, or suddenly abandoned ("retraits, prolongements, fuites"), and yet all this is achieved "leaving intact the ancient verse line, to which I ascribe dominion of passion and dreams." Mallarmé does not at all wish to break completely with tradition; he offers his poem not as a sketch but in a "state" where its presentation is "pushed forward in many ways not to the point of obfuscation but far enough to open people's eyes." The genre, he says, may eventually become one like the symphony—different from personal song—in which "to treat for preference (as in the poem that follows) subjects of pure and complex imagination and intellect, which there is no reason to exclude from Poetry: their only source."

Mallarmé is as difficult to translate as James Joyce. When one tries to parse and construe his sentences, the ambiguities encountered are sometimes like those encountered when trying to parse and construe a passage of late-nineteenth-century chromatic harmony. Music has long had the means of, as it were, changing the "case" of a note—the tonic of one phrase becomes the dominant, mediant, or whatever of the next—and of playing syntactical tricks far more complicated than that. Boulez probably went too far (and in a parenthesis allowed his combative youthful contempt for Wagner and for attractive melodies to color his thought) when, in a *Nouvelle Revue Française* essay of 1954, long before any of *Pli* had taken shape, he wrote, "Neither the Mallarmé of the *Coup de dés* nor Joyce was paralleled by anything in the music of his own time. . . . (If one thinks of what they loved: the one Wagner, the other Italian opera and Irish songs!)" But, he continued, "to see their investigations as having been marked by a search for a new musical poetics is not illusory." He aimed to create for music a poetic syntax of Mallarméan subtlety and flexibility ("I demand for music the right to parenthesis and italics") and to create structures that would not be self-sufficient, closed: "I want the musical work to be not that series of compartments which one must inevitably visit one after the other. I try to think of it as a domain in which, in some manner, one can choose one's own direction."

There are creators whose works seem to be installments in the continued creation of a single *Grand Oeuvre*—Mallarmé's term for the all-inclusive *Livre* he dreamed of writing. And others (Balanchine and Boulez among them) within whose oeuvres one can discern series of linked, mutually illuminating works, bound more closely than by the customary lines of development from one piece to the next. (Mahler's "Wunderhorn" songs and his first four symphonies form one such series; in a Mallarmé phrase, "ils s'allument

de reflets réciproques comme une virtuelle traînée de feux sur des pier-
reries.") Such creators are, on the one hand, constantly revising their earlier
works and, on the other, creating new ones in which previous ideas are re-
stated, extended, amplified, and led onward. The former process is illustrated
by Boulez's rescorings of "Le vierge, le vivace et le bel aujourd'hui" and of
his early cantata *Le Soleil des eaux* (whose latest version he conducted in
London this season), the other by the growth of his piano-solo "Don" both
into *Éclat* and then *Éclat-Multiples* and into the "Don" that opens *Pli selon
pli*—or by the flowering of the 1971 epitaph that he wrote for Stravinsky into
...*explosante/fixe*... (ten minutes long in 1972, over half an hour in 1973)
and by the close relationship of...*explosante/fixe*... to its successor, *Rituel*.
Ideas of Open Form—both as a domain in which an interpreter can choose
his paths and as a structure not so much complete in itself as an "ongoing
contribution" to a debate or to a body of congruent musical experiences—
were much discussed in the fifties. Composers had been practicing something
of the kind since music began. In his great B-minor Mass, his largest choral
work, Bach assembled suitable movements from seven cantatas, sacred and
secular, written during the two previous decades. Handel was forever repeating or recomposing his own—and other men's—music. Rossini, on a simple level, and Prokofiev, in labyrinthine ways, are "open form" composers. It
would be hard to draw strict defining lines between Prokofiev's devices of—
like Rossini—getting maximum mileage from a hit number, of salvaging apparently wasted music, of composing new music on existing material, and of
recomposing earlier works. Musical compositions, more fortunate in this respect than cathedrals, can undergo adaptation and reconstruction without
loss of the original: both the long and the short versions of Prokofiev's Fourth
Symphony—and both the chamber and the orchestral versions of Boulez's
"Une dentelle"—are still played. Boulez has not quite said, with Henry Ford,
that "history is bunk," but on occasion he has nearly said it. He lives and
works in the present, as if the present were all that mattered. What he wrote
specifically of Webern studies he demonstrates as a general belief when he
conducts works of the past: "They are useful only inasmuch as they have isolated the lines of force active at the present time." He has often declared that
"musicians have always been in the rearguard of the revolutions of others."
As one who lives his imaginative life in many centuries and can still be excited by hearing, say, what John Taverner and Christopher Tye made of and
around the "Westron Wynde" tune more than four centuries ago, I think that
Boulez is wrong, and that in his explorations he is not only making but also
repeating history—doing the kinds of thing that inventive musicians have always done even while advancing into new and uncharted terrain.

Sooner or later, composers seem to decide that an idea can be developed
no further or that a work has reached its final form. So far as I know, *Pli selon
pli* has not been altered in any significant way since 1962. It is now a coherent series of five distinct but related movements, cumulative in effect. The
history of its gradual construction is in itself an illustration of its subject. The
title is a phrase from a Mallarmé sonnet describing the stone of Bruges re-

vealing itself "fold by fold." In the same way, Boulez says in a program note, "as the five pieces unfold they reveal, fold by fold, a portrait of Mallarmé." The critic of the *Times* dismissed *Pli selon pli* after its Carnegie Hall performance as "a dead issue, at best an interesting reminder of the time about twenty years ago when the European music scene was breaking into partisan camps." It *is* such a reminder but also much more than that—and not "at best" that. It is the best piece that came out of those adventurous and prolific years—not just the work in which new techniques were most elegantly and lucidly refined and formulated but the most beautiful, most poetic, richest product of the time. On one level, it is indeed a "portrait of Mallarmé"—and, on another, a portrait of its composer. Maybe it also provides a portrait of anyone who seeks to understand it. (In one of his essays, Boulez quotes with approval the close of Michel Butor's essay on Baudelaire: "Some people may think that, while intending to write about Baudelaire, I have succeeded only in speaking of myself. It would certainly be better to say that it was Baudelaire who spoke of me. *He speaks of you.*") Beyond that, it is the result of an authentically Mallarméan act of creation: "The pure work implies the disappearance of the poet as speaker; he hands initiative over to the words." For *poet*, read *composer*; for *words*, *notes*. And it was achieved by what Boulez once described as "organizing delirium"—bringing Apollonian lucidity to bear upon, but not chill or destroy, a poetic musician's fine frenzy.

In his six years as music director of the New York Philharmonic, Boulez conducted none of his own music except the Improvisations I (chamber version) and II of *Pli selon pli* and, in his final season, *Rituel*. Reproached with depriving New York audiences of important twentieth-century music that other capitals were enjoying, he explained that he was reluctant to impose his own compositions on a subscription and therefore "captive" audience. There may have been a contributory reason: Would Philharmonic audiences have been willing to do the amount of homework that the composer expects? In his note on *Pli*, Boulez says, "In my transposition, or transmutation, of Mallarmé, I take it for granted that the direct sense of the poem has been acquired by reading it; I take it that the data communicated to the music by the poem have already been assimilated." That's taking a lot for granted. To prepare large audiences properly, the Philharmonic program books would have had to print, weeks in advance, *Un Coup de dés* (wherein are ordered many of the images—waves, whiteness, wings, shipwreck, stars, spume, abyss—of *Pli*) and the six relevant sonnets, in French and with as helpful an English translation as possible. Perhaps several translations. I have come across no single English rendering of a Mallarmé poem which provides more than glimmers of its full meaning. Untranslatable ambiguities in the French are both sonic and syntactical. Keith Bosley, translator of the Penguin Mallarmé, notes how the Faun's "Je tiens la reine" can mean at once that he holds the queen, the arena (*l'arène*), and the rein (*la rêne*); and only Boulez can tell us whether, in "A la nue accablante tu" (whose fourteen lines turn on a single verb, *abolit*), he has understood "le flanc enfant d'une sirène"—"the child-flank of a siren" (Allen Edwards), "the side-child of a siren" (record sleeve), "some young siren's infant flank" (Roger Fry)—to have been drowned (Edwards, Fry) or to have done the drowning (Bosley). The program of the Carnegie Hall concert contained the *Pli* texts and Allen Edwards's English translations—but it was too late to come across them when one was already in the hall. Only when one has the sonnets more or less by heart can one follow the words as they are sung. Only when one has the sense of the sonnets more or less by heart can one begin to hear the movements as a "transposition, or transmutation, of Mallarmé." In Boulez's words:

> I wanted to find a musical equivalent and that is why I chose the strictest forms. There are various levels of convergence between poetry and music. The simplest is the conveying of the sense of the words. Thus, when Mallarmé speaks of "absence," there is a musical sonority—a sound held for a long time—that can convey this idea. Another point of convergence is the form itself. The sonnet has a very strict form which calls for a certain musical structure. My purpose was to ascribe a kind of form to each verse according to the rules of the sonnet itself.

Moreover, to understand the work as a whole one needs to have read more Mallarmé than just the immediate texts. It also helps to have read some Butor.

For Mallarmé himself, music was a sacred mystery. On looking at a score, "we are seized by a religious amazement at the macabre processions of severe, chaste, unknown signs. And we close the missal unsullied by any profaning thought." That is a romanticized view of a perfectly specific notational system that anyone can learn. But Mallarmé's poems are filled with musical sounds evoked in a similar spirit of religious awe. In the sonnet to St. Cecilia, the wings of the angel who flies down to hear her become a sounding harp beneath the saint's fingers. In the Wagner sonnet, divine trumpet notes set down in liquid gold (written in the alphabet of the stars?) light up the inky hieroglyphs of old parchments. The dedicatee of "Don du poëme" has a voice "recalling viol and harpsichord." In "Une dentelle," there is a lute—musician with a hollow heart. Music comes down to earth with a bump in one of the prose poems: "The piano sparkles, the violin gives light to torn fibres, but the barrel-organ, in the twilight of memory, set me dreaming desperately. Now, while it was murmuring a cheerfully vulgar air such as brings gaiety to suburban hearts, an old-fashioned, hackneyed tune, whence was it that its refrain went to my soul and made me weep as at a romantic ballad?" Mahler could have answered that question in music; in the scherzo of the Fourth Symphony, perhaps he did. From Boulez it would surely draw no sympathetic answer. The "music" that Mallarmé himself created lies in his manipulation of motif, metre, and syntax.

"Don du poëme" is the dedicatory sonnet before *Hérodiade*, and foreshadows some of its imagery. In his "Don," Boulez sets just the first line of it, quite simply: "I bring you the child of a night of Edom." After an explosion, soft, slow, translucent sequences suggest Mallarmé's "glass burned with incense and gold, icy panes, alas! still dim." And then, through them, motifs of the succeeding movements begin to form—fragmentary instrumental allusions, isolated phrases of text. In the composer's words, " 'Don du poëme' . . . becomes here a 'don de l'oeuvre.' " In the next two movements of *Pli*, the musical form perceptibly follows the sonnet structure—octave in two distinct quatrains, sextet in two triplets. "The musical form may be found already determined if the finished, perfect structure that is the sonnet is taken into consideration. The necessary transposition demands the invention of equivalences—equivalences that may be applied both to the exterior form of the musical invention and to its quality or inner structure." I have no idea what specific systems of musical equivalences Boulez has devised. But in "Le vierge, le vivace et le bel aujourd'hui" the soprano's repeated rise to shining, sustained high A flats, each one louder and fuller than the one before, and each followed by a drop, forms a motif that seems to picture the swan-poet-composer trapped in the frozen lake while above him, unattainable, the stars of the Swan constellation mock his aspiration. The fluttering of the lace curtain in "Une dentelle," set against the long-sustained sonorities of absence, finds a more direct kind of musical expression. "A la nue accablante tu" is a poem of shocked, dreadful silence after some catastrophe. It opens with a long wordless vocalise. "Naufrage" and "furibond" may be the key words for the percussion toccata that follows. Then the first three lines of the poem are sung. At length, the piece ends in desolation. More of it was composed, in 1960, but the final section has been withheld from performance. The sonnet needs no more than there is here for its expression. "Tombeau" was Mallarmé's epitaph for Verlaine. Boulez's "Tombeau" begins with dark, dense sonorities: "Mourning oppresses with many a cloudy fold the ripened star of the future." Signals, strong and insistent, begin to sound: "A scintillation from that star will silver the crowd." As if in benediction, the soprano at last sings the last line of the sonnet in a long, clear line: "A shallow, slandered rivulet, death."

The Carnegie Hall performance was the boldest, the most confident and colorful, and therefore the most beautiful and moving performance of *Pli selon pli* that I have heard. *Pli* interpreters need to be not just delicate, accurate, and poetic; there are passages that call for heroic, exuberant, almost recklessly forthright playing. Mr. Weisberg had enlarged the Contemporary Chamber Ensemble, basically fifteen strong, with several of New York's best instrumentalists. His secure grasp of the piece enabled them to give of their best, without timidity or hesitation, without any of that sense of hanging on by the skin of the teeth which marked some earlier performances of it. The important balances within intricate chords, between different, superimposed sonorities, and between antiphonal groups across the platform were justly and eloquently achieved. Phyllis Bryn-Julson was the soprano soloist; the simple—if meaningless—accolade for her would be "the best American singer." To the precision, agility, and sure pitching of widely ranging notes which a contemporary soprano needs she adds beauty, firmness, purity, and evenness of tone, reaching to the highest and lowest extremes of the far-flung lines, and an instinctive command of expressive phrasing. She is, as it were, a fully equipped Bellini singer who sings Boulez as beautifully as if it were Bellini.

The Ensemble has plans for a series of similar concerts, presenting the important large-scale orchestral works that, for one reason or another, our regular large orchestras are not in a position to play. ("Performing difficulties," it notes, "have increased at a faster pace than the traditional format of weekly concerts can accommodate.") If its future concerts maintain the level of this *Pli selon pli*, they will be red-letter days of the New York musical scene.

March 20, 1978

Sound Track

Ivan the Terrible, the "oratorio for reciter, soloists, chorus, and full symphony orchestra" that Abram Stassevich assembled from Prokofiev's music for the Eisenstein movie, had what was apparently its New York première at the Philadelphia Orchestra's visit to Carnegie Hall this month. (A program note chronicled only St. Louis and Chicago performances.) Riccardo Muti conducted, and, in music well matched to his command of incisive rhythms, strong clear colors, full-toned playing, and precise balance, he made a great effect. It was an exciting concert. Boris Morgunov, who was the reciter at the first performance of the oratorio, in Moscow in 1961, repeated his role. His large, uninhibited, very imposing performance—besides narrating, he must enact both Ivan and the Holy Fool who disturbs Ivan's coronation—was in itself justification for doing the work in Russian, instead of in the English translation. Morgunov can also be heard in the new Angel recording of *Ivan the Terrible*, which Muti has made with his London orchestra, the Philharmonia; it was published here at the time of the concert. The Angel album contains a three-column libretto: Russian, transliteration, and English translation. The Carnegie Hall program book contained only the English translation—which was better than nothing but not enough—and the lighting in the hall was too dim for it to be followed with any ease. (What Carnegie saves on its lighting bill it might well spend on cooling; at the Boston Symphony's performance of Tippett's oratorio *A Child of Our Time*, at the Horowitz recital last week, and at Eve Queler's performance of *Tancredi*, it achieved temperatures that Shadrach, Meshach, and Abednego might have found comfortable but that seriously interfered with ordinary folk's attention to the music.)

Prokofiev's music for *Ivan* is graphic. It must be fifteen years since I last saw the two parts of Eisenstein's movie, but during the oratorio its images came back to me so insistently that at times I felt I was listening to a sound track and missing the visuals. And that's the trouble: it might make more sense to show the film—or, to a concert audience, even just the footage with continuous musical accompaniment. *Ivan* is not a score like *Petrushka* or *Agon*, which first took detailed shape in sound and then had spectacle added to it; Prokofiev watched Eisenstein's imagery and then wrote the accompaniment. Nevertheless, he did write music that proves worth hearing in its own right: choruses in the bold, stirring patriotic vein of his opera *War and Peace*, lyrical melodies in the long-breathed manner of Russian folk song, battle pieces, paeans, wedding songs, and boisterous, brutal music for the oprichniks, Ivan's private army. (Stalin suppressed Part II of the film.) In several scenes, comparisons with *Boris Godunov* are openly evoked. And all is achieved with Prokofiev's wonted vividness and flair; *Ivan* holds a worthy place in the long line of Russian historical epics.

Claudine Carlson was the splendidly smooth and steady contralto; I liked her even better than Irina Arkhipova, the more vibrant soloist of the Angel recording. The Mendelssohn Club of Philadelphia sang bravely. The orchestra was magnificent. The only miscalculation was campanological: the bells were amplified to a point where they drowned everything else.

In recent years, the work of Eugène Scribe has been much in evidence at the Met: in *Les Vêpres siciliennes*, *Le Prophète*, and *La Favorite*; in *Adriana Lecouvreur*, based on a Scribe play; and now in a revival of *L'elisir d'amore*, which, like *La sonnambula* and *Un ballo in maschera*, was composed to an Italian adaptation of a Scribe libretto. In 1831, when Felice Romani reworked a Scribe dance-drama as the text of *La sonnambula*, for Bellini, he translated some passages directly, he added the lovely soprano-tenor duet "Son geloso del zefiro errante," and in general he gave more warmth and depth to the characters while preserving the deftness of the original plot. Likewise in 1832, when, for Donizetti, he converted Scribe's *Le philtre* (set to music by Auber the previous year) into *L'elisir d'amore:* some passages are direct translations from the French; the lovely soprano-tenor duet "Chiedi all'aura lusinghiera" is an addition to Scribe's scheme; and Adina and Nemorino are drawn with more tender, more detailed touches than are Scribe's Térézine and Guillaume. When the curtain rises, Adina is reading "la storia di Tristano," and she bursts into merry laughter at the "bizzarra avventura." But *Elisir* tells a credible real-life version of the Tristan story: a potion not quite what it purports to be (in Donizetti it's claret, masquerading as the *Liebestrank*) breaks down inhibitions that have kept two loving souls apart. Under its influence, Nemorino becomes bolder, and Adina at length sheds her capriciousness and is won by his steady devotion.

Nathaniel Merrill's production, eighteen years old now, is rather too hard and bright for the piece, and Robert O'Hearn's costumes—skirts too short, heels too high—are also better suited to an opera buffa than to a comedy of sentiment. Instead of a realistic or prettily idealized depiction of village life, we have ballet girls flouncing and ballet boys prancing all over the scene. But once they clear off, Judith Blegen and José Carreras, as Adina and Nemorino, take us to the heart of the matter. There is plenty in *Elisir* to make us laugh—the score holds Donizetti's most sparkling music—but when the jokes are on Nemorino we should laugh *con tenerezza.* Miss Blegen is an exquisite Adina. Her voice seems to have grown fuller and sweeter, and she fills the role as completely and captivatingly as she does Mozart's Susanna. The sound is not large, but the notes are so clearly focused that even in the enormous Metropolitan they are all deliciously audible. Her grace notes, mordents, and other adornments are always distinctly sounded, unhurried, unsmudged, delicately in place. To charm of timbre she unites charm of manner, a winning and personal sense of phrase and of verbal inflection, impeccable musicianship, and a way of listening while others sing that makes her Adina alive at every moment. I cannot think why the record companies are not competing to engage her as Adina, Amina, Norina, Zerlina (both Mozart's and Auber's), and Susanna (both Handel's and Wolf-Ferrari's; she has already recorded Mozart's). Not even the young Scotto or the young Freni was so bewitching, or so beautiful, in Adina's "Prendi; per me sei libero."

On the first night, Carreras was oddly disappointing, graceless and ill at ease, in "Quanto è bella" and in "Una furtiva lagrima." Gigli, as record collectors know, sets the standard for the first, and McCormack, Tito Schipa, and Caruso, in different ways, set it for the second. Caruso is a dangerous model for Carreras, who is often tempted to sing more loudly than he should; but that Carreras can be melting, as Gigli was, and can command a Schipa-like delicacy was shown in all the rest of his performance. Except in those two arias, he was pretty well ideal—charming, rueful, funny, touching, limpid in tone, and individual in his phrasing. His recitative "Caro elisir! sei mio! Sì, tutto mio" was a high point of the evening; his "Adina, credimi" was a lyrical cry that went to the heart. Belcore and Dulcamara were played surely, skillfully, and without exaggeration by two veterans, Mario Sereni and Fernando Corena (who has been with the production from the start). Sarah Caldwell conducted. On the first night, there were one or two sleepy patches, but most of the time she was both spirited and warm. All the duets went well, but the stretto of the first-act finale was ill balanced.

Nino Rota's opera buffa *The Italian Straw Hat,* first heard in Palermo in 1955, was given its New York première this month by the Manhattan School of Music, and it was done in style. From Lowell Detweiler, there was scenery that any professional company might envy. Dona Granata's costumes, borrowed from Santa Fe, which performed the piece last summer, were lavish and attractive. Lou Galterio, one of America's best opera directors, put his cast through bright, busy, crisply executed paces. John Crosby, the president of the school, conducted. The work is a romp. Rota's score is lively, tuneful, and quite undistinguished. While comedies with better—and more adventurous—music by, among others, Offenbach, Bizet, Lecocq, and Wolf-Ferrari remain unrevived, there is no reason for any of our regular companies to take up *The Italian Straw Hat,* but it was a good choice for a student exercise. There is just one large role, Fadinard (which was played with brio and resource by Vincenzo Manno), and there are many small roles that provide chances for numerous members of an opera class.

March 27, 1978

Wronging a Rite

In an unusually interesting number of that interesting magazine *Opera News* [Vol. 42, No. 18], Winthrop Sargeant sets out some truths about Mozart's *Don Giovanni* which seem to have been forgotten by those responsible for the current Metropolitan revival: Don Giovanni himself is "not a character but an archetype," and "it is as an archetype that he comes into focus"; the opera "is a story of crime and punishment" and "a profound essay on the subject of morality." In the last sentence of his essay, Mr. Sargeant says, "The celebration of a myth is a rite, not a performance, and when I go to hear *Don Giovanni* I feel I am in the presence of a rite." At the Met, it is at best a rite heedlessly celebrated. In the very first bars of the overture, Richard Bonynge set the tone for a "performance" that is light where it should be grave, easygoing where it should be intense, and large only in the wrong sorts of way. In Gounod's words (quoted by Sargeant), "The first chords, so powerful and solemn with their syncopated rhythm, establish at once the majestic and formidable authority of Divine Justice, the avenger of crime. After the first four bars (rendered yet more terrible by the silence that completes the second and fourth) there commences a harmonic progression of which the sinister character freezes one with terror." But in Bonynge's reading the opening chords lacked force and majesty, and the chromatic progression slipped by without emphasis, as if it were an everyday thing. During the evening, I was seized with terror only twice: in the cemetery scene, when the music dropped into C major, and Giovanni himself was shaken (for no performance, not even a weak one, and no amount of familiarity can make that moment less than hair-raising); and in the penultimate scene, after Giovanni had given his hand to the Statue (for there James Morris, the protagonist, found in his fine voice the accents of both physical pain and spiritual dread).

Elsewhere in that issue of *Opera News*, George Marek reminds us how explicitly Molière's Don Juan, one of the models for Da Ponte's and Mozart's, is a freethinker and blasphemer who goes through life fearing nor God nor the Devil, since he believes in neither. In contrast, Theodore Fenner, in an article on Leigh Hunt as a music critic, cites Hunt's view of the piece, uncolored, in 1817, by the romantic awe in which the nineteenth century was soon to hold it:

> One has nothing to do but to reckon the songs in succession, and pane-gyrize them as they go by.... What [can be] more genteel on the one side, and hesitating and tremulous on the other, than the duet "Là ci darem la mano," with its ardent close and delicious symphonies?... What a prettier little irresistible piece of penitence than "Batti, batti, o bel Masetto"?

Hunt objects only to the penultimate scene: "The whole is too loud and crashing, and of too vulgar a description of the terrible. We know not that an apparition of stone has any particular claims to be noisy and bullying."

The nineteenth century's romantic awe may have been overdone. Edward Dent consciously provided a corrective when, in his *Mozart's Operas*, he stressed the *dramma-giocoso* aspects of the score. And Bonynge may have had a similar intention. But awe is—or should be—inescapable. I see what Dent means when he says that in the first scene, the killing of the Commendatore, "there is no note of tragedy; it is all planned from the standpoint of *opera buffa*"; that in the second scene "we know at once that we are not going to be allowed to take Elvira seriously for a moment"; that "the atmosphere of frivolity is kept up for several scenes"; that "the dramatic situation [in the serenading of Elvira] is the most repulsive ... endurable only if one takes a completely frivolous view of the whole play," since "taken seriously, Elvira's degradation is horrible." History—all that we have learned about eighteenth-century opera in general—tells us to laugh at Donna Elvira. So do many directors of *Don Giovanni*. Nevertheless, I do take her seriously and I weep for her: weep as she begins to sing "Ah taci, ingiusto core" (wept at her very first notes when she was Suzanne Danco, Sena Jurinac, or Elisabeth Schwarzkopf), and weep through the ensuing cruel, "horrible" joke that is played on her—while around me some of the audience is laughing, and even I am smiling, at the antics of Leporello as he imitates his master's amorous techniques. Elvira's degradation *is* horrible. And she *is* absurd—absurd and distressing at once, in a way that only cast-off mistresses still hoping and still importunate can be. I believe that Dent took her seriously, too, for he describes the spoof serenade as "perhaps the most beautiful number of the whole opera." And I am sure that Mozart did.

The *Don Giovanni* literature is immense [see page 503]. Mr. Sargeant cites Gounod's *Le Don Juan de Mozart* and Kierkegaard's *Either/Or*, whose first volume has considerable pages about the opera. His own essay (which contains observations like "Don Giovanni . . . is beautiful in precisely the way a flash of lightning is beautiful. He represents the *élan vital*, the life force that propels to growth, dominance, and mastery. And as such he is profoundly dangerous") joins my personal anthology. Required reading begins with E. T. A. Hoffmann's influential story "Don Juan, eine fabelhaftige Begebenheit," Pierre-Jean Jouve's *Le Don Juan de Mozart*, and—recently made available in English for the first time, published by Eulenburg as a separate book, *Mozart's "Don Giovanni"*—the long study of the opera that Hermann Abert wrote for his revision of Otto Jahn's Mozart biography. It should hardly need pointing out that a work that has so prominently occupied the imagination of philosophers, poets, novelists, playwrights (Shaw, in *Man and Superman*), and composers must be more than "the story of a gay blade who seduces an incredible number of women and is finally, and rather quaintly, thrown into hell by a stone statue because of his sins" (Sargeant's summary of the trivial way of considering and presenting the piece). But in the Met presentation—the production was created twenty-one years ago by Herbert Graf and is now directed by Patrick Tavernia—it is even *less* than that, not a story at all, not a drama, but a concert of individual numbers, almost unrelated, that happen to be sung, one after the other, in costume and amid Eugene Berman's heavy scenery. I must have seen about thirty different productions of the opera (and have reviewed perhaps a hundred performances). As I compiled my personal catalogue—*in Italia soltanto una, in Almagna cinque, tre in Francia,* and so on—I was surprised to find that from almost every one of them some vivid memory remained. The list starts in student days with the sane, beautiful Vienna production by Oscar Fritz Schuh, in neoclassical scenery, and runs to Peter Hall's powerful version for Glyndebourne last summer. Particularly keen impressions were left by Virginio Puecher's extraordinarily fierce staging for the Holland Festival (Giovanni's life was in danger from Elvira, from Ottavio, from Masetto; and, in the sextet, at the final cry of "Morrà!" Leporello escaped death by the skin of his teeth, for the stage direction "Don Ottavio fa l'atto di ucciderlo" was properly observed), and by Walter Felsenstein's extraordinarily realistic and sensual production for the Berlin Komische Oper. Such oddities as Franco Zeffirelli's huge, opulent production for Covent Garden (which worked only when the cast was also on the grandest possible scale) and Gian Carlo Menotti's curious Spoleto staging, amid reproductions of Henry Moore statues, made their mark. But from the current Met version I suspect no images will remain in a year or two but the grotesque one of Joan Sutherland's Anna sailing on like a galleon, dressed as if for an arts ball in an enormous black creation with a bejeweled front panel, and with tall plumes rising from her head. She seemed to belong to a different show. Perhaps one will also remember mistakes: in the first-act finale, Tavernia does not get the moments of unmasking right.

In a Mozartian's mind, poets and commentators conspire with successive performers heard and seen to add richness, depth, and color to his feeling for the great opera—although, of course, he accepts only those details that strike him as true. When I read Donna Anna's music on the page, it "sounds" for me with Lilli Lehmann's heroic grandeur (and, incidentally, with the appoggiaturas to be heard on her records of the two arias), with Frida Leider's breadth, and—here a visual memory comes into play as well—with Ljuba Welitch's bright flame. My Elvira is, above all, Elisabeth Schwarzkopf. My Leporello combines Erich Kunz's quick, sly cunning, a whiff of the garlic breath that Marcello Cortis seemed to breathe into the phrases, and something of the psychological complexity Lilli Lehmann writes about in her memoirs. And Giovanni? Mr. Sargeant's first point is proved, it seems to me, when I realize that, although one may recall individuals' touches of grace and courtesy (Emilio de Gogorza's serenade), of charm mingled with dangerous force, Giovanni is really brought to life by conductors'—Furtwängler's, Kempe's, Haitink's—handling of the overture, of the first scene, of the cemetery scene, and, above all, of the complementary first-act and second-act finales. (In the first, human intervention is powerless against the offender; in the second, divine intervention is decisive.) That may read as if one attended a performance of *Don Giovanni* expecting the impossible—the combined excellences of performers since recorded history began—and *difficilis, querulus, laudator temporis acti se puero, castigator censorque minorum. Difficilis,* yes, when it is a Met performance of one of the most important operas in its repertory, but, for the rest, not so. *Don Giovanni* is a self-renewing miracle, and renews its spectators. Lehmann has described how she approached the production that she directed for Salzburg in 1906 (when she was Anna, Gadski was Elvira, and Farrar was Zerlina):

An immense amount of material for each role lay garnered up in my memory. Had I not seen for almost fifty years all the *Don Giovanni* performances everywhere, with the most eminent Italian and German impersonators? Everything that was pregnant and subtle had stayed by me. My own individuality created, from the many admirable representations I had seen, ideal figures.

But four years later she had a new Leporello, the young Andrés de Segurola, who gave a different reading of the role from any she had known before and was "an illumination." (She regrets she did not have "cinematographic reproductions of each single gesture, so as to preserve what was there portrayed in fine observation of human character.") In my own experience I have always been glad to set out for a *Don Giovanni* production and, once there, have almost always eagerly enjoyed—with what has been sometimes deemed too promiscuous an appetite—performances on the most diverse levels. The opera was written for young singers—the first Giovanni, Luigi Bassi, had just turned twenty-one; the first Anna, Teresa Saporiti, was twenty-four—and student performances of it can be very fresh and powerful. Sometimes I have felt rage at, and felt that Mozart was outraged by, directors who did not share Lehmann's sane approach ("It was not my intention to create anything extravagant in equipment or scenery, nor to disfigure the opera by novel ideas"), but I have very seldom been bored, as I was by this Met *Don Giovanni.* It cannot be discussed as a rite, or as a drama, but only in terms of individual singers.

In nineteenth-century Paris, the star role was Don Ottavio when Rubini sang; audiences waited for the spectacular high F he would insert into "Il mio tesoro." The progression for nineteenth-century prima donnas was usually from Elvira to Zerlina to Anna; Lehmann advanced in that order, and so, it seems, did Eugenia Tadolini, the soprano whom Verdi did not want as Lady Macbeth. Elvira was the cadet role. Sophia Löwe, whom Verdi first wanted for Lady Macbeth, was deemed by the critic Henry Chorley to be a natural *seconda donna* and "the best Donna Elvira that I have ever seen." In Giulia Grisi's farewell season at Covent Garden, she sang Anna with a new-comer, Adelina Patti, as Zerlina, and thereafter during Patti's long reign there was no doubt which of the three *Don Giovanni* sopranos received top billing. For a while, when Christine Nilsson undertook Elvira (across the road at Drury Lane, not at Covent Garden), the balance of interest shifted some-what. In the words of a contemporary:

> The lamentations of the ill-used lady are not, as a rule, thought to form the most interesting part of Mozart's opera. But with Mlle. Nilsson in the character, Elvira, instead of being wearisome with her perpetual plaints, became highly interesting. The audience heard with sympathy her tales of woe, and felt that to deceive and, worse still, abandon so charming a woman was to combine crime with folly. Never did the public entertain so bad an opinion of Don Juan.

During the 1950s, a series of lustrous sopranos—their names have been men-tioned above—have similarly made Elvira the center of dramatic interest. After Welitch stopped singing Anna, Elisabeth Grümmer commanded the part (until challenges arrived from Birgit Nilsson and Joan Sutherland), but she was not a magnificent Anna, merely the best one around. Sutherland sang Anna at Glyndebourne in 1960, in a well-balanced production by Günther Rennert. She was very striking, particularly in "Non mi dir," where she seemed to be cradling her grief with a kind of fierce tenderness. There was more than spitfire heroics to her interpretation. A touch of this inner quality remained in her Met performance, but little of the quick, realistic intensity with which she used to observe and, in gesture, inflection, and accent, react to the murderous drama around her. Her voice sounded large but "shrouded" in timbre—which suits some of the music, not those passages where it should flash out like a sword. Elvira was Julia Varady, making her Met début. The sound was uneven; her registers were ill knit. She seemed to be doing her best, trying, not always successfully, not to go astray in the tricky passages. The Zerlina was Huguette Tourangeau, who appears in so many Sutherland-Bonynge shows. She had some curious, almost bizarre vocal moments, which might perhaps be considered piquant; but on the whole I thought her per-formance inept.

The best of the men was Allan Monk, the Masetto. It is not a negligible role. Giorgio Ronconi—Donizetti's Furioso and Torquato Tasso, Verdi's Nabucco—used to sing it, and Chorley, who devoted a chapter of his recollections to the great baritone, described it as almost the best of his creations. (Ronconi was a *baritono nobile* also admired as Dulcamara and Papageno.) In Monk's Masetto, honest love, truculence, and menace were justly blended. He sang well, and one felt the man's distress—one of the few emotions communicated from the stage during the evening. Gabriel Bacquier was a veteran, efficient, but unremarkable Leporello. James Morris's Giovanni is promising; a strong conductor and a strong, sensitive director might make much of it. The Ottavio of John Brecknock, another débutant, was limned in a decisive way but in tones more reedy than pleasing. Brecknock comes from the English National Opera, where Charles Mackerras has instilled an elegant, authentic *Aufführungspraxis;* this Ottavio graced his music, adorned his repeats, and alone of the cast sang all the necessary appoggiaturas.

April 3, 1978

Celebration

An encyclopedia assembled without grace and wit is a dull, heavy thing. The eleventh Britannica is good reading—any volume of the "Handy Volume" edition makes an ideal bedside book—while the fifteenth Britannica is something one consults (often in vain) for post-1911 facts but does not then go on and on reading simply because it is so well written and so entertaining. I hope the forthcoming sixth edition of Grove's Dictionary of Music and Musicians will have as many jokes as are tucked into unexpected corners of the fifth edition. Perhaps it will: an early editorial decision was to stress the importance of "Grove*heit*" (the quality of conveying accurate musical information in urbane prose)—as opposed to the *Grobheit* of Teutonic pedantry at its bluntest. The Mompou entry in the fifth Grove is one of the minor curiosities of musicological writing, and it is a nice point who was playing the joke on whom. Did its Dublin-born author, Walter Starkie, try to see what he could get away with? Or did he write in earnest, and the editor, Eric Blom, tongue-in-cheek naughtily allow the essay to stand? According to Starkie, the listener to Federico Mompou's music is reminded, even "irresistibly reminded," of many things, among them "the little Christmas plays written by Thornton Wilder . . . English music of the golden age of the Elizabethan virginalists . . . Galuppi, whose toccatas inspired Browning . . . the lovely lines of Enoch Soames:

> *Pale tunes irresolute,*
> *and traceries of old sounds,*
> *blown from a rotted flute,*
> *mingle with noise of cymbals*
> *rouged with rust."*

And of Debussy, who "paints nature coldly and objectively as if he were making a Japanese etching in the Hokusai style." Moreover, Mompou's music "may be described in the words Sir Thomas Browne wrote on the divinity of music: 'for even that vulgar and tavern-music, which makes one man merry, another mad, strikes in me a deep fit of devotion, and a profound contemplation of the First Composer. There is something in it of divinity more than the ear discovers.' "

I never thought to see Mompou plain, not because the calendar forbids it (he was born in 1893) but because Starkie tells us that he "is abnormally shy and shuns the world like the plague," and that "he lives a cloistered life dreaming of the quaint, primitive, sunlit world that we discover in the ancient miniatures of the fourteenth and fifteenth centuries or in the chronicles describing the lives of Pedro the Ceremonious or Martin the Humane among their Aragonese and Catalan subjects." But Mompou was in New York last week—a tall, impressive figure with a quick, searching glance—and he played a piano recital in Alice Tully Hall. He played three of his *Cançtos i dansas* based on Catalan airs ("No sooner does he pick up the popular tune than his musical daemon takes charge of it, transmogrifies it, illuminates it, and finally turns it by subtle magic into an entirely original tune"), a small set of variations, the five *Cants magics* of 1919, two Preludes, the *Suburbis* suite, and three of his *Escenes d'infants*. In addition, Alicia de Larrocha gave the first performance of a new *Cançto i dansa*, No. 14, which Mompou had composed for the occasion, and she accompanied José Carreras in four of Mompou's songs. The concert was put on by Lincoln Center, in its Great Performers series, together with the Spanish Institute, as an Homenaje a Mompou to mark his eighty-fifth birthday, which falls next week.

A little Mompou, occasionally encountered in recitals, or on records by Michelangeli, Gonzalo Soriano, and Victoria de los Angeles, goes a long way—if not quite all the way to the "unexplored regions of the subconscious," as has been claimed. Instead of being irresistibly reminded of Thornton Wilder, the virginalists, Galuppi, and the rest, I am reminded of Granados—but of a thinner, etherealized Granados in which veils of Debussyism break the harshness and directness of the Spanish sun. Mompou's music does have a character of its own. His harmony is diatonic, with added-note enrichments of a kind that cocktail-lounge pianism has long since debased; this pop element—for that is what it sounds like today—is part of a strangely fascinating, fastidious, poetic approach. Larrocha played and Carreras sang a St.

John of the Cross piece, *El cantar del alma*, with piano and voice in alternating meditations, so delicate and private that the public performance, to public applause, seemed almost a profanation. The composer himself played freely, fluently, and gracefully. Before each piece, he thought for a moment, and then embarked on music that he might have written anything up to sixty years ago as if he were improvising it on the spot for his and a few friends' pleasure.

I trust I am wrong, but sometimes it seems to me that when Elisabeth Schwarzkopf, Elisabeth Söderström, Peter Pears, and Dietrich Fischer-Dieskau retire, lieder singing will become a lost art. There is no one in younger generations who commands as they do the understanding and the technique that bring German songs to life. Centuries hence, when scholar-performers try to reconstruct the authentic style, they will at least have plenty of records by those artists and their great predecessors—Julia Culp, Elena Gerhardt, Elisabeth Schumann, Karl Erb, Gerhard Hüsch—to guide them, and thus be luckier than those who today venture upon troubadour songs or Burgundian ballades. Gundula Janowitz, with Irwin Gage as her supple, detailed pianist, gave her first New York lieder recital in Avery Fisher Hall last month, singing Schubert, Liszt, and Strauss. In the first half, she brought a touch of imagination to her tone in the opening words of Liszt's "Ihr Glocken von Marling," but the rest was lifeless, schoolroom singing, without interest.

Fischer-Dieskau and Jörg Demus have come to Carnegie Hall to give three Schubert recitals. At the first, they performed nine songs, nine more after an intermission, and then six encores. At the second, they did the *Winterreise*. As I write, the third is still to come. The main groups of the first recital, given unbroken by applause, were skillfully assembled to present a vision of Schubert at his most intimate and personal; no narrative songs or ballads, none of the great classical set pieces (no Schiller, and of Goethe only an erotic song from the *West-östlicher Divan*), no dramatic monologues or dialogues, but a sequence of tender, lyrical, and often melancholy pieces reflecting the Schubert who, in that strange allegory of 1822, wrote, "My heart filled with infinite love for those who scorned it, I wandered once more into distant lands. Through long, long years I sang my songs. But when I wished to sing of love it turned to sorrow, and when I wanted to sing of sorrow it was transformed into love." After the Goethe piece, "Versunken," Fischer-Dieskau sang "Des Sängers Habe"—take all else from me, but leave me the consolation of music—and then explored transitoriness and mortality, in "Wehmut," "Das Zügenglöcklein," "Abendbilder," "Auf der Donau," and "Totengräbers Heimweh." The second half began playfully ("Die Vögel") and included songs of consolation ("Am Fenster" and Leitner's "Die Sterne"), blitheness ("Fischerweise"), chivalric romance ("Liebeslauschen"), and pleasure in a lovely spring day ("Im Frühling," whose serene melody removes all smart from the words). Other themes that ran through this beautiful and moving anthology were those of moon and stars above, telling quietly of eternity ("Abendbilder," "Die Sterne," Schlegel's "Der Wanderer"); of busy waters and men's business upon them ("Der Strom," "Auf der Donau," "Der Schiffer," "Fischerweise"); and—perhaps most poignant of all, since every song could be deemed in some wise an illustration of it—of a poet's or composer's lonely striving (symbolically stated in "Des Sängers Habe," "Der Strom," and "Der Schiffer," and specifically in "Im Hochgebirge," alias "Heliopolis II"). "Im Hochgebirge," which closed the second group, pointed the way to the heroic Schubert, otherwise reserved for Fischer-Dieskau's third program—the Schubert of "Prometheus," "Gruppe aus dem Tartarus," and "An Schwager Kronos."

Fischer-Dieskau has recorded most of Schubert's songs that a male voice can meetly sing: one could assemble this anthology for oneself from his two rich Deutsche Grammophon volumes. But in the hall the juxtapositions, the new emotional colors that one song gained from another by contrast, continuation, or reminiscence of motifs, and the sense of an imaginative journey through Schubert's most private world made the recital far more than the sum of its items. Fischer-Dieskau sang with quiet, unforced intensity and in a free manner that could be described, somewhat paradoxically, as unstudied: one had the impression that he had studied the songs so long and so carefully that now, all intellectual and technical problems long since solved, he was bringing them to life through feeling alone. In fact, I have known him put a higher vocal polish on some phrases than he did on this occasion—but have never known him more intimate or more spiritually profound. Much the same could be said of the *Winterreise*. Fischer-Dieskau has sung it often. He has recorded it five times (thrice with Gerald Moore, once with Demus, once with Daniel Barenboim). Two seasons ago, he sang it in Carnegie Hall, with Alfred Brendel as pianist, and I remarked that by the end of that performance I hardly felt I had made the winter journey with poet and composer but, rather, had noted a hundred exquisite details of execution. Not so this time. Fischer-Dieskau sang it almost as if he were drunk—drunk, that is, both with rapturous contemplation of the great cycle and with the grief that had stolen from it into his soul. He began in numbed tones. Sometimes the words were blurred, and sometimes they were exaggeratedly distinct. Again one had the impression that any deliberate thoughts of technique and effect had been banished and that he had surrendered himself wholly to feeling. This is not to suggest that it was an uncontrolled performance—only that the control was now unconscious, the result of experiment and experience long since assimilated and transcended. It was an extraordinary account of the cycle, different from any I had heard Fischer-Dieskau give before. Even on a physical level: in "Erstarrung," at "Bis ich die Erde seh' " he gazed at the floor, and he continued to scan it during the next lines—"Wo find' ich eine Blüte, Wo find' ich grünes Gras?"—as if wondering why spring flowers did not burst forth between the boards of the Carnegie platform; in the second verse of "Die Krähe" he searched the air high over the heads of the audience, so intently that one's own eyes followed, half expecting to see the crow there. In description, these sound like the bad assumed tricks of a ham lieder singer miming out too fully what words, tones, and expression in the eyes—subtly seconded only by bearing and by tension in the hands—should be enough to convey. But I doubt whether Fischer-Dieskau knew he was "acting." He seemed oblivious of everything but that terrible winter journey, through the "agony . . . unending before insanity breaks in." He encountered as if unprepared "the overwhelming shock of each new manifestation of despair" and reeled—sometimes physically—beneath it. And when he reached the end of "Der Leiermann"—"the culmination of everything that Schubert ever wrote, for there is no escape from this agony"—he left his listeners paralyzed. (He seemed oblivious even of an audience some of whom made their presence distressingly evident, cawing and croaking, hacking and hawking.) The phrases just quoted are from Fischer-Dieskau's book *Schubert's Songs*, published by Knopf. In it he asks, "Should one perform *Die Winterreise* in public at all? Should one offer such an intimate diary of a human soul to an audience whose interests are so varied?" He decides yes—but only if the singer abjures any thought of charming, even of pleasing, and "is prepared to be criticized for his attitude." In this Carnegie performance, his almost mystical approach to the cycle found its complete expression.

The autograph of *Winterreise* has been published in facsimile. The sound—and the soul, too—of those painful, much-corrected, eloquent pages was made manifest by Fischer-Dieskau and Demus. Demus played a Bösendorfer grand; it was not the light, clear, singing, wood-framed instrument that Schubert would have known but had a rich tenderness, different from a Steinway's gleaming assurance, that was appropriate. During the *Winterreise*, one's ordinary critical faculties were quite suspended. During episodes of emotional calm in the earlier recital, one noted how lyrical, how sensitive both to harmonic pressures and to passing picturesque details, and yet how unassuming Demus's playing was; and that simply by the sound of pure, distinct vowels lovingly pronounced Fischer-Dieskau can cast a spell. In the first line of "Am Fenster" ("Ihr lieben Mauern hold und traut"), every word—even the lightly touched *und*—became a beautiful and appreciable object.

The program books were a slight cut above what New York recitals usually offer. Deutsch numbers and dates were given, and poets were named; texts were printed in German and in (anonymous) English translation. Still not enough. In any other city, three such important recitals, commemorating the hundred-and-fiftieth anniversary of Schubert's death, would surely be accompanied by a program book whose contents made a lasting contribution to Schubert understanding: perhaps a note on Michael Vogl, Schubert's foremost interpreter; an account of the circle of friends whose poems Schubert set; illustrations that would include the Schnorr von Carolsfeld lithograph musically depicted in "Liebeslauschen"; pointers to further reading (Richard Capell's and Fischer-Dieskau's studies) and to available editions of the songs. A dated discography of Fischer-Dieskau's Schubert records is something many Schubertians would be glad to have. In such a book, German texts would not be printed in fine, scarce-legible italic type. There would be notes on the songs beyond the isolated sentences lifted from Fischer-Dieskau's book which appeared in the program of the first recital. And the very proper request "Please do not turn page until end of song" would be matched by a careful layout in which a mid-song page turn did not occur.

A vivid little performer, Roswitha Trexler, well known at Europe's avant-garde festivals, made her New York début last week in recital at the Graduate Center of City University. She began with an astonishingly brilliant and expressive account of Berio's *Sequenza III* and provided further evidence of her vanguard virtuosity in works written for her by Milko Kelemen (unaccompanied) and the young East German composers Lothar Voigtlander (voice, tape, and piano) and Friedrich Schenker (voice and tape). In all these, the voice is amplified. In the second half, unmiked, she sang Brecht settings by Weill, Dessau, Eisler, and Brecht himself with sharp-cut words, a piquant rhythmic sense, but too slender a thread of tone to do justice to the lyrical moments. She was accompanied and the works were introduced by her husband, Fritz Hennenberg, music director of Leipzig Radio.

Montserrat Caballé was to have sung in a concert performance of Mercadante's *Virginia* last week, for Eve Queler's Opera Orchestra of New York, but she was ill, the event was canceled, and, alas, the major operatic novelty of the season disappeared. Last month, in Carnegie Hall, Miss Queler did Rossini's *Tancredi*, in the new edition by Philip Gossett, which had its première in Houston last year [see page 31]. Again Marilyn Horne sang the title role. Meanwhile, Peters International has brought out an American edition of the Arion recording, made in France by a young British cast with a French orchestra under an American conductor, John Perras. This is possibly the most limpidly and accurately sung account of a Rossini opera on records. A listener's reaction is likely to be "What a beautiful opera! How I should like to hear it done now by singers with the dash and brilliance of someone like Marilyn Horne!" Whereas a reaction to the *Tancredi* with Miss Horne in the title role might well be "How terrific she is! But I wish the opera were more dramatic." In New York, as in Houston, Miss Horne poured out prodigies of heroic bravura singing, throwing in flourishes and frills, scales and roulades, until scarcely a bar was left as Rossini wrote it. Katia Ricciarelli, the Amenaide, is a less accomplished mistress of Rossinian intricacy than Joan Carden, who did the role in Houston, but she is an honest, direct, and pleasing singer. She gave a touching account of the Act II preghiera, "Giusto Dio che umile adoro." Ernesto Palacio, a young Peruvian tenor, the Argirio, was more secure than he had been in Houston. In New York, he sang the original Act I aria, and he included more of the wonderful piece—"Ah! segnar invano io tento"—that opens Act II than he had in Houston. (It is exceedingly high and difficult, and since the première of *Tancredi*, in Venice in

1813, has usually been omitted, or replaced by an alternative aria.) Mariana Paunova, a Canadian mezzo, made something of the aria for Isaura, the heroine's confidante (it was omitted in Houston), but not much, for there is not much to be made of it—or of the other *aria di sorbetto*, for the hero's (mezzo) squire, a role to which Carmen Balthrop proved unsuited. Miss Queler conducted with spirit, and the Schola Cantorum provided a deft chorus.

A complete libretto, carefully prepared (apart from some mislineation), with indications of what is secco recitative, what not, and of which passages (mainly secco) would be cut in the performance, was distributed gratis. In parallel columns it provided the third English version of the *Tancredi* text to appear within six months. (Charles Whitfield made one for the record album, William Weaver made one for Houston, and the Opera Orchestra's was adapted anonymously from an 1848 Covent Garden libretto.) But no note in the program book told the audience that the ending they heard was unusual—the Ferrara "tragic finale," tried out at the opera's second production, in Ferrara in 1813, and thereafter unused until Houston revived it. When I heard the conventional happy ending again, on the Arion records, I agreed with Gossett that it is insipid and perfunctory. The tragic ending, a series of broken exclamations for the dying hero, is bold and strange. But—in New York, as in Houston—I felt that Miss Horne dragged it out to a point where it became ineffective.

The Metropolitan Opera's *Frau ohne Schatten*, last performed in 1971, has a new Dyer's Wife, Ursula Schröder-Feinen. On the first night, she gave an efficient and thorough, if somewhat prosaic and occasionally strident, account of the role. Empress, Emperor, and Barak were cast as before. Leonie Rysanek's reign as the Empress has lasted a quarter-century. She is still very delicate, tender, and touching, and she still rises to the long, moving scenes of the third act with warmth and freshness and in shining lirico-heroic tones. In her performance one could perceive, more clearly than anywhere else, what Strauss and Hofmannsthal intended their opera to mean. James King's Emperor was as wooden as ever. Walter Berry's Barak was honest, lovable, and very well sung. He remains within the story, whereas his great predecessors Ludwig Weber and Paul Schöffler transcended it, to become unforgettable type figures of simple human goodness. Mignon Dunn was powerful as the Nurse.

Having heard great things of the Met production, I was somewhat disappointed to find that in some respects it missed the clarity and the richness of the best *Frau* presentations. Clarity is missing in Robert O'Hearn's settings, which represent by tenebrous tangles what should surely be shown with the pure colors and the distinctness of a Persian miniature. However, he puts the Met's stage machinery to high spectacular use. Richness was missing in Karl Böhm's handling of the music. He gave the assured performance of someone long familiar with the score—so familiar that its marvels are no longer felt to require glowing, impassioned presentation. He also cut too much of the music. The Met sells an incomplete libretto, containing only as much of the text as is in the Böhm recording, and neither libretto nor program book reproduces the Hofmannsthal synopsis, which, as Norman Del Mar remarks in his Strauss study, "is an integral part of the whole work and as such utterly indispensable (containing explanatory information not to be found anywhere else)."

The City Opera's *Turn of the Screw*, one of its best productions, has returned to the repertory in excellent estate, again distinguished especially by Eileen Schauler's precise, penetrating study of the Governess and by Peter Fekula's subtle and strongly sung Miles. Against all expectation, Britten's chamber orchestration, instead of being lost in the large house, steals out to fill it; and Christopher Keene's conducting admirably combines dramatic incident with large musical form. A few things are wrong with Theodore Mann's staging: Mrs. Grose crosses herself as if she were an Irish housekeeper, and the children—who go to church in surplices—have picked up the Romish practice; Miles's miming at the piano is exaggerated. But almost everything else is right in this imaginative ensemble presentation.

April 10, 1978

I've not had The New Grove *(as it's called) in my hands long enough to have found many jokes, but there is some wit in its scholarly pages, and its very last line exemplifies the quality of Grove*heit. *Lionel Salter's admirable new entry for Mompou is less entertaining, less eccentric, and sounder than what it replaces.*

Damnation and Deliverance

Gounod's *Faust* is Goethe become a pretty love story. Hearing Boito's *Mefistofele* is like hearing a high-minded person talk about the play with intense feeling for it but in tones untouched by poetry—except at one or two moments of lyric inspiration. Listening to Schumann's setting is like picking up the well-loved volume to read, savor, and ponder some favorite passages. And hearing Berlioz's *La Damnation de Faust* is—to adapt Coleridge's phrase for Kean's acting of Shakespeare—like reading Goethe by flashes of lightning. As the pages fall open, a line or two may be misread; the imagination invents new details; and, through the eyes and mind of an eccentric genius, *Faust* is perceived with sudden new excitement.

Upon his first, tremendous discovery of *Faust* Part I, Berlioz set to music the songs, the Easter hymn, and the choruses—the passages to be sung even in a spoken performance of the play—and published them as his Opus 1. Then, still under Faustian influence, he embarked on the Fantastic Symphony. Seventeen years later, he returned to *Faust,* and amplified the earlier score as his "légende dramatique" *La Damnation de Faust.* It was composed in a series of "flashes," on a journey through Austria, Hungary, Bohemia, and Silesia. Bowling along in a coach, Berlioz began by writing the lines for Faust's invocation of "Nature immense" ("seeking," he says in his memoirs, "neither to translate nor yet to imitate Goethe's original but simply to take my inspiration from it and extract the musical essence it contained"). Lost in Pesth one evening, he set down the refrain of the peasants' dance by the light of a shop's gas flare. In Prague, he jumped up in the middle of the night to note the melody of Margaret's apotheosis, lest it be forgotten by morning. Ideas "presented themselves in the most unpredictable order." Back in Paris, he shaped his twenty scenes into four parts, each continuous and linked by recitative.

Part I shows Faust against military and pastoral backgrounds. Part II, closer to Goethe, contains the study scene, the Easter hymn, and Mephisto's entry; then, in Auerbach's cellar, the Rat and Flea songs; and, finally, a vision of Margaret. In Part III, set in Margaret's bedroom, Faust and Margaret meet. Part IV begins with the sad, lovely song of the deserted Margaret; Faust, in a craggy landscape, calls upon Nature, and then he and Mephisto mount black steeds "swifter than thought" for the wild ride that leads to the abyss. The gates of Hell slam behind them, and in three apocalyptic choruses there is infernal triumph in Pandemonium, shocked horror on earth, and tender rejoicing in Heaven as the soul of the redeemed Margaret is welcomed there. I set out the scheme because, although *La Damnation* does not have the completeness of a fully developed drama—Berlioz seized only on those parts of Goethe which lend themselves to musical realization—it is a well-shaped work, with its own kind of completeness. If anything seems an intrusion, it is the cellar scene, where Goethe is most nearly followed. For the rest, it is a searching picture of the questing hero, of his evil genius, and of the pure but passionate heroine—three figures vivid against a deep background of Life and Nature. Their portraits are achieved in a series of intense short numbers marked by the "passionate expression" that Berlioz considered a prevailing characteristic of his music. ("I mean an expression determined on enforcing the inner meaning of its subject, even when the feeling to be expressed is gentle and tender.") Not only Margaret's lament and Faust's invocation but also Mephisto's serenade, the dance of the sylphs, and the serene finale are in this sense "passionate."

La Damnation can be enjoyed on many levels. Beecham, who mounted it at Covent Garden in 1933, called it "a bunch of the loveliest tunes in existence." A nineteenth-century English critic wrote:

There is lovelier music in *Romeo and Juliet;* there are greater aims and larger effects in the Requiem; there is nobler drama in the *Troyens* . . . but in variety and completeness, in movement and romance, in life and color and charm, the *Damnation* is unrivaled, not only among the works of Berlioz himself, but, as it seems to us, by anything produced by the masters of symphony since Beethoven.

The masters of *symphony. La Damnation* is not an opera, and not a narrative oratorio, but a "concert opera," a "dramatic legend" related in a manner of Berlioz's own invention, kin to that of his "symphonie dramatique" *Roméo et Juliette.* In a libretto, localities are indicated, but only as settings in a theatre of the mind. The scenes shift "magically," in the space of a measure. The listener is moved "swifter than thought" from the plains of Hungary to Faust's German study; he is at once inside Margaret's room with the lovers and outside it with the mocking neighbors; he rides high over the earth on demon steeds. *La Damnation* is a dramatic experience realized in purely musical terms; the drama comes from the score, and not from the story. The piece was not meant for the stage. Yet it has been the most frequently staged of all Berlioz's works.

Raoul Gunsbourg was the first to mount it, in Monte Carlo in 1893, with Rose Caron (and later Melba, Calvé, and Farrar), Jean de Reszke, and Maurice Renaud, and it remained a staple of his repertory. In 1894, it was staged in Liverpool and New Orleans. In 1906, it reached the Met; in 1910, the Paris Opera. In that theatre, a new production, by Pierre Chéreau, held the boards from 1933 to 1959; then, in 1964, Maurice Béjart produced it there. The latest in a very long list of stagings is Sarah Caldwell's for the Opera Company of Boston. Ambitious directors evidently find the work irresistible. In every production I have seen, there have been exciting, rewarding, and affecting moments, but in the end the very graphicness of Berlioz's score has defeated all attempts to find a visual accompaniment for it and has fettered the lightning-flash movements of his mind and his music. As Richard Capell remarked after Beecham's Covent Garden version, the transfer must always involve mutilations and utterly needless visual effects—and, moreover, leave the spectator of them disappointed. But people go on trying.

Berlioz himself planned an operatic conversion of the work, to open the second season of the Grand English Opera company that Louis Jullien had formed at Drury Lane in 1847. Its productions were sung in English, but it was no narrowly nationalist enterprise: Julie Dorus-Gras, once prima donna of the Opéra, came out of retirement to lead the troupe; the first season's repertory was *Lucia, Linda di Chamounix, Figaro,* and Balfe's *The Maid of Honour;* and Berlioz was the conductor. In 1847, Her Majesty's and the newly established Royal Italian Opera at Covent Garden were already in cutthroat rivalry; the former offered Jenny Lind and Verdi, the other the greatest Italian singers of the day. Jullien's enterprise failed, he went bankrupt, and nothing came of Berlioz's intended *Mephistopheles.* What it might have been we must deduce from the composer's letters to Scribe, which were

published in a 1917 issue of the *Revue Bleue*. Scribe had been entrusted with
the dramatization. The garden scene, the church scene, and the death of Valentine were possible additions. Berlioz also wanted an assembly of the Prince
of Darkness to determine, by lot drawing from an urn, which of them should
seduce Faust; and his request for it suggests that the "color" of the music, if
not its actual notes, had already formed in his mind:

> Je voudrais ici un enfer très sombre, ténébreux et silencieux, pour con-
> traster avec le Pandaemonium de la fin. A la proclamation du nom de
> Méphistophélès, il y aura seulement une sorte d'illumination subite et
> brève comme un éclair et un cri terrible de joie infernale.

There could be spoken dialogue, except for Mephisto; he was to be played by
the Bohemian baritone Johann Pischek, who could sing in English but could
not speak it well. Pischek should have a grand aria, an *andante tendre et
douloureux* of three strophes in which the devil regrets that he cannot love,
weep, or die, followed by an *allegro furieux* to the effect that "since love,
tears, death itself are denied me, let an immortality of hate, vengeance, and
rage be my portion." The ride to the abyss, Berlioz said, was well within the
capacities of English stage machinery. (James Planché, the librettist of
Weber's *Oberon*, was both house poet and "superintendent of the decorative
departments.") For Pandemonium and Heaven, Jullien intended "to reproduce the effects of the marvelous pictures of the apocalyptic English painter
Martin."

Berlioz's *Mephistopheles* remains a might-have-been, but in a staging of
La Damnation Mad Martin would still be a good visual model for the final
scenes. Miss Caldwell staged them as a laser-beam light show, an extravaganza of flash and glitter, part disco, part *palais de danse* in effect. It seemed
uncontrolled, imprecise, and irrelevant. The evening began with Berlioz in
London at one side of an empty stage, penning his letters to Scribe, pondering how his score might be turned into an opera, and Miss Caldwell and
her team at the other side, pondering the same thing. As if in a rehearsal
directed now by Berlioz, now by Miss Caldwell, now by the ballet mistress,
the opening scenes took shape. We moved back and forth between, as it
were, conception and execution. The prima donna received "D'amour l'ar-
dente flamme" from Berlioz, began to sing it for him, and then, at the reprise,
moved into a set to finish the air in character. It was a high-spirited and ingenious production deployed through the whole of the theatre—stage, arena,
and balconies—to achieve effects of perspective; the Rákóczi march (in
which Miss Caldwell joined, and was cheered) and the students-and-soldiers
chorus came off particularly well. But along the way the work itself got lost.
This was a theatrical enactment of "Some Ideas About Possible Ways of
Staging *La Damnation*," and, as such, a stimulating, lively, and entertaining
demonstration. Someday, Miss Caldwell might put the ideas into practice
and stage *La Damnation*.

There was a good orchestra and a good chorus, and Robert Shaw conducted a strong, sensitive account of the score. Margaret was Evelyn Lear; she sang with feeling and color, but sometimes her tone was edgy. Faust was Alberto Remedios, intense if somewhat metallic in timbre; he seemed to have forgotten the legato that distinguishes his Wagnerian performances, and broke what should be smooth lines into disjunct notes. Mephisto was Donald Gramm, precise, pointed, and witty but not, in his final scene, terrible. The work was sung in English translations—a mixture of Geoffrey Dunn's, as used at the English National Opera, and Mr. Shaw's. Eugene Lee's scenery deftly and attractively combined the nineteenth and twentieth centuries, Berlioz and Miss Caldwell, theatrical illusion and theatre reality.

The third presentation of the Sacred Music Society, which began work in 1976 with Massenet's *Marie-Magdeleine* and last year did Refice's *Cecilia*, was a concert performance, in Avery Fisher Hall last week, of Rossini's "azione tragico-sacra" *Mosè in Egitto*, an opera unheard in New York, it seems, since Lorenzo Da Ponte (Mozart's librettist turned impresario) presented it here in 1835, and probably unheard anywhere else since about 1855. What *has* been heard is *Moïse et Pharaon*, Rossini's expansion, reordering, and recomposition for the Opéra of his earlier piece. In Paris, where Rossini had financial security, a stable company, a good orchestra, and plenty of rehearsal time, he was able to work out fully ideas and ideals that had been compromised in the haste and hurly-burly of Italian operatic life. *Moïse* (1827) is a clarification of *Mosè* (1818 and 1819). The two dramatic themes— Moses as leader of his people, and Elcia torn, like many an operatic heroine before and after her, between love and national loyalty—are more strongly presented. Musical practices pioneered in Naples—large-scale tonal organization, motivic dramaturgy, and adventurous orchestral writing—are carried out with determination and consistency. When fashioning *Moïse*, Rossini removed three *Mosè* arias, a brief conventional chorus, and two conventional concerted strettos; he added an overture, three extended ensemble scenes, dances, and a dramatic, unconventional aria. But since he had been a "reformer" from the first, many of the great things in *Moïse* were already present in *Mosè*. In his day, he was chided for giving the orchestra too much to do, for being too "learned," too musically elaborate—in a word, too German. Behind *Mosè* one hears Gluck and, again and again, the Mozart of *Don Giovanni*. Before it lie Verdi (whose *Nabucco* is demonstrably modeled after the 1827 score), Meyerbeer, and Wagner (whose orchestral perorations to *Das Rheingold* and *Götterdämmerung* are descendants of those in *Mosè*, *Le Siège de Corinthe*, and *Guillaume Tell*). *Mosè* was an influential work. It proved well worth hearing in its own right, not merely for its high historical importance. Balzac, who devoted the greater part of his story "Massimilla Doni" to an account of the opera, described it as an "immense poème musical." It is a progression from C minor to C major—from darkness to light, from captivity in Egypt to freedom in the Sinai Peninsula—richly conceived and richly executed on a very grand scale.

The richness and grandeur were revealed in a performance that should stand as a landmark in Rossini revival. So far as I know, there has been no comparable twentieth-century attempt to perform a Rossini opera with the sounds that the composer intended. The score was newly edited—from the autograph and from the Naples conducting copy—by Christie Tolstoy and Randolph Mickelson. The audience was supplied with a facsimile of the 1819 libretto, interleaved with a King's Theatre 1832 English translation, clearly printed in a well-chosen type. The orchestral and choral dispositions of Rossini's day were followed, providing strongly bassed, massive tuttis, as opposed to the top-heavy imbalance of modern choruses and orchestras. The military band was present and correct. The Jingling Johnny, or Turkish crescent, that Rossini called for had been found. So had a serpentone, which he specified to underpin Moses's tremendous brass-accompanied recitative "Eterno! immenso! incomprensibil Dio!" (But, in the event, it was replaced by the steadier and still appropriate sound of a cimbasso.) There were some ragged entries, but Angelo Campori's command of pace and balance was sure.

A similar care for the right sort of sound marked the casting. In the roles of Moses and Pharaoh, the heavy grandeur of a *basso profondo* and the brilliance and agility of a *basso cantante* were contrasted. Dimitri Kavrakos and Justino Díaz were both very impressive. The two soprano roles, Elcia and Amaltea, brought the contrast of a full, heavy, richly colored voice in the first (composed for Isabella Colbran) and a fleet, shining coloratura in the second. The Rumanian soprana Gabriela Cegolèa, making her American début, as Elcia, produced lustrous and beautiful sound; she should become an important singer. But her control of the splendid voice was uneven, and some of the passages were smudged. Marilyn Brustadt, as Amaltea, was quick, confident, and precise. She ran up to a sustained Queen of Night F. (The cabaletta of Amaltea's aria is the one Beverly Sills inserted into the Met *Siège de Corinthe.*) The two tenors, again, were strongly contrasted. Osiris, Pharaoh's son, was composed for Andrea Nozzari, a *tenore serio,* who seems to have been something like a modern dramatic baritone with the added abilities to reach down to a forceful G at the bottom of the bass staff and to sing brilliant coloratura up to high C. Impossible assignment today! The engagement of a heldentenor, James McCray, a Rienzi and a Siegfried, suggested something of what was required. Plainly, Mr. McCray found the coloratura a strain, though he struggled with it manfully. He did give the role the force and weight it needs, as a *tenore di grazia,* readier to cope with the fiendishly florid writing, would not be able to. Stephen Algie, as Aaron, provided the foil of a quick, keen, light, but incisive tenor. (In Rossini's *Otello,* the protagonist—another Nozzari role—and Rodrigo are a similarly contrasted pair.) Rossini's "scoring" for these very different kinds of voice—in duets, in canons, in the great prayer where three soloists sing the same melody in turn—was revealed in all its variety.

That prayer, "Dal tuo stellato soglio," did not form part of the original 1818 score; Rossini added it in 1819, and it became a hit number. "We seem to be watching the liberation of Italy," said Balzac. And, after hearing it at a

Rossini centenary concert at the Crystal Palace, in 1892, Shaw confessed that "I so wanted to hear it again that after a careful look round to see that none of my brother-critics were watching me I wore away about an eighth of an inch from the ferrule of my umbrella in abetting an encore." Why does it make so tremendous an effect? Partly, I think, because it sounds in definitive form, at last, a basic motif of the opera: a melody ascending by step from the first to the fifth degree of the scale, including an urgent stress on a sharpened fourth. It was an idea Rossini had used before: in a duet of *Tancredi*, and in the famous gondolier's song, "Nessun maggior dolore," in *Otello*, which floats up from the canal to chime with Desdemona's sad mood. In *Mosè*, it becomes a functional motif: adumbrated in the first duet for Elcia and Osiris, and alluded to in the orchestral parts of their second; heard in the duet for Pharaoh and Osiris; fully stated in the prayer; then referred to "in shorthand" (a simple, unison A sharp–B in E major) at the moment the Red Sea divides. The sharpened fourth is no more than a chromatic appoggiatura, sometimes harmonically amplified to force a transient dominant modulation. Its repeated employment in *Mosè* (and again in the aria that Rossini composed for *Moïse*) may not have been conscious, but it seems to be more than coincidental. Perhaps it reached Rossini as what Schoenberg calls "a subconsciously received gift from the Supreme Commander." In the prayer, it subconsciously fulfills a listener's long-aroused expectations, and seems to bring a closer gleam of the Promised Land. Harmonically, the prayer's minor-to-major structure is the simplest, grandest statement of the opera's basic progression.

It is tempting to embark on a long number-by-number description of this score, from the bold, *Zauberflöte*-inspired start and the tenebrous, winding theme, stated in C minor and then led through key after key, that depicts at once the dismay of a sun-bathed people plunged suddenly into darkness and the inexorable will to which they must eventually bow, right through to the radiant coda. Orchestration, harmony, form, colors, melodic invention, the fine control of textures, the contrast of mass and of solos, the "lighting effects" made manifest in the music—all deserve comment. But to do that would be merely to repeat what Balzac has so eloquently done. Enough, then, to praise a performance marked by seriousness, devotion, and a determination to discover and reveal what the composer intended (qualities sadly absent from the Met's trumpery account of *Le Siège de Corinthe*)—a performance to make it clear why the serious Rossini once had the world at his feet.

April 17, 1978

Introductions

Earlier this year, I wrote of Gunther Schuller's attempt to find a livelier, less conventional format for the discussion between composers, executants, and audience which Pierre Boulez established as an integral part of the Philharmonic's Prospective Encounters concerts. An American musician writes from Paris to tell me how Boulez is now managing public discussions there, at IRCAM (the Institut de Recherche et de Coordination Acoustique-Musique, attached to the Centre Georges Pompidou and directed by Boulez). In late February, Boulez conducted a concert with his Ensemble InterContemporain whose bill comprised five works that handle musical time in five different ways: Messiaen's *Modes de valeurs et d'intensités,* Stockhausen's *Zeitmasse,* György Ligeti's *Kammerkonzert,* Boulez's own *Éclat,* and Elliott Carter's *A Mirror on Which to Dwell.* On five of the six days preceding the concert, in the large hall of the Centre there were *séances de travail publiques,* each of them devoted to one of the works, with the Ensemble to play and Boulez to provide *présentation, analyse, et direction.* In the words of the bill announcing the *séances:*

> Les explications de Pierre Boulez et les nombreuses illustrations musicales apportées par l'Ensemble InterContemporain permettront d'isoler une composante essentielle des oeuvres choisies, d'en tracer le cheminement et de jeter un jour inhabituel sur le travail d'artisan du compositeur.

And then on the day of the concert, two and a half hours before it began, there was a *séance de synthèse,* with the IRCAM team and with Roland Barthes, Gilles Deleuze, and Michel Foucault as speakers. The critic of *Le Nouvel Observateur* began his notice, "Suppose that, about 1800, Kant, Schiller, and Goethe agreed to a public debate with Beethoven. Or, a century later, Bergson, Gide, and Claudel with Debussy." And my correspondent says, "Every *séance* was packed with people, and the concert could have been given twice. When Foucault and Barthes (who had come to all the *séances*) walked out to give their talks, the audience rose and cheered as if they were rock stars (where but in France?). . . . It all seemed a very worthwhile effort indeed, and everybody had a very good time, especially the crowded audiences."

They order this matter better in France. I'll leave the directors of the Philharmonic to ponder the moral, and consider instead another kind of preconcert discussion, practiced in New York, which it seems to me should receive wider publicity than it does. Two days before the Speculum Musicae's Tully Hall concert last month, two of the composers to be played at it, Charles Wuorinen and Frederic Rzewski, and one of the Speculum performers, Ursula Oppens, met in the studios of WKCR, the radio station of Columbia University, and for a couple of hours talked with two of its staff about contemporary music, its performers, and the public. The discussion was unscripted and evidently unrehearsed. It should have been recorded in advance and then edited to spare the radio audience the false starts, the stumblings, and a plethora of *I means*, *you knows*, and *sort ofs*. Nevertheless, one listened. Rzewski's remarks often had an elegant sharpness. (*"Protean and malleable* are not quite the same thing.") Wuorinen was concerned and interesting about the extent to which what he called the "automatic contempt" dished out to new works in the "journalistic press" made their subsequent programming difficult outside New York. He related how by the director of a New Jersey concert series he had been asked, not in any hostile way but with honest curiosity, "Do you set out to write cacophony?" He made the reasonable request that new serious musical compositions should, whether liked or not, be accorded the same serious, informed scrutiny by newspaper critics which new works of art in other forms receive.

On Sunday last week, Elliott Carter talked for an hour and a half with Ben Miller of WKCR, in anticipation of the Composers' Guild for Performance recital four days later at which Carter's Duo for violin and piano was to be played. This was a rather more shapely discourse. Mr. Miller began by putting a simple question that many friendly but puzzled listeners must have asked—"How much does it matter that when I listen to your pieces I don't *hear* the processes that you write about in the program notes?"—and Carter gave lucid, helpful answers, starting with the different possible ways of hearing and understanding Shubert piano sonatas, and pointing out that Beethoven sonatas could be enjoyed and understood without conscious hearing of their Schenkerian *Urlinien*. He discussed the practice of the WPA period, when composers aimed to produce readily accessible scores, and his resolve in the First String Quartet to write, for once, without considering the performers' or an audience's difficulties. He praised the educative role of the BBC, which, for example, after a poorly executed and poorly received performance of his Double Concerto went on and on billing the piece until it had gained both expert executants and an appreciative audience. He regretted the failure of Boulez's endeavor to create in New York an orchestral audience avid for contemporary music, and spoke of the recent Paris concert and the public excitement it had generated. His orchestral pieces, he said, had their best performances in England, France, and, recently, Italy. (Carter's music receives wider attention—and, probably, more frequent performances—in Europe than it does here; and the British branch of his publishers has marked his seventieth birthday by issuing a tributary pamphlet including a full list of his published works.) He spoke of the way compositions of his once deemed very difficult had become readily playable. Then, with an abrupt "Now let's listen to some music" from Mr. Miller, the Nonesuch recording of the Duo was played—to an audience unprepared for it in any way except by a remark of the composer's, early on, to the effect that he intended it to be heard as harmony. A long silence broken only by scratching followed the music (the technical competence of these WKCR programs was not high), and then in mid-sentence Carter was heard naming Mozart, Chopin, and sometimes Liszt as composers who had had an influence on him. There was more discussion: of his search to devise new forms of continuity; of the "inner checks" to insure that the careful working out of a process did not fetter the workings of imagination; of his keen interest in electronic music coupled to a conviction that a composer should master the medium—as he had not had time to do—before playing with it. When it was again time for a tune, and the Variations for Orchestra (in the Columbia recording, with Frederik Prausnitz and the New Philharmonia) was chosen, Mr. Miller, as if realizing that the Duo had been dropped in "cold," said, "So tell us about them." And Carter did, describing the inception, intentions, and construction of his Variations in a way that provided a model introduction for anyone about to hear the work. An account of practical considerations (such as the comparatively small string section but full brasses of the Louisville Orchestra, which commissioned the piece), of his large formal plan, and of his particular concern for effects of speed was mingled with pointers to some significant moments to listen for.

An *almost* model introduction, I should have said, for there were no musical illustrations, and it is the possibility of "live" examples which gives to radio talks an advantage over printed program notes. By BBC standards, these two WKCR programs were primitive. (No reflection on Mr. Miller, who, I understand, undertakes single-handed the tasks that the BBC would divide between an interviewer, a producer/editor, a sound engineer, and someone to play the records.) The sound quality was poor. The level fluctuated. Mr. Miller announced a recording of Wuorinen's *Grand Bamboula,* for string orchestra, as being his *Bearbeitungen über das Glogauer Liederbuch,* for flute, clarinet, violin, and cello. Anyone can put the needle down in the wrong track; but then after the piece had been played it was again misidentified—in detail, with the four instumentalists' names. More seriously, the programs lacked clear focus. Noncommercial broadcasting in this country cannot, it seems, afford to pay properly for carefully written and illustrated, carefully produced, carefully rehearsed and edited talks by the brightest and best musical minds. If I were Minister of Music and had money to spend, my first move would be to lure, say, Joseph Kerman, Edward T. Cone, and Jeremy Noble (musicians on the Berkeley, Princeton, and Buffalo campuses) into the studios at least once a month and make sure the whole nation could hear them. And my next, more difficult move would be to set up a proper music network to insure that important performances in Norfolk, San Antonio, Portland, Denver, Boston, and Baltimore—as well as in Paris, Palermo, or Prague—were carried from coast to coast. What we have at present is for the most part discrete, localized, sometimes hole-and-corner, and often last-minute enterprise—with the notable exception of Texaco's well-publicized nationwide Met broadcasts. New Yorkers, it is true, can hear the Philharmonic, Boston, Cleveland, and Philadelphia (on WQXR), Chicago (WNCN), and Baltimore (WNYC) orchestra concerts over the air, and also (mainly on WNCN and WNYC) a fair amount from the European festivals. But to discover the exact programs and dates well in advance requires scanning several separate publications and then some telephoning or letter writing. Elliott Carter's talk—an event, for musicians, of national significance—was announced in the radio section of the *Times*, but under "Concerts," on the morning of the day it was broadcast. I missed it there, and heard about it by chance only three minutes before it was due to begin—and by chance was free to listen. Such programs are important. If there is to be any radio preface to Speculum Musicae's May concert (at which the revised version of Boulez's *Polyphonie X* is due to have its American and Seymour Shifrin's *The Nick of Time* its New York première), prospective listeners should learn of it not just in the nick of time but far enough ahead to be able to make a note in their diaries. A schedule of related broadcasts would be a useful addition to Lincoln Center's monthly program book.

Words about new music—introductions, explanations, plans, and pointers—can be helpful. Hearing new scores more than once is yet more important. WKCR's Speculum program failed to include enough straightforward, attractive information about the composers and their forthcoming works, but it did provide a preliminary hearing of John Harbison's *The Flower-Fed Buffaloes (Reflections on the Spirit of Liberty)*, a work commissioned by the New York State Bar Association and given its official première at the concert. Harbison's starting point was a speech by Judge Learned Hand (which echoes lines that Wagner wrote to close *The Ring*): "Liberty lies in the hearts of men and women; when it dies there, no constitution, no law, no court can save it. . . . It is not the ruthless, the unbridled will; it is not freedom to do as one likes. That is the denial of liberty." The text of the composition is five poems—by Vachel Lindsay (two), Hart Crane, Michael Fried, and Gary Snyder—which Harbison has set for baritone soloist and small mixed chorus, accompanied basically by piano, with support, coloring, and counterpoints from an ensemble of clarinet and saxophone, violin, cello, and bass, and percussion. The poems treat of themes related to the judge's ideas about liberty. Ever present is the sense that white men are intruders on this land. At their best, they live on it and love it; at worst, in their greed for private gain destroy it and what and who lived on it before—the buffaloes, the prairie grass and flowers, the Blackfeet, the Pawnees. Snyder's trail clearer, resting from his work with cold drill, pick, and dynamite on a hill "snowed all but summer," suddenly notices the centuries-old shards of Indians' tools all about him. Their trails and his have converged. Harbison's central movement is a fierce, chilling, urban scherzo macabre of desperation, but his finale is Lindsay's affirmation "That flower-town, that wonder-town shall come." And so he lines himself with the poets who try to save us from despair and persuade us, if only for a while, that "these things shall be." Works like *The Flower-Fed Buffaloes* are precious and useful. Harbison's affirmations—and his final C pedal—are not glib but are achieved after delicate, even painful pondering, reflected in the rhythmic and harmonic tensions of the score. The musical imagery, like the verbal, is specifically American. The composer draws on several vernacular idioms, and inventively, precisely, eloquently shapes them into his own poetic statements. His clear-eyed economy brings the tone closer to Snyder's charged, precise, fresh, and flexible verse than to Lindsay's flowery rhetoric. I taped the broadcast and have discovered that the music, memorable at first encounter, gets better and better the more one hears it. At the concert, the soloist, David Evitts, sang the notes and pronounced the words clearly, without, however, leaving much impression that he understood the poems—as if Dionysus, mentioned by Crane, were nothing to him but four syllables. The Emmanuel Choir of Boston joined Speculum. The composer conducted. The piece lasts about twenty minutes, and deserves to become well known. [It is now recorded, on Nonesuch H-71366.]

A second hearing of Wuorinen's *Hyperion,* for twelve players, revealed a score that I underrated at its première, at the 1976 Adelaide Festival. It flowered as a bright, lyrical, and exuberant piece. From a first hearing of Rzewski's *Song and Dance,* for flute, clarinet, bass, and percussion, I remember only that it contains an effective vibraphone solo. Amid much concentrated music—Stravinsky's *Introitus* opened the concert and Varèse's *Déserts* ended it—it made an expansive, spun-out impression. [It does so again on the Nonesuch recording (it backs *The Flower-Fed Buffaloes*); but the Speculum virtuosity proves captivating.]

The three winning works of the East & West Artists' annual composers' competition were played in Carnegie Recital Hall last month at a satisfactory concert where the interest and vitality of the music were enough to keep Sunday-afternoon drowsiness at bay. (When I was a cub critic in London, cellists seemed always to give their début recitals on Sunday afternoon, and there were many half-dropt eyelids in the back row of Wigmore Hall.) The first prize had gone to Todd Brief's Fantasy for violin and piano, a complicated and arresting piece, but one, it seemed to me, gracelessly and uncouthly written for the instruments, against their natures and largely in extreme registers. Where Carter's Duo can persuade one that violin and piano are sounding almost as if of themselves, from their souls, Brief's duo suggested that the poor things were being put through an obstacle course plotted by a stern, uncompromising, not uninteresting mind. In Stephen Dembski's one-movement Trio for violin, cello, and piano, the difficulties were not so much those of producing acceptable sound as those of mastering complicated rhythms. The music sounded good to play and it was good to listen to—a discourse of ideas cogently and clearly developed. Gerald Levinson's two-movement Trio for clarinet, cello, and piano, first played over the French Radio, in 1976, is a captivating piece that combines a Crumb-like command of delicate, beautiful timbres and a sure grasp of form.

In addition, Bo Lawergren's *Farfar* (Swedish for "paternal grandfather") had its first performance. (The composer was a judge of, not an entrant in, the East & West competition.) Mr. Lawergren's *farfar* sailed the seas, kept sweet-smelling country stores, and recorded folk music on his fiddle. The piece is a brief, brilliant tone poem for piano solo. Most of the time, the right hand, on the keyboard, darts through small scraps of what sounds like fiddle melody while the left hand, inside the piano, damps the strings in ways that provide constant changes of tone color. The program was completed by Bruno Maderna's *Viola,* for unaccompanied viola, and Betsy Jolas's *Episode* and *Fusain,* for unaccompanied flutes (one player using in turn regular, piccolo, and bass instruments and also singing a bit). The ten young performers of the afternoon were adept; Karen Phillips, the solo violist, was especially impressive. These were seven pieces each of which I would be glad to hear again. It's not often one comes away from a concert of all new music saying that.

Christopher Keene brought the Syracuse Symphony Orchestra to Carnegie Hall last week with a bold, unconventional program—Barber's Essay No. 2 for Orchestra; Stephen Douglas Burton's Symphony No. 2, "Ariel"; and Janáček's Glagolitic Mass—and this was rewarded by a good house. The orchestra is able and alert. The strings were lithe, the woodwinds well balanced, and the brasses powerful without being pushy. The comments are general, but that is because the performances were of a kind to make one attend to the music rather than to the playing—which is as it should be. Mr. Keene, long admired both here and abroad as an opera conductor, was making his New York concert hall début. He showed his wonted, welcome care for proportion, for the long line and continuing sense of a composition. His detailing did not lack color or sharpness, but picturesque effects were not stressed for their own sake.

Burton's symphony, first done by the National Symphony and Antal Dorati in 1976, at the Kennedy Center, had its New York première. Mr. Keene's advocacy was eloquent but seemed to be misplaced. In casting the fifty-one-minute piece as a song cycle—five movements with alternating mezzo-soprano and baritone soloists, accompanied by large orchestra—Burton challenged comparison with Mahler's *Das Lied von der Erde.* In choosing as his text private, autobiographical (and, I think, rather awful, uncontrolled) poems by Sylvia Plath, he invited a disparity between means and message which proved fatal rather than fruitful. The lines "A smile fell in the grass./Irretrievable!" were followed by a crashing climax of early-Strauss immensity. The declamation was generally slow and oracular. Mahler, Strauss, and perhaps Shostakovich in their thumping veins were models for the musical style but were coarsely followed. There was a good deal of noise, including that of a thunder sheet. The vocalists, Diane Curry and Stephen Dickson, did not make much sense of the poems; I doubt whether in these settings of them any singers could.

Janáček's Mass, in which the Syracuse University Oratorio Society joined the orchestra, received an ardent and beautiful performance. Like Beethoven's Missa Solemnis, it is dedicated to an Archbishop of Olmütz. Mr. Keene's reading admirably combined its double aspect, of being at once a high ecclesiastical celebration and an almost informal outburst of popular fervor. Richard Taylor, outstanding in the solo quartet, sang the "Et incarnatus" and "Benedictus" with an ideal blend of smoothness, plangency, and passion. His sweet yet incisive tenor is one that should be heard in the Berlioz Requiem and Te Deum, in the Simpleton's Song of *Boris Godunov*. There is no real organ in Carnegie Hall, and one movement of Janáček's Mass is a big organ solo; Will Headlee did what he could on Carnegie's electronic instrument, but the sounds remained stubbornly synthetic.

Tully Hall does have a real organ, and at a Messiaen seventieth-birthday concert there last month Cherry Rhodes played sensitive, nondeafening performances of numbers from *La Nativité du Seigneur, Les Corps glorieux*, and the *Messe de la Pentecôte*. But the acoustics of the place are parched. Big chords drop dead, without a trace of reverberation, the instant fingers are lifted from the keys. Can nothing be done to make it a better hall for music? Pinpoint clarity is not all. The concert, put on by Continuum, the performing ensemble of the Performers' Committee for Twentieth-Century Music, offered a well-shaped, representative anthology of early and middle Messiaen chamber compositions—a duo, songs, piano and organ solos, and, finally, a keen, sharply colored account of *Oiseaux exotiques*, with the eighteen players conducted by Leon Kirchner. But—what price "continuum"?—nothing from the last twenty years of this still active composer.

Two other Tully events in brief. Joan Morris and William Bolcom, mezzo and pianist, billed just "A Very Varied Program," and gave one that ranged from Johannes Brahms ("Sandmännchen") to Mike Stoller. Miss Morris was as captivating (and Mr. Bolcom as rhythmic and eloquent) as ever. Is there anyone around able to handle words, phrases, inflections, and tone colors as well as she does? . . . The Ensemble for Early Music—two singers and three players, joined for the occasion by a narrator and two mimes—gave a fairly enjoyable account of its entertainment drawn from the early-fourteenth-century *Roman de Fauvel*. But—a "but" of the kind that always tends to crop up when medieval music is performed on anything but the highest level, and in inappropriate surroundings—the price of a ticket could perhaps more rewardingly have been spent on the EMI-Electrola record of *Fauvel* (distributed over here by Peters International), made by the Studio der Frühen Musik with slightly larger forces, superior grace, and a finer wit.

April 24, 1978

Mary in Virginia

Thea Musgrave's third full-length opera, *Mary, Queen of Scots*, given its first performances at the Edinburgh Festival last year by Scottish Opera, which commissioned it, was given its first American performances last month by the Virginia Opera Association, in Norfolk. It is an interesting, affecting, and important work, successful on many counts: as a poetic drama, as a presentation of characters and conflicts, as a study of history, as a long stretch of imaginative and excellently written music, and as a music-drama in which words, sounds, spectacle, and action conspire to stir a listener's mind and emotions. In short, it succeeds as a show, as a score, and as that fusion of both which creates good opera. In Britain today, the piece can also serve a social purpose, reminding people of what since 1603 they have been increasingly apt to forget: that Scotland is a country with a proud, independent history and culture of its own. Scottish independence of Westminster's lawmakers in several important fields is a matter of current political debate; while *Mary, Queen of Scots* is unlikely to ignite spontaneous demonstrations of popular patriotic feeling—of the kind provoked by Verdi's early operas in Risorgimento Italy, and Auber's *Masaniello* in Brussels—it does perhaps make an emotional contribution to that debate. Musgrave may be one of Shelley's unacknowledged legislators. Scottish nationalism is hardly a burning issue in Norfolk (though perhaps more there than elsewhere in this country, since Norfolk's Old Dominion University has an active Institute of Scottish Studies). But wherever it is done *Mary* has the distinction of dealing with serious events in a serious way. Its kinship is thus with Verdi's *Don Carlos* rather than with Donizetti's *Maria Stuarda;* moreover, it sticks closer to history than does Verdi's opera (which has Mary's sister-in-law as its heroine and one of the men she thought to marry as its protagonist). Like *Don Carlos*—and like Britten's *Gloriana*— *Mary* has both court scenes and popular crowd scenes. The people are brought on not solely to provide a colorful supporting chorus—although, of course, from the entertainment point of view they also serve that function. The responsibilities of rulers, the weal or woe caused by their decisions, the relation between their wills and desires and those of the people constitute one theme of the piece. The reception that *Mary* has been accorded, in Edinburgh (and then in Newcastle, Wolverhampton, and Glasgow, where Scottish Opera also did it) and in Norfolk, where it played five times to full houses, has been warmer than that most new operas win. [There have been further productions in San Francisco and in Hinsdale, Illinois; the opera is billed for the New York City Opera's spring 1981 season. The Virginia performance is recorded on Moss Music Group 301.]

The libretto is the composer's own, based on an unpublished play, *Moray*, by Amalia Elguera, the librettist of her previous opera, *The Voice of Ariadne*. The action opens in 1561, the year in which Mary, the eighteen-year-old Queen Dowager of France, returned to Scotland to assume her Scottish throne, and it closes in 1568, with Mary's departure for England, disgraced, dishonored, and uncrowned. Nineteen years as Elizabeth's prisoner, the plotting, the Norfolk conspiracy, Fotheringhay lie in the future. Those seven eventful years in Scotland saw Mary's marriage to the handsome, worthless Darnley, heir to both the Scottish and the English thrones; the rebellion of her bastard half brother Lord James, the Earl of Moray; the murder of the Italian minstrel David Riccio; the birth of James the future king of Scotland and England (for whom Jamestown, just up the James River from Norfolk, Virginia, is named); the murder of Darnley; Mary's rape by and marriage to his assassin, the Earl of Bothwell; her forced abdication; Moray's assumption of the regency—matter enough for a single opera. Musgrave's Mary is a role for a shining young soprano surrounded by male voices—Moray is a baritone, Bothwell a robust tenor, Darnley a lyric tenor, and Riccio a bass-baritone, and there are four other male roles of some importance—and her *Mary* is a drama about an intelligent, impetuous young queen and the three ambitious men each of whom hopes through her to rule Scotland. The first act closes with a ball at Holyrood. Against the background of a madrigal sung by Riccio and Mary's four attendant Marys, the Queen observes in turn Bothwell, Moray, and Darnley ("The three stars of my firmament/Which, which should I follow?"), and they her. She makes her disastrous choice of Darnley. (In the words of Swinburne's biography, "passion alone could shake the double fortress of her impregnable heart and ever-active brain.") Moray and Bothwell wait. At the heart of Act II is a powerful, extended duet for Mary and Moray, preceded by an aria for Moray ("Now I shall rule!"), followed by an aria for Mary, who has dismissed her brother ("Alone, alone, I stand alone"). After her aria, the madrigal of Act I is resumed for a while, and then cut short by the irruption of Riccio's murderers. Act III starts tenderly, with Mary singing a lullaby over her newborn child, and then follow in a rapid melodramatic sequence Bothwell's rude wooing, a duel between him and Moray, and a telescoped finale of Mary's cruel rejection by her people, Moray's assumption of power, Mary's farewell to Scotland, and—an anticipation of a later event, and possibly a miscalculation, since it packs too much into a few measures, takes the focus off Mary, and is unnecessary to the drama—the assassination of Moray.

Those are but a few of the scenes. Musgrave has given her libretto the dramatic form, the swift, flexible, and various gait, of a Shakespeare history play. The scenes are continuous; a staging is called for that will allow characters in Edinburgh to walk off on one side of the stage while on the other characters in Leith advance. This libretto, the composer has written, once drafted, remained in preliminary outline and was not worked out in detail until the music was being composed. There is a sure congruence between musical and theatrical proportions. Each episode has just enough words and just enough action to allow a full yet economical musical development. Nothing goes on too long. Dramatic and musical pacing, transitions, variety of tension, of texture, and of density, contrasts of expansive lyricism and quick-moving music are controlled in a masterly way. So is the exposition of the plot—conveying the necessary narrative information that older composers treated in secco recitative. Musgrave always plans a piece clearly and carefully. Everything she says and does is so sane, so lucid, so intelligent—she has worked wisely and effectively with electronic music, with aleatory devices, with peripatetic instrumentalists and fashionable deployments in space—that the listener struck primarily by her patent abilities may well miss her veins of romance, ambition, and poetic inspiration. Whenever I have been carried away by a Musgrave composition—as I was by *Mary, Queen of Scots*—it has nearly always been at second and subsequent hearings, once first-encounter admiration of her sheer competence, her effortless matching of means to ends and of demands to the executants for whom she wrote, has been registered and can be taken for granted.

A first hearing of *Mary* was enough to make it apparent how profitably Musgrave has pondered the problems of writing contemporary opera and found her solutions to them. Her debts are as unconcealed as were Mozart's, Verdi's, and Britten's; they consist not in copying but in finding suggestions, inspiration, and pointers to ways of treating a situation. When writing *Peter Grimes*, Britten drew sustenance from Verdi, Debussy, and Berg. *Mary* owes something to Debussy, much to Monteverdi, and much to Shakespeare, and in some ways it is a companion piece to *Gloriana*, that noble opera about Mary's English cousin. Darnley's wooing song recalls, in function if not in actual notes, Essex's lute song. Both operas contain a suite of sixteenth-century court dances counterpointed by keen, personal commentary that cuts through the antique harmonies—at once an attractive "period" spectacle and a potent dramatic device. At a second hearing, I found myself forgetting the careful planning, the parallels, the influences, and instead caring very much about Mary herself—move by move, event by event—and being at the same time rapt in the music, intent on the movement of the melodic lines, calmed or excited by the shifting patterns of harmonic tension, and stirred by the colors of the score. There is a visionary quality in *Mary*. The very start—where a motif associated with Mary clusters into shimmering, troubled string chords, and the tune "The Bonny Earl of Moray" marches in upon them—is a musical vision of the drama to come. One's first sight of Mary, a tall, lonely figure wrapped in swirling mists, come to take possession of her Scottish kingdom while across the waters there drifts the song in which Ronsard mourned her departure from France, and one's last sight of her, a tall, lonely figure leaving behind her people, her kingdom, and her son, are visions for which Musgrave has found eloquent music.

I did not see the Scottish production. It is hard to imagine *Mary* better done than it was in Norfolk. The title role, created in Edinburgh by Catherine Wilson, might have been written for Ashley Putnam, the Norfolk interpreter, so well does it suit her, and she it. Miss Putnam cannot be much older than the character she plays. She is tall, as Mary was, and beautiful. She is a commanding actress, with expressive features, a clever sense of timing, and the power to make men hang on her glance uncertain whether she will break into a sudden smile or a proud rebuke. She is the Mary of Swinburne's biography who "beside or behind the voluptuous or intellectual attractions of beauty and culture . . . had about her the fresher charm of a fearless and frank simplicity." Musgrave gives her heroine many chances—to be commanding, yielding, merry, melancholy, tender, severe, brave, broken—and Miss Putnam seized them all. The role is written very high, but her voice seems to flower more fully the higher it goes. Moray's role is written high, too, but Jake Gardner, who also sang it in Scotland, had its repeated F's, F-sharps, and climactic G's well within his voice. It could be objected that he cut too gallant, too dashing a figure for the ruthless politician and looked not at all like the gloomy, long-nosed Stewart that Hans Eworth painted. Against that, it might be claimed that, at any rate in an opera, political matter is most effectively conveyed with romantic ardor. Mr. Gardner is another very good actor. (The two principals are by way of being local heroes. Miss Putnam made her début with the Virginia Opera, in 1976, as Lucia di Lammermoor; Mr. Gardner came to national attention with his Norfolk Germont, in 1975, and returned the next year as Rossini's Figaro.) Jon Garrison was vivid as the dissolute Darnley. Barry Busse, in timbre and manner something like a smaller, slighter Jon Vickers, did not quite carry the weight and force for Bothwell, but he very nearly did. Kenneth Bell's Riccio was subtle and precise. David Farrar, the director, and Peter Mark, the conductor, achieved from all their cast a performance in which the details were sharp and exact and the whole was wonderfully impressive. With a few well-proportioned scenic elements—a jutting forestage platform, a raked and flared main stage, two galleries, a drop curtain and, for the Queen's supper room, hangings based on Mary's own embroideries, and a romantic backcloth—Miguel Romero housed the action in sets that were good to look at and dramatically effective. Alex Reid's costumes, borrowed from Scottish Opera, were authentic and very handsome. Martin Ross's lighting was supple and skillful. Wendy Hilton's choreography combined authenticity with dramatic aptness. The chorus, nearly forty strong, had been carefully prepared. Mr. Mark's orchestra—forty-four choice players, largely from the Norfolk Symphony—was excellent. The Norfolk Center Theatre, city-owned, a WPA building, holds more than twice as many people as Glyndebourne. In other ways, this *Mary* was rather like a Glyndebourne performance—one in which all the elements come together to provide a gripping and complete account of an opera.

It was a remarkable achievement by any standards, and an astonishing one for so young a company. The town itself seemed *Mary* mad; no one could be there and not know the opera was going on. An international conference on Scottish studies, devoted to Mary, Queen of Scots, and a regional conference of the Central Opera Service were both held in Norfolk to coincide with the production. The Virginia Opera Association began in 1975, with two performances of *La Bohème* and two of *La traviata*. Its 1975–76 season brought three performances each of three productions; the 1976–77, four each of three. This season, *Butterfly* had four performances, *Così* six (two of them in Richmond), and *Mary* five. The early history of Scottish Opera was rather similar: it began in 1962, with productions of *Butterfly* and *Pelléas*. But soon, in a theatre seating fewer than Norfolk's, it was doing *Otello, Boris, The Trojans*, and Henze's *Elegy for Young Lovers*. In 1971, it put on a complete *Ring* cycle. And now it is a year-round company, with an opera house of its own, holding 1,560, and makes regular tours of Scotland and England. *Mary* is but one of several new operas it has commissioned and brought to performance. Virginia is larger than Scotland—by ten thousand square miles. It has rather fewer inhabitants, but rather more if one adds in Washington. However, it is unprofitable to pursue the parallels. Things are too different. To the visitor, Norfolk seems a strange town. Most of its center has been razed; in 1975 it was and today it still is a wilderness of concrete, tar, and flattened rubble with a few isolated houses and churches left standing in the middle and some modern monster buildings around the edges. A few of us who wanted to gather and talk after the opera found that the only place open within easy walking distance was the bus terminal café—neon lit, noisy, friendly enough, but not quite what we had in mind. May opera exert its civilizing powers. May the "mall," running through a few blocks of the center which have not been demolished, blossom with bistros and late-night cafés. Next season, the bill is conventional—*Carmen, The Daughter of the Regiment*, and *Don Giovanni*—but five performances of each are scheduled. This season, Norfolk became for a while the center of America's operatic life.

May 1, 1978

Voyaging

When a musician today is heard talking of *ridim*, it doesn't necessarily mean that he's got rhythm and also a cold in the head. *Prunes* and *prism*, as Mrs. General told Little Dorrit, are very good words for giving a pretty form to the lips. *Rilm* and *rism* and *ridim* are familiar ways of referring to things that give a very pretty form to masses of musical information hitherto discrete and disorderly. The exhibition "The Music Ensemble, 1730–1830," set out in the auditorium foyer of the Graduate Center of City University (down the steps in the CUNY mall, between Forty-second and Forty-third Streets), gives graphic evidence of the work being done there by the Research Center for Musical Iconography, which is the American division of RIDIM, or Répertoire International d'Iconographie Musicale. RIDIM aims to provide for musical representations in paintings (and in sculpture, engravings, drawings, photographs, etc.) what RISM provides for *sources musicales* and RILM for *littérature musicale*—information gathered internationally on the widest possible scale, ordered, indexed, and made available to musicians. The viol player eager to know how bows were held in the mid-sixteenth century, the choirmaster seeking to dispose his singers as Heinrich Schütz did his, the maestro who when conducting Mozart or Mahler wants to arrange his strings and winds on the platform as Mozart or Mahler did, will discover where to look. RIDIM is concerned not only to collect but also to interpret the evidence. As David Munrow remarked in the introduction to his *Instruments of the Middle Ages and Renaissance,* while paintings of the fourteenth and fifteenth centuries may depict a dazzling variety of musical instruments in the hands of angels, "such angel concerts belong not to this world but to paradise, and they bear little relation to contemporary church-music practice."

The Nelson Gallery–Atkins Museum, in Kansas City, Missouri, houses a particularly musical collection of pictures. Last week, when I was in the city for a Beethoven festival, I had the lucky chance of being allowed to visit its rooms off-hours, alone, in silence. And into that silence I found there were stealing imagined sounds: not exactly melodies unheard, spirit ditties of no tone—not any specific melodies but, rather, faint yet clear intimations of timbres and of musical styles, and even of acoustic space, perceptible to the inner ear. The lute, dulcimer, portative organ, and harp held by a quartet of angels on a pair of Veronese organ shutters were little more than symbolic. The players' faces were blank; the picture remained silent. The organist and lutenist attendant on Memling's Madonna were evidently playing and also listening to what they played; a hint of harmony drifted across the flower-jeweled walled garden behind them. But the illusion of a real music captured in paint began with Sebastiano Ricci's *Marriage at Cana.* In the foreground, a young singer and recorder player are both intent on their scores, while a lutenist knows the music already; in the background, another trio—lute, archlute, and recorder—seem to be playing something completely different. The guests pay no attention to either ensemble; they eat and drink and chatter. It is a lifelike and almost Ivesian evocation of a party with music in the background.

Quiet music fills the frame of a deep, still Claude landscape where a goatherd pipes beneath a silvery evening sky. In music, poetry, and painting, the pastoral reed has long been a powerfully evocative symbol; there are still countries where it is a reality. And, since anyone who responds to any of the arts does so in a way in which personal experience mingles with the experience that artists through the ages have set down, I daydreamed away from Arcady to an afternoon in the modern world when, after walking for many hours across the hot Persian plain to visit the tomb of Darius, I rounded a corner of the holy mountain, Naqsh-i-Rustam, in which that tomb is hewn, saw below me a goatherd under a thorn tree, and heard him piping to his little flock. A year later, at night, I was among a crowd beneath that tomb who cried:

> *King of old days, Our Sultan! Come, appear!*
> *Stand on your tomb's high crest, King of our King,*
> *Robed in the royalty you used to wear.*
> *Darius, Father, Lord, Preserver, hear!*

And from the darkness of the tomb mouth, high on the cliff face, the Shade of Darius appeared to intone the lines that Aeschylus assigned him. (Peter Brook had staged the second part of his *Orghast* at Naqsh-i-Rustam, and it included an enactment of *The Persians*.) The great speech was declaimed in periods whose pitch rose step by step. Berlioz, I remembered, set the speech of the Shade of Hector, in *The Trojans*, in the same way. At the arrival of Berlioz, I returned to the Claude and to Kansas City, and realized that Berlioz, when he wrote the third movement of his Fantastic Symphony, must have heard piping in the Campagna such as Claude had pictured. Thoughts filled me of Ozymandias, of Darius' vanished splendor (some of his palace is now in Kansas City) and of the Iranian goatherd who might have been piping in Darius' day, and of the Beethoven who wrote both the blazing Missa Solemnis, which tells of royal ceremony in Cologne Cathedral and of glory around the heavenly throne, and the Pastoral Symphony, which tells tales of the Vienna woods. I remembered Ferdinand Ries's story of rustic piping in those woods which Beethoven could not hear, and Beethoven's despairing reference to the occasion in the heroic Heiligenstadt Testament.

The music changed to a Dionysian clashing and jingling and strumming, above a fat, coarse wind bass, in Castiglione's *Allegory on Vanity*, a very noisy painting, one which must surely seem to resound even when the gallery is filled with the hum of people; and then was stilled to a note from the harpsichord, a chord from the lute, before Jan Steen's nostalgic family group, a painting so detailed that one can read the harpsichord maker's name and almost read the score on the music rack. Since anyone who responds to any of the arts does so with all his senses, I began to feel hungry at this point—and then realized that I did so because in a kitchen opening off Steen's drawing room a maidservant is pouring a thin stream of oil over a delicious dish of hard-boiled eggs and beans. Music of a later age started to sound outside that luminous seventeenth-century Dutch room: somewhere in the museum the finale of Beethoven's Sonata, Op. 90, was being rehearsed. There was just time for a chef's salad—the museum restaurant's closest approach to the Steen dish—before the next festival event began.

This was a lecture by Edmund Frederick on the pianos of Beethoven's time. In a clear, straightforward style, he explained why the construction, action, and timbre of a modern piano make it an inadequate instrument for the interpretation of Beethoven's piano music (and, for that matter, of Chopin's and Liszt's). Robert Winter demonstrated the point by playing the Opus 90 finale on a Viennese piano of about 1820—a Hasska, which Mr. Frederick had brought with him—and then on a modern concert instrument. The point was made again, perhaps unwittingly, at a chamber recital that followed, given in the lofty museum atrium, when Cathy Waldman played the first of Beethoven's "Tre Sonate per il Clavicembalo o Forte-Piano con un Violino" (alias the D-major Violin Sonata, Op. 12, No. 1) on a big, modern Bösendorfer, while Marc Gottlieb, the concertmaster of the Kansas City Philharmonic, played the violin part on a fine modernized Andrea Guarneri.

The Beethoven Festival was given jointly by the Nelson Gallery–Atkins Museum and the Philharmonic. In the museum, besides lectures and chamber recitals, there was an exhibition. On one wall hung the ruddy, oft reproduced, seldom shown Beethoven portrait by Joseph Stieler which is referred to so frequently in the Conversation Books. There were autographs, a vivid little watercolor of the violinist Bridgetower, and an affectionate note to him from Beethoven (these from the Morgan Library). There were portraits of some of the composers who took part in the first performance of *Wellington's Victory*—Dragonetti, Spohr, Meyerbeer, Joseph Mayseder. There were instruments, paintings, and furniture of Beethoven's day, and in the center of the room stood the Hasska piano—not roped off but, with keyboard open and piano stool ready, inviting anyone who wished to to feel its light, shallow touch and hear its clear, energetic utterance with his own fingers and ears.

The Philharmonic concerts were held in the Music Hall of the Municipal Auditorium, a huge pile in the grandest PWA manner, massively marbled in its foyers and staircases, lit by wondrous modernistic constructions of crystal rods and brass bowls inset with cut-glass jewels. It is not a cheerful place, more fortress than fun palace; the architect allowed very few windows to pierce his limestone walls. But it is a monument of its kind, and has been very little spoiled. There is enough careful thirties detail to keep a visitor curiously occupied during intermissions. Roundels and friezes on the outside and murals within celebrate the brotherhood of man and the active, energetic virtues of agriculture, industry, and the arts. And so the building as a whole chimes not inappropriately with Beethoven's more earnest, affirmative, optimistic finales. It would be easy to rewrite the text of *The Ruins of Athens* in a form that could lead Minerva, horrified by the Turkish devastation of her beloved city, to find consolation in the new temple that has been raised beside not the Danube but the Missouri.

There were three full-scale concerts. At the first, *Fidelio* was done. The spoken dialogue was replaced by a well-judged, well-delivered English narrative. On an apron stage in front of the orchestra, the singers—in modern dress; Leonore in trousers—acted by glance, gesture, attitude, and movement. The entry of Pizarro's guards was suggested by file after file of the male chorus rising, with chilling Prussian precision, to its feet. For the prisoners' slow, stumbling entry into the light, the choristers rose one by one, at random. It was a successful production. In the heroine, Roberta Knie, one soon saw only Beethoven's Leonore—overhearing, horror-struck, the close of the Pizarro-Rocco duet; anxiously scanning the faces of the prisoners; striving, in Act II, to discern the features of the condemned man. Miss Knie is a true *ju-*

gendlicher Heldensopran, with a strong, clearly focused, and well-schooled voice, a cogent style, a manner in which warmth of feeling and determination are blended. Her fresh, fearless, candid interpretation reminded me of Christel Goltz's—and she sings the music more beautifully than Goltz did. Florestan was James McCracken, who was lyrical, ardent, and powerfully affecting. Robert Anderson was a sound, if not an exceptional, Rocco. Joshua Hecht, a seasoned Pizarro, sacrificed many of Beethoven's notes to declamatory emphasis. Carroll Freeman, the Jaquino, was a shade too perky in manner, but his singing was vivid and charming. Barbara Hocher was a pleasant Marzelline.

The second program was a re-creation of Beethoven's concert on December 8, 1813, in the great hall of Vienna University, when the Seventh Symphony and *Wellington's Victory* had their first performances and, between them, Maelzel's mechanical trumpeter, to full-orchestra accompaniment, played marches by Dussek and Pleyel. *Wellington's Victory* is not great music, but it can be great fun, and so it was in Kansas City. The cannon shots were left to the big bass drums (in 1813 Meyerbeer and Hummel were the drummers); there were no *Feuer Maschinen*. But for Beethoven's small-arms fire members of the audience had been enlisted; they had been provided with rattles, and were brought in on cue—Englishmen on the left of the house, the Frenchies on the right—by subconductors dressed as the opposed generals. *Wellington's Victory* is, of course, more than a jolly joke; it is also soundly and strikingly composed. The Dussek and Pleyel marches of 1813 have not been identified; for this concert, an appropriate martial air by each composer was chosen, the mechanical trumpeter was represented by a doll-like youth, and his synthetic trumpet tones were sounded by a Moog-synthesized clarion.

I could not stay for the final event, the Ninth Symphony, and heard only a rehearsal. All three programs were conducted by Maurice Peress, the music director of the Kansas City Philharmonic. His readings were spirited, sensitive, and sound. There was a vitality in the music making that lifted the spirits. There was no trace of routine in the orchestra's response. I had not seen Mr. Peress on the rostrum before—only heard his work when, out of sight in the pit, he conducted an alert account of Gottfried von Einem's *The Visit of the Old Lady* for the San Francisco Opera—so I do not know whether the authentically Beethovenian platform demeanor he displayed is habitual or is used only for Beethoven. Spohr first saw Beethoven conduct when he played in the première of *Wellington's Victory*, and recalled the occasion in his autobiography:

> Beethoven had accustomed himself to indicate expression to the orchestra by all manner of singular bodily movements. . . . At *piano* he crouched down lower and lower as he desired the degree of softness. If a *crescendo* then entered, he gradually rose again and at the entrance of the *forte* jumped into the air.

So did Mr. Peress. It looked ungainly but produced good results. Some of the tempi struck me as too brisk—for the adagio of Leonore's aria, for the allegretto of the Seventh Symphony. But they were of a piece with his committed, masculine, vigorous approach. This is not the whole of Beethoven; one missed the element of lyrical charm—exemplified at its most easygoing in the lazy, delicious bassoon tune of the Second Symphony larghetto, yet not incompatible with deep spiritual content, or absent from *Fidelio* and the Ninth Symphony. But energy, strength, and passion were not missing.

The Philharmonic is a good orchestra. There were some imprecisions that more rehearsal would doubtless have polished away, but the playing was fresh, lively, attentive, and intense—the kind of playing that seems to tell of, and communicates, enjoyment. The acoustics of the Music Hall, which holds about twenty-six hundred, are said to be uneven. I had been given seats at the front of the second balcony, and there the sound was strong and clear. Sometimes the winds swamped the strings, especially in the finale of the Seventh—a result, perhaps, of using four horns, three trumpets, and three woodwinds in a score that Beethoven wrote for only two of each. (With full wind doubling, the texture stays in proportion; this sesquialteral augmentation surely cannot ever be right.) The choir, the UMKC Civic Chorus, was a large, well-trained body of firm young voices; at the rehearsal of the Ninth, their fervent declamation of Schiller's ode made a great effect. Some things are more up-to-date in Kansas City than in the metropolis: the lights in the hall stayed on; the audience—as Beethoven would have expected—applauded each movement of the Seventh Symphony.

As one of the related events, I gave a little talk about the music, other than *Fidelio*, that Beethoven composed for the theatre. That night, during the intermission of *Fidelio*, a student came up to me to say that he had never heard any Beethoven before, and was overwhelmed by it. The orchestra hostess who drove me to the airport told me how moving she had found it to be stirred by, to be one of an audience stirred by, music that had been stirring people ever since it was composed. And I found the whole of my visit curiously stirring. Exhibition, recitals, and concerts had been planned together to reveal Beethoven as a living force, a source of joy, inspiration, and strength to men and women in nineteenth-century Vienna and twentieth-century Kansas City at once. "Meanings unknown before, Subtler than ever, more harmony, as if born here, related here . . . Sounds, echoes, wandering strains, as really here at home." Whitman was writing of Bellini and Donizetti in Dakota, not Beethoven in Missouri. He could have found uninhibited words to relate the adventure of voyaging as if across one swift span of a great bridge, from the East to the Middle West, and, once there, of voyaging swifter still across spans that led through space and time from Kansas City to Vienna, Rome, Athens, and Persepolis—with Egmont, Coriolanus, and Prometheus, Beethoven, Goethe, and Plutarch for company.

May 15, 1978

Enflam'd with Hope

It would have been a sorry opera season, with not one important new work created in the whole of this huge land, had not the Indiana University Opera Theatre, in Bloomington, given the première last month of John Eaton's *Danton and Robespierre*. Robert Ward's *Claudia Legare*, a version of *Hedda Gabler* set in Charleston, South Carolina, was created last month by the Minnesota Opera, but it proved to be a piece of small merit and no importance. It was commissioned by the New York City Opera and Julius Rudel, and rejected by them. *Danton and Robespierre*, on the other hand, is a large, exciting, adventurous, and vividly theatrical piece, one that James Levine and John Dexter should now acquire for the Met or Mr. Rudel for the City Opera. Contemporary works of such virtue are not common. It would be sad if this one were to disappear after just three performances of the admirable Bloomington production.

Eaton was born in Bryn Mawr, Pennsylvania, in 1935. He studied at Princeton with Milton Babbitt, Edward T. Cone, and Roger Sessions, and first came to attention in 1959, with his *Holy Sonnets of John Donne*, a cycle for dramatic soprano with orchestra or piano. In 1968, his full-length opera *Heracles*, libretto by Michael Fried, was broadcast by Italian Radio, and in 1972 it was staged as the inaugural performance in Bloomington's Musical Arts Center. The year before, Bloomington had done his one-act opera *Myshkin*, after Dostoyevsky's *Idiot*, and a television performance of this piece was shown by Public Broadcasting in 1973. A CRI record of his compositions (SD 296) contains *Blind Man's Cry* (1968), for soprano and an ensemble of synthesizers; Concert Music for Solo Clarinet (1961); and his Mass (1970) for soprano, clarinet, synthesizer ensemble, and tape. A Vox/Turnabout record of his Concert Piece for Syn-Ket and Symphony Orchestra—a work first heard at Tanglewood, under Gunther Schuller, in 1967 and then taken up by Zubin Mehta and the Los Angeles Philharmonic—and two Decca albums of Eaton pieces, entitled "Microtonal Fantasy" and "Electro-Vibrations," are no longer in print. In *Danton and Robespierre*, his varied concerns—dramatic music, vocal writing, electronic instruments played live, and microtonal enrichment of the thirteen notes making up the octave of Western music—are brought together in masterly fashion.

Eaton and his librettist, the Irish poet Patrick Creagh, thought at first of writing an opera in three acts which would deal with three pairs of contrasted revolutionaries: Danton and Robespierre, Trotsky and Lenin, and Che and Castro. That was just an idea, and one that they quickly realized would be unmanageable unless the real historical conflicts—of temperament and character as well as of political methods—were simplified and schematized to an extent that would make them both false to history and uninteresting as drama. So they decided to confine themselves to Danton and Robespierre, and deal with them fully. Eaton summarizes the subject matter as "the conflict between Danton, an idealist who sought just means to achieve realistic ends, and Robespierre, a realist for whom any means were justified to reach idealistic ends." He has written an urgent and topical opera. It had its inception during the student unrest of the late sixties; it reached the stage during days when "realists" in Italy were seeking to inaugurate a Reign of Terror; and all that its words and music say has bearing on what men are thinking and doing in a world most of whose nations are again seeking, at different speeds and in different ways, to achieve freedom, equality, and brotherhood in Socialist societies. *Danton and Robespierre* is an opera about idealism, about compromise, about kindness and love, about human weaknesses, and about the hideous strength of cold-blooded righteousness.

There is a passage in *The Prelude* which never fails to shock me—when Wordsworth, walking "over the smooth Sands of Leven's ample Aestuary," learns by chance from a passerby that Robespierre is dead, and exults in the news with fierce, uncharacteristic vindictiveness:

> *O Friend! few happier moments have been mine*
> *Through my whole life than that when first I heard*
> *That this foul Tribe of Moloch was o'erthrown,*
> *And their chief Regent levell'd with the dust. . . .*
> *Great was my glee of spirit, great my joy*
> *In vengeance . . .*

And although that glee is succeeded by calmer thoughts of "how . . . the mighty renovation would proceed," Wordsworth on his stroll is still moved by "uneasy bursts of exultation."

Most people, I imagine, have mixed feelings about the French Revolution. Wordsworth and Beethoven, born in 1770, both charted the years of enthusiasm when "Bliss was it in that dawn to be alive, But to be young was very heaven," and the disillusion that followed when, in the poet's words, "The sun that rose in splendour . . . put his function and his glory off," or, in the composer's words, Napoleon showed himself "nothing more than an ordinary human being," prepared to "trample on all the rights of man and . . . become a tyrant." Art enables us to apprehend the Revolution through many different eyes. Georg Büchner's play about one episode of it, *Dantons Tod*, has had a large influence on *Danton and Robespierre*. Büchner was born in the last year of the First Empire. In 1834, he published a fiery pamphlet, *The Hessian Messenger*, which begins, "Freedom for the huts! War on the palaces!" The next year, he wrote *Dantons Tod*. On one level, his drama seems like an attempt to rewrite *Hamlet* in a political setting. It casts itself readily with a *Hamlet* company: Hamlet as Danton, Claudius as Robespierre, Ophelia as Lucille Desmoulins, Laertes as Camille Desmoulins, Horatio as Lacroix,

Polonius as Saint-Just, and the gravediggers, scarce altered, as tumbrel driv-
ers and executioners. But Büchner intended more than a literary exercise. In
a letter about the play, he wrote:

> The dramatic poet is in my eyes nothing but a writer of history. . . . His
> greatest task is to come as close as possible to history as it actually hap-
> pened. His book must be neither more nor less moral than history it-
> self. . . . The poet is not a teacher of morality: he creates figures, he
> brings past times to life, and the public should learn from that, as well as
> from the study and observation of history, what is going on around them.

Eaton and Creagh do not set out to be teachers of morality, either. They
present but do not preach. It is a strength of their opera. To Büchner they
owe the general construction in short, kaleidoscopic scenes; the way the Paris
crowd episodes are handled, and some of their detail; and the vivid portrayal
of Robespierre in strange, visionary monologues. (In both play and opera,
Robespierre comes close to being the tragic hero of the action.) Some of the
parallels may derive from a common source: both Büchner and Creagh allow
Robespierre to speak in words that he actually spoke, and Danton's famous
speech to the Assembly on September 2, 1792 ("Il nous faut de l'audace, encore de l'audace, toujours de l'audace"), alluded to in the play, is delivered in
the first-act finale of the opera. The play covers the last months of Danton's
life. The opera starts a little earlier, on the eve of the September Massacres,
in 1792, and ends with Robespierre's execution, in July 1794, sixteen weeks
after Danton's. We lose the delightful grisette Marion, one of Büchner's most
memorable figures (she is reborn as Jenny in Brecht and Weill's *Mahagonny*);
we gain Gabrielle, Danton's first wife. In general, Eaton and Creagh's Danton is more uxorious, more domestic, less carefree than Büchner's. He is also
less witty, and does not go to the scaffold with a jest on his lips.

There has, of course, already been a very successful opera on *Dantons
Tod*—Gottfried von Einem's, performed first at the Salzburg Festival in 1947
and then widely for several years throughout Germany. Little of its music remains in my mind—only the impression of a strong play provided with an apt
and skillful continuous musical accompaniment. But while Büchner's *Dantons Tod* is indeed a strong play, Creagh's *Danton and Robespierre* is a better
dramma per musica. I must not give the impression that the libretto is simply
Dantons Tod remodeled. Although the debts to Büchner are plain, the historical incidents chosen and adapted for musical treatment, and the invented
episodes—their shaping and their sequence—have been worked out anew, to
form a scheme in which the musical developments are part of the dramatic
enactment. There are three acts. The first shows Danton as patriot and ora-
tor. The second contrasts Robespierre's Reign of Terror with Danton's brief
country retirement, and ends with his return to the Assembly, to speak mod-
eration. The third opens with a final, vain attempt at reconciliation between
Danton and Robespierre, and then moves swiftly to the double tragedy. Public scenes alternate with private episodes: on the one hand, arias, duets, and

ensembles involving, in different combinations, Danton, Gabrielle, Louise (his second wife), Lucille, and Camille; on the other hand, Robespierre alone with his single-minded obsession.

The form of the opera and the powerful Bloomington staging, directed by Hans Busch, designed by Max Röthlisberger, and lit by Allen R. White, can hardly be discussed separately. The composer's and librettist's visions—a single figure onstage, musing, and then, an instant later, an assembled crowd of hundreds; pitch darkness, and then, sounding through it, from every corner of the auditorium, a menacing whisper and a soft drumming that grow louder and louder until, with a sudden flash, the full Assembly in session is revealed, and, below it, the threatening crowd—were carried out to thrilling effect. On the large, deep stage of the Bloomington Musical Arts Center (a stage second only to the Met's, it is claimed), Mr. Röthlisberger had constructed a large, deep, exciting set, one that could contain within it a variety of other scenes—some small, some large, some shallow, some deep—in a way that quite avoided the monotony of unit sets such as the Met *Prophète, Aida,* and *Rigoletto* are played in. About five hundred students were used in the show—but that figure includes backstage workers and also the Singing Hoosiers, who appeared only in film sequences, marching against the Prussian invaders. In round figures, there were about two hundred people on the stage and a hundred in the pit.

A large orchestra is required: four each of flutes, oboes, horns, trumpets, and trombones; six clarinets, six bassoons; two tubas, three harps, two pianos; strings at a suggested strength of eighty-two; brass band onstage; electronic instruments. Half the winds and one of the pianos are tuned a quarter-tone below regular pitch. One of the harps is tuned at regular pitch, one a sixth-tone higher, one a sixth-tone lower. The strings and the singers—including the chorus—are called on to pitch in quarter-tones. (That is to say, between the notes C and D they must be able to sound not just the single note C-sharp/D-flat but the three distinct notes C-semisharp, C-sharp/D-flat, and D-semiflat.) My ear, corrupted by years of listening to singers whose natural vibrato often covers a quarter-tone or more, and to string and woodwind players with wide vibrato, was not fine enough, I confess, to discern how accurately the music was stated. (An old Beecham story seems relevant here: Leon Goossens sounds a rich oboe A as the orchestra's tuning note, and Sir Thomas remarks, "Gentlemen, take your pick.") Except in steady and exposed solo lines, it was hard to take conscious cognizance of the quarter-tones. One tended to "read" them as the nearest regular note, slightly "bent" for the purpose of expression in much the way that a singer singing traditional music will on occasion deliberately (or unconsciously) for the purpose of expression "bend" a note and pitch it a shade sharp or a shade flat. It may be that this is the way Eaton means us to hear them. So far as I can make out, he uses the quarter-tones not in any abstruse harmonic system but as an enrichment of expressive possibilities. Harmonies are "clean" or "dirty," pure or tainted, uncompromising or generously accommodating. A chord struck by the three harps quivers uneasily; on a single harp, it is precisely defined. In any event, the microtones cause no difficulty to the ordinary listener. At the start of the opera, there are opposed street cries from vendors of fish and loaves. The fishwife sings at regular pitches, accompanied by horns conventionally tuned; the baker's wife sings a quarter-tone "off," accompanied by clarinets similarly "off"; the bitonality, the opposition, takes on keener and readily apprehended edge. Microtones are also used to striking effect in the brief instrumental prelude. In just intonation, pure in the key of C major, an electronic organ plays a simple chorale that begins in C major and modulates, step by step, until it reaches F-sharp major, the furthest possible key—and in doing so the instrument becomes at first slightly, and at last excruciatingly, out of tune. It is a simple but effective symbol of an ideal—represented by an "ideal" tuning—that will fit one set of circumstances but becomes increasingly inapplicable to others. The chorale is associated with Robespierre. There is a moving passage in Act III where he sings it (to the words "O God, O great Creator, Look down on what we do") accompanied by strings—four solo cellos. And they, of course, as string players do, make constant microtonal adjustments, impossible on a keyboard instrument, which keep the harmonies perfectly in tune, all the way from C to F-sharp. There is a terrifying episode later in the act, after the death of Danton, where Robespierre tries to repeat his prayer and it goes horribly out of tune.

For all the intricacies of Eaton's score, it is direct and readily comprehensible. No more than Alban Berg is he afraid of big, straightforward, traditional theatre strokes: ostinatos, sudden outbursts, unisons, firm tonal anchors against which to measure degrees of dissonance and tension. His writing for the chorus is adventurous and exciting. His writing for the orchestra is varied and very colorful. Moreover, and perhaps most important of all, *Danton* is a mellifluous opera, composed with a command of lyrical vocal gestures that reveal character and are also good to sing. Without that quality, an opera does not live.

It would be hard to overpraise the work of Thomas Baldner, who conducted, the Bloomington student cast, the Bloomington student players, and all who prepared them. The difficulties of rhythm are scarcely less than those of pitching, but both the performances I heard were uncommonly assured. On the instrumental side, the brilliant brass players deserve especial mention; and, among the singers, James Anderson, Tim Noble, Gran Wilson, and Edith Vannerette (the Danton, Robespierre, Camille, and Lucille of the first cast), and Sally Wolf (the Lucille of the second cast). In the second cast, Michael Ballam and Robert McFarland (the Danton and Robespierre) were equally sure singers but rather less subtle actors. Mary Shearer and Debra Grodecki (the two Louises) and Nelda Nelson (Gabrielle in both casts) were also good. So were many other young artists in a cast far too large to list in detail. The challenge of the quarter-tones seemed to spur the singers to very precise, steady emission. At both performances, Louise and Lucille in a duet of canons, octaves, and unisons achieved an exactness of intonation such as I have never heard from Adalgisa and Norma on the professional stage. Score in hand, I have been listening to tapes—of both performances—with a kind of amazement at the sustained level of accomplishment. I urge the Public Broadcasting Service to secure a tape, to announce performances of *Danton* in good time for prospective listeners to buy the libretto (it is published by the Shawnee Press), and to let the whole land at least hear this remarkable work.

May 22, 1978

Thunder to the Tune of "Greensleeves"

Ralph Vaughan Williams, best known as a symphonic composer, wrote six operas. The first of them, the pastoral episode *The Shepherds of the Delectable Mountains* (1922), reappears in the fourth act of the last of them, the morality *The Pilgrim's Progress* (1951); the others are the romantic ballad opera *Hugh the Drover* (1924), the comedy *Sir John in Love* (1929), the romantic extravaganza *The Poisoned Kiss* (1936), and the lyric tragedy *Riders to the Sea* (1937). The dates are those of first performance, not composition: *Hugh, Riders,* and *The Poisoned Kiss* all waited about a decade to reach the stage. Four of the operas were created at the Royal College of Music, and *The Poisoned Kiss* at the Arts Theatre, Cambridge; Covent Garden staged *The Pilgrim's Progress,* but it was at a Cambridge University Musical Society production three years later that the composer remarked, *"This* is what I meant." In her biography of her husband, Ursula Vaughan Williams says, "It was perhaps a misfortune for Ralph's operas to start with student performances for . . . there was a danger that the general public might assume that the operas were works suitable only for amateurs. All his life and through the times of his greatest success as a writer of symphonies Ralph longed for his operas to be taken more seriously and to be given professional performances." *Riders to the Sea* is the only one of them which has had much of a career on the professional stage. There must be a band of enthusiasts for them, however, here as in Britain, for Angel recordings of *Sir John in Love, Riders to the Sea,* and *The Pilgrim's Progress* keep their place in the American catalogue. (In the British catalogue, there is also a reissue of the old 1924 excerpts from *Hugh the Drover.*) *The Pilgrim's Progress* is a powerful, profound, and beautiful opera. I had not seen *Sir John in Love* before the Bronx Opera's production of it this month. It was a performance that brought all the flaws of the piece to the fore and concealed most of its virtues.

Vaughan Williams retained all twenty characters of *The Merry Wives.* (Boito, in Verdi's *Falstaff,* reduced them to ten.) No one unfamiliar with the Shakespeare play can hope to keep tabs on who Shallow, Slender, Sir Hugh, Dr. Caius, Simple, Nym, and Rugby are or what parts they play in the intrigue. They crowd one another out. The libretto is clutter and confusion. From Boito, Vaughan Williams borrowed the device of the screen (but, tamely, he hides Mistress Page behind it) and the idea of a final ensemble, launched by Falstaff, to the effect that "Tutto nel mondo è burla." The words Vaughan Williams uses here ("All our pride is but a jest. . . . And the world is but a play") are from *A Book of Airs* (1601), by Philip Rosseter and Thomas Campion. Ben Jonson, Marlowe, Sidney, Middleton, and Shakespeare himself (in *Much Ado* and *Love's Labour's Lost*) are also among the poets called on to provide "additional lyrics." The music uses both genuine folk tunes ("Greensleeves" among them) and inventions in their vein. "When I could not find a suitable folk-tune," the composer writes in a preface, "I have made shift to make up something of my own." The result suggests a suite of Elizabethan lyrics set for voices and orchestra alternating with a partial performance of *The Merry Wives.* The play can't get going, because it keeps stopping for a song. The cantata *In Windsor Forest,* which Vaughan Williams fashioned from the opera, presents several of the choral songs in an apter context.

There is some beautiful music in the opera, however, and I can imagine being charmed by a performance that is light, graceful, various, and sweetly sung. Many critics have complained that *Sir John in Love* is heavy—and not only by comparison with Nicolai's lyrically high-spirited *Die lustigen Weiber* and Verdi's miraculous, quicksilver *Falstaff.* Some of it, to be sure, is deliberately galumphing. There is nothing Mendelssohnian in Vaughan Williams's final scene; he said that he wanted the dances there "to be a bit rough and grotesque—they are village boys *playing* at fairies, not real fairies." In the Bronx performance (which I saw in Hunter College Playhouse), passages smooth and rough, romantic and rumbustious, lyrical and lumbering, all came out much the same. There was a dour, gruff Falstaff. The others were caricatures or approximations—except Mazzelle Sykes's Meg Page and David Koch's Nym (a tiny role), who behaved like real people. Neither Michael Spierman, who conducted, nor Sebastian Russ, who directed, seemed to have much understanding of the romance that might save the clumsy *Sir John* from being a trudge. Inferior to *Die lustigen Weiber* and *Falstaff* in just about every way, *Sir John* has one quality those works lack: Englishness—a feeling for the English countryside, English character, and English song. After *Falstaff,* Boito wrote that "Shakespeare's farce is led back by the miracle of sound to its clear Tuscan source." (In a sense, the librettist was congratulating himself, since his text is self-consciously Boccaccian; the young lovers' refrain, "Bocca baciata," is taken directly from the *Decameron,* where it has a very different significance.) But Vaughan Williams set *The Merry Wives* as what John Masefield called it—"the only Shakespearean play which treats exclusively of English country society." That is not enough, in my view, to make *Sir John in Love* a successful opera, but it does give it particularity. The particularity was missing in the Bronx production.

Since a sparkling double bill of Offenbach's *Ba-ta-clan* and Schubert's *Die Verschworenen*, early in 1975, directed by Lou Galterio, none of the Bronx productions that I have seen has been in really sharp focus. So appreciation of the company's enterprise, its enlargement of the repertory, etc., has been tempered by regret that much energy, talent, enthusiasm, etc., have not been used in the most effective way. The *Sir John* program lists the many organizations (state, city, and borough councils and departments; commercial enterprises; foundations; the National Opera Institute) and individuals whose support made the production possible. Companies like the Bronx Opera, Brooklyn's New Opera Theatre, Eastern Opera, and the New York Lyric Opera are important and deserve support. They fill gaps—as do the student productions at the Juilliard and the Manhattan Schools—between Met and City Opera shows, broom-closet, piano-accompanied productions of out-of-the-way works, and grand concert performances. To draw up a coherent plan, acceptable in Washington, Albany, and New York, of how the public money available for opera could most advantageously be spent would be difficult; harmonizing the ideas of headstrong individual company directors is tricky. But it should be tried. There is a need for cooperative endeavor, for the elimination of unnecessary productions (yet another *Traviata* or *Bohème*), and for giving the successful shows a wider circulation.

Soon after the première of *Sir John in Love*, in 1929, Vaughan Williams and Gustav Holst, with the composer Rutland Boughton, drew up a scheme for the establishment of a small opera company to tour villages and small towns, drawing on local enterprise for supers and extra chorus:

> We do not advise operas which audiences may have seen on a large scale with all the glitter and tinsel of a large crowd and showy costumes etc. . . . We suggest everything on a small scale to start with—no orchestra but only a piano. . . . A company of about 20—everyone willing to take a hand at everything: e.g. the principal soprano of Monday would walk on on Tuesday, help mend the costumes on Wednesday and be noises off on Thursday.

A half century later, the British government, through its Arts Council, has taken on the principal cost of providing opera throughout the country. There are seven established, subsidized companies playing year-round—or, at any rate, extended—seasons, not just presenting a production three or four times and then dropping it, as the Boston, Bronx, Brooklyn, and many other companies here do. And the appetite for opera has grown to an extent where just about the whole of operatic history is being brought to life in sight and sound by smaller troupes, like the Handel Opera Society and Opera Rara (who receive Arts Council support provided their ideas and direction are judged adventurous and sound), and by the university operatic societies. A list of the pieces done during the last year or so in or within reach of London would be very long. Here—omitting the numerous first performances, the Handel, the German, Italian, Slavonic, Brazilian, and Portuguese works—is a selection of offbeat French operas I read about: Rameau's *La Princesse de Navarre* and his *Les Fêtes d'Hébé*; André Philidor's *Le Jardinier et son seigneur* and his *Tom Jones*; Grétry's *Richard Coeur de Lion* and his *L'Amant jaloux*; Cherubini's *Médée*; Hérold's *Zampa*; Offenbach's *Le Pont des soupirs, Mesdames de la Halle, La Grande-Duchesse, La Fille du tambour-major*, and (a Bicentennial pasticcio revived) *Christopher Columbus*; Bizet's *Don Procopio*; César Franck's *Hulda*. (I omit more standard French fare, such as *Les Troyens*—Carthage at Covent Garden, Troy from the Chelsea Opera Group—and Kent Opera's *Iphigénie en Tauride*.) A New York list would include Meyerbeer's *Les Huguenots* and Auber's *Manon Lescaut*, presented by Bel Canto Opera—but the one with piano accompaniment, the other with a thirteen-piece band, and both done in a small church hall, unsuited to grand opera.

After the Soviet invasion of Hungary in 1956, Vaughan Williams, writing to console Rutland Boughton, thitherto a staunch Party member but now disillusioned, remarked, "It seems to me that all right-minded people are communists, as far as that word means that everything should be done eventually for the common good." In 1937, the year *Riders to the Sea* was produced, Marc Blitzstein brought out in New York his tough, tuneful opera *The Cradle Will Rock*, which is about wrong-minded people acting for their own good. (It is also the theme of his grand opera *Regina*, based on Lillian Hellman's *The Little Foxes*.) *The Cradle Will Rock* has been revived by the Lyric Theatre of New York, in the Eighteenth Street Playhouse. There is an able young company, crisply directed by Neal Newman, and accompanied at the piano by Bruce Coyle. (The first production was piano accompanied; so is the recording of a 1964 production, available now on CRI SD 266. With orchestra, the piece was staged by the City Opera in 1960.) Blitzstein's libretto is a black-and-white morality play, as direct in its statements as a broadsheet ballad, and with none of the ambiguities of Brecht's political fables. Formally, it is a wry, fierce comedy, conceived in the comic spirit as Goldoni defined it:

> Comedy was created to correct vice and ridicule bad customs; when the ancient poets wrote comedies in this manner, the common people could participate, because, seeing the copy of a character on the stage, each found the original either in himself or in someone else. But when comedies became merely ridiculous, no one paid attention anymore, because, with the excuse of making people laugh, they admitted the worst and most blatant errors. But now that we have returned to fish comedies from nature's *mare magnum*, men feel their hearts touched again. They

can identify with the characters or passions and discern whether a character is well observed and developed, and whether a passion is well motivated.

The specific issue of *The Cradle Will Rock* is the drive for industrial unionism—part of the attempt under FDR to shape a juster American society. The opera remains undated, no mere period piece, for two reasons: the audience can still recognize the characters portrayed, in themselves or in others; and Blitzstein's music is powerfully affecting. The Eighteenth Street Playhouse is small; the Lyric Theatre production is scaled to make that a virtue.

The Goldoni sentences above are quoted in the program notes for Bel Canto Opera's latest show: Wolf-Ferrari's *Le donne curiose*, the first (1903) of five lyric comedies he based on Goldoni plays. It is a piece about a men's club—the rhythm of the club's motto, "Bandie xe le donne" ("No women admitted"), is rapped out by the orchestra as a motto theme—and some inquisitive women's successful penetration of it. In his memoirs, Goldoni revealed that he intended a covert representation of a Freemason's lodge. We need not strive to find much topical significance in the piece; in this age, when, I read the other day, it has been estimated that "more than half of all American wives have suffered at least one beating at the hands of their husbands," Goldoni's and Wolf-Ferrari's gentle suggestion that husbands should treat their wives a little better is small beer. It is a pretty play, slight but not trivial, neat in its observations on human behavior.

There were two casts. In the one I saw, no one was outstanding, but an acceptable performing level was maintained. June Marano, at the piano, was efficient but not quite lilting or charming enough. (Wolf-Ferrari had as happy an instrumental touch as Rossini; much is lost in a piano reduction.) Nicholas Deutsch, the director, had rightly based his staging on quiddities of character, not clowning. A custard-pie joke at the end was not his fault: a stage direction says, "The amusement is increased when Pantalone gives Arlecchino a good-natured blow on the head, which sends his face down into a large dish of whipped cream." This is an unhappy attempt on the part of the composer and his librettist to give adventitious vivacity to a flagging close. *Le donne curiose* falls off in its final scene, which perhaps keeps it from being in the very top—the *Quattro rusteghi*—flight of Wolf-Ferrari's operas. But the five previous scenes display to admiration his captivating blend of easy, exquisite lyricism, high spirits, musical wit, and unforced inventiveness. He is a composer who can keep listeners happy in ways that Mozart, Rossini, Schubert, and Smetana understood.

May 29, 1978

All American opera companies—and orchestras—are, in effect, largely supported by public funds, if the tax unpaid on individual contributions

*to them is regarded as such. In this country, a rich opera lover can under-
write the production of a favorite work of his with a tax-deductible contribution. In Britain, he pays the tax, and the Arts Council determines
how the public money can most usefully and rewardingly be spent.*

Harmonious Numbers

Speculum Musicae, in Alice Tully Hall last month, played two twentieth-
century classics, Edgard Varèse's *Octandre* (a gleaming, secure performance)
and Alban Berg's Chamber Concerto (with Ursula Oppens, piano, and Rolf
Schulte, violin, as the cogent, impassioned soloists). And between them it
gave what may have been the first public performance of Henry Cowell's
Quartet Romantic (composed 1915–17) and the first performance of Seymour
Shifrin's *The Nick of Time* (completed earlier this year and dedicated to
Speculum). The Quartet Romantic and its companion work the Quartet Euphometric (composed 1916–19) are early experiments in what Cowell called
"rhythm-harmony" compositions. Harmonies can be expressed as rhythmic
ratios. If A is sounding at 440 cycles per second, the E a perfect fifth above it
will sound at 660 cycles per second; and if that perfect fifth is lowered in
pitch and slowed down so far that the original A and E can be heard no
longer as tones but only as pulsations, the pulsations will be rapping out a
rhythm of three against two. A perfect triad—A, C-sharp, E; or C, E,
G—similarly lowered will produce a rhythmic "knocking" of six against five
against four. And, provided that one overlooks the adjustments needed to
produce equal temperament (for the purposes of these pieces Cowell did
overlook them), any combination of notes can be expressed as a ratio of pulsations. If the value one is assigned to the C below the bass staff, the C above
that, the first harmonic, will be two; C-sharp will be two and two-fifteenths,
D will be two and a quarter; D-sharp two and a third; and so on. To each
note of the chromatic scale a figure can be assigned: nine against seven and a
half against six will correspond to a G-major triad on the treble staff.

To create the first section of his Quartet Romantic, Cowell composed an
eight-bar chorale theme in C major, harmonized it in four parts very simply,
and then repeated it with rhythmic variations and in rich chromatic harmonies. The first measure of the chorale is a chord of C major four beats
long—C on the bass staff, middle C, the E and G above that—corresponding
therefore to a pulse pattern of six against five against four against two. Each
beat of the chorale is expanded into a measure of the quartet: in the first

measure, the top part plays six equal notes, the next five notes, the next four, and the bass voice two. It is as simple—and schematic—as that. But it is not at all simple for the performers. The fifth beat of the chorale melody is an A, whose ratio to the unitary fundamental C is six and two-thirds; and so into the fifth measure of the quartet the player of the top line must fit in six and two-thirds quarter-notes. The value of the F-sharp above middle C is five and three-fifths. The first time this F-sharp occurs in the chorale, the quartet player is required to divide the corresponding measure into twenty-eight parts, and play six notes whose lengths correspond to 5, 5, 5, 5, 5, and 3 of those twenty-eight divisions. (Two further complications. That five and three-fifths is not always laid out with the fractional part at the end; the patterns 2-5-5-5-5-5-1 and 4-5-5-5-5-4 also occur. And when a single beat of the chorale is divided into two eighth-notes of different pitch, the corresponding measure of the quartet is similarly divided; half the measure may have to be distributed between, say, two and a half notes, and the other half between two and a quarter.)

In short, Cowell has mechanically converted his chorale into a rhythmic matrix, waiting to be filled with notes whose lengths—but not pitches—have been determined in advance. (One could do the same with a Bach chorale, with any hymn tune, with the sixth movement of Beethoven's Opus 131; the more chromatic the harmony, the more complicated the resultant rhythmic patterns.) Cowell's choice of pitches to be played seems to have been governed by no system but only by an ear concerned to make agreeable, interesting sounds, shapes, and melodies. In a preface to the score (which was published by C. F. Peters in 1974), the composer says, "Since I used all twelve tones freely, the pieces are atonal. But unlike the atonal styles then developing abroad (with which I only became acquainted later), the melodic lines are more often conjunct than not, and the vertical combinations use consonance as well as dissonance. . . . The musical intention was flowing and lyrical, not severe or harsh, or ejaculatory."

His intention is realized in a flowing and lyrical piece. The four parts were scored for two flutes, violin, and viola. Since the lines in the chorale never cross, it follows—from what has been said above about the process of converting harmony into rhythmic patterns—that the top line, the first flute, must always play in shorter note values than those of the second line, the second flute, which in turn plays in shorter note values than those of the violin, below it, while the viola moves in longer notes still. Since there are no rests in the chorale, all four instruments move nonstop in a kind of moto perpetuo. (To be precise, the top two lines of the chorale coincide on a unison, halfway through, and at the corresponding point in the quartet Cowell does allow each flute in turn a measure's rest.) Since the beginning of most measures is marked by simultaneous entries on three or all four of the instruments, and since the measures are of equal length, the listener can follow them, hear where the bar lines fall, and enjoy an attractive effect as of four companions keeping abreast as they proceed—but one (the viola) taking long slow strides, and the three others increasingly short and rapid steps. If just the viola and first-flute lines were played, the result might suggest a man and a frisky terrier moving together, each with uneven gait, across a meadow.

This account of simultaneous but not synchronous motion, of varied pacing within the same measures, is likely to bring Elliott Carter to mind, and certainly some of the time experiments that have sounded in Carter's music since the Cello Sonata (1948) are kin to those that Cowell was trying in 1915. (There is the difference that Cowell's elaborate rhythms are arrived at by a simple system whereas the source of Carter's elaborate rhythms remains—to me, at any rate—mysterious and beautiful.) By comparison with the metrical intricacies of Carter's Third String Quartet, those of the Quartet Romantic may seem slight, but in fact they are pretty well comparable. For a metrically precise performance of the last measure of Carter's quartet, the four players must divide the one and a quarter seconds it lasts into, respectively, seven, five, nine, and six equal parts. A machine controlling the ensemble would divide the measure into 630 equal parts, bringing in first-violin notes on the counts of 181, 271, 361, 451, and 541 and cello notes at the counts of 106, 316, and 526. Choosing at random a measure of the Quartet Romantic, measure 29, I find that the first flute must divide the two and two-fifths seconds it lasts into twenty-eight equal parts, the second flute and the viola into nine, and the violin into ten. A machine controlling the ensemble would divide the measure into 1,260 equal parts, bringing in first-flute notes at the counts of 1, 226, 451, 676, 901, and 1126, and viola notes at the counts of 1, 567, and 1121. The Carter quartet, which has far greater variety of rhythmic figurations and frequent changes of time-signature and metronome marking, must be the harder to perform. The first movement of the Cowell is ruled out in a basic 4/4 (variously subdivided) throughout, at a steady quarter-note = 100.

At the time he composed them, Cowell realized his "rhythm-harmony" quartets were "obviously unperformable by any known human agency" and "thought of them as purely fanciful." But in 1964, when he wrote the preface for the score published ten years later, performances no longer seemed inconceivable: "If the day should come when the first movement of the 'Romantic,' with all its rhythmic complications, is actually playable, I should like to point out that it was conceived as something human that would sound warm and rich and somewhat *rubato*. Whatever the electronic or other means used for it, its composer hopes that it need not sound icy in tone nor rigid in rhythm." It was brought to performance at last by the human agency of four members of the Speculum ensemble (Paul Dunkel and Susan Palma, flutes; Rolf Schulte, violin; John Graham, viola) assisted by a mechanical device: a "click tape"— a four-track tape clicking out to each of the players his or her rhythmic patterns. With their metrical paths, as it were, thus clearly plotted before them, the Speculum quartet recorded the work for New World Records (NW 285); in the studio, the players could not hear one another; balance was supervised in the control room. There are no indications in the score, for the first movement, of dynamics, phrasing, expression, or accent; the players must supply them of their own musicianship, and the Speculum players did so convincingly. (Flutists have to draw breath at times; flute lines that Cowell left unbroken for pages on end were given articulation.) In the Tully Hall performance, each player had a track of the click tape playing into just one ear, while the other ear could be attentive to balance and ensemble. And it was, I think, an even more romantic and "human" performance of the work. It did sound "warm and rich and somewhat *rubato.*"

The Quartet Romantic as plotted on the tape lasts seventeen minutes and six seconds. It is in two unequal movements. The first, and longer, begins with the transformation of the chorale. Then there is a central section metrically derived in similar fashion from a little contrapuntal exercise in 4/4 and in G. Again, each beat of the exercise becomes one measure of the quartet. (The first note is a B, the fifth harmonic above a fundamental G, and so in the corresponding measure of the quartet a single instrument plays five equal notes.) In choosing the free pitches to fill this new rhythmic matrix, Cowell writes a free canon, on a theme that opens with a distinctive octave leap and constantly changes its note values to fit the rhythmic matrix. Then there is a third section; decoding a few measures to discover the underlying progression that supplies its rhythms, I found a toccatalike piece with an active top line over simple harmonies. (The chorale in C and the contrapuntal exercise in G are set out in the preliminary matter to the score.) First and second sections are then repeated, and there is a brief coda. As the underlying harmonies become simpler, so, of course, do the corresponding rhythmic relationships—and in that way the harmonic tensions and resolutions of the original pieces *can* be sensed in the quartet as rhythmic tensions and resolutions. The coda of the "toccata" ends with repeated tonic octaves, four deep, and so the quartet movement ends with a simple rhythmic pattern of eight against four against two against one. Rhythm and harmony satisfyingly coincide when Cowell leads his free part-writing to close in final octaves. The short second movement is a span of calm four-part counterpoint, lyrical, atonal, conventionally notated, and built on a theme that is slightly altered at each entry.

The Quartet Euphometric, composed for string quartet (and recorded by the Emerson String Quartet on New World Records, NW 218), lasts just under two minutes. It represents the transformation of a simple C-major four-chord sequence (with passing notes) into rhythms by a different method. The first chord—C, G, E—sounds the second, third, and fifth harmonics of a fundamental C; the quartet begins (after a largo introduction) with the metres 2/4, 3/4, and 5/4 superimposed. But in this work the notes retain their "real" values: five notes are not squeezed into, or three notes stretched across, a fixed 4/4 measure, but in each part the bar lines themselves are shifted; after two measures of 5/4 in the first violin and five measures of 2/4 in the cello, the two instruments coincide again on a first beat. Again, the choice of pitches is free; only the rhythmic patterns are predetermined.

Enough of mathematics. Bruce Archibald, in notes that accompany the record of the Quartet Euphometric, calls these compositions "essentially student works that systematically explore a particular new musical idea." Are they more than that? Are they worth performing? It seems to me that they are. They produce pleasing and beautiful sounds.

Shifrin's *The Nick of Time* is a substantial, two-movement piece—lasting about twenty minutes—for flute, clarinet, piano, violin, cello, bass, and percussion. It takes its title from *Walden:*

> In any weather, at any hour of the day or night, I have been anxious to improve the nick of time, and notch it on my stick too; to stand on the meeting of two eternities, the past and the future, which is precisely the present moment; to toe that line.

The composer suggests that that may cast some oblique light on the composition—but continues the Thoreau quotation: "You will pardon some obscurities, for there are more secrets in my trade than in most men's, and yet not voluntarily kept, but inseparable from its very nature." *The Nick of Time* is one of the most "difficult" yet one of the most arresting and engrossing of Shifrin's compositions. (I wish Speculum had played it twice.) Through most of the first movement, there runs a long line, a lyrical thread. It can be followed—but not easily, for it passes from instrument to instrument. The performers would probably have to play the work many times—and listeners hear it many times—before it began to yield all its secrets. At the Tully Hall performance, most of the individual phrases were sounded in an eloquent, lyrical fashion—especially by Ben Hudson, violin, and Jerry Grossman, cello—but (or so it seemed to me) the effect of the long progress was sometimes abrupt and ejaculatory when it could have been smooth and continuous. Shifrin is fond of suddenly disturbing his surface with a ripple, of throwing a sudden flash or flicker across his scene. It means that his music is full of incident; it can also make it seem scrappy, incoherent, if the performers do not present all its details in very precise balance. Although it is absurd for a critic after one hearing to try to assess a performance by expert players who have studied the work carefully, I cannot quite suppress a feeling that Speculum will in time play *The Nick of Time* still better; and I hope the ensemble is invited to record it. Admiration for the piece was increased when I got hold of a score. What the performance did make clear was the eventfulness, the sharp colors, the intensity—the "knife edge" quality—of the music. The first movement comes to an end, through an almost Bartókian episode for soft solo percussion, in quietness and stillness. The second movement begins as if in the same still moment. Strands of gentle melody begin to form. Then the attention is drawn to individual details—represented by solos or duos—of the scene. At last, everything clusters toward a climax.

In his program note, the composer remarks on the difficulty of finding words to tell of music: "Everything set down mocks all that is left unsaid and, in the process, more often than not, the effort that is the piece dwindles and may be belittled." Finding words to describe *The Nick of Time is* hard. Let me end with a simple affirmation. It seemed to me a rich and imaginative stretch of music, one I would like to hear again.

June 5, 1978

Master of All Music

Bernard Haitink, born in Amsterdam in 1929, did not come suddenly before the public as a glamorous young conductor with the full force of a record company's publicity machine behind him. After some years with the Netherlands Radio Philharmonic, first as a violinist and then as its conductor, he went to the Concertgebouw Orchestra in 1961. In 1967, he became, in addition, the conductor of the London Philharmonic—a post he has just relinquished—and took it to first place in the shifting hierarchy of London's five full-time symphony orchestras. Last year, he was appointed musical director of Glyndebourne, where he has been conducting since 1972; did his first Wagner opera (Covent Garden's new production of *Lohengrin*); and was knighted. Gradually, he has become the most solidly and consistently esteemed conductor of our day. Among his many recordings are the complete symphonies of Beethoven, Brahms, Bruckner, and Mahler, all of them on the Philips label. I remember well the occasion when I realized that Haitink was not just a thoroughly sound and satisfying conductor but a great one: it was during a performance of Bruckner's Seventh Symphony, ten years ago, in his first season with the London Philharmonic. It must be a common realization now; there have been standing ovations at his recent Carnegie Hall concerts with the Concertgebouw Orchestra. Haitink and the Amsterdam orchestra came to Carnegie last month to play six Beethoven programs—all the symphonies and, with Vladimir Ashkenazy as soloist, all the piano concertos. I went to four of the concerts and wished I could have gone to all six. Beethoven's even-numbered symphonies are not very often done now in New York, it seems; I have not been keeping exact statistics, but I have the impression that Bruckner's Fourth is played more often than Beethoven's Fourth, and Mahler's Sixth far more often than the Pastoral. (This season, the Philharmonic played Beethoven's First, Third, and Seventh Symphonies; in Carnegie, before the Concertgebouw visit, the First, Seventh, and Ninth had been done.) I had not heard the Second, Fourth, or Sixth Symphony for years. Nor for years had I heard *any* Beethoven symphonies, in live performances, quite so well performed.

Haitink needs to be heard with an orchestra that he knows, and one that plays as if it loved music. Earlier this season, in Avery Fisher Hall, he conducted some concerts in the Philharmonic subscription series which were respectable but unremarkable. There was a Haydn symphony, No. 96, the "Miracle," that was very agreeably turned; there was a substantial and coherent account of Shostakovich No. 15, that wry, disturbing, bitter testament, part cynical, part sentimental, and tragic in its final effect; and there was a Tchaikovsky "Pathétique" handled with passion and power. But in none of those performances did one feel that the conductor's intentions were fully realized by all the players, that their hearts were beating as one with his. In any case, Fisher Hall—a long, rectangular, gilded box—is not designed, as Carnegie Hall is, to catch up an audience in communal rapture. (The floor of Fisher Hall has forty-three rows of seats and that of Carnegie only twenty-nine. Fisher to Carnegie is roughly what Tully Hall is to Town Hall; in each case, the latter holds more people but seems more intimate.) The Philharmonic this season has been a characterless orchestra. (Next season, we will hear what Zubin Mehta can make of it.) But the Concertgebouw has as marked, as instantly recognizable a character as the Philadelphia, the Chicago, or the Vienna Philharmonic, and, like those three orchestras, it seems to carry the sound of its home hall with it wherever it goes. It does not have the Philadelphians' velvet opulence, the Chicagoans' fierce virtuoso brilliance, or the deep, rich, Viennese patina. Positively, it has full, well-balanced, well-blended, "active" sound. (The same can be said of the acoustics of the Concertgebouw building itself.) Middle-of-the-road epithets seem appropriate to it, as they do to Haitink; neither it nor he is extremely anything—except extremely good. *Auream mediocritatem diliget,* but "golden mediocrity" must be understood in its old sense—that ideal golden mean, in pursuit of which an interpreter may be required to follow a creator's most extravagant flights but must not exaggerate them. Haitink and the Concertgebouw *can* be hectic, impassioned, turbulent, violent, when the music calls on them to be so. Most London orchestras are protean; blindfold, one could tell more easily whether Solti, Abbado, Boult, Muti, or Haitink was conducting than whether the London Symphony, the London Philharmonic, the Royal Philharmonic, the Philharmonia, or the BBC Symphony was playing. But I feel I would recognize the sound of the Concertgebouw Orchestra after a few measures whoever held the baton. That may be because in its ninety-five-year history it has had only four permanent conductors: Willem Kes, Willem Mengelberg, Eduard van Beinum, and now Haitink. The continuity of its sonorous ideals is documented by the phonograph. In the early forties, Beethoven's nine symphonies conducted by Mengelberg were recorded live in the Concertgebouw. Of Mengelberg's orchestra, a colleague wrote:

> Immaculately groomed and tuned, its playing . . . is always immensely accomplished, section luminously blended with section, from the strong but wonderfully malleable cellos and basses up to winds which can play with devilish accuracy yet in something like the Adagio of the Fourth

Symphony conjure a heart-rending pathos. Time and again the ensemble playing is breathtaking in its ardour and beauty.

Exactly the same—with one small reservation to be mentioned later—could be written of Haitink's orchestra as we heard it last month. And, though he is a less grandly wayward, a steadier conductor than Mengelberg, he has a similar power of holding listeners rapt on every turn of the music and of building to a finish that crowns each opus.

The great performances I heard were of the Sixth, Seventh, and Fourth Symphonies. (The works were not played in chronological order.) Haitink's Pastoral is not quite as liltingly playful as was Beecham's—there is a stiller light in the bright sky—or as graciously charming as was Walter's, but in its unforced intensity, poetic beauty, cheerfulness, hushed happiness in the brookside scene, exuberance, and rainbow serenity in the final hymn it is a complete and wonderful performance. The Concertgebouw woodwinds are a special glory: clear, pure flutes untroubled by the throbbing and wobble that many American players affect; the first bassoon an artist of great sensibility who, like all Concertgebouw soloists, never forces his accomplishments upon the listener. In the Allegretto of the Seventh Symphony, these woodwinds were matchless. The first movement was filled with growing excitement. The finale—Tovey's "triumph of Bacchic fury"—brought a sense of physical exhilaration; the tempo was fast, but Haitink justified it. As the slow introduction of the Fourth (first bassoon again superb) yielded to the Allegro vivace, darkness was invaded by light; that, of course, happens in every performance, but not always is it accompanied by such a leaping of the spirits, a feeling that a tangible weight has been removed. Nor is the finale always as thrilling as it was on this occasion.

When affixing a metronome marking to one of his songs, Beethoven added the note "100 according to Mälzel; but this must be held applicable to only the first measures, for feeling also has its tempo, and this cannot be entirely expressed by a figure." Beecham claimed that for a natural, affectionate reading of the first twelve measures of the Eighth Symphony four slightly different metronome markings were needed. Haitink's Beethoven has this naturalness; he knows that "feeling also has its tempo." His golden mean lies between metrical rigidity and metrical caprice. His account of the Eighth Symphony was a delight, and his performance of the Ninth the revelation that performances of the Ninth always should be. That reservation mentioned earlier concerns the woodwind intonation in the Adagio of the Ninth; it was not quite true. But this was the orchestra's third big concert in three days, and the last of a heavy tour that had taken it to Washington, Minneapolis, and Ames, Iowa, as well as New York. One sign of tiredness could be forgiven; there was no lack of energy, fervor, or jubilation in the playing.

The piano concertos were less remarkable. I wish Haitink had chosen instead to do some of the Beethoven music we hear too seldom: the *Prometheus* ballet, the *King Stephen, Ruins of Athens,* and *Consecration of the House* overtures, the 1790 cantatas. (One program did include the *Egmont* overture.) Haitink has recorded the piano concertos both with Arrau and with Brendel as soloist; Ashkenazy has recorded them with Solti as conductor. Haitink and Ashkenazy did not mate well. The pianist does not have the same command of Beethoven counterpoint, of large-scale structure, or of "molded" tempo; he was not metrically rigid, but the fluctuations seemed to be caused less by apt, beautiful feeling than by a tendency to scamper through runs. Haitink, after setting out expositions clearly, in a somewhat neutral fashion, remained content to accompany, yet occasionally pianist and orchestra got out of time.

The symphonies were memorable: a late and splendid climax to an orchestral season whose other high points for me have been Mahler's Fourth by the Philadelphians under Abbado and Boulez's *Pli selon pli.*

The Juilliard Theatre Center has revived John Gay's *The Beggar's Opera*, one of the hit works of all time, using an edition that Frederic Austin made for a famous production at the Lyric, Hammersmith, in 1920, which ran and ran. For the tenth-anniversary (and sixteen-hundred-and-eighty-fifth) performance, A. P. Herbert wrote a prologue:

> *Ah, Mr. Gay, I wonder, would you write*
> *A different play, if you were here tonight?*
> *Your admonitions have a modern touch,*
> *And politicians have not altered much.*

In the opening air of the piece, Peachum, who directs a band of thieves and occasionally peaches 'em, sings:

> *The Priest calls the Lawyer a cheat,*
> *The Lawyer beknaves the Divine;*
> *And the Statesman, because he's so great,*
> *Thinks his trade as honest as mine.*

On the day of the third Juilliard performance, one could read in the *Times* of a senator who admitted to lying under oath, of a representative sentenced to jail for using his influence improperly, of a priest who confessed to concealing 2.2 million dollars in secret bank accounts while fund-raising for his order, of a broker who conspired to create a fraudulent 27 million-dollar tax loss. A gaming house was also front-page news. Call girls, corrupt lawyers, judges, and prison officials were missing from the columns that day, but there was still enough to show that Gay's "admonitions have a modern touch."

The Juilliard production, directed by Eve Shapiro, was not quite fierce or bitter enough. *The Beggar's Opera,* according to Pope, owed its origin to a remark of Swift's: "What an odd pretty sort of thing a Newgate Pastoral might make." In modern revivals, there is always a temptation to stress the prettiness at the expense of the political and social content. (A Boston libretto of 1854, made for the Pyne and Harrison troupe, presents the text with "the objectionable matter expunged.") Use of the Austin twenties score abets this approach; the accompaniments are arranged in a deft but genteel fashion for a small ensemble in which the harpsichord plays no functional role but adds "quaint" touches of period color. For the original *Beggar's Opera*, Gay wrote new words to sixty-nine well-known airs, and John Christopher Pepusch wrote basses to them. Later editions and "realizations" of their work have been numerous: Arne, Milhaud, Edward Dent, Bliss (for the 1953 movie), and Britten are among those who have made them. Austin made two; his later, 1940 version (used in the Argo recording) is fresher and more stylish. Elliott Carter set the brothel chorus "Let's be gay" for the young ladies of the Wells College Glee Club. Kurt Weill's *Die Dreigroschenoper* and Duke Ellington's *Beggar's Holiday* are independent new compositions, not arrangements. By all accounts, the most stylish edition of all is Manfred Bukofzer's, which was performed at Columbia in 1954. Dent could not resist some learned contrapuntal elaborations. Bliss scored richly and added passages of *Fortspinnung*. Britten's version (which the Juilliard performed in 1950) is a delectable anthology of his cunning harmonic and instrumental devices, and a masterpiece in its way, but such things as the luscious, heavenly-choir treatment of two of the loveliest melodies, "O Polly, you might have toy'd and kist" and "Cease your funning," take it far from the original.

It was rather feeble of the Juilliard students not to make their own edition, choosing for themselves which airs to include and which to omit. (For Macheath's scena in the condemned hold, Gay ingeniously strung ten tunes together, running his rhyme scheme through them, and ending with "Greensleeves"; Austin retains only four of them.) It is my impression that *The Beggar's Opera* would be best served by an instrumentally plain accompaniment of eighteenth-century disposition (perhaps oboes and flutes in alternation, a bassoon, strings, and continuo; but with many airs accompanied by continuo only), which would throw all attention on the actors delivering the airs. The Britten score is one for "real musicians" to perform. At the Juilliard, the Austin version was played by music students, conducted by Ronald Braunstein, but enacted and sung by drama students. Their singing was less accomplished than that of the drama students who did Brecht's *Mann ist Mann* last year, but it was confident and pretty well in tune. Michael Redgrave (who figured in an abridged recording of the opera) and Laurence Olivier (who stars in the film version) have provided precedent for actor Macheaths, but the Juilliard performance almost foundered on a miscasting of this role. The student who played him looked wrong. More important, his characterization was callow. But otherwise it was a trim, capably executed show. Denise Woods's Lucy was especially vivid. The movement staff of the Theatre Center was listed in full, and deserved to be: Miss Shapiro had included plenty of rough-and-tumble in her staging—too much for the good of the piece—and it was carried out with gymnastic virtuosity.

·   ·   ·

The New Opera Theatre at the Brooklyn Academy of Music, directed by Ian Strasfogel, produced this season an Offenbach double bill, his late, lyrical *Pomme d'api* (wrongly claimed as an American première; it was done at the New York Academy of Music in 1880) and his early, hilarious *Ba-ta-clan*. *Pomme d'api*, Englished as *Wild Rose*, was attractively performed, even if Noelle Rogers in the title role tended to be kewpie-cute. Tonio DiPaolo sang with beautiful tone and clear, expressive words. Mr. Strasfogel turned the elegant, sparkling *Ba-ta-clan* into a buck-basketful of pratfall humors. In the Hortense Schneider role he had a star, Kate Hurney. He could have relied on her twinkling eyes, her witty timing, and her beguiling way with the music to carry the day; instead, she was set to compete with a pair of nonstop mimes, with a narrator who kept getting in the way, with "subtitles" in the form of bubbles held over her head to translate what she sang. (She sang in French, although there is published an admirable English translation of *Ba-ta-clan*— by one Ian Strasfogel.) The other singers fell in with the coarseness of the general presentation. It says much for Miss Hurney—and for Offenbach's genius—that one couldn't help enjoying *Ba-ta-clan* all the same. Richard Dufallo conducted a young orchestra, the St. Luke's Chamber Ensemble, which played with a smile in its tone and in its phrasing. And the Academy's Helen Carey Playhouse, holding about eleven hundred, makes a good home for the opera.

The Trial of the Gypsy, Gian Carlo Menotti's latest opera—more specifically, "a dramatic cantata for a boys choir," with piano accompaniment—composed for the Newark Boys Chorus and given its first performance as the centerpiece of the Chorus's concert in Tully Hall last month, is trashy music, and not even tuneful or tearjerking, the way that *Amahl* is. It *is* "singable"— skillfully laid out for the young voices. The four anonymous soloists (a large role for the gypsy, small parts for three judges) and the chorus were firm and clear. They deserved something better to exercise their talents on.

I was down South, at Spoleto-in-Charleston, when Philip Glass and his ensemble gave their first Carnegie concert, last week, but had been able to spend many hours of Memorial Day Monday listening to music by Glass and by Steve Reich. WKCR put out twenty hours of their works, starting at six in the morning and continuing until two the next morning. There were two hours of Glass's score for the opera *Einstein on the Beach* (which has been performed thirty-five times in Europe and twice at the Met)—part of a recording due to appear in the fall [Tomato TOM-4-2901]. There were both published recordings and private tapes lent by the composers. There was an advance hearing of Reich's Music for Eighteen Musicians in a recording due soon on the ECM/Polydor label [ECM-1-1129], and I was glad to catch up with a composition that has achieved some fame. (It was first played in New York in 1976, and soon afterward was taken round Britain on the Arts Council's Contemporary Music Network.) Music for Eighteen Musicians has been well described as "an unbroken hour-long stretch of scintillating sounds in joyous patterns." The ensemble is violin, cello, two clarinets alternating with bass clarinets, four female voices that blend into the clarinet tone, and ten players with an array of marimbas, xylophones, pianos, maracas, and a metallophone. The colors are bright and surprising, the harmonies often rich. Both Glass and Reich call for patient listeners. Their works contain much repetition. There is no hurrying the slow shift of the rhythmic phases. The beat may remain steady for an hour on end. Glass's Music in Twelve Parts contains a plagal cadence repeated in various rhythms over an ostinato for about ten minutes, and it doesn't ever reach a close; a new sound and a new chord suddenly break in, with an effect as if one wall of a room had suddenly disappeared, to reveal a completely new view.

The WKCR retrospective was well presented. Between the compositions, there were brief, focused interviews with the composers, setting their pieces in context. It was interesting to hear Reich describe how his early tape piece *Melodica* (1966) was constructed from a brief musical pattern that he had dreamed; and how, after assembling it in the course of a day, he had felt it necessary to get back to work with live performers. Introducing Music for Eighteen Musicians, he named Bach, Stravinsky, Charlie Parker, and Miles Davis as his main Western mentors, and he told how into that rich work are gathered the devices tried in some of his earlier compositions.

Both Glass and Reich are important, and internationally acclaimed. At the 1976 Paris Autumn Festival, where *Einstein* was performed, there were four full-scale Reich concerts in the Salle Wagram. In their own country, they have enthusiastic followers but not yet any central position; there has been little overlap, I imagine, between their audiences and those of the Philharmonic and the Met. The Met *Einsteins*, the Carnegie concert, and this ambitious WKCR broadcast may help to change that.

June 12, 1978

Spoleto of the South

In 1958, Gian Carlo Menotti launched the Festival of Two Worlds in Spoleto, Italy—an ancient Umbrian city on Etruscan foundations which recalls in the name of one of its gates the inhabitants' repulse of Hannibal in 217 B.C. Last year, Menotti inaugurated a New World branch of the festival, in Charleston,

South Carolina—a modern city, founded in 1670, which retains many of its eighteenth-century and early-nineteenth-century buildings. Last year, I described some of the likenesses and differences between the two places. In brief, Spoleto is a steep hill town, while Charleston, on a peninsula between the Ashley and the Cooper, rises nowhere more than twenty feet above the rivers. Each town is picturesque, and therefore a good festival site. In the words of the eleventh Britannica, "there are . . . few medieval towns with so picturesque an appearance" as Spoleto, while in Charleston "the quaint specimens of colonial architecture" and the abundant and beautiful flora— live oaks and lindens, magnolias, palmettos—"give the city a peculiarly picturesque character." The churches of Spoleto are larger and more striking, but those of Charleston are numerous and not without interest. Charleston's principal theatre, the Gaillard Municipal Auditorium, which seats more than twenty-seven hundred, is much larger than Spoleto's, the Teatro Nuovo, which seats less than nine hundred. Each has a smaller theatre: Spoleto's Teatro Caio Melisso, a miniature opera house with horseshoe tiers, seats about four hundred, and Charleston's Dock Street Theatre, a WPA reconstruction of a Georgian playhouse, seats about four hundred and fifty. In both places at festival time, the days and nights are filled with music, dance, drama, and exhibitions. This year, the Charleston festival has grown from twelve days to eighteen. Last year, two operas were done; this year, five. The midday chamber music concerts in the Dock Street Theatre, a big success with the public, have been supplemented by afternoon chamber recitals in the Garden Theatre, a 1918 movie house bought by the city, done up, and now brought into festival use: it also housed a full retrospective of Luchino Visconti's films and a series of country music concerts. The recitals were timed not to clash with the afternoon "Intermezzo" concerts held in the various churches. Most days, there was jazz, afternoon, evening, and night, at Charles Towne Landing, a park some miles up the Ashley. Tennessee Williams's *Crève Coeur* had its première. The Ballets Félix Blaska and the Netherlands Dance Theatre danced. The Phe Zulu Theatre Company played *Umabatha*, a tribal version of *Macbeth*. Restaurants stayed open late, and a large, cool, elegant disco was added to the extracurricular attractions. Everything I attended in churches and in the Dock Street Theatre was packed, but at *Vanessa* and *La traviata*, in the huge Gaillard Auditorium, there were rows and rows of empty seats.

La traviata was a restaging by Gianfranco Ventura of a production that Menotti directed for the Fenice, Venice, three years ago. There was a different cast: in Venice the principals were Maria Chiara, Gianni Raimondi, and Mario Zanasi; in Charleston, Luciana Serra, a Kitty in Spanish and Italian performances of Menotti's *The Last Savage*, Maurizio Frusoni, a Lensky in Menotti's production of *Eugene Onegin* at the 1975 Florence Maggio, and David Holloway, of the New York City Opera. The show was dull and dead, as a secondhand staging is apt to be unless the individual interpreters reanimate it. Miss Serra is not negligible. The voice is very sure: it is even and precisely focused throughout its range and at all dynamics; she sings real notes, free of fluff and flutter. In "Parigi, o caro" and in "Prendi, quest'è l'immagine" she traced a delicate and moving line. But otherwise her interpretation was no more than competent—and Claudie Gastine's costumes did not flatter her figure. Mr. Frusoni was a stick, unromantic in timbre and in bearing. Mr. Holloway, miscast as a heavy father, forced his splendid young baritone and turned every grace note of "Di Provenza" into a bump. Cal Stewart Kellogg II's conducting was stiff, metronomic, and unfeeling.

Samuel Barber's first opera, *Vanessa*, to a libretto by Menotti, was created at the old Metropolitan, with Eleanor Steber in the title role. It is twenty years old now and has not worn well. Both plot and score are synthetic. In a richly appointed drawing room "in a northern country," Baroness Vanessa awaits the return of her lover Anatol, unseen for twenty years. The mirrors are shrouded. She is veiled. With her are her mother, who does not speak to her, and her niece Erika. Erika orders the next day's dinner, and Vanessa amends it; they decide on potage crème aux perles, langoustines grillées sauce aux huîtres, palombes rôties nature, gâteau d'amandes au miel, a bottle of Montrachet, and two bottles of Romanée-Conti. Not Anatol but his son, another Anatol, arrives. That night, he seduces Erika. Then Vanessa falls in love with him. She unshrouds the mirrors. In Act II, she gives a ball to announce their engagement; during it, Erika rushes out into the snow, toward a frozen lake, and has a miscarriage on the way. Vanessa and Anatol, married, leave for Paris; Erika covers up the mirrors again and settles down to live with the old Baroness, who now won't speak to her, either. "Now it is my turn to wait."

I saw the original production when it came from the Met to the Salzburg Festival, and remarked that "it is a slightly less awful libretto than it seems." Beneath the staginess and contrivance, Steber, Rosalind Elias, and Nicolai Gedda found hints of three interestingly self-aware characters. Erika is pitilessly clear-sighted. Anatol, an adventurer, is honest with her, honest with himself, and clever in his handling of Vanessa. Vanessa, perceiving more of the true situation than she allows herself to admit, grasps eagerly at a love from which, after all, she can hope to extract a certain amount of enjoyment. But Johanna Meier, the Vanessa of the Charleston production, missed the touch of deliberate self-deception which makes the character mildly interesting and individual. In voice and in manner, she is warm, generous, dignified, and spontaneous, and therefore she is an attractive performer in whatever part she plays; but there is a tendency for all her roles to come out seeming much the same—incarnations of a likable all-purpose heroine who would fit equally well into *Arabella*, *Die Fledermaus*, and *Die Meistersinger*. Henry Price did not have enough voice to fill the role of Anatol in so large a theatre. The star of the evening was Katherine Ciesinski, as Erika. Wide-eyed, with a clear, open brow and a clear, firm voice, Miss Ciesinski is the latest in the line of admirable young mezzos from whom much can be expected. She was both an eloquent, touching, credible actress and an excellent singer.

Barber's music is a weak syrup apparently brewed from Cilea, Giordano, Tchaikovsky, and Richard Strauss. It flows along agreeably enough, pausing now and again to crystallize around an aria, a duet, or an ensemble. Menotti staged the opera as if he had lost any confidence in his collaborator's ability to hold the listener's attention. During a long, important dialogue for Erika and the old Baroness which opens the second scene, the focus of attention was shifted to a blond footman arranging six roses in a vase, stepping back to appraise the effect, rearranging them, stepping back again—and so on until the dialogue was done. During the Doctor's aria in the final scene, the focus of attention was shifted to Vanessa fussily painting her face before a little glass held up by her maid. At the ball, the old Baroness suddenly appeared in her nightdress, and none of the guests even seemed to notice her. Christopher Keene, the musical director of the festival, was an able conductor. Instead of the Victorian Gothic of Cecil Beaton's scenery for the original production, there was turn-of-the-century rococo, designed by Pasquale Grossi. The show looked good. The opera itself seemed unnecessary.

In Spoleto, Menotti kept his own music off the bills for ten years. But in Charleston we had *The Consul* last year and, this year, a double bill of the little church operas *The Egg* and *Martin's Lie*, played in the Circular Congregational Church, an 1891 building. *The Egg* is slight, silly, ethically shallow, and musically worthless. The level of taste can be gauged from an incident when a blundering cook misaims his cleaver and chops off a cookboy's finger; this is meant to be funny. *Martin's Lie* was commissioned for Canterbury Cathedral but denied performance there as being theologically shaky—which it is. But at least it is an efficient tearjerker. A dear little fatherless boy persists in a courageous lie while a torturer brings a red-hot poker closer and closer to his eyes; then he dies of fear, and the other little orphan boys mourn him. Sean Coogan, of the Newark Boys Chorus, was accomplished in the title role.

The fifth opera was an abridged version of Donizetti's *Il furioso all'isola di San Domingo*, done in the Dock Street Theatre. *Il furioso*, first performed in Rome in 1833, was once a famous piece: within six years some seventy Italian theatres had produced it; within a decade it had traveled round the world. (Mexico City and Havana produced it in 1836, New Orleans in 1842.) The first modern revival was in Siena in 1958, the next at the Spoleto festival in 1967. It is an opera semiseria. [The subject matter is discussed in reviews of the Brooklyn (page 327) and the Washington (page 437) productions in 1979.] Some of the opera's success must have been due to the exotic setting and the unconventional characters and plot; there are storms, a shipwreck, and the piquancy—as in *The Tempest* and in Metastasio's much-set *L'isola disabitata*—of unexpected island encounters far from home. And much of its success must have been due to the liveliness of Donizetti's score, which combines the fresh, graceful inventions of *L'elisir d'amore*, its immediate predecessor, with elements of his high dramatic manner.

The merits of the piece were faintly perceptible in the Charleston production. As in Spoleto, it had been condensed from three acts into two and heavily cut. If the Gaillard Auditorium is too big for anything but grand opera with grand singers, the Dock Street Theatre is too small for anything but chamber opera. Donizetti's orchestration was reduced to mainly single winds, and his décor to a single scene (by Lorenzo Mongiardino, as in Spoleto). The staging, by Richard Pearlman, was clumsy, and the conducting, by Clayton Westermann, was stodgy. The festival published no libretto, and so it was doubly idiotic for an American cast to be singing an unfamiliar work to an American audience in Italian. When Menotti produces his own works abroad, he has them translated into the language of the country; at Spoleto in 1961 he gave *Vanessa* in Italian. Donizetti's opera deserves to be treated with equal seriousness. Brenda Boozer was attractive as Marcella, the planter's daughter; otherwise the singing was mediocre.

A poor year, then, for Spoleto-in-Charleston opera—except in the "discovery" of Katherine Ciesinski. Excuses can be found. One theatre is too big, the other too small. The Westminster Choir, a student body, sings in both big operas and also gives concerts. The Spoleto Festival Orchestra, of largely student recruitment, plays for all the operas and also gives concerts. So how can one expect carefully rehearsed, consistently polished performances from them? Am I being too severe? I think not. Even at a festival, some roughness is acceptable provided that the works, the directors, the conductors, the principal artists have been very carefully chosen and provided that the performances are as good as in the circumstances they can be. But a second-rate *Traviata* is not festival fare; nor is a *Furioso* that bears so little relation to what its creators intended.

The midday concerts I heard followed their familiar pattern: excellent young artists, most of them known in New York; middle-of-the-road repertory; Charles Wadsworth as a cheerfully philistine host. The audience—to judge from a show of hands Mr. Wadsworth asked for—was mostly local; it was decently served, and at times with distinction. (Spoleto-in-Spoleto is a more adventurous and international affair, and at the midday concerts there Jessye Norman, Pinchas Zukerman, and Christoph Eschenbach first came to international attention.) I think that more might be done to tie the festival to the place, and to recall the days when Charleston vied with New Orleans and Boston as a glittering cultural center. One reads that the first opera performed in North America was *Flora, or Hob in the Well*, produced in Charleston in 1735. Is that something that might be revived in the Dock Street Theatre? (It held the boards in London for much of the eighteenth century.) There is a local composer, Edmond S. T. Jenkins (1894–1926). Would any of his compositions merit revival at the midday concerts? (His symphony *Charlestonia* was first played in Ostend, Belgium.) Some of the happiest hours I spent at the festival this year were in the grounds of Middleton Place, an eighteenth-century plantation up the Ashley, with magnificent terraces, allées, and ornamental lakes—a formal European garden on the grandest scale unexpectedly re-created in South Carolina with great live oaks, magnolias, and crêpe myrtles beneath American skies. The Spoleto Festival Orchestra was due to give a concert there. Who on earth decided that an all-Tchaikovsky program would be apt?

June 19, 1978

Trees and Music

Last year, the Opera Theatre of St. Louis, then in its second season, impressed me as being one of the best companies in this country. This year, the impression was confirmed. In the course of a three-week season, three operas were done—*L'arbore di Diana*, by Vicente Martín y Soler, *Albert Herring*, and *La Bohème*—and the Spielplan was so laid out that all of them could be seen on a three-day visit. (I stayed four days, because *L'arbore di Diana* is no longer a repertory staple and is a piece worth hearing more than once.) The company performs in the Loretto-Hilton Theatre of Webster College, about eight miles from downtown St. Louis. The theatre, with an airy, light-filled foyer, stands on a tree-studded lawn. This year, a tent in which dinner was served before the shows and drink during the intermissions and afterward was an addition to the civilized, friendly atmosphere that prevails. There were also a few picnickers on the lawn. Opera Theatre is not a copy of Glyndebourne, but it does have some points of resemblance. In fashioning a company specifically for St. Louis, Richard Gaddes, its director, borrowed good ideas from Glyndebourne, from Santa Fe, and perhaps from Wexford, and added several of his own. The theatre, holding nine hundred and fifty people, is larger than Glyndebourne's but has a smaller orchestra pit, and it is not quite ideal for opera. The listeners sit on three sides of a thrust stage (though most of them are frontally placed). The acoustics are patchy and not as warm as they might be. But the productions are devised to make a virtue of the intimacy and designed to minimize the disadvantages of the protruding stage—indeed, to take positive advantage of it wherever possible. The theatre has a lively feel to it, and so does the whole enterprise. The casts are chosen from among America's best young artists (except in a few roles where the ballast of maturity is needed). A concern for detail and for all the aspects of opera giving and opera going is everywhere apparent—from the assembling of keen, expert musical and stage staffs, so that the works will be as well prepared and as well presented as possible, to the casting of young people both efficient and attractive to be ticket sellers, ticket takers, barmen, and barmaidens. (The Met could learn a lot from St. Louis about the art of making visitors feel welcome the moment they step into a theatre.) The program book is well printed. The company photographer is excellent. These front-of-house merits are not just trimmings but contributory evidence of an approach to opera which is at once serious, zestful, and complete. All operas, of course, are sung in English. The orchestra, drawn this year from the St. Louis Symphony, was better than before.

Recent stagings of *La Bohème* have focused attention on matters of time and place in this veristic opera. The Met's latest production claims to be set in 1880, and the Statue of Liberty looms over the second scene—complete with her right arm, which in 1880 was really standing in Madison Square Park, having preceded the rest of her over here, on a fund-raising drive. In the English National Opera's new staging of the piece, the Café Momus is on the Right Bank, which is where it was in life—despite Puccini's heading "In the Latin Quarter" to Act II. The director and the designer of the St. Louis *Bohème*, Bolen High and Gerald Allen, had noted that, although the opera is commonly given a late-nineteenth-century setting, the score specifies "about 1830." One doesn't usually think of the action of *La Bohème* as being before that of *La traviata* (which in most librettos is dated "about 1850"; the 1953 score, however, "revised and corrected," says "about 1700"). An 1830 date for *La Bohème* is puzzling, because in that year Henry Mürger, from whose *Scènes de la vie de bohème* the libretto is drawn, was only eight. Mürger wrote about himself and his friends; the 1840s are indicated. The *Scènes* were running in *Le Corsaire* in 1848, the year Dumas's novel *La Dame aux camélias* appeared. So Mimì and Marguerite Gautier, the original of Violetta, are contemporaries. To a director who wants to get the background right, it matters whether Louis Philippe or Louis Napoleon is on the throne. It matters even more to one who views Violetta or Mimì as the victim of a particular society. I have not yet encountered a production of *La Bohème* that attempted to present the piece as "a triumph of Socialism," which is what the Goncourts called Mürger's work, but no doubt the attempt has been made. Any detailed fidelity to the original would be inappropriate. Puccini and his librettists made their changes deliberately. The director who consults Mürger discovers as Rodolphe

> a young man whose face could hardly be seen for a huge, bushy, many-colored beard. To set off this prognathic hirsutism, a premature baldness had stripped his temples as bare as a knee. A cluster of hairs, so few as to be almost countable, vainly endeavored to conceal this nakedness.

He would not cut a romantic figure in the opera.

There was no silliness or misguided authenticity in the St. Louis *Bohème*. It differed from a conventional presentation of the piece in ways determined by the nature of the theatre and of the company. The six principals were all young, scarcely older than the characters they portrayed, and that lent both freshness and poignancy to the drama. Sheri Greenawald was a delicate, intelligent Mimì, aiming at truth of expression rather than vocal or physical glamour; she was touching, credible, and musically precise. Vinson Cole, a Rodolphe bearded but not bald, was a tenor much improved since last I heard him—smoother, more shapely in his phrasing, more of an actor. He must still guard against Pavarotti-like moments of sacrificing character and sense to sound. Sheila Barnes was a bright, unexaggerated Musette, and Stephen Dickson a cheerful, unexaggerated Marcel. (Since the opera was sung in English, Italian names are not apposite.) James McKeel and Joseph McKee were Schaunard and Colline. It was an unusually even performance; one was aware of six characters brought together, and of the way they lived—not just of a soprano and tenor with supporting cast. Mr. Allen's simple, open settings, against a backdrop of Paris, looked good. There were no walls: Stephen Ross's skillful lighting defined spaces, but, inevitably, dramatically important entrances—Mimì's in Act I, Musette's in Act IV—lost their effectiveness. The size of the pit imposed a more serious limitation: there was room for only thirty-six players, and Mario Parenti's reduced instrumentation was used. One became aware how much Puccini's emotional eloquence depends on the orchestral sound. Bruce Ferden's conducting was lyrical and lively.

One need not go to St. Louis, however, to see *La Bohème*. The two other works were the attraction of the season—complementary comedies, one from the twentieth and one from the eighteenth century, both of them spun around the serious theme of chastity. I'll write about *Albert Herring* next week. *L'arbore di Diana* was the third of five operas that Martín composed to librettos by Lorenzo Da Ponte. It had its first performance, at the Vienna Burgtheater, in 1787—twenty-three years after the settlement of St. Louis. The second Martín–Da Ponte collaboration, *Una cosa rara* (1786), had appeared six months after, and been far more successful than, the Mozart–Da Ponte *Le nozze di Figaro. Rara est concordia formae atque pudicitae.* Lilla, the heroine of *Una cosa rara*, is that rare thing, a woman both beautiful and chaste. She is firm as rock, *come scoglio*, in her love for Lubino, even though the Infante of Spain himself (in the tender accents of Mozart's Ferrando), his friend, and the local Podestà all woo her. Da Ponte is not a disinterested witness, but other accounts—and the Burgtheater annals—confirm the one he gives in his memoirs of the first night of *Una cosa rara*:

> From the rising of the curtain, everyone praised such grace, such sweetness, such melody in the music, and therewith such novelty and interest in the words, that the audience was caught up in an ecstasy of pleasure. On an attentive silence never before lent to any Italian opera there followed a frenzy of applause, cries of delight and joy.

The following year, Salieri, Martín, and Mozart all wanted Da Ponte librettos. Salieri asked for an Italian adaptation of his French opera *Tarare* (and so once again, as in *Figaro*, Da Ponte Italianized a Beaumarchais text). For Mozart, Da Ponte says, "I chose *Don Giovanni*, a subject that pleased him mightily." For Martín, "I wanted an attractive theme, adaptable to those sweet melodies of his, which one feels in one's soul but which few know how to imitate." At random, he gave the composer a title, *The Tree of Diana*, but "had not the slightest idea what that tree was to be." When Martín called for his scenario, the poet stalled him for half an hour and then produced a plot. *Una cosa rara* had dealt with women's fidelity; *L'arbore di Diana*, like *Così fan tutte*, shows their frailty. The goddess Diana has in her garden a wondrous tree. Its fruits glow with mystic radiance and sweet music sounds from its branches when nymphs chaste in deed and thought pass beneath them. But that fruit turns blacker than coal and rains down upon any lass who has been lax in observing her vows—"disfiguring her face, bruising her body, or breaking her limbs in proportion to her crime." The god of love will have none of this. Disguised as a girl, he enters the garden, incites the gardener to seduce Diana's nymphs, and brings to the grove two more young men, the huntsman Silvius and the beautiful shepherd Endymion, who wins the goddess's heart. When the Rite of the Tree is next celebrated, storm and earthquake ensue; the Reign of Chastity is ended and that of Love begins. The subject, Da Ponte remarked, combined "some merit of novelty" with "the timeliness of fitting admirably with certain policies of my august patron and sovereign." Joseph II had lately issued "a decree, holy indeed, abolishing the barbarous institution of monasticism" throughout his dominions. There were some shocked comments after the première of *L'arbore di Diana;* it was remarked that such a libretto could never have reached the stage in Maria Theresa's day. But Joseph, it seems, both got the point and enjoyed the piece. Almost as successful as *Una cosa rara*, it was soon being played all over Europe.

Once his three subjects had been decided, Da Ponte settled down to work twelve hours a day with a bottle of Tokay on his right hand, a box of Seville tobacco on his left, and an inkhorn between. His Calliope was the housekeeper's sixteen-year-old daughter, summoned by a bell, whenever inspiration flagged, to bring a biscuit, coffee, or other consolations of which she was *perfetta maestra*. Mornings he devoted to Martín, afternoons to Salieri, and evenings to Mozart—as if, he remarked, he were absorbed in turn by Petrarch, Tasso, and Dante's *Inferno*. (So much for the assertion that *Don Giovanni* was intended to be merely a comedy!) *L'arbore di Diana* and *Don Giovanni* were produced in October 1787, and *Assur*, the new version of *Tarare*, three months later. Da Ponte thought *L'arbore di Diana* his best libretto. He was wrong—right to think it graceful, piquant, amusing, and "voluptuous without being lascivious," wrong to consider it interesting from beginning to end. The promising initial idea is dissipated in a flurry of scatterbrained flirtation; what might have been a *Love's Labour's Lost* or a precursor of *The Princess* becomes something like an untidier *Princess Ida*. Comings and goings for the eight characters are unmotivated except by a determination to shuffle and deal the eight voices in as many patterns as possible. Diana has three principal nymphs: Britomartis, Clytie, and Chloe.

When they sing with the gardener, Doristus, they are like the Queen of Night's Three Ladies with Papageno. One of them joins the three men to provide a quartet of different texture. Besides many pretty arias, in many veins, there are duets, trios, quartets, quintets, sextets, and a septet, and, of course, finales written to the formula that Da Ponte described so vividly:

> Everybody sings and every form of singing must be available—the adagio, the allegro, the andante, the intimate, the harmonious, and then—noise, noise, noise. . . . The finale must produce on the stage every singer of the cast, be there three hundred of them, and whether by ones, by twos, and by threes or by sixes, by tens, and by sixties; and they must have solos, duets, terzets, sextets, thirteenets, sixtyets; and if the plot of the drama does not permit this, the poet must find a way to make it permit, in the face of reason, good sense, Aristotle, and all the powers of heaven and earth!

L'arbore di Diana is no *Figaro* or *Così fan tutte* in its dramatic working or its delineation of character. It is not even a *Cosa rara* (which has an unusual shape: in the first finale, all knots are apparently neatly tied, and then in Act II their strength is tested). Its libretto, like Da Ponte's for *Così fan tutte*, provides the framework for a sequence of attractive musical numbers; unlike it, it goes no further, no deeper. Da Ponte evidently knew his composers' strengths, and Martín was no Mozart. (If he had been, he would hardly have won such immediate success.) In music his characters are charmingly portrayed, but not profoundly. *Figaro* and *Così* take their listeners to the brink of tears; *Una cosa rara* and *L'arbore di Diana* remain untouched by even the possibility of tragedy—except at one point in each opera. In Act II of *Una cosa rara*, Lilla has an aria, "Consola le pene," that strikes deep. In the second finale of *L'arbore*, Diana sings a larghetto, "Fra quest'ombre taciturne," owning to herself that she loves Endymion. It begins like a Mozart concerto slow movement. Through gently pulsing string triplets, two flutes play and then the goddess sings a rapt, beautiful melody. But it is all over in twenty-two measures. None of the numbers in *L'arbore di Diana* is extended—except Diana's allegro maestoso bravura aria "Sento che Dea son io," in Act I. With its huge leaps and its brilliant coloratura running up to high D, it sounds as if it were composed for Mozart's first Fiordiligi, Adriana Ferraresi del Bene (who was Da Ponte's inamorata). But although Ferraresi did make her Vienna début as Diana, that was only in 1788. The first Diana was Anna Morichelli—and one contemporary critic remarked that in this showstopping aria Martín merely assembled all her favorite pieces of spectacular vocalism. The first Amor was Luisa Laschi-Mombelli, Mozart's Countess in *Figaro*—the one who ran up to the high C's in the second finale. (Later, he adjusted the part for Cavalieri, and gave the top line to Ferraresi, the new Susanna.) In 1787, Doristus was Stefano Mandini, Mozart's Count, and Britomartis was Maria Mandini, his Marcellina. Vincenzo Calvesi, the first Endymion, went on to become Mozart's Ferrando.

Don Giovanni's supper band plays an air from *Una cosa rara* (improving on the tune as it does so). Those are not the only measures of Martín which reappear in Mozart's music. Some of the shared figures and turns of melody are mere tags, the small change of the later eighteenth century; others suggest a more direct derivation. Borrowing seems to have been mutual: Martín evidently found ideas in *Figaro* besides providing them for *Così* and *Die Zauberflöte*. He could write melodies, but he had none of the commands of expressive harmony, expressive counterpoint, and searching development which set Mozart above him—and above Paisiello, Anfossi, Cimarosa, and all those whose tuneful, thin-textured scores delighted the Viennese public. At the least, *L'arbore di Diana* affords a measure by which to judge Mozart's genius in transforming the commonplaces of opera buffa into something specific. It tells us more about Da Ponte, and shows how strongly Mozart must have influenced the dramaturgy of the operas they worked on together. It throws new light on the abilities of the singers for whom Mozart composed. But, beyond that, the opera in its own right provides a good deal of innocent pleasure by its graceful tunes, its Rossinian high spirits, and its exquisitely deft, sometimes adventurous orchestration. One of Amor's arias is accompanied by the extraordinary sound of violins scrubbing out an arpeggio figuration *sul ponticello* beneath an oboe and flute melody; I can think of nothing in Mozart or Haydn quite like it.

The St. Louis cast was lively. Elizabeth Hynes was a clear, bright, touching Diana. She needs to work on her trills. The three nymphs, played by Erie Mills, Brenda Warren, and Susan Quittmeyer, were attractive and witty; Miss Mills made much of Britomartis's minuet aria, and Miss Quittmeyer made even more of the catchy, heady ländler in which Chloe decides to throw discretion to the winds. Sunny Joy Langton was a twinkling, accurate Amor. The three men were not quite on the same level. John Aler, the Endymion, has a sweet tenor and a refined style, but he is no kind of actor. Gimi Beni, a mature, ripe, and, admittedly, accomplished buffo, was miscast as the lusty young gardener. He suggested Don Pasquale where a young Papageno is needed; the girls refer to Doristus as a "garzon." Ronald Raines portrayed Silvius in a confident musical-comedy manner—effective enough, but not quite right for the piece. For that matter, the whole style of the production was not quite right—but the women were more skillful than the men in reconciling its demands with those of Martín and Da Ponte. Colin Graham, who directed, and John Kavelin and John Carver Sullivan, who designed, displayed an unworthy lack of confidence in the opera's ability to entertain on its own terms. They decided to deck it out with additional, irrelevant jokes, derived from the choice of a chic Edwardian setting. The women's dresses were 1910 neoclassical; Silvius was kitted up for cricket; the décor was Fabergé built large. The effect was pretty—and would have been prettier still if Mr. Kavelin had not mounted the comedy against a backcloth and wings of funeral black—but inappropriate. In every opera audience, there seem to be people who prefer not to listen to the music, and Mr. Graham played up to them: whole sections of the score were drowned by applause for stock comic antics. All the same, the execution was dapper, and *L'arbore di Diana* survived. Claude White conducted, neatly and ably, but sometimes a little too fast, as if he shared the director's insistence on pushing ahead with the jokes. Comic operas become more, not less, animated when the music is given space to breathe, when lyrical melodies unfold slowly and fast numbers dance along with a lilting, supple gait. The orchestra's playing was neither loving enough nor always quite in tune.

A Martín revival was inaugurated by Roy Jesson, a scholar and conductor whose career was cut cruelly short by a fatal illness just when it was beginning to flower. For Opera 61, one of the British troupes specializing in off-center repertory, he edited, translated, and conducted *Una cosa rara*, in 1967; it was broadcast, and the work was taken up abroad. In 1972, he did the same for *L'arbore di Diana*. St. Louis used the Jesson score and translation. One hopes that the work he began will be continued; curiosity is whetted about the two operas Martín wrote in St. Petersburg with Catherine the Great as his librettist (one of them is said to be a five-act satire on Gustavus III, the hero of *Un ballo in maschera*) and the two he wrote in London with Da Ponte.

June 26, 1978

What Harbour Shelters Peace?

Most of Benjamin Britten's operas grew from local roots. The singers for whom he composed—Joan Cross, Jennifer Vyvyan, Margaret Ritchie, Kathleen Ferrier, Janet Baker, Peter Pears, Owen Brannigan—left their mark on his scores as surely as the singers for whom Handel, Mozart, Bellini, Donizetti, and Verdi composed did on theirs. *Peter Grimes, Albert Herring,* and *The Little Sweep* are set in the Suffolk country where Britten lived. The textures of *Noye's Fludde* and of the three church parables are determined in part by the acoustics of Orford Church, where they were first performed. In *Curlew River,* Britten and his librettist, William Plomer, moved a No play, *Sumida River,* from Japan to Suffolk. In *Albert Herring,* he and his librettist, Eric Crozier, moved a Maupassant story, "Le Rosier de Mme. Husson," across the Channel to an imaginary Loxford, which seems to correspond to the real Woodbridge, a small Suffolk town not far from Aldeburgh. (It was from Woodbridge, one is told, that a real Mrs. Herring, who kept a greengrocer's shop, wrote to the authors to protest that she didn't really treat her son badly.) They also changed the ending of the tale. Maupassant's Isidore is crowned with roses, and Britten's Albert is crowned May King, because no virtuous girl can be found for the feminine title. Isidore goes off on a week's debauch in Paris, spends all his prize money, returns to become a hopeless drunkard, and dies in a fit of delirium tremens. Albert pedals off to Ipswich, a town with rather more limited possibilities of sin, where he spends only a night away and only three pounds of his 25-pound prize. Isidore is ruined by his coronation. Albert is saved. He had been shy, bullied, and something of a booby; he returns confident, at ease with himself and with life, quite ready to stand up to Mum, and even to Lady Billows, the formidable local tyrant. *Albert Herring* is the happy counterpart, the bright verso, of *Peter Grimes*, which preceded it by two years. In *Grimes*, a tragedy, the hero is destroyed by the forces of convention ranged against him and by his inability either to come to terms with or to conquer them; in *Herring*, a comedy, the hero wins. Almost all Britten's protagonists pose a question that runs through *Grimes* as a musical motif: "What harbour shelters peace? ... What harbour can embrace terrors and tragedies?" Grimes, Owen Wingrave, and Gustav von Aschenbach can find an answer only in death; Albert, like the Three Holy Children and the Prodigal Son, is fortunate enough to find an answer in life. When he considers the stars, he echoes Grimes in both verbal and musical imagery. Grimes sang, "But if the horoscope's bewildering, like flashing turmoil of a shoal of herring, who can turn skies back and begin again?" To similar music, Albert, eschewing an eponymous simile, sings, "Embrace till stars spin round like Catherine-wheels." Albert's central monologue, with its chains of distorted reminiscences and free-association musings on his life, is another version of Grimes's mad scene. Its climax—"The tide will turn, the sun will set"—is utterly serious and utterly Grimesian.

It is sometimes forgotten that few of Britten's operas after *Grimes* were greeted with full, generous praise—that acclaim for them was slow to come. "Opinion is divided about *Albert Herring*," says the 1954 Grove; and the author of the entry, who was the critic of the London *Times*, often made it clear on which side of the division his influential opinion fell. It was nearly twenty years before it was generally discovered that there is more to *Albert Herring* than entertaining caricatures and a comedy with some poignant—and some tiresome—touches; the early presentations of the piece stressed its jokiness. But, just as Colin Davis and Jon Vickers, at the Metropolitan and at Covent Garden, showed *Peter Grimes* to be a more violent and disturbing opera than had been apparent at earlier performances, and rather as later productions of Henze's *Elegy for Young Lovers* and *The Young Lord* brought to the surface a fierceness that was but latent in the first, good-humored presentations, so later directors have revealed that *Albert Herring*, beneath all the charm and the coziness, has a tough, resilient core. In 1966, Anthony Besch staged for Scottish Opera a production of the work which dug beneath the larky humors of the libretto to lay bare the psychological situation beneath. That *Herring* turned on a knife-edge between comedy and tragedy. The pressures on Albert were like those on Janáček's Kát'a Kabanová. They might easily have destroyed him, as they did her. It was only luck—Sid's prank of lacing the lemonade with rum—that saved him. (The unexpected forms in which salvation may come constitute another recurrent Britten theme—but one best discussed in connection with *Billy Budd,* due at the Met next season.) Four years later, at the Wexford Festival, Michael Geliot went further—too far, in fact—and staged a harsh, angry version of the comedy. There was no affectionate parody in the portrayal of Lady Billows. She was ogress through and through, a sinister symbol of the conservative, repressive forces in English society. This cannot have been Britten's conscious view of her, but it is a possible view of the character he created. And the same year, in *Owen Wingrave,* he was creating Lady Billows's dark counterpart—the equally formidable, equally destructive, and not at all amusing Miss Wingrave. (Scarcely by coincidence, Miss Wingrave was composed for Sylvia Fisher, who had succeeded Joan Cross as the foremost interpreter of Lady B.)

It is perfectly possible to find in *Albert Herring* an allegory of the new, Socialist Britain breaking joyously from fetters of tradition, superstition, and unthinking conservatism. It is also possible to "read" it in another way. It has often been suggested that Grimes's inner struggle—like Claggart's and like Captain Vere's in *Billy Budd*—is against a homosexuality that neither he nor, for that matter, his creator is consciously aware of. (Not often suggested in print, however: I touched on the subject in a note for the New York City Opera *Herring,* in 1971; Philip Brett dealt with it in a thoughtful article in *The Musical Times* for last December.) Similarly, Albert can be considered an apt symbol for someone "coming out." Such interpretations are not necessarily untrue (they are among the things that the opera could be about), but they are unnecessarily restrictive and specific. *Albert Herring,* like *Peter Grimes,* is at once a particular drama, held strictly and artistically within the bounds of its period and topographical frame, and a presentation of a general human plight—that of an outsider at odds (for whatever reason) with those around him, trying to find a way to be accepted by them and at ease with himself. Like all the best comedies, it is based on a real and recognizable predicament. The allegory is of varied applicability to the thought and experience of its spectators. Moreover, *Herring* is a work that, again like *Grimes,* has grown from its local, particular sources to be enjoyed the world over, and one whose characters, independent now of their first performers, can be illumined by many different interpretations.

The Opera Theatre of St. Louis staged *Albert Herring* two years ago, and this season revived it. The production, directed by Lou Galterio, maintained a well-nigh perfect balance between seriousness and comedy. There were a few social solecisms—the mayor, chewing on a cheroot, became a sheriff; the children adopted stage-Cockney accents and demeanor; men kept their hats on when they shouldn't have—but there were no mistakes in characterization. It was a tender, loving, and musically sensitive presentation, executed in fine detail. And in the protagonist, James Hoback, it had the best Albert yet, one who looked right, sang right, did all things right. The young tenor showed more than a touch of the genius that can give life and light to every gesture and every inflection of an operatic portrayal. Whenever he was on the stage, one watched and listened intently—and felt and understood. The way *he* listened when others were singing made their music more vivid. It was not at all a self-seeking or look-how-well-I-do-it kind of performance; its greatness lay in his quick yet quiet comprehension of what every phrase could mean and in his vivid yet unobtrusive projection. The not inconsiderable vocal difficulties of a role tailored for the young Pears had been solved, and not even Pears himself sang Albert so well. The dramatic difficulties had been faced and mastered. There is no ready explanation of how Albert's transformation and liberation were achieved by, in his words, "a night that was a nightmare example of drunkenness, and dirt, and worse." No ready verbal explanation, that is—but, as often happens in operas where the libretto is ambiguous or elliptical (the close of *Götterdämmerung* is a celebrated example), music can supply what is missing in the textual argument. The trouble with that assertion is that the point cannot be demonstrated in words. By his delivery of the *lento e tranquillo* phrases ("It seems as clear as clear can be . . .") in Albert's first monologue, Mr. Hoback, prepared us for the well-adjusted, capable youth revealed at last in the thrice-sung *amabile grazioso* phrase ("And I'm more than grateful to you all . . .") of his last monologue. With the four notes of "That'll do, Mum!" and perfectly judged gesture and expression in which tenderness and resolution were combined, he seemed to convey all the keen, complicated emotions of the moment when a son breaks the apron strings.

Pauline Tinsley was Lady Billows. She was grand, dignified, and imposing. She did not guy the role; like a good comedienne, she took herself very seriously. But she did not sing the music quite fully enough. Evelyn Petros was Nancy, one of the most likable, unaffected characters in all opera, and was excellent. Stephen Dickson gave Sid an acceptable touch of cocky vulgarity. Judith Christin as Mrs. Herring, David Ward as Police Superintendent Budd, and Dale Moore as the Vicar provided precise, cleverly observed performances. So did Elizabeth Pruett as Miss Wordsworth and Joyce Gerber as Florence, but their words were not always clear. John Kasarda's sets and Dona Granata's costumes were attractive and appropriate. John Moriarty conducted with a sure feeling for the *Falstaff*-like quality that *Herring* has of being able to express in a few phrases—even in a single phrase—what elsewhere might be the matter of a full-scale aria. The orchestra, members of the St. Louis Symphony, played well.

After the close of the main season, a special performance was given for television. (At regular performances, there was none of the camera distraction that Charleston audiences complained of at one *Vanessa* there, or of the special television lighting that sometimes spoils Met shows.) WNET and the BBC collaborated to catch this *Herring* for broadcast through America (in

August) and Europe. It must be difficult to catch on a small screen enough of this ensemble performance, alive and alert in every detail on the stage. When Sid and Nancy were singing at one side of the stage, Albert listening at the other deserved equal attention. I hope enough has been caught to show all the world what good work is being done in St. Louis.

Britten's last major composition, his Third String Quartet, Op. 94, was given its first American performances earlier this season at two recitals of the Chamber Music Society of Lincoln Center; the second of them was taped and later broadcast by WNCN. (After the quartet, Britten completed only some folk-song arrangements and the brief "Welcome Ode" that greeted Queen Elizabeth on her Jubilee visit to Ipswich, in 1977.) The quartet had its first performance, in Aldeburgh, on December 19, 1976, fifteen days after the composer's death. The players, as in New York, were the Amadeus Quartet; the piece was written for them. The quartet, in five movements, is laid out in a symmetrical plan, with a slow movement at its center. Two scherzos, one "very fast" and the other "fast—*con fuoco,*" flank it; the first movement and the finale move at a moderate, flowing pace. It is hardly being wise only after the event to discern in the piece a valedictory tone. The finale, headed "Recitative and Passacaglia," is subtitled "La Serenissima," which is how Venice is hailed in Britten's opera *Death in Venice.* The Third Quartet is in some sense a parergon to *Death in Venice,* rather as the Second Quartet (1945) was to *Peter Grimes.* The finale, like so much of Britten's music, presents an image of the ever-changing yet essentially unchanging sea in whose quiet depths, "away from tidal waves, away from storm," Grimes and Budd find their sheltering harbor. In the quartet, not wave motion, which lends itself so readily to musical transcription, is pictured but a tranquil swell and the contrast between a moving surface and the still profundities. The basic passacaglia theme is an alternation between E and F-sharp, oscillating and then climbing to G-sharp, oscillating and then falling to D-natural. Above it, another oscillating theme moves slightly more swiftly, sounds an untroubled E major, but then falls to D-natural at the moment that the passacaglia theme does. This is not the Suffolk sea of *Peter Grimes.* It is something closer to Plato's "vast sea of beauty," on which Gustav von Aschenbach at the moment of death embarks—summoned thither, it seems to him, by the beautiful messenger standing at its edge. Yet it is not quite tranquil, not quite "serenissima." Although in the long final chord the second and first violins play a consonant E and G-sharp, the cello has fallen to the D-natural, and the viola plays a middle C-sharp. Britten's last word is not untroubled. This is a poignant envoy.

The writing in the earlier movements is spare, even terse. The first movement, "Duets," has a nagging, nudging opposition of repeated-note themes a tone apart as first subject, and a lyrical melody, opening with a rising sixth, as second subject. In the second movement, "Ostinato," a flying fig-

ure leaping upward or downward by sevenths appears (in some form) in almost every measure. The slow movement, "Solo," is a rhapsody for the first
violin—a long, musing, Shostakovich-like melody sung over, in turn, a slow
A-flat arpeggio from the cello, a slow F-major arpeggio from the viola, a
slow A-major arpeggio from the second violin. The harmonic progression
is reversed in some central bars of busy strumming, and then the solo
continues, "smooth and calm," while the other instruments climb slowly, in
C major, to a sustained high E. The second scherzo, "Burlesque," recalls
another Shostakovich vein with its scraps of trite "popular" melody, rhythmically insistent but metrically teasing. Accompanied recitative, passing
from player to player, leads into the quiet, slow pulsations and soft, full
texture of the finale. The ear grasps the piece as a whole, and the passacaglia
as a fulfillment of the earlier movements; study of the score (which is published in pocket format by Faber/G. Schirmer) reveals the detailed motivic
relationships.

In April, the American Friends of the Aldeburgh Festival and the Oratorio
Society of New York joined to celebrate Britten's life and work in a Carnegie
Hall concert. The first half was the Mozart Requiem. Then Janet Baker sang
the American première of *Phaedra*, the solo cantata that Britten wrote for
her in 1975—speeches from the Robert Lowell translation of Racine's play
set as a powerful, passionate sequence of recitatives and arias. The concert
closed with the *Spring Symphony*, which Britten composed in 1949 because,
in the words of Grove, "he believed that some more positive evangel of joy
should be used to overcome the strain and discouragement of the time." Its
bright message of joy, of delight in the spring's return, raising spirits in both
town and country, is unfaded. The music is copious, and abounds in exuberant, ingenious, unforced strokes of instrumentation and counterpoint.

  The Britten memorial concert that the American Friends presented last
year in St. Thomas Church, on Fifth Avenue, has been preserved on a two-
record album (Hessound S-1001–02). The program is a retrospective of Britten's choral music, from the *Hymn to St. Cecilia* (1942) to *Sacred and Profane*
(1975), eight medieval lyrics set for unaccompanied voices. Those works are
sung by the Yale Concert Choir. The boys of St. Thomas Choir sing the Missa
Brevis (1959) and join with the Manhattan Chorus in *Voices for Today* (1965),
a United Nations anthem. All sing together in "The spacious firmament on
high," the finale of *Noye's Fludde*—Addison's hymn and Tallis's noble canonic melody in an arrangement by Britten that fills a large space with glorious sound. The recording successfully captures the atmosphere of a particular, and moving, occasion in a particular place. Another recorded performance of *Sacred and Profane* appears on London OS 26527, which also
includes Janet Baker's wonderful singing of *Phaedra*.

. . .

I had hoped to write about Schubert this week. Carnegie Hall presented a five-day "Schubert Fest," at which the eight symphonies were played by the American Symphony, under Sergiu Comissiona. Before each concert there was chamber music; after it, a lieder recital. I went to the first two days and then gave up. The symphonies were woefully underrehearsed. Schubert was ill served.

August 3, 1978

PART II

1978–1979

Landmarks

In London this summer, I saw, night after night, faces familiar from the Lincoln Center foyers. It was not surprising, for there was much to attract any eager operagoer. Although on any day of July only one of the two major companies was playing (the Royal Opera ended its 1977–78 season on July 27; the next day, the English National Opera opened its 1978–79 season), in and around the capital some thirty different operas could be heard during the month, and they included Monteverdi's *Orfeo* and *Ulisse* (done by the Kent Opera), Rameau's *Hippolyte et Aricie* at Covent Garden, Handel's *Orlando*, Verdi's unrevised *Macbeth*, four of Mozart's operas, two of Stravinsky's, and three of Britten's. Also *Lucrezia Borgia, Parsifal,* and Nicolai's *Merry Wives.* Over the air, the BBC offered about a dozen more operas, among them Luigi Ricci's *La serva e l'ussero* and Debussy's *La Chute de la maison Usher,* in a longer version than we have heard in America. August was scarcely less busy; some of the rarities were Marc-Antoine Charpentier's *Médée* and Chabrier's *Gwendoline* in radio performances, and Schoenberg's *Die glückliche Hand* and Rameau's *Les Boréades* at the Proms. Janet Baker sang Gluck's Orpheus. The English National staged Weill's *Seven Deadly Sins.* At the Edinburgh Festival, crossing into September, there were *Carmen* (a revival of the Berganza-Abbado performance I reviewed last year), *Pelléas,* Monteverdi's three operas (done by the Zurich Opera), *Kát'a Kabanová,* Luigi Nono's *Al gran sole carico d'amore,* and Peter Maxwell Davies's *Le Jongleur de Notre Dame.* The Welsh National Opera began the new season with Janáček's *The Makropulos Affair,* and the Royal Opera with *The Ring.*

At Glyndebourne, the new productions were both of Mozart. *Così fan tutte* completed a Mozart–Da Ponte trio directed by Peter Hall. (His *Figaro* first appeared five years ago. Last year, there was *Don Giovanni;* it was revived this year, and Brent Ellis was admired in the title role.) Lilli Lehmann in her autobiography regrets that every single movement of the Leporello, Andrés de Segurola, in her Salzburg production of *Don Giovanni* in 1910 was not filmed, to preserve for posterity a performance not stock or clowned but based upon "observation of human character." Happily, Hall's *Figaro, Giovanni,* and *Così* are preserved (the first two by Southern Television, *Così* by the BBC)—music and movement together, as was not possible in 1910. Music and movement are as one in these three productions, which have made manifest more freshly, more precisely than any others I have seen what is so often written about Mozart's miraculous insight into the workings of the human heart. In *Così,* all the stale, standard jokes—Alfonso's "Morti [pause for reaction and laughter] non sono," a Despina who brandishes an outsize magnet, a Ferrando who yells coloratura in the first finale and has to be shushed—are banished. The easy adventitious laughs are forgone. Everyone behaves like a real person; the suitors' and Despina's disguises are believable; "observation of human character" determines each movement and each inflection. Exceptional in an age of directorial vanity and foolishness, Hall asks not "What can I do to be new, different, and surprising?" but "What did Mozart do?" The orchestra, he says, dictates his direction, and the London Philharmonic under Bernard Haitink, in superb form, gave no false instructions. Hall has an extraordinary way of reconciling realism and convention; he makes it seem the most natural thing in the world for someone to embark on an aria. The listener feels the harmonic tensions of the score as emotional tensions, and in the finale holds his breath through the whirl of keys and dramatic crises until C major returns. There was firm, simple, and very attractive scenery by John Bury. Bozena Betley sang Fiordiligi with exquisite phrasing and line. Maria Ewing, making her British début, was an irresistibly impulsive, credible Dorabella. Max-René Cosotti was a lively Ferrando, and Håkan Hagegård a bonny Guglielmo. (In Act I, Guglielmo sang the extended display aria "Rivolgete" in place of "Non siate ritrosi"—not recommended for general use, but very enjoyable to hear on occasion. In the finale, measures 67–124, usually omitted, were reinstated. In fact, this was the fullest *Così* I have ever encountered in a theatre.) Nan Christie was a lively Despina, and Stafford Dean a wise, witty Don Alfonso. There have been fuller-voiced Fiordiligis, more mellifluous Ferrandos, neater Despinas in our time—but never, I'll wager, a whole *Così* so honest, sensitive, direct, stylish, and truthfully "Mozartian" in all its details.

Glyndebourne's new *Zauberflöte* was less wonderful. David Hockney's designs, which received much advance publicity, were distinguished and pretty, but as scenery they proved undramatic. Their effect was slight—merely decorative—and the strength of the opera was lost. John Cox's direction was similarly lightweight: at the start of Act II, to Mozart's solemn music, the Priests assembled informally and squatted down as if for a Glyndebourne picnic. One does not want the *Flute* to be heavy; the English National version (a 1975 production, directed by Anthony Besch, designed by John Stoddart, and revived to open the new season) showed how it should combine entertaining spectacle, simple jollity, and mysterious grandeur. At Glyndebourne, Haitink's conducting showed that, too (there is pageantry in the score), and showed up the staging as insubstantial. I heard a well-nigh ideal Pamina, Felicity Lott, and a brave, forthright Tamino, Leo Goeke.

Lott, Goeke, and Samuel Ramey led the cast of a *Rake's Progress* revival—a production in which Hockney's elegantly inventive designs, Cox's clever production, and Haitink's alert, lucid conducting *are* in perfect balance. *La Bohème* introduced two young American sopranos to Europe, but neither of them—Linda Zoghby as Mimì, Ashley Putnam as Musetta—made much impression. The honors of the evening went to an Italian débutant, Alberto Cupido, a Rodolfo whose fresh flow of bright, lyrical tone and forward, limpid words recalled Pavarotti's British début in the role, fifteen years ago. Cox's direction was weak in characterization, fussy in detail, and sometimes absurd: the toy seller Parpignol became a Messenger of Death, crying his wares in an eerie green spotlight on a suddenly darkened stage. But the director, the artists, and the conductor, Nicola Rescigno, get high marks for having insured, by timing and inflection, that the sequence of "Che gelida manina . . . Mi chiamano Mimì . . . O soave fanciulla" would flow uninterrupted by applause.

Hippolyte, Rameau's first grand opera, was the final presentation of Lina Lalandi's glorious English Bach Festival, which does not limit its activities to England and to Bach but also visits Versailles and this year did Handel's *Rinaldo*, a divertissement from Rameau's *La Princesse de Navarre*, and the first modern revivals of Handel's *Terpsicore* (1734) and Vivaldi's *Griselda* (1735). In recent years, Miss Lalandi has been building a baroque operatic troupe in which players of authentic instruments are matched by singers, directed by the American scholar Dene Barnett, who seek to pose and gesture as Rameau's singers did, and by dancers, directed by Belinda Quirey and Michael Holmes, who seek to move as Rameau's dancers did. The designs for her resplendent wardrobe are by René-Louis Boquet, who worked for Louis XV. She cannot yet run to baroque stage machinery: in Versailles the royal theatre has a permanent eighteenth-century setting, and in London the Royal Opera's *Ballo in maschera* ballroom was used for *Hippolyte*. Covent Garden, built in 1858 to house nineteenth-century opera, proved slightly too large for the presentation. *Hippolyte* seems to have made more of an effect in Versailles, where singers, players, and audience are all in one unified acoustical space and projection is easier. The French hailed the show as a revelation. In London, it was enthralling to watch the quick, disciplined passions of Rameau's music incisively defined by the actors, and to see the rhythms and patterns of his dances take form in space. Miss Lalandi needs a stronger musical director than Jean-Claude Malgoire, who led some coarse, out-of-tune instrumental playing. Some of her singers have still to master both telling French declamation and confidence in the striking of extravagant attitudes. This "authentic" *Hippolyte* complemented rather than eclipsed the "unauthentic" modern production, with Janet Baker as Phaedra, that provided my introduction to the great opera thirteen years ago. But it was a landmark in our age's excited discovery of baroque opera—the first production of its kind, and a splendid one.

Another landmark has been the discovery of *Les Boréades*, Rameau's last opera. He died, in 1764, while it was in rehearsal at the Opéra. The work was abandoned and remained unknown for two centuries—unedited until in 1972 M. Térey-Smith submitted a critical score for a University of Rochester doctorate, and unheard until in 1975 John Eliot Gardiner, with his Monteverdi Choir and Orchestra, brought it to performance, in his own edition. (The Choir, formed in Cambridge in 1965, has few rivals in the vivid performance of large-scale seventeenth- and eighteenth-century scores. Its account of Handel's "Dixit" and Purcell's "Welcome, welcome glorious morn" during the City of London Festival was another musical high point of London's summer.) Rameau, like Mozart, tempts his listeners to declare that the most recently heard of his operas is the greatest of all. *Hippolyte*, the first of his *tragédies*, is perhaps the grandest. *Castor* the most affecting, and *Dardanus* the most fanciful. (I have never heard *Zoroastre*. I wish the Juilliard would do the piece: it has the theatre, the musicians, the dancers, and in Albert Fuller and Wendy Hilton two enthusiasts to direct and inspire their work.) *Les Boréades*, composed when Rameau was eighty-one, seems to comprehend all their merits, and, in addition, a vein of high spirits and fecund invention is explored with new mastery. One listens with mounting astonishment and rapture. There are numbers as sensuously beautiful as any Rameau wrote. And there is a Gluckian feeling for drama-in-music (*Orfeo* was published, in Paris, in the year of *Les Boréades*), for continuity, contrast, and cumulative form, which makes *Les Boréades*, so to speak, Rameau's *Otello* and *Falstaff* in one. Instrumentally, Gardiner celebrates a practical marriage between musical competence and musical authenticity. Modern fiddles are played on by eighteenth-century bows, with eighteenth-century bowing; conical-bore flutes and boxwood C-clarinets are used when they are available. The stars of the Prom performance were the tenor Paul Elliott, a bright, elegant, and affecting Abaris, and the French soprano Anne-Marie Rodde, as Sémire. (Miss Rodde also shone in *Hippolyte*, and as a lieder singer in one of the BBC's almost daily recitals.) Eiddwen Harrhy, Jennifer Smith, Marilyn Hill Smith, Carolyn Watkinson, Ian Caley, Ian Caddy, and Stephen Varcoe are other names to note in the corps of young British singers schooled and increasingly experienced in the execution of eighteenth-century music.

The last new production of the Royal Opera's 1977–78 season was of Verdi's *Luisa Miller*, unheard at Covent Garden since 1874, when Patti sang it. It was directed and designed plainly, rather dully, by Filippo Sanjust. The Miller home was acceptable; the castle scenes were in stark monochrome. Katia Ricciarelli was sensitive and touching in the title role, but she cannot open out on a big, swelling phrase. (Rosa Ponselle, who certainly could, reestablished the opera in our century.) Pavarotti sang the first Rodolfos; I heard José Carreras. His Verdi heroes—Jacopo Foscari, Corrado, Alfredo, Riccardo, Don Carlos—all come out much the same, cast in a mold of generalized ardor, in a way that is, however, always a pleasure. Lorin Maazel conducted with crude, bright emphasis. Then *Pelléas* and *Norma* were revived. The former had a subtle, arresting Mélisande in Anne Howells, a magnificent Pelléas in Thomas Allen, a vigorous Golaud in Thomas Stewart, and strong, beautiful orchestral playing under Colin Davis. Two prima donnas quarreled over *Norma*. Montserrat Caballé arrived wanting to sing her big duet with Adalgisa down a tone (the common transposition; on a blank staff of Bellini's autograph there is already sketched a way of effecting it). Grace Bumbry, the Adalgisa, wanted to sing it in the original keys. A compromise was reached by which Caballé got her way for five of the eight performances and then ceded the title role to Bumbry for the last three. Josephine Veasey stepped in as Adalgisa for the last two Caballé performances—while Bumbry prepared for her elevation—and continued in the part, competently but unremarkably, to the end of the run. Bumbry, as Norma, also chose the low keys for the duet—but now, of course, she had the upper line in it. (Both ladies sang "Casta Diva" down in F.) With Caballé in the title role, the best seats cost seventeen pounds fifty (thirty-five dollars); with Bumbry, only fifteen pounds. But Bumbry was the better Norma. Caballé on her opening night was often strident, uneven, and perfunctory. Of both Adalgisa and Norma, Bumbry gave serious, carefully studied interpretations. Coloratura—as Hanslick remarked in his account of Lilli Lehmann's Norma—"was never a coquettish intrusion but remained noble, serious, subordinate to the situation." But her timbre was not unfailingly pure and beautiful. There was a rough, coarse Pollione, Pedro Lavirgen; a threadbare Oroveso, David Ward; and a routine conductor, Jesús López-Cobos.

The first month of the Royal Opera's new season was devoted solely to three cycles of *The Ring*. The show should have been carefully rehearsed. Yet at the first *Rheingold* and *Walküre*—all I caught of it—the scene changes made a racket and the scene shifters were visible. That *might* just have been the deliberate intention of the director, Götz Friedrich—to reinforce his assertion that the settings of the *Ring* action are not mythical landscapes, not nineteenth-century factories and boardrooms, not any places of today or tomorrow, but precisely the boards of the theatre on which the cycle is being performed. But what it suggested was that Sieglinde had a butler and footmen to lay her supper table. The Covent Garden *Ring*, designed by Josef Svoboda, is a stunning piece of stage engineering. An enormous square platform supported on a single piston fills the stage. It can revolve, sway, heave, slant in any direction to create vertiginous aeries. Its louvred upper surface can suddenly flip open, completely or in selected strips, to create a giant staircase, leading toward Valhalla. Its mirrored underside reflects the Rhine bed and the deep pits of Nibelheim. During preludes and symphonic interludes, it is put through its paces to divert us. It serves in spectacular fashion to illustrate Friedrich's tendentious commentary on how *The Ring* might be performed, but it does not serve Wagner's work well. The cast was largely that of Bayreuth: Gwyneth Jones (Brünnhilde), Donald McIntyre (Wotan), Jean Cox (Siegfried), Peter Hofmann (Siegmund), etc. But the singers appeared at a disadvantage. Friedrich's personal dislike of the Gods—his Froh is a mincing queen, his Donner a seedy dodderer, his Loge a cheeky house-boy—inhibits them from expressing much. The Wotan of *Das Rheingold* is concealed behind a half-mask; the Wotan of *Die Walküre* is a *Gauleiter,* and the Brünnhilde a metallic robot. Only Hunding, hailed in Friedrich's program note as "the first 'real' man," seems to win his approval, and in the person and voice of Aage Haugland—the first "real," majestically commanding Wagnerian voice to be heard in the cycle—Hunding was certainly the hero of the show. Colin Davis's conducting had lost some of the confidence and conviction it had two years ago.

In our age of directorial vanity and foolishness, from which Wagner has been the chief sufferer, the Metropolitan *Tannhäuser,* directed by Otto Schenk and designed by Günther Schneider-Siemssen, shines out as a beacon of good sense, romance, beauty, expressiveness, and concern for the composer's intentions. It was revived last week to open the 1978–79 season. The orchestral playing, under James Levine, was richer than any I heard in Europe's theatres this summer. There were a new Elisabeth, Venus, Tannhäuser, and Hermann. Teresa Zylis-Gara's heroine was impetuous yet dignified, admirably conceived. Her German was not quite sharp cut, and since the voice was sometimes slow to "sound," sustained notes tended to become swells, and the Prayer lost impetus. But her tone was fresh and full, and the performance as a whole was very pleasing. Tatiana Troyanos's Venus was roundly voiced, not quite incisively enough declaimed. There are few Tannhäusers around today, and when James McCracken fell out the Met was lucky to get Richard Cassilly. Although his tones sometimes develop an ugly snarl, his intellectual and dramatic command of the role is complete. Kurt Moll, in a Met début, as Hermann, sang with authority and grandeur. Bernd Weikl's Wolfram, apart from a few mispitched notes, was as nobly ardent as before, and Kathleen Battle's Shepherd was even more sweetly and truly sung. The choral sound was big and bold, if not quite as smooth and rich in tone as it has been. All in all, I doubt whether one could today hear Wagner's opera better sung and played than it was here. And I'm sure one could not see it better staged.

On the second night of the season, Britten's *Billy Budd,* directed by John Dexter, designed by William Dudley, and conducted by Raymond Leppard, joined the Metropolitan repertory. There is also a new production of the piece in San Francisco; I hope to see it, to see the Met version again, and then write about this important, arresting, and in some ways puzzling opera [page 230]. In brief, the Met performance is at once a spectacular show and a highly intelligent, cogent presentation of the dramatic conflicts—a successful and striking achievement, not to be missed. Peter Pears reassumes the role, Captain Vere, that he created twenty-seven years ago, and brings even greater subtlety to its portrayal than he did then. James Morris's extraordinary Claggart makes full sense of the part for the first time. On the opening night, Richard Stilwell had not yet quite got the measure of Billy. Leppard's conducting was eloquent.

. . .

The City Opera season opened with a run of Victor Herbert's operetta *Naughty Marietta*. The first new opera production of the season was of Giordano's *Andrea Chénier*. Formally, harmonically, emotionally, and in its political thinking, the work is all over the place—a sprawl of the ingredients that four years later Puccini tidied into *Tosca*. Full-blooded, committed singing of its principal numbers has kept it alive. The City Opera version, with Marilyn Zschau, Ermanno Mauro, and Richard Fredricks in the principal roles and Emerson Buckley as conductor, is a decent, straightforward account of the piece but contains little to stir the pulses. Nathaniel Merrill's direction and Robert O'Hearn's décor are plain, even bleak, in a way that might suit a serious French Revolution opera; *Chénier*, which treats the great issues as local color, needs rather more help than they give it.

October 2, 1978

Projection

Within six days last month, Zubin Mehta conducted four different programs with the Philharmonic: two in the regular subscription series and two as special benefit concerts. I missed the first of them (*Leonore* No. 3, Samuel Barber's new Third Essay, and Mahler's First Symphony). I heard the others—and still have no clear notion what kind of a conductor Mehta really is. The regular Thursday concert began with Webern's Six Pieces and included Varèse's *Intégrales*, and the Webern also opened the Sunday-afternoon benefit (at which Horowitz played Rakhmaninov's Third Concerto)—as if to declare from the start that our new music director, like his predecessor, intends to do twentieth-century classics as standard repertory. In fact, Boulez's and Mehta's favored fields overlap more than one might suppose. With the Los Angeles Philharmonic, Mehta has made good Varèse and Schoenberg records. Elliott Carter's Piano Concerto and a clutch of Messiaen appear on his later bills, and next week he is introducing to America Peter Maxwell Davies's hour-long new Symphony—a vast, romantic, and very beautiful composition, which was a great hit with London's Prom audience this summer and is formidably difficult to play.

Both the Webern and the Varèse were eloquently done. These were not like Boulez performances. Where Boulez would set out sounds carefully and exactly in time and space, Mehta sought to *project* them, to make the music shine out so that listeners would feel as well as perceive and understand it. In the Philharmonic's playing there was a more loving concern for expressive colors and for emotional phrasing than I have heard in a long time. Projection is what *Intégrales* requires; Varèse used the word when writing about the composition, and his "beams of sound" producing "the feeling akin to that aroused by beams of light sent forth by a powerful searchlight" were brightly emitted. There was also great vitality in the dance rhythms. The sense of dance in Varèse is often strong—a fierce dance, as of surging waves, of tree-tops tossed by a gale, sometimes of people who remain close to nature, not the dance of the theatre or the ballroom. He is a universal composer; his is the only Western music I have heard played in Persepolis and thought nei-ther unfitted to nor diminished by the immensity and antiquity of the place. Yet he is also the particular poet-in-sound of New York. It makes special sense to hear him here, and he can help listeners to apprehend the romance, the distortions, the pressures, and the challenges of his chosen city.

In each of the three programs, there was a piano concerto. On Thursday, it was Beethoven's Third, with the young Soviet-Israeli pianist Yefim Bronf-man as soloist. He gave a fluent but featureless performance. The fingers moved evenly, and the phrasing was shapely, but there was a lack of accent, impetus, musical verve. (By chance, there turned up on my desk the next day a new Angel recording of the piece, made by Sviatoslav Richter, Riccardo Muti, and the Philharmonia. Richter also adopts a gentle, unassertive ap-proach to the music, and shows that this is not incompatible with youthful high spirits and energy.) On Wednesday, at a pension fund benefit, Rudolf Serkin had played the "Emperor" with his wonted decisiveness and intensity. Some of the runs ran away with him. But he is still a musician who holds one intent on each of the themes and on all that happens to them. His interpreta-tion had a strength and a beauty that made one glad to be listening again to the familiar work and led one to follow it as if it were being created afresh.

I first heard Horowitz in 1951, playing Rakhmaninov's Third Concerto in London's Festival Hall, and then not again in person until he gave a recital in the Metropolitan Opera House in November 1974. Through the years, his playing of the twenty-four bars in simple octaves which open the concerto remained with me—a memory of magical piano sound to be treasured beside memories of Michelangeli's repeated notes in "Le Gibet" and his "Scarbo" flurries (in Ravel's *Gaspard de la nuit*), of Gieseking's crystalline trills and runs in the "Waldstein" finale, of Kempff's celestial twittering and chirrups in "St. Francis of Assisi Preaching to the Birds" (the first of Liszt's two *Leg-ends*), of the sonorities that Cortot, late in his career, could still draw from Debussy's "La Cathédrale engloutie." Every concertgoer, I imagine, amasses a similar little hoard of cherished sonic jewels that glow undimmed through the years—individual moments of intense aural delight, as distinct from whole interpretations that also prove unforgettable. They are garnered directly in the concert hall, not from records. The great pianists I grew up hearing regularly "live" were Fischer, Backhaus, Gieseking, Kempff, and

Serkin. Horowitz, that single concerto appearance apart, remained a sound on discs. Much of his repertory was not of the music that meant most to me; his Beethoven and Brahms were exotic to someone who revered Schnabel; and I found more poetry in Rakhmaninov's own recording of his Third Concerto. The 1974 re-encounter was disconcerting. Horowitz's playing was brilliant but mannered, with passages so boldly struck that at times the piano began to clatter. It was at the White House recital in February of this year that I fell completely under his spell. The opening work was Chopin's B-flat-minor Sonata. By the time the second subject was reached, I was unconscious of the exceptional surroundings and audience, and lost in a world of sounds that, as the recital proceeded, ranged from soft melodies stealing out like a benediction to thunderous quasiorchestral tuttis. From what was more a dream adventure than anything to which cool analysis can be applied, I recall, first, the extraordinary sense of "visible" sonorities: thick darkness that might slowly brighten or might be pierced by rays of tender light; wisps of fleeting cloud and mist; sudden, exquisite glitter; the finale of the Chopin sonata passing like a swift wind. Second, the clarity of voice against voice, the balance of color against color, making the piano seem not one instrument but many, from an aeolian harp breathed upon, not struck, to a Berliozian massed orchestra. Third, the free, plastic molding of the melodies. Horowitz played Chopin as if unaware of listeners—not a superfluous movement, not a trace of showmanship. Then, in a merry Rakhmaninov polka and his own *Carmen* fantasy, he allowed his wit and exuberance to bubble forth, irresistibly.

At a Carnegie Hall recital last March, he played Liszt's B-minor Sonata. A few months earlier, his new recording of the work had appeared, on RCA; he first recorded it in 1932. In January, he had played Rakhmaninov's Third Concerto with the Philharmonic and Ormandy; the performance (with some later retouching) has been issued on disc by RCA, and can be compared with his 1930 and 1951 versions. From RCA there has also come a long series—"The Horowitz Collection"—of recordings from the forties and fifties. I have been listening to him with mounting wonder, and the "new" Horowitz seems to me an even greater pianist than the old. In the words of a British colleague writing about the Liszt sonata, "In the new account there may be a volt or two less of manic electricity, but the current, in the main, has been refined, not calmed. There is greater depth of coloring, richness of subtle detail, and pointing; the movement is broader, at once grander and more intimate." So, too, with the Rakhmaninov concerto: this year's performances, with Ormandy and now with Mehta, revealed new delicacies of shading, in timbre and in rhythmic placing. After Horowitz, Berman sounds blunt, and Ashkenazy tame.

Mehta's contribution to the concertos was not noticeable. He accompanied. He didn't get in the way, but he played no positive part in what should be, if not contests, at any rate joint achievements. For classical music, he seems to favor rather thick, blended orchestral timbres, not luminous detail. In Beethoven's Third, the orchestra's playing was as devoid of sharp-cut incident as was Bronfman's. In the "Emperor," on the other hand, one had the curious sense that Serkin's mind was directing things even during the orchestra's long opening ritornello—communicating to the players as if by telepathy the initial shaping of the themes on which the soloist would later be discoursing. The development section was a true dialogue: Serkin retired to an accompanying, coloring role whenever the composer asked him to. Things were different in the Rakhmaninov. There is an extended episode in the intermezzo when clarinet and bassoon—joined later by flute and oboe—are the soloists and the piano's role is to shed a light sparkle around their singing. But the Philharmonic players remained in the background, content to accompany what should have been the accompaniment to their phrases.

The Wednesday concert began with the *Rienzi* overture and continued with excerpts from Prokofiev's *Romeo and Juliet*. The Thursday concert ended with Ravel's *La Valse*. In all of these, Mehta showed his ability to secure playing that is very loud and rich without being raucous. In all of them, he also puzzled me, as he often does, by his rhythms. His tempi are not eccentric; it is a matter of pulse and rubato. Just when I believe I am "with" him, have been persuaded by him to feel the progress of a composition as he does, he can hold back at a moment of climax and thus destroy the effect he has been building toward. Or else when everything seems to have been prepared for a slight broadening he will suddenly contradict the apparent implications of his own phrasing. To put it drastically, I found in these interpretations the oddest compound of the commonplace and the inexplicable. The account of Beethoven's Eighth Symphony which preceded Horowitz's concerto performance was merely commonplace: there was nothing in the utterance of the themes, the movements of the harmony, or the juxtapositions of timbres which made one want to listen. On the other hand, the orchestra is playing for Mehta with a will. And there *were* those memorable performances of the Webern and the Varèse.

October 9, 1978

Summer Retrospect

If Edinburgh's climate were better, its theatres more fully equipped, and its hotels less disagreeable, the Edinburgh Festival might have no rivals. Rudolf Bing's judgment was right when in 1947 he chose the northern capital as the place for a great annual international celebration of music, drama, dance—all the arts. The city—medieval, Adam neoclassical, and grandly Victorian—

is so romantically beautiful, substantial, picturesque, and various that simply to be there is a festival in itself. ("I walk about . . . feeling as though I am listening to *Figaro* from morning till night," Bernard Levin wrote this year.) On a fine day, it can seem the fairest town in the world, and beneath stormy skies the most dramatic. But there are many Edinburgh days when an even, gray, dampy light moves the soul to melancholy; then one is glad to enter the halls, theatres, and galleries. Three weeks are filled daylong and nightlong with the busy Festival program, and round those official offerings is a "fringe" woven by adventurous little troupes from all over the world. This year, there were some four hundred and fifty different fringe productions. The big art shows were of the Armand Hammer collection and of Giambologna's bronzes. The Chicago Symphony and the Dresden Staatskapelle headed a list of eight orchestras; Abbado, Boulez, Giulini, and Solti were among the conductors. The most important (though not the best-attended) event was the British première of Luigi Nono's second opera, *Al gran sole carico d'amore*, brought to Edinburgh by the Frankfurt Opera. *Al gran sole*, commissioned by La Scala, was first performed in Milan in 1975, and was revived there in a revised edition last February. Abbado conducted it (the score is dedicated to him and to the pianist Maurizio Pollini); the staging was by Yury Lyubimov and David Borovsky, the chief director and designer at Moscow's Taganka Theatre. The Frankfurt production was directed by Jürgen Flimm, designed by Karl-Ernst Herrmann, and conducted by Michael Gielen; in Edinburgh it was done in concert form, in the King's Theatre. The drama of the piece lies chiefly in its musical confrontations and contrasts, not in any conventional plot, and it came across strongly.

The title is a line of a Rimbaud poem, *Les Mains de Jeanne-Marie:* "Dark hands that summer tanned . . . they have paled, wondrous, in the great sun charged with love, on the bronze of the machine guns through a Paris in rebellion." A madrigal-like setting of the poem, in French, forms one "scene" of the opera. The libretto, the composer's own, is compiled from many sources, among them Marx, Lenin, Brecht, Cesare Pavese's "Deola" poems, popular revolutionary songs, and sayings of revolutionary leaders. As a prelude, soprano soloist and chorus proclaim first Che Guevara's "La belleza no está reñida con la revolución." It can stand as a motto for the piece and as a summary of the belief in which Nono has been composing some of the most sensuously beautiful and politically fervent scores of our day: "Beauty is not a denial of the revolution." In *Al gran sole*, he has sought and hymned the beauty of emotions that revolutions have brought forth in women. The basic setting of Act I is the Paris Commune of 1871. (Marx's declaration "The Paris of the workers, with its Commune, will be celebrated through eternity as the glorious herald of a new society" is also sung in the prelude.) The chief character in this act is Louise Michel, schoolmistress turned Communarde, but her spirited statements are intercut with some by the twentieth-century guerrilla Tania Bunke. Favre, Thiers, Bismarck, and the choruses take lines from Brecht's *The Days of the Commune*. The act ends with an ensemble setting of Lenin's "In different situations and in other conditions, the Russian revolutions of 1905 and 1917 continued the work of the Commune." Cool historians have questioned the correctness of that view. The 1871 Commune was an unmethodical muddle. But it has also been a continuing source of social and artistic inspiration, and Nono treats it as such here. Act II continues the tale in Russia in 1905: "Day after day, the siren howls in the oily, steamy air above the working-class suburb"—from the Gorky-Brecht *The Mother.* The Mother is followed by the prostitute Deola, bravely affirming that "life will be beautiful" so long as clouds keep moving above Turin. To scenes of industrial strife in Russia in 1905 and Turin in the 1940s and 1950s there is then added the attack on the Moncada Barracks, in Cuba, in 1953 (texts by Haydée Santamaria and Celia Sánchez). In the penultimate scene, the mourning of Vietnamese mothers (lines from actual letters) is followed by words of hope from prison, by Antonio Gramsci, Georgy Dimitrov, and Fidel Castro. The act is punctuated by episodes representing "the massing of the forces of oppression." In the finale, it seems at first that those forces have triumphed, but then the song they have crushed rises again and swells into a couplet from the Internationale: "No more slaves or masters! Up, let us continue the struggle!"

This politico-dramatic program, however morally admirable, would not be enough to insure merit for the music. But Nono's score is active and dramatic in itself, not merely illustrative. It does illustrate, as music readily can, such things as the crude massing of brute force, and opposition to it, in the form of snatches of revolutionary song. More subtly, it draws its listeners into a network of feelings about its central theme: the parts women have played in the social struggle, not just in their traditional roles as mothers, mourners, mistresses, helpmeets, and muses but as participants in the history of progressive thought, action, and emotion. In a program note, Nono contrasts his heroines with Violetta, and his opera with *La traviata.* Verdi's opera, he reminds us, is, among other things, a didactic piece: in the conflict of a prostitute with the society that destroys her, she is "on a higher moral plane than the society." But *La traviata* is "a self-contained story . . . the result of a historical situation," while in *Al gran sole* the prostitute "belongs to an enduring developmental process." The Russian Mother of Gorky and Brecht could also be a mother of the Turin strikers, and she sings again in the Cuban struggle. The Mother is an alto role. (The part was movingly sung in Edinburgh by Sona Cervena.) For all the other women, there is no simple voice-to-role identification. The songs of each are assigned to one or more of four high-soprano soloists, joined sometimes by ten women of a semichorus and by the women of the full chorus. The "Deola" poems are at the heart of the work. Pavese "is for me a kind of prism breaking light up into different colors," Nono writes. "And when Pavese's poems are put beside other texts, they take on a completely different light, and themselves cast a totally different light on the others." Pavese's lyricism, so to speak, plays upon the heroines' scenes taken from *The Days of the Commune*, from *The Mother*, and from history, and they, too, break into lyrical music. The work is tautly and potently constructed. It is composed for very large forces (several small male solo roles besides the major roles for women; semichorus of twenty; big full chorus; big orchestra; four-track electronic tape projected through the theatre) and employs a very wide range of textures and dynamics. Strongly staged, as, by all accounts, it was in Milan and in Frankfurt, it must be overwhelming. In Edinburgh, it made a great impression. The Frankfurt cast was led by two principal sopranos—Deborah Cook and June Card—able to sustain very high lines with uncommon sweetness and purity of tone. From all his performers, Gielen obtained an amazingly confident and eloquent account of the very difficult music, in which Nono's expressive use of voice against voice, timbre against timbre, and rhythm against rhythm is explored both on larger and on more exquisitely delicate scales than in previous compositions.

The Zurich Opera's celebrated Monteverdi "cycle," which is making the rounds of Europe (Hamburg, La Scala, etc.), came to Edinburgh. It consists of *Orfeo* (1607), which is a court opera, and *Il ritorno d'Ulisse in patria* (1641) and *L'incoronazione di Poppea* (1642), which were composed for public theatres—Monteverdi's three surviving operas—"arranged" and conducted by Nikolaus Harnoncourt; directed and designed, all three in the same basic set, by Jean-Pierre Ponnelle; and accompanied by a band of baroque instruments. I saw *Ulisse* and *Poppea*. The shows did Monteverdi no service and were deplorable in almost every way. Harnoncourt's latest "arrangements," which are even more questionable than those he has recorded, and are disfigured by cruel cuts, throw the focus of musical interest again and again on the orchestra pit. The final duet of *Poppea* emerged as a virtuoso two-recorder concerto with vocal backing. There was just one Italian in the casts—Maria Minetto, the Nurse in both operas. She had no more than a worn thread of a voice, but she was almost alone in declaiming the words as if they meant something. Many of the principal singers were dull and inexpressive (Ortrun Wenkel drooped through the part of Penelope like a pallid marionette); sometimes they had been grossly overdirected, to a point where Monteverdi's apparently surefire music made no effect. In *Ulisse*, the stringing-of-the-bow scene brought three pratfalls for Pisander; Irus made such a protracted meal of his big aria—jumping down at last into the pit to weep on Harnoncourt's shoulder—that all the simple fun of it was lost; Penelope and Ulysses celebrated their reunion by singing the final duet lying flat on the stage, heads where the prompter's box would have been had there been one. In *Poppea*, the cute little Cupid of the Prologue stayed onstage much of the time, as master of ceremonies; Seneca's disciples played their mourning chorus for laughs; the formidable Octavia became an absurd hennaed hag; and in the final duet Poppea sang "Pur ti miro . . . pur ti stringo" gazing at and pressing not Nero but Octavia's discarded crown. Ponnelle has been described as a director for whom too much is never quite enough. Sad that so much effort should have been put into these comic-strip perversions of operatic masterpieces! Monstrous, if the traveling circus should inhibit wide-spread appreciation of their greatness and persuade audiences that this is what Monteverdi is about!

This year is the fiftieth anniversary of Janáček's death. The Frankfurt Opera also brought to Edinburgh its new production of his *Kát'a Kabanová*. Once again, a meddling director—this time he was Volker Schlöndorff, better known as a movie maker—got between a composer and the intended effect of his piece. Janáček's Kát'a is a tragic heroine, destroyed by her own accept-ance of the harsh judgment passed on an adulteress by a bourgeois society. Everyone around her has in varying ways come to terms with it, learned to live with or evade it. Kát'a cannot. Schlöndorff imposes a different plot, about an elegant, neurotic Kát'a prey to sick, sexy imaginings. In the final scene, she steps out of her dress to sing the monologue and the duet with Boris in her shift, as a mad scene; Boris is reduced to a motionless apparition in a blue spotlight; the veristic dialogue makes little sense. There were other glosses. As Michael Ewans says in his *Janáček's Tragic Operas*, there is little doubt that Janáček brings down the first curtain of Act II on "the sadomaso-chistic prelude to lovemaking." Schlöndorff doesn't leave it as a prelude. To the end—whose extraordinary effect, unprecedented and unparalleled in opera, is so vividly described by Mr. Ewans—Schlöndorff adds a drunken Ti-chon, sloshing his schnapps over Kát'a's corpse, and a hostile crowd advanc-ing upon Kabanicha. Hildegard Behrens's Kát'a was clearly, sometimes lus-trously, sung. Kabanicha lay high for Sona Cervena. Gielen's conducting was keen. The other singing was routine German provincial.

Scottish Opera and the Welsh National Opera have joined forcces to produce a Janáček cycle. It began with *Jenůfa*. I traveled south from Edinburgh by way of Cardiff to catch the second co-production, *The Makropulos Affair*. Elisabeth Söderström was the heroine—intelligent, exact, clever in her han-dling of the first and second acts, but not quite ample enough of voice to fill the big utterances of the last. The direction—thoughtful, sensitive, and thoroughly musical—was by David Pountney, who established his Janáček credentials with Wexford's *Kát'a*, some years ago, and with the Welsh/Scot-tish *Jenůfa*. The sweet, touching Kristina was misplayed as a pert, feather-brained floozy, but otherwise the numerous smaller parts were accurately and vividly taken. Richard Armstrong's conducting was both delicate and impassioned.

And so to London, for the last week of the Proms. It began with a highly ac-complished and aptly incantatory performance of Stockhausen's *Stim-mung*—that "natural" chord on a fundamental B-flat sustained for some sev-enty-five minutes and enhanced by the chanting of magic names, by the recitation of short poems, by the adoption of rhythmic motifs that spread from member to member of the ensemble, by slow, subtle shifts of vowel color. The vocal sextet was Gregory Rose's Singcircle. Its performances of *Stimmung* are the first not to be based on those of the Collegium Vocale of Cologne, which created the work and recorded it. *Stimmung* is a piece that sounds ridiculous when described and yet proves enthralling in performance. The Singcircle believes in it, and hopes to sing it a hundred times; the Prom performance was its sixth. Stockhausen had his fiftieth birthday in August, and so there were articles and talks, and many of his works were done, four of them at the Proms. Leonard Bernstein was sixty that month, and George Rochberg was sixty in July; BBC concerts marked both anniversaries. There was much tercentenary Vivaldi; some bicentenary Thomas Arne and Fernando Sor; not enough centenary Franz Schreker; and sesquicentennial Schubert everywhere. Every day of this year, Radio 3's broadcasting ends with a Schubert song, and so most of my summer days were ended delightfully, often instructively. There is much to be said for focusing attention on a single Schubert song billed well in advance. If one doesn't know it, one can read the poem in preparation. The performances are culled from all ages of record history and from the BBC's own rich store of previous recitals on tape and disc. Sometimes the song chosen reflected the main musical event of the day—as when the "Lied des Orpheus" provided a late-night pendant to the Prom of Gluck's *Orfeo* sung by Janet Baker.

In summer, London devotes itself to festival. There were festivals everywhere. Festivals of old music, of new music, of British music, of Handel. Festivals in the City, in the Wigmore Hall, in the South Bank halls, and in Riverside Studios, the latest addition to London's arts centers (performing spaces, galleries, a restaurant, beside the Thames at Hammersmith). Festivals in St. John's, Smith Square, a beautiful baroque church by Thomas Archer; in Christ Church, Spitalfields, a baroque masterpiece by Hawksmoor; in St. Bartholomew's, Smithfield, a Norman priory. Meanwhile, the BBC relayed festivals from the rest of the country and from Europe. The biggest festival of all is the Proms: fifty-five concerts in eight weeks, given by twenty orchestras and eleven choirs—Boulez, Gielen, Haitink, Muti, and Solti among the conductors. Some highlights, apart from Rameau's *Les Boréades*, reviewed two weeks ago: the Rakhmaninov Vespers, in Westminster Cathedral, imaginatively interspersed with brass music by Barber, Ives, and Ruggles; Glyndebourne's *Così*, losing some stylishness but not its high spirits in the transfer from its home theatre; Liszt's long oratorio *Christus*, in what may have been its first complete performance since the composer himself abridged it (rightly, in my view) after he first heard it; Brian Ferneyhough's Missa Brevis (in St. Augustine's, Kilburn), an early and astonishingly beautiful composition by a composer long familiar on the avant-garde international scene but only recently come to general prominence in England—fiendishly difficult to sing, and brilliantly sung by the John Alldis Choir. And perhaps most exciting of all, Peter Maxwell Davies's new Symphony, conducted with passion, precision, and romance by Simon Rattle, the new young hero of the Prom audience. (His Stravinsky, Dvořák, Mozart, and Haydn were marvelously buoyant and musical.) The symphony is being played here by the Philharmonic this week.

October 16, 1978

Saved

The Metropolitan and the San Francisco productions of *Billy Budd* were complementary. Between them, they sustained a view long held by several of my friends but only recently mine, that *Billy Budd*, the sixth of Britten's fifteen operas, is musically the richest and most arresting of them all. Comparisons need not be odious: in brief, New York's version was scenically the more spectacular and emotionally the more romantic, while San Francisco's was musically in sharper focus—the clearest and keenest account of the opera I have ever heard. In both places, the conjunction of artists coming to the piece for the first time and artists who had long been associated with it resulted in performances of uncommon freshness, accuracy, and power. In New York, Captain Vere was sung by Peter Pears, who created the role, twenty-seven years ago, at Covent Garden; and Peter Glossop, a former Billy, played Mr. Redburn, his first lieutenant. In San Francisco, Vere was Richard Lewis, who has been singing the part since 1964; the director was Ande Anderson, who worked on the original production, with the composer, and has staged several of its revivals; and the designs derived from those John Piper created for the première. Outstanding among the new minds playing upon the piece and revealing new aspects of it were those of, in New York, James Morris, the Claggart, and, in San Francisco, David Atherton, who conducted, and Dale Duesing, the Billy.

The New York staging, directed by John Dexter and designed by William Dudley, is a big-house amplification of the version they put on in Hamburg in 1972. (That production, like the Met's, had Richard Stilwell in the title role.) It is based on quick, penetrating appreciation of the work itself, of the Herman Melville story on which it is based, and of differences between the story and the opera. Against a black backcloth and wings, H.M.S. *Indomitable* (the opera was composed before Harrison Hayford and Merton Sealts established a definitive text of Melville's tale, in which the vessel is named the *Bellipotent*) is shown in lateral cross-section. Individually or all at once, its levels can rise and fall to create the different settings of the drama—main deck and quarterdeck, captain's cabin spanning the ship from side to side, berth deck. For the chase at the start of Act II, the whole structure rises hugely to reveal four decks fully manned for battle, and the towering visual effect mirrors the mounting excitement of the music. An illusion of five decks is created for Billy's soliloquy, and he lies in irons on the lowest of them. Here the designer has possibly erred. His scene does suggest Melville's "levels so like the tiered galleries of a coal mine"—but Billy should be on the second of them, just below the luminous night on the spar deck. His gun-deck Gethsemane is the most beautiful of Melville's many allegorically charged prison scenes. The gun bays suggest side chapels of a cathedral, branching from "the long dim-vistaed broad aisle between the two batteries." Flickering splashes of dirty yellow light from two swinging battle lanterns pollute the pale moonshine that struggles in through the open ports. Lying amid the black machinery of war, Billy in his "white jumper and white duck trousers, each more or less soiled, dimly glimmered in the obscure light of the bay like a patch of discolored snow in early April lingering at some upland cave's black mouth." The snow will soon melt. Billy's perfect beauty will soon be no more. Already it is smutched by his "generous young heart's virgin experience of the diabolical incarnate and effective in some men": "The skeleton in the cheekbone at the point of its angle was just beginning delicately to be defined under the warm-tinted skin. In fervid hearts self-contained, some brief experiences devour our human tissue."

In this last work of Melville's, left uncompleted at his death, in 1891, whiteness and blackness are symbols held more closely to their traditional values than they were in *Moby Dick*, forty years earlier. But nothing in Melville is quite unambiguous, and after Billy's funeral the *Indomitable* sails on under light airs into a whiteness so bleak, so blank, unmarked by good or ill, that it seems more chilling in its indifference than even the terrible Whiteness of the Whale. "The circumambient air in the clearness of its serenity was like smooth white marble in the polished block not yet removed from the marble-dealer's yard."

Not an image, not a word in Melville is lightly or carelessly chosen. (Vere's name tells of truth and also of vacillation; *Bili* and *Budd* were appellations of the Celtic Apollo; to *clag* is to adhere as with the touch of pitch or a spider's web.) Nor is a note, timbre, or harmony in Britten's score. And so discussion of any detail in a thoughtful, sensitive performance of *Billy Budd* leads toward speculation about the nature and meaning of the work. The design of Mr. Dudley's set obviates the five mid-act curtains—two in Act I, three in Act II—that Britten specifies; the scenes change before our eyes. Between scenes, Mr. Dexter has caught the principal characters—one, two, or all three of them—in shafts of light, on levels and in attitudes that brilliantly represent the ambiguities and changing tensions of the drama: Vere alone on his knees, invoking Authority; Billy and Claggart on the starry deck, each destined to be the other's destroyer, one carefree and the other racked; Vere between Billy and Claggart, a man caught between a Bright Angel and Lucifer; Billy between Claggart and Vere, innocent victim of, on one side, a passion that envy has perverted to hate and, on the other, a temperate judgment that—too late—is warmed by love. Explicatory tableaux uncalled for by the creators of an opera are usually to be deplored, but these added tableaux are not merely explicatory; they are at once dramatic and disturbing in the right way. On the surface, *Billy Budd*—Melville's or Britten's—is a fable of diagrammatic simplicity. The plot can be told in a few sentences—such as these from E. M. Forster's 1927 lectures published as *Aspects of the Novel:*

> The scene is on a British man-of-war soon after the Mutiny at the Nore. . . . The hero, a young sailor, has goodness. . . . On the surface he is a pleasant, merry, rather insensitive lad, whose perfect physique is marred by one slight defect, a stammer, which finally destroys him. . . . Claggart, one of the petty officers, at once sees in him the enemy—his own enemy, for Claggart is evil. . . . He accuses Billy of trying to foment a mutiny. The charge is ridiculous, no one believes it, and yet it proves fatal. For when the boy is summoned to declare his innocence, he is so horrified that he cannot speak, his ludicrous stammer seizes him . . . and he knocks down his traducer, kills him, and has to be hanged.

Yet by the force of Melville's imaginative thought and by the force of his language, both drawing vitality from Shakespeare and Milton, the simple black-and-white fable explodes in a bewildering moral rainbow. And, as the author exclaims in the course of his tale, "who in the rainbow can draw the line where the violet tint ends and the orange tint begins?" *Billy Budd* is an unsettling opera to attend, and its power derives in the first place from Melville. To the writing desk on which Melville composed *Billy Budd* was attached the precept "Keep true to the dreams of thy youth." Those dreams were often terrible. In "Pierre, or, The Ambiguities," the tale of a nineteenth-century New York Hamlet, Melville observes how the trail of truth too far followed can lead to Hyperborean regions where "all objects are seen in a dubious, uncertain, and refracting light," to a barren pole, where the hitherto guiding compass points indifferently in all directions. No moral judgments are made in *Billy Budd*, but, in Forster's words, "Melville—after the initial roughness of his realism—reaches straight back into the universal, to a blackness and sadness so transcending our own that they are indistinguishable from glory." Such incandescent blackness is hard to distinguish from the whiteness that in *Moby Dick* strikes panic to the soul and in *Billy Budd* obliterates the temporal tragedy. In practical terms, one may regret the unrelieved blackness against which the drama is played at the Met; an unrelievedly white backcloth might serve as well—or as badly. What the opera needs (and received in San Francisco) is surely an evocation of the isolating sea, to define the *Indomitable* moving through night and days, through blackness and whiteness, as a "fragment of earth," and to affirm the important metaphor of the world in a man-of-war.

Forster's 1927 account of *Billy Budd* appears in a chapter titled "Prophecy." To illustrate that particular aspect of the novel, he cites Dostoyevsky,

Melville, D. H. Lawrence, and Emily Brontë—and "Melville is at the center of our picture." Hardy, "a philosopher and a great poet," is excluded, because "Hardy's novels . . . do not give out sounds"—whereas in Melville "we catch the song" even when "we cannot catch the words of the song." Here Forster is speaking specifically of *Moby Dick*, but what he says is true of *Billy Budd:* "As soon as we catch the song in it," the easy yarn "grows difficult and immensely important." More than twenty years later, when an operatic collaboration between Britten and Forster was proposed, Melville's *Billy Budd*—P. N. Furbank tells us in his Forster biography—occurred to both men almost simultaneously as the ideal subject. Forster was unversed in operatic writing; Eric Crozier, the librettist of Britten's *Albert Herring*, was co-opted to help with the stage mechanics. When he raised practical objections to the idea of an all-male opera, Britten and Forster swept them aside. The story filled some inner need in them. F. O. Matthiessen, at the close of the Melville section of his *American Renaissance* (1941), declared that "Melville could feel that the deepest need for rapaciously individualistic America was a radical affirmation of the heart." That chimes with Forster's famous remark "If I had to choose between betraying my country and betraying my friend, I hope I should have the guts to betray my country." Matthiessen says, "After all he had suffered, Melville could endure to the end in the belief that though good goes to defeat and death, its radiance can redeem life." That chimes with a belief proclaimed in many of Britten's works. It is a more optimistic reading of *Billy Budd* than mine, but is the reading expressed in the opera. Back in 1927, Forster wrote that in Melville, at last, "the balance righted itself, and he gave us harmony and temporary salvation." In the tale, Billy's death is signaled by a moment of temporary equilibrium—"The hull, deliberately recovering from the periodic roll to leeward, was just regaining an even keel when the last signal was given"—and is decked in the radiant imagery of redemption:

> At the same moment it chanced that the vapory fleece hanging low in the East was shot through with a soft glory as of the fleece of the Lamb of God seen in mystical vision. . . . Billy ascended; and, ascending, took the full rose of the dawn.

Britten and Forster seized on this theme and extended it. In Melville, Vere dies soon afterward, with Billy's name on his lips. In the opera, he lives on to become an old man, at peace with himself and the world, proclaiming that Billy "has saved me, and blessed me, and the love that passes understanding has come to me." It is a legitimate extension, perhaps, of the "salvation" implied by Melville's description and also by his bold stroke of sexual metaphor: when Billy was hanged, the customary spasm in the body was miraculously absent but, as if in mystic transference, Vere himself "stood erectly rigid as a musket." By Billy's sacrificial death Vere is saved, as Tannhäuser was saved by Elisabeth's, and Faust by Gretchen's. Forster gave up writing novels in 1924. He had protested "weariness of the only subject I both can and may treat—the love of men for women and vice versa." But Melville in the mid-nineteenth-century wrote fearlessly of passions in the all-male world he knew from his four years of seafaring, and at the end of the century—true to the dreams of his youth—he returned to that world. Of course, *Billy Budd* is not simply a homosexual yarn, but its imagery is strictly homoerotic. Billy is a glorious young Adam without an Eve. Claggart, a new Satan stirred by the sight of the paradise he cannot enter and is driven to destroy, sometimes watches the "cheerful sea-Hyperion" with feverish tears in his eyes and "a touch of soft yearning, as if [he] could even have loved Billy but for fate and ban." Even Captain Vere mentally strips Billy, as "a fine specimen of the genus *homo*, who in the nude might have posed for a statue of the young Adam before the Fall." For Melville, the tale continued his discoveries that *Lear, Hamlet,* and *Paradise Lost* were works relevant to life intensely lived on a whaler or a man-of-war, that he could treat again of their tremendous issues in terms of his own experience, and that he could reshape their high language to serve his expression. For more than thirty years (since *The Confidence Man,* in 1857), he had published no prose. Like his own John Marr, a sailor stranded in a humdrum world, he was thrown "more and more upon retrospective musings . . . lit by that aureola circling over any object of affections in the past, for reunion with which an imaginative heart passionately yearns."

Billy Budd is a distillation of themes, thoughts, images, and characters encountered in *Redburn, White-Jacket,* and *Moby Dick*. It began as the ballad soliloquy of a sailor condemned to death for inciting a mutiny. A prose introduction then told of Claggart, the master-of-arms who preferred the charge against an innocent Budd. In a further expansion, Captain Vere was added, to complete the allegory of Innocence, Evil, and Responsibility—of Adam before the Fall, the envious and destructive Tempter, and an inadequate man called on to play the part of all-powerful Judge. Melville's last revisions, it seems, were concerned with dramatizing what was formerly narrated, thus leaving readers to draw their own conclusions. Forster and Britten completed the process, but they also made some significant changes. Melville does not judge Vere; he shows him. In *The Confidence Man,* he had already observed how "the moderate man" can be "the invaluable understrapper of the wicked man"; in a sense, Vere completes Claggart's unfinished work of destruction. But Melville allows Vere powerful arguments—the strict letter of the Articles of War, the danger of mutiny—to justify his action in condemning Billy to death. Forster rejected those arguments. He did judge Melville's Vere, and determined "to rescue Vere from Melville." In the book, Vere plays prosecutor and, by his speeches, sways a drumhead court that is inclined to acquit Billy. In the opera, he plays Pilate. He is silent when Billy cries "Captain Vere, save me!" He refuses to take responsibility, and, to his officers' "Grant us your guidance," answers, "No. Do not ask me. I cannot. . . . Pronounce your verdict." It adds a new mystery of human behavior. It complicates the drama. And it leads to the peripeteia of Vere's aria "I accept their verdict. . . . Beauty, handsomeness, goodness, it is for me to destroy you." We move into a drama of redemption and salvation. The stage remains empty as Vere goes off to tell Billy of the sentence, while a sequence of thirty-four common chords, differently scored and spaced, mystically represents Melville's "sacrament . . . wherever under circumstances at all akin to those here attempted to be set forth two of great Nature's nobler order embrace." In performances, this bold and wonderful stroke is sometimes nervously handled. The Metropolitan conductor, Raymond Leppard, underplayed the passage; the chords slipped by too easily. In San Francisco, David Atherton was eloquent—each chord did sound like a new statement, the gleam of a new possibility, in some close, solemn argument—but the director diminished the force of the sequence by leaving Vere onstage for the first half of it.

The opera makes its deepest statements through harmony. Those chords resolve into the untroubled, lapping F major of Billy's gun-deck ballad, and they recur at its close: "I'm strong . . . And I'll stay strong." The very opening bars of the work—introducing Vere as an old man, musing on the great crisis of his life—present a B-flat/B minor opposition that clears only in the long B-flat pedal at the very end of the work. These harmonic meanings are not at all obscure; audiences can appreciate them without any conscious analysis. And the whole work, for all its subtle, intricate networks of motivic relationships and developments, and its wondrously delicate, adventurous, and unconventional scoring, has a similar directness. In *Peter Grimes*, Britten created magnificent sea music—seascapes seen from the land. In *Billy Budd*, there is another kind of sea music, in which the movement of the ship—the sense of the long, straining timbers, of the vessel's living response to wind and wave—seems to live in the music itself. The absence of women's voices passes unnoticed; the score is often bright with clear, busy shipboard signals. Ship and sea provide a picturesque background—and foreground, too, for ship and sea enclose the action, to make intense the crisis set on "this fragment of earth, this floating monarchy" of which Vere is king. Britten thought that there was too much shipboard detail in Piper's 1951 settings. When Covent Garden revived the opera in 1964, they were stripped and simplified. I think the composer was probably wrong; the most powerful *Budd* décor I have seen—Roger Butlin's for the Welsh National Opera—is also the most realistic. But Piper's settings, further remodeled to Mr. Anderson's ideas, rebuilt in San Francisco on a larger scale and provided with projections of changing sea and skies, worked very well.

Since 1951, it has been customary to portray Claggart as a big, blustering bully. Forbes Robinson, who took the role under Solti in 1964, and then in the Welsh production, found more subtlety in the man, and in San Francisco he again gave a striking and impressive performance. But he is slightly too ponderous, in manner as well as appearance too conventionally a "heavy," to be altogether convincing in the role. James Morris, at the Met, is the first Claggart of my experience to express fully the Lucifer-like beauty, sorrow, and passion of the Evil One, and to embody the occasional hint that in Billy and Claggart we have a final projection of the twinned bright and dark angels—Taji's Yillah and Hautia (in "Mardi"), Pierre's Lucy and Isabel—who recur in Melville's work. And Mr. Morris sang the role matchlessly. Except in the literal sense (for his low G and G-sharp were not strong), he plumbed Claggart's great monologue and made of it just what Forster hoped for:

> I want *passion*—love constricted, perverted, poisoned, but none the less *flowing* down its agonising channel: a sexual discharge gone evil. Not soggy depression or growling remorse.

No subsequent Billy has quite recaptured the freshness and naturalness of Theodor Uppman, who created the part and might have been born to play it. In Richard Stilwell's stage personality, there is usually a hint of patrician reserve; as Billy, at the Met, he doffed it almost too resolutely, and slightly forced the brightness and bounciness. In the ballad, he gave equal stress and length to each of the eighth-notes. But on the whole he was very good. Dale Duesing, in San Francisco, was even better. The ballad flowed, in phrases. During the confrontation with Claggart, he had expressed with marvelous intensity Billy's agony at this revelation of "the diabolical incarnate," and, during the trial, his further agony when Vere refuses to save him. Without exaggeration, he suggested the new understanding that comes to Billy, and carried the redemptive burden of the role as reshaped by Britten and Forster. His singing was strong and beautiful. Peter Pears's Vere, in New York, was subtly and powerfully acted, and sung with many fine, moving inflections. Richard Lewis's, in San Francisco, was more strongly voiced, and Vere's big solos—every word clear—rang out more keenly. Clarity was the hallmark of the San Francisco presentation. Not even Solti conducted so sharp-cut, rhythmically precise an account of the score as David Atherton did. Everything was in focus; everyone was confident. And in the quick acoustics of the War Memorial Opera House I heard more of the scoring, more of the words, more of the choral part-writing (admirable chorus, prepared by Richard Bradshaw) than ever before. The casts are too large to review in detail. In general, the smaller parts were more precisely played in San Francisco. In particular, the excellence of the New York Novice, James Atherton, and of the San Francisco Novice's Friend, Samuel Byrd (who has a very beautiful baritone), should be mentioned. In both places, *Billy Budd* proved overwhelming.

October 23, 1978

Island Symphony

There are several ways of approaching Peter Maxwell Davies's Symphony, which was given its first four American performances by the Philharmonic, under Zubin Mehta, this month. It is a major contemporary composer's deliberate—and yet, with hindsight over Davies's scores of the last decade, one might now say predestined—return to the tradition of the full-scale concert-hall symphony: it has four movements, is for full orchestra with triple wood-winds, and lasts fifty-six minutes; symphonies of Sibelius, Mahler, Schumann, and Beethoven played a part in its making. It is a romantic and picturesque work that holds evocations of sea, sky, and storm, of bright-edged light and unpolluted natural sound on the Orcadian island where since 1970 Davies has lived. It is the largest manifestation of its composer's almost medieval devotion to "secret" structures governing details of pitch and duration, his rapt transformations of plainchant melodies in a way to make modern listeners one with the ages, and his professed concern "to evolve a musical language simple and strong enough to make the complex forms with which I have become involved meaningful and audible—particularly with regard to functional harmony operating over and relating large spans of time." It is his most extended piece of big-orchestra writing, an essay in harmonizing the bright, spare, luminous sonorities projected in his chamber works of recent years and the sonic surge and tempest that can be summoned by a full symphony orchestra. And it is a "visionary" piece: in a program note for the London première (on February 2 this year) the composer said, "Perhaps it would help to put listeners in a frame of mind to be at least sympathetic to the intention, if not the result, to know that possibly the creative artists I admire most are two twelfth-century writers, whose language, to my mind, builds the only sound structures parallel to the statement made by the medieval cathedrals—Dante and St. Thomas Aquinas."

In the New York program book, the note was abridged and that sentence was omitted. The Philharmonic had prepared its performances thoroughly but had done less than it should have to prepare its audiences to receive the exacting composition. It might have hired and shown to its subscribers the Arts Council of Great Britain's fifty-minute film *One Foot in Eden,* an introduction to Davies's later music in its Orcadian setting. Besides the trinkets for sale at the new "gift shop," there are now serious books and records—but among them was not the Nonesuch recording of *Dark Angels* (1974), one of Davies's Orkney song cycles; or the Argo recording of the Second Fantasia on John Taverner's "In Nomine" (1964), Davies's earlier composition on a symphonic scale; or even the study score of the Symphony itself, which Boosey & Hawkes put into print before its first performance. The Philharmonic might have invited the Music Project to play, as one of the "preconcert" recitals favored by Boulez, *A Mirror of Whitening Light*, which it introduced to America earlier this year; this chamber-orchestra work, which Davies wrote immediately after the Symphony, is one of the most attractive and readily accessible examples of his recent style. The composer, it is true, did talk about the Symphony at one of the Friday-morning lectures held in the chorus room of Fisher Hall, and provided an introduction valuable to the handful of people who attended it. But those lectures are not widely publicized. (Davies's comparable talk before the London Prom performance of the Symphony this summer filled the large concert hall of the Royal College of Music.) It was adventurous of Mehta to bill the piece. His opening run of concerts with the Philharmonic has made it clear that his first care, like that of his predecessor, is for contemporary music. And that is good. Less good that in the week before the Symphony his Schubert (*Rosamunde* music and Fifth Symphony) and his Richard Strauss (Four Last Songs and *Salome* closing scene, with Montserrat Caballé as soloist) proved not worth writing about. But if he is to carry his listeners with him, and continue Boulez's endeavor to create a Philharmonic audience eager to discover, understand, and enjoy what today's composers are writing, his efforts need to be seconded by something like the British pizzazz and high-pressure, insistent publicity for contemporary music, coupled with ready availability of information, rather than the gentlemanly American reticence that prevails in Fisher Hall. New York's serious radio stations might be roped in. Would, say, WKCR be reluctant to carry repeats of the Friday-morning lectures and other related programs, which could be prominently billed in the Philharmonic program books? The program book for the Davies Symphony did not even tell audiences the date and station on which the concert could be heard again. [The Philharmonic *has* now taken to telling its audiences when concerts are to be broadcast.] If the Symphony did not, except among a band of enthusiasts, become quite the smash-hit and talk-of-the-town event it was in London, the reason was partly that it was not heard in context, and as a climax and summation, by audiences familiar with Davies's music of the last eight years. There had been *some* preparation for it. During the 1976 Celebration of Contemporary Music (that "inaugural festival" which has so far had no successor), the Orcadian song cycle *Stone Litany* was performed in the Juilliard Theatre. Later that year, the Fires of London, the ensemble that Davies directs, played his *Ave Maris Stella* in the Brooklyn Academy of Music. And in April this year there was the Music Project's *A Mirror of Whitening Light*, in Town Hall. But those were all single events, unrepeated, and the Philharmonic audience may have missed them.

A Mirror of Whitening Light, or *Speculum Luminis Dealbensis*, is a twenty-two-minute composition for fourteen players. Two plainsongs underlie its melodies, and a "magic square"—a device that, the composer says, "suitably used, can generate perfectly recognizable and workable sequences of pitches and rhythmic lengths"—acts as an agent in their transformations. The connotations of the title are part alchemical, referring to the process whereby base metals and, by metaphorical extension, the soul may be whitened and purified, and part scenic: "Fancifully, perhaps, I often see the great cliff-bound bay before my window where the Atlantic and the North Sea meet as a huge alchemical crucible, rich in speculative connotations, and at all times a miracle of ever-changing reflected light, and it is this which is the physical Mirror of the title." The opening section presents in quick succession five vividly atmospheric, mercurial, and contrasting "impressions" of light, of transformation processes, and of harmonic adventures grounded on a fundamental C; and from these the work grows, rising to a brilliant *jeu de vagues*, subsiding in a long, beautiful coda. The Music Project is a lively, talented young ensemble, New York's bright, fresh alternative to the established Chamber Music Society of Lincoln Center. (This season, the Project's regular concert series is on Sunday afternoons in St. Stephen's Church, on West Sixty-ninth Street; on each bill there is a Schubert chamber work.) Its performance of the *Mirror*, conducted by Gerard Schwarz, was alert, sparkling, and sensitive.

I have never been to the Orkneys, but have heard and read much about them since Davies went to live there, and have "heard" and "seen" them in his Orcadian scores. Orkney literature—from the twelfth-century *Orkneyinga Saga* to the poems and prose of Edwin Muir and George Mackay Brown—is strong and distinctive. One believes Muir when he says, "Strange blessings, never in Paradise known, Fall from these beclouded skies." Sober music critics return from the midsummer St. Magnus Festival, in Orkney, to write with rapture of "the light and the landscape of the far North," where "well after midnight, sea and sky meet in clear blue and copper, the land a thin black shape of the swathes of color," and of the paradoxes in "a beautiful but treeless rustic landscape, at once lush and austere; a land of midnight sun and midday dark, of grand and tragic history and gentle, Liberal politics." On the island of Hoy, living without electricity, drawing water from a spring, and hewing wood for his fire, Davies has rediscovered and reaffirmed human scale in his recent music. It sometimes reminds me of a remark made by the Northern symphonist Carl Nielsen: "The glutted must be taught to regard a melodic third as a gift of God, a fourth as an experience, and a fifth as the supreme bliss." It is not surprising that plainchant continues to provide the inspiration for Davies's themes, or that an almost reverent feeling for interval makes them memorable. The composer has said, "Living in London, and travelling, one's sense of hearing becomes dulled and distorted; a single jet taking off blurs one's hearing for hours afterwards. . . . But after a few days of solitude at Hoy I begin to hear again." By attentive listening to Davies's music, ears dulled by subway, siren, and aircraft sounds, by the cacophony of New York streets, "begin to hear again." Of course, there can also be violence in his music, and there is in the Symphony: "Boulders that must be ten to fifteen feet across are there grinding on each other three hundred feet below the house. It's a kind of physical pulsation that you hear with your whole body." Behind the human actions and dreams, there is the terrible impersonal grandeur of the Atlantic storms—and also the long, violent history of the islands. In Davies's recent scores, the past is a living element in the present. *Stone Litany* was inspired by a Neolithic Orkney monument. The opera *The Martyrdom of St. Magnus* treats of incidents in the *Orkneyinga Saga*, takes musical inspiration from the thirteenth-century Hymn to St. Magnus, and was first performed, last year, in the twelfth-century cathedral where Magnus is buried. (The American première was given at the Aspen Festival last July.) The moment of the martyrdom is set in the present day and wherever the opera is being performed: "It is no longer possible to persuade ourselves that 'such things couldn't happen here.' " The score becomes a nightmare phantasmagoria of distorted dance music through centuries from the twelfth to the twentieth; transformation and parody techniques pioneered in Davies's Expressionist compositions of the sixties become alarmingly potent. Then, in the final scene, the twelfth century and the present are merged: monks chant a litany that Magnus himself might have sung, but the resonances around that melody and the visionary solo song of a timeless Orkney woman are heard and set down with a twentieth-century ear.

Death sentences on the symphony and the symphony orchestra have often been pronounced. (At a Cheltenham Festival debate in 1971, Davies himself seconded the proposition that the extinction of the symphony orchestra was inevitable.) Both refuse to die. This summer, in London alone new symphonies by Lennox Berkeley (No. 4), John McCabe (No. 3), Andrzej Panufnik (his *Sinfonia di Sfere*), and Michael Tippett (No. 4) were performed and broadcast. The première of Anthony Milner's Second Symphony, in Liverpool, was broadcast, and so was Panufnik's *Sinfonia Mistica*. A series of thirteen BBC Tuesday-afternoon programs, "Symphonies from the North," provided a survey of busy symphonic activity in Scandinavia since Carl Nielsen. For some years, a full-scale symphony seems to have been forcing itself on Davies. His *Worldes Blis* (1969)—as Stephen Pruslin points out in the March issue of the magazine *Tempo*—is in effect a symphonic first movement containing hints of a scherzo and slow movement; *St. Thomas Wake* (also 1969) is a symphonic scherzo, and *Stone Litany* could be likened to a symphonic slow movement. Davies's Symphony began life, in 1973, as an orchestral piece called *Black Pentecost*, commissioned by London's Philharmonia Orchestra; according to the Philharmonic program note, Mehta was to have conducted it with the Philharmonia. Although finished, it was withdrawn before performance, because, the composer said, "I felt very keenly that this single movement was incomplete. . . . It was, as it were, budding and putting out shoots, and although I had firmly drawn a final double bar-line, the music was reaching out across it, suggesting transformations beyond the confines of a single movement." That piece, refashioned after the first movement of Sibelius's Fifth, became a lento evaporating into a scherzo and is now the second movement of the Symphony. The first movement is a series of charged developments and transformations, articulated by climaxes and "holds" that open out in the succeeding sections, and unified by a theme of emphatic rhythmic outline. The third movement is "another invocation of the extraordinary, almost unearthly, treeless winter land and seascape of the Orkney island where I live," but it is not "merely descriptive and atmospheric"; it is also a slower, more relaxed example of the transformation processes found elsewhere in the work. The finale is a kaleidoscope of changing textures, including suggestions of gull cries and birdsong; a mysterious duet for harp and timpani, with touches of added color from marimba and double-bass; rapid trumpet signals piercing a dense web of slow-woven melodies; and, at the last, a long, fierce crescendo abruptly cut short, as Sibelius's Fifth Symphony is, by some stabbing chords. Descriptions are apt to stress section-by-section construction. Repeated hearing is needed to disclose the long continuous thought that runs through the movements and unites them one to another. At a first hearing, the sheer eventfulness and beauty of the music—melodies that seem to stretch out toward some far horizon, the soaring song of a solo violin, slow surging and massing, swift, sudden flurries—can hold a listener enthralled.

The Symphony is very difficult to conduct and to play. Young Simon Rattle, who conducted the London première, learned its secrets by bringing it to performance point with his own orchestra, the BBC Scottish, before doing it in public with the Philharmonia. With the Philharmonia, he has recorded it, for London Records (HEAD 21). Mehta and the Philharmonic's interpretation, I think, was not quite as exciting, picturesque, or committedly energetic and loving as Rattle and the Philharmonia's; but the Philharmonic became more and more confident during the run. I "just listened" to the first and third performances, followed the second and fourth with the score, noted no more than a few small inaccuracies and inadequacies, and admired very much not only the professional competence of the players but also the increasing eloquence with which they sounded the long melodies and the bright, clear colors.

October 30, 1978

Patterns

Steve Reich and Musicians, an ensemble of eighteen players, gave a concert of Reich's music in the Wollman Auditorium of Columbia University the week before last. It was presented by WKCR, the university's radio station. The place was packed with a young and enthusiastic audience. In Europe, Reich is nearer to the center of the musical scene than he is here (two years ago there were four Reich concerts in the Salle Wagram during the Paris

Autumn Festival; both *Drumming* and Music for Eighteen Musicians have toured on the Arts Council of Great Britain's Contemporary Music Network), but he is not without honor in his own country. I enjoyed the Columbia concert. I was interested by the musical events of the compositions—fascinated by the processes that had gone into their making, engaged and attracted by the results, and admiring of the executants' high musicianship. And yet, as so often happens at concerts where the hypnotic effect of much repetition or near-repetition moves a young audience to rapture—during music as different as Satie's *Vexations*, a full-length Indian recital, Stockhausen's *Stimmung*, and Philip Glass's *Einstein on the Beach*—I felt at moments a certain uneasiness. What was this audience really hearing and responding to? And what was I, who the night before had thrilled to Peter Maxwell Davies's Symphony and brought to bear on it all I knew of the ten centuries of history on which it stands? Was it indecently promiscuous to surrender so soon and so readily to simple harmonies and a steady beat, even if they were enlivened by rhythmic intricacies and pretty timbres?

The concert began with *Clapping Music,* a duet written in 1972—a straightforward "phase" composition. One performer claps out an unchanging rhythmic pattern; the other, starting in unison, then displaces the pattern, a beat at a time. It is rather like a game, and an entertaining one to overhear: the basic pattern is so composed that its superimpositions produce catchy, beguiling effects. Moreover, the fact that it *is* a game of skill—it was expertly played by Russ Hartenberger and Reich himself—gives it a lively quality that would be lost in a machine performance. A machine could accurately reproduce the kaleidoscope of rhythms, but one would lose the moments of give and take, the small human adjustments, and—not unimportant—the infectious zest in a tricky task successfully accomplished which animated the Columbia performance. Then there was *Violin Phase,* a 1967 piece. Here the basic pattern and its out-of-phase superimpositions are on tape. A live performer—the fiddler who made the tape—sometimes adds still another "phase," and sometimes he does something yet more interesting. To the patterns-in-time of the monotone *Clapping Music* have been added melodic patterns-in-pitch; and when a rapid melody sounds against itself in double or triple canon, new motifs and new melodies soon emerge from the combination. The soloist—he was Shem Guibbory—hears them, chooses ones that catch his fancy, and reinforces those by sounding them on his own instrument. Thus he shares or guides the listeners' perceptions. When he ceases, their ears continue to trace the indicated new melody or motif; a figure in the sonic carpet is discerned for a while, and then gradually fades as the patterns alter. *Violin Phase* is a work that seems to make its auditors concerned participants in what is happening. Reich's pieces have the merit of not going on too long. There comes a moment when a listener says to himself, "Yes, I see how it works; it's ingenious; and now there's no need to spell it out all the way." At that point, the piece usually ends. The first half of the concert closed with Music for Mallet Instruments, Voices, and Organ, of 1973, for an ensemble of eleven. Here new contrasts are brought into play—of timbres, of sustained notes against rapid patter or pulsing, of patterns that speed up against patterns that slow down—and harmony is used as a structural element.

The three works formed a good introduction to the main piece of the evening, Music for Eighteen Musicians, of 1976, Reich's largest and most ambitious composition to date. In the recently issued recording (ECM-1-1129), it lasts very nearly an hour. The Columbia performance was shorter by about ten minutes; it was perhaps less steady, spacious, and limpid than the recorded version but had the charge of extra excitement provided by a live event. Here all Reich's experiments with rhythmic canons, with sedulous patter against long-held tones, with new melodies emerging from a composite of others, with shifts of timbre across a large, varied body of players and singers, with moves of harmonic plane now gradual, now sudden come to fruition in a rich, carefully organized composition. There is a new idea— using the span of a human breath as a measure of certain durations, set against the sustained "bickerin brattle" of the percussions' moto perpetuo. (In a program note, the composer writes of "one breath after another gradually washing up like waves against the constant rhythm of the pianos and mallet instruments.") The metallophone signals changes of section: the "conductor's cues," as in some Balinese and African music, become part of the music itself. One of music's oldest expressive devices lies in likenesses with perceptible differences. Patterns from one section of Music for Eighteen Musicians reappear, differently scored, in other sections; Reich suggests the simile of "resemblances between members of a family," in which "certain characteristics will be shared, but others will be unique." Another device is showing that things exactly the same can nevertheless be different. The first and third bars of the introduction to Act II of Fidelio are exactly the same, an octave F from the strings. But in the second and fourth bars the winds sound different resonances above F, and thus make the two F's different. Seven bars later, the middle strings sound exactly the same motif three times, but each time through a different harmony. Immediately after that, Beethoven starts to use pulse patterns in an almost Reichian way.

Reich's work has been called "minimal music." It is a label that can fairly be attached to some of his earlier compositions, such as Clapping Music, which are based on the rigorous working out of a single idea. It does not apply to his increasingly thoughtful and elaborately eloquent later pieces. The reflection that Beethoven and Reich seem to have worked at some of the same "problems" can calm the uneasiness voiced in my first paragraph. His music has a joyful, very attractive surface; it may be that some of his admirers do not get beyond it. (Ditto with much Stockhausen.) But there is substance beneath.

In September, I listened to a radio performance of Fidelio, from Munich, which whetted the appetite for the Metropolitan Opera's revival of the work with three of the same principals—Hildegard Behrens, James King, and Kurt

Moll, as Leonore, Florestan, and Rocco—and with the same conductor, Karl Böhm. In the flesh, Miss Behrens fulfilled the marvelous promise of the broadcast. She was urgent. She sang the role as keenly, declaimed and acted it as vividly, as if she were playing a verismo heroine, and yet never transgressed the bounds of apt style. Her voice, very well schooled and accurately focused, compassed the extremes of the role without trace of strain or impurity. Her words, sung or spoken, were given full value. And she looked the part. Mr. King was, as ever, a reliable, if somewhat wooden, Florestan. Mr. Moll's Rocco, laid out on sound traditional lines, was as admirably sung a performance as one could hope to hear. But the Met orchestra under Dr. Böhm was rough and raucous: the brasses brayed, the drums were banged, the ensemble seesawed, and chords that call for a unanimous attack spattered into life. The eminent conductor got a great reception; people must have been hearing through to the carefully paced, classical *Fidelio* that underlay the rude execution. Siegmund Nimsgern was a dapper, precise Don Pizarro. Arleen Augér's buxom Marzelline and James Atherton's Jaquino lacked incisiveness, and Bernd Weikl seemed to have no idea what to do with Don Fernando. *Fidelio* is an opera that should be performed annually; next season, the Met must mount a worthy performance around Miss Behrens's remarkable heroine.

Massenet's *Werther* is cropping up all over: in San Francisco (with Maria Ewing as its heroine), in Houston (with Frederica von Stade), in Chicago (with Yvonne Minton), in London (with Teresa Berganza, at Covent Garden, in the English National production made for Janet Baker), at the Opéra-Comique (with Jane Rhodes), in Florence (with Lucia Valentini Terrani), in Munich (with Brigitte Fassbänder), and at the Met (with Elena Obraztsova, and later Régine Crespin). *Werther* is a good opera but one difficult to bring off. Goethe described the book from which it is drawn as "a creation that I fed, like the pelican, with my heartblood," and told Eckermann that he had reread it but once and would not do so again, for "here are incendiary bombs." French nineteenth-century librettists were adept at defusing—reducing the wilder, more romantic flights of man's imagination to safe operatic platitudes, house-training Benvenuto Cellini, Faust, Werther, Wilhelm Meister, and Hamlet. (In this context, *Carmen* was something of a miracle; no wonder it had a rough passage to success.) But Massenet once declared that he put into *Werther* all his soul and all his artistic conscience. There is soul in the music of the lovers' first meeting; in the moonlit orchestral interlude of the first act, leading so tenderly into Charlotte's "Il faut nous séparer" and the subsequent duet; and in all of Act III. A sterner artistic conscience might have jibbed at spinning so much of Act IV around a Chopinesque tag too slight to carry its dramatic burden. What *Werther* needs is that French combination of precision with romance—and a grace and charm of manner which do not preclude more serious emotions. The Met principals did not supply them. Miss Obraztsova, a heavyweight, domineering singer—a natural Amneris—made a serious attempt to subdue her voice and style to the character of Charlotte, but the result could only seem crude to anyone brought up on the sound and the delicacy of Ninon Vallin in the role. And she did not pronounce the text beautifully. Placido Domingo's Werther was forceful, not graceful; his new, powerful "dramatic" timbre—a fine Othello sound—was suited only to the more vigorous outbursts. Frankenstein's monster wept when he read of Werther's death; I think Mr. Domingo would have left him dry-eyed. Julius Rudel, in his Met début, conducted with complete understanding of the style. There is a horrid modern touch in the staging: instead of cutting pieces from an enormous loaf for the children's supper, Charlotte hands round a plate of ready-sliced bread.

November 6, 1978

Town and Country

In much the way that Handel can be claimed as Britain's greatest opera composer, Kurt Weill might be claimed as America's: a master musician, master musical dramatist, and large soul who found song for the people of his adopted country, learned its idioms, joined them to his own, and composed music of international importance. Langston Hughes, the black poet who wrote lyrics for Weill's *Street Scene*, remarked perceptively (in an article about his collaboration with Weill) that the first solo of that opera, the janitor's "I got a marble and a star," is composed in a specifically black-American national idiom and yet in such a way that a German or anyone else could sing it without seeming out of place or exotic. Hughes also recalled how he and Weill would spend hours in the streets of New York waiting for children to break into spontaneous play, so that they could catch the right style, verbal and musical, for the children's game that begins Act II.

Street Scene, after an absence of twelve years, is back on the boards of the City Opera, and it is very well done: directed by Jack O'Brien, conducted by John Mauceri, and sung and acted by the large cast (nearly sixty named soloists) with an accomplishment and an accuracy of style which make it a powerful and moving experience. Elmer Rice's play *Street Scene*, the source of Weill's "book," was first done, on Broadway, in 1929; the opera was first done, also on Broadway, in 1947. Much of the spoken dialogue was taken over from play to opera unaltered, but a few verbal changes indicate a post-war setting for the latter: the liquor described in 1929 as "t'ree parts dynamite an' one part army mule" is in 1947 "t'ree parts high octane, one part atom bomb." Also, understandably, Weill could evidently not bring himself to set the contemptuous terms by which in the play the members of the Jewish family are referred to by the rest of the cast. The general anti-Semitism (shown by the characters, not by the play) is toned down, and the language of racial disdain is also softened. Rice filled his New York tenement with types: an ebullient Italian, a fat, comfortable hausfrau, a thick-skulled Swedish couple, a left-wing Russian Jew, and hard-shell "real Americans" despising the foreigners. Their strife is the stuff of tragedy, but they verge on caricature. In the opera, where the playwright's pungent, accurate language is softened, they would be caricatures had Mr. O'Brien's touch been less sure. The war has left no mark on the drama; the decision to set it back in the original period of the play is surely right.

David Drew, in the long, important foreword to his anthology *Über Kurt Weill* (a Suhrkamp paperback), provides one of the very few attempts to see Weill whole. In the course of it, he observes that Weill's art

> is consistently and tellingly equivocal. . . . Ambiguities of structure and expression, together with apparent anomalies of tone and idiom, are . . . exploited with such merciless accuracy that no formal or emotional expectations are secure. Methodical in this as in its deliberately outrageous breaches of etiquette, the music declares itself to be the enemy of most orthodoxies and of all systems. Hence it prefers to leave unanswered the social and moral questions that it has raised, unless the answers happen to suggest themselves in terms of the simplest and least partial appeals to humanity and justice. In short, it is the expression of an essentially romantic sensibility, awakened by new perceptions and reacting to changed circumstance, but in no sense the expression of a legislator or ideologue.

That is true of *The Threepenny Opera, Mahagonny,* and *Der Jasager,* and equally true of *Lady in the Dark, Street Scene,* and *Lost in the Stars.* The ambiguities of structure and expression and the apparent anomalies of tone and idiom in *Street Scene* raise many questions, and one comes up with different kinds of answers to them. Is the "ice cream sextet" over the edge of caricature? Maybe—but it's as beautifully composed as a Mozart ensemble. Is the structure off balance, since Act I contains fourteen numbers, mostly solo, and seldom sequentially related, while Act II is dominated by two big "operatic" choral ensembles? Maybe—but there seems to be something almost Greek in the slow preparation for tragedy and then the sudden, swift catastrophe. Are the lyrics too banal to bear the charge of full-voiced musical emotion in the passionate episodes? Yes and no: the listener's resultant uneasiness is something Weill intends. Is the setting of lines from Whitman's Lincoln elegy ("In the dooryard fronting an old farm-house near the white-wash'd palings, Stands the lilac-bush tall-growing") eloquent enough for its purpose? Well, maybe not: the listener must add knowledge of the whole poem if he is to

share the note of hope that, in both finales, shines through the sordid mess—
to catch the shorthand allusion to Lincoln's vision of what America might be,
and respond to Whitman's assurance of renewal, of healing after tragedy.

Catherine Malfitano's Rose is a well-nigh ideal performance in every
way. Alan Kays's Sam is lyrical, sensitive, affecting, and unaffected. Eileen
Schauler, in the dramatic-soprano role of Mrs. Maurrant (created by Polyna
Stoska, who can be heard in the Columbia recording), is natural and very
moving; one would like a richer voice but could hardly hope for a more convincing interpretation. William Chapman's Frank Maurrant is very sure.
There are also exact performances from Kathleen Hegierski (Jenny), Diane
Curry (Mrs. Jones), Lynn Cohen (Shirley Kaplan), Bronwyn Thomas and
Daniel Levans (Mae and Dick), Alan Titus (Mr. Easter; but he needs a haircut
for the prewar setting), Jonathan Green (Lippo), and, indeed, from almost everyone in the enormous cast. John Mauceri's pacing of the music is precise,
and the orchestral playing is first-rate. Many of the words are unclear, especially during the first forty minutes. It is partly Weill's fault (his music always
catches the sense of the lines but is not always a good match for their natural
sound), but the sheer size of the State Theater is chiefly to blame. A pity that
the publishers do not allow the libretto to be put on general sale.

"A full and just appraisal of Weill's work for Broadway," Mr. Drew
writes, "will become possible only when his early work has been fully reap-
praised, and not before." However, chances of hearing that early work are
infrequent. A few days before *Street Scene* opened, the Greenwich Philharmonia, conducted by David Gilbert, provided one when it came into town, to
Avery Fisher Hall, to give a Weill program that included the New York première—and American troisième—of his First Symphony (two Greenwich
performances had preceded it), the seldom heard *Quodlibet*, Op. 9 (1923),
and *Der neue Orpheus*, Op. 15 (1925). Those three works represented the
early, pre-Brecht Weill. The fourth piece on the bill, the *Kleine Dreigroschenmusik*, is music from a Weill-Brecht theatre collaboration recomposed
for concert performance; Otto Klemperer conducted the première, in 1929.
Lotte Lenya was the guest of honor at the New York concert. A week before,
she had had her eightieth birthday; at the end of the program, artists and audience joined to sing to her in celebration.

The collaboration between Weill and Brecht, from the *Mahagonny
Songspiel* (1927) to *The Seven Deadly Sins* (1933), produced a group of mas-
terworks that have tended to throw their shadow, backward and forward,
over a career that extended from the First Symphony (1921) to *Lost in the
Stars* (1949) and the unfinished *Huckleberry Finn*. One line that runs right
through all Weill's music is the influence of Mahler. Weill's First Symphony
is a turbulent, wonderfully inventive piece. Beethoven, Liszt, Mahler, and
Schoenberg bear on it; there seems to be an eventful program, part political,
part religious—visions of violence, victory, and peace—just below its surface.
Mahler appears "in person" in one of the variations at the center of *Der neue
Orpheus*, conducting his Philharmonic. In this "concertino" for voice, violin,
and orchestra, Weill—with characteristic ambiguity, humor, and human-

ity—considers the various roles that music is called on to play in the modern world. The *Quodlibet* is a suite for full orchestra drawn from the 1922 children's ballet *Die Zaubernacht.* (It was done in New York, at the Garrick Theatre, in 1925.) The suite is subtitled "Eine Unterhaltungsmusik," and it *is* entertaining, but is also a substantial, elaborately composed four-movement work filled with rare musical inventions.

I was unable to attend this important concert but managed to hear the Greenwich Philharmonia's own tape recording of it. To judge by that, the Philharmonia's playing of the symphony was accomplished, if less polished in detail than that of the BBC Symphony or of the Leipzig Gewandhaus Orchestra (who have recorded Weill's First and Second Symphonies for, respectively, Argo and Philips, under Gary Bertini and Edo de Waart), and David Gilbert gave an exceptionally coherent and cogent reading of a piece not easy to hold together. In all four works, he showed himself an expert and persuasive Weillian. Barbara Martin was the singer and Richard Young the violinist in *The New Orpheus.* (It was sung in an English translation by Lys Symonette.) To the orchestral *Quodlibet* was added, from *Die Zaubernacht,* the Queen of the Toys' aria, orchestrated by Mr. Gilbert from the piano score. It was interesting to hear, although it does not really belong in what, like the *Kleine Dreigroschenmusik,* is a self-sufficient concert work. I hope the admirable Greenwich pioneering venture bears fruit. It is high time that Weill's two symphonies enter the regular concert repertory.

The Metropolitan Opera's new production of *The Bartered Bride,* directed by John Dexter, designed by Josef Svoboda, and sung to a new English libretto, by Tony Harrison, is a disaster, to be shunned by anyone who knows and values Smetana's lovable opera and equally by anyone whose first acquaintance with it would be blighted by the horrid travesty. Although Smetana's *The Brandenburgers in Bohemia, Dalibor,* and, especially, *Libuše* deal with more patently patriotic matter, *The Bartered Bride,* as the Met program note remarks, has become the Czechoslovak national opera and is done "whenever the embattled Czech identity is in need of celebration or defense." It is a repertory cornerstone of the National Theatre, to which Smetana devoted so much of his life, composing for it national operas in every genre, from light comedy to visionary epic. Its opening chorus celebrated the end of the Nazi Occupation, in 1945. After a summer when everyone who loves Czechoslovakia and its music turned in thought to that heroic and indomitable country, remembering that ten years ago its new-won freedoms were again brutally extinguished, it was doubly distressing to encounter this crass and unworthy representation of *The Bartered Bride.* When the show is revived, it must be with a new cast, new scenery, and a new translation.

The Bartered Bride had its hundredth Prague performance in 1882, and on that occasion the composer described it as "only a plaything"—an opera he had "tossed off" to confound those who thought him a heavy Wagnerian, and one that at the time of its writing he had deemed more spirited than Offenbach. He was probably reacting against adulation too solemn. No one needs telling that *The Bartered Bride* is no mere operetta but an opera semi-seria, or that, although its plot is resolved by a Gilbertian twist, it is concerned with real people in real plights. There is scarcely a modern director who does not begin by observing that Mařenka is the victim of a mercenary contract, Jeník a villager dispossessed of his rights, and Kecal a sinister, evil force. What is more likely to need stressing today is that *The Bartered Bride* is also a picturesque folk opera of abundant charm, tender, romantic emotion, high spirits, and humor. One would hardly guess it from the Met performance. The setting there is essentially a bare stage against a plain blue backcloth with slits in it to allow mass entrances. Some orange palings and white housefronts deck it from time to time, and in Act III there is a merry-go-round for Vašek to ride on. The casting is peculiar. Mařenka and Jeník call for singers of at least the weight of Agathe and Max in *Der Freischütz*. (Destinn, Gadski, Maria Müller, and Rethberg were all Met Mařenkas.) Teresa Stratas and Nicolai Gedda do not fill their music. That she presents a hard, pinched, shrewish little heroine and he a gauche, Vašek-like booby of a hero may be a directorial decision. Jon Vickers, who does Vašek, might make a telling Jeník; he plays Vašek as a Holy Fool, a Parsifal circled by children in· place of flower maidens. In incomprehensible accents, Martti Talvela barks his way sternly through Kecal's patter and misses all the fun of the role as Smetana wrote it. James Levine's conducting is spirited, but on the first night he pushed the score too hard. He didn't give his players, especially his wood-wind players, time to enjoy the marvelous music that Smetana wrote for them. But there were signs that he loves the piece—how could anyone not love it?—and so he will probably relax into giving a performance of it tender as well as brilliant.

There seem to be two John Dexters on Lincoln Plaza: the Dexter who directed *Lulu, The Carmelites, Billy Budd*—and, in London, Penderecki's *The Devils*—precisely, potently, astutely, and with a just sense for revealing the composers' intentions; and the Dexter who made such a hash of *Les Vêpres siciliennes, Aida, Rigoletto, La Gioconda, La forza del destino*, and *Le Prophète* that one wished the Met would send him to opera school to acquire some understanding of nineteenth-century opera and ways of staging it. The latter Dexter has directed *The Bartered Bride*. His staging is an odd mixture of what look like beginners' mistakes (doing the first scene for Mařenka and Jeník with one or the other atop a teetering stepladder; setting Mařenka scurrying around to collect eggs, scattered about the almost bare stage, during her scene with Vašek) and sheer perversity. The heady furiant—that joyful outburst in Act II when the girls pour into the inn and start dancing with the young men—is turned into a squabble between two flighty waiters. Jeník and Kecal strike their bargain *coram choro*. Directors whose concern is to "strip away" charms that they consider incidental—but that are often an essential and significant part of a work—tend to end up inventing new, irrelevant nonsense, lest they be left with a concert performance.

As a translator myself—even though one without any designs on Slavonic opera—I feel some diffidence about condemning the work of a colleague, but indignation at what has been done to Smetana's piece tempts me to speak out. Let me put it thus: Tony Harrison evidently does not share a belief that a translator should aim at an audibly intelligible syntax (if he did, he would hardly pen lines as hard to parse by ear alone as "Women workers, husbands boozers" or "Feast day's feast day, don't forget it") and should try to convey the sense of the original. The first Jeník-Mařenka duet begins "Jako matka požehnáním,/takž kletbou macecha zlá," rendered almost literally by Rosa Newmarch's "Though a mother is a blessing,/a cruel stepmother's nothing but a curse." Mr. Harrison makes this "Home's Moravia, farm and family,/but here I sleep in the straw." Mrs. Newmarch's words fit the music well and are audible in performance; I quote them from memory. Mr. Harrison's don't and aren't; I quote them from the printed libretto that G. Schirmer has published. In the English version by Joan Cross and Eric Crozier, Vašek enters, stammering, with "M-m-m-mother said/tha-tha-that I must wed," which proves effective and comprehensible. What Mr. Vickers sang at his entry was unintelligible; the printed libretto reveals "M-m-m-m-mama th-th-th-thinks it's time/Vašek h-h-h-heard ch-ch-ch-church bells chime." And "church bells chime" is a mouthful that not even Mr. Vickers can get out clearly to three short eighth-notes. An essay on the translation, in the Met program book, claims that "all of Smetana's textual repetitions are ... retained rather than add new words." Not so. The opera begins, "Proč bychom se netěšili [sung twice],/když nám pán bůh zdraví dá, zdraví dá [sung thrice]!" It means "Why shouldn't we be happy, when God gives us health!" Newmarch has "Come, then let us all be merry,/since God gives us health today!" Cross and Crozier, less literal but more singable, have "Now's the time for fun and laughter,/we have earned a holiday"—and their "holiday" fits the repeated "zdraví dá" well. Life is gloomier at the Met: the repeated first line is expanded into "Still got strength to face the worst with,/well-brewed beer to beat a thirst with," followed by "we've all earned this holiday!" To avoid "weevil earned the solid A," the chorus must adopt an exaggerated staccato.

A new English translation was needed. There are unacceptable passages of translatorese in the Newmarch and Cross-Crozier versions, and even more of them in the Marion Farquhar version (found in Schirmer's vocal score). I have not heard Graham Jones's old translation, used by the Met in 1936 and by the Juilliard in 1973, or David Pountney and Leonard Hancock's new translation, made for Scottish Opera earlier this year. Mr. Harrison's libretto, besides so often misrepresenting the sense, does not sing well. "He's taken leave of *all* his senses" is translatorese. Jeník yearns for "my *new* wife," with an inflection to suggest that he has or had an old one. Mařenka's lovely threefold "Chci věčně věrně žít" ("I want to live faithful forever"), marked to be sung *dolce*, then *con intimo sentimento*, then *lento, mezza voce e dolcissimo* with a pause on the penultimate note, is translated as "My life's all finished now." The tender sentiment is altered; the soprano is required to sustain three D's on the short *i* of "fi," then one on the short *i* of "nished," and to close a smooth cadence through the consonant cluster *shdn*. I have never before caught so few words of an English *Bride*. Even in the huge Los Angeles Shrine, holding sixty-five hundred people, I could hear, in 1964, what the San Francisco Opera singers were saying—in yet another translation, Craig Hankenson's.

November 13, 1978

Aristocrat

Jacob Druckman's Viola Concerto, which had its first performance, in Avery Fisher Hall, the week before last, is the latest in the series of pieces that the Philharmonic has commissioned, with funds provided by Francis Goelet, for its own principals to play with the orchestra. And to my mind and ears it is the best work in the series so far. The concerto lasts twenty-five minutes. The soloist was Sol Greitzer, who has been with the Philharmonic for twenty-five years and has been its principal viola since 1972. In his performance, beauty, virtuosity, and fancy were combined. Druckman is a composer who often expects his interpreters to play a creative part—to seize a line he has written for them and add something of their own temperaments to its delivery. This Mr. Greitzer did. On his instrument he created a "character" of romantic, poetic sensibility, witty and resourceful. Aware that he stands no chance against what the composer in a program note describes as "the terrible power of the full orchestra," he retires before its tempests to reappear, dauntless and freshly inventive, when they are spent. In the long run, the viola is master of the situations. His ideas are what the orchestra players take up, elaborate, amplify. Thrice, they proceed from these to an immense, mindless outburst of their own; thrice, the soloist proposes a return to orderly, civilized discourse. Thus, the work, which plays without break, has four main sections, led by the soloist, divided by three orchestral tutti. To the violist's fourth set of proposals the orchestra players offer no eventual opposition. They subside at last on a unison A, initiated by him; and then he, having tamed the unruly gang, flies off and away on a chromatic arpeggio suggesting A minor. The concerto presents the viola as the aristocrat of the orchestra and reminds one that the violins, who usually dominate it today, are, historically speaking, nothing but jumped-up violas. The soloist's kindred souls are his fellow-violas; they are the first to make any independent contribution to his opening statements, seconding them with a golden halo of soft, melancholy harmonics after other instruments have merely aped his motifs. The other player whom the viola can regard as an equal is the alto flute, with whom he sings two lyrical duets. And it is the alto flute who first understands the viola's suggestion that things should come to a close on A.

At a first hearing, Druckman's concerto, like his *Chiaroscuro,* which the Philharmonic played last year, disturbed me a little by seeming to lack sustained thematic argument based on sequences of pitches which in repetition, variation, or development can be recognized—to put it simply, tunes. It is possible to write enjoyable music in which the themes are not tunes but timbres, densities, colors, contrasting kinds of motion, etc.; György Ligeti and several Poles have shown how. But it tends to be a limited kind of music. The demonstration of being able to "do without" prompts the question: Yes, but *why* do without what is most music's nearly essential ingredient—except as an experiment, an exercise? However, at a second hearing of the concerto it began to sing—often across thirds, fourths, and sixths. Druckman has long been a master orchestrator, adept at creating thin, luminous washes of sound, thick, rich impastos, and transformations of texture sudden or slow. A clear sonic sky may swiftly blacken, grow dense with menace, and be rent by lightning bolts. Darkness almost visible may begin to sparkle with twinkling points of light. The Viola Concerto demonstrates all the big-orchestra virtuosity of *Chiaroscuro,* but that is not all the piece is about.

The concert was conducted by James Levine, whose command of the concerto seemed to be complete. The evening began with the *Rienzi* overture—a substantial performance with rich string tone and vivid brasses, a deeper, less flamboyant, more securely paced account of the piece than the one Zubin Mehta conducted with the orchestra earlier in the season. The second half was Brahms's Fourth Symphony, and this was slightly disappointing; neither the first movement nor the finale found the easy, convincing, natural stride that marks Levine's recorded performance with the Chicago Symphony.

In a generous view, Lincoln Center could be deemed to extend from Sixty-sixth to Fifty-ninth streets, from the Juilliard School to the Church of St. Paul the Apostle—a forum bounded by an academy on the north and a basilica on the south. The church is occasionally used for concerts, and I wish it were used more often when music calling for a big, resonant acoustic is to be played. Between the Center proper and the church lies the Lincoln Center campus of Fordham University, one of New York's few public buildings with lawns and trees around them. Fordham has a useful little auditorium, seating about five hundred and bright in sound. Here, a few days before the Druckman concerto was done, Henry Cowell's Piano Concerto had its New York première and (apparently) North American deuxième. The composer played it with the Havana Philharmonic in December 1930; earlier that year, he had played just one or two movements of it (authorities disagree) in New York with the Conductorless Orchestra. The score was published in Paris in 1931, but—astonishingly—the work seems to have been neglected until Doris Hays played it last month with the Omaha Symphony, and then in New York with the New Amsterdam Symphony, conducted by Victoria Bond. Miss Hays is a Cowell specialist; a recorded recital on the Finnadar label demonstrates her command of his exuberant, extravagant piano techniques and her feeling for his exuberant yet poetic musical personality.

The concerto has three movements, titled Polyharmony, Tone Cluster, and Counter Rhythm. A good deal of the piano writing is for forearms. When a forearm is brought down on the white keys, it suggests C major; on the black keys, F-sharp major. But Cowell avoids simplistic bitonality by using his forearm clusters as color above or below a chromatic melody, or by alternating distinct notes and clusters with a sort of rapid oompah effect in which the *ooms* define a tune and the *pahs* punctuate it. Miss Hays is also adept at playing tunes with her right elbow—striking the top note of a cluster precisely. It's not easy. Just try it. The concerto is a dashing experiment rather than an important composition. It is quite short—about seventeen minutes—and is exhilarating to listen to. It might be a hit at a Philharmonic concert.

The New Amsterdam program began with a somewhat rough performance of Liszt's *Orpheus*, a companion piece to Kurt Weill's *Der neue Orpheus* in that—though in romantic rather than Weill's realistic strains—it hymns the power of music and treats Orpheus as a symbolic figure. In the words of Liszt's preface, "Orpheus, that is to say Art, needs to spread his waves of melody, his chords vibrant like tender, irresistible light, over the warring elements that rend one another and bleed in every individual soul, as in the entrails of every society." Two days later, Orphic strains sounded again at Lincoln Center, in Alice Tully Hall. For the opening concert of its tenth-anniversary season, the Chamber Music Society of Lincoln Center had commissioned a new piece from William Schuman, the Center's first artistic director. It is *In Sweet Music*, a "serenade on a setting of Shakespeare, for flute, viola, voice, and harp."

In the early 1940s, Schuman embarked on incidental music for a production of *Henry VIII*. The production was abandoned, but "Orpheus with his lute" had already been set, and it was published for voice and piano. In 1961, the song became the starting point for Schuman's *A Song of Orpheus*, a fantasy for cello and orchestra. (There is a Columbia recording by Leonard Rose and the Cleveland Orchestra under Szell.) *In Sweet Music* is a descendant of both the song and the fantasy. The first "singer" is an alto flute. Shakespeare's lines are printed beneath the notes of her part (the performer was Paula Robison), and she declaims the melody as if "thinking" the words. When the mezzo-soprano (Jan DeGaetani) enters, she announces the title, musingly, and then becomes an "instrument," threading a line of colored vocalise, to syllables like *loo* and *la* and *lee*, through the texture. The central section is a scherzo, with scat syllables for the singer. Then the viola (Walter Trampler) becomes a "singer," and finally the mezzo becomes articulate and adds the words—the words of "Orpheus with his lute"—to the melody that in various shapes has underlain all the serenade. The harp (Osian Ellis) has as important a role as the pair of harps in Liszt's tone poem, sometimes accompanying the song, sometimes carrying the main strain, as if Orpheus' voice ceased while his fingers played on. The harp writing is adventurous and delicate. *In Sweet Music* is a cultivated, attractive, and finely worked piece.

Tully Hall is not an ideal place in which to enjoy chamber music. It is dull to the eye, and the sound, though clear, is dry. The Church of Christ and St. Stephen's, on West Sixty-ninth Street, provides a more attractive—and acoustically satisfactory—setting. Hearing music by natural light becomes a pleasure increasingly rare. (There was an outcry at the Edinburgh Festival this year when audiences discovered that the windows of Leith Town Hall, used for daytime chamber recitals, had been blacked out.) In Christ and St. Stephen's, the sunlight passes through richly colored glass, and so electric light must be added to it if scores are to be clearly legible. But one is still in touch with the outside world, not closeted deep in a concrete bunker. In a concert intermission, one steps out into a garden. One sunny Sunday afternoon last month, I dropped in to a concert there to hear the Music Project play Schubert's B-flat Piano Trio, Hindemith's Kleine Kammermusik, Op. 24, No. 2, for wind quintet, and Dvořák's String Quintet in G. The pleasures afforded by the place itself may be—apart from the good acoustics—no more than incidental. It's not great architecture, merely an unpretentious late-nineteenth-century church with a friendly, village-hall feel to it. But those pleasures are real, and they can make one receptive to the music. During that Schubert trio, of course, a listener attends to nothing but the miracle of the music. The performance by William Henry, Bonnie Hartman, and Dan Berlinghoff, violin, cello, and piano, was fresh, buoyant, and sensitive.

About the aptness for music of St. Peter's, the striking modern church by Hugh Stubbins nestling in the shade of his Citicorp Center, I feel less sure. I paid my first visit there the other day to hear the Baroque Music Masters—a quartet of baroque violin, flute, and cello, and harpsichord—and the tenor Paul Sperry give a modest recital of English seventeenth- and eighteenth-century music. Perhaps the place looks better by day, when light must pour through the tall bands of window. Under artificial light, it seemed bleak. The huge sweeps of cream-colored wall seemed to be awaiting decoration. One wall was animated occasionally by the shadows of passersby or peerers-in on Lexington Avenue; that's not the sort of distracting animation a listener wants. But it's an interesting space, and the sound there seems to be good.

The students' café of the Manhattan School of Music, that airy modern pavilion added to the Broadway side of the former Juilliard buildings, up at One hundred and twenty-second Street, was packed last week for a concert given by the Group for Contemporary Music. Admission—or, rather, specified contribution—was only a dollar for students, three dollars for the general public; for another dollar one was invited to visit, between numbers, a table at the back of the room laden with punch bowls and flagons of wine. We sat around at tables. The lighting, from candles, was enough to read texts by. This was what a concert of contemporary music should be: a pleasant social occasion, providing a chance to talk to old friends and make new ones, in circumstances that do not preclude—that positively foster—careful attention to the music. The program included three premières. Ernst Krenek's *They Knew What They Wanted*, Op. 227, is a set of three sexy tales: of Ginevra and the handsome young clerk in the municipal office (from the *Decameron*), of Tamar and her father-in-law, Judah (from Genesis), and of Pasiphaë and the bull (recounted here in Krenek's own elegant cinquains). They are told in tempo (Rheda Becker was a vivacious, accomplished narrator) and accompanied by oboe, piano, percussion, and tape. Krenek himself directed the performance. The work is an entertainment executed with a master's touch: witty, laconic, neatly understated, not unserious. Andrew Violette's *Black Tea*, the setting of a poem—a Vietnamese widow's lament—by Gladys Brown, for soprano, harp, percussion, and double-bass, seemed to me earnest and carefully made. Tobias Picker's Rhapsody, for violin and piano, introduced a young composer who should be worth watching: a genuine creator, with a fertile, unforced vein of invention and the ability to hold one's attention on everything that he made happen. That expression of approbation is vague. I would need to hear the Rhapsody again and study the score before saying anything more specific. At any rate, it is certainly a piece that I want to hear again. It was performed by Benjamin Hudson, violin, and the composer.

November 20, 1978

For more about Tobias Picker, see page 284. His Rhapsody has stood up well to further hearing. It is recorded—together with his When Soft Voices Die, Sextet No. 3, *and* Romance for violin and piano—*on CRI SD 427.*

Still Fairer Hopes

The once familiar features of great composers have been changing with bewildering rapidity. It happened with Bach, with Rossini, with Verdi; now it has happened with Schubert. Who is this practical fellow who turns out—

churns out—the bulk of his cantatas during the first three years of a twenty-seven-year Leipzig appointment? Can he be the hebdomadally pious composer, praying in notes, whom we were brought up to revere? Who is this earnest operatic reformer striving in work after work to rescue the Italian lyric theatre from frivolity and formula? Surely not the "cynic amused" that Francis Toye once wrote about? And this carefully educated, cultivated, Paris-influenced, largely Paris-based man who has set his sights on an Opéra success, who insists on adding spectacular elements to the scenarios submitted to him? Is he recognizable as the self-taught peasant from Roncole, the bear of Busseto, the contemner of the Opéra and all its works?

And who is this prosperous and popular Viennese composer of the 1820s, the first musician in history to earn an independent living by his pen alone, without official post, princely patrons, or pupils; winning from his publications an average salary scarcely less than that of the Hofkapellmeister, Vienna's highest musical dignitary; second only to Rossini as the favorite of Vienna concert audiences? Can he really be the Franz Schubert who (according to Tovey) "never heard his own mature orchestral music at all," who (according to Sir George Grove) was dragged down into an early grave by "his privations, his absolute poverty, and the distress which he naturally felt at finding that no exertions could improve his circumstances"? Look here, upon this picture, and on this. Has the modern study of documents, of sketches and drafts, of watermarks in the paper on which they are written, of "compositional procedures," and of precise contours in the foothills from which the peak composers emerge made so great a difference? It has. The touch of exaggeration, even caricature, in the new portraits is forgivable in an endeavor to correct the old counterfeits.

Twenty years ago, Maurice J. E. Brown, in his *Schubert: A Critical Biography*, made an attempt "to present the composer in the light of a century of discovery and research," to substitute truth for the fairy tales of earlier biographers, to paint a "true picture of how he appears to the musical world of the mid-twentieth century." Brown—a science master by profession, a great Schubertian by calling—disposed of the sillier stories: that "Hark! hark! the lark" was written on the back of a menu, dashed off in a sudden moment of inspiration amid the hubbub of a beer garden; that half a dozen of the *Winterreise* songs were composed in a single morning and sold to their publisher for tenpence each. More important, he refuted the view that "Schubert is conspicuous among great composers for the insufficiency of his musical education," that "he had no great talent for self-criticism, and the least possible feeling for abstract design, and balance and order," and "no taste for the patient balancing, considering, and rewriting again and again, which was characteristic of Beethoven." Those phrases, from Hubert Parry's 1894 essay on the composer, express received ideas that ran on well into the twentieth century and still appear in popular books and unconsidered program notes. Most important, Brown made—and supported—the positive assertions that Schubert, so far from being a natural muses' son who created with carefree inspiration, was a dedicated, hardworking, and earnest musician, "the professional composer *par excellence,"* driven by "utter self-devotion to his genius"; that he should be regarded as an exemplar of the "grand style"; that (here Brown employs some of the exaggeration referred to above) "the very elements which many music lovers find most congenial are either absent altogether in his music, or only briefly encountered: wit, understatement, sophistication, picturesqueness, delicacy, bravura"; and that "his expression is full-blooded, personal, extravagant."

In his foreword, Brown remarked that "Schubert has been for thirty years, and will be for forty years to come, spared the attention of centenary celebration, with its unavoidable exaggerations and distortions." He did not reckon with sesquicentennial observance. Schubert died on November 19, 1828, and so 1978 has been a Schubert Year, with congresses, conferences, and performances in numbers numberless. In Detroit, from November 2 to 15, there was Schubert every day—a series of fourteen concerts, in a festival titled "Schubert/Vienna," put on by the Detroit Symphony Orchestra. The concerts ranged from symphonies and the opera *Alfonso und Estrella* in the big Ford Auditorium to chamber music in the Institute of Arts and in the Community Arts Auditorium, on the Wayne State University campus. Within the festival, there was a three-day international Schubert congress sponsored by the orchestra and the university. Vienna was further represented by Brahms, Wolf, Schoenberg, Berg, and Webern. The excellent Bern String Quartet played Alexander von Zemlinsky's Quartet No. 3 along with Schubert and Schoenberg. There were master classes, a course in Schubert and his poets, exhibitions, the B-flat Mass in liturgy. Everyone seemed to be joining in—except the Michigan Opera Theatre, which was playing *Show Boat*, not *Des Teufels Lustschloss, Die Freunde von Salamanka,* or *Fierrabras.* At the final concert, after "Der Wanderer," Schubert's "Wanderer" Fantasy, and the Schubert-Liszt "Wanderer" Fantasy, Antal Dorati conducted the orchestra in dances and marches by Schubert, Joseph Lanner, and Johann Strauss I and II. In 1828, Schubert, Lanner, and the elder Strauss were adjudged to have written the most successful dance music heard that year in Vienna.

Schubert and Detroit, it must be admitted, are as oddly matched in scale as are the little Schubert and the towering baritone Michael Vogl in the well-known caricature of the pair "setting out for battle and victory." I find Detroit a gaunt and hideous city, on the whole, but one filled with architectural excitements—most of them very big, and widely separated. The congressists were kept busy within three quarters where there are clusters of good buildings and where the civic determination to make Detroit a good place to live in—the "renaissance" that its inhabitants speak of with justified pride—can be seen and felt. The Ford Auditorium is in the riverside Civic Center, laid out on lines devised by the Saarinens—a good Yamasaki building opposite, and the soaring, glittering cylinders of the Renaissance Center, a modern Ilium, off to one side. The congress hotel was in the New Center, beside Albert Kahn's majestic General Motors Building and his breathtaking Fisher Building. Ten blocks away, in the Cultural Center, which includes the

Institute of Arts, Cass Gilbert's Public Library, and the Wayne State campus, the Schubert meetings were held in the airy pavilion that is Yamasaki's McGregor Memorial Conference Center.

It was a good congress; everyone seemed agreed on that. Admittedly, it had its bad quarter hours when a point that was either true—and evident the instant it was pointed out—or so farfetched that no amount of Bellman iteration ("What I tell you three times is true") could make it acceptable was labored. In 1958, Brown wrote:

> Both Tovey and Capell dwell affectionately . . . on the wonderful way in which the main key of C major is held back in the song "Dass sie hier gewesen," so that the preliminary remarks of the poet are given ambiguous harmonies, and the diatonic C major is not used until at length the words "I know that she has been here" are sung.

The familiar observation, which Tovey (in a famous essay on Schubert's harmony) and Richard Capell (in his eloquent *Schubert's Songs*) dwelt on fifty years ago—and which is also made in the song chapter of Gerald Abraham's Schubert symposium (1946), in Dietrich Fischer-Dieskau's book *Schubert's Songs*, in Gerald Moore's newly published *Farewell Recital*, and probably in fifty other places—received a protracted classroom exposition in Detroit.

The most startling biographical news came from Otto Biba, one of the two chief archivists of Vienna's Gesellschaft der Musikfreunde. An article in this month's *Musical Times*, a Schubert issue, summarizes what was formerly believed of the composer's less than close relations with the Gesellschaft; and it is all upset by Dr. Biba's revelations that in 1821 Schubert became a member, in 1825 an associate director, and in 1827 a full board member of the society. Leopold von Sonnleithner's statements that the Great C-major Symphony (usually dated 1828) was presented to the Gesellschaft in October 1826 and that "soon after it had been composed it was rehearsed by the Gesellschaft in the practices at the Conservatoire" now receive confirmation, Biba said, in the form of orchestral material dating from 1827; extra parts were made in 1830, and in 1836 the finale was publicly played in Vienna— three years before Schumann and Mendelssohn, in Leipzig, conspired to bring the "totally unknown" piece to light. (Sonnleithner is proving to be the most reliable of the early Schubert witnesses. Brown doubted his statement that the slow movement of the E-flat Piano Trio is based on a song by Isaak Berg: "It is hard to take Sonnleithner's suggestion seriously"; the song "has never been traced." But now it has been traced; and Sonnleithner is perfectly right.)

Does it matter whether the Great C Major was composed in 1828 or 1825? As John Reed, in his *Schubert: The Final Years* (1972), said, "the answer can only be that nothing can matter more to our idea of Schubert's development, indeed that no consistent account of his development can be given until the question is resolved." Reed argued passionately for 1825, after adding to his weighing of the contradictory evidence of documents his perception of the music: "One needs only the evidence of one's ears to agree that its energy and exuberance, Terpsichorean drive and generosity of scale all suggest a date pre-*Winterreise,* even if no account is taken of the many specific cross-references which link the symphony in style and idiom with other works of 1824 and 1825." That 1825 date has now been supported by Dr. Biba's archives, by Robert Winter's examination of the paper on which the symphony is written (see the *Musical Times* for last June), and by Ernst Hilmar's persuasive demonstration that the apparent *1828* on the autograph can be read as *1825* (see the *Österreichische Musikzeitschrift* for last June). Thus, satisfyingly, the varied disciplines of modern musicology conspire to support "the evidence of one's ears," and the crucial question *is* resolved at last: the Great C Major was begun in 1825, on 1825 paper, and completed the following year.

Back in 1867, Grove and Sullivan had already noted in detail the plentiful revisions that Schubert made. (Grove's excited, delighted, and detailed account of examining the manuscripts of the nine symphonies must be one of the first things of its kind in musicological history. He brought them all to performance—all but two from manuscript—at the Crystal Palace; and in 1880–81 they were done as a cycle, in chronological order.) The latest of the C Major revisions, Winter tells us, are on paper that Schubert used in the autumn of 1826, and presumably they were made just before he presented the score to the Gesellschaft. (At last week's New York Philharmonic concert, a program note continued to assign the work to the last year of Schubert's life, assured us that the composer had had no chance of hearing it, and suggested that the "high-spirited, jubilant symphony was probably an escape from the unhappy circumstances of its creator's life, Schubert finding solace in a world of his own making" at a time when he was "living on charity, ignored by the Viennese music public, cheated by unscrupulous publishers.")

Satisfyingly, too, the Detroit Schubert congress brought into focus much of the news about the composer that has been turning up in this sesquicentennial year—published in various periodicals or filtering back from the big Vienna congress held in June. We could hear with our own ears and assess the effect of expressive alterations and additions that Vogl, Schubert's favorite interpreter, would make to the plain written text of the songs: Walther Dürr, one of the editors-in-chief of the New Schubert Edition, sang them to us, with commentary. Arnold Feil, the other editor, joined Professor Dürr in a brilliant comic turn: a presentation of "Erlkönig" first as composed by Reichardt, Zelter, and other lesser lights and then as composed by Schubert, and recomposed after Schubert by Feil in a way to reveal the subtlety of Schubert's paragraphs and periods. They do their piece in different voices—Dürr in his singing, Feil (aided by eyebrows, popping eyes, and a hand that has language in it) in his commentary. Would that all musicologists had their realization that presenting a serious paper *viva voce* should be a performance, an entertainment; otherwise, just publish it. Other performers at the congress meetings were Elisabeth Schumann (enrolled via the phonograph), whose exquisite interpretation of "Nacht und Träume" stole through the room like a benediction, and Malcolm Bilson, who moved between a Viennese fortepiano and a Steinway to demonstrate how much Schubert's piano writing loses—in timbre, rhythmic incisiveness, clarity, vigor, and sodality with voice or strings—when it is played on a modern monster. Such demonstrations should hardly be necessary any longer. Yet a week earlier, in the music room of the Frick Collection—a domestic setting—Charles Rosen had played Schubert's last three sonatas on a thickly sonorous modern Steinway. He left no doubt that they were composed in the "grand style." He demonstrated the "streak of violence" that Hugh Macdonald discusses in "Schubert's Volcanic Temper," an article in this month's *Musical Times.* He made his points incisively—but as if to calloused ears. We can forgive a Serkin, Curzon, or Richter for sticking to the instrument he grew up with and learned to love and master: but how much longer must we go on listening to Mozart, Haydn, Beethoven, Schubert on the wrong instrument?

One star billed to appear at the Detroit festival failed to turn up. This was Robert Smith's replica of an early-nineteenth-century fortepiano by Conrad Graf. At the last moment, its maker decided that it was not yet ready for a début. So Mr. Bilson played Schubert on his Philip Belt replica of a late-eighteenth-century fortepiano by Gabriel Anton Walter. The program had to be changed: Schubert's A-minor Sonata, D. 537, and the B-flat Trio, originally announced, need the bigger instrument. But the Walter (whose clarity, sweetness, and immediacy can be enjoyed on two Advent cassettes that Mr. Bilson has recorded) was a perfect match for the sweet, pure soprano of Susan Robinson and for Sergiu Luca's violin in the D-major Sonatina. When it accompanied Charles Roe in a big song such as "Antigone und Oedip," it could be struck hard and sound forceful without becoming thick and without drowning the singer. Mr. Roe, a baritone with a tenor extension, and a dramatic artist versed in lieder, as Vogl was, sang a group of nine Schubert songs using Vogl's embellishments. He was impressive. In Mr. Bilson's playing, intimacy, poetry, and strength were combined.

The Great C Major has been shifted back to 1825, but we have gained a new piece to represent Schubert's last symphonic thoughts. A batch of symphony sketches, numbered D. 615 and dated 1818 in the old Deutsch catalogue, has now—on the basis of watermarks, handwriting, and style—been divided into three: symphony sketches of 1818, 1821, and 1828 (numbered D. 615, D. 708A, and D. 936A in the revised Deutsch catalogue, which has just appeared). They are set out in two-staff particella. For the Detroit congress, Peter Gülke, a conductor of the Dresden Staatskapelle, had orchestrated and recorded them. They contain some of the most adventurous music Schubert ever penned. D. 615 shows him experimenting with a new kind of material. D. 708A shows him pushing more conventional material down astonishingly bold and unconventional paths. From the sketches for D. 936A, Gülke built a full-scale Mahlerian Andante in B Minor which may well come to be loved as Schubert's *Abschied.* Its opening oboe theme (cited on page 218 of Brown's biography) had already suggested Mahler. Gülke claimed, and his versions seemed to confirm, that Schubert's great stride between the Sixth Symphony and the "Unfinished" is no greater than that between the Great C Major and this final unfinished symphony, cut short by death—that these fragments advance far beyond any of his previous essays in the form. The sketches are now published in facsimile by Bärenreiter, and no doubt they will soon attract other orchestrators. (Gülke's reading and realization did not go quite unquestioned.) There is precious music here that is worth hearing. To another rich store of precious Schubert music, contained in his operas, I hope to return.

November 27, 1978

Otto Biba's "Schubert's Position in Viennese Musical Life," Maynard Solomon's "Schubert and Beethoven," and Walther Dürr's "Schubert and Johann Michael Vogl: A Reappraisal" appear in 19th Century Music *3, no. 2 (November 1979).*

A Rich Possession

In the first act of Schubert's opera *Alfonso und Estrella*, Troila, the exiled king of Leon, places a chain around the neck of his son Alfonso as a pledge of his promise that one day the youth will be allowed to leave the valley in which they live; and Alfonso sings, several times, "May this chain shine like a star on my path, in every sorrow be my treasure, my talisman." Later in the act, Mauregato, the usurping king, declares that, according to a sacred vow, "only he who returns the chain of Eurich, still missing from the ancient regalia," may win the hand of his daughter Estrella. In Act II, Estrella is lost: "Who will point out the path to me, surrounded by crag and forest?" she sings, six times. Alfonso answers her question, and a sequence of three duets divided by two arias ensues—probably the longest love scene in opera before Act II of *Tristan.* Alfonso begins the last duet with "As memento of the most lovely moment, please accept this chain," and Estrella accepts it. Two scenes later, Mauregato is astonished to see his daughter return to court wearing the chain of Eurich. In a beautiful aria, she reveals that it was given to her by a golden-haired stranger; further explanation is cut short by the irruption of rebels led by Adolfo, Mauregato's generalissimo, who wants Estrella, and the throne, for himself. Such a series of events would be perfectly acceptable in a magic opera—even one in heroic vein—where chains of coincidence can reassure us that mighty spirits are guiding mortals toward a happy ending. And they are appropriate enough in comedy. (In Henri Rabaud's *Mârouf*, for example, we are charmed when Mârouf stumbles upon a genie and a treasure just in time to save his neck from the Sultan's axe.) But they make a slightly ridiculous effect in a high drama of chivalry and adventure laid in medieval Spain. The difference between chance and destiny may be one only of tone (in Calderón's comedies, Wagner once remarked, chance plays the role allotted to fate in the tragedies), but it is essential to get the tone right. The librettist of *Alfonso*, Schubert's friend and companion Franz von Schober, got it wrong. In later years, he confessed that his text was "such a miserable, stillborn, bungling piece of work that even so great a genius as Schubert was unable to bring it to life." Schubert, hoping for a Berlin production, sent *Alfonso* to the great soprano Anna Milder—Beethoven's first Leonore, and famous as Gluck's Iphigenia, Alcestis, and Armida. With mingled tact and perception, Milder replied that it would not quite suit the tastes of the public "accustomed to the grand tragic high opera [as composed by Spontini, the musical director of the Berlin Opera] or the comic opera of the French." She advised Schubert to tackle a one-acter on an Oriental subject. *Alfonso* remained unstaged until Liszt mounted it in Weimar in 1854, twenty-six years after Schubert's death. That was in a heavily abridged form. So far as I know, *Alfonso* has never been staged in a complete edition. Last month, in Detroit, there was a concert performance that was billed as the American première. About three-quarters of the score was done, perhaps a little more: there was two and a half hours of music.

Schubert wrote two grand romantic operas, *Alfonso* (1821–22) and *Fierrabras* (1823), and worked on a dozen or so other stage pieces, some of which he finished, some not. In the complete edition, his dramatic works form the bulkiest section. From about 1812, when he was fifteen, to 1823, he nearly always had an opera on the stocks. Only the one-act Singspiel *Die Zwillingsbrüder* reached the stage in his lifetime (it was done six times at the Kärntnerthortheater in 1820); yet not until 1823—after the rejection of *Fierrabras* and *Die Verschworenen* and the failure of the musical play *Rosamunde*, which was withdrawn after two performances at the Theater an der Wien—did he renounce his ambition to be a dramatic composer. (And then not completely: *Alfonso* was sent to Milder in 1825; and in his last years there was some sporadic work on a piece called *Der Graf von Gleichen*.) Three questions suggest themselves. Why did Schubert, in the face of repeated frustration, continue year after year to try to write for the theatre? Why were his pieces not done at the time? And why today, in this age of operatic exploration, when the works of Handel and Haydn and such pieces as Beethoven's *Leonore*, Weber's *Euryanthe*, and Schumann's *Genoveva* are performed from time to time, are these thousands of pages by one of the world's greatest and best-loved composers left largely unheard and almost entirely unstaged?

I don't think there are any simple, single answers. Since opera then as now was the most profitable kind of composition—provided the piece got done—financial inducement may supply a partial answer to the first question. But it seems to me that Schubert also had a vision of a kind of opera he wanted and felt qualified to write—one derived in part from the magic entertainments of which *The Magic Flute* is a transcendent example, in part from the heroic, elevated dramas of which *Fidelio* is the transcendent example, and in part from the tunefulness and picturesqueness of Rossini's serious operas. In 1820, when *Die Zwillingsbrüder* appeared at the Kärntnerthor, Schubert's musical play *Die Zauberharfe* was staged at the Theater an der Wien, and his theatrical future may have seemed bright. Early the next year, he composed extra numbers for the Kärntnerthor production of Hérold's *La Clochette*, and for a while he was a repetiteur at the theatre. (There he coached Caroline Unger, later the prima donna of Donizetti's *Belisario*, *Maria di Rudenz*, and other operas, for her Vienna début, in *Così fan tutte*.) In December 1821, the great Neapolitan impresario Domenico Barbaia took over the management of the Kärntnerthor and the Theater an der Wien. Rossini and Donizetti were at various times Barbaia's house composers and musical directors; he launched Mercadante and Bellini on their careers; for a while his empire stretched from the San Carlo in Naples, through La Scala in Milan, to Vienna. And this Diaghilev of his day was no foe to German opera. Once in Vienna, he commissioned new pieces from Weber and Schubert, put on the famous 1822 revival of *Fidelio*, and asked Beethoven for another opera. Beethoven's conversation books of the time produce a flurry of suggestions about possible subjects. (What kind of piece might he have written for Sontag, Fodor, Colbran, Unger, Rubini, Davide, Donzelli, Lablache—the Barbaia stars who sang Rossini, Donizetti, and Bellini?) Weber, although he had been specifically asked for "an opera in the style of *Der Freischütz*," produced the chivalric farrago *Euryanthe*, which was not a success, and which has obstinately resisted later attempts to bring it to life. Schubert submitted *Alfonso*, and it was rejected.

A one-word answer to Schubert's lack of operatic success in his lifetime might be "Rossini." In Vienna, as in Italy, Paris, and London, Rossini was all-conquering. His music first reached Kärntnerthor in 1816, with *L'inganno felice*. *Tancredi*, *L'italiana*, *Ciro in Babilonia*, *Elisabetta*, *La gazza ladra*, *Otello*, *Il barbiere*, *Il turco*, *Cenerentola*, *Armida*, *Mosè*, and the rest followed in a steady stream, flowing through both the Kärntnerthor and the Theater an der Wien, done sometimes in German, sometimes in Italian. Rossini fever reached its height with the composer's visit to the city, in 1822, and continued to rage. On the bill of a Beethoven concert, in 1824, "Di tanti palpiti," the hit number from *Tancredi*, appears between the Kyrie of the Missa Solemnis and the Ninth Symphony. (It was sung by Davide, while Sontag, Unger, and Donzelli, Bellini's first Pollione, sang in the Beethoven works.) In the 1824–25 season, Fodor starred in *Semiramide* sixty times. Schubert's admiration for Rossini is documented, and Rossini's powerful influence on Schubert's music has often been noted. In 1951, Alfred Einstein remarked that "there is much that is accepted as purely Schubertian which would be better described as pseudo-Rossini"; and today, when Rossini's serious operas are better known than they were then, the source of such things as the canonic trio in the first finale of *Alfonso* and of several episodes of romantic scene painting is more easily recognized. Moreover, today, when Rossini is no longer considered beneath respectable musicological concern, the debt that the finale of the Great C-major Symphony owes to the stretto of the first-act finale in *Il barbiere* can be acknowledged without embarrassment. What need stressing, rather, are differences between Schubert's operas and Rossini's, if one attempts to discover why the former had no success with a theatrical public whose enthusiasm for the latter was boundless. Differences are not hard to find. Schubert had no command of the *convenienze*—the tested and successful formulas that determined the vocal distribution, the form, and the sequence of numbers in Italian opera. Rossini's command of them was absolute, and though he departs from them often, it is always with deliberate mastery. But when Schubert begins the third act of *Alfonso* with six ensembles all employing the soprano, the effect is clumsy, amateurish, and undramatic.

Alfonso sounds direct echoes not only of Rossini but also of Gluck, Mozart, Beethoven, and Weber. In addition, there are more complicated echoes—of Mozart as reflected in Rossini, Cherubini as reflected in Beethoven, perhaps Gluck as reflected in Salieri. The aim in *Alfonso* and *Fierrabras*, it seems to me, is to unite the high seriousness of Gluck, Cherubini, and Spontini (whose *Vestale* and *Cortez* were played in Vienna), the directness of Beethoven, the picturesqueness of Weber, and the ready appeal of Rossini. It sounds an attractive formula, but the result is slow moving. Promising dramatic ideas—there are several of them—are worked out with untheatrical diligence for page upon page. Just about every action is treated to large-scale musical exposition, repetition, development, restatement, and emphatic coda. There is no feeling for stage time. One might say that Schubert, like Haydn, was far too thorough and expansive a musician to be a successful opera composer. Yet, like Haydn, in his operas he wrote page upon page of music that is well worth hearing. So one might also say that no one knows Schubert who does not know his operas. For one thing, although the orchestration is nearly always too massive for its purpose, it contains some of his most colorful and adventurous instrumental inventions.

Maurice J. E. Brown, writing in 1959, declared of *Alfonso* and *Fierrabras* that "the only reason why these operas continue to be unstaged today is the inaccessibility of the music." The full scores—soprano, alto, and tenor lines in C clef—appear in the complete edition. "How different the problem would be," Brown said, "if the two works were available in vocal scores." Since then, performing materials have been made: *Alfonso* has been done at the Edinburgh Festival, in concert, and by the Italian Radio (in Detroit the Italian parts were used), and last year it was staged by Reading University; *Fierrabras* was done by the BBC in 1971. Those performances, and now the Detroit *Alfonso*, produced confirmation of the old verdicts, rather than reappraisal. I agree with Brown that the actual plots are perhaps not as silly or as uninteresting as is often said; the action of *Fierrabras*, based loosely on Calderón, has some merit in it. But they are very clumsily handled, and, as I have suggested, the musical manner is often inappropriate to the matter. The true test, however, will come when the pieces are staged in style by a major company. It is disappointing that the Schubert sesquicentennial should pass in this country unmarked by any important stage productions. Massenet's *Esclarmonde* has reached the San Francisco and Met stages; surely *Alfonso*, for all its evident faults, has a larger claim to be heard on them? The City Opera has done Korngold's *Die tote Stadt;* why not *Fierrabras?* Only the little one-acter *Die Verschworenen* gets played from time to time. Otherwise, we must listen to Schubert's operas on records and in the occasional broadcast or concert performance. *Die Verschworenen, Die Zwillingsbrüder,* and *Der vierjährige Posten,* a lively little Singspiel of 1815, are already available on Electrola recordings, distributed in this country by Peters International. The singers are good; Helen Donath, Peter Schreier, Dietrich Fischer-Dieskau, and Kurt Moll are among them. And an *Alfonso,* with Edith Mathis and Schreier in the title roles, is due from Angel early next year [SX 3878].

The Detroit *Alfonso* made an excellent case for the music. It was very much a concert version: the piece was sung not in English but in German; no libretto was on sale, and the houselights were dimmed to a point that discouraged close attention to the synopsis in the program. Antal Dorati, who conducted, deployed the Detroit Symphony at a fuller strength than Schubert can have envisaged, but then he was performing in a much larger house—the Ford Auditorium—than any the composer would have known. Elisabeth Söderström was a wonderful Estrella. The part lies ideally for her: her voice was lustrous, clear of focus, and beautiful in timbre. She sang the music as if she loved it, in a way to make listeners love it, too. Curtis Rayam, the Alfonso, is a young-heroic tenor with fresh, well-formed tones; they were a little raw to start with but then warmed into a winning sound. William Parker, the Troila, is a fine young-heroic baritone, with the timbre and manner, at once romantic and noble, of Wagner's Wolfram. (Rayam can be heard, briefly, on New World Records NW 220, as the undervoice in C. A. White's "Trusting"; Parker sings Indian cycles by Arthur Farwell and Charles Wakefield Cadman on NW 213, and a recital of twentieth-century American songs on NW 300.) Peter Lagger as a vigorous Adolfo, Steven Kimbrough as Mauregato, and Catherine Grimshaw, Thomas Parker, and Bruce Hall in small parts completed an admirable cast. The Kenneth Jewell Chorale and the Detroit Lutheran Singers made a strong chorus. Dorati conducted with spirit, with appreciation of the colors and verve of the music, and also with feeling for the lyrical episodes. There were some delicately molded instrumental solos. One would have liked a performance in rather more intimate surroundings; at times conductor, singers, and players seemed to be forcing the piece out into the huge space, determined to make it go. It did go. The cuts were mainly of repeats. A few of them were regrettable—for Schubert sometimes seems more long-winded when his very long, elaborately balanced periods are curtailed—but they had been carefully considered. And cuts, we are told, are inevitable nowadays when long operas—except those by Wagner—are revived. Riccardo Muti, in Florence, seems to be the only conductor both able and willing to do pieces like *Guillaume Tell* and *Les Vêpres siciliennes* unabridged.

December 11, 1978

Theme Sublime

Once, twice, sometimes thrice a year, an opera by a composer of international reputation is given its world première. Intendants, directors, publishers, critics, and other interested parties gather from all over the world to attend the dress rehearsal, the first performance, and perhaps the second. A few months later, there comes the second production, in another city, and with it a round of comparisons and second appraisals. These events happen more often in Europe than in America: Puccini's *Trittico*, at the Metropolitan in 1918, and Prokofiev's *Love of Three Oranges*, in Chicago in 1921, were the last important international commissions and creations here until, last month, the Lyric Opera of Chicago brought Krzysztof Penderecki's *Paradise Lost* to birth. *Paradise Lost* was the third big première of 1978. In April, there was György Ligeti's *Le Grand Macabre*, in Stockholm; the second production followed in Hamburg, in October, and the English National Opera plans to mount it next year. In July, there was Aribert Reimann's *Lear*, in Munich; the second production followed in Dusseldorf, in October. The Chicago production of *Paradise Lost* travels to La Scala in January; next spring there will be a new production in Stuttgart; and another has been announced by Dusseldorf. *Paradise Lost* is Penderecki's second opera. His first, *The Devils of Loudun*, "created" in Hamburg in 1969, notched up eight different productions and a recording in four years.

The new work is a less sensational piece than *The Devils*, that dramatic but rather distasteful opera. Without questioning Penderecki's sincerity of purpose, one could question his sense of decency in making theatrical capital of scenes of sexual hysteria, purgation by enema, and prolonged torture. Even Puccini didn't go so far. And the music that accompanied those scenes had no redeeming power; rather, it seemed to aim no higher than to be an added means of titillation. *Paradise Lost* has an altogether solider and weightier score. An attempt in the opera house to justify the ways of God to men could hardly be anything but serious and substantial, and of all the many musical works based on Milton's poem Penderecki's is the most ambitiously Miltonic.

The earliest attempt at such a work was initiated by Dryden. In the words of Aubrey's brief life, "John Dryden, Esq., Poet Laureate, who very much admires [Milton], went to him to have leave to putt his *Paradise Lost* into a Drame in rythme. Mr. Milton received him civilly, and told him he would give him leave to tagge his Verses." The resulting five-act "opera written in heroique verse" was aptly titled by an iambic pentameter, *The State of Innocence, and Fall of Man.* Although Dryden imposed order as well as rhymed couplets on an epic that ranges hugely through space and backward and forward through time, his work did not reach the stage, and it was probably never set to music. A musical *Paradise Lost* did get done at both Covent Garden and Drury Lane in the latter half of the eighteenth century. The words, "altered and adapted to the stage from Milton," were by Benjamin Stillingfleet, and the music was by John Christopher Smith the younger, Handel's pupil and amanuensis. This *Paradise Lost* is an oratorio to a libretto cast in dramatic form, as Handel's oratorio librettos were. Lines of or after Milton alternate with songs such as Adam's

> *Sweet partaker of my toil!*
> *Partner of each pleasing care!*
> *We have duly till'd the soil,*
> *Sleep shall now our strength repair.*

The three acts, all set in Eden, traverse an evening, dawn the next day, and the final hours in the Garden. No Satan or Serpent appears to disturb us. Eve falls in the wings and then leads Adam offstage toward his fall. The other characters are angels. Stillingfleet does not flinch from raising knotty philosophical problems but does so in pretty verses, as when Eve asks:

> *Glittering stars, resplendent moon,*
> *To what purpose are your rays?*
> *Sleep will close our eyelids soon;*
> *None will then upon you gaze.*
> *Why? oh! Adam, tell me why,*
> *All this glory in the sky?*

There have been several other oratorios and cantatas on *Paradise Lost.* Anton Rubinstein's *Das verlorene Paradies* (1855) is termed an opera, but the vocal score reveals an oratoriolike composition; the three acts represent the Rebellion in Heaven, the Creation, and the Temptation and Fall. Enrico Bossi's oratorio *Il paradiso perduto* (1903) seems once to have been popular.

Its three parts are set in Hell, in Paradise (signifying Heaven, not Eden), and on Earth. Penderecki and his librettist, Christopher Fry, however, preserve an epic movement through time and space. Their work begins with Milton himself onstage, speaking fragments of the first-person apostrophes that open Books III and I. There is a "flash-forward" to the Adam-and-Eve postlapsarian squabbles of Books IX and X, jumbled together. Milton speaks again: "Who first seduced them?" The scene changes to the fiery gulf of Hell; the Satanic rally and great debate begin. When Satan mentions "a place, another World,/The happy seat of some new race called Man," there is an "inset" of Adam's creation. Satan's brave journey to that new world, past Hell Gate guarded by Sin and Death and on through Chaos, is "intercut" with a scherzo during which Adam names the animals (an unhappily cute little number, with children going "Baaa, baaa" and "Urrp, urrp," and a quotation from *Lohengrin* when the swan appears) and an intermezzo during which Eve is created (to the pretty sound of sonars—tubes that when whirled through the air on a string sound sweetly and mysteriously the notes of a major triad, changing harmonics as the speed of whirling alters). After Satan's arrival on Niphates top, events proceed more or less chronologically. The Messiah's intervention on man's behalf is represented. As in Milton, the unfortunate consequences of Eve's and Adam's lapse—murder, maladies ("inductive mainly to the sin of Eve"), warfare, flood—are revealed to Adam by St. Michael in visions while Eve lies quietly sleeping. Milton's order is not followed exactly, but there is a bold attempt, unmatched in any of the earlier *Paradise Lost* reworkings I know, to present things on the Miltonic scale, though far more briefly.

Is it possible to justify the ways of God to men? That is matter too large for a mere music critic to tackle. But if a reader of Milton's *Paradise Lost* says no—if all our woe cannot be reconciled with belief in a loving, omnipotent God; if Adam's tremendous, reproachful questions in Book X are inadequately answered; if, in Adam's words, "inexplicable Thy justice seems"— then Milton has failed in his specifically stated purpose, despite all his great incidental achievements. Many sage, sensitive minds have deemed that he did so fail, while creating hugely, greatly, as a poet. The question of belief— or, at the least, of a suspension of disbelief, willing or unwilling—cannot quite be evaded in an account of Penderecki and Fry's *Paradise Lost.* Unlike Stillingfleet, they have not simply handled Milton's argument in a decorative way. They expect of their listeners more than just aesthetic appraisal of and emotional response to their music and their spectacle. Of course, the events they portray no longer have to be understood as a representation of what really happened. Milton may have believed that our universe, with all things in it—except that unfortunate afterthought woman—was created in the space of six days, and that it hangs suspended from Heaven on a golden chain. For Penderecki and Fry, Milton's cosmography and history are (I take it) a myth, a spiritual and philosophical allegory, a poetic and potent way of expressing deep theological truths. One of the tenets central to Milton and therefore carried over into the opera, if less insistently stated there, is that woman is an altogether lower sort of creature than man. Today, there are people who find the historical jump to even a temporary acceptance of belief in woman's inherent inferiority harder to make than the jump to acceptance of belief in a loving Creator and a Saviour who lived on earth for a while in Palestine. One part of Milton's myth they denounce as pernicious; the other they can allow to be, at the least, acceptable for artistic purposes. I don't want to make too much of the point, but it does exemplify a large difficulty in recomposing *Paradise Lost* today: the need to separate what for Milton was all literal truth into essential allegory, picturesque incidental detail, and ideas to be rejected except as, perhaps, an illustration of ways in which people once thought.

Still, anyone who seeks to understand a large work of art follows the White Queen's advice: draws a long breath, shuts his eyes, and practices believing impossible things until he can manage six of them before breakfast. I was prepared to go along with Penderecki's *Paradise Lost* until, after the scene in which the Son offers to lay down his life to redeem man, the chorus sang the first chorale of Bach's St. John Passion, "O grosse Lieb', o Lieb' ohn' alle Masse." It did so in the translation of the Reverend J. Troutbeck, D.D.: "O wondrous love, whose depths no heart has sounded. . . . We live, the pleasure of this world enjoying,/And Thou art dying." But the actual words were not important; what mattered was Bach's harmonies and, beyond them, the associations of that chorale which are bred into anyone who has had a Christian upbringing. When I listen to Bach's Passion music, I am able to embrace a creed that has obtained in just a part of the world, during just a short twenty centuries of that world's long history. When I read Milton's *Paradise Lost,* I side with Adam, thrill to Satan's tragic grandeur, and feel admiration for the poet Milton—for his wide-ranging mind, his control of form, and his command of words whose weight, sounds, rhythms, and syntax conspire to picture the world and its works which I know, and worlds unknown. But when in Penderecki's *Paradise Lost* I heard Bach's chorale I felt that it showed up the inadequacy of Fry's text and, even more, of Penderecki's own music—in weight, sounds, rhythms, and syntax—to deal with the tremendous subject.

Fry's libretto is constructed from phrases, sometimes whole lines, abstracted from Milton. A single, fairly lengthy example can serve to show his method. Forty-seven famous lines from Satan's great invocation near the start of Book IV are condensed into eight short lines. Milton's Satan begins:

> *O thou that with surpassing Glory crownd,*
> *Look'st from thy sole Dominion like the God*
> *Of this new World; at whose sight all the Starrs*
> *Hide thir diminisht heads; to thee I call,*
> *But with no friendly voice, and add thy name*
> *O Sun, to tell thee how I hate thy beams*
> *That bring to my remembrance from what state*
> *I fell, how glorious once above thy Spheare. . . .*

Thirty-four lines later, he reaches:

> *Me miserable! which way shall I flie*
> *Infinite wrauth, and infinite despaire?*
> *Which way I flie is Hell; my self am Hell;*
> *And in the lowest deep a lower deep*
> *Still threatning to devour me opens wide,*
> *To which the Hell I suffer seems a Heav'n.*

Fry's Satan says:

> *O Sun, to thee I call*
> *How I hate thy beams*
> *That bring remembrance*
> *From what state I fell.*
> *Which way shall I fly?*
> *Infinite wrath, and infinite despair?*
> *Which way I fly is Hell*
> *Myself am Hell.*

Reduction, of course, was inevitable. Fry's is skillful. A librettist is usually re-quired to reduce the verbal music of his original, in order to make way for new music that will clothe it. (Few successful Shakespeare operas have been composed to Shakespeare's words. Britten's *A Midsummer Night's Dream;* what else?) Fry has fashioned a language whose vocabulary is Milton's but which moves in shorter, manageable periods. He has, as I have suggested, preserved something of Milton's epic form. The stage presence of the poet himself parallels the first-person interventions of the earlier books. The inter-mission (the opera is in two acts, each of about ninety minutes) falls between Satan's first, nocturnal and his second, successful temptation of Eve—be-tween which events in Milton four whole books provide an "interlude." But the diction can be disconcerting to anyone who knows Milton well: when Fry leaps a score or scores of lines, and even from book to book, in mid-sentence; when for no apparent reason he changes "thou" to "you," and even gives us things like "thou has" (Adam addresses Eve as "thou" but adopts a chummy "you" in dialogues with God); and, above all, when the stage Milton declaims the famous opening lines of the epic and gets three of the words wrong—"whose" becomes "where," "woe" becomes "woes," "with loss" becomes "and loss." The changes must be deliberate, else they could hardly have sur-vived the first rehearsal. But what is the point of them?

Penderecki, by his own admission, has an odd approach to words: he prefers to set languages that he does not know very well. As a result, his notes alone have to carry a heavy expressive burden. Because the word setting is not vivid, the singers cannot "use" the text, and it tends to be inaudible any-way. (It will be interesting to discover if this is so when Stuttgart does the piece in German translation; translators are often more scrupulous about making the words fit the music than the original composers are). *Paradise Lost* is not an opera that lives along the vocal lines and enters a listener's understanding through eloquence of vocal gesture. Milton is a speaker (he was electrically amplified in the huge Chicago auditorium). The Voice of God (in Chicago the same voice, Arnold Moss's, that spoke Milton) descends through loudspeakers most of the time, but some of His utterances are assigned to an ensemble of six male voices in the pit, singing in an antique manner that was suggested to the composer by hearing Samaritan chant. When Adam, in his first solo, delivered the tremendous questions "Did I request thee ["you" in this version], Maker, from my Clay/To mould me Man, did I sollicite thee ["you"]/From darkness to promote me?" in an unemphatic way, to phrases that had no sharply defined melodic or rhythmic profile, one began to wonder what Penderecki was at. No score of the opera was available for study; what the composer intended and what one actually heard may not be quite the same thing. William Stone, the Adam, is a young lyric baritone with a pleasant voice, but he was a bland, inexpressive performer. Ellen Shade sang Eve, and she is a lustrous, colorful performer. So was it Penderecki's intention or a chance of casting that made Eve register far more strongly than Adam? Miss Shade's rich, complicated timbre was better suited to the knowing than to the innocent Eve. Her aria and rapturous vocalise after tasting the fruit provided the lyrical high point of the evening. With Satan, the difficulty of distinguishing between intention and execution became most acute. In the libretto, the role looks very important, and Satan certainly has a great deal to sing. He was portrayed, by Peter Van Ginkel, as a plump, comfortable burgess: take off the feathered headdress and he might have been Kothner. A dramatic baritone is specified; Mr. Van Ginkel did not have the tones of command, and when he essayed force he was apt to woof about without defining exact pitches. But to what extent was this unimposing Devil the product of a resolve on Penderecki's part that Satan, for once, shouldn't steal the show, and to what extent of a feeble interpretation?

As in his Magnificat, Penderecki uses three countertenors: for Death, Ithuriel, and Raphael. Paul Esswood as Death and John Patrick Thomas as Ithuriel were good; Dale Terbeek delivered Raphael's warning so weakly that it was not surprising it went unheeded. Sin is a mezzo, and Joy Davidson, especially in a splendidly solid contralto range, was very impressive. Zephon, who keeps angel guard in Eden with Ithuriel, is a high soprano part, and it was sweetly sung by Susan Brummell. Among Satan's princes, the two tenors Michael Ballam and Melvin Lowery, as Beelzebub and Belial, were outstanding. The most sharply defined singing of all—and the only consistently intelligible words—came from Frank Little, as Michael, who dominates the final scenes of the opera. I nearly forgot to mention the Messiah, another baritone role, taken by Alan Opie. Penderecki plays down His part in things. When He visits Eden, after the Fall, to question and sentence man, the Voice of God that Adam hears is still the speaker's. In the Chicago staging, presented as the milksop, auburn-haired, white-robed figure of a child's illustrated Bible, Christ became an almost insignificant role.

What of the score? Much heavy, portentous orchestral writing; long, long pedals; thumping drum figures to indicate that something important is going to happen; ponderous brass progressions; grandiloquent organ; clusters building up and then "decaying." All the old, tricksy devices, for chorus and for orchestra, that one knows from Penderecki's earlier large pieces, and then some new ones. Some very pretty sounds, especially when Eve is around: the ensemble of sonars, already mentioned, during her creation, and a gamelan-like episode to accompany her dance through the Garden. A great deal of motivic construction, so insistently employed that everyone seems eventually to be singing much the same sort of music. Penderecki is in some ways the Puccini of our day—a fundamentally conservative composer able to assimilate and master whatever techniques are in the air and to serve up modern music without tears. He is a less individual and inventive musician than Puccini was, but he aims higher. When he misses the mark, the distance between aim and achievement produces an effect of bombast, even vulgarity. The end of this *Paradise Lost* is peculiar, almost irrelevant. Instead of Milton's movingly human close

> *They hand in hand with wandring steps and slow,*
> *Through* Eden *took thir solitarie way*

there is a moral:

> *Through the world's wilderness*
> *Long wanders man,*
> *Until he shall hear and learn*
> *The secret power*
> *Of harmony, in whose image he was made.*

The idea is touched on elsewhere in Milton, but it seems an intrusion into *Paradise Lost,* even in a musical version. Fry's words, astonishingly, prove to be adapted from Satan's suggestion to Christ, in Book IV of *Paradise Regained,* that, since He seems to be more a scholarly than a political type, He might take a course in composition and creative writing at Athens. The music closes with a long D-major triad, *tutta forza.* Wagner denounced the electric sunblaze that ends Act III of Meyerbeer's *Le Prophète* as an effect without a cause. The D-major affirmative blaze at the end of Penderecki's opera seems to me a musical counterpart.

I have been calling the work an opera. In the published libretto, Penderecki terms it a *rappresentazione,* but when talking about it he refers to it quite simply as an opera, too. *Rappresentazione* is not a genre; it simply means a "representation," though usually of something not commonly staged. (Emilio de' Cavalieri's *La rappresentazione di anima e di corpo,* put on in St. Philip Neri's church in Rome in 1600, is the most famous example.) The Chicago representation of *Paradise Lost* was inadequate scenically—but not, so far as one could judge, orchestrally or chorally; Bruno Bartoletti, who conducted, seemed to be in secure control. The shortcomings of two of the principals have been mentioned above. The staging was a last-minute endeavor to cobble a performance from ingredients that had begun to fall apart. *Paradise Lost* had a long and troubled birth. It was commissioned back in 1973, for Bicentennial performance. Sam Wanamaker was to direct it, and Josef Svoboda to design it. The score was not ready in time; a two-year postponement was agreed on. Virginio Puecher was then engaged to direct it, and Ezio Frigerio to design it. Nine days before the première, Carol Fox, the general manager of the Lyric Opera, announced that she had accepted Puecher's resignation, "following areas of disagreement between him and the composer." And Penderecki said, "As rehearsals progressed, I found that my own vision of the opera I have created was in conflict with Mr. Puecher's directorial concepts." Igal Perry, the young Israeli ballet master of Dennis Wayne's Dancers, had been working as an assistant on the show. He was called in to put it on. If one did not know the circumstances—had not been told that the elaborate scenery, which had been built in Milan, could not be got to function safely and silently, and was therefore reduced to near-immobility—one would say damning things about the failure to realize even the simplest of the visions described in the libretto, let alone the large ones. Eve didn't eat an apple. Satan never changed his costume.

One thing led to another. Because the towers in which the chorus sat in caged tiers had to be anchored, one at each side of the stage, there was no possibility of sidelighting. The composer insisted on an obscuring gauze between the stage and the audience; and so Duane Schuler, who usually lights so well, had to fall back on overhead spotlights, which fell on the singers' foreheads, noses, and chins while leaving their eyes and lips in shadow. And so on. Having learned these things, all I can do is suggest that Mr. Perry made an intelligent attempt to save something from the wreck. It was not his—or perhaps anyone's—fault that Eden was a black-painted disco with a glitter roof; that no heavenly radiance shone; that the stasis of the chorus destroyed any sense of epic movement. Only one element seemed to come off as had been planned—the important dances, choreographed by John Butler in his familiar manner. The singers of Adam and Eve have dancing doubles, who were well portrayed by Dennis Wayne and Nancy Thuesen; even more important than the sung duets in Eden are the danced duos, one before and one after the Fall.

December 18, 1978

Moral Mirth

Late in 1842, Donizetti composed *Don Pasquale*, his last and in many people's opinion his best comedy, for the four singers who were generally reckoned to have the most beautiful voices and most accomplished techniques of their day: Giulia Grisi, Mario, Antonio Tamburini, and Luigi Lablache. Mario, who had made his Théâtre-Italien début in 1840, was the new boy of the famous quartet, in which he had replaced Giovanni Battista Rubini. For Grisi, Rubini, Tamburini, and Lablache, in 1835, Donizetti had composed *Marino Faliero*, and Bellini *I puritani*. At the time of *Don Pasquale*, Grisi and Mario, the young lovers of the plot (and lovers in life), were in their early thirties; Tamburini, the Malatesta, was in his early forties; and Lablache, the Pasquale, was nearly fifty. Grisi had been singing for some fifteen years, Tamburini and Lablache for some twenty-five. All four were in their prime and still had many years of glory on the stage before them. All were celebrated in both tragedy and comedy: Grisi was the leading Norma of the age, and Lablache the noblest and most powerful Oroveso.

For its new production of *Don Pasquale*, the Metropolitan has chosen three veteran singers whose voices are worn and not beautiful and a dapper young débutant whose timbre became metallic and a shade raw when, in his aria, he pushed up the volume in an endeavor to fill the enormous house. And so the vocal rewards of the evening were few. Beauty of sound is not everything, though it counts for a good deal. Beauty of style, wit, musical and verbal resourcefulness, and delicate acting can go a long way toward carrying the day. (Late in his career, Mariano Stabile was still a matchless Malatesta.) *Don Pasquale* is such a delightful opera that once the execution passes a certain point it is easy to be indulgent to any shortcomings. But if that point is not reached it is hard to be forgiving—and it is hard to forgive the Met its new *Don Pasquale*. One can try to find excuses: the sheer size of the house; the difficulty of playing a domestic comedy in a language not that of the cast or the audience. But the difficulty was compounded rather than overcome by the casting, the direction, the designing, and the conducting.

The Lincoln Center program book for December contains a penetrating essay by Conrad L. Osborne in which he traces what *Don Pasquale* has in common with the regular commedia dell'arte plot of the amorous old man outwitted and in what ways it represents something new. The librettist, Giovanni Ruffini, adapted an earlier text, by Angelo Anelli. Both men had been political prisoners. In 1833, Ruffini and his brother Iacopo, ardent followers of Mazzini, were condemned to death. Iacopo committed suicide in prison; Giovanni managed to escape. *Don Pasquale* was created in the Paris circle of

Italian political exiles. (So was *I puritani*. Its librettist, Carlo Pepoli, had passed a term in the Venetian prisons, where his sight was impaired. I own a sketch of the *Puritani* libretto in Bellini's hand with a later marginal note by Pepoli explaining that he had dictated it "when the infirmity of my poor eyes absolutely prevented me from writing.") One doesn't go to *Don Pasquale* expecting the performance to make a patent and emphatic political statement. If it did, I would be quick to denounce it as a traduction of the essential nature of the piece. But I did go to this *Don Pasquale* having been reminded by Mr. Osborne of the atmosphere in which it grew, and at a time when the newspapers had set me reflecting on parallels between Iranian drama today—both comic and serious—and Italian drama of the nineteenth century. (At the Shiraz Festival, I used to meet playwrights who worked within restrictions much like those Donizetti's and Verdi's librettists had to suffer.) Any opera worth its salt is more than an entertainment or a divertissement. Opera almost from its inception has been the most potently political form of art, in its courtly days hymning and then with increasing frequency challenging the status quo. And, as Mr. Osborne puts it:

> The libretto's description of Pasquale as an "old celibate, old-fashioned, tightfisted, credulous, obstinate," while Ernesto is a "young enthusiast" and Norina "of a volatile nature, impatient of contradiction," defines a conflict that echoed in the streets. Pasquale must be taught a lesson not only to fulfill a *commedia* intrigue or to re-enact one of society's ruling myths, but to strike a blow for social and sexual equality. These are the same blows struck by the heroes of so many operatic tragedies of the nineteenth century.

If *Don Pasquale* proves so much more moving than *Il barbiere*, it is because Donizetti's work is more than the standard comedy of manners and character. In the rondo-finale of the piece, Norina sings, "The moral of all this is easy to discern. . . . It is foolish for old men to get married." But a deeper moral has been sounding in Donizetti's music: that the conflict between the old, conservative ways and the revolutionary new thought need not have a tragic outcome. Crabbed age and youth *can* live together, and, in Mr. Osborne's words, "we must forgive the old the blindness that comes of the need to preserve, as we must forgive the young their insensitivity." Donizetti's score—his bold new inventions on traditional foundations, his unconventional treatment of familiar stagecraft, even his demonstrations that themes on restatement should reflect new ideas, and not just be unthinkingly repeated—tells of reconciliation between the best of the old and the best of the new. His moral needs no directorial stressing. It emerges naturally from a performance that is musically resourceful, presents the characters as the composer conceived them, and holds a just balance between hilarity and tenderness. An audience should find Don Pasquale at once ridiculous and deserving of sympathy, and should feel—as Norina herself feels—that she has gone too far when she strikes him.

At the Metropolitan, the designer, Desmond Heeley, has for what seem to have been purely cosmetic reasons shifted the action forward from the Risorgimento to the early years of our century, and so Ernesto and Norina are no longer—not even lightly and obliquely, within the comic context—representatives of Mazzini's Young Italy. Sensibly, Mr. Heeley has blocked down the immense stage opening, but he has done so by using black borders and backcloth and coarse gilded frames decked with heavy, full-blown roses which suggest an expensive funeral parlor. Norina redecorates the house in execrable taste, and the garden of the last scene is on a ducal scale that makes nonsense of the middle-class milieu. John Dexter's production eschews broad clowning—and for that one is grateful—but it is fussily focused upon stage properties. Nos. 1 and 3 of the score are apparently about the mounted butterflies that Don Pasquale collects. No. 2 brings the first statement of the overcoat joke—Do put it on and leave; No, I won't—that then dominates No. 4, the duet "Prender moglie." No. 5, Norina's "Quel guardo, il cavaliere," becomes an aria of which a vamp's long cigarette holder is the central feature. In No. 6, Norina and Malatesta's rehearsal duet, business with wineglasses is prominent. No. 7, Ernesto's "Cercherò," is about his false starts at writing a poem in a notebook. And so on. There is a long and honorable tradition of stage business in *Don Pasquale*. Lablache's enactment of the simple direction "raccogliendo un foglio," in Act III, was a turn that kept audiences laughing for minutes on end; his enormous bulk made it hard for him to pick up the letter that Norina had dropped, and repeated attempts were necessary. That was business of a kind that arose naturally from the physique of the man, and it was in character. But Mr. Dexter has obscured character, motivation, and the simple sense of what the actors are saying beneath a crust of intrusive, irrelevant, finicky inventions.

Beverly Sills's portrayal of the heroine was especially distressing, for Miss Sills is usually a deft and intelligent actress. Has any previous Norina failed, in the Act II trio, to distinguish between her own sparkling asides and the timid utterances in her assumed role of Sophronia? And do Mr. Dexter and Miss Sills really think that a demure young lady "from the convent fresh emerging" would plonk herself down in a drawing room with legs widely straddled; or that Pasquale would for a moment entertain the idea of marriage to such a hoyden? On the first night, the soprano's tones were brittle and insubstantial until in the rondo-finale they found a freer, fuller flow. Nicolai Gedda's stage demeanor can suggest Vašek even when he is playing Benvenuto Cellini, so perhaps Mr. Dexter was accepting the inevitable when he changed Ernesto from a romantic young lover to an owlish booby. (As a recurrent joke, Ernesto wore glasses but whipped them off whenever Norina appeared or was mentioned.) Gabriel Bacquier is on record as saying, "I don't believe Pasquale can be played in a comic way," and he certainly brought no great sense of humor to the role. In a dry, unexuberant, misguided manner, he gave a rather polished performance, and marshaled his voice skillfully. Only Malatesta was done along traditional lines, by Håkan Hagegård;

and, once an undervoiced "Bella siccome un angelo" was over, he was perfectly acceptable. Under Nicola Rescigno, the orchestra sounded rather loud and heavy.

Things may improve a bit when the performers can take the elaborate business in their stride and start thinking about their roles and how to express them. The first night was a glum affair. I came home and listened to Ferruccio Corradetti and Giuseppe De Luca's ebullient recording of the Act III duet "Cheti, cheti" (made in 1907; most recently reissued in the EMI album "The Record of Singing"). There is a good deal of spontaneous fooling about—perhaps more than a modern audience would accept—but it is all improvised on a basis of secure, elegant command of the music, and the authentic characters of Pasquale and Malatesta shine out in every deliciously funny inflection. That ancient recording has more life in it—and more gaiety—than the Met's live show.

December 25, 1978

Famous Orpheus

Elliott Carter's latest composition, *Syringa*, is a twenty-minute piece for mezzo-soprano, bass, and an ensemble of eleven players. It might be called a chamber cantata. The top layer of its text, sung by the mezzo-soprano, is a poem—of eighty-seven lines, most of them long—by John Ashbery, which was written for Carter to set. The title is unexplained. It carries the associations of reflorescence, of recurrence, of a sight reawakening emotions from a poignant past, which have long been attached to the lilac by Whitman's Lincoln elegy. To paraphrase the prose sense of an Ashbery poem is seldom easy. His *Syringa*, as I read it, has an autobiographical starting point in some keen loss suffered long ago, something comparable to Orpheus's loss of Eurydice, which changed the burden of his song from celebration of "the glad personal quality Of the things beneath the sky"— Eurydice being "a part Of this"—into passionate lament. That is just the starting point; the themes of the poem are a poet's possible ways of dealing with grief and continuing with life, and the legend of Orpheus provides a precedent. Precedent can become vivid and personal when in the tale of "a totally different incident with a similar name" there are discerned "hidden syllables Of what happened so long before that In some small town." Ashbery uses images that seem to enshrine memories from that small town:

> *Singing accurately*
> *So that the notes mount straight up out of the well of*
> *Dim noon and rival the tiny, sparkling yellow flowers*
> *Growing around the brink of the quarry, encapsulizes*
> *The different weights of the things.*

But memories cannot be caught in "a single snapshot." Life flows as music flows, and the value of one moment or one note cannot be known until all is done: " 'The end crowns all,' Meaning also that the 'tableau' Is wrong." So long as Orpheus' songs dwelt only upon his lost Eurydice, he was as the reeds in a river or grasses beneath the wind, stirred by life but not a participant. *Syringa* is also a poem about the making of a poem (or a song) while "the whole wheel Of recorded history flashes past." It proves apt for musical treatment.

Along with Ashbery's lines, Carter has set a second text, a Greek anthology of his own compilation, which is sung by the bass. In a program note, the composer talks of expressing "the subliminal background that might be evoked in the mind of a reader [of Ashbery's poem]"—a background that includes Plato, Attic tragedy, and thoughts of a possibly historical Orpheus who was more than an incantatory singer and founded an important religion. Carter begins in the beginning, with the Creation story of Orphic writings, including some lines attributed to Orpheus himself. But when the bass arrives at the birth of Eros, fairest among the immortal gods, he breaks down on the word ἀθανάτοισι (immortal), and moves into exclamations of lament. The priest becomes the bereft husband; Gluck's famous "Che farò senza Euridice?" finds a counterpart in a line from *Alcestis*, "σὺ γάρ, ὦ μόνα, ὦ φίλα γυναικῶν" ("For you, O only one, O dear wife"). It coincides with the sentence in Ashbery's poem "Then one day, everything changed." While the mezzo tells how Apollo came to Orpheus and bade him cease lamenting, the bass sings Mimnermus's version of "Gather ye rosebuds while ye may," as if opposing to the passionate "What is life to me without her?" (an old translation of "Che farò") Mimnermus's "What is life without Aphrodite . . . without stolen meetings, lovers' gifts, and lovers' union?" (Mimnermus mourned his lost flute girl, Nanno, in graceful measures.) When Orpheus was killed, his head, still singing, down the stream was sent until it reached the Lesbian shore. For a hundred and fifty bars, the bass sings love songs by Sappho and then a springtime love song by Ibycus while the mezzo tells of Orpheus' later life, his death, and his philosophy; Carter makes the natural images in Ibycus and in Ashbery coincide. The bass then recounts (from the *Symposium*) Phaedrus' version of Orpheus' descending into Hell—that he was sent empty away, with only a wraith of Eurydice, because, mere minstrel that he was, he did not dare, like Alcestis, to die for love. This coincides with a difficult stretch of the Ashbery poem, a meditation on illusion and comprehension which is ascribed to horses—and comes rather close to being Thoughts We Doubt Each Horse Thought.

The play of ideas between the English and the Greek texts is analogous to the play of musical ideas so often found in Carter's chamber works. The two strands may be independent or related; one may seize upon and adopt elements of the other; related passages may be presented simultaneously or lapped, or even widely separated, leaving the listener to make the connections. In *Syringa*, there is also an occasional interplay of similar sounds between the two languages: an Aeschylean pun on *Apollo* (from the *Agamemnon*) is followed by a Carterian diglot pun when the bass's cry of "στέλλου, κομιζου" (or "stelloō, komizoō," "Begone, go away," from *Prometheus Bound*) is taken up by the mezzo's "Stellification Is for the few." Carter's Greek text ends with a musing on "σῶμα, σῆμα," from Socrates' reflection, in the *Cratylus*, that in Orphic doctrine the body (σῶμα) is but the sign, or even the tomb (σῆμα), of the soul—as if the soul, buried in its present existence, could make signs only through the body. The mezzo's last word, *summer*, echoes the bass's "sōma, sēma." Although the words are unrelated in meaning, the congruence of sounds, the music made by consonants with varied vowels, provides a satisfying cadence.

From all this, it must be clear that *Syringa* is not just the latest in the long, long line of compositions celebrating music's power of stirring men to mirth, melancholy, compassion, and awe. Carter invites us to move between "some small town" and the ancient world where—in the words of W. K. C. Guthrie's *Orpheus and Greek Religion*—"we find ourselves among men to whom [Orpheus] meant much more than a kind of superior snake-charmer, who understood the power of melody to sway the creatures of animate or inanimate nature to his will." His spirit left its mark on Greek philosophy, thought, and religion, crossed to Rome, and was known to the early Christians. The intellectual content of *Syringa* is rich and dense. I would recommend anyone approaching it—may it soon be recorded—to read in advance not just the Ashbery poem (several times) and the Greek texts but also Guthrie's book, I. M. Linforth's *The Arts of Orpheus*, and the further studies and the poems to which those books will lead him. Not that *Syringa* cannot be enjoyed without such preparation. At the first performance, which was given in Alice Tully Hall last month by Jan DeGaetani, Thomas Paul, and the Speculum Musicae, conducted by Harvey Sollberger, the audience was handed a sheet containing only the Ashbery poem, not the Greek texts. The English could be followed. As for the subliminal background: those that understood Mr. Paul smiled at one another; but, for mine own part, it was Greek to me—a Greek in which cries on Apollo and Eros and cries of despair ("ὤ," "ἔα," "ὀτοτοτοῖ") that need no translation, but not much else, could be comprehended. *Syringa*, however, is musically eloquent independent of its texts. The patterns of line, gesture, and timbre, the sound of the two languages interacting, and the rhythmic tensions and releases made sense—not the full sense that only study of the words can reveal, but enough.

Syringa sounds beautiful. Orpheus's lute is here a guitar (it was wonderfully well played by Scott Kuney), and the instrument opens the piece as if exploring the first mysteries of musical language: the jar of adjacent semitones sharply twanged, the impulse that propels a leading note toward its resolution, the resultant pang if that resolution is delayed. When the bass enters to take up the line, this "lute" strikes chords in accompaniment. Cello, bass clarinet, viola, alto flute, violin, English horn, double-bass join in, one by one. The piano and the drums are held back until the moment when "everything changed" as Eurydice was lost. Then the trombone enters, to add force to Orpheus' violent, rock-rending cries of despair. (*Fissures* is a word Ashbery might perhaps have avoided in a text intended for singing; the ear hears *fishers*, even *fishes*, and is distracted for a moment.) The appearance of Apollo is heralded by a still moment, a solo signal on the alto flute, and then soft, limpid vibraphone chords. The alto flute comes to the fore in the Sappho fragments. Ashbery's passage about "The way music passes, emblematic Of life," coincident with Sappho's "Cool waters from above sing as they flow through the apple orchard," inspires some of the most seductive pages that Carter has penned, a soft web of lilting yet elusive rhythms and tender, lapped melodies. The final pages seem to be a mystic transfiguration of this passage.

The two singers were admirable. Miss DeGaetani has acquired a new way with words. To her old command of an exquisite, profoundly expressive musical line she has added a power of inflecting that line with verbal sense, and—aided, of course, by the composer's delicate, incisive word setting—she caught to perfection the varied tone of Ashbery's verses, which ranges from the conversational to the elevated. Mr. Paul, called on to be in turn hieratic, rhetorical, impassioned, lyrical, and pensive, fulfilled every demand. The Speculum playing lived along every line.

Syringa was done in an all-Carter program—Speculum's only New York concert of the season—on the eve of Carter's seventieth birthday. The concert began with the Brass Quintet (1974), played by the American Brass Quintet, and ended with the Double Concerto for harpsichord and piano (1961), in which Paul Jacobs and Ursula Oppens were the soloists and Richard Fitz was the conductor. After *Syringa*, Carter's Elizabeth Bishop song cycle, *A Mirror on Which to Dwell* (1975), was done by its dedicatees, Susan Wyner and Speculum, under Mr. Fitz. Like *Syringa*, the two recent works and the earlier one were performed with superlative accomplishment; the concert was the climax of the Carter septuagenary celebrations that made New York's musical life rich during the final months of 1978. This "Carter festival" began in late October with a League-ISCM program, in Carnegie Recital Hall, which included early chamber music and songs. In November, there was chamber music in the Juilliard Theatre played by the Juilliard String Quartet (the Second Quartet, of 1959), by the Atlantic Woodwind Quartet (the Eight Etudes, of 1950), and by the pianist Gilbert Kalish (joining the cellist and then the leader of the Juilliard Quartet in the Cello Sonata, of 1948, and the Duo for violin and piano, of 1974). In Tully Hall, the Juilliard Orchestra, under Sixten Ehrling, gave the New York première of the suite made in 1941, and revised in 1969, from the ballet *Pocahontas* (1936). The Gregg Smith Singers, in the same hall, revived some of Carter's early choral settings. At the end of the month, the Philharmonic, under Zubin Mehta, gave the New York deuxième of the Piano Concerto (1965), with Miss Oppens as soloist. In December, two days before the Speculum concert, the Composers String Quartet played Carter's three string quartets in one program, up at Columbia. On his birthday, the American Composers Orchestra, under Dennis Russell Davies, played the Variations for Orchestra (1955). The next day, Michael Boriskin played the Piano Sonata, and four days after that Richard Sher and Bernard Rose played the Cello Sonata, both in Carnegie Recital Hall. Which left unheard a few small pieces and, of the larger compositions, the Symphony No. 1 (1942, revised in 1954), the ballet *The Minotaur* (1947), the Woodwind Quintet (1948), and the two orchestral pieces written to Philharmonic commissions: the Concerto for Orchestra (1969) and the Symphony of Three Orchestras (1977). However, recordings of all but the first and last of these were broadcast in a set of five WNCN programs devoted to Carter. From the English office of his principal publishers there came a booklet with a perceptive essay by Bayan Northcott, tributes, and a catalogue. No. XIX of J. F. Weber's Discography Series, dealing with Carter and William Schuman, gave details of the fifty-eight recordings of Carter's music. (It is obtainable, for one dollar, from 310 Genesee Street, Utica, New York 13502.) The last two Carter entries are Columbia recordings of the *Mirror* and the Symphony of Three Orchestras, the latter made as long ago as February 1977, but both of them still unreleased.

I attended most but not quite all of the celebrations. They provided not so much revaluation of Carter's music as confirmation of the value long attached to it. Six years ago, when his Third String Quartet appeared, I wrote that "internationally, Elliott Carter . . . is now America's most famous living composer," and chose words carefully at a time when Ives's music, too, was prominent in Europe and Carter's was less frequently played in America than it is now. The pieces that have appeared since then—the Duo for violin and piano, the Brass Quintet, the *Mirror*, the Symphony of Three Orchestras, and now *Syringa*—and, equally, increasingly revelatory performances of earlier works once but imperfectly executed prompt a less cautiously limited affirmation. In a "world view" there are perhaps six established very important composers active today: Carter and Tippett, now in their seventies; Boulez, Henze, and Stockhausen, in their fifties; and Maxwell Davies, in his forties. (If I omit Messiaen, who is one day older than Carter, it is because I am thinking of composers not only distinguished by the creation of a large body of substantial works in many forms, and by an individual, quickly recognizable voice, but also "active" in the sense that each new work of theirs breaks new ground.) Any attempt to order the six would be silly; each of them has different things to offer, on which various listeners place different values. But I do think it at least likely that if there were to be an international poll to nominate "the greatest living composer" Carter's name would lead all the rest.

The basic musical facts of his career have been set out often enough to need no restatement. The clearest account of his development is probably his own essay "Music and the Time Screen," published in *Current Thought in Musicology* (1976) and reprinted in *The Writings of Elliott Carter* (1977). It recounts his thoughts about rhythm, time, and metre; about harmony; and about musical "character" implicit in instruments themselves. (Although Carter taxes the musical intelligence of his executants to the utmost and stretches their traditional techniques, he never asks them to produce outré, unmusical noises foreign to the nature of their instruments.) But toward the end of the essay he confesses that what he has discussed is only

> the outer shell, the wrapping of the music. The reason for writing it—for developing it in the way described, for weighing every note, chord, rhythm in the light of their expressive intention and their living, spontaneous interrelationships, and the judging of it all, almost unconsciously, against a private standard of what gives me genuine sensuous pleasure, of what seems fascinating, interesting, imaginative, moving, and of urgent importance—cannot be put into words.

A little earlier, he remarks ruefully that "the artistic horizon of the American composer is not expanded by life in a society that is unable to furnish him with artistic and intellectual ideas and critiques of sufficient depth, clarity, and quality to be of much use." And yet his isolation, his independence of vogue, and his sturdy insistence on remaining an essentially American composer when he could have been—was, is—an idol of enthusiastic European audiences have surely been a source of his strength. He cannot be fitted into any movements or modes. The companions on his voyages of exploration into a world of new music have been not other composers but imaginative writers whose imagery has suggested to him structure, texture, even "content" for compositions; some inspiring executants who bring his notes to life with love and intelligence; and also—or so it seems to me—natural phenomena: patterns made by wind, water, and light, the maculation on a birch trunk, the striations of a shell. For these last I have no evidence but that of my feelings—not while I listen (there is seldom overt "tone painting" in Carter's music; the wheeling gull flight of the trumpet solo near the start of the Symphony of Three Orchestras is a graphic exception) but afterward, when, trying to find words, I resort to similes from nature to describe the mysterious satisfaction of senses and spirit which the music has afforded.

Carter himself points to the First String Quartet, of 1951, as the work in which he found his individual voice. He went into the wilderness, literally, to create it. For the first time, he composed without considering what difficulties he might be putting in the way of both performers and listeners. Paradoxically, the piece was played more widely than anything he had written before. From the quartet, the richly branching lines to the later compositions are easy to follow. But in the earlier compositions heard during the birthday celebrations the accents of that voice were already sounding. In the 1945 song "Voyage" (admirably sung and played at the League concert by Susan and Yehudi Wyner), the vocal line, floating above and free of the piano part, adumbrates the two kinds of motion, simultaneous but not synchronous, heard in so many of his later works. The first and last of "Three Poems of Robert Frost" (same performers, same comment), of 1942, reveal the wit and the sparkle that often make Carter's music lovable. These qualities could be heard again twinkling in the Sonata for flute, oboe, cello, and harpsichord, of 1952 (played by Mr. Sollberger, Steve Taylor, Eric Bartlett, and Mr. Jacobs to close the League concert), in the Brass Quintet, and in the Double Concerto. Carter, like Haydn, can bring a smile of pure pleasure to a listener's lips, but interpreters who have long since mastered his rhythms and his notes, who can play with the music as well as play it, are needed to reveal the charm and humor—mischief, even—of the musical working. In *Pocahontas* one finds a composer familiar with Stravinsky and Hindemith, and some measures not far from the "American pastoral" vein of Copland or Barber, but also, and more often, a characteristically Carterian kind of rhythmic motion. *Elegy,* which was played at the League concert, in its viola-and-piano version, by Guillermo Figueroa and Alan Feinberg, may date back to the thirties, according to David Schiff's program note; its long, lyrical span already looks to the shapely, self-generating melodies of the latest works.

At the Composers String Quartet recital, concentration—on works that call for very great concentration—was made difficult by the presence of glaring lights beating down into the audience's eyes and of an obtrusive film crew walking about the hall, and even across the platform, during the music. But, so far as I could tell, the Quartet played the pieces—especially No. 2—with even more eloquence than it brought to its earlier, justly celebrated performances. The Composers Orchestra account of the Variations was excellently vivid and balanced. Miss Oppens was a thoroughly satisfying soloist at the second and third of the three Philharmonic performances of the Piano Concerto. At the first, she had seemed a shade reticent, but at the others she was both commanding and very expressive. However, the seven-instrument concertino, intermediary between the soloist and the full-orchestra mass, did not stand out clearly, and the three big woodwind solos of the second movement lacked sharpness of characterization. It was better than the old recording. But I feel I have still to hear the whole piece as lucidly and lovingly rendered in all its details as the Double Concerto was at the Speculum concert.

What next? One Sunday afternoon in December, there was a three-hour Carter program on WKCR, during which the composer revealed that before the summer is out he hopes to have finished a piano piece for Miss Oppens, Mr. Jacobs, Mr. Kalish, and Charles Rosen (who played the Piano Concerto in London last year)—not an eight-hand piece but a response to requests from each of those four notable Carter pianists. [This piece, *Night Fantasies,* was given its first performance, by Miss Oppens, at the Bath Festival, in June 1980; Nicholas Kenyon reviewed it in *The New Yorker* of September 1.] Similarly, the Fires of London, the London Sinfonietta, and Boulez's IRCAM ensemble, in Paris, which have all asked for a new composition, may be given one to share among them. Meanwhile, the feast of recent months has still to be digested. Thank heavens for the phonograph: the only way to understand Carter's music is to listen to it, and listen again. But the real performances, the play of so many different fine musicians upon music that was written to live on the breaths and under the fingers of its executants (the account of the Brass Quintet, for example, was not note perfect, but it was freer and more vivid than the one on the Odyssey recording), and the cumulation of so many sensuously pleasing, imaginative, moving, and important compositions brought new understanding and new enjoyment.

January 8, 1979

Intuitions

Tobias Picker's Octet, dedicated to the ensemble Parnassus and its director, Anthony Korf, had its first performance, in Carnegie Recital Hall, last month. The nine-minute work happily confirmed the favorable impression made by Picker's Rhapsody, for violin and piano, at a Group for Contemporary Music concert the month before. The forces of the Octet are oboe, bass clarinet, and horn, violin, cello, and double-bass, harp and vibraphone/marimba; and they are skillfully and imaginatively handled. The start of the piece suggests that of *Tristan* in the way motif steals upon motif to build into chords, but instead of Wagner's clinging semitones there is a gentle, open whole-tone flow—or, rather, a series of flows so directed that, while a cross-section through any point of the opening measures may reveal a common triad, one hears a web of lines and timbres instead of a chord progression. The scoring is smooth. Voice laps over or enters upon voice; coincidence on crossing points lends color and emphasis to the moments of unison; the texture is active but not dense or lumpy. A whole-tone melody implicit in the opening measures, later drawn out in a single thread by the horn, is never far away, but the moods and the motion of the music change freely, as if in a set of improvisations spun from that basic theme. The ending comes suddenly, perhaps too suddenly—but better that than a welcome outstayed. I find Picker's music hard to describe. I can't point to influences. Sometimes I think he may have been listening to Varèse timbres. Carter may have encouraged his feeling for inner rhythmic vitality. (Picker's music "keeps going" in an organic way, generating its own energy, not relying on motor or moto perpetuo pulses.) The harmony seems to have been arrived at by intuition. My intuition tells me that he is one of the most gifted, individual, and unschematic of our young composers. He is twenty-four.

I wasn't able to get to the Parnassus concert and am writing about it on the strength of a very clear tape I borrowed from the ensemble. Picker's Octet was preceded by a poised and yet passionate account of Varèse's *Octandre*. A trenchant performance; special praise for the oboe, Gerard Reuter. The concert ended with Charles Wuorinen's *The Winds*, composed for Parnassus in 1977 and here receiving its second performance. This is a brilliant, animated stretch of music, lasting fifteen minutes. The forces are five woodwinds (flute, oboe, clarinet, bass clarinet, bassoon), three brasses (trumpet, trombone, tuba), and piano. A repeated-note signal recurs to define the structure; some episodes are whirling, some lyrical. There is exuberance both in the invention of incidents and in the scoring, which makes striking use of different combinations, of timbre contrasts when a note moves from instrument to instrument, and of lines moving in and out of unisons. Perhaps Picker found some ideas here.

The prolific Wuorinen is in good form, and December was not only Carter month but also a Wuorinen month in New York. Besides *The Winds* and the Second Piano Sonata (a Bicentennial piece, which Jeffrey Swann played in Carnegie Recital Hall), there were two premières. First, the American Composers Orchestra, under Dennis Russell Davies, played Wuorinen's Two-Part Symphony, in Alice Tully Hall. This is a neoclassical composition; in a program note, the composer suggested that he might have called it Symphony in C or Short Symphony had not those titles already been used by Stravinsky and Copland. Stravinskian the piece certainly is, but with a difference, for, like *The Winds*, it is twelve-note music with an emphatic tonic—E-flat in *The Winds*, C in the symphony. Wuorinen says that he "had a very good time writing it"; and people will have a good time listening to it. (The performance was recorded by CRI, on S-410.) Nevertheless, it struck me as being one of Wuorinen's larger but not one of his "major" or most intensely imagined compositions. In the last few years, I have heard more new works by Wuorinen than by anyone else, and have been bored by only one of them (the piano duet *Making Ends Meet*—and that may have been the performers' fault). [It is recorded on Desto 7131.] He brims with lively ideas. He effortlessly commands—and combines—a diversity of techniques. A big, generous creativity pours through even the overschematic channels he sometimes devises.

The second Wuorinen première was of *Archangel*, a short piece (about twelve minutes) for bass trombone with string quartet, played at a Group for Contemporary Music concert up at the Manhattan School. It's a severe, concentrated work with apocalyptic overtones, opening with noble, lyrical declamation. Toward the end, the trombone, muted, grows hoarse—more dark angel than archangel—and finally it sounds those pedal tones that Messiaen has made into a symbol of abyss. The work was commissioned by David Taylor, who played it most tellingly. Wuorinen is already well represented on disc. If I had to pick three more works to illustrate in small space and as vividly as possible the variety of his achievement, they might be the somber *Archangel*, the glittering *Arabia Felix*, and the high-spirited *On Alligators*.

I asked a friend what "media hype" means, and learned that it means the creation of a reputation and of box-office success by high-pressure, insistent publicity, and that by extension the term is sometimes applied to the object of such a campaign. "Like Lazar Berman?" "Yes, or like Youri Egorov." Now, certainly the kind of yucky publicity with which the young Russian-émigré pianist Egorov has been promoted might be enough to deter sober musicians from taking him seriously. He studied with Jakov Zak at the Moscow Conservatory. In 1976, on a tour of Italy, he asked the Dutch authorities for asylum, and now he lives in Amsterdam. When he didn't make the finals of the Van Cliburn International Piano Competition, in Fort Worth, in 1977, indignant members of the audience raised for him an equivalent of the ten-thousand-dollar grand prize. He has the kind of looks that sell records with his face smiling out shyly from the sleeve. "Women seem to fantasize about hugging him," one read in *Musical America*. EGOROV: THE NEXT HOROWITZ? was a Chicago headline. About his Carnegie Hall recital last month, the *Times* reported him as saying, "The wonderful thing about this program is that I can combine the music of Bach, Mozart, Chopin, and Schumann with myself, with my own fantasies." Well, there was a good, serious cello recital in Carnegie Recital Hall that night. I decided to start in the big hall and at any rate sample the prodigy. And stayed on till his last encore to admire—now let me add my mite to the hype—the biggest and most poetical young pianistic talent I have ever encountered.

The program was Bach's Chromatic Fantasy and Fugue, Mozart's C-minor Fantasy (without the sonata it was written to introduce), Chopin's F-minor Fantasy, and Schumann's C-major Fantasy. The Bach began with a blurred, pedaled, Schumannesque run—a pianist's Bach, not a purist's, but beautiful, warmly and lovingly molded. The Mozart was bravely expressive in phrasing and never aggressive in timbres. In the Chopin, Egorov's special merits began to shine. Both it and the Schumann, which was played as the second half of the recital, are unorthodox structures (their titles were intended to indicate as much), and both were accorded exceptionally coherent performances—and that despite an employment of large-scale rubato uncommon today.

Egorov is evidently an intuitive interpreter, and all his instincts in Chopin and Schumann were right. His playing confirmed an argument put forward in *The Chopin Companion*, a collection of essays edited by Alan Walker (Norton Library, 1973). In an early chapter in which the Fantasy and form are discussed, Alan Rawsthorne remarks, with a composer's authority, that "Chopin's instinct rarely errs, and it is instinct conditioned by experience and reflection that will ultimately solve the problems of musical form." In a later chapter, Walker chooses the Fantasy for his demonstration that an extended work containing an astonishing diversity of ideas can nevertheless express a unity. Such a demonstration, Walker rightly insists, is something that should come *after* understanding: "Musical understanding is essentially intuitive." Having made the "leap in the dark," the listener can then try by analysis to gauge what has been jumped. And, of course, there is no suggestion that Chopin consciously patterned the multifarious melodies of his Fantasy to redefine precisely thematic boundaries established in the first two measures of the *tempo di marcia.* "The musical intuition of a genius obeys unconscious laws. We are more likely to catch a glimpse of them in Chopin than in many other composers precisely because he worked intuitively." The operation of unconscious laws is subtler than that of imposed, consciously worked thematic identities of the Lisztian type. The interpreter determined to impose unity upon great diversity, or to demonstrate his perception of it, may give an arresting "lecture," but he will not bring the music to life. Two remarks in Alfred Brendel's collection of essays *Musical Thoughts and Afterthoughts* (Princeton, 1976) are apropos. "*Feeling* must remain the Alpha and Omega of a musician." And, "The moment an audience feels that a performer wants to teach them, his case is lost." I must stress that Egorov's feelings, intuition, and instincts are right. If they were wrong—if what he calls "my own fantasies" had distorted or obscured Chopin's and Schumann's fantasies—playing as free as his would degenerate into shapeless rhapsody. Instead, a long line ran unbroken through each work. Of two performances now past, this can be only one listener's assertion. But there is a "demonstration" of his capacity for long, linear thought in his recording (on Dutch EMI) of the "eight fantasies" that make up Schumann's *Kreisleriana.*

Schumann was twenty-six when he composed the C-major Fantasy. Egorov is twenty-four. He seems to be made of different stuff from most young pianists. (Was that why he got nowhere in the Cliburn Competition?) Not for a moment did he show any wish to impress the audience with how fast, how loud, or even how beautifully or how intelligently he could play. His technical ability is apparently boundless, but he revealed no more of it than was needed for the piece in hand. Even his last encore, Liszt's *La campanella,* was treated not as a display piece but as a stretch of fleet, delicate poetry in which miracles of virtuoso execution could be taken for granted. He played a Baldwin—a very beautiful instrument, whose clear, unboomy bass, soft-shining, unglittery treble, and warm evenness through the whole range proved ideal for Romantic piano music and for Egorov's unshowy, romantic, tenderly fervent approach to it. He played as if he were unaware of his audience, although in fact he could not have been. There were many noisy, unmusical people there (drawn by the media hype?), and open, unstifled coughing sometimes drowned the piano. After the march section of the Schumann Fantasy, during what should be a stilled, breath-catching moment into which the *lento sostenuto* arpeggios then steal, some brute bawled out "Marvelous!" It *was* marvelous—majestic, energetic but quite unhurried, grandly powerful at the climaxes without any harshness or hardness of tone—but more marvelous still was the sense that this "Trophies" section remained unfulfilled until it was followed by the soft benediction of "Palms."

Egorov is more than a young man with a pretty face, fast fingers, and a headline-catching history of defection in Rome and failure-become-triumph in Fort Worth. His platform manner is modest, his personality self-effacing. He seems to be a Baryshnikov, not a Nureyev, of the concert world. May he survive unspoiled.

January 15, 1979

A recording of Egorov's Carnegie Hall recital—but without the Schumann Fantasy that was so rudely interrupted—appeared on Peters PLE-121. The Schumann Fantasy, coupled with his Arabeske, *then appeared on PLE-122.*

Viva Vivaldi

The lasting memorials of Vivaldi's tercentenary year are recordings—chief among them the three albums containing the operas *Tito Manlio* (Philips), *Orlando* (RCA), and *L'Olimpiade* (Hungaroton). When Alfredo Casella launched the Vivaldi revival, in Siena in 1939, he included an opera, *L'Olimpiade*, in a week-long festival. That revival got under way after the war, but when, on long-playing records, Vivaldi swept the world it was as an instrumental composer. Concerto performances poured out by the dozen; some attention was paid to the church music, but only one opera, *La fida ninfa*, was published, and until last year it was the only one available on disc. I have never seen a Vivaldi opera on the stage—only dramatic representations of his oratorio *Juditha triumphans*. While operas by Steffani, Alessandro Scarlatti, Caldara, and Vinci were being revived, it was surprising to encounter none by the composer whose name had become a household word. Vivaldi once claimed to have written ninety-four operas. That figure presumably included serenatas, intermezzos, and pasticcios, for only some fifty operas by him have been identified. The music of some sixteen survives in a reasonably complete state. In 1978, at least eight of them were brought to performance: besides the three recordings, there was a concert *Griselda* in London, a staged *Orlando* in Verona, a French Radio *Fida ninfa* in Paris, an *Incoronazione di*

Dario from Clarion staged in Siena and given a concert performance in Castelfranco, and a *Farnace* at a Clarion Concert in Alice Tully Hall. Nothing that I read about them showed the sort of enthusiasm that revivals of Caldara and Vinci have kindled. After attending *Farnace* and then listening, on consecutive days, to the three recordings, I suspect that the fault is not Vivaldi's. Each of these performances revealed some of his strengths, but not one did justice to all of them.

Vivaldi's operas are long—as long as Wagner's. *Tito Manlio*, the most nearly complete of the three recorded performances, takes ten sides, as do *Tristan*, *Die Meistersinger*, and *Parsifal*. And only this *Tito Manlio*, with its sequence of thirty-six well-contrasted arias, two duets, accompanied recitatives, and much secco recitative (here abridged but still abundant), gives an adequate idea of how a Vivaldi opera is made. There is rather a good plot—a seventeenth-century libretto, by Matteo Noris, first musicked by Carlo Francesco Pollarolo in 1696, drawn from Livy, and set in 340 B.C., during a Latin rebellion against the Romans. The Roman consul Titus Manlius condemns his son Manlius to death for disobeying orders and slaying a Latin foe, Geminius, in single combat. The conflict between paternal fondness and impartial severity provides the central crisis; Titus's recitative as he hesitates to sign the warrant is eloquent. The sister of the slain man comes to Titus to plead for the life of Manlius, whom she loves. Manlius' own sister comes to her father to insist on her brother's death, for she loved Geminius, and he her. But each heroine is divided between love and sororal affection. All would end in tragedy had not Noris (in defiance of history) allowed Titus to accept, at last, a plea for acquittal by Manlius' fellow-officers. "The will of the army is law to the law," he declares. There are three further characters, and two of them are also in love with Manlius' sister; nevertheless, it is a tight, well-motivated, and not uninteresting drama. Vivaldi noted on the score that he had written the music in five days. "It sounds it" would not be a fair comment—unless one meant that the work flowed with unlabored brilliance and effortless felicity of invention. *Tito Manlio* was composed for the Archducal Theatre in Mantua, which had a well-stocked orchestra. Trumpet, recorder, cello, oboe, and violin each provide the obbligato to arias otherwise accompanied only by continuo. Some textures are rich; one is bare to the point of being simply violins in unison with the voice. The opera gains by being heard in extenso: a heroic aria is followed by one still more heroic, with trumpet obbligato; a lovely "slumber" aria for the imprisoned Manlius is followed by one even lovelier, with violin obbligato, for his beloved as she watches his slumbers. The conductor is Vittorio Negri, who doesn't let things grow slack but sometimes keeps fast arias jogging along with a Tigger-like bounciness. There is beautiful playing by the Berlin Chamber Orchestra. The singers are an accomplished team—smooth, refined, and flexible in their vocalization. But only two of them are Italians—the basses Giancarlo Luccardi, in the title role, and Domenico Trimarchi, as a servant (a welcome seventeenth-century survival into eighteenth-century opera seria)—and they are the only ones who utter the text with due vividness. The others sometimes sound as if they were on their best behavior; one wants a stronger whiff of the theatre. Rose Wagemann, a Met Leonore, sings the mezzo role of Manlius.

Tito Manlio dates from 1719. *L'Olimpiade*, fifteen years and twenty-four operas later, has an even better libretto—one of Metastasio's most celebrated, written for Caldara the year before Vivaldi set it, and used again by more than fifty composers, right up to the young Donizetti. This time, Herodotus provides the basic material. His account of the competition for the hand of Agariste, the daughter of Cleisthenes of Sicyon (Pericles' great-great-grandfather), is one of the funniest episodes in the *Histories*, and could make a fine opera buffa. Metastasio's version is more serious. No one dances on a table or stands on his head, beating time to the music with his feet. The competition takes place at the Olympic Games, at which Cleisthenes is referee and Megacles victor ludorum. Megacles, not knowing that the prize is to be the girl he loves, has enrolled for the games under the name of his friend Lycidas, who is no athlete but desires Agariste. By the workings of a rational and admirably constructed plot, Megacles, having won, is thus forced to choose between his love for Agariste and his loyalty to Lycidas; unable to resolve the conflict, he attempts suicide. Lycidas, disgraced when his scheme is discovered, is ordered into exile, but instead of obeying he attempts to kill Cleisthenes and is sentenced to sacrificial death. Cleisthenes pronounces the sentence with reluctance, expressed in the famous lines that begin "Non so donde viene" (lines that were twice put to music by Mozart). The final scene inhabits the world of *Idomeneo*. The priests chant; the smoking altars await the victim; he advances, brave and unfaltering; the ritual begins—but is interrupted by a heroic woman offering to die in place of the man she loves. Instead of a deus ex machina or an oracle, there comes the revelation that Lycidas is Cleisthenes' long-lost son, and although this turn of events may sound Gilbertian, it is simply and soberly achieved. In any case, Cleisthenes, having embraced his son, prepares to continue the rite: the father must yield to the judge. But Megacles declares that Cleisthenes' sway does not extend beyond Sicyon; in Olympia the people have the last word. They do so, pronouncing forgiveness and a happy ending.

The last act of *L'Olimpiade* as here recorded makes a tremendous effect. There are seven fine numbers: a strange and very beautiful quintet of contrasted emotions; a strong aria for Argene, the woman who loves Lycidas; a chromatic aria for a subaltern character, Lycidas' tutor; a ritual chorus not far from Gluck; a noble setting of "Non so donde viene"; a powerful accompanied recitative; and a coro finale that is not the usual perfunctory jubilation but a solidly worked stretch of music containing surprises. "As here recorded," I say, because the edition used is the one that Virgilio Mortari made for Siena in 1939, and the album note does not tell what relation it bears to Vivaldi's original score. In his 1939 program notes, Mortari wrote of "cuts, reorderings, and substitutions" and of additions from the 1734 opera *Dorilla*. Vivaldi's score is in Turin, the nearest 1734 libretto is in Washington, and I have not checked to discover what's what. I do feel pretty sure that the roles of the two young men, Megacles and Lycidas, are sung an octave too low. That is something that should not happen today. It spoils Vivaldi's music, much as using a baritone Cherubino or Octavian would spoil Mozart's or Strauss's, much as using a baritone Caesar does spoil Handel's. (In *Tito Manlio*, the young heroes' roles are sung by women, untransposed.) Mortari's pioneering edition, which takes six sides, is, I suppose, based on an anthology of what he considered the best numbers in *L'Olimpiade*. But forty years have passed since he wrote of not "demanding of the public that they should suffer austerities and conventions which today would doubtless be intolerable." Today's public is surely readier to enjoy Vivaldi on his own terms. (I hear that a new scholarly edition of *L'Olimpiade*, by Francesco Degrada, is on its way.) A heaviness in the recorded performance is due often to the downward transpositions, and sometimes to the conductor's slow tempi. In the pronunciation, there is a good deal of *kvesta-* and *kvell*ing. Da capos are undecorated, and blunt endings instead of appoggiaturas are plentiful. On the credit side, all concerned seem to believe that the music is beautiful and expressive, and show it to be so. Despite everything, this is finally an eloquent performance.

I have gone into the plots because these Vivaldi operas need to be followed, not just listened to. The Vivaldi experts disagree about the significance of the recitative. Walter Kolneder, in his book on the composer, speaks of "long recitatives, whose dramatic purpose we find hard to understand today because we know that as a rule they were not listened to at all. . . . Obviously the recitatives had the purpose of resting the singers and spreading out the raisins well in the cake." But of *L'Olimpiade* Hellmuth Christian Wolff writes in the *New Oxford History of Music*, "The first priority . . . was that Metastasio's affecting poetry should be heard, expressively declaimed and acted. The arias were only in the nature of interludes." Both scholars seem to me to be wrong. Recitatives and arias *both* call for attention, even though the poet's contribution to the former may be more important than the composer's. With what pleasure one listens to them depends on how well the singers declaim them. Of Mozart's *Il re pastore*, which has a Metastasio libretto, Edward Dent once wrote, "The whole of the real drama is in the recitatives; and every word of them must be savored like sips of an Imperial Tokay." The recitatives in the *Orlando* recording are treated by the singers in this spirit. In the very first of them, Victoria de los Angeles is so limpid of tone, shapely of phrase, and eloquent in her handling of words that when it was done I moved the needle back to enjoy it all over again. This *Orlando* set provides something missing in the two others—virtuoso singing. In the title role, Marilyn Horne offers prodigies of bravura. Sometimes there is a touch of coarseness in the way she sends her chest tones flying through quicksilver divisions. But she is never less than astounding. And all the singers are very able—even Sesto Bruscantini, though he is much hampered by being made to sing mezzo music an octave too low. Claudio Scimone conducts brightly, and there is fine playing from the Solisti Veneti. Da capos are decorated; cadenzas are elaborate. In the continuo, there are too many obtrusive Technicolor effects. *Orlando*, which dates from 1727, is a picturesque opera, a "spectacular" after Ariosto, calling for a flying horse and elaborate transformation scenes. (The record box is decorated with a large helmet, which reminds one that in 1725 the Hamburg Opera paid a composer only fifty florins for his score and spent a hundred florins on a helmet for the principal singer.) Unlike *Tito Manlio* and *L'Olimpiade*, it is neither a very sensible nor a noble drama, and what shape the original may have had has here been destroyed by wholesale cutting and reshuffling. (In an album note, Scimone provides a frank, detailed account of his rearrangement.) But there are scenes passionate, violent, tender, and pathetic, and they are all vividly performed.

The Clarion *Farnace* was not very well sung, and Tully Hall is unsuited acoustically and in atmosphere to baroque opera. (Town Hall would have provided a better shape and a better feel.) The opera dates from 1726, and was revised the following year. The plot is one of those in-and-out-and-roundabout intrigues, concerned with dynastic difficulties in a Pontic kingdom set up by Pompey. The fierce, vindictive ambition of the ex-queen Berenice—Pharnaces has both seized her husband's throne and abducted her daughter, Tamiri—gives it some continuity, and Elaine Bonazzi played Berenice with spirit. Otherwise, I carry from the performance memories of a very pretty nightingale aria sweetly sung by D'Anna Fortunato; an excellent simile aria ("Burned by scorching rays, I am a wretched plant") sung by Joy Zornig; a capital aria for Pharnaces, using material from "Winter" in *The Four Seasons;* and a high-tension recitative before the happy ending. Newell Jenkins, who had made the edition, conducted.

During the year, I Virtuosi di Roma, some good soloists, and the Italian Radio-Television Chorus, conducted by Renato Fasano, brought a performance of *Juditha triumphans* to Avery Fisher Hall. This *sacrum militare oratorium* has been called Vivaldi's best opera. It is a magnificently rich work, accompanied by perhaps the most colorful orchestra Vivaldi ever assembled. No libretto was provided, so many people may have missed the points of the drama. (Wise virgins brought a text from one of the three recordings there have been.) Two of the singers were exceptional: in the title role, Carmen Gonzales, a smooth and beautiful young contralto with a good feeling for words (she is also an excellent Bradamante in the *Orlando* set, and has sung with the City Opera), and, as Bagoas, Nucci Condo, long breathed, even, and fluent in divisions. About two-thirds of the work was done: recitatives were shortened, and the aria da capos were shorn to ritornello restatements (which made the numbers lopsided). Philips has a complete recording, conducted by Negri.

Largest-scale Vivaldi was represented by the first installment of the recording of the complete sacred choral music promised by Philips. It contained five double-choir, double-orchestra pieces: the *Dixit dominus* (with its introduzione for solo soprano), a Kyrie, "Beatus vir," "Lauda Jerusalem," and "Domine ad adiuvandum me." Negri conducts. The British soloists, choir, and orchestra are admirably accomplished. The whole effect is splendid. All the same, I began to wish for a more Latin tang and bite in their sound.

Of concerto records, of course, there was a torrent. (There are now thirty-two versions of *The Four Seasons* in the Schwann catalogue.) I made no attempt to keep up, but can recommend the latest oboe concertos that Heinz Holliger has recorded with I Musici (Philips). They are enough in themselves to show that Vivaldi was not the "dull fellow" Stravinsky called him. Vivaldi, in my experience, becomes dull only when one isn't really listening—or when he is dully played.

January 22, 1979

Classics

The New Music Consort devised three good programs for its series in Carnegie Recital Hall: French, Austrian and German, and Italian evenings, each built around one or two of the twentieth-century "classics" that established themselves about a quarter of a century ago—Boulez's *Le Marteau sans maître*, Messiaen's *Oiseaux exotiques*, Stockhausen's *Zyklus*, Berio's *Circles*, Nono's *Polifonica-Monodia-Ritmica*. Just listing the titles makes me feel old; I remember discovering and writing about those pieces with excitement when they were new. An early version of *Le Marteau*, with just six of the nine movements it now has, appeared at the 1954 Donaueschingen Festival. Hans Rosbaud introduced the full piece at the 1955 ISCM festival, in Baden-Baden. A few weeks later, he conducted a deuxième, at the Aix-en-Provence festival, and that was the only time I've seen an audience come to blows after a new work. A few hours later, the Aix casino band pattered out a parody of *Le Marteau*. The surface sounds of the piece are readily imitable; within a few years the concert halls of the world were filled with *petits marteaux* emulating the high, delicate timbres created by the Maître. The Marteau ensemble—alto flute, xylorimba, vibraphone, guitar, viola, percussion, alto singer—is one without a bass voice, except for a few strokes from deep and even deeper gongs in the finale. In a preface to the score, Boulez says that Far Eastern and African sounds influenced his instrumentation, though not in any way his musical vocabulary: "It's more a matter of European musical vocabulary being enriched by non-European hearing." The work wears well. It is instantly alluring to the ear, even pretty. Beyond that, it is exquisitely, satisfyingly constructed, number by number and as a coherent sequence. While most of the tinkling pieces of the fifties which it influenced now seem no more than dainty, faded finery, *Le Marteau* stays strong. The Consort's performance, given at the first concert of the series, and conducted by George

Manahan, was well balanced. What the composer called the "chain"—its links the single characteristic each instrument shares with another—running through the ensemble held firm. But violence of emotion was missing. *Le Marteau* is also a fierce piece, if fierce with a controlled, inner passion. Its texts are by René Char, a poet to whom Boulez was drawn by what he discerned as "a contained violence, not the violence of many gestures." (*Le Visage nuptial* and *Le Soleil des eaux* also have Char texts.) Although the Consort's rhythms were precise, the players did not sound indignant or angry. In the four movements with voice, the alto part was sung by Beverly Morgan, true and exact in the lower and middle reaches, not cleanly focused on the high notes. The other "classic" in this French bill was *Oiseaux exotiques*, also of 1955, played with spirit and accomplishment and making a brave, bright sound in the little hall. Aleck Karis was dashing and secure in the important piano part. The programs are planned to reach both forward and backward. This one included the *Inventions* (1959–61) of Gilbert Amy, a Boulez pupil, which was billed as a New York première. I'd heard the piece before but can't remember when or where. It is early and unmemorable Amy. The evening began with Debussy's Sonata for cello and piano, played by Madeleine Shapiro as if it were a cello solo with accompaniment, and more eloquently by Mr. Karis.

Why do cello-and-piano duos so often sit in a way that prevents the players' eyes from meeting? (String quartets don't arrange themselves on the platform facing out, back to back.) The new concert hall in Abraham Goodman House, the Hebrew Arts School, on West Sixty-seventh Street, was inaugurated last month by a cello-and-piano recital given by Nathaniel Rosen and Samuel Sanders. Mr. Sanders is an able pianist, but in Chopin's Sonata, where the piano should be at least an equal and probably the dominant partner, he let Mr. Rosen take the lead. Mr. Rosen's tone is large and golden, his manner broad and confident. The recital began with a François Francoeur sonata, played in what might be called the full-blooded conservatory prize-pupil fashion rather than with any nice appreciation of French baroque style, and the music had evidently passed through the hands of a modern editor. Since this was one of those December nights when Elliott Carter called, I did not stay for the whole recital and must delay a detailed report on the new hall till I have heard more music in it. First impressions were favorable: the sound was warm, the shape pleasing, the feeling intimate. The place has four hundred and sixty seats—about twice as many as Bruno Walter Auditorium (in the Library of Performing Arts) and half as many as Tully Hall. Lincoln Center lacks such a hall, and so Abraham Goodman House, which is two blocks north of it, just off Broadway, should have a useful part to play.

Meanwhile, Christ and St. Stephen's Church, on West Sixty-ninth Street, remains my "local" for chamber music. On Sunday last week, I dropped in there not as a critic (the accident of an event's proximity to where a critic lives shouldn't determine what he reviews) but simply for the pleasure of listening to some chamber music in friendly, informal surroundings. The ensemble called For the Love of Music has a Sunday-night series in the church. I review the concert after all because I heard a young artist of rare quality—Frederick Zlotkin, a cellist with passion that never became splurgy, a big, strong, gleaming tone that never became fat, and a personality that held me intent along every line as he unfolded it yet remained that of a true chamber-music player, taking as well as giving color. Schumann's three Fantasiestücke, Op. 73, are a cellist's warhorse; Mr. Zlotkin and Pamela Mia Paul, the pianist, played them with enthusiasm, fancy, and, in the third, sizzling brilliance—as if the music had just leaped from Schumann's fiery pen. Richard Sortomme, a poised, thoughtful violinist, and Mr. Zlotkin played Kodály's Duo with full appreciation of its attractive quiddities and musing exchanges. Then the three players joined in a happy performance of Mendelssohn's C-minor Trio.

Wagner, in his memoir of Ludwig Schnorr von Carolsfeld, the first Tristan, recalled that when Schnorr sang the third-act monologue the rich, immensely complicated orchestral writing, a symphonic web such as no composer had woven before, "completely disappeared—or, more accurately, appeared to be subsumed in his delivery." It was not so at the *Tristan* that Eve Queler conducted in Carnegie Hall on New Year's Eve. The Tristan was Herbert Becker, a stalwart but unromantic and unimaginative sounder of the notes—not Miss Queler's first choice for the role, a replacement when Jess Thomas fell ill. Isolde was Berit Lindholm, replacing Roberta Knie, and she was good to hear. The voice is bright, not ample; it lacks the timbres of tenderness but not those of command, anger, and passion. Purely and sharply focused, it has plenty of power. Notes are hit dead center, without strain and without gustiness. Moreover, Miss Lindholm is a keen, intelligent, and often affecting interpreter; since Nilsson, she has been the most consistently reliable of Brünnhildes and Isoldes. In the theatre—and even on the concert platform—her slim, erect presence is an added advantage. Miss Queler and we were lucky that she was free.

Richard Clark was a strong, clean Kurwenal. Marianna Busching was Brangäne. Louis Lebherz was Marke. Curtis Rayam was the Young Sailor, Melot, and the Shepherd. Most important, the orchestra was that of the National Opera Orchestra Workshop, established at the University of Maryland last summer, with Miss Queler as its music director, to introduce young instrumentalists to the techniques and the musical rewards of playing for opera. *Don Giovanni, Rigoletto, Tosca, La Bohème,* and *Cavalleria rusticana* were rehearsed at the summer session, and its climax was a concert performance of *Tristan,* with Miss Knie and Mr. Thomas in the leading roles. It was a success. From some twenty states, the young players reassembled to do it again, in Carnegie Hall. This performance, too, was a success. I stayed for three or four calls and then walked a good block from the hall, Wagner-drunk, not noticing the rain, before remembering that I'd left an umbrella behind. When I got back there to retrieve it, the place was still ringing with cheers. The playing had the warmth, vitality, and commitment that are hallmarks of a good young orchestra. It was also accomplished. Solo lines were expressive, the balance was good, and Miss Queler's handling of the huge drama was sure.

January 29, 1979

Contented and Charmed

Erismena, a happy product of Cavalli's middle-period mastery, was a happy choice of work for the New Opera Theatre of the Brooklyn Academy of Music. Tastes change, and Cavalli's day has come again. In 1789, Burney wrote of *Erismena*, in his *General History of Music:*

> It is amusing to see how contented, and even charmed, the public is at one period with what appears contemptible at another. For this drama, which was not only often heard with rapture at Venice in 1655, the year of its performance, and at Bologna 1668, thirteen years after, but revived again at Venice in a different theatre in 1670, is so deficient in poetical and musical merit, compared with those in present favour, that no perfection of performance could render it palatable.

Burney could have added earlier Bologna productions and others at Milan, Florence, Ferrara (twice), Brescia, Genoa, Ancona, Lucca, and Forlì. *Erismena* was one of Cavalli's most successful pieces. There may even have been a London performance, for there survives a seventeenth-century score with an English translation; it has been suggested that *Erismena* may be the "Italian opera in musique, the first that had been in England of its kind," that Evelyn saw in 1674. After some three centuries' sleep, *Erismena* was revived again in 1967, by the BBC, in that early translation. Seven years later, the Holland Festival brought it to the modern stage, very successfully, in Italian. The Brooklyn performances (two of them, last month) were in English. The musical leader of the Holland presentation, Alan Curtis, led it again, and four of the singers were the same.

Erismena, with a libretto by Aurelio Aureli, has a complicated plot. Roughly, *A* loves B, who loves *C*, and *C* is also loved by D and E. (Italics indicate women.) *C* falls in love with *A*, not knowing that she is a woman disguised as a warrior. *A*, B, and *C* all have assumed names—as it were, X, Y, and Z. In fact, they are three long-lost royal children; A is E's daughter, and B and C are brother and sister. As in several Venetian seventeenth-century plots, flickers of sexual equivocacy and incestuous desire lend piquancy to the situations. But before any harm can be done, the revelations of a royal nurse and the timely discovery of a locket make all identities plain and effect a happy ending: A + B, C + D, with E (a bass, while all the others are high-voice roles, soprano or castrato) bestowing his fatherly blessing on the young people. The 1655 libretto has a three-page prologue recounting the events that led up to the point where the action begins. In the theatre, as so often happens, the lines of an intrigue that sounds impossibly tangled in the telling soon become clear. The drama is not merely a Gilbertian masquerade. Strong emotions are brought into play; death sentences are passed, and death is faced with noble stoicism or sweet regret. Besides the five exalted principals, there are five subaltern roles: a confidante, the nurse, a page, a sergeant, and a general. The first four comment perkily on their employers' plights and indulge in their own lighthearted amorous play. I enjoy the noble formality of eighteenth-century opera seria, appreciate the reforms wrought by the librettists Apostolo Zeno and Metastasio, and marvel at the musical richness with which a Jommelli, the melodic sweetness with which a Caldara, the verve and dramatic intensity with which a Handel could invest the traditional plots. But there is a special pleasure to be gained from returning to the mid-seventeenth century, when opera was still young and supple. In Monteverdi's three surviving operas we find him tackling head-on all the conflicts that have made opera the form absorbing most musicians' attention since first it was invented: between words and music, closed forms and a progressive plot, vocal and instrumental eloquence, convention and realism, spectacle and sound. He balanced intensity with expansiveness, tragedy with comic or pastoral relief, solos with ensembles, recitatives with arias. Over the centuries, the great reformers stepped in to right those balances when any of them went awry, but opera was still in balance when Cavalli began. The plot still mattered as much as the prima donna or the primo uomo. The arias did not carry all the emphasis. In Grove, Egon Wellesz wrote that "Monteverdi and Cavalli stand in the same relation to each other as Richard Wagner and Richard Strauss," and that "Monteverdi is unquestionably the greater genius, but Cavalli is the more brilliant of the two." Jane Glover, in her excellent little study of Cavalli, published last year by St. Martin's, ventures another parallel: "It is perhaps true to say that Cavalli was to Monteverdi as Handel was to Bach." She summarizes his achievement:

> He composed with spontaneity and fluency, and his immediate reaction to his texts revealed sensitivity, wit, and understanding. He always obeyed the effect, as Handel did, and as Bach did not. . . . His greatest successes were in his handling of the most extreme emotions: passion (with rapturous love duets), desolation (with tragic laments and intensely chromatic recitative), fury (in turbulent and aggressive out-

bursts), and insanity (wild arioso passages with ungainly leaps and bizarre dissonances). He also had a flair for comedy, and he excelled in lively burlesque.

So no wonder the public is once again contented, and even charmed, with Cavalli's operas and ready to hear them with rapture. Wellesz, who was writing in 1954, doubted whether any of them could be restored to the modern stage, but since Glyndebourne revived *Ormindo*, in 1967, at least eleven of them have been brought back to life. Manhattan's two regular opera houses are monsters that only the largest works of the late-nineteenth and twentieth centuries and only the largest voices can adequately fill. Brooklyn is luckier: its Academy of Music contains, side by side, a grand-opera house of reasonable size and a smaller theatre well suited to Cavalli. Curtis's orchestra was perhaps a little larger than Cavalli had at the Teatro Sant' Apollinare, where *Erismena* was first done, but it was one he would have recognized: a handful of baroque strings, two recorders, two harpsichords and a lute, and two trumpets to sound offstage fanfares. Curtis was both editor of the text and musical director of its execution, and that is as it should be, for the two functions are hardly separable. He does not believe in writing out elaborate set parts for continuo accompaniments that should be improvised. He does not orchestrate the arias for singing strings, recompose and reorder passages in the light of Romantic practice, add hit numbers from other operas, play fast and loose with tonality, or turn solos into duets and duets into trios. Positively, he assembles players—here they were the Baroque Music Masters Chamber Orchestra—whom he can inspire to be bold and free, eloquently to the fore when Cavalli requires it (as in the violins' pedal C that pierces the exchanges of an affecting prison duet), yet always servants of the singers and their emotions. Curtis has become a very good conductor. He knows that recitatives should be sung—as Monteverdi once put it—"in time to the beating of the heart and not to the beat of a hand." Lightly, unobtrusively, yet surely, he guided the fresh flow of invention as Cavalli slips from recitative into arioso or aria, shifts between three-time and four-time, edges his cadences through exquisitely poignant chromatics, varies his accompaniment textures, and juxtaposes scenes of high sentiment with songs of direct, earthy good sense. *Erismena* moved at varied paces. Mingled with predictable twists of the plot was a piquant, paradoxical feeling that anything might happen next, both in the adventures of the characters and in Cavalli's lively response to them. Seventeenth-century librettos often have a more wayward charm than those of the eighteenth century.

Onstage, there was a kaleidoscope of vocal colors. The title role was taken by Mary Burgess, direct, forthright, clear of tone, delicate of nuance. Carmen Balthrop was Aldimira, the much-courted "C" of the plot, and she is well suited to play an irresistibly attractive and variously attracted heroine. (There is another such in Cavalli's *Ormindo*.) But she must work at her English pronunciation and learn to give vowels their true color and full value. Jeffrey Gall, one of the two noble countertenors, was both stylish and romantic. The other, Daniel Collins, was in disagreeable voice and is no actor. John Ferrante, a third countertenor, grossly overplayed the nurse—described in the old English score as an "ancient bawd"—but he did so with skill. The role of the page was possibly written for a boy; it was brightly and deftly taken by Peter Becker, a fourth countertenor.

The opera was played in costumes borrowed from the Holland production, but without scenery. The staging, by Ian Strasfogel, w︰s coarse, clumsy, and unworthy. Instead of teaching his performers to act, and to declaim English dramatic verse as if it meant something, he set them to carrying out all manner of blunt, crude business. One lesson that the numerous Cavalli productions of the last twelve years should have taught is that the serious scenes of the operas deserve to be taken seriously. Günther Rennert in the Glyndebourne *Ormindo* overdid the comedy. Filippo Sanjust in the Holland *Erismena* began elegantly but then embarked on a crescendo of jokiness which climaxed in outright vulgarity. At least, he had the excuse, not available to Mr. Strasfogel, that he was seeking to enliven a foreign-language libretto that his audience was not following in detail. Contrariwise, Peter Hall in the Glyndebourne *Calisto* demonstrated that stylish, sensitive, musical direction makes the emotions more affecting and the jokes far funnier. There was a good deal of rubbish in the Brooklyn staging. In Act I, whenever anyone thought of or mentioned someone else, that person made a "spectral" stage appearance—a set of visual footnotes that merely confused the action. Act III degenerated into slapstick and an invitation to belly laughs. If Mr. Strasfogel believed in the work, he should have trusted his librettist, trusted his anonymous seventeenth-century translator (whose work is both accurate and deft, an inspiration to anyone who today essays to turn a Cavalli opera into English), and drilled his cast to get all the words across more effectively.

Someone asked me in what genre *Erismena* should be placed. Is it tragedy averted, romantic intrigue, or comedy? All and none. It should be accepted—and presented—for exactly what it is: a fascinating (and oddly lifelike) mingling of tragedy, romance, and humor. The Romantic reformers looked to Shakespeare to justify their breaking down of stage conventions into something more human. Burney found something Shakespearean in the manner of *Erismena* (and did not approve it, for he deemed Shakespeare's dramaturgy barbarous). So can we—and delight in it.

Janet Baker has sung only two Cavalli roles: Diana and Jupiter-disguised-as-Diana in *Calisto*. In them, and as Penelope in Monteverdi's *Il ritorno d'Ulisse* and as Purcell's Dido, she has provided a paragon of seventeenth-century operatic manners, being passionate without romantic excess, witty without grossness, direct and "realistic" without breaking the frame of the classical dramas. She gives full value to words, colors lines with emotion, and commands all gradations of dramatic rhythm from a measured beat to free declamation "in time to the beating of the heart." (In a sense, the Cavalli and Monteverdi roles were composed for her; at any rate, in Raymond Leppard's editions they were extensively retailored to take advantage of her voice and temperament.) She excels as a dramatic singer, and although so far she refuses to take the boards in America, not liking the conditions of American opera giving, in her Carnegie Hall recital last month there could be heard—and seen—something of her Penelope, her Vitellia (in *La clemenza di Tito*), her Charlotte, and even her Dorabella. The first half of the recital reached its climax in Haydn's cantata *Miseri noi, misera patria*, a scene for, it seems, Cassandra (the author of the verses has not been identified)—a vision of a proud city shattered and burned by invaders. (The score is in the Library of Congress.) After a fierce recitative, the dark, tragic color and the smooth line that Dame Janet brought to the first line of the aria, "Funeste orror di morte," were overwhelming. Duparc's "Au pays où se fait la guerre" was sung in a very full, dramatic way, and his "Extase" in so fine-drawn a thread of tone that on one word it snapped for an instant. Baker's singing is always brave; she will push her considerable technique to its very limits rather than play safe, and that is one of the things that make her so exciting an artist. Lia's air from Debussy's *L'Enfant prodigue* (quaintly described in the program as a song) was another full-voiced dramatic scena. She sang a Delius group—three songs from the Norwegian, by Bjørnson and Ibsen, in less than happy English translations, and the Shelley setting "Love's Philosophy"— and, to end the billed program, a Stanford ballad, which was new to me, "La Belle Dame sans merci." It is a kind of English "Erlkönig"-cum-"Waldesgespräch," and it was vividly done. The single encore was Thomas Pasatieri's cabaret song "Vocal Modesty" (which he wrote for Joanna Simon). Dame Janet sang it with the delicate mischief that makes her Dorabella memorable. Martin Isepp was the pianist.

The program book was a disgrace: a Handel cantata, which opened the evening, comically mistranslated; several translations missing; most of the poets unnamed; mislineation all over the place; and the foreign verses printed in a tiny italic type quite illegible in the dim-lit hall. When will the people who put on concerts start to treat New York audiences as grown-up, intelligent people, interested in music and not just in the noises it makes, able to read, and some of them even able to read scores?

Since I have not heard all of Massenet's operas, I cannot tell whether *Sapho*, which was given a concert performance in Carnegie Hall last week by the Friends of French Opera, is musically the least interesting of them, but it is certainly the least interesting and attractive of the dozen I have heard. Staged, it makes some effect. The leading role—an aging model who grasps at a last chance of happiness with an innocent young student from Provence—is a vehicle that can carry a clever actress to success. But the score is tawdry, second-rate, and (in its dependence on Bizet, Tchaikovsky, and earlier, better Massenet) secondhand music. Elisabeth Söderström, who has not sung opera in New York for fifteen years, returned to give a lustrous, very intelligent, and fully acted performance. She takes all opera in her span. Her characters range from Monteverdi's Nero (1642) to Clitoria in Ligeti's *Le Grand Macabre* (1978). Celebrated as Mozart's, Richard Strauss's, and Janáček's heroines, she has also created more modern roles than any other diva of our day. She is always a delight to hear and see, and whatever could be done for *Sapho* she did. The student was Donald Grobe, looking younger and sounding a little less dry than he did twenty years ago. Robert Lawrence conducted.

February 5, 1979

Questions

George Rochberg can be a rum composer, but I have never known him to be a dull one. His latest work is a set of three string quartets, Nos. 4, 5, and 6, intended to be played in sequence at a single concert. They are called "The Concord Quartets" and are named not for the Transcendentalists (as Ives's "Concord" Sonata is) but for the Concord String Quartet, long associated with Rochberg's music. The Concord has recorded his first three quartets. No. 3 was written for it, and No. 4 is dedicated to its members. The Concord played all six Rochberg quartets in a small "festival" of his chamber music last month at the University of Pennsylvania, where he teaches, and then brought the three new works to Alice Tully Hall. The concert was a belated celebration of the composer's sixtieth birthday, last July. The title proved apt in other ways, for many a true concord of well-tuned sounds was heard during the evening, and it ended with six perfect cadences in G major. In brief, "The Concord Quartets" embrace manners of string-quartet writing from Haydn's to Schoenberg's. Their harmonic language covers a still wider span—three centuries—since a variations movement in No. 6 begins with a Pachelbel transcription. The eclecticism was disconcerting. It also provided diversity and surprises. Rochberg's expressed aim—"to ensure maximum variety of gesture and texture and the broadest possible spectrum I could command, from the purest diatonicism to the most complex chromaticism"—was certainly fulfilled.

There is a pastime called "Dittersdorf," which consists of putting on a record of an unfamiliar piece of music and inviting friends to guess the composer. (Music that sounds like Haydn—but not quite—often turns out to be by Dittersdorf; hence the name.) The BBC plays a grander variant in its program "The Innocent Ear," which consists of large works unidentified until they have been performed. (Tuning in last summer, I recognized Busoni's Violin Concerto, but not at once, and was quite foxed by Edmund Rubbra's First Symphony.) The music of Rochberg lends itself to rounds of Dittersdorf. In 1972, he composed a piece for cello and piano, *Ricordanza,* whose central section begins with a direct quotation, transposed, of the main theme of Beethoven's Cello Sonata in C, Op. 102, No. 1. In the outer sections, over mainly I–IV–V harmonies, the cello unfolds a long and beautiful melody, its shapes somewhat reminiscent of Beethoven's "Spring" Sonata. The tonality moves by classical third-shifts—A, F, D-flat, A. (The piece is recorded on CRI, along with the First String Quartet and the Duo Concertante.) It's hard to guess when and by whom *Ricordanza* was written. Equally hard, the when and by whom of such a movement as the finale of Rochberg's Sixth Quartet. Someone who didn't know—who came to the work with an innocent ear— might date the impassioned slow introduction, in E-flat minor, to the 1890s, and then be baffled by the Haydnish (or Dittersdorfish?) G-major exposition that opens the allegro.

Of course, Rochberg isn't simply playing games. For some twenty years, he has been asking and, as a composer, finding his answers to questions of a kind that occur to most musical people. Put very simply, they might be: What does the music of the past really mean to me today? What do the multifarious musics of the present mean to me, who was brought up to love Bach and Beethoven? In what ways do I listen similarly, and in what ways differently, to Binchois, Buxtehude, Bartók, and Jean Barraqué, Ciconia, Cavalli, and Elliott Carter, Dunstable, Dufay, Jacob Druckman, and Peter Maxwell Davies? Am I being sadly promiscuous or healthily catholic in embracing many discrete styles so readily? When there are already more great string quartets (or symphonies, sonatas, whatever) than in a lifetime I can get to know well, why should I bother to listen to/play/create further string quartets (or whatever), which may or may not be great? Do rock, Rochberg, and Steve Reich add something to my life which I can't find in Monteverdi and Mozart? Some of the answers are easily found. Some of them are sounded: when, for example, Davies composes his wind sextet, *Alma redemptoris mater,* based on a motet of Dunstable, and when he leaps back over the centuries to make plainchant—the origin of Western music in its melodic aspect—the foundation of a symphony saying things only the twentieth century could say. An awareness—more, a demonstration—of the past as a part of the present informs much of the art that is being made today. Sometimes it expresses simple nostalgia for the familiar and comfortable after a period of wild, bold experiments and rigorous quest. Sometimes it takes the form of pastiche. At its lowest, it aims at no more than an easy success with the part of the public which likes what it knows. On higher levels, it may test the applicability of medieval, Renaissance, and classical techniques to modern material, find new links between mathematics and music, and discover how far the old representational methods can serve to capture and communicate sights, sounds, and ideas of the twentieth century. I have never felt myself to be a person who lives solely in the present, and when Rochberg, in a note accompanying the Nonesuch recording of his Third Quartet, writes "We are filaments of a universal mind; we dream each other's dreams and those of our ancestors," I respond to the thought.

A direct approach to Rochberg's way of musical thinking is through his attractive orchestral piece *Music for the Magic Theater*. (It is recorded on Desto.) The title is suggested by Hermann Hesse's *Steppenwolf*—that very musical novel in the course of which Mozart, in various guises, offers glimpses of a serene order into which the chaotic and contradictory pieces of modern life may seem for a moment to settle. In one of the more disturbing passages of the book, the Master plays chess games with fragments of the hero's personality, and the metaphors are musical: "The second game . . . was the same world built of the same material, but the key was different, the time changed, the motif was differently given out, and the situations were differently presented." For his musical purposes, Rochberg reproduces the sense of time past bearing on the present and of other men's thoughts providing not solutions but at least glimpses of possible solutions to present plights. In the book, Goethe and Mozart converse with the hero; in the score, Mozart, Beethoven, Mahler, Webern, and Varèse are heard speaking. Rochberg's three movements are called "acts," and in a preface he sets out the scenario. In Act I, past and present are confused. In Act II, "the past haunts us with its nostalgic beauty," and the music is the slow movement of Mozart's Divertimento K. 287, quoted not directly but in a transcription to make it sound as if it came from a great distance, its unearthly beauty and perfection still recognizable but crystalline. What can it mean now? Act III is an affirmation that "only the present is really real," and in his preface the composer quotes from Hesse's last page: "I knew that all the hundred thousand pieces of life's game were in my pocket. A glimpse of its meaning had stirred my reason, and I was determined to begin the game afresh." *Music for the Magic Theater* was composed in 1965. After listening to it, one hears the *Ricordanza* of 1972 as a sojourn in a room of the magic theatre where for a while the old rules and tables of kindred and affinity—the relations of IV to V to I and of tonal centers a third apart—have not yet been confused and thrown into question.

The master of collage composition was Bernd Alois Zimmermann, who in 1970, aged fifty-two, conscientiously completed some commissions he had accepted and then, defeated by life's cruel game, killed himself. Rochberg's collage compositions do not, it seems to me, have the heroic quality of Zimmermann's. Their musical intensity is lower. Back in 1953, in music for William Saroyan's *Sam Ego's House*, Zimmermann superimposed the Schumann Piano Concerto on Duke Ellington. His *Monologe* for two pianos (1964) is built of Bach, Beethoven, Debussy, Messiaen; he described it as "a dream association between the past and present epochs of music which surround us daily . . . a microfilm of the card index of our consciousness." His ballet *Présence* (1961) is a collage on various levels: at once a trio for violin, cello, and piano, a pas de trois for three characters (Don Quixote, Molly Bloom, and Ubu Roi), and a score in which Strauss's *Don Quixote*, Prokofiev's Seventh

Piano Sonata, Stockhausen's *Zeitmasse,* and Debussy's *Jeux* are combined. This work "is the thin ice on which one's foot can rest only until it breaks," he said. "In front is a view of the future—but the ice is certain to splinter, and the constant attempts to find a foothold are futile." Zimmermann opened Act IV of his powerful, tragic opera *Die Soldaten,* first performed in 1965, with *twelve* simultaneous scenes. (In practice, they have been reduced to three enacted on the stage while nine are represented in film projections.) The finale of his *Requiem for a Young Poet* (1969), dedicated to the memory of three poets who killed themselves, piles up Beethoven's Ninth and the Beatles, the voices of Ribbentrop, Stalin, Goebbels, and Churchill, and tape recordings of political demonstrations. Suddenly, the terrifying din is cut short. A text by Konrad Bayer, one of the poets, breaks into the silence, and there is a last, despairing, massed cry of "Dona nobis pacem." Zimmermann's last work, completed five days before his death, was *So I returned, and considered all the oppressions that are done under the sun,* for two speakers—representing Christ and a formidable, aged Grand Inquisitor—a singer in lament, and orchestra. It ends with a quotation from Bach's "Es ist genug," cut short.

Collage was employed in some of the works done at three concerts that the Reich Music Foundation presented last month at the Guggenheim Museum. A collage—more precisely, a confrontation—of liturgy and Wilfred Owen war poems supplied the text of Britten's *War Requiem,* which was performed by the National Symphony in Carnegie Hall last month. Collage is a technique effective for throwing received ideas into question. Sometimes it seems to be the recourse of a composer with nothing of his own to say—not in Zimmermann's case, however, for he could be an eloquent and generous inventor in his own right. Zimmermann's Requiem comes to a climax of agony; Britten's, after agony and contrasts not less violent but less violently sounded, finds peace at last, and concord.

Rochberg's First String Quartet (1952) stands on the verge of commitment to a twelve-note method of composing. It is a well-made and engaging piece, rhythmically alive, lyrical, expansive, yet orderly. The Second Quartet (1961), in which a soprano voice joins the four strings, is a serial composition and an expressive one. (The Concord's recording, with Phyllis Bryn-Julson, on Turnabout, is out of print but is still around in some stores; there is also a CRI recording made by the Philadelphia String Quartet and Janice Harsanyi.) In a note for the Concord's recording of the Third Quartet (on Nonesuch), Rochberg wrote:

> By the beginning of the 60s, I had become completely dissatisfied with [serialism's] inherently narrow terms. I found the palette of constant chromaticism increasingly constricting, nor could I accept any longer the limited range of gestures that always seemed to channel the music into some form or other of expressionism.

Serialism, he continued, was "a style which made it virtually impossible to express serenity, tranquillity, grace, wit, energy." And so:

I have been engaged in an effort to rediscover the larger and more sweeping gestures of the past, to reconcile my love for that past and its traditions with my relation to the present and its often destructive pressures. This has been an almost impossible task; it has taken many forms; all of them have led me back to the world of tonal music.

First, there were the collage pieces such as the *Music for the Magic Theater.* Then, in the Third Quartet (1972), came a collage of manners if not of actual matter. The central movement is a serene A-major adagio that César Franck would have deemed harmonically unadventurous. The finale includes a Mahlerian D-major serenade and a B-flat scherzo but ends in energetic dissonance. The way to "The Concord Quartets" lay open. It led through the Violin Concerto that Rochberg composed for Isaac Stern (1974)—a piece that seemed to me to show too ready a yielding to the lure of the Romantic past and to be little more than amiable platitudes strung out in sequences. (I've heard it only once, and perhaps I'm being unfair.) There is more matter in the new quartets. No. 4 begins with a fantasia and continues with a slow, sweetly euphonious fugue with Victorian harmonies; a serenade that is a fragmented waltz movement reminiscent of Berg; and a final fantasia of declamatory recitatives and emphatic gestures. No. 5 begins with an allegro marziale in A major—active, contrapuntal, ingenious, and Haydnish. The slow movement is an E-flat-minor elegy, an eloquent stretch of romantic musing. One of music's oldest devices, a major-minor alternation, is very beautifully spaced and scored at its close. Memories of Beethoven seem to have been coming to the fore, and the subsequent scherzo is written in Beethoven rhythms; its trio section is imitation Mahler. Then comes a serenade in which a brief reiterated motif much like that dominating the opening exchanges of Janáček's *Kát'a Kabanová* (where it carries the words "Oh what nonsense!") is prominent. There is a big, vigorous C-minor finale in late-Viennese vein. No. 6 opens with a rhetorical fantasia. Then there is a scherzo that carries hints of Tchaikovsky. In the central movement, the set of variations after Pachelbel, the harmonic idiom gradually swells to a Mahlerian richness. There is a serenade, again Bergian, and then the Romantic-into-classical finale already mentioned. The Fourth and Fifth Quartets last each about twenty-six minutes, and the Sixth lasts thirty-three.

On the positive side, there is everywhere evident what Rochberg once described as "an urge to compose the most beautiful melodies I could imagine and an obsession with creating a sense of rightness of harmony and harmonic progression." That was in a sleeve note for the CRI record of the nearly atonal First Quartet, the twelve-note Duo Concertante of 1955, which is a graphic and inventive work of strong character, and the blamelessly A-major *Ricordanza;* the same urge and the same obsession mark "The Concord Quartets." Next, there is unfailingly "grateful" writing for the instruments—and perhaps this is the place to praise the Concord String Quartet's performances. Its players provide the kind of quartet playing I admire and enjoy most—lean, lithe, alert, and colorful, unconcerned with displaying a fat, full sound for its own sake. (If I were a composer, I would want the Concord Quartet or the Composers Quartet to play my works.) Rochberg's quartet writing is marked by an evenness of assignment among the players. Second fiddle is every bit as important as first. The special characters of viola and cello are seldom stressed. The composer writes "on" the four instruments as if they all lay under his fingers, distinguished only by pitch. It is not a failing but a manner, and it is very much suited to the Concord—four exceptionally well matched, even players. I particularly admired their handling of the dramatic and emotional kaleidoscope of the scherzo in the Sixth Quartet—and throughout the evening enjoyed their quick, sensitive response to what Rochberg was doing.

Now some doubts that crept in must be expressed. In the fugue of the Fourth Quartet, I suddenly seemed to hear an echo of the sweet, slack, ingenious imitations that in my organist days I was taught to improvise while the congregation dispersed. (Of course, my efforts weren't as elegant or as neat as Rochberg's are, but they did have the same quality of *Fortspinnung*—self-indulgent spinning out of counterpoint.) There were episodes that recalled those student exercises: "Continue in the style of . . . ." There were passages that sounded more like pastiche than like original composition. In theory, there is no reason a modern composer shouldn't write a Monteverdian madrigal as good as any Monteverdi wrote (or an artist paint in Vermeer's manner a *Christ at Emmaus* as moving as if it had been painted by Vermeer himself). In practice, it doesn't happen. And when Rochberg essays a development section in the manner of Haydn or Beethoven, it becomes apparent not only that he is not their peer but also that he has donned fancy dress.

I enjoy masquerades. And I respect a creator who genuinely feels that clothes of the past are more comfortable and more expressive garments than those of today. Over "The Concord Quartets" I would leave a question mark. Beside Elliott Carter's, or Britten's last, or Shostakovich's late string quartets they may seem insignificant. Almost irrelevant. Yet, in addition to raising questions about what music *is* "relevant," they are attractive, tunable, never dull, and often moving.

February 12, 1979

Now with Noble Wrath,
Now with Love

When performers learn to master, and their audiences to understand, an idiom previously unfamiliar or imperfectly understood, fashions change, critical assessments become out of date, and history books have to be rewritten. The range of music available for the public to enjoy is increased, since there is more that it can "read in the original," not in the rough-and-ready construe obtained by applying the syntax of another age's music. It is a long while since Bach was considered too barbaric and Palestrina too Simple Simon to be worth listening to. The music of the seventeenth, sixteenth, fifteenth, and fourteenth centuries is now open to modern audiences. So, nearer home, is Italian opera written in the first half of the nineteenth century, which to our fathers was a deliberately closed book.

Burney owned scores of Peri's *Euridice*, Caccini's *Euridice* (both 1600), and Monteverdi's *Orfeo* (1607), which can be regarded as the first three operas ever written, and in Book IV of his *General History of Music* (1789) he wrote that he was "unable to discover Monteverdi's superiority," since "more forms of phrases of musical recitation still in use may be found in Peri and Caccini than in Monteverdi." In 1907, Romain Rolland took Strauss to hear *Pelléas et Mélisande,* and in his diary Rolland wrote:

> He wholly misses the point of the last scene. For my part, I find it a scene of emotional brilliance. I do not think that, since Monteverdi, anything in music has achieved such intensity with such modest means. . . . For Strauss there is no music.

After the opera, Rolland, Strauss, Ravel, and a few others gathered in a café:

> The conversation turns to ancient music, a subject in which Strauss is profoundly uninterested. He says somewhat disdainfully that he knows nothing of Frescobaldi or of Monteverdi, indeed nothing before Bach, and that the subject does not interest him—certain little things by Rameau perhaps. We try to make him understand that there are works of quite modern genius like Monteverdi's *Orfeo*. He listens politely, but he is bored.

Rolland knew *Orfeo* in d'Indy's edition, which omits the first and last of the five acts and contains about half the music, provided with a rich, full con-

tinuo realization. The opera had to wait more than three centuries for a revival in anything like its original form. Then, in 1925, the newly formed Oxford University Opera Club did it uncut, in a careful new edition prepared by
Jack Westrup. The club celebrated its jubilee by reviving *Orfeo*, in a new
edition by Jane Glover. In 1925, Westrup had used modern instruments,
oboes and clarinets among them. In 1975, Miss Glover could use instruments
of Monteverdi's day. She wrote:

> Knowledge of seventeenth-century performing practice and style has
> grown considerably. Cornetts and chitarrones have become ever more
> popular and are played with increasing excellence; and singers special-
> ize in and perfect the art of Caccini's *nuove musiche*. Audience tastes
> have similarly swung back to the pure Renaissance and Baroque styles.

In Britain, *Orfeo* has been played almost as a repertory piece, up and
down the country, ever since Sadler's Wells (now the English National
Opera) took it up, in 1965, in an edition by Raymond Leppard; in 1976 Kent
Opera made it the first panel of its Monteverdi "trilogy," in an edition by
Roger Norrington. New York first heard *Orfeo* at the Met in concert in 1912,
in a much abridged and modernized version by Giacomo Orefice. In 1960,
the City Opera opened its season with *Orfeo*. Stokowski conducted. Paul
Henry Lang, in his *Tribune* review, described the edition used as "the best
available score," without further identification, and the program provided
none. But there were gamba, lute, chitarrone, recorders, and small organs in
the orchestra. The work was much shortened (Harold Schonberg, in the
Times, called it "a digest version"), and was played on a double bill with
Dallapiccola's *Il prigioniero*. It was dropped after three performances and
has never been revived. What seems to have been New York's first full staging of *Orfeo* was given by the Juilliard American Opera Center this month.

The show was played thrice, to packed houses. It was an important occasion. *Orfeo* was revealed to be the masterpiece of musical drama that—
pace Burney, *pace* Strauss—it is. In the prologue to the opera, the allegorical
figure of La Musica comes forward:

> *I am Music, who in sweet accents*
> *Know how to calm every troubled heart,*
> *And, now with noble wrath, now with love,*
> *Can inflame the most frigid minds.*

That, one might say, is a declaration of what opera is about; and it was Monteverdi who showed how *all* Music's devices—not just the new recitative
style of dramatic utterance, which had brought opera into being, but also
closed forms, repetitions, variations, and affective instrumental colorings—
could be combined into a harmonious balance (or sometimes a fruitful opposition) in the cause of expressiveness. The Orpheus legend, which is about the

power of music, is a "self-illustrating" subject. Monteverdi's *Orfeo* is a perfect opera, number by number and in its pacing, its proportions, its control of tensions and contrasts. *Ulisse* and *Poppea*, written three decades later, for the public theatres of Venice, are operas of a kind different from *Orfeo*, which was composed for the Mantuan court—they are swifter, less formal, more modest in instrumental resource, more "human." But who would seek to range the three in any order of merit?

No reviews survive of the 1607 première. We know a little more about the staging of Peri's Orpheus opera, *Euridice*, in 1600. The instrumental players were "within" the stage, presumably concealed amid the scenery, where they could see and follow the singers. (There are careful instructions for such placing in the preface to Gagliano's *Dafne*, produced in Mantua a year after *Orfeo*.) Well-disposed lamps produced an effect of bright daylight in the outer scenes, while in the Underworld there was a coppery glow, and tongues of flickering flame could be glimpsed through rifts. On either side of the stage, statues of Poetry and Painting were represented—apt symbol of Opera's comprising all the arts. Similar painted statues could be discerned on the Juilliard stage, but only just; the décor (sets by Alfred Silbermann, costumes by Anna Anni) was lent by the Gulbenkian Foundation of Lisbon, whose theatre has a wider opening than the Juilliard's. The scenes were at once handsome and simple. The transformation from Hades to the Thracian fields was surprising, effective, and beautiful, and the grand, cloud-borne descent of Apollo shone with splendor. Sandro Sequi, who directed, had plainly worked long and carefully with his cast. This was a sensitive and finely achieved production, and in style one of the most satisfying Monteverdi stagings I have seen.

The Juilliard had perhaps given a little less hard thought to the musical side of things. The edition used was that of Denis Stevens, which is a scholarly and practical score devised to make *Orfeo* accessible to companies or music schools that lag behind the times in not being able to muster a full complement of original instruments. Modern oboes replace the cornetts; a modern brass quintet takes over from Monteverdi's five trumpets and his five trombones. Stevens also rebars all Monteverdi's recitatives and ariosi and some of his choruses (the greater part of the music, in fact) to indicate where "a slight stress is called for by the natural flow of the text." Personally, I think that Monteverdi's own longer, "unmeasured measures" further a more eloquent recitation, and that the singers should be trusted—or coached—to discover where the natural accents lie. Be that as it may, Stevens is not to be held responsible for what happened at the Juilliard, where the recitatives and ariosi were actually *conducted*. (It would make as little sense to have a conductor onstage at a lieder recital, indicating tempo and accents to the singer and the accompanist.) Peter Herman Adler beat time, and he did so with a heavy hand in the measured episodes and a dulling one in passages where it is up to the individual singers to set the paces and determine the phrasing. The opera was sung in Italian. It is plainly a good thing that student singers should have exercise in performing that language, but they—and the audience—would have learned more about Monteverdi's directness and affecting power if a good English translation had been used. Most of the time, the singers declaimed the text as if they understood it. Sometimes, but not quite often enough, they seized it, molded it, and let it determine the flow of the music. More attention to Caccini's *nuove musiche* prescriptions for the varied declamation of dramatic recitative was needed, and probably longer rehearsal with the continuo accompanists, so that they could have phrased, breathed, attacked as if with the singers' own breaths.

The singing was never less than agreeable, and was a good deal more than that from Zehava Gal (an eloquent Messenger) and Hei-Kyung Hong (a beautifully pure, steady, and expressive Proserpine). In the title role, Ronald Raines had the right ideas but not always the vocal technique to carry them through. Roseann Del George (La Musica), James Justiss (a stylish counter-tenor Shepherd), Pamela Coburn (Eurydice), Mischa Ferenzov (Charon), Robert Briggs (a sonorous Pluto), and Brian Schexnayder (a bold Apollo) all deserve mention. The principal dance, featuring a bounding Pan, looked rather silly. Michael Rice's lighting was fidgety and out-of-period.

Before leaving the subject of Orpheus, let me add a word on behalf of Peri's opera. So often we are told that Monteverdi's *Orfeo* is the first *real* opera, that its predecessors consist—as Lang put it in his 1960 City Opera review—of "dull recitatives." Not so. I've not heard Caccini's *Euridice;* in score it does look, well, somewhat plain—though perhaps impassioned performers would bring it to life. Peri's *Euridice* is not only dramatic but also melodious—more melodious in its recitative periods, in fact, than Monteverdi's *Orfeo*. It is not as powerfully or purposively shaped a dramatic score as Monteverdi's. (I don't go as far as Burney did.) It doesn't have the same rich variety of forms and of instrumentation. But it is well worth staging. The Juilliard should do it—without a conductor, and with continuo players in the wings, alert to the phrases as they fall from the singers' lips.

Textbooks tell us that Verdi's *Otello* drove Rossini's *Otello* from the stage, but that is not quite true. The annals of performance in Giuseppe Radiciotti's big Rossini biography show that by the mid-century Rossini's opera was already beginning to lose its popularity; Radiciotti's list of productions grows thin there and peters out in 1880, seven years before Verdi's *Otello* appeared. (In Prague and Berlin, the opera lingered on for a decade.) It is true, however, that Verdian *canto d'azione*—the direct, declamatory style of singing pioneered by Bellini, developed by Donizetti and Mercadante, and perfected by Verdi—ousted Rossini's florid, highly decorated manner of utterance as an acceptable medium for Italian operatic tragedy. Rossini's *Otello* was composed, in 1816, for Isabella Colbran, celebrated for what Stendhal once described as her "lava-stream of roulades," and the coloratura tenor Giovanni Davide. Verdi's *Otello* is the culmination of "the new style," recognized as such in the 1840s and propagated by singers like Giuseppina Strepponi, Erminia Frezzolini, and Gaetano Fraschini. And it is also true that in our age, when the submerged landmarks of early-nineteenth-century opera are beginning to re-emerge, Rossini's *Otello*, an arresting and beautiful work, might be done more often were it not shadowed by Verdi's towering masterpiece on the same subject. What seem to have been its first performances in this century were those given in Town Hall by the American Opera Society in 1954 (with Jennie Tourel as Desdemona) and in 1957 (with Eileen Farrell). Then London staged it in 1961, and Rome in 1964; the Rome production came to the Met in 1968. There have been other revivals; Wexford's, in 1967, is one I recall with pleasure. Most recently, the Academy of Vocal Arts, in Philadelphia, gave two performances in the Walnut Street Theatre.

Otello, the third of the ten operas, nine of them serious, that Rossini composed for Naples, is in its way a reform piece. A first glance at the score shows many pages of display music for voices adept in divisions and accurate in leaps; a closer examination shows only three set arias, and only one, Roderigo's, in regular form. Othello's aria, a tender andante between a vivace marziale and a fiery allegro, is embedded in the opening sequences, and in some scores it is headed "duetto," because of Iago's frequent asides. Desdemona's aria, shaped as the second-act finale, punctuated by choral entries, and propelled by offstage action, has a long, freely composed arioso, the brief, beautiful "L'error d'un'infelice" (whose delicately falling filigree, over andante sostenuto triplets, Bellini recalled when composing "Casta Diva"), and a final cadence of quicksilver roulades prolonged for four pages. Even Roderigo's aria has its surprises: the voice enters before the clarinet introduction has run its course.

Henry F. Chorley has a wise chapter about Rossini in his *Thirty Years' Musical Recollections* (1862). In the 1830s, Chorley recalled, "the sagacious, the scientific, and the sour set their faces against [Rossini] as a mere flimsy tune-spinner." But thirty years later "his wondrous grace, his fertility of invention, his admirable treatment of the voice, his simple and effective taste in arrangement of the orchestra" became more apparent than ever. (The 1930 and 1960 views of Rossini were in similar contrast.) "The day may never come," Chorley continued, "in which commentators will wrangle about his outer forms and inner meanings." That day has come. *La Cenerentola* has been assessed—and even staged—as a moral parable, and Rossini's forms have been carefully studied. "It would be difficult to name any more forcible example of musical expression than the third act of *Otello*," Chorley said. Not *very* difficult today, but there is still uncommon force and pathos in the great sequence. After the soft, richly scored prelude, whose strains recur to accompany the gentle conversation of Desdemona and Emilia, there is the gondolier's song—just fifteen offstage measures (but designated for a primo tenore), a snatch of Dante, the unhappy Francesca's "Nessun maggior dolore," drifting up from the lagoon, over a moonlit string shimmer, to chime with Desdemona's sad thoughts. Magical passage! Then the exquisite Willow Song; Desdemona's innocent, touching prayer; the extended, abrupt music of

Othello's entrance, elaborately annotated, as in Verdi, with stage directions; a storm that is not merely picturesque but whose lightnings streak and whose thunders shake the desperate vocal lines of Othello and Desdemona; the four-octave tumble after the murder; the tense silence pierced by single notes (precursors of the gruesome double-bass cries in Strauss's *Salome*); the ironically joyful music as Roderigo, the Doge, Desdemona's father, and the chorus burst in to congratulate Othello, restored to favor now that Iago's perfidy has been revealed; the sudden, shocking close. Verdi and Boito evidently knew this act well. In Rossini's autograph, it is set out in a single span, not broken into numbers (and the Philadelphia audience was sensitive enough not to interrupt it with applause). The Willow Song provides the full statement of a melodic cell from which much of the music has budded, and is a lovely example of the tender melodies, adorned with delicate, unobtrusive embroidery, and subtly accompanied, that the true Rossinian holds dearer than all the verve and brilliance. Here, in "L'error d'un'infelice," and in Desdemona's Mozartian duet with Emilia is found the poetic Rossini who can join hands with the Berlioz of the duo-nocturne in *Béatrice* and the garden scene of *Les Troyens*.

The libretto, by the Marchese Francesco Berio di Salsa, observes the unities by being set in Venice within a day. It is far from Shakespeare. Stendhal in two devastating chapters laid bare its weaknesses, but he added, "We are so electrified by the magnificent quality of the songs, so spellbound, so overwhelmed by the incomparable beauty of the theme, that we invent our own libretto to match."

The Philadelphia production had a cast of young, fresh, unforced voices, flowing out effortlessly into a theatre of moderate size (but one whose potentially good acoustics were spoiled by the noisy bourdon of a projector fan). In the Rome production, the music of Acts I and II had seemed hardly substantial enough to fill the opulent, romantic staging, which was by Sandro Sequi, and Giorgio de Chirico's big, colorful scenery; Act III, however, came off splendidly. The Philadelphia performance, in modest yet effective décor by Robert Yodice, was more even, more of a piece. Dino Yannopoulos's staging had its ill-judged moments, but on the whole it moved well enough, and unobtrusively. Cecelia Dempsey was a touching Desdemona with a very good sense of Rossinian phrase. Josephine Mozzani was a delightful Emilia. Gary Burgess's Othello was vividly declaimed. Richard Brunner's Roderigo was bright (Roderigo has the most brilliant of the four primo tenore roles), and William Austin's Iago was lively. Only a Sutherland or a Horne can today accurately define Rossini's fiendishly taxing divisions, but this cast did pretty well. There was perhaps rather less fudging, smudging, and snatching, and rather more sweet suppleness, than in the Rome performance. Best of all, there was the most impressive, sensitive, shapely, and stylish Rossini conducting since Vittorio Gui's. Alessandro Siciliani, a young Florentine making his American début, showed himself a master of the manner, naturally eloquent in his shaping, timing, molding, balancing. Everything seemed to happen at exactly the right speed, with the right emphases, and in the right timbres. There was a good orchestra, drawn from the Concerto Soloists of Philadelphia. Rightly, the opera was sung in English; the dramatic sense of Rossini's inventions could be followed.

February 19, 1979

The Shakespearean Truth

The Metropolitan's new production of *Don Carlos* provides a long, serious, and elevating account of the long, serious, and elevating opera by which Verdi intended, he once wrote, to transform the lyric theatres of his day. The show was neither as handsome nor as handsomely sung as Karajan's production at the Salzburg Festival or the Scala production directed by Luca Ronconi and conducted by Claudio Abbado (two of the major stagings in recent years), but in some ways it came closer than either of those to achieving a faithful execution of the opera. The choice of text does much to determine the tone of a presentation. Reviewing the Scala production, in January last year [see page 80], I gave some account of the opera's intricate history, so here I will be summary. Karajan chose Verdi's short, revised, four-act 1883 score and made it shorter still by savage cuts. Abbado put together a very long, composite text, a patchwork of the 1883 score, the five-act 1867 score, and earlier scenes that Verdi had removed while the opera was still in rehearsal. At the Met, James Levine does 1883 uncut and prefaces it with the Fontainebleau act, which Verdi dropped in his 1883 revision. This act is also presented without cuts; in fact, it is extended—by the Prélude et Introduction, excised after an 1867 dress rehearsal when the opera ran too long. The production, with two intermissions, lasts about four and a half hours.

In a weakly directed performance, *Don Carlos*, however well sung, can seem to be a series of discrete historical tableaux. But in a performance inspired by Verdi's conception of the piece—he described it as an opera "made of ideas," not of "duets, cavatinas, finales, etc.," and one in which every musical, scenic, and even choreographic detail should be part of an ensemble—it is revealed as a tightly constructed drama, on a very large scale. Here are the fullest, noblest statements of the themes that dominated Verdi's thought: his detestation of ecclesiastical and political tyranny, his championing of personal and national liberty, and his vivid, tragic vision of men and women in extreme plights, compelled by honor and duty to sacrifice their hopes of personal happiness. The action of *Don Carlos*, based (not strictly) on

Schiller's great play, is not historically precise in detail. In 1559, when Elizabeth of Valois was married to Philip II, she was but fifteen; Philip was thirty-two, and Carlos but fourteen; Charles V, who in the opera emerges from his monastic retirement, *imperator ex machina*, to effect the dénouement, had been dead for nine months. But, as Verdi remarked in an (unpublished) 1883 letter to Giulio Ricordi, although the drama is not historically accurate, "it contains the Shakespearean truth and profundity of characterization."

The characters most fully felt are Philip, a lonely monarch, loving but unlovable and unloved, upright and honorable in action according to his own terrible lights, and the gentle, pure, dignified Elizabeth, whose lineaments Verdi traced with a tender and delicate hand. These are two full-scale tragic portraits. In a performance of Schiller's play, Philip tends to be the dominant figure. In Verdi's opera, the five principal roles are evenly balanced, and each of them must to some extent be portrayed by the others: we behold Carlos through the eyes of Posa and Eboli; Posa through the eyes of Philip (and of the Grand Inquisitor); and so on. If in a particular performance of the opera one person is pre-eminent, it is likely to be for the paradoxical reason that she or he abjures any self-seeking and devotes all efforts to being a part of the composer's "l'insieme, il tutto." In the Met *Don Carlos*, Renata Scotto's Elizabeth is thus pre-eminent. Not only is her presentation of the Queen's character complete; the characters of Carlos, Eboli, and Philip are by her made more vivid, and the great social themes of the drama become manifest in her singing and her acting. This is a nobly "Verdian" account of the role. In Act II, Elizabeth sings, with deep emotion, "Le devoir, saint flambeau, devant mes yeux a lui, Je marche guidée par lui." All Miss Scotto's performance was marked by this sense of ardent dedication. If on occasion she pushed her tones beyond the limits of their natural beauty, she had the composer's warrant for doing so: writing to Charles Nuitter about the Elizabeth-Philip confrontation in Act IV, Verdi said that he wanted to give the actress a chance for "a strident outburst [*una strillacciata*] that would not be beautiful, either poetically or musically, but would be theatrical." Her soft singing was limpid, and the phrases were tenderly molded. Even when she sang *very* softly, the lines were purely and distinctly projected. In the Act II romance, "Ô ma chère compagne," the English horn and the flute could not have been listening to her intently enough, for they nearly drowned her. After the Act V *stances*, her artistry and magnetic presence prevented the solemnity of the scene from being shattered by general applause. She is the only Elizabeth I know who has managed it.

Nicolai Ghiaurov's Philip was not on this exalted level. I first heard Ghiaurov eighteen years ago, in *Don Carlos*, at La Scala, as the Grand Inquisitor in a new production by Margherita Wallmann; his chief care seemed to be to show that he could sing three times as loud as the Philip, Boris Christoff. Two years later, in the same production he was the Philip, and since then he has been doing the part prominently, regularly, and impressively. The voice is no longer the massively sonorous instrument it once was, but he can still nurse very big sounds from it at climaxes. His performance is not profound or fine drawn, and is imposing rather than affecting. Toward the end of the air, he became histrionic; when it was over, he got up from his chair to bow to the audience's applause and then sat down again to await the announcement of the Inquisitor. The two-octave descent after the Inquisitor's departure, "L'orgueil du roi fléchit devant l'orgueil du prêtre," was a magnificent, sustained fortissimo outburst, not Verdi's forte cry dying to an intense, bitter pianissimo.

The "active" roles, as so often in Verdi, are assigned to the middle voices—the mezzo and the baritone, to Eboli and Posa. They cause things to happen—even if, strictly speaking, Eboli's two solos are not necessary to the action. The Veil Song is a divertissement; only the last two lines of "O don fatal" ("Un jour me reste! . . . Je le sauverai!") affect the plot, and during numerous rewritings of the air the fact that it is Eboli who incites the insurrection at the close of Act IV was obscured. But musically Eboli matters. She provides variety of texture. She sings in two trios and a quartet. (Moreover, until Verdi removed it in 1866 she had a tender duet with Elizabeth, and until 1883 a second "Veil Song," a voluptuous solo in Act III.) She adds a dash of brilliance and sensuality to the prevailing sombre drama. Verdi composed the first three acts of *Don Carlos* for a mezzo Eboli, Rosine Bloch, who had recently made her Opéra début as Azucena, but he completed the role for Pauline Gueymard, the Opéra's first Leonora in *Il trovatore*, a Donna Elvira, but also a Fidès in *Le Prophète*. For Gueymard, the Veil Song, originally written in G, was lifted a tone. There is no reason an Eboli who feels happier in the lower key should not revert to it. "O don fatal" was always in A flat—*pace* some curious statements in the press consequent on Marilyn Horne's choosing to sing it down a minor third, in F. Verdi revised the air several times before it reached its present form but did not put it up; one early version of its final section reaches to the high C. Like many modern interpreters of the part, Miss Horne adopted rather too massive and majestic an approach to it. In the cast list of the *Don Carlos* production book, Eboli is characterized as "very elegant, frivolous, capricious, and readily excitable"; Verdi said that she was essentially a *coquine*. One wants a highborn cousin of Carmen and Preziosilla, not a sister to Amneris. Miss Horne, retaining the higher key, did some seductive and attractive things with the Veil Song. She spat out the "woman offended" lines of the Act III trio with venom and vigor. Verdi regularly forbade any transpositions of his music which he himself had not made, less through tonal convictions, I think—for in 1883 he lifted the final duet of *Don Carlos* by a semitone, and then ended the opera in B instead of A—than out of general insistence that no one should tamper with his scores. (His contracts usually specify heavy penalties if any transpositions, cuts, or reductions of orchestration are made.) In principle, singers should be free to sing arias at the pitch where they can most readily do justice to themselves and to the music. In practice, Miss Horne's low "O don fatal" proved too dark, heavy, and chesty. If she were to learn the role in the original language, it might suggest the way to a lighter, brighter, more twinkly approach. The Met *Carlos* was sung in an Italian translation, alas; more of that later.

Posa has one very important duet with Philip (Verdi composed it three times, in 1866, 1872, and 1882), expressing his vision of a world in which all men are free, and two expansive, almost effusive solos expressing his love for Carlos, which are the most old-fashioned numbers in the score. At the Met, Sherrill Milnes was partly but not wholly successful in portraying the ardent, idealistic dreamer. Sometimes he seemed just a baritone with a good presence and a very fine voice, and in the Act III finale his cry of "Votre épée!" (translated as "A me il ferro!") was absurdly exaggerated—a self-seeking display of big, sustained, ringing sound. Giuseppe Giacomini, the Carlos, produced strong, well-filled tones, but his interpretation was wooden. He did little to suggest the prince's quick, impetuous, unstable character. Domingo, Vickers, Carreras, and Carlo Cossutta are more vivid performers of the role; perhaps the Met should have scheduled its production for a time when one of them was available. James Morris was a potent Grand Inquisitor. Charles V needed grander tones than those of John Cheek. *Don Carlos* taxes a company's bass strength to the utmost, and taxed the Met's too far. The six Flemish deputies were played, not nobly enough, by six unnamed choristers. No one was unnamed at the 1867 première—not even the Act III supers or the two mute Dominicans who support the Grand Inquisitor—and that immense cast list seems to symbolize Verdi's insistence that everyone who appears in the drama has an important and personal contribution to make to it.

The scenery is disappointing. David Reppa's set is a rectangular platform, variously decked, and flanked by two tall, unattractive towers that seem to be made of plywood patches. Verdi laid out his three central acts in two scenes each: a shallow scene followed by a deep one. (There was a further scene change in Act III for the ballet sequence, but that no longer concerns us.) The scheme was practical: scene changes were effected instantly, in full view, and during intermissions the built-up scenery of a deep set could be prepared behind the backcloth of a shallow one. The drama was devised and the music was composed to this plan, and virtue was made of the contrasts in scenic depth it afforded [see page 86]. Reppa's décor is also practical. It is changed quickly, behind a front drop painted with the Spanish imperial stemma. Two of Verdi's four intermissions are done away with. But because all the scenes are much the same size they do not reflect the tensions and shaping of the drama. Or of the score: Abbado has remarked how study of Verdi's stage plans helped him to understand Verdi's musical intentions. The costumes, by Ray Diffen, are handsome, but the scenery looks as if it were run up on the cheap. This *Carlos* suggests not the Metropolitan but a small German provincial house; and even of its kind the décor is an undistinguished example.

Act I is always a problem. It is a bleak winter scene, yet it must house the rapturous idyll that Elizabeth and Carlos treasure as the happiest hour of their lives. Somehow, Carlos's ecstatic cry "Naked boughs, ravines, briars, to my enchanted eyes you seem to be covered with flowers!" must find a visual counterpart. Luciano Damiani, Ronconi's designer at La Scala, suggested the enchantment with a shimmering snow-cloth and effects of moonlight.

Reppa's scene looked merely bleak. In his third scene, when the court ladies and Tybalt sang of the shade from immense firs, the thousands of flowers covering the ground, and the murmuring pines that they were enjoying, they did so in what looked like a concrete municipal "park" where a few seedling cypresses were the only flora. In the coronation scene, there was no cathedral; there were no great doors to swing open for Philip's solemn entry; and a bolt of cloth spanned the public square from side to side—a sure way of shrinking an imagined great space to the dimensions of a tent.

John Dexter's staging seems to have been blocked out in full knowledge of the production book. Sometimes he departs from it ineffectively. (The Act III trio makes better musical and dramatic sense when the three singers are stationed and shifted as there prescribed; Elizabeth's *marziale* episode in the final duet, "Oui, violà l'héroïsme," is surely not music to be sung sitting down.) Sometimes he improves on the composer's directions. (When the French peasants press in on Elizabeth, delaying her first exit, the urgency of their plight is made vivid to her, and to us.) At the close of Act III, the auto-da-fé procession reaches its end station too early. No one should seem to hear the Heavenly Voice, Verdi said. (There is nothing supernatural about the action of *Don Carlos;* the Voice—at the Met it was beautifully sung by Leona Mitchell—is hardly more than an illusory, almost ironic musical comment on the cruel proceedings.) But here the crowd sat or stood around listening to it. In the next scene, Philip read a paper while the Inquisitor was talking to him. At the very end of the opera, Charles V failed to put in his appearance. His voice was heard, and Carlos stumbled through the gates toward the tomb. This was tame. Of detailed direction—getting the chorus to bear themselves like Frenchmen in Act I and thereafter like Spaniards; instilling into the ladies-in-waiting a proper sense of court decorum; teaching the monks to move as monks do—there was little trace. Gil Wechsler's lighting, too often dependent on follow spots, did little to suggest place or time of day.

Don Carlos was composed in French and revised in French. Verdi wrote some of the most important lines himself, and every line passed under his attentive scrutiny. The Italian translation used at the Met is uncredited either in the program or in the newly printed libretto. It was originally made in 1867 by Achille de Lauzières; in 1883 Angelo Zanardini translated the newly composed passages and revised some of his predecessor's least felicitous lines; in 1973 Piero Faggioni translated the Prélude et Introduction into Italian when he included my "new" scenes in his production for La Fenice. De Lauzières could not decide whether to call the heroine Elisabetta or Isabella (either is possible) and used sometimes one, sometimes the other. Zanardini changed one *Isabella* to *Elisabetta* but otherwise let the confusions stand. Faggioni compounded them: the French peasants first call their princess Elisabetta and then, a few pages later, Isabella. But that muddle is the least of the faults of this translation. Again and again, it falsifies the sense. It blunts Verdi's keen rhythms and doesn't fit his phrasing. In "O don fatal," it allots the word *furor* to notes Verdi wrote for *du ciel* and the words *il cielo* to his angry outbursts on *colère.* It makes fancy what is clear and direct. Verdi's

Elizabeth sings "Fontainebleau! mon coeur est plein de votre image," but the Italian translators give her the equivalent of "Fontainebleau! t'ward thee opes my thought its pinions." When Philip sings the simple phrase "Voici le jour!" the very sound of the words suggests the light of a cold gray dawn filtering through his windows; "Già spunta il dì!" is a big, fat sound. There are people who say they prefer to listen to *Don Carlos* in Italian. They can't have heard it in French. The Italian translation casts a film of rich, thick sludge over the clarity of the original. There is, of course, the practical point that singers who sing French well are hard to find. Argument on those lines applies with equal force to *Faust, Carmen, Le Prophète,* and *Werther*—works that the Met expects its artists to learn in the original language. When an opera is translated from one foreign language into another, the audience suffers all the losses of translation and reaps none of the gains in communicativeness. An exotic translation must be accepted if it is the only expedient by which a decent cast can be assembled. Let it not be defended on any other grounds.

James Levine's conducting is large, impassioned, colorful, potent. He feels the movement of the piece, and its meaning. The pacing is right, and so are the proportions. It is perhaps not for me to champion the restoration of the Prélude et Introduction. Let me quote Joseph Kerman on the subject, in a *Musical Times* review of its first public performance, given in 1971 by the Chelsea Opera Group:

> The original [opening] is stronger, more shapely, and more coherent. It is right for *Don Carlos* to start not on a personal note (like *Aida*) but on a theme of national import, for in no other opera did Verdi work harder or more successfully to fuse the fates of individuals with the destiny of nations. Once we have heard the hunt music following the peasant chorus—the sport of kings set against the hunger of their subjects—we realize how arbitrary, in dramatic terms, the huntsmen sound all by themselves at the beginning of the cut version. . . . I do not believe anyone can doubt that this opera should be sung in French, and that the original beginning should be restored.

The three Elizabeth-Carlos duets also gain immensely from being performed in full. Carlos and Posa's prayer was sung with quiet intensity, not blared. (It will be more moving still when the singers "stretch" the triplets.) The coronation-cum-auto-da-fé scene, for once unshortened, seemed grander than ever, and Levine's ardent handling of it made it what Verdi once declared it to be, the heart of the opera.

February 26, 1979

Island Emperor

In Gatti-Casazza's day, the Metropolitan Opera was an important company that performed contemporary operas both European and native. In the 1933–34 season, there were three American operas: Howard Hanson's *Merry Mount* was new; Louis Gruenberg's *The Emperor Jones* was a revival from the previous season; and Deems Taylor's *Peter Ibbetson* was in its third season. All three were conducted by Tullio Serafin and starred Lawrence Tibbett. At its première, *The Emperor Jones*—according to Olin Downes, in the *Times*—had drawn "one of the largest audiences the Metropolitan has ever known" and had won an "instant and sweeping success." (It was first given at a Saturday matinée, on a double bill with *Pagliacci;* in the evening Maria Müller, Göta Ljungberg, and Friedrich Schorr sang in *Die Walküre.*) Gruenberg, born in Brest Litovsk in 1884, brought to this country at the age of two, was a Busoni pupil. He came to international prominence with his *Daniel Jazz* at the 1925 ISCM Festival. Like Korngold, he ended up in Hollywood and wrote a violin concerto for Heifetz. Kleiber had planned to do *The Emperor Jones* in Berlin in 1932, but that place and time were unpropitious for an opera by a Jew about a black. Serafin revived it in Rome in 1951. The Michigan Opera Theatre, in Detroit, gave five performances of it last month—the first full production in this country, it seems, since the Chicago Opera Company's in 1946.

The Emperor Jones has a place in operatic history. It was hard to judge from the score what sort of effect it might make in the theatre. Tibbett's record of the spiritual in it, "It's a-me, Oh Lawd, standin' in de need of prayer," contains little except a powerful climax built on a three-note motif: F, E-flat, D-flat above the staff, then repeated an octave lower. I went to Detroit, heard and saw an accomplished production of the work, and thought the music neither as admirable and potent as Downes thought it nor as meretricious as Paul Rosenfeld, in *Discoveries of a Music Critic*, declared it to be.

The libretto is Eugene O'Neill's play slightly abridged, provided with some offstage choruses between scenes, and altered at the end. Gruenberg made the adaptation himself. After the first scene—an expository conversation between Jones and Smithers, a Cockney trader—the opera is a monodrama for the protagonist. Schoenberg's monodrama *Erwartung*, produced at the 1924 ISCM Festival—the year before *Daniel Jazz*—may have been in Gruenberg's mind. In one, an obsessed soprano wanders through a dark wood; in the other, an obsessed baritone wanders through a dark forest. Brutus Jones, ex–Pullman porter, murderer, escaped convict, and now ex-emperor of a Caribbean island, is on the run. The "bush niggers" (the word is all over the libretto), whom Jones despises, brutalizes, and has grown rich from, have now rebelled against him. In a series of jungle hallucination scenes, or "ha'nts," he relives first his crimes and then "hereditary" experiences—the slave market, the slave ship bringing his ancestors to America, and, finally, a Congo rite at which he is to be sacrificed. Calling on Jesus, he spends his ammunition firing at the ghosts, and thus leads the pursuing rebels to him. In O'Neill's play, his last shot is fired at a crocodile god, and the finale is a veristic, chilling, deliberate anticlimax—after the night of vivid horrors, a dawn scene in which Jones is shot, almost casually, offstage. But in the opera the Congo rite and the Caribbean pursuit are merged; Jones commits suicide, and the opera ends with a savage triumph dance over his corpse.

In 1950, a proposed NBC television performance of *The Emperor Jones* was canceled lest it offend blacks. In language, both play and opera seem to me pretty offensive still. The last words of the play, spoken by Smithers, are "Stupid as 'ogs, the lot of 'em! Blarsted niggers!" Smithers is not presented as an admirable character, but some of his attitudes are reflected in O'Neill's own stage directions. The rebel leader is "a heavy-set, ape-faced old savage of the extreme African type." Jones's "features are typically negroid, yet there is something decidedly distinctive about his face. . . . His eyes are alive with a keen, cunning intelligence." Gruenberg carried that "yet" into his directions. In Detroit, the text was not bowdlerized; the performers were evidently willing to accept the language as authentic to the period. It is harder to accept the play as the Sophoclean tragedy Downes deemed it to be. Brutus Jones is no Macbeth. His ambition has been to get rich at his fellow-blacks' expense, bank his money abroad, and escape when his subjects will suffer his despotism no longer. In America, he has picked up enough white-man smartness to know how to exploit the credulous West Indians. Suffering and retribution following on commerical sharp practice can provide a moral spectacle; but it is not quite the stuff of high tragedy. There is no suggestion that Jones is a potentially great or good man corrupted or led astray. Moreover, there seems to be no particular reason why the memory of his crimes should recur in the jungle and destroy him. One could say: O'Neill demonstrates that back in the jungle a sophisticated black reverts to savagery as swiftly as Jones's Western clothes fall from him and leave him almost naked—and that, I fear, is the plain surface reading of both the play and the libretto. One could add: And by this the playwright intends a parable of what can happen to any man, whatever his color, who has founded his career upon crime—but that reading must be forced on the text. Alternatively, one might say: This is simply a striking and effective piece of theatre without any special significance—and leave it at that. On any reading, the tone of the play seems pretentious for its matter.

Toward the end of O'Neill's first scene, a drumbeat starts up offstage, and it continues throughout the play, increasing its pace and volume until in the Congo rite it "grows to a fierce, exultant boom whose throbs seem to fill the air with vibrating rhythm." Gruenberg takes over this device, but it loses some of its force when it is but one element of a musical score. This score puzzles me. It is bare—much of the time just two opposed lines, each of them thickened with block harmonies. It is almost athematic. The only tune is the three-note spiritual, and that lasts only eleven measures. The rest is declamation, cries, plain speech, rhythms, and sounds. And yet the first impression, that there is "no music" (as Strauss said of *Pelléas*), is soon modified by the discovery that *something* is holding one's attention—propelling, shaping, and articulating the drama, and making it vivid in a way that a plain spoken performance would not be. Probably, it is Gruenberg's control of timbres, density, and rhythmic tensions.

In successive Detroit performances, I heard two singers in the title role. David Arnold's words were clear and his projection was vivid. He looked a little young and slender to be the "powerfully built, full-blooded Negro of middle age" O'Neill and Gruenberg called for. Andrew Smith was much, much heavier—almost too bulky. His presence was imposing. His words were less clear. Both men gave arresting performances in different ways. The chorus was offstage, and its brief interjections were piped into the auditorium by way of loudspeakers; such canned sound is never effective. Onstage, there was a corps of sixteen accomplished and beautiful black dancers, miming all the roles, black and white, of the hallucination scenes, and representing décor, forest fears, soldiers, savages as required. It was a skillful and imaginative production, designed by Neil Peter Jampolis, directed by Rhoda Levine, and choreographed by Clifford Fears. But Mr. Fears's final dance was not a success; it looked too neat and too calisthenic. Robert Willoughby Jones, who had edited the score (including a new version of the finale, which Gruenberg made shortly before his death, in 1964), conducted a sensitive and well-prepared performance.

The Michigan company performs in a large theatre, the Music Hall, seating nearly eighteen hundred people—more than the Hamburg, Frankfurt, or Stuttgart opera houses, almost as many as Bayreuth. Each year, it does an American opera. *The Emperor Jones,* which lasts about seventy minutes, was given, as in 1933, on a bill with *Pagliacci.* This was sung in English, and therefore came across with unusual emotional force and directness. Marianna Christos, as Nedda, was outstanding. Her pitch was perfect. Her tone poured out pure and unforced at every level. Her words were eloquently uttered. She looks dramatic, and she can act. Her future should be bright.

March 5, 1979

Lulu at Last

Alban Berg's *Lulu*, composed between 1929 and 1935, was given its first complete performance, at the Paris Opera, last month. Berg died untimely, on Christmas Eve 1935, before he had finished setting out Act III of the opera in full score; until now, only two acts and some fragments of the third have been available for a performance. Helene Berg, his widow, who in 1936 had hoped that Schoenberg would complete the scoring, later decided to suppress Act III as far as she could. She died in 1976, and in her will reiterated her objections to anyone's even seeing the autograph of Act III or the photocopy of it held by Berg's publishers. But those publishers, Universal Edition, had already engaged the Austrian composer Friedrich Cerha to prepare a score. The Alban Berg Foundation—set up to execute the terms of Frau Helene's will—has sought but so far not obtained an injunction against its performance. The day after the Paris première, the BBC broadcast a deuxième, piano accompanied, of the final sequences. The American première of the full *Lulu* is due in Santa Fe this summer [see page 420].

In all previous productions, *Lulu* has been misrepresented by truncation. In Paris, the opera was misrepresented by malinscenation, the prevailing operatic sin of our day; the chance of presenting a *Lulu* accurate in staging as well as in musical text was not taken. Nearly fifty years ago, Schoenberg complained to Webern about "the new despots of theatrical art, the directors," and what he said then—"This side of things is in a very bad way nowadays; the high-handedness of these minions and their total lack of conscience are surpassed only by their lack of culture and their feebleness"—is still true today. The Paris *Lulu* was put on by the team that perpetrated Bayreuth's centenary *Ring* extravaganza: Pierre Boulez conducted, Patrice Chéreau directed, Richard Peduzzi designed the scenery, and Jacques Schmidt designed the costumes. The final scene of their *Lulu* was set not in the London garret prescribed by the composer but at the foot of a monumental staircase leading down into a lofty, magnificent public lavatory, cased in malachite, towering into the flies. In this improbable edifice, Lulu and her cronies had taken up quarters. The mechanics of Berg's action depend largely on doors, degrees of privacy and intimacy, surprise entries, and various forms of concealment; most of what he wanted was impossible in Peduzzi's grandiose, open halls. In the first scene of Act II, a huge party was going on. Odd of Dr. Schön to express surprise at finding visitors in his house: an immense coatrack was full; posses of waiters and waitresses in musical-comedy formations kept crossing the stage and prancing up and down another immense staircase. Lulu shot her husband with dozens of people looking on. At the close of the previous act, another party turned up, to watch the taut, tense, very private scene in which Lulu compels Dr. Schön to write a letter breaking with his fiancée; the fiancée herself even watched some of it. Dr. Schön wrote the letter crawling about the stage on all fours, and Lulu rode triumphantly on his back. This was but one of several vulgar extra touches that Chéreau had added to an already sensational libretto.

The musical design of Act III was familiar; George Perle published a detailed account of it fifteen years ago. What was needed—and what Paris did not fully supply—was confirmation in the theatre, through the senses, of what the mind knew: that neither the music nor the drama of Acts I and II makes full sense without the developments, recapitulations, parallels, and correspondences to be found in Act III. In this act, there are restatements of earlier passages as literal—and as revelatory, as "transfigured" in effect—as Isolde's Liebestod is of a passage from Act II of Wagner's opera. Through Berg's music there runs a paradox: it sounds spontaneous and direct, yet all its elements—even the metronome markings and the number of measures in a movement—reflect aspects of patterns. The score of the three-act *Lulu* is also a two-part structure, dividing at the palindrome interlude at the center of the central act. Berg imposed further dramatic patterns and symmetries on the two Wedekind plays, *Earth Spirit* and *Pandora's Box*, from which he drew his libretto. For example, by doubling roles he brought back the three husbands whom in Part 1 Lulu drove to their deaths as the three clients whom in Part 2 she leads to her London garret. The third husband, Dr. Schön, returns as the third client, Jack the Ripper, who puts an end to her. The music recurs, supporting new words; sometimes there are verbal affinities as well. It is disconcerting and rather horrible to hear the glowing, passionate, almost effusive love music of Lulu and Dr. Schön return to accompany Lulu's encounter with the Ripper. If Lulu possesses any attractive or "redeeming" quality, it is her true emotion for Schön, the man who was kind to her when she was small and tried to steal his watch—"the only man I loved." But that emotion is soured by Lulu's ardent wooing of Schön/Jack—"I like you so much! Don't let me beseech you any longer"—to the point where she pays him to take her. It has been said that Helene Berg gave as a reason for her suppression of Act III Alban's regret (communicated from another world) that he had ever dealt with such squalid subject matter. Seeing *Lulu* whole gives one a certain sympathy for the widow's viewpoint. It *is* a painful and sordid drama pushed to the point of sensationalism. If there is a moral, it must be that desire degrades everyone who feels it. Even the lesbian Countess Geschwitz, whose final love song is set to a flood of "noble," beautiful music, ending the opera, has been reduced to an amorous spaniel. People talk of her self-sacrificing love; in fact, like all Lulu's victims, she is dragged low by unquenchable lust.

Chéreau views Lulu not as a femme fatale but as a woman who more specifically attracts self-destructive men (and women). I'm not sure how much sense this makes, or how it squares with the reversals of role in Berg's final scene. (Must the destroyed always be destroyers as well?) The doubling of Lulu's first husband and first client was not made in this production; here the first client was a bouncy little dwarf—which merely added a pointless kinky gloss to Berg's drama. Franz Mazura gave a substantial, subtle, and detailed portrayal of both Schön and Jack. Teresa Stratas, in the title role, showed herself, as ever, a plucky, intelligent, and determined little soprano. She does not have the high, sweet, pure tones the part requires, and became rather pinched and squeaky when the pitch rose, but she had some charming, vivid, and individual moments. Yvonne Minton's Geschwitz, strongly sung, was a shade undercharacterized. Alwa Schön calls for singing more lyrical in timbre than Kenneth Riegel's. The other performers were without exception efficient, and sometimes more than that. Boulez's conducting was lucid, rhythmically keen, but not emotional enough for the romantic Viennese music. The orchestral playing lacked warmth, glow, passion.

This Paris première was a big occasion in that "all the world"— at any rate, the directors of a dozen or two opera companies, the international press, many other well-known faces—was there. But it did not provide the revelation one had hoped for. The truncated Met *Lulu* two seasons ago, sensitively directed, lovingly conducted, and intelligently and aptly designed, gave a truer account of Berg's piece—so far as it went—than this pretentious and somewhat perverted presentation.

March 12, 1979

Tableaux

Ezra Laderman's opera *Galileo Galilei* was given its first performance last month, by the Tri-Cities Opera, in Binghamton, New York. The piece was expanded from a ninety-minute oratorio commissioned by CBS television and filmed in Riverside Church in 1967. The libretto is by Joe Darion. It is not so much a drama, like Brecht's *Leben des Galilei*, as a dramatized documentary—facts of Galileo's life laid out in a series of tableaux. There are three acts, of increasing length: roughly twenty-five, forty, and fifty minutes. In the first of them, Galileo, in youth, falls foul of his hidebound colleagues at the University of Padua and then hears a chorus of the mindless, threatening mob. In the second, a Papal council considers his unorthodox teaching; the women in his life—his mistress, his daughters, his bawds—sing of him; and Cardinal Bellarmine establishes the terms by which the Church will allow him to publish: he must propound the Copernican theory as a hypothesis only. In Act III, under a new Pope, Galileo is hauled before the Inquisition;

after a long, distasteful dance of torture, he recants. In an epilogue, old and blind, he defiantly sends off his last book to Holland for publication. There is no theatrical action. There is little conflict except in dialogues between Galileo and his Friend, a mezzo-soprano role and less a character than a sharer of what would otherwise be soliloquies. Nevertheless, *Galileo Galilei* worked well in the theatre and held the attention securely. The score is arresting, and the staging was brilliant. The libretto is less cogent, being at once glib and humdrum. In a program note, Darion and Laderman say, "Galileo Galilei had within him everything that is good and noble in mankind and everything that is weak and mean and ignoble—which is to say that he was a human being like all the rest of us. But . . . his genius lit up the skies, and his weaknesses brought him before the Inquisition and under the shadow of the rope and the flames." That is fluffy, and inapplicable to both the historical and this operatic Galileo. It was hardly the man's weaknesses that brought him before the Inquisition. He was never in serious danger of torture. And in the character as represented there is nothing particularly good and noble, and nothing particularly mean and ignoble except, maybe, a lack of emotional generosity in dealings with women.

The opera invites comparisons with others based on historical personages: Pfitzner's *Palestrina*, Hindemith's *Mathis der Maler*, and, above all, his *Die Harmonie der Welt*, which is about Galileo's contemporary Johannes Kepler. When the comparisons are made, the plainness of Laderman and Darion's opera and their reluctance to transcend the documentary framework become apparent. Pfitzner's Palestrina is a musician wrestling with style, tradition, and the contradictory impulses of personal weariness and artistic duty. Hindemith's Mathis is an artist discovering whether he can better serve suffering mankind with a sword or with his art. Hindemith's Kepler is at once a philosopher seeking (like Hindemith) to descry a harmonious order beneath the muddles of life and a scientist reluctant to serve employers who may harness his discoveries to destruction. In all three operas, a listener senses and shares the creators' concerns. The conflicts and affirmations of the plot inspire and are made manifest in the music. The subjects are important and of personal application to anyone who ever wonders how he should spend his days in this world. Not so *Galileo Galilei*, which does not go beyond a this happened and then that happened. The creators point no parable, pronounce no judgment, explicit or implicit, and do not invite their listeners to define and judge. Nevertheless, what happens happens in a lively way.

Laderman's forte is writing catchy jingles: "Seven is a holy number" (a scherzo for a trio of professors), "The Anonymous Beast of Rome" (a scherzo macabre for the mob), "The Holy Mother Church" (a chromatic chorale), "Simple as a sword, Clean, clean, clean as a flame" (a Carl Orff–like rhythmic chant for the torturers), "He took us and used us and gave us away" (a lilting lament that punctuates the women's scene). From these jingles, chants, refrains, brought back to underpin the free passages of recitative or lyrical arioso, extended scenes are built. Jingles apart, the music is hard to describe. It is decent, satisfying, intelligently and strongly made. But I hear no note of passion in it. Good sense, not inner necessity, seems to have said "Cast the Friend as a mezzo-soprano, and add the central scene of bawds, etc., so that women's voices may provide some variety in an otherwise all-male drama." The disagreeable song-and-dance torture sequence is there as if in response to the question "How can we introduce action into Act III?" At the last, in Galileo's final solo, some emotion does shine out, in the setting of "The earth moves! The truth is the truth! It is God's truth, and to deny it is to deny God! . . . I abjure my abjuration!"

The performance, given by the Tri-Cities Opera in collaboration with the State University of New York at Binghamton, where Laderman teaches, was excellent. Carmen Savoca, who directed, and Peyton Hibbitt, who conducted, founded the Tri-Cities Opera thirty years ago. Their company has been the nursery for several admirable young singers—among them Cynthia Clarey, Louise Wohlafka, and Jake Gardner. Although the repertory has been pretty conservative—*The Barber* the only Rossini, *Lucia* the only Donizetti, *Carmen* the only Bizet, no Marschner or Moniuszko, Keiser or Handel, Fauré or César Franck—there are two previous world premières in the annals: Myron Fink's *Jeremiah* and Richard Brooks's chamber opera *Rapunzel. Galileo* had a lofty, light, handsome set, by John Bielenberg—an airy construction, open to Galileo's starry skies, that could hold all the chorus and allow them to move about on various levels. Staging, lighting, and costuming were intelligent, stylish, and helpful to the piece. Kenneth Bell was impressive in the title role, and others of the large cast who deserve mention are Catherine Allard (one of Galileo's daughters), Gerald Grahame and Bruce Reed (Interrogator in the alternate casts), Randolph Messing (Bellarmine), and Robert Lischetti (Urban VIII). The chorus of fifty sang their important and not easy music with clarity and confidence. The three cities served by the company are Binghamton, Endicott, and Johnson City. It plays in the Binghamton Forum, a large theatre, seating fifteen hundred, but one in which just about every word was clear.

Mathis der Maler heads my list of unjustly neglected twentieth-century operas. Neither the Metropolitan nor the City Opera has yet got round to producing it. (London's two big companies have been equally remiss.) Hindemith's preceding opera, the comedy *Neues vom Tage*, was given its New York première by the Manhattan School of Music this month. This was a stylish, accurate, and spirited presentation of one of the best twentieth-century comic operas. The plot is slight as can be—a set of connected sketches satirizing the sensational press and the public taste to which it panders. The title could be translated *The Daily News;* in fact, the piece was done in a bright English translation, by Don Moreland, as *News of the Day*. Beneath the fun and foolery there is sharpness and twinkling, clear-eyed observation. The music, wonderfully resourceful, affords pleasures like those of listening to Bach at his most exuberantly inventive. Neatness, energy, wit, and variety of motion, texture, and color conspire to delight one.

The staging was by Lou Galterio, who strikes me as the best American opera director. Maxine Willi Klein's scenery and Steven Feldman's costumes were smart, pretty Art Deco—a style that may have become a designer's cliché but was here used freshly, elegantly, and with distinction as a perfect match for the late-twenties music. I heard—twice over, for the opera was almost new to me (and far more enjoyable here than I had found it in a fussy Vienna Volksoper staging)—trim performances from Lauren Wagner and Richard Harrell, as Laura and Edward, the principal roles; from Marc Krause, as Mr. Herman, the professional co-respondent; from Mikki Shiff, as a reporter; from just about everyone in the large, well-prepared cast. How many professional companies could muster a chorus of a dozen young, pretty blond secretaries all looking exactly alike and precisely in period? Bruce Ferden, conducting, moved rather jerkily, and he was very prominent, for he had been jacked up waist-high out of the pit, but he kept the music flowing and sounded lines as well as rhythms. There was good playing from the student orchestra. Dorothy Uris had coached the cast to sing English properly. Hindemith's revised score, of 1953, vocally less florid than the 1929 original, was used. The production was a high point of New York's operatic season so far—something to set beside the Met's *Billy Budd* and the City Opera's *Street Scene.*

In 1833, the year after *L'elisir d'amore,* Donizetti brought out four unusual and very successful operas. All four could boast distinguished literary origins: *Il furioso all'isola di San Domingo* is after—a long way after—an episode in *Don Quixote; Parisina* is after Byron; *Torquato Tasso* has Goethe, Goldoni, and Byron in its ancestry; and *Lucrezia Borgia* is after Victor Hugo. Three of the four operas are set in Ferrara, at the Este court. Two of them, *Il furioso* and *Tasso,* were composed for a twenty-two-year-old baritone, Giorgio Ronconi (later Verdi's first Nabucco), who seems to have inspired both the librettist, Jacopo Ferretti, and the composer to venture beyond the bounds of Ottocento formula and write psychologically far-ranging dramas. Cardenio, the hero of *Il furioso,* has been driven mad by his wife's unfaithfulness; subject to fits of violence, he wanders through the lush Caribbean island. There is no subplot: the opera is concerned with the effects of his encountering his wife and his brother, and his eventual return to sanity. So far as I know, neither of these two baritone operas has received a worthy revival in our day; no new young Ronconi has appeared to bring them back into the limelight. A Siena production of *Il furioso,* in 1958, with Ugo Savarese and Gabriella Tucci, had no immediate issue. Then the opera was cut to shreds in Spoleto, Italy, in 1967, and again in Spoleto U.S.A., alias Charleston, last year. Last month's production, by the New Opera Theatre of the Brooklyn Academy of Music, restored some but not all of the missing music. Once again, a reduced orchestration was used. Even so, the small orchestra played too loud; Richard Dufallo, conducting, drowned singers whom he should have accompanied. The scenery and costumes were borrowed from Spoleto. The direction, by

Ian Strasfogel, did not extend to getting the chorus to move competently. The result was village-hall opera with a mixture of some accomplished elements. Although Stephen Dickson lacked the vocal resources to do justice to the richness of the title role, he seemed to feel the force of the music. Pamela Myers, the soprano, had her moments; her voice is a potentially exciting instrument, as yet unschooled. The tenor, Richard Barrett, was painful, and the buffo, Donnie Ray Albert, unpolished. Nevertheless, something came across. It was not an evening wasted. One got an idea of what this picturesque, passionate opera might be when properly done. Sensibly, it was sung in English, but the cast needed Mrs. Uris's attention. From the protagonist we had things like "I'm-a in-a love-a with-a you."

March 19, 1979

Champions

The Manhattan School production of Hindemith's early comedy *Neues vom Tage*, last month—its New York première—and then the all-Hindemith concert given in Carnegie Hall by the Philharmonia Orchestra of Yale were important occasions. Since his death, in 1963, Hindemith has lacked champions among those who plan concert programs and opera seasons, and as a result some of the most noble, substantial, and nourishing music of our time has been going unheard. *News of the Day* showed what high-spirited, heady delights we have been missing, while the concert revealed the "permanence, grandeur, deliberation, lucidity, and calm" that mark Hindemith's serious music. Those "paramount virtues" of art, ascribed to Braque by Patrick Heron, are attributed equally to Hindemith by Ian Kemp at the close of his valuable little monograph on the composer. The Yale concert began with the *Symphonia Serena*, composed for the Dallas Symphony Orchestra in 1946, and unheard in New York for fifteen years. From the very start of the symphony, with the broad horn theme flung out across the busy patterns of the upper strings, the music displays the beauty of ideas—melodic, instrumental, and formal—for which Hindemith is to be valued. There is variety in it, and wit, and tenderness. Much has been said about Hindemith's excellent craftsmanship; often his music is described as manufactured, dry, even mechanical. Mr. Kemp wonders whether if the composer had not written that primer called *The Craft of Musical Composition* his reputation would now be higher. Yet beside that exposition of technical "craft" there should be set the eloquent pages about inspiration in his book *A Composer's World*. I hear Hindemith's music, and especially the scores of his American years, as inspired, warm, joyful, even passionate. John Mauceri, who conducted the Yale concert, also seems to hear it that way. Without any loss of rhythmic verve, he stressed the lyricism, singing quality, and expressiveness of the *Symphonia Serena*. His phrasing was flexible, not metronomic. There was mirth in the second movement, romance in the third, and joy in the finale.

Then Phyllis Curtin sang the six songs from the *Marienleben* cycle which Hindemith provided with orchestral accompaniment—four in 1939 and two in 1959. When *Das Marienleben*, for voice and piano, first appeared, in 1923, it was hailed as, in the words of Hindemith's pupil Franz Reizenstein, "a shining example of *Neue Sachlichkeit*"—that plain, "prose," matter-of-fact manner of putting things which was opposed to the excesses of Expressionism and hyper-Romanticism. From 1936 onward, Hindemith revised the cycle, purified and refined it. He made the vocal lines plainer still. Yet with passing years the poetic quality of *Das Marienleben* and its emotional intensity became ever more apparent. The cycle is intimate. It should be heard whole, and a listener must have in front of him the Rilke poems, with, if needed, a translation. These "concert versions" of just six of the fifteen songs, sung in the gloomy half-light that the Carnegie management continues to favor, did not make a great impression, and Miss Curtin's voice sounded worn. But after the intermission there was the great *Harmonie der Welt* symphony, and, except in the literal sense, all was light again.

The opera *Die Harmonie der Welt*, which was first performed in Munich, in 1957, is an undervalued composition; *unvalued* might be a more accurate word, since opportunities to form any estimate of it have been rare. It has seldom been staged in Europe and never in America; and even the related symphony had not been heard here for twenty-six years. Hindemith's opera *Mathis der Maler* probably has a more urgent claim to be part of the international repertory; it is more patently dramatic. But *Die Harmonie der Welt* is his most affecting testament to the power of music. The final passacaglia, during which the characters of the piece, transformed into planets, move through a *musica mundana*, is a vision that even in the imperfect Munich staging proved overwhelming. The symphony, which appeared before the opera, in 1951, has the same finale, and it works out the same themes. Its three movements present music as an emblem of events, conflicts, strife, outward drama; then as a mirror of love and understanding between human souls; and, finally, mysteriously, as a symbol of a harmonious order that sometimes can be glimpsed beneath the disproportioned, harsh din of our life. At Yale, where Hindemith taught from 1940 to 1953, Willie Ruff, who studied with him, and a colleague have created a "harmony of the spheres" based on the notations and calculations of Johannes Kepler, the seventeenth-century astronomer who is the protagonist of Hindemith's opera. With the help of a computer, the data corresponding to a century of planetary motions have been compressed and synthesized into a thirty-minute "celestial song." In Hindemith's score, there is no such direct attempt to turn Kepler's calculations into sound. Here the *musica mundana* is symbolically suggested. The E-major chord at the end of the passacaglia is hard won, and it has been well said that "the real Harmony" begins only after that major triad.

The Philharmonia Orchestra of Yale is the symphonic descendant of the Yale Collegium Musicum, which Hindemith himself founded. Mr. Mauceri, a Yale graduate, is a former conductor of the Yale Symphony. Their performance of *Die Harmonie der Welt* was large, grand, and very well shaped. Beyond that, it was stirring, exalting. As in the *Symphonia Serena*, Mr. Mauceri made the counterpoint sound lyrical and poetic, not dry.

Last season, the Metropolitan Opera put on a bold, imaginative production of *Tannhäuser*, directed by Otto Schenk—one in which all the resources of modern stagecraft were brought to the service of Wagner's vision. This season's *Flying Dutchman*, directed by Jean-Pierre Ponnelle, is a sorry step backward; it is one of those modish personal perversions of a Wagner opera which have become common elsewhere but are not yet endemic in New York. For both ill and good, the Met under James Levine and John Dexter has hitherto gone its own way, and, except in the matter of star soloists, avoided the international operatic mainstream. The new artistic directors have not obtained Claudio Abbado, Bernard Haitink, Georg Solti, Carlos Kleiber, or Riccardo Muti to conduct. They have not employed those fashionable stage directors Götz Friedrich, Joachim Herz, Luca Ronconi, Jorge Lavelli, or Patrice Chéreau; until now they have even managed to do without Mr. Ponnelle, whose work is so hard to escape elsewhere. (This year, three of Salzburg's six operas are directed by him.) Mr. Ponnelle was last at the Met in 1973, for an *Italiana in Algeri*. For a while, a *Don Carlos* by him was threatened, but the danger was averted and it went off to Hamburg. As a result of this sturdy independence, New York has lost something on the musical side on nights when Levine himself has not been conducting but on the staging side has probably been spared a good deal of expense, elaboration, and irritation. Mr. Dexter's own record as house director may be deplorable (two and a half twentieth-century successes—*Lulu*, *Budd*, and *Carmelites*—to set against a string of nineteenth-century messes), but even his weakest work has not moved a Met audience to so violently vocal a repudiation as that which exploded when the curtain fell on the first night of Mr. Ponnelle's *Flying Dutchman*. Angry booing is an ugly sound, yet it must be welcomed if managements accept it as a sign that the public wants no more of such jejune rubbish as was here served it. The program book for the *Dutchman* includes a note by the director, which begins:

> I wanted to tell the story on a different level than the primitive legend, so I decided to turn the entire opera into a dream of the Steersman. In that way, it can reflect all of his frustrations and complexes as well as become more theatrically believable. I think it's quite believable that a little sailor should project himself, in this dream, into a profession that is

completely contrary to his own. In this production the Steersman and Erik the huntsman are the same person, the latter being the former's fantasy of himself.

Like the modern soldier or astronaut, the Steersman and all the men on Daland's ship have been compelled to leave home without women. This dream, therefore, reflects the young sailor's loneliness and jealousies.

The trouble with that idea—one trouble—is that Wagner didn't write an opera about a hysterical, sex-starved little sailor in love with the boss's daughter. It would make as much sense to present *Salome* as Narraboth's dream, *Tosca* as the Sacristan's dream, and *La traviata* as Dr. Grenvil's dream. Narraboth could be doubled with Herod, the Sacristan with Scarpia, and Dr. Grenvil with Giorgio Germont, so that by these fantasy projections into characters with completely different professions all their frustrations and complexes could be reflected. At the end of the respective operas, Narraboth, Sacristan, and Doctor would wake up to discover that nothing had really happened—they had imagined it all.

Wagner, as he explained in "A Communication to My Friends," wrote an opera whose plot embodied, in a new, composite legend of his own devising, three potent, related myths: of Ulysses, yearning through long wanderings for home, hearth, and wife; of the Wandering Jew, longing for death to end his sufferings; and of the Flying Dutchman, that myth in which "a primal trait of human nature speaks out with heart-enthralling force . . . the longing for rest amid the storms of life." (Monteverdi's *Il ritorno d'Ulisse* and Britten's *Peter Grimes* are two related dramas.) Wagner's own stormy sea adventures in the Norwegian fjords lent picturesqueness to his score: the musical images for wave, wind, and storm are vivid; the sailors' cries rebounding from the granite cliffs echo from actual shipboard memories. Wagner's unhappiness when he wrote the opera, in Paris, and his revulsion from the artistic tastes of a bourgeois-capitalist capital lent emotional keenness to his drama. And his own complicated yearning not just for repose and security but for some as yet unformulated future achievement inspired the search for a heroine who would be, in his words, "no longer the home-tending Penelope of Ulysses, as courted in the days of old, but the quintessence of womankind, the still unmanifest, the longed-for, the dreamed-of, the infinitely womanly woman . . . in a phrase, *the woman of the future.*"

Mr. Ponnelle has mislaid the myth that gives Wagner's opera its power. In the director's words, "The sexual relationship between Erik, Senta, and the Dutchman is infinitely more significant in this version than the Dutchman's arduous quest for a pure woman." All the action is made to take place aboard Daland's ship, which seems to be a tramp steamer. Its helm also serves as a giant spinning wheel. The Dutchman's vessel is represented by some spectral shrouds, in which bodies are tangled, and a suggestion of red sails in the backdrop. The Steersman is present throughout, writhing in his heated dream, sometimes mopping and mowing and dancing about. (The role is shared by the tenor who sings the Steersman's and Erik's music—William Lewis on the first night—and a smaller-size, mute double. During one episode, the pair dance a mirror pas de deux.) This staging is not merely silly, willful, and pointless. Besides destroying the large drama of the opera, it renders ineffective theatrical passages that one thought were surefire: the first appearance of the Dutchman's ship; the moment when the Dutchman sets food on solid land (in this version he doesn't); above all, his entry, in the second scene, as a living incarnation of the picture Senta has been contemplating. There is no picture at the Met; during Senta's ballad the Dutchman himself is revealed, standing in a kind of closet at the back, until Mary closes the doors on him. When they open again, the surprise effect of his appearance has been dispelled by the anticipation. Dramatically, the evening makes the effect of being a prelude to—or, at best, a curious commentary on—Wagner's opera. When it is over, one wants the opera itself to begin.

The music is not unscathed by the scenic travesty. It could hardly escape being spoiled: in his "Remarks on Performing the Opera *The Flying Dutchman*," Wagner makes it clear—sometimes with a detailed, bar-by-bar commentary—that his music and the stage action as he conceived it should be treated as inseparable. Mr. Levine conducted, and the performance did not move as convincingly as his *Tannhäuser;* it must have been hard for him to decide which drama, Wagner's or Mr. Ponnelle's, he should express. In what has here become the principal role, Mr. Lewis was very efficient. In what should be the principal role, José van Dam sang with beauty of tone, poignantly, and powerfully. His is not a big, commanding bass-baritone of heroic amplitude; it was lyrical, pure, unforced, and always excellently audible. One would like to hear Mr. van Dam in a proper performance of the opera. As Senta, Carol Neblett made her Met début. On the first night, she tended to be unsteady and uneven in the lower ranges and strident above, and her words were not clear. In the second part of the duet with the Dutchman, however, around "Wohl kenn' ich Weibes heil'ge Pflichten," the voice began to flow more easily and fully. Paul Plishka was a capable Daland. But no one stood much of a chance against Mr. Ponnelle's staging. At Daland's "Wie? Hört' ich recht? Meine Tochter sein Weib," Mr. Plishka was made to don the Dutchman's mantle, displaying its thick lining of golden trinkets, and do some waltz-strutting in it. At the Dutchman's talk of treasure, a little earlier, golden spangles had poured down from the flies. The spinning chorus looked ridiculous, for the girls were apparently all harnessed together, with old Mary holding the reins. This production is shared by the Met and San Francisco. It had its première in San Francisco in 1975. What a pity it was ever brought to New York!

Last month, in the Bruno Walter Auditorium, Michael Ingham and Carolyn Horn, baritone and piano, performed two song cycles by Ernst Krenek, *Gesänge des späten Jahres* and *Spätlese*. At a reception afterward, I learned how the composer earlier this season had gone over to Darmstadt to attend a production of his opera *Karl V.*, had been to two rehearsals, and had then set out for the airport and returned to America, refusing to witness or by his presence to imply approval of, even acquiescence in, a staging that contradicted both the spirit and the details of his opera. Living composers are in a position to protest against directorial pretension and destructiveness. In Paris, the critics had to do so on Berg's behalf after Mr. Chéreau's maltreatment of *Lulu*. At the Met, the audience itself was moved to take up Wagner's cause.

April 2, 1979

Fire in April

Miss Havisham's Fire, Dominick Argento's fourth full-length opera, was given its first performance last month by the New York City Opera, which had commissioned it (the company's seventeenth world première and thirteenth commission). The work proved easy and attractive to listen to; it is skillfully composed, and it was well performed. The libretto, by John Olon-Scrymgeour, Argento's collaborator on four previous pieces, is described as being "after Dickens," but *Miss Havisham's Fire* is not a straight operatic version of *Great Expectations*. The title continues, *Being an Investigation into the Unusual and Violent Death of Aurelia Havisham on the Seventeenth of April, in the Year Eighteen Hundred and Sixty*. Joe Gargery, Mrs. Gargery, Biddy, Mr. Wopsle, Wemmick and the Aged Parent, Abel Magwitch, and Herbert Pocket are omitted; Mr. Pumblechook speaks only his name and two sentences, as he delivers Pip to Satis House. It is not Pip's story but Miss Havisham's, extracted from Pip's first-person narrative and then elaborated. None of the marsh, forge, or London events are represented; all but one of the sixteen scenes are set in Satis House or its garden. The frame of the drama is an inquest in the library; testimony given during the inquest by Nanny Broome, Sarah Pocket, Mr. Jaggers, Pip, Raymond Pocket, and Old Orlick is dramatized in a series of flashbacks. Nanny Broome, Miss Havisham's former governess, and an unnamed Examiner officiating at the inquest are inventions of the librettist; Old Orlick and Bentley Drummle draw their names but not their characters from Dickens. Pip, Estella, Miss Havisham, and her Pocket relations play in the flashbacks much the roles that they do in the novel. Mr. Jaggers is reduced to a cipher. It might be best to forget Dickens altogether, but no one who has read *Great Expectations* can hope to do so. As Angus Calder remarks in his introduction to the Penguin edition of the book, Miss Havisham is "one of the many Dickens creatures . . . who are as much part of the permanent furniture of the private and public rooms of the Western mind as Ulysses and Sinbad."

The opera falls into two acts, each of about eighty minutes. It also falls clearly into two parts, differently divided. The second part is a long scena (lasting about half an hour) for Miss Havisham; described as an epilogue, it is a freely invented fantasia on the Dickens character, and is not drawn, as much of the first part is, from the events and the actual dialogue of the novel. In fact, in dramaturgy as in language this closing section differs so much from the preceding scenes that it comes as no surprise to discover—from an essay in the program book, by Hans Heinsheimer—that originally the epilogue had an independent existence, as a monologue entitled *Miss Havisham's Wedding Night*. In 1974, Argento composed a forty-five-minute monodrama for baritone or tenor called *A Water Bird Talk*; *Miss Havisham's Wedding Night* was written as a companion piece for soprano and orchestra. Argento set it to music, but when he and the librettist "discussed it between themselves and also with others it seemed too short; and it was also felt that Francis Poulenc in *La Voix humaine*, Arnold Schoenberg in *Erwartung*, and Hugo Weisgall in his Strindberg opera *The Stronger* had already covered similar exasperated ground in their monologues. So back to Dickens they went, and a full-length version emerged."

There was already in existence a work even more similar in the ground it covered—Peter Maxwell Davies's *Miss Donnithorne's Maggot*, a monodrama for soprano, based not on Miss Havisham herself but on the woman who was probably Dickens's principal model for her, Miss Eliza Emily Donnithorne, of Newtown, New South Wales. One morning in 1856, Miss Donnithorne dressed for her wedding; the wedding breakfast was laid out; the guests assembled; but the groom did not appear. For thirty years thereafter, Miss Donnithorne shut herself in her house, allowing nothing to be disturbed, while the wedding feast decayed into dust. According to a contemporary, she found her only solace in books. (She could have read *Great Expectations*, for she died only in 1886.) Both Davies's work, which has a text by Randolph Stow, and Argento's epilogue are a series of contrasting episodes in which the character's disordered fancies range freely, madly, with sudden, keen moments of self-awareness, between her present and that disastrous bridal day. *Miss Havisham's Wedding Night* is a striking and effective piece that, like *Miss Donnithorne's Maggot*, might well be performed with success on its own—even as a work of concert-hall music theatre. A tattered wedding dress could provide theatrical setting enough.

Whether the preceding scenes are really necessary, how much they add to the drama of Miss Havisham, and, by extension, whether so much time, money, and talent were well spent on the excellent City Opera production are open to question. The expansion from a monodrama to a full-scale opera with a large cast was deftly achieved, but there is something schematic about the result. The donnée is that a mystery attended Miss Havisham's death: "This lamentable event has given rise to very grave suspicions, rumors, innuendoes," the Examiner says, and Mr. Jaggers says, "What we want are facts. Nothing but facts." Hence the inquest. Nanny Broome, the first wit-ness, says, "You are all guilty of her death!," adding, to Estella, "You, a vam-pire, who took her blood, her breath, her soul!" Old Orlick, the last witness, says, "I killed her. I killed the witch before her bridegroom could touch her! . . . She loved me! . . . I hurled the fire with heaven's blessings!" But that makes no sense in terms of the novel, and very little in terms of the operatic drama. Miss Havisham is not Estella's victim. The operatic Orlick is deranged; what he says isn't evidence, and Mr. Jaggers, that clear-minded lawyer, steps incomprehensibly out of character when he insists on hearing it ("Let him be. He's inspired"). On the narrative level, there is no special mys-tery about Miss Havisham's death. In a prologue to the opera, we are shown the cause of it more or less as Pip describes it in the novel:

> I looked into the room where I had left her, and I saw her seated in the ragged chair upon the hearth close to the fire, with her back towards me. In the moment when I was withdrawing my head to go quietly away, I saw a great flaming light spring up. In the same moment, I saw her run-ning at me, shrieking, with a whirl of fire blazing all about her, and soaring at least as many feet above her head as she was high.

In other words, the dramatic structure of the whole when closely examined seems contrived and even flimsy—a concoction to fill out an evening in the theatre. Olon-Scrymgeour has included versions of two crucial Dickens chap-ters—Chapter 38, the interview between Miss Havisham and Estella, and Chapter 49, the last interview between Pip and Miss Havisham—and by in-cluding them he draws attention to the central theme of the novel: the self-knowledge, understanding of others, and compassion that come not only to Pip and Estella but also to Miss Havisham herself. But in invoking that theme without developing it, in surrounding it with theatrical effects, and in letting it all lead back to a mad Miss Havisham as finale, he has made *Miss Havi-sham's Fire* seem empty, unsatisfying—a mere entertainment. *Great Expec-tations* is a beautiful and moral book. One can understand that in an opera there might be no room for Dickens's impassioned indictment of a society where "justice" is something that must be bought with money, and of a city of terrible contrasts, where the rich may waste in an hour what the poor labor a year to win, where the powerful and greedy flourish while poverty and despair drive their victims to crime. In an opera, there might not be room for Dickens's intricate ironies. (The haughty, ladylike Estella is the daughter of a convict and a murderess; Pip, so ambitious to be a gentleman, becomes one only when he is ready to return to the humble life he strove to escape from.) Or for the elaborate symbolism represented by Wemmick and his divided life and divided loyalties between Walworth and Little Britain. Or for the playful counterpoints to Pip's progress represented by Mr. Wopsle's career. All the good characters of the book—Dickens's affirmation that even in this wretched world some people find it possible to live a decent life—have been omitted. But in a full-scale opera where Miss Havisham, Pip, and Estella loom large there should have been room to show that these characters develop at last from coldness, cruelty, and self-absorption. I find Olon-Scrymgeour's libretto lacking in humor, human richness and warmth, and moral vision. Argento's music does not go very far toward supplying those qualities (except in one aria). But, on a lower level, it does supply an evening of arias, ariettas, and ensembles that, as I said, are easy and attractive to listen to.

The title role was originally intended for Beverly Sills. In the event, it has been divided between Gianna Rolandi, who plays Miss Havisham on her bridal day, and Rita Shane, who plays the mad Miss Havisham. Miss Rolandi has a joyful, brilliant D-major aria, "The sun has risen," reminiscent of Jenifer's coloratura music in Tippett's *The Midsummer Marriage.* She sings it brightly, buoyantly. She acts the impetuous young bride well, and makes poignant the moment when she is stricken. Miss Shane has a tremendous role—a series of arias, duets, and dialogues culminating in what is surely the longest "mad scene" in all opera—and she gives a stunning account of it. Her voice tells at every level, across a very wide range. Her coloratura is accurate, powerful, and dramatic. Her words remain audible even when the writing is high, and she uses them effectively. It is a virtuoso performance, resourceful, vivid, subtle, and varied. Alan Titus gives a romantic account of Pip as a young man. (His principal aria, "One memorable day," opens with the memorable oboe phrase from the "Abschied" of Mahler's *Song of the Earth.*) Robert Sapolsky, who plays the boy Pip, sings extremely well—though he gives the appearance of being rather more of a little gentleman than the child Estella does of being a young lady, which disturbs the plot. Susanne Marsee, as the grown Estella, is aptly cold, clear, and beautiful. Others who deserve special mention are Elaine Bonazzi, as Nanny Broome; RoseMarie Freni, as Sarah Pocket; and Paul Ukena, as Old Orlick. The cast is without serious weakness. Most of the playing is keen and intelligent. Most of the singing is highly accomplished. Even the smallest roles—the two maids who assist the young Miss Havisham to dress, the brief appearance of Orlick as a young man—are excellently sung. The production, like that of *Street Scene* last fall, shows the company at uncommon strength. Only Mr. Jaggers and the Examiner are disappointing, for they do not sing meaningful English.

The easiest way of describing Argento's music, which is tonal, and largely tuneful, is to say that it often recalls Britten's. The spiteful Sarah Pocket seems to be a new version of Mrs. Sedley, in *Peter Grimes.* When Nanny Broome sings "Orlick, it's Nanny . . . come to take you home," the rhythm, the texture, the very notes of Ellen Orford's "Peter, we've come to take you home" are remembered. The textures of the *Grimes* mad scene—the pedal points, the unaccompanied fragments, the bitonal oppositions—are frequently brought to mind. And Britten is a good model. So is Verdi: the luminous octave play of the *Aida* Nile scene opens Argento's second act. Argento's lines sing well. His orchestra is picturesque. He uses offstage choruses and semichoruses skillfully to provide color, atmosphere, and emotional scene setting. In Dickens, there is a blacksmith's song, "Old Clem," which

Pip, Joe Gargery, and Orlick sing at their work, and which Pip then sings to Miss Havisham. It catches her fancy; she, Estella, and Pip sing it at Satis House. Argento has found a good, catchy tune for "Old Clem," and builds his first finale on it. In Act II, there is a ball scene at the assembly rooms where Estella and Bentley Drummle meet. For this, Argento has devised a kaleido-scope of dance-tune fragments. The scene is irrelevant to the main drama—it seems an intrusion, too obvious an attempt to provide variety, to escape from Satis House for a moment—but it is cleverly composed. The finest passage in the score, I think, is Miss Havisham's aria "I see you in a looking-glass." An underlying, limpid diatonicism seems to reflect her returning grasp on sanity and reality. Each change of harmony corresponds to a new effort at under-standing on her part. But sudden flights of chromatic coloratura disturb her mind again. The words are largely from Dickens, and here one gains an idea of the Dickens opera that Argento might have composed. So one does else-where from time to time, but in no sustained way.

These impressions I formed after attending the opera twice. The second time, I heard more in it and admired it more. By any reckoning, it is a not inconsiderable achievement. In *A Water Bird Talk*, there is, I think, a happier match of form and content, of matter and means, and in Argento's *Voyage of Edgar Allan Poe* a stronger, stranger fancy is at work. But *Miss Havisham's Fire* is more clearly shaped than the Poe piece, and I imagine it has a future. The staging, by H. Wesley Balk, the designing, by John Conklin, and the lighting, by Gilbert Hemsley, contain some strokes of high imagination. The problem of getting the members of the inquest on and off has been too simply solved: a curtain is lifted and a wagon advances or recedes. Julius Rudel con-ducts an expert performance.

April 9, 1979

Crusaders

In preparation for Meyerbeer's opera *Il crociato in Egitto*, which was given its North American première last month by the Sacred Music Society, in Carnegie Hall, I dipped into the composer's *Briefwechsel und Tagebücher* (three volumes of which have so far been published), and some sentences by Gaetano Rossi, the librettist of *Il crociato*, caught my eye: "La Scala is de-serted—the public is irritated, disgusted—Only one new opera in four months!" Rossi was writing in October 1826. (The novelty in question was

Nicola Vaccai's *Il precipizio, o Le fucine di Norvegia,* and it was done twenty-four times—a pretty good run, even for those days.) Earlier that year, *Il crociato* had had its Milan première. Ever since its creation, in Venice in 1824 (where it was the third new work of the Fenice season), it had been a success opera of the day, acclaimed not only throughout Italy but also in London, Paris, Munich, and Barcelona; soon it was to sweep the rest of Europe and cross the Atlantic to Havana and Mexico. In the nineteenth century, people wanted to hear new operas. In our day, however, there is no outcry from an irritated and disgusted New York public nor is the Metropolitan Opera House deserted because Ligeti's *Le Grand Macabre,* Nono's *Al gran sole carico d'amore,* and Henze's *We Come to the River* are still unperformed there, or because twelve years have passed since the company mounted a première. It should be stressed that nineteenth-century audiences wanted more than simple, copious provision of well-loved fare, more than mere variations on the familiar formulas. *Il crociato* had something new to offer them, and what it was can be traced in the series of excited reviews that accompanied the work's progress from city to city. Such a series runs through *The Harmonicon* in the 1820s. A report from the magazine's Trieste correspondent, one P.V., is characteristic. From other places, the news of *Il crociato* and its triumph had arrived; in Trieste itself there had been "no less than thirteen full rehearsals, and as many separate ones of the choruses"; and both the composer and the librettist had come to town to supervise the latest production of their piece.

> Expectation and impatience were therefore on the tiptoe, and its appearance was at length crowned with unanimous and tumultuous applause. I shall not easily forget the enthusiasm which this moment produced, an enthusiasm which a calmer review of the merits of the piece has fully justified. For myself, I frankly acknowledge that of all the operas I ever heard, the music of *Il crociato* has touched me the most, as well by the novelty of its motivos, as by the sweetness of its melodies, and the grandeur and lofty character of its accompaniments. As I am of opinion that *Der Freischütz* is the first modern German music, so is *Il crociato* the first of the modern Italian: or rather I would correct myself and say, that of all living composers, Meyerbeer is the one who most happily combines the easy, flowing, and expressive melodies of Italy, with the severer beauties, the grander accompaniments, of the German school.

Meyerbeer was a magpie, but a clever and industrious one, with a huge talent for skillful assembly. His career proceeded by a series of reactions, and *Il crociato* was one of its peaks. As a composer, he was German trained, notably under Abt Vogler, but he first made his mark as a pianist. When he went to Vienna to play, he chanced to hear Johann Nepomuk Hummel on the evening of his arrival (we are told) and as a consequence retired for several months to reform his own piano technique entirely before appearing to the

Viennese public. Similar reformations punctuated his progress as a composer. In Vienna, his comic opera *Alimelek* failed to please, and Salieri (we are told) advised him to visit Italy and learn to write for the voice. Meyerbeer went to Venice and there succumbed to Rossini's *Tancredi*—but again I must parenthesize a "we are told," for the older biographical accounts of the composer, such as that in Grove, don't always tally with facts in the new document volumes. What we are told does, however, accurately reflect the stylistic development shown in the scores. On hearing *Tancredi*, Meyerbeer "surrendered spellbound to the genial charm," says Grove. "He had no style of his own to abandon, but he abandoned Vogler's without regret and set to work to write Italian operas." A series of five (two of them with Rossi librettos) appeared in quick succession, the last two at La Scala. Then came *Il crociato*, an ambitious attempt to do now what Rossini had been praised—or reproached—for doing in *Semiramide* the year before: to Italian melodiousness adding German science, German formal strength, German richness of orchestration. After *Semiramide*, Rossini had gone north, leaving the way clear for the northerner to triumph. Meyerbeer was composing for the same theatre, La Fenice, and engaged the same librettist, Rossi. Then, after *Il crociato*, he followed Rossini to Paris, and there, after a new, long period of diligent study, assimilation, and consolidation, he produced *Robert le Diable*, seven years after *Il crociato*, and set grand opera on the track that led to *Lohengrin* and *Aida*. Beside the direct line of influence between Rossini and Verdi, and the subsidiary line with connections at Bellini and Donizetti, there is a third route, which starts from *Semiramide* and passes through *Il crociato* and Meyerbeer's French operas. In "Opera and Drama," Wagner made the case against Meyerbeer:

> He was like the starling who follows the plowshare down the field and merrily picks up the earthworm just uncovered in the furrow. . . . He became the weathercock of European operatic music. . . . In Italy, he composed operas *à la* Rossini, precisely until the larger wind of Paris began to chop. . . . With one bound, Meyerbeer was in Paris.

Wagner allowed Meyerbeer "cosmopolitan capacity." He underrated the industry, the thoroughness, and the determination that won for Meyerbeer a success not just with the big public but also with men of taste and discernment; the energy that modern revivals of his pieces have revealed; and the fact that—as Henry Chorley remarked of a greater composer, whose *Trovatore* he trounced for "the essentially superficial and showy nature of its effects"—"by new combination known materials make a new whole."

The basic situation of Rossi's libretto for *Il crociato*, derived from a French source, is interesting in a Voltairean way. A band of Knights of Rhodes was defeated near Damietta, during the Sixth Crusade. Armand d'Orville, a Provençal knight left on the field for dead, escaped enslavement by concealing himself in the spoils of a fallen Egyptian soldier. Chance brought him the opportunity of saving the life of Aladdin, the Sultan of Damietta, and winning his favor. Living at the Egyptian court, under an assumed name, Armand has learned to respect pagan virtues, and also to love Palmide, the Sultan's daughter. In the words of the Argument affixed to a London libretto:

> Afar from his country, with scarcely a hope of ever returning to it again, young, and of an ardent mind, Armand forgot himself, his duties, the faith he had plighted to Felicia, a noble maiden of Provence, and yielded to the love of Palmide. He instructed her by stealth in the mysteries of his faith; they were secretly united, and the product of this union is a son. But the call of honour, the love of country, and the sense of a dereliction of duty, were ever present to his mind, and threw a gloom over his happiness.

Now an embassy of Knights of Rhodes, whose Grand Master is Armand's uncle Adrian, has arrived in Damietta to negotiate an exchange of prisoners and a peace treaty. With them is Felicia, disguised as a knight, seeking her beloved Armand's tomb. So there are tense confrontations, and the outcome is complicated by a palace insurrection led by the wicked vizier Osmin, who desires Palmide for himself. Once again, Armand is able to save the Sultan's life, and all ends happily—except for poor Felicia, who has generously renounced her prior claim on the Crusader.

Rossi and Meyerbeer did not expound their action in full—at any rate, not in any edition of *Il crociato* that I have seen. Perhaps on the first night there was more explanatory recitative. From the second night onward, the piece was cut. For productions in Florence, Trieste, London, Paris, Milan, and Turin, new numbers were composed or numbers were added from other Meyerbeer operas to suit the specific casts. In an 1826 Reggio production, there were interpolations of music by Rossini, Mercadante, Pacini, and Donizetti. The Dresden première began at six thirty and ended about nine, so the piece must have been heavily abridged. From the start, composer and librettist were concerned less with a drama fully worked and convincing in all its details than with the general setting and the opportunities it provided for picturesque, novel décor and for, above all, numbers that would display the singers, alone and in combination, to striking effect. Wagner's charge against Meyerbeer of "effects without causes"—his example was the sunburst that closes Act III of *Le Prophète*—applies here, since by "causes" Wagner meant characterization and action that inspire, demand, find their inevitable outcome in the music. From one point of view, *Il crociato* appears to be an almost abstract composition—a series of impressive musical movements scored for singers, orchestra, and scenery. In the handsome libretto prepared for the Carnegie Hall performance, the first-act finale was designated and in a program note analyzed as a theatre transformation, for very large forces, of a four-movement classical symphony. Not only Rossini but also Mozart, Haydn, and Beethoven can be discerned in its contents and construction. Beethoven's popular *Wellington's Victory* symphony, at the première of which, in 1813, Meyerbeer banged the bass drum, evidently played its part, but the program note went too far in citing Beethoven's Ninth as another example of classical influence on this finale: the Ninth had its first performance two months after *Il crociato*. (Beethoven's soprano was Henriette Sontag, for whom Meyerbeer happened to compose new *Crociato* numbers—but that's another story.)

The most celebrated number in *Il crociato* is the trio in Act I, "Giovinetto cavalier," for Armand and the two women who love him. Meyerbeer had set his sights on an unusual trio, for the combination of soprano, castrato, and contralto. (Giovanni Battista Velluti, the last of the great operatic castrati, was engaged as the hero of the new piece.) Tracing the history of the trio through the almost daily letters Rossi wrote to Meyerbeer while *Il crociato* was being planned tells us much about the composer's work methods. Among the subjects discussed were a *Vespri siciliani* and a *Cavalieri di Rodi*, as *Il crociato* was at first called. Rossi's scheme for *Vespri* contained such a trio, while his *Cavalieri/Crociato* trio was planned for soprano, tenor, and contralto. When Meyerbeer settled on *Il crociato* as his subject, he extracted from Rossi a solemn promise that *Vespri*, now assigned to the composer Francesco Morlacchi, would no longer contain a high-voice trio: that effect he wished to reserve for himself. Then it was Meyerbeer's idea that the trio should be built on a "vera romanza alla provenzale." And so the number took shape. In the palace gardens, Felicia sings to Palmide the song with which Armand, back in Provence, won her heart. Palmide says that she knows it, too, for with it she was serenaded beneath her harem walls. She sings the second strophe, and the two voices twine in the refrain: "O youthful heart, do not trust the sighs of love." Offstage, a third voice is heard: Armand is singing his favorite song as he walks through the garden. When he enters, the three voices join. Unaccompanied cadenzas *a tre* in the coda include an octave-and-a-half descent in parallel triplet roulades of 6-3 chords. Rossi, when he sent Meyerbeer the words, declared that this number would be the high point of their opera; after the première, the *Gazzetta privilegiata di Venezia* reported that it was. When gently, purely, and beautifully sung, and exquisitely in tune, as it was in Carnegie, this trio still ravishes the senses—and it does so even though the graceful melody itself, like so many of Meyerbeer's, is unmemorable after its first two measures. The rest depends on finespun vocal embroidery, tender phrasing, and the contrast of voices different in character yet harmonious. The instrumentation, for a consort of harp, flute, clarinet, English horn, French horn, violin, cello, and double-bass, lends an added charm. The *Gazzetta* review named the 1824 players individually. Let me name the New York players, for they, too, "provided delicious accompaniment": Susan Jolles, Trudy Kane, Joseph Rabbai, Diane Lesser, Earl Chapin, Marilyn Wright, Frederick Zlotkin, and Alvin Brehm.

The genesis of the other numbers is less amply documented, but a similar care for situation, balance, and novelty of effect marked all the planning. At one point, Velluti weighed in with a letter describing in detail what sort of role and what sort of scenes would make the most of his talents, and what his current particular strengths were. The other notable numbers in *Il crociato* are a *coro dello sbarco* at the arrival of the Knights of Rhodes in a splendid vessel, oars keeping time to the cello figures, the Nile bank thronged by an eager crowd, and a military band in attendance; the first-act finale already mentioned, with its two military bands, Egyptian and Christian; and a tense, tuneful muster of conspirators in Act II. The solos and duets contain much lyrical tracery and much bravura that provide "instant effect" in perform-ance, but in memory the details fade, leaving a generalized impression of pa-thos, energy, and vocal brilliance. Palmide's "D'una madre sventurata," written as if for Mozart's Constanze, is an aria one remembers. The recita-tive, some of it secco but most of it in the elevated style, elaborately accom-panied, is always remarkable.

Like all Randolph Mickelson's Sacred Music Society presentations, this *Crociato* was prepared with care, scholarship, understanding, love, and en-thusiasm. The orchestra, like that deployed in last year's *Mosè in Egitto*, was not a modern top-heavy ensemble but a richly based one, some sixty strong, with the instrumental disposition of the 1820s. The important military bands—including eight trumpets and nine clarinets—came from West Point. There were some forty players: a forty/sixty ratio for *banda*/orchestra is more or less what one finds in librettos of the time where the players are listed and can be counted. The fierce military snap in the bandsmen's playing and drumming provided the intended contrast to the sound of the classical orchestra. (When the Met next revives *Le Prophète*, or mounts *Rienzi* or *Na-bucco*, it should enlist the West Point men.) The secco recitatives were ac-companied on an early-nineteenth-century piano, and that, too, was authen-tic and apt. The important chorus—all male, as in several Venetian operas—was strong. Gianfranco Masini, conducting, brought excitement, delicacy, and an excellent sense of style to the music. His command of color and texture contrasts within numbers and of the progress and proportions of the whole was admirable. *Il crociato* is one of the earliest opera scores to have metronome markings. Some of the indicated speeds prove surprising, but Mr. Masini showed that the composer knew what he was about. Although Meyerbeer calls for virtuoso singing, fine singers alone cannot bring his operas to life. They need—and *Il crociato* here received—a musical execu-tion in which all the details are sharp.

Sopranos and contraltos have both tackled the principal, castrato role. (In Venice, the same prima donna was understudy for the soprano and the castrato.) The New York edition included Armand music composed for Vel-luti, for the contralto Carolina Bassi, and for the soprano Giuditta Pasta. (Meyerbeer described Armand as a mezzo-soprano role, and said that it really lay too low for Pasta.) *Il crociato* had its first twentieth-century performance in London, seven years ago, and there Armand was the mezzo Patricia Kern. In New York, he was the soprano Felicity Palmer, a Pamina, an Elvira, and a Countess in *Figaro*. (Both singers can be heard in the recent RCA recording of Purcell's *Dido and Aeneas*, Miss Kern as the dramatic-contralto Sorceress and Miss Palmer as the soubrette, Belinda.) Miss Palmer, a young star of the English National Opera, was making her New York opera début. She showed herself to be a potential dramatic soprano, an exciting singer who may perhaps in time follow the Lilli Lehmann path to Norma and Isolde while continuing to sing Violetta, Fiordiligi, and Handel's heroines. Her voice was distinguished by range, power, flexibility, and a ring of bright metal in the timbre. There was dramatic force and emotional beauty in her phrasing. She was commanding. Palmide was sung by Yvonne Kenny, a young soprano, making her American début, who came to prominence a few years ago in London performances of Donizetti's *Rosmonda d'Inghilterra* and *Il castello di Kenilworth*, and is now a star of the Royal Opera, the Ilia of its *Idomeneo*. She has a beautiful voice—a warm, limpid lyric soprano, fluent, even, and malleable. In duet, Miss Palmer's and Miss Kenny's runs, graces, and cadenzas were sweetly and accurately tuned.

Adrian, the Grand Master, is the tenor. He is called on for high C's, C-sharps, and D's set in a context at once heroic and fiendishly florid. Rockwell Blake was at hand to fulfill all the demands. For good measure, he even threw in a strong, sustained high E. (It wasn't a pretty sound, but it was securely there.) The role also reaches low—down into the baritone register, and right down to the bottom G on the bass staff—and there Mr. Blake was equally effective. He is the wide-ranging, high-flying, heroic-coloratura tenor phenomenon we have been waiting for since the Ottocento revival began. Felicia's role was diminished by the omission of her aria—of both arias, according to the early Simrock score I was using. Dana Krueger sang what remained of it—notably the solo launching of the trio—with smooth accomplishment. Although Aladdin has no solo (or, rather, had none in this edition), the casting of a major bass in the part, Justino Díaz, brought rewards. Almost every number of the opera is punctuated and propelled into its next movement by sultanic pronouncements, which Mr. Díaz delivered with authority. In the comprimario role of Osmin, James Atherton was given a few brief moments to show his mettle. In the tiny role of Alma, Palmide's confidante, Carol Cates was not. Carnegie Hall has a shape, a sound, and a feel far better suited to opera than those of Fisher Hall, where the earlier Sacred Music Society presentations were held. The lighting was not strong enough, either on the singers, whose eyes were in shadow, or—my usual grumble—in the body of the hall, where the libretto *could* be followed, but not at a glance.

The society interprets the *sacred* in its title freely. Massenet's *Marie-Magdeleine*, its first presentation, was described by its composer as a "drame sacré," and Refice's *Cecilia*, its second, as an "azione sacra," but with *Mosè* and *Il crociato* it has moved unabashed into opera. The only requirement seems to be that the operas concerned should be on subjects that in their day were allowed Lenten performance. Rossi did call his work "a sacred opera, so to speak, a *Triumph* of *Religion!* an opera for Lent." One need not be nice over terminology. What matters is that *Mosè* and now, even more prominently, *Il crociato* have been New York landmarks of the international Otto-cento revival. Although neither of them was staged, in several important ways they came closer to the sound of the "real thing" than many of the British or Italian revivals have done.

April 16, 1979

Models

At the Philharmonic earlier this month, Alfred Brendel played two Mozart piano concertos—the E-flat, K. 271, and the C-minor, K. 491—and I have seldom heard them, or any Mozart concertos, more admirably played. Brendel, like Artur Schnabel, has been called an "intellectual" pianist, but when I listen to Schnabel on records, and hear Brendel today in concert, the thing that strikes me first is the *beauty* of the playing—beauty of sound, phrasing, and balance put at the service of the music. Objections to a modern Steinway as an instrument for Mozart were forgotten while Brendel drew from it lines that were fresh, cleanly articulated, energetic yet unforced, "singing" in clear, sweet tones. Of special note in these two performances where every detail held one on the miracles of the music were the thrilling control of densities, emotional and harmonic, in the slow movement of K. 271 and a touch of unexpected solemnity, even majesty, about the announcement of the minuet in the final rondo. If Brendel reads his reviews, he must grow tired of finding Schnabel's name in them. No one could confuse the two pianists, and attribute (if by some trick the recording characteristics could be got to match) records made by one of them to the other. They share intentness, gravity that does not preclude charm, and a communicative, joy-giving quality that springs from truth of conception joined to justness of execution. The "classic" recording of K. 271 is Walter Gieseking's, and of K. 491 Edwin Fischer's. Again, one could not confuse their performances with Brendel's, but in his Philharmonic interpretations Brendel was, like Gieseking, exquisite and, like Fischer, tender. Zubin Mehta conducted. He did not rise to the same heights. But when Brendel accompanied the Philharmonic players, as in the C-minor he was often called on to do, he seemed to turn base metal to gold.

I first encountered Brendel in 1952, as a young virtuoso; he was soloist in a recording of Prokofiev's spiky Fifth Concerto. As a virtuoso, he played, in Carnegie Hall earlier this season, Liszt's "Fountains at the Villa d'Este," in a program that also included some of Liszt's strange, somber late pieces, Schoenberg's Six Little Pieces, and then the Busoni Toccata and the Brahms-Handel Variations. And it was there I observed that he is now playing better, more beautifully, than ever before. About his all-Schubert recital last year (there was another this year, but I missed it), I had some reservations. I first encountered Brendel as a mature Beethoven pianist in 1969, when at the York Festival he did the last three sonatas in a single program. It was one of the great recitals of my life. Then I followed him through a period of speculation and experiment, when his work *could* perhaps have been called "intellectual" in a pejorative sense, and out into the sunlight—and ethereal radiance—of the same Beethoven program in Carnegie in 1977. Today, the virtuoso, the poet, and the thinker combine in perfect harmony.

Another pianist whom I have, so to speak, grown with, and heard from his first appearance on the international scene onward (though less often than Brendel), is Maurizio Pollini. He won the Warsaw Chopin Competition in 1960, played Chopin beautifully, and that year made a fine recording of the First Concerto; retired for a while; reappeared (his United States début was in 1968); in 1972 recorded a dazzling album of Chopin's studies; and now has a very high reputation. Last year, in Carnegie, he, too, played Beethoven's last three sonatas in a single program. I admired his smoothness, poise, polish, dexterity, and also his carefully considered interpretations. But "nothing happened." I didn't write about the concert, for I felt that the fault must be in me, failing to respond to something that everyone else was applauding. But when Pollini played Beethoven's Fourth Concerto with the Philharmonic last month, again "nothing happened." On this occasion, simple technical things were perceptibly wrong: although the conductor was Claudio Abbado, with whom Pollini has long been associated, the ensemble between the soloist and the orchestra was often imprecise. The piano, a Steinway, sounded thick in the middle, wooden in the bass, and marimba-like at the top. But the chief disappointment was Pollini's blandness in a work that can be the most moving of all piano concertos.

The previous Philharmonic program was also conducted by Abbado. It consisted of Mahler's Sixth Symphony, and one went with high hopes, for Abbado is perhaps the most poetic and vivid Mahler conductor of our day. He has made fine records of the Second Symphony with the Chicago Symphony and of the Fourth with the Vienna Philharmonic; in New York, he has given memorable performances of the Second and the Fourth with the Philadelphia and of the Sixth with the Cleveland. But those hopes were disappointed. Abbado wasn't able to get the right sound from the Philharmonic. In Boulez's day, the orchestra lacked spirit and used to sound dry and plain except when it was rising to the challenge of some difficult new score (Elliott Carter's Symphony of Three Orchestras, Boulez's *Rituel*). Now, in Mehta's day, it seems to have become coarse, noisy, and intractable.

The Rochester Philharmonic, which visited Carnegie Hall last month under its music director, David Zinman, played with more zest. The concert brought the New York première of Dominick Argento's *In Praise of Music*, composed two years ago for the Minnesota Orchestra. The subtitle is "Seven Songs for Orchestra." Each "song" is dedicated to a musician (David, Apollo, Pan, Orpheus, Israfel, Cecilia, Mozart) and headed by a quotation pertaining to him or her. The first six are also headed by musical quotations (strains of a Sephardic incantation, a Delphic hymn, a Japanese melody, a fragment of Monteverdi's *Orfeo*, an Arabian street song, and a plainchant), on the basis of which Argento builds his music; Mozart is honored by a free monody, not in Mozartian style, played by the violins. A large orchestra is used in a colorful and resourceful way. The piece is deftly and fluently made, undemanding and agreeable to listen to; it lasts about half an hour. Some passages suggest Britten—but a Britten working at reduced voltage. A schoolmasterly comment along the lines of "Very gifted indeed, but must try harder, not be too easily satisfied" came to mind. The concert opened with a fizzing account of Berlioz's *Benvenuto Cellini* overture; Mr. Zinman's conducting looked flashy, but the orchestra responded to the show he put on. There followed a routine, perfunctory account of Beethoven's Third Piano Concerto, in which Misha Dichter was a workaday soloist.

Seiji Ozawa's podium antics are equally animated; dance critics should really go along to review him. I've never seen him rehearse; perhaps then he takes things more calmly and seems to listen to what's happening in the performance, instead of just miming out the score so elaborately. He brought the Boston Symphony and the Tanglewood Festival Chorus to Carnegie this month to give two performances of Schoenberg's massive *Gurrelieder* (in German—which is not what Schoenberg would have wanted). The big orchestra poured to the very edges of the platform. It was disposed in the modern, lopsided way—all the violins clumped on the left, the basses way out to the right—and the instrumental sound was not well balanced either internally or against the soloists. (I heard the first performance; the second was said to be better.) James McCracken, striving with Waldemar's heroic music, sacrificed lyricism of tone to force. He was clear and powerful. Jessye Norman was a calmly majestic Tove. Schoenberg wrote his vocal lines without phrasing slurs, but surely he did not mean them to be sung—as they were here—nonlegato, in a series of unjoined notes. Tatiana Troyanos was the Wood Dove; much of her low-lying music sounded toneless, but richness came in when the line rose. The chorus was excellent. *Gurrelieder* cannot fail to make an effect, and the vigorous, enthusiastic performance was cheered; but I felt that Ozawa's account of the work's content had been superficial. Boston program notes and program books regularly put those of New York to shame, and Michael Steinberg's long essay on *Gurrelieder* made rewarding— if not, when packed down into the mean format of a Carnegie Hall program book, physically easy—reading.

The Metropolitan Opera made amends for its deplorable *Dutchman* by putting on a noble, serious revival of *Parsifal* at Passiontide. The score was given uncut; the performance began at seven and ended at midnight. Yet the evening did not seem long, for James Levine, conducting his first theatre *Parsifal*, led a performance that was broad, flowing, and unforced (his act timings were close to those of Hermann Levi, who conducted the first *Parsifal*, in 1882); Jon Vickers, in the title role, sang with a poetic force and intensity that kept one rapt on each of his phrases; and all the cast was strong. The production, directed by Nathaniel Merrill and designed by Robert O'Hearn, dates from 1970 and was last done five seasons ago. It was new to me, and I admired it. It owes much to, and might even be described as a free transcription of, Wieland Wagner's great Bayreuth staging—less calmly austere in general tone and more colorful in the donjon and flower-garden scenes. The flower maidens are ridiculous—a gaggle of Las Vegas showgirls, décolleté, wearing tall spangled headdresses and gauzy chiffon dresses. But a touch of light relief at this point does no harm; in fact, it may have been Wagner's intention. In general, his stage directions suggest a far more spectacular and picturesque show than we generally see today, and the 1882 designs, even of the Grail Hall, were brightly colored. (In 1923, Felix Weingartner was already regretting that scenic designers seemed to have lost the technical abilities and command of illusion he had admired at Bayreuth in 1882.) There was nothing in the Met transformation scenes to make one catch one's breath with amazement. But the staging never got in the way of the music or the drama, and much of the time positively supported them. In these days, especially where Wagner is concerned, that is something to be grateful for. Some things are wrong that could easily be put right. During Parsifal's long "Nein, nein! Nicht die Wunde ist es," Kundry did not "gaze at him with terror and astonishment" but turned her back and then embarked on a slow, distracting prowl along the horseshoe-shaped mound that circles the forestage. In Act I when Gurnemanz said "The sun stands high" and in Act III when he said "Midday," there was not nearly enough light in the sky.

In the earlier scenes, Mr. Vickers was a little too determinedly boyish in bearing; the Met libretto may translate Kundry's "tör'ger Reiner" as "foolish virgin," but the young Parsifal shouldn't suggest Albert Herring. In the later scenes, Mr. Vickers acted and sang as one inspired. Christa Ludwig's voice became somewhat shrill and shallow in the more strenuous passages of Kundry's music, but her performance in the role remains wonderfully moving. Martti Talvela, the Gurnemanz, and Bernd Weikl, an Amfortas of incisive and passionate tones, both needed more legato. Vern Shinall's Klingsor told strongly. In the Met, the enchanted, transfigured, mystically eloquent sounds that Bayreuth's acoustics make possible cannot be achieved, but Mr. Levine drew rich, deep tone from the orchestra. The sound was full but never clogged; the Good Friday music was luminous.

The Juilliard School's production of Mozart's early romantic comedy *La finta giardiniera* will have served some educational purpose if the students concerned in it regard it as a demonstration of how eighteenth-century opera should *not* be performed. Still, music so skillful and delightful managed to shine through the layers of stale, silly, insensitive (and ineptly executed) business which the director, David Ostwald, had imposed on it. The wonderful Act II finale survived his onslaught upon it. Calvin Morgan's set reached out right over the orchestra pit into the house proper, and this allowed young voices to have an impact they lose when the Juilliard Theatre is used in a traditional way. (In its concert hall formation, the place has excellent acoustics, but as an opera house it is unflattering to voices.) The orchestra had to be stationed at the back of the stage. Roger Nierenberg conducted admirably. He was buoyant, unforcing, and stylish; he got the Juilliard Symphony to play like true Mozartians. The singers could see *him*, reproduced on large television screens attached to the front of the circle. But—what matters far more—he couldn't see *them*, and so the performance couldn't have the right living, give-and-take quality.

There were some promising artists in the first of the alternate casts. The Ramiro, Susan Mentzer, was especially impressive. The Serpetta, Lisa Sakas, was, in addition, a good actress. To the rest, one would recommend more study in Juilliard classes of drama, movement, and eighteenth-century deportment. The abridged edition of the English Music Theatre Company was used, which has spoken dialogue. (Mozart's recitatives for the first of the three acts were long thought to be lost; in sung-recitative performances, people generally used those of Pasquale Anfossi, who set the libretto a few months before Mozart did. But the Mozart recitatives turned up recently in a Brno convent and are published in the Neue Mozart Ausgabe score of the opera.) The cast made the worst of Edmund Tracey's English translation, stressing wrong articulations like "I am so angry that/How shall I ever ree/Gain peace of mind."

April 23, 1979

Not Without Honor

Ernst Krenek, born in Vienna in 1900, has in some two hundred and thirty compositions traced the musical history of the twentieth century; he has set down in notes (and in words, too, when basing compositions on his own texts) the autobiography of a very intelligent, keen-minded, ever-curious man; and he has given to the world a large quantity of adventurous, interesting, and beautiful music. The first two assertions are standard commentary on Krenek; the full truth of the third was revealed during an eight-day Krenek Festival, from Palm Sunday to Easter, organized by the Music Department of the University of California at Santa Barbara. There were twelve concerts; some fifty Krenek compositions were performed. The earliest of them was the First String Quartet, Op. 6, of 1921, and the latest *The Dissembler*, a monologue for baritone and chamber orchestra, Op. 229, completed last year. Orchestra pieces, band pieces, choruses, chamber music, instrumental solos, songs, a chamber opera, and a television opera were done. Only Krenek as a composer of full-scale operas (he has written nine of them) was unrepresented. Admission to all the events was free. A carefully edited program book contained all the texts, with translations, so that charged poetry by Karl Kraus and dense, charged poetry by Krenek himself could be conned in advance of concerts at which it was sung. Lecturers from America, Austria, and Germany came to talk about particular aspects of Krenek's work. Six of the concerts were held in the excellent Lotte Lehmann Concert Hall, on the campus, and six in the Lobero Theatre, in the town. The Santa Barbara Museum of Art housed an exhibition of Krenek's musical sketches and of his precise, elegant watercolors. Krenek was present, active from early morning till late at night, conducting, playing, rehearsing, coaching, talking, and answering questions that arose as we traversed—and he, hearing some early works for the first time in many years and some recent works for the first time ever, retraversed—the last sixty years of music's history and the oeuvre of a musician who both reflected and helped to shape them.

The reflective aspect of Krenek's musical personality is the better known. His career is commonly divided into five periods: atonal, neoclassical, neoromantic, twelve-note, and serial. In his "Self-Analysis," published in 1953, he remarked, "It is quite possible that the unusual variety of my output has baffled observers accustomed to more homogeneous phenomena. It is my impression that this confusion has surrounded my work with an unusual obscurity—almost anonymity." In that long essay, he discerned two opposed forces affecting his music:

> From an early stage of my career, I have been attracted by the idea of pure, uncompromising creation, independent from the trends of the day, or at times explicitly opposed to them. . . . At the same time I was constantly tempted by the achievement of practical results in terms of "this world," whose current problems were a permanent challenge to me. . . . This presupposes a fair degree of adaptability, which proves to me that I have not really the makings of either a crusader or a hermit.

The adaptability has on occasion called forth scornful comment. As a student, I heard Egon Wellesz—another Vienna-born composer, Schoenberg's pupil, and fifteen years Krenek's senior—say, "Poor Ernst, always a year behind the avant-garde." Twenty years later, when Krenek had added a master's command of total serialization and of electronic composition to his expressive resources, Pierre Boulez said much the same. There may be chronological truth behind the gibes, but three other things need saying, too.

First, a vanguard position affords no automatic guarantee of musical merit. (Mozart is not derided for his enthusiastic adoption of musical devices he discovered in Mannheim; nor are Berg and Webern for walking Schoenberg's twelve-note path. The imaginative use made of inventions, not their novelty, is what matters in music.) Second, Krenek's atonal, neoclassical, and neoromantic periods lasted only a few years each; the opera *Karl V.*, completed in 1933, begins a forty-five-year "period" of steady, consistent development, unbroken by any willful or violent adoptions of a new manner. (Moreover, boundaries between those earlier periods cannot be hard drawn: one of the things the Santa Barbara festival made plain was an adumbration of each new manner in works of the preceding period.) Third, it is now evident that Krenek's adoption of the twelve-note system was not like the donning of a modish new suit but was an emotional and musical necessity prescribed by his ear and his imagination before his analytical mind began to wrestle with it. By embracing the method, he was sacrificing, not courting, public favor. Perhaps a fourth point should be added: that Krenek *has* been a pioneer. *Karl V.* is the first completed twelve-note opera (I put it that way because Schoenberg began *Moses und Aron* and Berg began *Lulu* at much the same time), and Krenek had no precedent for using a twelve-note method on so vast a scale; the finale of the Sixth String Quartet (1936) anticipates serial procedures that came to prominence only in the postwar years.

The Santa Barbara festival was not ordered as a dryly didactic demonstration with works done in chronological sequence. Compositions new and old appeared side by side; songs, choruses, instrumental solos, and chamber and orchestral music were built into enjoyable, varied programs whose diversity of forces would hardly be possible in the commercial music world. But, to simplify discussion—and with apologies to the admirable orchestras, ensembles, and soloists consequently left unnamed—let me draw out two particular strands from the rich fabric: the sequence of Krenek's seven string quartets, all of which were played, and a series of five song cycles. The former illustrates in closeup Krenek's musical development, and the other carries his autobiography.

The First Quartet was composed in 1921, while Krenek was still a student of Franz Schreker at the Berlin Hochschule. It brought his name before the public when it was introduced (without Schreker's knowledge) at a German Musicians' Festival in Nuremberg. The piece, which owes nothing to Schreker's ripe musical style but much, it would seem, to his strict contrapuntal training, suggests a young modernist's musing on the matter and the form of Beethoven's Quartet in C-sharp minor. The first three notes enounce that key, but the harmony then becomes assertively polytonal. Beethoven began with a fugue; Krenek ends with one, appending a reminiscence of his opening. His themes are athletic, exuberant expansions of the BACH motif. Bartók, whose first two string quartets and Allegro Barbaro had appeared by the time, may have inspired the forceful gait of the music and the vigorous string writing. The Second Quartet (also 1921) is even more Bartókian in its insistence on rhythmic energy. The work is less compact than its predecessor: invention doesn't flag, but the movements do seem to last a long time.

The Third Quartet (1923) bridges Krenek's first and second periods. It is dedicated to Hindemith and was first played, at the 1924 ISCM Festival, by the Amar-Hindemith Quartet (who recorded a movement of it). It is a shapely, engaging piece—an excellent, closely argued discourse (sometimes the Britten of the Bridge Variations is foreshadowed), with a poignant adagio. Krenek began composing it on a train, between Frankfurt and Berlin. The fourth movement of the Fourth Quartet (1923–24) was also begun on a train, between Vienna and Winterthur—on the journey that took Krenek decisively into his Swiss, neoclassical period. The neoclassical goal is reached in the finale that owes something to Stravinsky and something to the "Jupiter" Symphony, but the approach to it rambles through six oddly assorted movements. This incoherent yet striking work remained until recently unpublished.

The Fifth Quartet (1930) is a happy product of Krenek's next, neoromantic, Viennese period. The hit opera *Jonny spielt auf* had brought him fame and fortune. He settled in Vienna, "charmed," in his words, "by the city, the country of Austria, and the style of its life, as if I had never known them before." And, in the words of Grove, "he gradually drifted into the stylistic backwaters of a kind of neo-Schubertian romanticism." Backwaters are pleasant places. The Fifth Quartet is Schubertian, and attractively so—the central movement a long set of leisurely variations, the finale a fantasy that flows on as if by free association. The envoy of *Alice* comes to mind:

> *A boat, beneath a sunny sky*
> *Lingering onward dreamily*
> *In an evening of July . . .*

But then it is time to end. With swift, sure strokes, the composer pulls through an unexpected harmonic channel and brings the quartet back to the E-flat whence it started.

Soon those backwaters were troubled: outwardly by Nazi clouds gathering in the west and scudding toward Vienna, and inwardly by the composer's newly restless, questing spirit. The large result was *Karl V.*, commissioned by the Vienna State Opera but withdrawn after it had been put into rehearsal. I saw it in Munich in 1965; it is at once a grandly, nobly humane political vision and a grandly energetic muster of newfound forces. The sense of struggle in Krenek's handling of the unfamiliar twelve-note material makes the subject the more vivid. The Sixth Quartet represents mastery of the new method; I think it is the strongest and most beautiful of the seven, and one of Krenek's finest works. There is something Beethovenian in the seemingly inevitable cut of the themes and the indelible impress they leave; in the force and eloquence of the arguments; in the rapt adagio that begins the work; in the heroic concluding fugue, on four subjects, which is never merely ingenious but moves through passages serene, strenuous, and trans-figured to reach the affirmatory unison close. In 1937, Krenek first visited, and in 1938 emigrated to, America. In 1944, in St. Paul, he composed his Sev-enth Quartet, "dedicated in gratitude to the vivifying spirit of my American students." It is an exuberant, joyful discourse for the four instruments—Krenek's Opus 135, as it were.

The seven quartets were played, not in sequence, by the Thouvenel String Quartet (Eugene Purdue, Michael Rosenbloom, Sally Chisholm, Jef-frey Levenson), formed on the Bloomington, Indiana, campus and currently resident in Midland, Texas—a young, expert, alert ensemble, very well bal-anced, lithe, musical, sweetly and truly tuned. When the festival was over, the quartet set about recording a Krenek cycle, and I look forward to the publication of the discs. All seven works meet without question that simplest of a critic's criteria: Do I want to hear the piece again? The Third and the Sixth are compositions that deserve a regular place in the string-quartet rep-ertory. The First, the Fifth, and the Seventh would be strong inducements to attend any recital that billed them. And although the Second and the Fourth seemed, at first hearing, imperfectly fashioned works, they were interesting and rewarding to hear. One of New York's concert-giving bodies—the 92nd Street Y, the Metropolitan Museum, Abraham Goodman House, or the Frick Collection—should invite the Thouvenel to play the whole cycle here next year, which is Krenek's eightieth-birthday year.

In 1929, Krenek sang of his native land in *Reisebuch aus den österrei-chischen Alpen*, a travel diary in the form of twenty songs to his own texts—picturesque, lyrical, funny, reflective. The work was written in a burst of twenty days, in Vienna, on his return from an Alpine tour; it is one of Krenek's most spontaneous compositions. The verbal and musical images are keen and are surely matched. Schubert and his *Winterreise* provide the model. The underlying theme is one that runs through Krenek's work (it had been movingly sounded in the opera *Leben des Orest*, which preceded the *Reisebuch*): Where, both spiritually and physically, is "home"? If one's na-tive land is politically or culturally intolerable, where can one live and work and be content? A resolute "I set forth, to discover my home," in an un-clouded E-flat, begins the cycle. Scenery, natives, and tourists are viewed with a sharp yet tender, a sympathetic yet sometimes satirical, eye. At one point, "Southland," that country of untroubled, classical beauty, is glimpsed in the distance: "Not my home, yet sometimes it seems to me as if I would rather have been born there." The final song starts uncertainly (and propheti-cally) with twelve-note melodies before rediscovering the E-flat home key.

Durch die Nacht (1931) is a darker cycle, a setting of seven lyrics by Karl Kraus, the untranslatable Austrian poet whose independence and purity of mind and insistence on purity of language were an inspiration to Krenek. Musically, the cycle shows a twelve-note way of thought forcing itself upon the romantic idiom. So does the cycle *Gesänge des späten Jahres*, composed later that year, to Krenek's own poems. These songs are darker still; the last of them ends with an apparently deliberate allusion to the Farewell in

Mahler's *Song of the Earth.* In both cycles, the words and the music mourn what is being lost, are shaken by foreboding of more terrible destruction—and yet affirm that not *all* is or will be lost forever. The following year, in an essay in the magazine *Anbruch,* Krenek wrote:

> Man's wealth of happiness and sorrow, the fact that from time immemorial he has been lost in the impenetrable chaos of life on earth, his heroic and vain attempts to brighten the hopeless obscurity, the beauty and nobility of the human heart, the indestructible greatness of nature—these are the subjects we want to turn to. . . .

And these are subjects that his music, so often called merely smart or cerebral, has sung and continues to sing.

In the last of the *Gesänge des späten Jahres,* there is a passage now glowing, now crystalline, to the words "One day, I will perhaps arrive in places that mine eyes have not yet seen, where the images of childhood will be exalted to luminous essence . . . where in incorruptible splendor fantasies will surround me, and I will dare to trust the radiant vision without fear of disillusionment." This touches again on the northerner's romantic dream of clear, classical skies untroubled by cloudy speculation, fever, and fret. In America, the Pacific coastal ranges sometimes play a role analogous to that of the Alps in Germanic art: although California has no classical past, it, too, is a land where lemon trees bloom, where golden oranges glow in the dark foliage. Krenek, as I said, emigrated to America in 1938. In 1945, he became an American citizen. (Křenek was respelled Krenek). In 1944, he had composed *The Ballad of the Railroads,* a cycle of ten songs to his own English words. In content, this takes up from the last song of the previous cycle. The composer writes in a program note, "The highly emotional text reflects the sentiments of the exile who is about to find a new home at the shores of the Pacific where at Christmas the gentle breezes wave through the palm trees." Images of childhood return. The music is vivid, but the verses are unskilled:

> *All night I hear the trains from far away*
> *Roam by the house like animals of prey.*
> *With heavy breath they labor up the hill,*
> *They howl in triumph when they reach the peak—*
> *My heart stands still—*
> *They roar down the curve, and away they sneak.*

Krenek's latest cycle, *Spätlese,* to his own German text, gathers up the strands of his life and work in a composition both moving and masterly. The poems, it seems to me, are Krenek's best (and untranslatable into English; in the title itself, ideas of "late harvest" and "late reading" are combined). There are allusions, verbal and musical, to earlier songs. The content is autobiographical:

Late harvest, still on the vine,
while the young wine is already fermenting . . .

Late writing, ridiculed as a poor imitation of the swift present,
late recognized as model of an unknown future . . .

In another song, a late guest, "esteemed but uninvited, honored but not in demand," enters—as Krenek himself re-entered the postwar Darmstadt scene—where "the boys are squatting fiercely around the new wine," and "he who won't sprain his throat will win no laurels." There is neither rancor nor arrogance in the tone but a mature, mellow confidence, as in work that has been well done and will one day, like the fine Spätlese waiting patiently in the cellar, be appreciated. The final "Warte . . . warte" is another echo of Mahler's Abschied.

The *Reisebuch*, the *Gesänge des späten Jahres*, and *Spätlese* were sung by Michael Ingham and played by Carolyn Horn (who have recorded the last two cycles for Orion, a company with a good deal of Krenek in its catalogue). He can sound like a young Fischer-Dieskau; she is a pianist who seems instinctively to find the full meaning of a phrase. Everything they did was expressive. Other outstanding festival performers were Constance Navratil (soprano in several songs and chamber pieces), James Ostryniec (oboe), Joe Kucera (percussion), and Ernst Krenek (conductor and pianist). At the final concert, on Easter Day, the University Singers sang the Mass "Gib uns den Frieden" (1970); the Santa Barbara Symphony, under Lawrence Christiansen, gave the American premières of two substantial orchestra pieces, *Auf- und Ablehnung* (1974) and *Fivefold Enfoldment* (1969), and then wound things up with the charming, chipper, neoclassical Kleine Symphonie (1928).

In Krenek's latest piece, *The Dissembler*, written for Mr. Ingham and performed by him in the opening program, the protagonist dons a series of mental masks (playing, in turn, actor, scientist, philosopher, judge, tarot reader, preacher, jester), drops them, makes a personal avowal of faith, and slips away with a light "All this was just pretense." It is a witty, brilliant, and disturbing piece, a flickering reflection of Krenek's own versatility, his cleverness, his skill, and his habit of cool, quizzical self-perception. [There is an Orion recording.] Krenek as a commentator has sometimes seemed not to take himself quite seriously. That as well as his facility and prolificness may have told against him. But during the festival programs, carefully chosen from the huge oeuvre, a "real" Krenek in all his richness, variety, and, it can now be added, consistency of aspiration could be discovered. Nearly twenty years ago, Stravinsky said (in *Dialogues and a Diary*), "Krenek will be honored one day even at home."

April 30, 1979

In the 1980–81 season, the Thouvenel Quartet played Krenek's String Quartets at the Y.

British Worthy

Purcell's *Dido and Aeneas* has not lacked praise, but I don't think it has been praised enough. Jack Westrup, in the Master Musicians volume on the composer, calls it "a masterpiece, but not, as is sometimes claimed, a flawless masterpiece." Robert Etheridge Moore, in *Henry Purcell and the Restoration Theatre,* calls it a "dramatic masterpiece" and yet not "by any means a flawless work." Joseph Kerman, in *Opera as Drama,* speaks of its "dramatic perfection" but finds the recitative "impersonal, courtly, and bombastic." All three commentators suggest that the expression of Aeneas' agony on receiving the apparently divine command to leave Carthage, desert Dido, and found Rome is somewhat perfunctory. And I, who sometimes think that *Dido and Aeneas* is just about the only flawless opera—well, remembering *Così fan tutte,* perhaps I should say the only flawless operatic tragedy—ever written, would claim that Aeneas's soliloquy at the end of Act II is a perfectly proportioned piece of composition, exactly what is called for at this crisis in the drama. The harmonies are wrested as violently as the hero's heart; his E-major cry of "Yours be the blame, ye Gods, for I obey your will" sounds an ironic echo of his boast in Act I that he will "defie the Feeble stroke of Destiny." Here Aeneas, in Acts I and III a suppliant, comes into his own. The outer acts belong to Dido, but in Act II she sings only a single couplet. The words ("The Skies are Clouded") are ominous; the harmony, decorated fanfares of D major, points to the G minor of her final entrance and lament; the figuration adumbrates the violent phrases in which she is to dismiss Aeneas.

Nahum Tate's libretto has come in for its share of scorn. His seven-line stanza for Dido's lament, it's been said, doesn't scan:

> *Thy Hand,* Belinda, *darkness shades me,*
> *On thy Bosom let me rest,*
> *More I wou'd but Death invades me.*
> *Death is now a Welcom Guest.*
> *When I am laid in Earth* [may] *my wrongs Create*
> *No trouble in thy Breast,*
> *Remember me, but ah! forget my Fate.*

These are verses of a kind that Dryden, in the preface to *his* libretto for Purcell, *King Arthur, or The British Worthy,* described as "rugged to the Reader, that they may be harmonious to the Hearer." He knew that "the Numbers of Poetry and Vocal Musick ... are sometimes contrary." And Tate plainly

355

knew it, too. Purcell sets Tate's first four lines in recitative; the skillful construction of the last three (Purcell added the *may*) allows him to expand them into that great lament declaimed in spans of four, five, six, or seven bars over a regular five-bar ground bass. Dido's first air has a five-line stanza:

> *Ah!* Belinda, *I am prest*
> *With Torment not to be confest.*
> *Peace and I are Strangers grown.*
> *I Languish till my Grief is known,*
> *Yet wou'd not have it Guest.*

Here Purcell sets the first two lines as arioso, the last three as an air in periods of four, five, or six bars; and he binds arioso and air together by placing both of them over a four-bar ground bass. In both the air and the lament, the vocal and the ground-bass cadences seldom coincide: the repeated bass treads on inexorably, while the song flows and surges with the heroine's thoughts, falls silent for a moment, rings out again, repeats words with a new, fierce intensity. In both pieces, when the singer is done—in Westrup's words, "when the heart is so charged that there is nothing more to add"—the strings alone take over the burden. Neither piece comes to a full close but flows on into the next number. Tate's libretto seems to me at once settable, subtle, and beautiful. The Trojan sailor's lusty, insouciant farewell to their Carthaginian lasses forms a potent prelude to and commentary on Aeneas' desertion of Dido. Less obviously, the epithalamic wish so brightly sung near the start of the opera, "*Cupids* Strew your path with Flowers," finds its tragic fulfillment in the final chorus:

> *With drooping Wings you Cupids come,*
> *To scatter Roses on her Tomb.*

Purcell must have known both Lully's and Carissimi's music. He commanded both the French and the Italian manners, and to them he added a mastery of English declamation which has never been excelled. He discovered for himself operatic secrets known to Monteverdi: the balance of free declamation and formal structure, the matching of dissonance and resolution to emotional tension and release, a control of dramatic tempo—knowing when to bate, when to press on—and a feeling for melodic contour and vocal register that make inner emotion explicit. Moreover, he and Tate anticipated what Gluck and Calzabigi, seventy years later, were to strive for in *Orfeo*: directness of dramatic expression, an absence of frills, the presentation of a coherent drama that moves swiftly—but variously, through scenes of changing emotion—to its tragic close, and a protagonist who, with dignity and passion, sings from the heart to touch the hearts of all who listen.

This masterpiece was composed, probably in 1689, for performance at a boarding school for young gentlewomen in Chelsea. (Would that all girls' schools, boys' schools, mixed schools, and music schools regularly commissioned end-of-term operas from the leading composers of their countries.) Purcell did not have to provide the pomp, the spectacle, the elaborate divertissements expected by the Dorset Garden or Drury Lane audiences. *Dido* is still done by schools (the first modern staging, in 1895, was by the Royal College of Music, and the first American staging, in 1932, was by the Juilliard), but as early as 1700 it was taken into the professional repertory. It is one of those necessary works—like Handel's *Semele, Fidelio,* and Mozart's operas from *Idomeneo* onward—that an opera lover grows hungry for if much more than a year passes without a performance to nourish him. A long procession of Didos is likely to fill his memory. (In mine, Kirsten Flagstad, Joan Cross, Teresa Berganza, Kiri Te Kanawa, and Janet Baker are among the more famous—the first the most heroic and majestic and the last the most passionate of all.) *Dido* had been missing from New York for six years—since the Mini-Met presentation of 1973—when the City Opera mounted its new production. Alas, it was a performance almost without merit, put on by a team—Cal Stewart Kellogg as conductor, Frank Corsaro as director ("pantomine scenes directed in collaboration with George Balanchine"), Rouben Ter-Arutunian as designer, and Peter Martins as choreographer—none of whom showed any feeling for the style and structure of Purcell's opera.

The first mistake was probably to choose the "realization" of the score by Benjamin Britten and Imogen Holst rather than a cleaner, less richly elaborated edition. Some of the harmonies and some of the verbal underlay in the Britten-Holst version seem to me dubious—but that's a matter for musicological debate. In other ways, the score is a dangerous one to put into the hands of performers unversed in Purcell. The profusion of added expression marks, the shifts of tempo and dynamics, the exhortations like "forceful," "more intense," "animated" represent the ideas of two master Purcellians— tips, hints toward an eloquent performance—but in my experience they have invariably led (except in performances by Britten's own company, the English Opera Group) to slow, heavy, overrhetorical execution. The very look of the pages in the edition edited by Margaret Laurie and Thurston Dart is lighter, less emphatic, less fulsomely romantic. "Interpretation" is already written into the Britten-Holst text; when performers go on to "interpret" that text still further, the results can be disastrous. *Dido* is announced for revival next season. When it returns, the conductor must be urged to put down his baton and, a harpsichord in front of him and a cellist at his elbow, in the continuo-supported recitatives and airs accompany the singers. These passages no more need "conducting" than a lieder singer and her accompanist do. This season, Mr. Kellogg beat out recitatives in 4/4, sometimes with subdivisions. Almost all his tempi were too slow; often they were lugubrious. Almost all his rhythms plodded. Each movement closed with a broad ritardando. (Ritardando was even practiced by the offstage echoes, with comic effect.) The life was drained from number after number. Some rehearsals at which the text is spoken, not sung, and the singers' faults of emphasis, inflection, and speed are corrected might be helpful.

The set and the staging are unfortunately beyond repair. The set has a gaudy disco floor and at the back a flimsy triple portico, shop-windowy classical. Dido is wrapped in transparent shower curtains, one trimmed with black and another with flowers, and she goes to her death wearing only gold smallclothes and a tall crown. "See your Royal Guest appears," Belinda cries in Act I; "How God-like is the Form he bears"—and Aeneas slopes on wearing a nightdress and a necklace. The two Witches are deaf, and use ear trumpets to catch what the Sorceress says. In an epilogue to the Chelsea performance, Lady Dorothy Burk said: "Like nimble Fawns, and Birds that bless the Spring,/Unscarr'd by turning Times we dance and sing." The City Opera chorus didn't dance. Cloaked and masked, as if for Stravinsky's *Oedipus Rex*, it stood motionless on either side of the stage and sang like a well-drilled choral society, not like courtiers, sailors, and witches cackling with melodious laughter. Dancers played at being courtiers, witches, trees, animals, sailors.

The heroines of the three principal *Dido* productions staged in Britain this season were Janet Baker (whom, many years ago, in the Great Hall of Hampton Court, I heard as a memorable Sorceress), Sandra Browne (a Trinidadian mezzo who made her début as Man Friday in Offenbach's *Robinson Crusoe*, six years ago), and Ann Murray (who also came to prominence as Man Friday, five years ago). There are surely many American sopranos or mezzos who would be good in the role. The City Opera imported Miss Browne, who was not very good. A London colleague had complained, rightly, of her "weightily romantic style." In the huge, unresonant space of the State Theater, and at Mr. Kellogg's snail's-pace tempi, she seemed to be pushing for sound and altogether missing the sense of the great role. David Holloway's Aeneas was a hangdog cipher. Janice Hall's Belinda and Rose-Marie Freni's Sorceress were promising but needed instruction.

Dido lasts less than an hour (except when Mr. Kellogg conducts it; he made it last about ten minutes over the hour). Finding an apt companion piece (or pieces) is not easy. This season, Scottish Opera played it on a triple bill with Gustav Holst's *Savitri* and Edward Harper's *Fanny Robin*, based on Hardy. English National Opera North, Britain's latest full-scale opera company, in Leeds, played it with Poulenc's *Les Mamelles de Tirésias*, and so did the English National Opera, in London (same staging, different cast and conductor). Opera Integra, also in London, played it with Monteverdi's *Il ballo delle ingrate*. The City Opera paired it, not happily, with a feeble ballet, *Le Bourgeois Gentilhomme*, choreographed by Balanchine and Jerome Robbins to some of the Strauss incidental music for Hofmannsthal's adaptation of the Molière play.

If Purcell's school opera is something professionals have taken up, his large professional operas have become something hardly performable today except by schools that have departments of singing, playing, acting, dancing, and stage design. A typical stage direction (from *The Fairy Queen*) is:

> The scene changes to a great wood; a long row of large trees on each side; a river in the middle; two rows of lesser trees of a different kind just on the side of the river, which meet in the middle, and make so many

arches; two great dragons make a bridge over the river; their bodies form two arches, through which two swans are seen in the river at a great distance. . . . While a symphony's playing, the two swans come swimming on through the arches to the bank of the river, as if they would land; these turn themselves into fairies, and dance; at the same time the bridge vanishes, and the trees that were arched, raise themselves upright.

King Arthur, The Fairy Queen, The Indian Queen, and (whoever composed it) *The Tempest* are none of them what Purcell himself, in a preface to *The Fairy Queen,* considered a real opera in the Italian or French sense—"a story sung with proper action." *Dido* is such a real opera. In the others, the principals don't sing; they speak. Music is allotted to fairies, magicians, rustics, warrior bands, and the like, and consecutive sketches of music are in the main reserved for masques dropped more or less appropriately into the action. They are odd, extravagant works. Attempts to "rescue" them for the modern stage by drastic reordering and by such expedients as adding scenes of Shakespeare to *The Fairy Queen* and *The Tempest* have seldom been successful. These baroque entertainments were not carelessly or cynically composed. They are carefully balanced. The genre is unfamiliar, and what John Evelyn called "a mercenary theatre"—or even a state-supported theatre— might balk at engaging threefold casts led by the best actors, singers, and dancers of the day. But I wish the Juilliard would mount a full-scale, uncut Purcell-Dryden presentation, one in which the students in every division would have a chance to show their mettle. Properly co-ordinated, directed by someone with a real understanding of what English baroque opera was meant to be, such a show might be a revelation. *King Arthur* can hardly be unstageworthy. It was first put on by Betterton, with him in the title role, in 1691, and it held the boards for a hundred and fifty years. Garrick revived it in the late eighteenth century, and Macready in the mid-nineteeth. Kemble played Arthur. Mrs. Siddons played Emmeline. There was a New York production, at the Park Theatre, in 1800—and an Atlanta production in 1968. Concert performances of the musical sections—introduced by brief narratives and mere scraps of dialogue, and shorn of their essential scenic element—afford no more than a hint of what a complete *King Arthur* might be. But they do allow us, at least, to enjoy Purcell's fine theatre music in its musical aspects.

The 92nd Street Y Chorale, conducted by Amy Kaiser, performed the music from *King Arthur* last week, and it was good to hear it. The chorus, composed of dedicated amateurs, was alert, lively, and accomplished. There were twelve soloists, and to a woman or man they sang in a fresh, forthright, unfancified way that was most taking. The sopranos Nadia Bach and Rosemary George, the tenor Robert Guarino, and the bass Phillip Sneed must have special mention. Sometimes there was too little feeling for Dryden's verse. Two sirens "arise from the water," "show themselves to the waist," and sing cajolingly to Arthur:

Come Bath with us an Hour or two,
Come Naked in, for we are so;
What Danger from a Naked Foe?

But in this performance their words went almost for nothing; I doubt whether anyone not using a text even caught them. Miss Kaiser set apt tempi. There was none of the heaviness that distorted the City Opera *Dido,* but some of the numbers in dance rhythms were too jerky, not lilting enough in their flow. The performance was given in the Buttenweiser Hall of the Y. It is not an elegant or a distinguished piece of architecture. Unlike the Great Hall of Hampton Court, Inigo Jones's Banqueting House, or Thomas Archer's St. John's, Smith Square, it lends no incidental charm to Purcell's music. No café, no buffet in the building provided cheer during the intermission or after the show. (Even after six years here, I'm surprised at the graceless conditions New York concertgoers accept as a matter of course.) But it was the right size for the performance. Every detail told.

May 7, 1979

Riches in a Little Room

I first heard the Juilliard String Quartet nearly thirty years ago, in a drawing room—the drawing room of a large house that had become the London Music Club. I have heard it often since, but never in quite such intimate surroundings. The economics of music making usually drive world-famous string quartets into fairly large halls (at any rate, in large towns where large audiences can be expected); to hear their chamber music in a chamber one must usually have recourse to the phonograph. But not always. The Juilliard is quartet-in-residence at the Juilliard School, and twice a year it gives a free concert in the Juilliard Theatre. This is a large "chamber"—it seats over nine hundred—but it is a well-lit and thoroughly agreeable place whose shape, sight lines, and sound make it one of New York's best homes for chamber music.

The centerpiece of the Juilliard's April recital there was the New York première of Fred Lerdahl's First String Quartet, composed last year, in memory of Sarah H. Joslyn, for the quartet to play at the Joslyn Art Museum in Omaha, Nebraska. The Omaha première was in March; the Juilliard has also done the work in Washington and in Boston. Lerdahl (who was born in 1943) was known to me as the composer of *Eros*, a rich and beautiful set of variations for mezzo and chamber ensemble, introduced by the Chamber Music Society of Lincoln Center in 1977 and now available on a CRI record. (Another CRI record contains his String Trio and Piano Fantasy; the trio was played here in March at a Composers' Guild recital.) The String Quartet is also a set of variations, but not on a theme. The starting point is an open-fifth chord, G-G-D-G. This is the first of fifteen sections; each subsequent section is a variation and expansion of—approximately one and a half times as long as—its predecessor. Section No. 2 is just two chords, that of No. 1 preceded by a differently spaced G-G-G-D. In No. 3, a new chromatic chord, built of semitone, appoggiaturalike displacements of G and D, intervenes between the two chords based on G. In No. 4, two such chords intervene. In No. 5, further displacements yield a sequence of eight chords, still opening and closing as Nos. 3 and 4 did. So far, all has been in strict homophony and played nonvibrato at an unvarying *piano*, each chord a half-note long. In No. 6, a small rhythmic independence, created by appoggiaturas from the first and the second violin, creeps in. It grows in No. 7, and here there is also a single, sustained vibrato chord within the nonvibrato progression. No. 8 introduces the first dynamic nuance. The most insistent of the intruder notes has been C-sharp, a tritone from the tonic G, and at the close of the next four sections this C-sharp lodges itself in the basic G-D harmony.

All this sounds schematic, and of course it is, but the effect is not dry or mechanical. The quartet sounds like a composition that demanded to be written, not a clever construction. I recount the details from the score, but the composer's claim, in a program note, that "the process of expansion is . . . audible" is justified. Gradually, from his very simple start, he amasses his material. Gradually the harmonies, the rhythms, the variations of timbre, and the range of dynamics grow more intricate, and the listener can hear how they grow—through the first ten sections or so. Nos. 10, 11, and 12 can be heard starting with the same melody in an ever richer form. But, because of the sesquialter increases, detailed following of the process becomes harder, although developments of earlier melodies, moods, and kinds of movement can still be recognized. The first chord lasts less than a second; the final section lasts some six minutes and is subdivided into contrasting sections of its own. From the seed, stems, branches, and blossoms have sprung. The pit is no longer discernible in the peach tree. But that vegetable metaphor suggested by the quartet's "organic" growth is not wholly apt. The finale is not the inevitable, the only possible outcome. Throughout the work, one feels that improvisation played a part in its making, that in the earlier sections each progression—and in the later sections each episode—was chosen from many that would have been possible within the schema established for the piece. (Once the selection is made, of course, it becomes a fixed quantity affecting the range of subsequent possibilities.) Moreover, there is what the composer calls a "psychological" progress running through the quartet, "from simplicity and repose to their opposites." The easy, conventional formal ending would have been a restatement of the start; the actual ending is stranger. For a moment, there is a hint of a shining, almost *Lohengrin*-like, A-major apotheosis. Then echoes of the cadence that closed the earlier sections are heard—but after the preceding adventures a return to that simple affirmation cannot be entertained, and the work dissolves instead into disjunct, disturbed chromatic sighs.

The quartet met that first, simple critical criterion I wrote about last month: "Do I want to hear the piece again?" Through the courtesy of the Juilliard School, which tape-records Juilliard Theatre concerts for its archive, I was able to do so, and it rewarded further listening. There are still some episodes—notably, a long passage of "wave motion" in the finale—whose sense eludes me, but as a whole and in most of its details the quartet, like *Eros*, reveals an individual and striking voice, a fertile yet disciplined mind, and a finished, confident technique. The piece is composed for the four instruments as a piano piece might be for ten fingers: by which I mean that it makes the effect less of a dialogue between four individual players than of a single discourse set out in four—or, with divisions, in up to eight—parts. The composer suggests a timing of twenty minutes; the Juilliard performance lasted about fourteen. I used a stopwatch over the whole, not a metronome to check individual passages, but have the impression that the earlier sections might profit from a more deliberate, spacious exposition, and that, in general, the Juilliard, while already evident masters of the music, may give it a longer breath in subsequent performances. Lerdahl is working on a Second Quartet, commissioned for the Pro Arte, which "will continue the expanding variational process but reverse the psychological course of the First Quartet back to its beginning." I'll be watching for it. The First Quartet, he says, "is both a complete piece in itself and first half of a larger work."

The Juilliard recital began with Schubert's Quartettsatz, which was given an unsettled performance. The playing of the leader, Robert Mann, was nervous and edgy, and it was as if he had set the basic tempo a shade too fast for the natural flow of the music. The recital ended with Schoenberg's First Quartet, magnificently well done. I think this was the first work I ever heard the Juilliard play, and it's a work I learned from Juilliard performances. The Quartet recorded a Schoenberg cycle in the early fifties, and again two years ago. A booklet accompanying the new album includes a conversation in which the players discuss their altered approach to No. 1. Mr. Mann recalls that Schoenberg himself intimated, through a disciple, that the early Juilliard performances were a shade too intense for his taste:

> We *were* smackin' it away in those days in terms of rhythmic drive, maybe a lot more as if it were a Bartók quartet. Today, I'm sure our performance is quite as driving as it ever was but with perhaps a lot less of that pungency and acerbic character.

Samuel Rhodes, the viola, adds, "When you remove the pungency and bite, you have to substitute something else that fits the music." The LaSalle Quartet—as it were, a Léner to the Juilliard's Busch—has since then brought us a sweeter, more delicate, more exquisite Schoenberg, but in Schoenberg's First the Juilliard (the "new" Juilliard, for Mr. Mann is the only player who has been a member of the ensemble since its inception) combines strength with beauty in a way that strikes me as unmatched. Its account of No. 1 remains a great performance of our day.

The music room of the Frick house, where concerts are given on Sunday afternoons, free except for the two-dollar admission to the collection, is another New York place where celebrated artists can be heard in intimate surroundings. It is a good room for chamber music, but it could be better still: the audience is packed in uncomfortably tight. An overflow audience listens through loudspeakers in the garden court outside; a larger audience can listen over WNYC. Since those actually in the music room are inevitably an élite, there can be little objection to making the events more "élitist" yet: by taking out a few rows of chairs and removing all impediment to full enjoyment.

The Sunday before last, the Borodin Quartet played there. It began with the D-major Quartet of its titular composer, which it played with its wonted sweetness and beauty. But only the viola was willing to employ in full the emotive portamento that must have been standard in Borodin's day. The cello brought touches of it to the famous tune ("And This Is My Beloved") of the Notturno; the first violin, echoing him in the canon episode, played those richly drooping fourths cleanly. The Borodin's specialty is Shostakovich. That composer's own closest alliance was with the Beethoven Quartet, which gave the premières of his Quartets Nos. 2 to 14, and to members of which Nos. 11 to 14 are dedicated, but it is the Borodin Quartet that has most prominently played Shostakovich cycles the world over, and its Shostakovich recordings remain in the catalogue while the Beethoven's Shostakovich recordings are allowed to disappear. At the Frick recital, the Borodin played Nos. 8 and 15. No. 8 is signed again and again with the composer's initials, Д. Ш.—in German D. Sch., or the notes we call D, E-flat, C, B—treated as a terse, tragic motto. The work is the first in the series of quartets which enshrines the composer's private brooding, grief, bitterness, and (reaching its climax in No. 13) anguish. No. 15, formed of six adagios, is a sequence of reflections on death. By contrast with the Beethoven Quartet or with the Fitzwilliam Quartet (which has recorded all but the first two of the fifteen quartets), the Borodin romanticizes the compositions. Which is to say only that it plays them with a beauty of tone and inflection which would remove the pangs, the keenness, the bitterness, if anything could. But nothing can. In one way, the Frick recital was a profoundly depressing occasion, for it compelled one to think about the stricken, unhappy artist, confiding his sorrow to these intimate pages. And, in another way, it was a profoundly inspiring occasion—a manifestation that the human spirit is indestructible, a *de profundis* from a voice that could not be silenced. These works contain utterances as moving, as poetic, as those in despairing Psalms, and are beautifully wrought, strangely imaginative music. The Borodin's playing was fine drawn, tender, exquisite.

Earlier in the season, the Emerson String Quartet, four Juilliard graduates, winners of last year's Naumburg Award in Chamber Music, gave a recital in Alice Tully Hall. The program was Mozart's "Dissonanzen," Smetana's *From My Life*, and Bartók's Fifth Quartet. There was a large and enthusiastic audience. The playing was graceful, well balanced, and well mannered—phrasing always sensitive, tone pure. The players excelled in dance movements—Smetana's polka and the start of his finale, Bartók's Scherzo alla bulgarese—for they have an elegant, cultivated sense of rhythm. But the Mozart lacked force. Although all four movements are marked with emphatic contrasts of *p* and *f*, the Quartet might have been using an edition from which the dynamic indications had been expunged; its range was *mp* to *mf*. The opening measures were altogether too smooth (as in the Guarneri recording): the dissonances weren't pressed; the cello's *sf* appoggiaturas were underplayed. And so on. A Minuet and Trio that should make its points by almost startling alternations of soft and loud was flattened. Of course, it is a pleasure to listen to sweet-toned, well-tuned quartets in the classical repertory—even in Tully Hall, which is really too big and too dry for eighteenth-century chamber music. I enjoyed the Emerson's gentleness and its eschewal of sleek, plummy, overnourished sound. But in violent episodes it remained gentle to the point of blandness; places in the "Dissonanzen" call for grit and a fiercer kind of playing. The Emerson showed vividness of thought but not of timbre. In the Smetana quartet, a lack of bite, a reluctance on the viola's part to hit the *sf* hard in the opening theme, and on the leader's part to hit the *rfz* even harder at the climax of the finale, muted the cruelty of the tragedy. But the lyrical episodes were captivating. Bartók brought out the best in the players; they became colorful, uninhibited; they rose to the challenge of the writing and were spurred, perhaps, by emphatic markings—*ff, stridente; ff, marcatissimo; strepitoso*—to play full out and not bother about politeness.

The regular thoughts about live, public performances versus private phonograph performances arose. In Tully Hall, I disturbed my neighbor by turning the pages of a pocket score—silently, but not invisibly. He disturbed me—more seriously, in my opinion—by beating time with his hand and then, worse, tapping with his toe in tempi that contradicted the Emerson's whenever it used rubato (which was often, for, as I said, its sense of rhythm is notable). At the Juilliard concert, there were seals scattered through the audience. In London, the South Bank program books for many years carried a notice that read:

> During a recent test in the Hall, a note played *mezzoforte* on the horn measured approximately 65 decibels (dB [A]) of sound. A single "uncovered" cough gave the same reading. A handkerchief placed over the mouth when coughing assists in obtaining a *pianissimo*.

And a loosely balled handkerchief stuffed into the mouth can reduce a cough to an almost unoffending volume. At the Juilliard recital, Lerdahl's quartet was punctuated by audience participation as loud as *mezzoforte* horn calls from a lusty hunting party. There are times when one wishes New York concerts began with a little lecture-demonstration, kin to those given by air hostesses before takeoff: an exhortation to refrain from obtrusive bodily movement; an instruction on how to stifle coughing and on techniques for delaying it during passages when the music is very quiet; perhaps an observation that after certain pieces a brief moment of silence can show truer appreciation of a work and its interpreters than a "Bravo!" bawled while the last notes are dying away. It might be a good idea to have a special foot tappers' section (heavily carpeted) on the lines of the smoking section in an airplane. It would certainly be a good idea to have a score readers' section (more brightly lit than the rest of the hall). Carnegie Recital Hall used to have one, in the balcony, and I'm sorry it has been abolished.

The Juilliard School's presentation of Britten's *A Midsummer Night's Dream*, though described as only an "opera workshop production," was finished, sensitive, and beautiful. Stephen Colvin, conducting, knew well how to cast the instrumental "spells"—the warm midsummer forest sighs of the first act; the four soft chords, each with a different timbre, that spread their nocturnal magic through the second act; the sense of ceremony, growing from the tiny fairy pageantry of Tytania's bodyguard to the hunting-horn march that leads to the finale in Theseus' palace—drawing listeners into a world of dreams and enchantment that waken to a dawn of healing. The Juilliard Symphony brought color, intentness, and vivacity to a score whose fineness can seem slight unless the playing is brave. The outstanding singers at the second performance were Roseann Del George, a Tytania whose timbre remained pure and sweet into the highest reaches of the role, one who was at once delicate, charming, and formidable; Robert Briggs, a substantial, forthright Bottom whose cheerful earthiness was touched by romance, as Britten intended; and, best of all, James Justiss, as Oberon. Although traces of harshness entered Mr. Justiss's countertenor tones when the volume rose, he displayed a feeling for the sounds of consonant and vowel, for the relative weights of words, for poetry-in-song which has become rare even on the professional stage. He moved sensitively. All the cast—lovers, fairies (boys from the Church of the Transfiguration choir), and tradesmen—sang firmly and showed character. Only Henry Stram's Puck—a shaggy satyr, not Britten's touching adolescent, half boy, half fairy, moved by the mortals' pangs even while mischievously amused by them—struck a false note, and that was chiefly the fault of the costuming and the direction. Fancy asking a Puck to mime lion, bear, wolf, bull, meddling monkey, busy ape in lightning succession while Oberon mentions them! More than once, Norman Ayrton's staging was overactive. (Echoes of Peter Brook's acrobatic *Dream* still linger.) It scarcely touched on the cruelty and the grossness (lady with donkey) that lie just beneath the romantic surface of the play. But it was poetic. So were Calvin Morgan's décor and Paul Gallo's lighting.

May 14, 1979

Choirs and Places
Where They Sing

Early this season, there was a big choral concert in Carnegie Hall to celebrate five centuries of publishing by the Oxford University Press. The program was drawn from music of those five centuries which Oxford has printed. Seven choruses took part—the New York Choral Society, the Cappella Nova, the Canticum Novum Singers, the Sine Nomine Singers, the Oratorio Society (the choir that sang Berlioz's Te Deum at the Carnegie inaugural concert, in 1891), the St. Cecilia Chorus, and the Dessoff Choirs. They performed individually and, eight hundred strong, joined in massed performances of Walton's Coronation Te Deum and Vaughan Williams's *Serenade to Music* (which was originally composed for sixteen soloists). Debarred by a cough from attending the concert, I listened over the air. The event was broadcast by WNYC, and later by other National Public Radio stations. The level of execution ranged from the competent but lackluster, through the capable and committed, to vivid Byrd and Josquin from the Canticum Novum and vivid Binchois from the Cappella Nova. Such a jamboree inevitably loses something over the radio, but the slow, massive sweep of "Spem in alium," Tallis's forty-part tour de force, sung by groups from all the choirs, did not fail to produce a very grand effect. John Alldis, one of Britain's best choral conductors, made his New York début directing the massed items. This celebration displayed a cross-section of New York choral singing. There follow notes on a few of the season's choral events, large and small.

The Cathedral Church of St. John the Divine was begun in 1892. Building continued for fifty years, and then broke off. It has now been resumed, and in celebration a performance of Liszt's large oratorio *Christus* was held there on the last Sunday of April. Richard Westenburg, director of music at the cathedral, conducted; Musica Sacra singers and players formed the bulk of his forces. Admission was free. In 1977, *Christus* provided the climax of the Liszt Festival of London; it was given in Westminster Cathedral, a very resonant building, and aroused great enthusiasm. I heard *Christus* the following year, broadcast from an Albert Hall Prom, and was not overwhelmed. The oratorio was done complete, possibly for the first time since Liszt himself abridged it; I suggested that he had done well to shorten it. But it was an improper suggestion. *Christus* is long, and many of its numbers are repetitive. But when it is performed in such a building as St. John's, and conducted with the passion and precision that Mr. Westenburg brought to it, its movements do not seem too long. In fact, longer seems shorter: the Prom performance was billed as a hundred and fifty minutes of music, while the St. John's performance, paced to cathedral acoustics, lasted twenty minutes more. Incomplete, St. John's already claims to be the largest Gothic church in the world. It is very reverberant, and lends amplitude and grandeur to voices that sing in it. For *Christus*, the performers were stationed where choir and crossing meet; the listeners sat in the crossing, beneath the immense dome, and in the eastern bays of the tremendous nave. I attended a rehearsal, not the performance, and thrilled to the grandest and most affecting choral tone I have ever heard in this city. The voices of the soloists—Alpha Floyd, Diane Curry, Vincenzo Manno, and Bruce Fifer—rose and rang. Mr. Manno did not abjure emotional portamento. Mr. Fifer sang "Tristis est anima mea," the Gethsemane scene that opens the third part, with nobility, fervor, and steadiness. In such acoustics, the slow pacing of the harmonies, the long preparations, and the unhurried establishment of each new key attained are essential—and beautiful. In such a building, the repetitions in the score seem kin to the architectural repetitions, bay upon bay, that give a great cathedral its grandeur. Despite the reverberation, the sound was not mushy but firm. One could hear what was happening. The shepherds' piping, small, pure, and clear, stole through the building. The clarity of the pizzicato strings at the start of the Three Kings' March was astonishing. During the "Et ecce stella" section of that number—the starry shine of the high strings and the brave peal of the trumpet melody winging out as if beneath a sonic as well as the actual dome—the acoustics revealed the sense of Liszt's orchestral writing in a way that no concert hall can do.

Christus spans a wide variety of styles. The text of the outer sections juxtaposes the Vulgate and medieval hymns; the central section, concerned with Christ's ministry, includes the Beatitudes, the Paternoster, Christ's charge to Peter, and a triumphal Entry into Jerusalem. The textures range from chamber ensemble to a full-scale Wagnerian orchestral tempest on the Sea of Galilee, and from choral writing with a minimal organ accompaniment to all the forces in full cry. The styles range from neo-modal harmony to, in the Stabat Mater, a chromaticism like that of early Schoenberg. As the Liszt scholar Robert Collet has written, "the work is significant because it reveals so much of the complexity and many-sidedness of Liszt's personality, with the significant exceptions of the erotic and the diabolic." The composer called *Christus* his testament. When I heard this St. John's performance, I understood why. Here, again, was proof that some scores cannot be fully understood or appreciated until they have been brought to life in a setting something like that the composer intended. St. John's is the place where New York performances of Berlioz's Requiem and Te Deum should be held.

The Cathedral maintains a busy musical life. So do I, and it happens that I have not yet got round to hearing medieval or Renaissance music sung there in the main church (but only in St. James's chapel). And I have never heard Guillaume Dufay's three big papal motets—composed to celebrate Eugenius IV's coronation in 1431, his treaty with King Sigismund in 1433, and his consecration of the Duomo in Florence in 1436—sung in really big buildings.

But grandeur can also be achieved in smaller space when the sound is good, and the first two of those motets sounded very splendid when the Elizabethan Enterprise (with guests to bring the ensemble up to nine) did them in Corpus Christi Church early this year. Corpus Christi—on One hundred and twenty-first Street just east of Broadway—is a small church, built in the thirties, holding about five hundred. The design is neither medieval nor Renaissance but on late-seventeenth-century lines, with pews and galleries. The sound is very good, warm and resonant, intimate yet open. Here there is held a Sunday-afternoon concert series called "Music before 1800"; I get to it whenever I can, for it is probably the most reliably rewarding of New York's early-music series.

Early Dufay working at full stretch was an inspired composer. The Elizabethan Enterprise, directed by Lucy Cross, was just a shade too polite in timbre for my taste—if Luca della Robbia's choristers on the Florence Cathedral *cantoria* were modeled from the life, their singing must have poured from open throats—but it showed a fine command of rhythm and phrase and was well tuned. The music breathed, flowered, moved decisively without being driven or straitjacketed. The program, which presented early Dufay in the context of his predecessors and contemporaries—Ciconia, Guillaume Legrant—included the "catalogue motet" of Jean Brassart, "Romanorum Rex." There were three such motets—works in which composers name and honor their colleagues—on the bill of a later Corpus Christi concert given by the Cappella Nova, directed by Richard Taruskin. "Arms and the Man" was its title. It was a composite Mass, whose Ordinary was drawn from five different "L'Homme Armé" Masses (Dufay was represented by the Sanctus) and Proper from Heinrich Isaac's *Choralis Constantinus.* The "honor-roll motets" could be regarded as sung, contemporary program notes on Renaissance composers. (Modern program notes, texts, and translations were also provided.) This sounds too artful an idea, perhaps, but it worked well, producing a coherent tapestry of Renaissance music woven on a firm liturgical frame, not a patchwork. It was particularly enlightening to hear numbers from Isaac's monumental volumes put to use in context (well, more or less; but it was a concert, not a service). His great sequence "Ad laudes salvatoris" almost stole the show. Not quite: at the end, Dufay's "Ave regina," the motet he wanted to hear during his dying moments, was given an impassioned, beautiful, and wonderfully moving performance. The Cappella Nova has twenty singers, who make a good sound. Mr. Taruskin tends to dance around while he directs them, but he elicits nicely athletic, flexible phrasing. And they sing as if they knew what the texts mean; on such a line as "Gaude Virgo gloriosa" the tone became radiant.

Good music in its full liturgical context can be caught at the Church of St. Mary the Virgin, on West Forty-sixth Street. Indeed, a critic who attends High Mass there is tempted to review the whole production—direction, acting, costumes, lighting, libretto, smoke effects—and not just the music. (The church would be unlikely to object; it bills a special Votive Mass as "our usual—and then some!") Earlier this year, the Mass that Méhul composed for

Napoleon's coronation was sung at St. Mary's. For some reason, it was not sung at the imperial coronation, and it was apparently not published before 1879—so although Beethoven (for his C-major Mass) and Verdi (for his Requiem) both seem to have borrowed ideas from it, coincidence, not influence, must be the reason. It is time some Méhul operas were revived in America—by the campus and small-town companies that so seldom lift their sights beyond *Figaro, The Barber, Don Pasquale, La Bohème,* and other staples. He was a good composer. Beethoven admired him. Grove calls him "the man who carried on Gluck's work with more than Gluck's musical skill." And the Mass (done with organ accompaniment, not orchestra) revealed all his neatness, his accuracy in invention, his unaffected seriousness coupled with lively grace. McNeil Robinson, music director at St. Mary's, led a captivating and dignified performance. St. Mary's, a lofty Gothic building dating from 1895, is shaped like the chancel of a large medieval church. The musicians sing and play in a gallery on the west wall, and fill the space with warm, bright sound. The choir was good, and so were the soloists: Hedi Klebl, Judith Malafronte, Gordon Shannon, and Jan Opalach.

The Winchester Cathedral Choir, touring North America in celebration of the nine-hundredth anniversary of the new cathedral—one of the longest churches in the world—might have done well to choose a church, and not Carnegie Hall, for its New York appearance, in March. The bill announced a program of church music from John Taverner (born about 1500) to John Tavener (born in 1944), with Mozart's F-minor Fantasia for clockwork organ as an interlude. Carnegie Hall is an admirable place, but it is hardly numinous. It has excellent concert-hall acoustics but not the reverberation of a great cathedral. Although the light there is often far too dim, it's not a dim *religious* light. Moreover, at concert time the Carnegie organ, a synthetic, electronic instrument, wouldn't start, and three works that had particularly drawn me to the concert—S. S. Wesley's noble cantata *The Wilderness,* Britten's Antiphon, and Tavener's Little Requiem—couldn't be performed. A new program was improvised, with unaccompanied or piano-accompanied music to fill the gaps. James Lancelot, the cathedral suborganist, moved from console to Steinway keyboard; Martin Neary, organist and master of the music, introduced the pieces. The occasion became informal. Stanford's fine unaccompanied motets "Justorum animae" and "Coelos ascendit," smoothly and sensitively sung, were a bonus. Mr. Neary's choir is a body of "professionals," able to pull pieces from its repertory and at short notice perform them on a high level. Taverner's "Dum transisset" and Purcell's "Jehovah, quam multi sunt," prepared as part of the original bill, were done in a polished fashion. Britten's difficult *Hymn to St. Cecilia* was not quite polished.

Britten's *War Requiem* was composed for the new Coventry Cathedral, which rises beside the ruins of the cathedral destroyed, as most of the town was, by the Germans. I heard it there, and had heard it only in very large churches before the Carnegie Hall performance with the National Symphony under Mstislav Rostropovich, earlier this year. (In New York, three of its previous performances were in St. Bartholomew's.) Resonance, space, and distance effects are intended to play a part in the score, and associations have played a part in listeners' experience of it: apt associations in Coventry, which, like the *Requiem*, is dedicated to peace and reconciliation; ironic— but still apt—associations in abbeys and cathedrals where faded banners hang as proud memorials of battle. (In this specifically pacificist work, the opening prayer of the Latin Mass, bell accompanied, yields to Wilfred Owen's "No mockeries for them from prayers or bells"; the "Quam olim Abrahae" phrase of the Offertory is followed by Owen's poem that ends, "Offer the Ram of Pride instead of him. But the old man would not so, but slew his son,—And half the seed of Europe, one by one.") In Carnegie Hall, imagination had to work hard to supply the associations. The boys' choir was stationed in the second gallery, but that provided only an approximation of the effect intended at the end—an "In paradisum" stealing in from afar. The performers were eloquent. The *War Requiem* should have had a Russian, an English, and a German soloist at its first performance, in 1962, but, in the event, Galina Vishnevskaya could not attend. She sang the soprano part in Carnegie with shining, soaring tone, better controlled, steadier than I have heard from her in years. Peter Pears, in his original role, was profoundly moving, and so was John Shirley-Quirk, in music originally written for Dietrich Fischer-Dieskau. The finale is a tender dialogue, set between the "Libera me" and "In paradisum," for a dead English soldier and the German soldier he killed, and it is one of Britten's high inspirations. The chorus was the Choral Arts Society, and the boys' choir that of the Washington Cathedral. Rostropovich, a conductor often more emotional than shapely, here led an intense but not uncontrolled performance.

Women are but a poor second-best in music written for boys. The women of the Elizabethan Enterprise and the Cappella Nova subdued their femininity—perhaps even too much so, for although they were clear, pure, and steady, they seldom caught the tangy, passionate timbre of trebles in full cry. At the Met and the City Opera, America seems to have the best boys in the world: little Yniolds, Fyodors, shepherd lads in *Tosca*, and Mileses in *The Turn of the Screw* who sing the prima donnas off the stage. So far as I know, there are five New York churches where boys sing regularly on Sundays: St. Thomas's (where sometimes they sing on weekdays, too), the Church of the Transfiguration, Grace Church in Manhattan, Grace Church in Brooklyn Heights, and St. Luke in the Fields. The women of the Sine Nomine Singers, conducted by Harry Saltzman, sounded too womanly in Morley's Burial Service and Purcell's G-minor Evening Service, the substantial items in a concert entitled "In Praise of Music," given in Tully Hall in March. The first half was a patchwork of sixteenth-, seventeenth-, and eighteenth-century items in praise of music. Twenty-three voices seemed rather too many for the madrigals. Tully Hall, unflattering to voices, cruelly revealed some patches of off-pitch singing. The editor of the program book overrated the audience's ability to follow sung Latin without the original words before it.

Singing more discordant than one expects to hear at a public concert came from Vox Humana, conducted by Sandra Goodman, in a complete performance of the Elizabethan madrigal collection *The Triumphes of Oriana* given at St. John's Church in the Village in March. There were fifteen singers, deployed in various formations. There should have been a lute, virginals, or a harpsichord at hand to help them maintain pitch. In the *Triumphes*, the poetry matters almost as much as the music, but in this performance all words, even of such lines as "Ere beauty's splendour all their eyes had dazed" and "To see such bright stars blazing," were given much the same weight, intensity, and tone. Clear, intelligible pronunciation is not the same thing as bringing words to life. I'm delighted that Harry Plunket Greene's splendid *Interpretation in Song* has been put back into print (by Da Capo Press), with a new, enthusiastic introduction by Dorothy Uris, whose own *To Sing in English* is another necessary primer on the subject. Let the word *stately*, Plunket Greene says, be uttered "as though the speaker acknowledged a curtsey." Let Vox Humana remember this next time it gets to the line "You stately Nymphs draw near," in Morley's "Arise, awake." Thomas Hunt's "Hark! did ye ever hear so sweet a singing?" came off best; the group rose to the challenge of the strong clashes and cross-accents.

The choral singing of the Temple University Choir was just about the most accomplished feature of the Beethoven Ninth that, preceded by the *Egmont* overture, formed the first of three concerts given by the Los Angeles Philharmonic in Carnegie Hall this month. The orchestra is touring with its new music director, Carlo Maria Giulini. Although Giulini came to prominence as a Verdi conductor—at Covent Garden's new productions of *Don Carlos, Falstaff, Il trovatore*, and *La traviata*, between 1958 and 1967, and an annual Requiem with the Philharmonia—he also made a mark in the German Romantic repertory: a notable *Freischütz* at La Scala; strong, supple Schumann symphonies with the Philharmonia. But he has not—on the evidence of this concert—matured into an inspiring conductor of the Ninth. The interpretation stayed on the surface. It showed a kind of simple piety—all the obvious things were sincerely and reverently done—but the result remained prose. Orchestras, like pianos, are often shaken out of tune by travel; the Los Angeles woodwind chording was woefully inharmonious. The soloists formed an ill-matched, unbalanced quartet.

May 21, 1979

Words for Music Perhaps

John Harbison's second opera, *Full Moon in March*, was done in Cambridge last month by the Boston Musica Viva. The libretto is an abridgment, the composer's own, of Yeats's play *A Full Moon in March*. For two distinct reasons, it was a bold choice of text. First: although *A Full Moon*—which is but seven pages long and consists of four songs and a dance framed in blank-verse dialogue and choric commentary—does call for music, it calls for no more than a few passages chanted or sung to balladlike tunes, with some supporting notes or chords plucked on a zither, drumbeats, and perhaps a hint of melody piped on a simple flute. Yeats had very definite ideas about the role that music should play in his works. And second: it is hardly a self-sufficient, comprehensible dramatic action but the barest, sparest presentation of an idea, image, vision, that runs through Yeats's work. *A Full Moon* (1935) is one of the late dance plays Yeats wrote when the dancing of Ninette de Valois had rekindled his interest in ritual plays influenced by Noh. He persuaded de Valois to revive his earlier plays for dancers, at the Abbey Theatre. For her, he rewrote *The Only Jealousy of Emer* (1916) as *Fighting the Waves* (performed in 1929), turning the role of the Woman of the Sidhe into a purely danced one, since de Valois was unwilling to speak on the stage. (Anyone who has heard Dame Ninette's clear, incisive, beautiful voice ringing through Covent Garden to reprove some fault at a Royal Ballet rehearsal, or in speeches from the stage of that theatre reaching easily to the gods, must wonder why.) For her, he wrote *The King of the Great Clock Tower* (1934). Then, for Margot Ruddock, he reworked it as *A Full Moon in March*, adding spoken passages for the Queen but arranging the action so that the actress could be replaced by a dancer at the climactic scene. At the same time, he chiseled and refined the play, making it more intense and more mysterious. Even in the earlier, fuller form, it had not been easy to understand. In her memoir *Come Dance with Me*, de Valois recalls the day of the last rehearsal and first performance:

> I arose from my throne and removed my mask, behind which I had sunk for an hour, lulled to peace by the voice of that great actor [F. J. McCormick, who played the King]. Within the folds of his costume of the heroic age, he looked at me, sighed and shook himself like a dog. "Well, may the spirit of Mr. Yeats be with us tonight, and may it spread itself a bit and give a clue to the audience as to what it all is that we be talkin' about."

And, as Richard Taylor says in his study of Yeats's drama in relation to Noh, "the plays for dancers and those later works based upon them rarely provide enough dramatic context to render them significant, at least not without reference to associations and parallels in other plays." The Old Man who speaks the prologue to *The Death of Cuchulain,* the last play in the series, tells his listeners that the piece is intended for people who "know the old epics and Mr. Yeats' plays about them." Yeats made no bones about writing for a select, educated audience of connoisseurs. "Realism is created for the common people and was always their peculiar delight. . . . In the studio and in the drawing-room we can found a true theatre of beauty." *A Full Moon* is intended for people who recognize the epitome of the author's long, oft-expressed obsession with Muse and Poet: aspects of Maud Gonne and W. B. Yeats; the lovely, lonely virgin and the ardent, aspirant man who both is sacrificed to and fructifies her; Leda "mastered by the brute blood" and engendering the epic of Troy. Commentaries on *Clock Tower* and *A Full Moon* have been numerous and diverse. The interpretations are not mutually exclusive. The action of *A Full Moon* is a brief, concentrated rite that can represent many related and compatible things. There are but two characters, attended by a chorus of two. The Queen has promised hand and kingdom to him "that best sings his passion." A coarse Swineherd who approaches her is beheaded for his presumption. The Queen dances to his severed head. It sings. The Queen dances again, "a dance of adoration." "She stood all bathed in blood. The blood begat." The stage directions of the published play are terse. In a draft, Yeats was more explicit:

> She takes up the head and lays it upon the ground. She dances before it. Her dance is a dance of invitation. She takes up the head and dances with the head to drum taps which grow quicker and quicker. Her dance expresses the sexual act. She kisses the head. Her body shivers. She sinks slowly down, holding the head against her breast. . . . The song at the end of *Clock Tower* with the line "Their desecration and the lover's night."

During the play, the First Attendant has sung the tale of another severed head, set upon a stake by an ancient Irish queen, and singing; Yeats had already told this tale in an 1896 story, "The Binding of the Hair." (The imagery goes back to Orpheus.) *The Death of Cuchulain* reaches its climax in another dance by a queen before a severed head. Behind the play lie Mallarmé's *Hérodiade,* Wilde's *Salome,* Puccini's—and therefore Schiller's and Gozzi's—*Turandot,* and also, as Harold Bloom pointed out in his *Yeats,* Keats's *The Fall of Hyperion,* which is evoked by a quotation from it. "A poetical passage," Yeats once wrote, "cannot be understood without a rich memory."

In *Clock Tower* and *A Full Moon,* critics have found, among other things, "the poet triumphant after death through his magical and enduring art"; a "dramatization of the Oedipus complex, further complicated by streaks of sadism, masochism, necrophily, and also a certain 'nostalgie de la boue' "; a "reconstruction of the Platonic myth of the relation between spirit and matter"; the *poète maudit* and the "Image that costs the artist personal happiness, indeed life itself"; a "symbolic enactment of the complete, the 'perfect' life"; a "simple account of the Saviour-God myth"; an opposition of the "eternal feminine" and "the masculine principle in nature, brutal, violent, and disruptive"; and "only a hollow image of fulfilled desire, a gross aberration prompted by the quester's weariness, or pseudo-apocalypse caused through the aged impatience that wills what it despairs of imagining."

Harbison—and perhaps this was as well—set to work without worrying too much in advance what the play might *mean*. His concern was to bring it to life in the theatre in his own way, not to interpret it. According to his program note, "this opera was written in a nonreflective state, well before any effort had been made to understand the matter, beyond the absorption of the images." Seized by the mystery and power of the rite, he "enacted" it with vivid and beautiful music. Only after composition, he says, did he realize that he had thrown certain themes into relief: "the problem of reconciling our physical and spiritual natures, the image of the artist suitor to a cruel and all-powerful Muse." This intuitive response by a composer with a fertile yet disciplined imagination and a natural command of dramatic music (that is, of pacing, gesture, "color," and, above all, communicative melody) created from *A Full Moon* a self-sufficient opera that needs no explanation. Harbison composed not just the songs and the dances but also the dialogue. In his note, he says that "Yeats declared that he wanted the entire text of his later, Noh-like dance plays to be sung." I have found no evidence of that declaration. Harbison cites only the poet's notes on *Clock Tower*:

> The orchestra brings more elaborate music and I have gone over to the enemy. I say to the musician "Lose my words in patterns of sound as the name of God is lost in Arabian arabesques. They are a secret between the singers, myself, yourself. The plain fable, the plain prose of the dialogue, Ninette de Valois' dance are there for the audience. They can find my words in the book if they are curious, but we will not thrust our secret upon them."

The passage must be read in context. Elsewhere in those notes, Yeats remarks that his earlier dance plays, made for the élite audience of "the studio and the drawing room," had seemed "out of place" at the Abbey. Their successors, *Fighting the Waves* and now *Clock Tower,* are deliberate compromises, made for a public stage and outwardly effective for a common audience, while still holding a "secret" for connoisseurs to discover by reading his words. The passage Harbison quotes continues, "I can be as subtle or metaphysical as I like without endangering the clarity necessary for dramatic effect." *Fighting the Waves* had a fierce score by George Antheil, for an ensemble of flute, clarinet, trumpet, trombone, piano, two violins, cello, double-bass, and percussion. But what has been published of the *Clock Tower* score, which is by Arthur Duff, has the simplicity, directness, and spareness of the scores that Edmund Dulac and Walter Rummel wrote for the earlier dance plays. The words are not lost in patterns of sound. They must have been easily heard. Drum and gong are the only instruments mentioned. In *A Full Moon*, only drum, flute, and zither are specified.

Yeats is a poet to fascinate anyone interested in the wedding of words and musical notes. Like the theorists of the Florentine Camerata, whose speculations led to the invention of opera, he dreamed of Greek poets declaiming to harp or lyre. In the *Clock Tower* notes, he wrote:

> I am not musical; I have the poet's exact time sense, only the vaguest sense of pitch; yet I get the greatest pleasure from certain combinations of singing, acting, speaking, drum, gong, flute, string, provided that some or all the words keep their natural passionate rhythm.

As a child, I thrilled to the *sound* of "The Lake Isle of Innisfree," which Bloom calls "the most renowned (and now deprecated) of Yeats's early lyrics." I still use its first stanza, recited and chanted, as a student exercise in rhythms, weights, and distinctness of vowel colors. In 1901, apropos of the first production of *The Countess Cathleen*, George Moore wrote of "the author's theory that verse should be chanted and not spoken." In 1902, there appeared Yeats's essay "Speaking to the Psaltery":

> I have always known that there was something I disliked about singing, and . . . now at last I understand why, for I have found something better. . . . A friend . . . has sat with a beautiful stringed instrument upon her knee, her fingers passing over the strings, and has spoken to me some verses. . . . Although she sometimes spoke to a little tune, it was never singing, as we sing today. . . . Nor was it reciting, for she spoke to a notation as definite as that of song, using the instrument, which murmured sweetly and faintly, under the spoken sounds, to give her the changing notes.

Yeats appends in musical notation some poems as that friend, Florence Farr, and some as he himself, spoke them. But when he heard poetry fully set and sung to music, "I did not hear the words, or if I did their natural pronunciation was altered and their natural music was altered, or it was drowned in another music which I did not understand." In "Plays and Controversies" (1923), he asks for songs in which "every word . . . every cadence, is audible and expressive as if it were spoken . . . for music that shall mean nothing, or next to nothing, apart from the words." In the first paragraph of the *Clock Tower* notes, he complains that "the singer, shrill from conflict with the violins, loud from the strain of great concert halls, trained by some voice-producer to turn language into honey and oil, cannot sing poetry." (Mrs. Yeats retorted that if he had heard Elena Gerhardt or Gervase Elwes sing he would "know that's all nonsense.")

So Harbison, it would seem, errs in claiming Yeats's "sanction" for a full musical setting of A Full Moon. But he does not need that sanction. His own excellent score asserts and justifies the musician's prerogative to rape a poem or play, to invest "the plain fable" with his own kind of "secret." Like the poet, the composer, provided he has Harbison's dramatic gifts, can be as subtle or as metaphysical as he likes without endangering the clarity necessary for dramatic effect. Yeats would no longer hear *his* music in Harbison's score for A Full Moon; he no longer heard it in Antheil's score for Fighting the Waves, the work in which he had for a while "gone over to the enemy." In that enemy camp, the composer commands. The choreographer, director, and designer are his adjutants. The poet remains in a back room, nursing his secrets, visited by only a few.

In Harbison's opera, the attendants are a soprano and a tenor. (Yeats suggested a soprano and a bass, and in an earlier draft a tenor and a bass.) They sing the stanzas of the first song, with its "Crown of gold or dung of swine" refrain, in octaves, to a strong melody of bold outline and sensitive rhythm, around which the orchestra spins chorale-variation-type accompaniment of a somewhat Stravinskian cut. The soprano sings the first two stanzas of the second song, about the ancient Irish queen, in quasi-ballad style, while the tenor "improvises" melismas in accompaniment; in the two subsequent stanzas the roles are reversed. The melody is developed in successive stanzas but remains recognizable; the soprano's final burst of high vocalise after "heard the dead lips sing" makes vivid the miracle. (And throughout the opera there are such moments where the sense of the words flowers into music of keen eloquence.) The third song, the Queen's "Child and darling, hear my song," voiced by the soprano—a dancer has now taken over the role of the Queen—is the most schematic. The second line is audibly a palindrome of the first, and the fourth of the third; the third line is an inversion of the first, and the fourth of the second. In the first stanza, the melody moves in even, deliberate steps, as if defining triads. In the second stanza, those steps are filled in with semitone passing-notes or portamento. An outburst of free, quasi-extempore coloratura on the refrain "virgin cruelty" becomes more expressive after the measured pacing that precedes it. Harbison, I suspect, knew as little what to make of the fourth song, the Head's trivial nursery rhyme ("I sing a song of Jack and Jill. Jill had murdered Jack"), as most critics have done. He sets it simply, for the tenor, over a lilting bass, with the "full moon in March" refrain as a slow, high, plangent cry. The final, lofty choric stanzas ("Why must those holy, haughty feet descend") recall the chorale at the end of Britten's The Rape of Lucretia—in motion, in the soprano-tenor octave texture, even in harmony, as the emphatic, carefully shaped melody is solemnly intoned over a pedal C and pauses on a prominent tritone G-flat. (For the first time, it strikes me that André Obey's play Le Viol de Lucrèce, the source of Britten's libretto, contains Noh elements.)

For Swineherd and Queen, baritone and mezzo-soprano, Harbison has fashioned from the dialogue an aria apiece and a duet. The Swineherd's aria ("Queen, look at me") is a moving and powerful piece of music, arresting and declamatory in its outer sections; arabesques from the bass clarinet add a magical, musical resonance to the singer's bold, direct statements. The Queen's aria is wound with a sinuous oboe line. She seems to be a cousin of Szymanowski's Queen Roxana; there are even touches that recall Rimsky's Queen of Shemakhan. The two lines of the duet are excellently opposed, and so led that even when they combine for a moment in octaves or tenths they seem to be in emotional conflict. The wind doubling of the Queen's voice obscures her words but gives force and color to her line. The dance is animated, intense, and graphic without being at all vulgar.

The opera lasts thirty-five minutes. The orchestra is an ensemble of eight: flute, oboe, bass clarinet, violin, viola, cello, piano, and percussion. (The piano is "prepared" so that it serves as a protean, exotic percussion instrument, a *jeu de timbres*.) Yeats's setting is outside time and place, despite localizing references to the Irish queen and a Byzantine empress. The timbre of Harbison's music often has a slightly Oriental tinge, lent it by the chromatic arabesques, the soft melodious clonk (not quite gamelan, not quite tuned gong) of the prepared piano, and the block-chord ostinatos as of *Butterfly* and *The Mikado.* The harmonies are Western based. The music sounds as if it had been written without preconceptions, under the inspiration of the play, directly and fluently, and had then been carefully refined in its working. *Full Moon in March* is an opera that holds the ear and stirs the mind. It moves surely and it sounds beautiful. It should have a future.

The Boston Musica Viva performance, conducted by Richard Pittman, was well played and well sung. David Arnold, as the Swineherd, was outstanding. He had stage presence and vocal presence; he displayed an instinctive authority. D'Anna Fortunato sang the Queen with delicate phrasing, dignity, expressiveness, and accuracy. Cheryl Cobb and Kim Scown made an expert chorus. But the presentation as a whole did not show the work to full advantage. It was played in Sanders Theatre, which has tricky acoustics, and the instruments tended to drown all voices except Mr. Arnold's. A more careful disposition of players and singers was needed. The words were seldom audible. The staging, designed by Campbell Baird and directed by Nicholas Deutsch, was commonplace, not subtle or exquisite. Micki Goodman, the dancer, lacked the resource and personality to carry the climax of the rite. The opera was recorded by WGBH for distribution by National Public Radio, and this enthusiastic account of it is based on not just the single Cambridge performance but a tape recording, which, better balanced, reveals the music's merits more clearly. CRI has announced a recording.

May 28, 1979

Unpropped

The Metropolitan has not done Richard Strauss's *Die ägyptische Helena* for fifty years—not since Gatti-Casazza put it on there, within five months of its première, as the first novelty of his 1928–29 season. His Helen was the glamorous Maria Jeritza, who had been Strauss's and his librettist's, Hofmannsthal's, first choice for the role. (In fact, Gatti had three Helens available in his company: Elisabeth Rethberg, who created the role, in Dresden; Jeritza, who sang the part in Vienna five days later; and Maria Müller, Berlin's first Helen.) The work lasted only one season. The concert performance brought to Carnegie Hall in April by the Detroit Symphony was welcome, even though *Die ägyptische Helena* needs the stage, needs all the help it can get from lustrous acting and captivating scenery. With that help, as Munich and Vienna revivals have shown, it can provide a magical evening in the theatre—even if the effect of the enchantment proves as fleeting as that of the potion on which the plot depends. Yet, precisely because it is not inherently strong and good, one cannot urge companies to mount it while more important operas remain unstaged. An occasional concert performance (before Detroit's, there was one by the Little Orchestra Society, in Philharmonic Hall, in 1967) or broadcast provides the chance of hearing some rich, beautiful music and of discovering what happened between the grandiose *Die Frau ohne Schatten* (completed in 1917) and the domestic *Arabella* (1933), two Strauss-Hofmannsthal operas that have found a place in the repertory. The collaborators began, as so often, by planning a light piece—lighter than *Ariadne*, almost an operetta—and ended by producing an inappropriately weighty one. But there are passages that look forward to the simpler lyricism of *Arabella*.

The plot is worked up from new twists on Stesichorus' suggestion that not Helen but only a phantom image of her went off to Troy, on Herodotus' tale that during the Trojan War Helen was really in Egypt, and on Euripides' wry *Helen*, which combined those ideas to enshrine a bitter moral—thousands of men slaughtered and a great city destroyed in pursuit of a phantom—in a romantic comedy of reconciliation between Helen and Menelaus. Hofmannsthal's libretto owes rather more to Euripides than has been stated: his Aithra, a kindly sorceress, derives in part from Euripides' Theonoë, a kindly seer; his Altair—demonstration of the power of Helen's destructive and corrupting beauty—derives in part from Euripides' Theoclymenus. (Hofmannsthal himself made the connection between Helen and Wedekind's Lulu.) The first twist is that Menelaus, fuddled by Aithra's drugs, is induced to believe the tale of the phantom and accept the woman he intended to kill.

Act I is, in Hofmannsthal's words, "a short frivolous comedy of a husband duped by two women after undergoing terrifying adventures." But, he continued, "surely these characters were meant for more than this?" He skirted the *big* issues. Even a Shakespeare, he said, could not begin to portray Menelaus' feelings about his loved and hated, guilty, irresistible wife, regained amid the carnage she and he had caused. And Euripides' moral, crystallized in the servant's question "You mean it was for a cloud, a nothing, we did all this work?," was not matter for an operetta. (*Helen* appeared in 412 B.C., just after the Sicilian Expedition, Athens's Vietnam.) Hofmannsthal's second twist is that Helen—although "a demon," a type of "ever-deceitful womanhood"—in Act II prefers reality to a husband kept under sedation. Serene, confident in her beauty, she gives Menelaus a draught of remembrance. He raises his sword to her, and then embraces her instead. Around those situations Hofmannsthal amassed decorative elaboration in a libretto at once trivial, pretentious, elegant, and clever. The program book in Detroit included the long, important essay in which he explained and defended his "treatment." The Carnegie program book, touching a new low, offered merely a skimpy, two-hundred-word outline of the intricate plot. In neither place was it noted that this was a rare chance to hear the original *Helena*, not the 1933 revision used in most modern revivals.

The performance, conducted by Antal Dorati, stressed vigor and volume at the expense of beauty and delicacy of sound. Gwyneth Jones, its heroine, was very loud, but in the octaves of the invocation "Erde und Nacht, Mond und Meer" the Menelaus, the Finnish tenor Matti Kastu, showed that he could make even more noise than she until the line rose above the staff. His singing was strong but quite unpoetic. Hers was warm and generous but often strident. There were radiant notes in the rapturous aria "Zweite Brautnacht" but also some harsh, ugly sounds. Barbara Hendricks's soprano was too light for Aithra. She had to force. (The first Vienna Aithra was Margit Angerer, later a famous Octavian, who was considered for Helen when in Dresden Jeritza proved unobtainable.) Birgit Finnilä, Curtis Rayam, and Willard White sang the Omniscient Mussel, Da-Ud, and Altair, unremarkably. The same forces have recorded the opera, for London Records (OSA 13135), and in the recorded performance they give rather more attention to pure focus, phrasing, expression, and sense.

Next season, contemporary opera at the Met is represented by a revival of Benjamin Britten's *Billy Budd,* a 1951 work, and, to some extent, by a new production of Kurt Weill's *The Rise and Fall of the City of Mahagonny,* which will be nearly half a century old when it reaches the house, in November. The other new productions are of *Die Entführung, Manon Lescaut,* and *Un ballo in maschera.* Things were not ever thus. In that 1928–29 season, *Die ägyptische Helena,* almost brand-new, was followed by the American premières of Respighi's *La campana sommersa* (with Rethberg, Martinelli, De Luca, and Pinza), which was a year old; Krenek's *Jonny spielt auf* (with Florence Easton, Michael Bohnen—later Tibbett—and Friedrich Schorr), two years old; and Pizzetti's *Fra Gherardo* (with Maria Müller and Pinza), less than a year old. From the previous season, Deems Taylor's *The King's Henchman,* which the company had created, was carried over (with Easton and Tibbett), and so was *Turandot,* another modern opera. A contemporary parallel could be a 1979–80 Met season including productions of Ligeti's *Le Grand Macabre,* Penderecki's *Paradise Lost,* Henze's *We Come to the River,* Nono's *Al gran sole carico d'amore,* and Tippett's *The Ice Break*—with Scotto and Caballé, Domingo and Pavarotti, Sherrill Milnes, Yury Mazurok, James Morris, and Kurt Moll in the casts. Most of Gatti's 1928–29 repertory was newer then than *Mahagonny* is now; *Pelléas, Butterfly,* and *La rondine* were newer then than *Billy Budd* is now. Twelve works—*Aida, Carmen, Cavalleria, Gioconda, Hänsel, Lohengrin, Manon Lescaut, Pagliacci, Parsifal, Rigoletto, Rosenkavalier,* and *Tosca*—are common to both seasons. Both contain five operas by Verdi and one by Meyerbeer. But whereas in 1928–29 nine operas by Wagner, six by Puccini, and seven by Frenchmen could be heard, for 1979–80 only two by Wagner, two by Puccini, and two by Frenchmen are billed.

Many morals could be drawn, not all of them unfavorable to the present management. It is hard to believe that those earlier productions were thoroughly rehearsed. In a twenty-four-week season, Gatti did forty-seven different operas and several concerts; in the forthcoming thirty-week season the Met is to do just twenty-five. But one thing does need stressing: the present directors' reluctance to put on new operas, the leading singers' failure to clamor for them (in 1927 Hofmannsthal could report that Jeritza "pines for a *new* part"), and the public's preference for the familiar are mutually reinforcing. Until the vicious circle is broken, things can only get worse. The postwar Met circled down to become the most backward of the world's big opera houses. James Levine's task is not easy. He will have to act if he is not to be remembered as the musical director of a major company who never conducted a new opera.

Bellini's *I Capuleti e i Montecchi* is a tricky piece to bring off. Eve Queler, the conductor who made even Berlioz's *Lélio* seem shapely and coherent, didn't quite manage it, at the Opera Orchestra of New York concert performance in Carnegie last month. She is in distinguished company. Maazel, Abbado, and, on the Angel recording, Giuseppe Patanè were no more successful. In my experience, only Sarah Caldwell, at a 1975 Boston production, has led a *Capuleti* gripping from beginning to end. The opera came at a turning point in Bellini's career. Some numbers are in the forceful, declamatory manner that first brought him into prominence; others display the vein of long, lovely, tender melody for which he is esteemed today. Miss Queler, uncharacteristically, did not give enough brio to the bold, brash numbers, and she allowed her singers to drag the recitatives, with emphatic tenutos on almost every appoggiatura. (A rehearsal at which the text was spoken, not sung, might have helped to keep the show moving.) Romeo's soliloquy in the tomb lost all momentum.

The Romeo was Tatiana Troyanos, who is experienced in the part: she sang it for Miss Caldwell, and just before the Carnegie performance she had been singing it in Washington. Her account of it was serious, ardent, and impressive, but the vibrato in her heroic tones and the breathiness in her soft attacks were disturbing. Vibrato and breathiness applied with care can be valuable and potent expressive devices; when persistent, they suggest an affliction rather than an accomplishment. Ashley Putnam was in most ways an accomplished Juliet, but her tone color had too little variety, and taste deserted her when she shrieked an unwritten E-flat *in alt* at the close of the first act and when, at the end of the second-act aria, after a similar E *in alt,* she clung to a high tonic through tonic and dominant harmonies alike. The Tybalt was Fausto Tenzi, a young Swiss tenor Germanic in timbre and callow in style. In the small parts, Boris Martinovich, the Capulet, made much of his best notes, recurrent middle C's and D's, but faded when the line went lower, and Julien Robbins was an admirable and powerful Laurence.

The ballad opera *The Duenna* has a libretto by Sheridan and a score partly composed and partly assembled by his father-in-law, Thomas Linley, Sr. Like Sheridan's plays *The Rivals* and *St. Patrick's Day,* it appeared at Covent Garden in 1775 (the year of Mozart's *Finta giardiniera* and *Il re pastore*), and it had a long run. Mrs. Green, the first Mrs. Malaprop, took the title role. Soon the opera was sweeping the country; in 1779 it crossed the Atlantic, to Jamaica; in 1786 it reached New York, and the next year Philadelphia and Baltimore. Its extraordinary success is hard to understand; several other ballad operas have prettier tunes and funnier plots. The book of *The Duenna* is a fairly entertaining tangle of amorous intrigue (Prokofiev and Roberto Gerhard have based lively operas on it) but no miracle of wit or neatness. The score is a series of commonplace ditties, many of them in the jiggety-joggety 6/8 that marks English music through the centuries. When a Tommaso Giordani air lifted from *La marchesa giardiniera* arrives, late in Act II, it brings the first breath of able musical invention.

The concert performance of *The Duenna*—music only, linked by narration—that the Federal Music Society put on in Alice Tully Hall last month did little to commend the work. The singers were handsomely costumed but undirected; they showed almost no spark of dramatic imagination, little sense of how to put over a theatre song. Most of their words are inaudible. Only the Carlos showed any liveliness. The role was played *en travesti* by Judith Otten, a soprano, but it was created by the rather important Jewish tenor Michael Leoni, Giordani's partner for a while at the English Opera House in Dublin, and later chazzan at the Jamaica synagogue. On the bill with *The Duenna* was Paisiello's *Barber* overture, Haydn's "La Reine" symphony, and an ineptly composed cantata, *The Military Glory of Great Britain*, attributed to James Lyon and first done at Princeton in 1762. It is good that New York has an orchestra specializing in music of Colonial and Federal times, trying to produce the right sounds with the right forces. The Society's historical wind instruments made a delightful sound when they were played in tune, but often they were played badly out of tune. The conductor, John Baldon, tended to reduce all tempi and all dynamics to a moderato and mezzo forte, and all rhythms to a plod. Tully Hall was not an apt setting. Lincoln Center is celebrating its twentieth birthday: the present it needs most is a music room suitable in size, sound, and appearance for eighteenth-century music.

Without the activities of the Opera Orchestra and the Sacred Music Society, New York's operatic life would be poorer. *I lombardi, Le Cid, Gemma di Vergy, Aroldo, Mosè, Il crociato*—the list of what they have brought us is long. There can be several good reasons for doing an opera in concert form: to present a work unjustly neglected by the opera companies; to revive a work perhaps justly neglected—one historically important, one worth an occasional airing if not the expense of a full production; to introduce to a city fine new singers (Montserrat Caballé made her New York début in a concert. *Lucrezia Borgia*) or familiar singers in unfamiliar roles; and to present even a familiar masterpiece on a higher musical level, with a more distinguished cast, than those of the regular opera companies. One or more of those reasons justified the concert performances so far considered. The last justified most of the concert performances that Solti and the Chicago Symphony have brought to Carnegie—but not their *Fidelio* last month. Its heroine was Hildegard Behrens, who sang the role at the Met this season. It was good to hear her again, for she is the most moving, eloquent, and accomplished Leonore of our day, and even on the concert platform the opera came to life in and through her. She has the two high virtues that distinguish a singer from singers who may have an equally fine, or even finer, voice: vivid words, and a way of moving from note to note, and on through a phrase, that excites rapt attention. She was always in tune, and, though she seemed impetuous, spontaneous, she never lost control. Hans Sotin was an admirable Rocco; his sound was beautiful and his characterization firm. But the performance had no other shining merits. Peter Hofmann, the heldentenor who came to prominence at Bayreuth's centennial *Ring*, made his New York début, as Florestan, and did not please. His voice was strong but dry, his phrasing untouched by imagination. The others—Theo Adam as Pizarro, Sona Ghazarian and David Kuebler as Marzelline and Jaquino, Gwynne Howell as Don Fernando—were ordinary. The work would have sounded more truthful with an orchestra and chorus half the size. On both the human and the transcendental level, Solti failed us. The notes of *Fidelio* were there, but, except when Miss Behrens or Mr. Sotin was singing, not its charm, its heroism, its spiritual grandeur. It was surprising to hear the Chicago strings turn the grace notes of the Act II introduction into smudges, but that was a small detail in a performance that became mechanical, unaffecting, unworthy whenever Leonore was "offstage." From a practical point of view, the presentation was unskillful: the singers were kept back by a row of music stands set up like a police line, and were so stationed in Act II that, depending on where one sat, either Leonore or Florestan was hidden by the convulsive conductor. Solti is horrid to watch, and the blank-visaged Mr. Hofmann wasn't worth watching, but Miss Behrens, Leonore in stance and in every glance, certainly was.

June 4, 1979

Living Opera

The Opera Company of Boston, whose twenty-first season has just ended, with the American première of Michael Tippett's *The Ice Break*, has at last acquired a home of its own: the Savoy Theatre, on Washington Street—downtown, large, handsome, handily close to three subway lines. The company in its early years, as the Opera Group, did most of its work in the Donnelly Memorial Theatre, later renamed the Back Bay Theatre. From 1965 to 1968, it stayed there; Luigi Nono's *Intolleranza* and Schoenberg's *Moses and Aaron* had their American premières. The Back Bay was demolished in 1968; after a season in the Shubert and two peripatetic seasons, the troupe perched for seven years in the theatre called sometimes the Aquarius and sometimes the Orpheum. There I watched and heard Sarah Caldwell, on a small, shallow stage and with an orchestra spilling over into what in this country is also termed the orchestra, work her miracles: produce in *I Capuleti*, *Benvenuto Cellini*, the uncut 1867 *Don Carlos*, and Glinka's *Russlan and Lyudmila* some of America's most exciting operatic evenings; give the long-awaited American première of Roger Sessions's rich, noble *Montezuma*. The Orpheum was a shabby, not unattractive place. Miss Caldwell learned how to turn some of its limitations to dramatic advantage. But it was cramped and uncomfortable both in sound and for the spectators. The Savoy, a Thomas Lamb building of 1928, is a very grand affair of marble and gold and rich red stuffs, of columns and mirrors and glittering chandeliers. Lamb's best-known palaces in New York tend to show Babylonian exuberance (Loew's 175th Street is the most opulent, and the Pythian Temple, on West Seventieth Street, the oddest), but the Savoy is in his French manner; it owes something to Jules Hardouin-Mansart and something to Charles Garnier—a people's Versailles on the Opéra scale.

The Savoy, called the B. F. Keith Memorial Theatre when it opened, lasted only a year as a "live" theatre—Al Jolson and George M. Cohan were at the first night—and then went over to movies (largely but not entirely; I met Bostonians there who remembered hearing their first Gilbert and Sullivan from its balcony). It stands on the site of the old Boston Theatre, built in 1854, where Grisi and Mario sang, where later the Met gave its first out-of-town performances. The grand entrance is on Washington Street, but there is also an approach from the Common; an arcade runs through the building, past the stage door, shopfronts, and offices, and divides the box office and the grand foyer. On one of the plate-glass windows, the company's rehearsal schedules were crayoned. The "opera arcade" should become a regular shortcut taken by Bostonians eager to follow the activities of their company. Perhaps the whole quarter will now, like Covent Garden after the vegetable market moved out, sport attractive restaurants, cafés, exhibition galleries open late, even gardens. (There's an empty lot opposite the Savoy that could be made into a pleasant garden.) Boston has always seemed to me a rather civilized sort of city, where such things could happen.

Theatres like the Savoy—and Loew's 175th Street, Loew's Paradise in the Bronx before it was "doubled" and then "tripled," Loew's Kings in Brooklyn, the Brooklyn Paramount, which is now a basketball court, and a hundred others—are to America what the abbeys are to Britain. Thomas Lamb, John Eberson, George and C. W. Rapp, Timothy L. Pflueger, and B. Marcus Priteca are in a way America's William of Sens, William of Wynford, and Henry Yevele. Short-term commercial greed was their Henry VIII. (C. W. Rapp's 1925 remark "Balaban & Katz theatres are put up to last forever" makes wry reading today.) Their works that remain face the same problems as Britain's remaining abbeys: When congregations and audiences have shrunk, who is to pay for the upkeep of the huge edifices? In some cities, the performing arts have been able to take over where the movies failed. The Oakland Paramount (Pflueger, 1931) is now the home of the Oakland Symphony, Loew's Penn (Rapp & Rapp, 1927) of the Pittsburgh Symphony, Loew's Ohio (Lamb, 1928) of the Columbus Symphony, the St. Louis Theatre (Rapp & Rapp, 1926) of the St. Louis Symphony, the Vancouver Orpheum (Priteca, 1927) of the Vancouver Symphony. Loew's State in Providence (Rapp & Rapp, 1928) has become a performing arts center.

The orchestras I have heard in some of these places have sounded fine—sometimes distant, but no more so than in modern concert halls of comparable vastness. But over the Savoy as an opera house there does hang a question mark: it is too big for opera on anything but the grandest scale to make a quick, immediate impact right through the house. It seats about twenty-eight hundred people. Fifteen hundred (the capacity of Venice's Fenice, Palermo's Teatro Massimo) was as many people as Walter Felsenstein ever wanted any of his productions to play to; his own house, the Berlin Komische Oper, held 1,338. Eighteen hundred (Bayreuth) is acceptable. The Paris Opera and the Munich State Opera hold around two thousand, and the Bolshoy holds a hundred more. When one goes much over that figure, difficulties begin, and the twenty-two-hundred-odd houses (Kennedy Center, Covent Garden) just about reach the limit of places where both Mozart and Wagner can satisfactorily be played. Of course, these are rough generalizations. Much depends on individual acoustics and also on the way an audience is packed in. (The Vienna State Opera is listed as a 1,642-seater, but the *Stehplatz* brings its capacity up to just over two thousand. The Scala is variously listed as seating twenty-two hundred and holding thirty-six hundred; the latter figure is no doubt reached on those nights when the top two tiers can seem like the subway at rush hour.) It's not just a matter of being able to *hear*. In the very large New York State Theater and in the enormous Met, one can usually hear what is going on, but few voices set the whole of those huge spaces ringing. Moreover, glances, fleeting facial expressions, form an important part of opera. *The Ice Break* had a production last year in Kiel, whose opera house seats 984, and by all accounts it told strongly there. In Boston, I was sitting near the front and so could admire some delicate acting whose details could hardly have reached to the back rows. The voices were pepped up with a discreet touch of electric amplification—not obtrusive, not really noticeable. This is a controversial matter. The Met uses amplification in the bigger houses it plays on tour. Julius Rudel proscribed it in the State Theater, and sometimes I have thought him too rigorous. Is there any moral objection to thus rectifying the acoustic faults of a place? Is it wrong to use any means available to make a performance more vivid, more enjoyable? I'll leave those difficult questions, and note merely that the Savoy is a theatre, like the Orpheum, in which Miss Caldwell found it advisable to use some amplification. However, there are plans to make the stage larger and the auditorium smaller. Perhaps then it will no longer be needed. All the same, Miss Caldwell deserves a fifteen-hundred-seater, and I hope one day she gets it. Some may declare an opera house of that size uneconomic, but "Menotti's Law"—an axiom I once heard Gian Carlo Menotti expound—has, so far as I know, never been disproved: the larger the theatre, the larger the subsidy it requires.

I wrote at length about *The Ice Break* after its première, two years ago, at Covent Garden (which commissioned the work, and which last month revived it for five performances) [see page 3]. In brief, the work rises from a visionary composer's contemplation of the violence, oppression, and strife that rack the world and of the limited yet intense consolations, the small occasions for hope, that can save mankind from despair. The characters are, as it were, versions of Solzhenitsyn, confronting the Western world after years in a Soviet prison camp, and of Muhammad Ali, proclaiming a simple creed of Black is Beautiful and Best; the variously bewildered, questing, and easily swayed young; an émigré housewife lifted by suffering to rapt, poetic utterance; and a young black nurse whose natural compassion (her name is Hannah, "grace") makes her the instrument of a healing more than physical. Most serious operas proceed by historical analogy or mythological metaphor, but three of Tippett's four operas (*King Priam* is the exception) deal with contemporary themes in a contemporary setting. *The Midsummer Marriage,* a song of joy, is an abundant lyrical outpouring of natural and archetypal imagery as an expression of essential human nature. In *The Knot Garden,* seven characters bring their cares to a private place and there, in conflicts and combinations, weave patterns of the outside world. *The Ice Break* is set squarely in that world. Three crowd scenes, different presentations of unthinking, stereotyped emotion—a popular idol's welcome, a race riot, a hallucinatory mass "trip"—form its three acts; at the same time, we enter the minds and interlocked lives of six individuals affected by and trying to comprehend the events around them. It is a very difficult opera to sing, to play, and to stage.

The Covent Garden première was an elegant, polished production, with expert individual performances and a brilliant conductor (Colin Davis, to whom the piece is dedicated). Ralph Koltai's set was a complicated, ingenious, and beautiful construction. Sam Wanamaker's staging was deft. I admired it, but there were people who missed the searing, tender drama beneath that smoothly accomplished presentation. ("A schema of contemporary dramatic cliché" was one colleague's phrase.) The Boston production, staged and conducted by Miss Caldwell, was tough, violent, direct, and accurate, yet no less tender or poetic. And one seemed to hear more of what was happening in the music. Perhaps the playing *was* more expressive, the instrumental balance more carefully handled. Perhaps the force and truth of the staging illumined the sense of the score more clearly. Certainly I felt that Miss Caldwell had gone deeper into the work than Mr. Wanamaker. Herbert Senn and Helen Pond's scenery was plain and serviceable. Marcia Dixcy's and Polly P. Smith's costumes were strong. Everything came together in a production that included some touches of high technical wizardry but never drew unseemly attention to them. Moreover, the vision that an English composer shaped as American scenes—even though they are formalized, not meant to be realistic—took on new aspects in this American performance. The racial street battle that in London had seemed so formal became in Boston something closer to verismo—a ritual enactment of what had happened and might happen again in the Boston streets. [That October, the New York *Times* front page carried a picture of white students, black students, and police in riot, outside East Boston High School, showing a scene close to Act II, Scene 8 of *The Ice Break*.] The acid trip was plainly closer to the understanding of the young Boston choristers than it had been to the ladies and gentlemen of the Covent Garden chorus. The last of the four performances was broadcast by WGBH and carried in New York by WNYC. I listened to it here, while fog swirled over the city, and Hannah's central aria—a song of love and distress, "Blue night of my soul, blue-black within this city's night," with memories of Bessie Smith deep within it, and the fierce, terrifying music of hate and anger before and after it—made an overwhelming effect.

Hannah was Cynthia Clarey; she was warm, grave, and beautiful. All in the cast—Arlene Saunders and Richard Fredricks as the Russian couple, Nadia and Lev; Jake Gardner as their American son; Leigh Munro as his silly, enthusiastic girl friend; Curtis Rayam as the black popular hero; Bruce Reed as the doctor; Jeffrey Gall and Adelle Nicholson uniting their voices in the utterances of Astron, the psychedelic messenger—gave precise and communicative performances. Miss Saunders's tender, radiant death scene, exquisitely judged, never overdone, and Mr. Fredricks's delivery of the final lines (a noble passage from Goethe's *Wilhelm Meister,* nobly set) were especially eloquent. *The Ice Break* is brief: there was seventy-five minutes of music in London, eighty-three in Boston. Every phrase has to tell. And in this performance every phrase did tell. Other soloists who should be mentioned are Chris Krueger (flute), André Lizotte (clarinet), Steven Young (bassoon), Richard Burgin (violin), and Winifred Mayes (cello). In this extraordinary, inspired piece, timbres, harmonies, melodic steps, and stage actions conspire to affect a listener in a way that defies cool analysis. At the end of Act II, Tippett sketches the possibility of some reconciliation between races, cultures, and generations by bringing together electric guitar, bass guitar, solo violin, and solo cello, accompanying two silent figures, Hannah and Lev. It seems schematic in prescription, but the sounds prove wonderfully moving.

Can I find anything about the production to criticize? Only that in the crowd scenes the sharp distinction between singing chorus and dancing corps (choreography by Talley Beatty) was awkward. But the reason for that was plain: more choral motion, and the singing would have been less accurate. The force, expressiveness, and rhythmic incisiveness of the crowds (chorus master William Huckaby) was one of the great strengths of the evening. In every way, Tippett's opera was memorably revealed. This *Ice Break* is one of Miss Caldwell's and the Boston company's high achievements.

Peter Maxwell Davies's opera *The Two Fiddlers* was composed for the children of Kirkwall Grammar School, Orkney, and first performed at the St. Magnus Festival last year. The Orcadian children took it on a tour of Italy. In London, the Royal Opera presented a Christmas run of eighteen performances (not in Covent Garden) with children from Pimlico School. The American première was given in April by the preparatory division of the Manhattan School of Music.

The Two Fiddlers is based on Orkney matter and on Orkney music. They still fiddle on the islands. (During each St. Magnus Festival, the Orkney Strathspey and Reel Society has held a concert; a record of Orkney fiddle music is distributed in this country by Peters International.) In the opera, the fiddlers Gavin and Storm, on their way home from a wedding, are surprised by trolls. Storm plays tunes for them, and as a reward they offer to grant him a wish. Orcadian life is hard; Storm wishes "that my people may never have to work again, so that they can enjoy themselves, always and forever!" The trolls seize on it: "No more crofting, no more fishing, no more work at all! If they're granted this we shall have them in our power." During Storm's minutes in the troll mound, twenty-one years have passed outside. He returns home to find the islanders grown fat and lazy, spending hours and hours in front of television sets, and eating commercially prepared food. Gavin has acquired a house (bought with a mortgage), a car, a life insurance policy, a paunch; for exercise, he plays golf. "We don't have fiddle music anymore— We just put on the record player, very loud." So Storm says:

> *I must make up a new tune,*
> *To break the spell,*
> *And make them work again,*
> *A new piece of music,*
> *To make them dance*
> *And work for their daily bread.*

With a lively set of reels on his fiddle, Storm wakes them. A haggis is piped in to celebrate the occasion. But the trolls add a warning to the festive finale: they have insidious ways of returning, of regaining control.

The libretto, the composer's own, is elaborated from an old Orkney tale retold by George Mackay Brown (whose powerful novel *Greenvoe* tells in realistic terms of an Orkney isle and its ancient, living culture under invasion from the new technological destroyers). The plot has connections with Stravinsky's *The Soldier's Tale*. That work, too, plays tricks with time; it, too, asks "What shall it profit a man, if he shall gain the whole world, and lose his own soul?" and uses fiddle tunes as a symbol of the soul. The subject matter is topical at a time when oil is replacing fish as the richest North Sea harvest, when multinational corporations are coming to Orkney; and it lies close to the heart of a composer who has gone to live on Orkney to escape the physical and moral corruption of big-city life. On the Upper West Side, some of the references must have seemed exotic. On the simplest level, there is the line, from an islander bored by "telly" commercials, "Switch to the *other* station—it must be better than that." (It isn't; Davies's catchy commercial jingles, for Trollo Pills to cure all ills, Trollomatic vacuum cleaners, Trollup to eat, Trollka to drink, are replaced by a soap opera, "Trollville Place.") And a cure for the curses of capitalism is a shade too easily stated. Still, although *The Two Fiddlers* is charged with a moral, the message is not spelled out didactically. As Kurt Weill said of *Mahagonny*, another anticapitalist opera, the piece is meant to be fun as well as "an experience."

In the Manhattan production, directed and conducted by Cynthia Auerbach, the cast, of over a hundred, aged from five to eighteen, plainly enjoyed itself. But the presentation was slightly low-voltage. In previous productions, the title roles were taken by boys who could both fiddle and sing; here the fiddling came from the pit, and the actors of the parts were somewhat pallid—too careful, too polite. Miss Auerbach should have urged them to hit their lines harder. The set designer, Linda Conaway, got some things wrong (against the tenor of the tale to make the record player, belching hard rock, a windup Victrola). Yet, on the whole, this was a big, enthusiastically mounted show. The piece is a "real opera" for children to create (there is no condescension in the score), and one that may possibly set them questioning aspects of life which elsewhere they are taught to take for granted.

June 11, 1979

Manifest

The Juilliard School, I notice, has a new (noncredit) class, in platform deportment. So I must have been wrong in thinking for all these years that American conservatories did give platform deportment classes, and that their tenor was never let an audience guess from the expression on your face that music making might be an enjoyable business or that you actually like the work you're playing. Dour demeanor is so regular in New York that I had assumed it must be inculcated and carefully maintained. Watch Speculum Musicae, Parnassus, or the New Music Consort play some tricky, delightful modern composition: how often do the players' faces light up in pure pleasure at felicities in the music or in their execution of it? Watch British, French, or Italian musicians of comparable achievement play the same piece: although they may not play it any better, their manner is likely to invite the audience to share their appreciation of it.

Such reflections occurred to me, not for the first time, at the performance—a musically good performance—of Luciano Berio's *Circles* given in Carnegie Recital Hall earlier this season by the New Music Consort. *Circles,* composed in 1960, is an immediately attractive modern classic. When Cathy Berberian, for whom it was written, sings and acts it, a deaf man can take pleasure in the piece. Judith Bettina, the protagonist of the Consort performance, sang the work accurately, sweetly, and brightly, but she enacted it in a deadpan fashion. At the end, the audience was enthusiastic. Miss Bettina and the two percussionists, Claire Heldrich and Gary Schall, accepted the applause gravely, almost grimly. Only the harpist, Alyssa Hess, intimated by her expression that *Circles* had been fun to play and that she was glad that we, too, had enjoyed it.

I don't want to make too much of this. *Circles* is a special case—in its composer's words, "a structure of actions, to be listened to as theatre and to be viewed as music." The singer also directs the piece, beating time, clacking her claves, ringing her little finger cymbals, jingling glass chimes and wood chimes, changing her command post. One doesn't want all music to be elaborately mopped and mowed through by its executants. A conductor who dances out an elaborate, obtrusive platform choreography can be distracting. A page turner for Dame Myra Hess told me that he was once surprised during rehearsal to see the words LOOK UP! writ large in her score over a tender second subject. Dame Myra didn't look up—not until the performance that night, when her eyes rolled soulfully to heaven. It's not really an unkind story: that soulful glance may well have helped some listeners to understand the expressiveness that she intended the melody to carry. Similarly, Lotte

Lehmann's primer *More Than Singing* provides many tips about glances, gestures, and postures that can help a singer to communicate the sense of a song.
Harry Plunket Greene's *Interpretation in Song* even suggests that the singer
of "Er, der herrlichste von allen" may at the turns in the vocal line "clasp her
hands or clutch at her heart or throw her arms out to the beloved image." But
I'm thinking of something less carefully considered: unstudied, spontaneous
communicativeness, a bond of shared enjoyment, unconcealed, between performers and audience. And I'm deploring the apparently deliberate cultiva-
tion of a stern, puritan platform manner—as if it were bad form to admit to
delight. Sometimes, I think, the result "sounds": the inhibited demeanor inhibits expression. Even when it doesn't, it is likely to inhibit an audience's
response and dull its appreciation. There are phonograph records on which
one can "hear" the twinkle in Elisabeth Schumann's, Horowitz's, or Gerard
Schwarz's eyes.

Circles closed the third of the three national programs (French, Austrian
and German, Italian) that the New Music Consort gave this season. Luigi
Nono's *Polifonica-Monodia-Ritmica* (1951) began it, in a delicate and beautiful performance, conducted by George Manahan. There were also Bruno
Maderna's *Honey-rêves* (1961), Berio's set of folk song arrangements (1963),
which call for more diverse characterization than Miss Bettina gave them,
and Luigi Dallapiccola's exquisite *Piccola musica notturna* (1954). It was
something of a down-memory-lane program—nothing from the last sixteen
years—and that was a pity, for in this town we hear precious little of what
Italian composers are up to, while all those works are on disc (and all but the
folk songs in the current catalogue). But it was a coherent evening of cultivated, finely wrought, and—in the Nono and in *Circles*—inspired music, performed on a high level of accomplishment. Next season, the Consort plays
three concerts of American chamber music in its Carnegie series; I hope the
programs include the best of the new pieces it has been introducing at York
College, in Queens.

The League-ISCM concerts, which a few years ago I used to attend, I confess,
more as a matter of duty than with any great keenness, have again become an
important element in the musical life of the city—not least because the
works presented come from all over the country. This season's seven programs, performed in Carnegie Recital Hall, were varied and were imaginatively, intelligently, and purposively assembled. In the course of two of them,
four of the six winning works in the League-ISCM 1978 competition were
done. The competition was held to choose six compositions, by six composers,
to go forward as the national submission to the international jury of the
World Music Days—the new name for the ISCM Festival—which this year
will be held in Athens in September. (Two of the winning pieces were for
large forces that would not fit a recital format, so their composers were represented by pieces that would fit.) The American judges spanned the country:
John Harbison (Cambridge), Paul Lansky (Princeton), Roger Reynolds (San

Diego), Ralph Shapey (Chicago), and Harvey Solberger (New York). So did the winners: Laura Clayton (Ann Arbor), John Heiss (Auburndale, Massachusetts), Michael McNabb (Stanford), Frank Retzel (Chicago), Maurice Wright (New York), and Scott A. Wyatt (Urbana). Three of the six winning pieces use tape, and in a fourth the instruments are amplified.

I caught three of the pieces submitted to Athens and particularly liked two of them: McNabb's *Dreamsong* and Heiss's Chamber Concerto. McNabb works at Stanford University's Center for Computer Research in Music and Acoustics; his *Dreamsong* is for computer-generated stereo tape, with recorded soprano. A few weeks later, at The Rockefeller University, I heard the computer-generated score in somewhat similar vein which McNabb and William Schottstaedt had composed to accompany Elliott Levinthal's three-dimensional film of Martian landscapes, assembled from signals that the Viking spacecraft sent back to Earth. The sounds were strange, romantic, and picturesque, evocative of an otherworld landscape. They made a good sound track. Much electronic composition (the term is intended to cover both synthesized sounds and natural sounds recorded and electronically processed) suggests background music—accompaniment to odysseys or travelogues that call for something more special than the mock-Delius habitually added to images of familiar pastoral scenes. And I own that at the League concert, which happened before I knew about the Martian movie, *Dreamsong* at first seemed to me an invitation to roam in imagination through long, unfamiliar landscapes. But soon, or so I thought, it was revealed as music in its own right—music to attend to, not to dream through—for interesting, arresting things were happening, and the shape was making sense. When the mysterious sounds suddenly coalesced into articulate words, the effect was potent. To put it another way, McNabb is plainly a real composer, apprehensible as such—not a stunt man or a mere dabbler in technical tricks. Heiss's Chamber Concerto was closer to common musical experience, for although it starts scrappily, it then turns to ordered musical discourse, pleasing and holding the mind and the ear as voice responds to voice and theme plays upon theme. The piece is a clarification, now for four players (flute, clarinet, piano, and percussion), of the Flute Concerto, for soloist and ensemble of ten, which Speculum introduced two years ago. The flute still has the dominant role, of which Carol Wincenc was a striking interpreter. I didn't *dislike* the third Athens piece on this bill—Wyatt's *Menagerie*, a four-channel electronic composition, in three sections entitled "Tree Clams," "Air Stones," and "Moonsheep." Indeed, "Tree Clams" began and ended captivatingly. But I felt that I'd missed the point of it, that I was somehow on the wrong wavelength.

The Wright work that went to Athens was *Stellae*, for orchestra and tape. At the League concert, his Chamber Symphony, for piano and electronic sound, was played—an animated and cogent, and eventually witty, dialogue. Robert Miller was brilliant in the live role. The concert began with Eric Stokes's *Eldey Island, In Memoriam Homo Sapiens*, for flute and tape. The title may be dog Latin, but the piece is surefire, partly because it must be almost impossible to write an unattractive work for solo flute, or even for solo flute with tape effects, and partly because the subject (the subtitle is "An elegy on the extinction of the Great Auk at the hand of man through greed, folly and arrogance") has listeners on its side as soon as they have read the program note. It tells how, in 1844, three men spotted the last surviving pair of auks. As the men approached, the birds "ran along under the high cliffs, their heads erect, their little wings somewhat extended. They uttered no cry of alarm, and moved with their short steps as quickly as a man could run." But they were caught, and strangled, and then their egg, the last egg of the great auks, was wantonly smashed. Given that matter, who could fail to write an effective and moving composition? Stokes has done it skillfully. The New York première of Jean Eichelberger Ivey's *Prospero*, for bass, horn, percussion, and tape, completed the program. This struck me as a dull piece—"Ye elves of hills, brooks, standing lakes, and groves," the epilogue, and some other scraps of *The Tempest* declaimed to pitches against sound effects.

June 18, 1979

Prima Donna

Stephen Paulus is a New Jersey–born, Minneaplis-based composer who will be thirty in August. Richard Gaddes, the general director of the Opera Theatre of St. Louis, heard a tape of his *North Shore*, a work for soloists, chorus, and orchestra; liked the way Paulus wrote for voices; thought he detected in him a born opera composer; and (with the New Music Circle of St. Louis) commissioned a one-act piece for the St. Louis company. The result, *The Village Singer*, had its première this month and proved bright testimony to Mr. Gaddes's flair, Paulus's ability, and the prowess of the admirable St. Louis company. Accounts of a successful first opera are usually qualified by the remark that its promising young composer still has a lot to learn. (By the time they were Paulus's age, Mozart was embarking on *Figaro* and Bellini on *Norma*, and Rossini had written all except the last of his thirty-three Italian operas; but today composers can be called "young" till they are thirty.) What was striking about *The Village Singer* is how *little* its composer still has to learn about dramatic timing, balancing musical forms and theatrical discourse, creating melodic curves that reveal character or convey emotion, and the other specifically operatic skills. His score is at once fresh and masterly.

The libretto, by the poet Michael Dennis Browne, who also lives in Minneapolis, is drawn from Mary Wilkins Freeman's short story "A Village Singer" (1891). For forty years, Miss Candace Whitcomb has been the leading soprano of the church choir in a New England village. Her upper notes have become unreliable. The other members of the choir give her a surprise party and an album of photographs, and she, suspecting nothing, is touched by their tribute. But when they have gone, she finds in the album a letter telling her that her services are no longer needed; a younger soprano, Miss Alma Way, has been engaged. Next Sunday morning, Alma embarks on a solo:

> Her voice rang out piercingly sweet; the people nodded admiringly at each other; but suddenly there was a stir; all the faces turned toward the windows on the south side of the church. Above the din of the wind and the birds, above Alma Way's sweetly straining tones, arose another female voice, singing another hymn to another tune. . . . Candace Whitcomb's cottage stood close to the south side of the church. She was playing on her parlor organ, and singing, to drown out the voice of her rival.

The minister comes to remonstrate with her, but in vain. "I'm goin' to let folks see that I ain't trod down quite flat, that there's a little rise left in me." During the afternoon service, the same antiphonal battle is fought. Now Candace's nephew Wilson Ford, who is engaged to Alma, comes to remonstrate with her, and also in vain. But the fires of ambition and resolution that suddenly blazed in Candace destroy her. Fevered, she takes to her bed. The next Sunday (in the opera, three Sundays later), she asks for Alma to come to sing to her after the service.

> Candace lay and listened. Her face had a holy and radiant expression. When Alma stopped singing it did not disappear, but she looked up and spoke, and it was like a secondary glimpse of the old shape of a forest tree through the smoke and flame of the transfiguring fire the instant before it falls. "You flatted a little on—soul," said Candace.

That is all, but it is more than a tragicomic anecdote. Both the story and the opera trace a delicate, touching portrait of "this obscure woman, kept relentlessly by circumstances in a narrow track, [to whom] singing in the village choir had been as much as Italy was to Napoleon." Her tender feeling for William Emmons, the elderly leader of the choir, who was wont to walk home with her after rehearsals and sing duets with her to the parlor organ, and who has now acquiesced, even taken a leading role, in her dismissal, adds poignancy to the tale. Thoughts of Prospero, of Verdi's Falstaff, of Isak Dinesen's Pellegrina Leoni, of Strauss's Marschallin, of aging masters in whatever art who find it not easy to hand over leadership to the young deepen a reader's or a listener's apprehension of the story or the opera. It is a good subject for musical treatment, since it can be vividly realized in musical terms, and a fine subject for an American opera with a universal theme and particularity of setting and local color.

The scenes move between Candace's parlor and the church, visible side by side on the stage, and finally to Candace's bedroom. The score starts as the story does: "The trees were in full leaf, a heavy south wind was blowing, and there was a loud murmur among the new leaves." For "this soft sylvan music—the tender harmony of the leaves and the south wind, and the sweet, desultory whistles of birds," Paulus has borrowed, developed, and built upon the murmuring figuration that begins the *Così fan tutte* trio "Soave sia il vento." The hymn tunes and their words are traditional: Isaac Watts, Thomas Moore, and Sabine Baring-Gould have contributed to the libretto, and Samuel Webbe, Sir Joseph Barnby, and John Bacchus Dykes to the score. At her surprise party, Candace, asked to sing, obliges with J. S. Fearis's hymn "Beautiful Isle" ("Somewhere the sun is shining"), with words by Jessie B. Pounds. It was copyrighted in 1897, and so when Candace says "I always did like that song" there is a slight chronological awkwardness: since the opera is set "at the turn of the century," the piece cannot have been in her repertory very long. But the sentimental tune (William, at Candace's request, joins in the refrain) fits the occasion well, and the other hymn texts are carefully chosen to point the situations. Alma's first solo is Watts's "In vain we tune our formal songs, In vain we strive to rise," sung to Dykes's "St. Agnes," in G; the supporting harmonies go terribly awry under the onslaught of Candace's "Gracious spirit, dwell with me," sung to Richard Redhead's "Rock of Ages" tune first in E-flat and then soaring up into B-flat. Likewise, the choir's and Alma's "Come, ye disconsolate" (words by Moore, tune by Webbe), in C, quails before Candace's ringing "To God my earnest voice I raise," proclaimed to the "When I survey" tune in A-flat. In each case, one hymn is in 4/4 and the other in 3/4, but the quarter-notes march at the same tempo, and the result is a carefully controlled, not a chance, cacophony. All Paulus's score is marked by a similar command of harmonic tension that defines the dramatic tensions. The opera is not exactly "in" any key, but the beginning and the end, where the leafy murmur grows slower and dies at last on the sound of a bell, suggest D major or G major poised above an uneasy tritone alternation of E and B-flat.

The title role was composed for Pauline Tinsley, a soprano who made her début as Rossini's Desdemona, in 1961, and now sings Lady Macbeth, Elektra, and Turandot. I have heard her in a wider range of roles—Rossini's and Verdi's Desdemona, Mozart's and Verdi's Elvira, the Queen of Night, Tosca, Wagner's Irene (in *Rienzi*), Weber's Clarissa (in *The Three Pintos*)—than any other soprano, and feel that Candace Whitcomb is her finest achievement yet. Not a note, not a word, not a glance or a gesture was out of place. She was funny, spirited, potent, and profoundly moving—a whole character, and never a caricature. Elizabeth Pruett's gentle, attractive Alma was precisely and sensitively played and sung. The other principals—David Hillman as Wilson, Melvin Lowery as the minister, Marc Embree as William—were pretty good, but not so exact in every detail. Although Colin Graham, who directed, got the big things and most of the little things right, he admitted (both in *The Village Singer* and in *La traviata*, another production of the St. Louis season) some awkward, stagy behavior with hats, hands in pockets, etc. In such a piece, everything must ring true. The denomination of the church is left vague, even distractingly contradictory, by all concerned. In the story, the services are called meetings, and Candace refers to the church as a "meetin' house." The choir's three hymns in the opera (the third is an offstage "Now the day is over," accompanying Candace's last monologue) appear, words and music, in the Episcopalian hymnal. Candace's words, however, are taken, no doubt with intent, from Dissenting hymnals. The choir is unsurpliced, informal, but the minister chants the Grace with a positively Tractarian flourish. It is a nice touch that in his fluster at Candace's interventions he leaves out the words "and the love of God." There are several such little subtleties, verbal and musical, in the piece. Candace's triumphant last note, on *soul,* is a long, steady G above the staff, *mp-f-pp.* But Alma's note for *soul* had been the A above it.

The Village Singer has a cast of ten. In St. Louis, the five smaller parts (with Alma, Wilson, and William they make up the eight-voice choir) were neatly characterized and well sung. There is an orchestra of twenty-two—six woodwinds, horn, two percussions, harp, keyboard (organ and piano), and eleven strings—which Paulus handles with uncommon skill and variety. The conductor was William Harwood, who ever since his Yale *Idomeneo,* in 1975, has seemed to me the best of America's young opera conductors, for he has an instinctive command of dramatic pace, vocal phrasing, and telling instrumental commentary. Maxine Willi Klein's scenery elegantly outlined the structure of the buildings, beneath a leafy sky border. Her furniture and John Carver Sullivan's costumes looked both attractive and authentic. Arden Fingerhut's supple, imaginative lighting unobtrusively seconded the drama. The stage turntable was discreetly used.

An operatic treatment of *A Village Singer* could easily have gone wrong—become broad, larky, or mawkishly sentimental. Paulus's opera is none of these. It shows an uncommon niceness of taste, and delicacy and depth of feeling. The challenge posed to his skills is perfectly met. The piece makes a sure start to an operatic career. Now one would like to see him venture more boldly, into matter still more challenging to his musical invention. Preceded by some New England melodrama or tragedy, and followed by a high-spirited comedy, *The Village Singer* could well become the central panel of an American *Trittico.* In St. Louis, the opera was given on a double bill with *Gianni Schicchi,* the comic panel of Puccini's *Trittico,* conducted by Victor DeRenzi. This was a revival and refinement, in new décor (by the same scenery-costume-lighting team as in the Paulus), of Lou Galterio's brilliant 1977 production. The action is shifted from the Middle Ages to the 1930s; provided one accepts the slight legal anachronisms that result, everything is real, true to character, mercurial, and irresistible. Spiro Malas was the new Schicchi, and first-rate. Erie Mills was a pretty Lauretta. Vinson

Cole, the Rinuccio, is a tenor who has suddenly taken the step from high promise to high accomplishment. His tone was free and beautiful, all his words were alive, and his acting was ardent. Rinuccio's *stornello* can seldom have sounded more charming or more stirringly romantic.

June 25, 1979

Excursions

The Opera Theatre of St. Louis plays in the Loretto-Hilton Theatre of Webster College, in Webster Groves, a suburb of the city. After the opera, one can pluck ripe mulberries, enjoy the scent of honeysuckle, hear crickets chirrup. Across the lawn from the theatre is an open-sided tent—this year it was called a pavilion—where for the five central days of the season good food was served before the shows: Austrian on *Ariadne* night, French on that of *La traviata,* Italian on that of *Gianni Schicchi,* and Spanish on those of *The Three Pintos.* Every day, picnic fare was on sale. After the performances, the audience did not scuttle home but gathered on the lawn or in the tent, drinking, talking, discussing the show, mingling with the casts and the crew. Operagoing in St. Louis is a civilized and enjoyable experience. In some ways, the place recalls Glyndebourne—a younger, less formal Glyndebourne, without the long dresses and the black ties. No downs, cows, lake, croquet lawn, or gardens, it is true, but the same feeling that an opera is more keenly appreciated in agreeable surroundings and that an audience should be made to feel welcome and wanted. The Glyndebourne parallels run deeper, for the St. Louis troupe is also an ensemble, not a company subscribing to the idea of opera once defined by Angelica Catalani's husband: "Ma femme et quatre ou cinq poupées—voilà tout ce qu'il faut." The emphasis is not on famous, familiar singers flying in to do their thing but on a team of young artists carefully chosen, carefully rehearsed, and playing a repertory season. Mostly, they are at a "pre-Glyndebourne" stage; one must not make reckless comparisons. The troupe is in its fourth year. I have known it for three, and one of the pleasures it affords is to watch young singers grow there: the tenor Vinson Cole, for example, who has been with Opera Theatre from the start, in successive years Ernesto, Ory, Rodolfo, and then, as I wrote last week, as good a Rinuccio as one could hope to hear and see; or the soprano Sheri Greenawald, in successive years Norina, Galatea (in Rameau's *Pygmalion*) and Despina, Mimì, and Violetta; or the baritone Stephen Dickson, in successive years Sid (in *Albert Herring*), Guglielmo, Sid again and Marcello, and then the star of *The Three Pintos*. (Next year, he goes to Glyndebourne.) The St. Louis repertory is another powerful attraction. In 1977, it included *Pygmalion* and *Le Comte Ory;* last year Vicente Martín y Soler's *L'arbore di Diana;* and this year, the première of Stephen Paulus's *The Village Singer* and the American première of *The Three Pintos*, begun by Weber in 1820 and completed by Mahler in 1887.

The *Pintos* is a problem piece. Weber began work on it within days of completing *Der Freischütz*. In the words of his son Max:

> His productive spirit, after its flight into such mystic and romantic regions, yearned for lighter, brighter scenes, where genial humour reigned. Weber conceived a great longing for the composition of some little comic opera for a small orchestra into which he might pour the endless stream of pretty, rippling melodies which he felt constantly springing up in his brain.

But the commission for *Euryanthe* intervened, and then that for *Oberon*, and although the *Pintos* had possibly been completed in its composer's mind, only seven of its seventeen musical numbers (Act I and the first number of Act II) had been committed to paper—and then only in his musical shorthand—when he died, in 1826. More precisely, only those seven draft numbers were found; Weber's widow, Carolina, and his pupil Julius Benedict believed that a full score had been made. Carolina asked Meyerbeer to complete the opera, and in 1827 a Berlin paper looked forward to hearing it. Between 1836 and 1841, Meyerbeer dickered with completing the piece for the Opéra-Comique; Scribe was approached about preparing a new libretto, since the original, Meyerbeer said, was "the silliest, stupidest stuff in the world." (Karl Winkler, alias Theodor Hell, the original librettist, wasn't pleased.) In 1836, Carolina wrote to Meyerbeer's mother asking her to use her influence with her son to get the opera finished. In 1837, Winkler sent Meyerbeer, at his request, some other Weber compositions, to help him to fill the gaps. (Among them was the early opera *Peter Schmoll*, an attractive piece that awaits its American première.) The Weber scholar F. W. Jähns sent him a version of the *Pintos* drafts set out in a two-color full score—black for undisputed and red for questionable readings—so that for Act I he had merely to complete the instrumentation. In 1839, the work was reported ready; performances in Paris and to inaugurate the great new opera house that was rising in Dresden were predicted. But it wasn't ready. In 1845, Meyerbeer commissioned a new libretto for it, called *The Two Pintos*, from Charlotte Birch-Pfeiffer. In 1846 and 1847, he worked at the score. Nothing came of all this, but I set out these details, culled from the recently published Meyerbeer diary and correspondence, to clear the oft-maligned composer of the charge that, having been entrusted by the widow Weber with the *Pintos* sketches, he simply let them gather dust for twenty years.

In 1887, Weber's grandson Carl showed the sketches to Mahler, then a young Leipzig Kapellmeister, and early in 1888 a Weber-Mahler *Three Pintos* had its première, in Leipzig. It was a success, and on German stages was played frequently for a few years; then it all but disappeared. The first modern revival was mounted by the music society of John Lewis, a London department store, in 1962. Pauline Tinsley was the heroine; John Cox, now director of production at Glyndebourne, was the director; and David Lloyd-Jones, now musical director of English National Opera North (Britain's latest full-time, full-scale opera company), was the conductor. (Would that Macy's or Bloomingdale's had the same good habit of doing operas—enriching a city's repertory annually with important revivals and at the same time fostering important talent!) Since then, there have been a few other *Pintos* productions and a recording, published in this country by RCA. The common appraisal—justified, I believe—has been: What attractive music, but what an incompetent opera! It was what I felt at John Lewis and after the recording, and again at the first St. Louis performance. But at a second performance I tried to listen "through" the Mahler rearrangement to the first act of the *Pintos* as Weber had planned it, for it had struck me that a better job of reconstruction than Mahler's would be possible and desirable—not musically, number by number, since the freshness and aptness of Mahler's orchestration have never been in question, but dramaturgically. Weber's grandson altered Winkler's libretto, and Mahler altered it again, and while it can never have been a strong thing, the alterations present the original musical numbers in an awkward and ineffective sequence. As it stands, the action of the Weber-Mahler *Pintos* is: Act I: Gaston meets Pinto, who is on his way to Madrid to marry Clarissa; he steals Pinto's letter of introduction and decides to marry Clarissa himself. Act II: Clarissa laments the impending marriage, for she loves Gomez; she and Gomez swear fidelity. Act III: Gomez persuades Gaston to give *him* the letter; as "Don Pinto" he marries Clarissa, and when the real Pinto turns up it is too late for changes.

Mahler arranged Weber's six Act I *Pinto* pieces in the order 4, 5, 6 (a substantial finale), intermission, and then (as Act II) 1, 2, 3, and he added irrelevancies from other Weber compositions. (The first edition of the score bears the odd but essentially accurate ascription of the "dramatic" part to Weber and the "musical" part to Mahler.) Mahler's Act II begins with the traditional introduzione—a chorus establishing the basic situation and introducing some of the characters in solo utterance—that should open a whole opera, and it ends without a proper finale. The original No. 2, Clarissa's aria—a fairly light piece that would work well as the first solo of a comic opera—has more weight thrown on it than it can bear where Mahler placed it, at the center of Act II. (He tried to make it function as the more substantial "Leise, leise" does in *Der Freischütz*—to the point of prefacing it, as "Leise, leise" is prefaced, by a soubrette aria.) At a stroke, a modern director could put all this right—produce a better shape, a better story, and a properly balanced sequence of numbers—by playing Mahler's Act II before his Act I, without intermission, and striking out all his interpolations. Some of the struck pieces the director should keep up his sleeve to use in the reconstruction of a second act—or even, if he felt brave enough, of a second and then a third act, based on Weber's original scheme. There a skillful librettist and a sensitive musician, versed in early-nineteenth-century practice, could probably work in the best of the Weber-Mahler and the Mahler-freely-after-Weber numbers, for several of them are brilliant; and the adapters might also do what Mahler deliberately didn't do—use numbers from other Weber operas, either unfinished or now unfamiliar: *Peter Schmoll, Rübezahl, Silvana.* Moreover, among Weber's numerous "insert arias" for other men's operas and his abundant incidental music for plays they might find some pieces more effective and apter for their purposes than the Weber compositions Mahler chose.

I'm proposing two things here. First, that the Weber-Mahler *Pintos* would be strengthened by simply playing the acts in the order II, I, III. That can easily be tested by listening to the recording in that order. But, second, that what we really need is a Weber–Mahler–A. N. Other *Three Pintos*, in which Weber's Act I is respected and the rest is boldly reconstructed in a version that retains the best of Mahler's extra ideas.

The St. Louis production was lively, jolly, enjoyable, not exactly distinguished. Richard Pearlman's direction didn't suggest that he loved the work, believed in it, and believed in his cast. It was efficient and competent for the most part but sometimes dropped into coarse, careless cliché. Stephen Dickson in the Leporello role of Gaston's servant, Ambrosio, was outstanding. In the penultimate number of Act I, Weber requires him to sing in falsetto, in drag, and Mahler, oblivious of diminishing returns, employed falsetto excursions in three other numbers. Mr. Dickson achieved it all with discretion, manfully, without camp. He sang as if he loved and admired Weber's music, launching the canonic trio in Act III—brilliant of Mahler to have perceived that this early (1802) exercise of Weber's would prove irresistible on the stage—in a way that combined wit of utterance and beauty of tone. Alan Kays excels in roles of straightforward, unaffected sentiment (such as Sam in Kurt Weill's *Street Scene*); Gaston needs more dash and sparkle than he could provide. Neil Rosenshein, a naturally romantic, naturally elegant tenor, was well cast as Gomez for his St. Louis début. As the real Pinto, Joseph McKee was too fussy, a caricature. The men were stronger than the women. They also get more chances. Sheryl Woods was a pretty Clarissa. Faith Esham was a twinkling Laura, Clarissa's maid. Jane Kamp had not been shown how to make the most of Inez's cat song. Bruce Ferden conducted. All St. Louis performances are (with a partial exception noted below) sung in English, and rightly so. For *Pintos*, the version Rodney Blumer—better known as Rodney Milnes, an associate editor of *Opera*—made for John Lewis was used.

The Loretto-Hilton, which seats 925, is an attractive theatre but not an easy one to use for opera. The stage thrusts forward into the auditorium, and many of the audience have but a sideways view of things. The arrangements for flying are meager. Most of the light must come from above. The pit is small and deep, and the acoustics are patchy. In the matter of theatre resources, St. Louis is not at all like Glyndebourne. But the St. Louis directors,

designers, and conductors are learning ways to mitigate the disadvantages of
the house while making the most of its intimacy, directness, and friendly atmosphere. This year, the season was extended to four weeks; four bills were
given; and all performances were well attended. *La traviata* was brashly
conducted by Mr. Ferden. Colin Graham's direction was often unstylish. Miss
Greenawald played Violetta with care and intelligence, and she looked
beautiful, but she was oddly unmoving. There was an unromantic Alfredo,
Jon Fredric West. *Ariadne on Naxos* was more striking. Lou Galterio's direction was detailed, inventive, and amusing in the right ways, never off-key.
Naiad and Echo, Elizabeth Pruett and Miss Kamp, were especially vivid.
Miss Esham played the Composer ideally, but her tone was not limpid or
pure in focus. Erie Mills was a sparkling and accurate Zerbinetta. There was
luster in Pamela Myers's Ariadne, and David Hillman's Bacchus had its moments. Leonard Slatkin, the music director–elect of the St. Louis Symphony
(which plays for the St. Louis opera), conducted—his début in a professional
opera house. Strauss's bewitching score was deftly and charmingly played
(the St. Louis woodwinds are especially good), but at times Mr. Slatkin
leaped on its delights with too much alacrity. There are moments when an
Ariadne conductor should cede to a singer, as if saying, "Now comes *your*
moment to hold the audience spellbound; handle the phrases as if you had all
the time in the world at your disposal, and I'll follow you"—at the Composer's "O du Knabe, du Kind," Zerbinetta's "Ein Augenblick ist wenig,"
Ariadne's great scena. But here one was always conscious of Mr. Slatkin's
hands on the reins. As at the New York City Opera, the prologue and the
commedia dell'arte parts of the opera were sung in English, while the opera
seria was done in German. This is not a good idea. (If the opera seria is to be
given in a foreign language, it should surely be Italian.) It unbalances the
piece, and lends philistine support to a Zerbinetta view of the high operatic
art, suggesting that what Ariadne and Bacchus actually say is unimportant.

Caramoor, forty-five miles north of New York, in Westchester County, is a
house poorly sited and lavishly, expensively furnished with a bewildering
profusion of objects good and bad. On summer weekends, a series of musical
events, the Caramoor Festival, is held there—some of them in the courtyard
of the house, which holds about six hundred people, and others in the mos-
quito-ridden open-air "Venetian Theatre," which can hold nearly two thousand people. The programs can be adventurous, but nothing I've ever heard
at Caramoor has been quite first-rate. (Even first-rate ensembles don't sound
their best in the open air.) Hitherto I have passed over the seasons in silence.
But the American première of Ottorino Respighi's opera *Lucrezia* calls for at
least a few words. Caramoor opened last month with a double bill of Respighi's *The Birds* and *Lucrezia*—two-thirds of the 1937 triple bill at La Scala
(the opera *Maria Egiziaca* was the third work) on which *Lucrezia* had its first
performance. Before the show, there was a jolly party in the courtyard and
dinner in a tent. These were enjoyable. A festive feeling was created. But it

faded during the performance, and a critic must ungratefully bite the Caramoor hand that wined and fed him.

Respighi, who died in 1936, would have been a hundred this month. In this country, the centenary is passing almost unobserved except at Caramoor: the day after *The Birds* and *Lucrezia*, the Music Project played his *Deità silvane*, for voice and fifteen instruments, and *Il tramonto*, for voice and string quartet, in a chamber recital. (Maybe our radio stations do have plans for *Re Enzo*, *Semirâma*, *Belfagor*, and *La fiamma*, for chamber concerts, for learned centenary appraisals, but news of them has not reached me.) *The Birds*, Respighi's colorful elaboration of six baroque avian fancies, was danced to dull, pointless choreography by Robert Weiss. *Lucrezia*, Respighi's last composition—a few pages were orchestrated after his death by his widow—is a spare, sustained, and pleasing essay in the grave, soberly beautiful poetic vein that surfaces from time to time even amid the glittering orchestral pageantry of his famous tone poems *The Pines of Rome, The Fountains of Rome, Roman Festivals*. The libretto, by Claudio Guastalla, is based on André Obey's play *Le Viol de Lucrèce*, which Britten used ten years later for his opera on the subject. In Respighi's version, the Chorus is a single voice, a mezzo-soprano (Ebe Stignani at the first performance, Diane Curry at Caramoor), whose narrative manner and music recall the Testo in Monteverdi's *Il combattimento*. The title role was conceived for a commanding young dramatic soprano, Maria Caniglia, who must have been grandly impressive in the heroine's long, dignified, and moving final speech. In Caramoor's open air, Eleanor Bergquist sounded insubstantial; her manner lacked grandeur; and an animated frieze of posturing boys competed for the audience's attention. Fred Hartmann's direction was generally feeble and insensitive. Laszlo Heltay conducted. Carlos Serrano was Tarquin, David Britton was a vivid Collatinus, and James McCray was Brutus. The opera was done in Italian. Contained by a theatre, strongly directed, and powerfully yet chastely sung, *Lucrezia* should be an impressive piece. Even in this unsatisfactory performance, it threw some new light on a thoughtful, cultivated, earnest composer who deserves to be remembered for more than his exuberant instrumental mastery.

July 2, 1979

Affirmation

At least three compositions by Ralph Shapey were played in New York this season. Abraham Stokman gave the world première of Twenty-one Variations for Piano (1978) in Alice Tully Hall in January; Robert Black gave the world première of Thirty-one Variations for Piano (1966–73) in Carnegie Recital Hall in May; and the next day the Juilliard School gave the New York première of the cantata *The Covenant*. Last year, recordings appeared of Shapey's Seventh String Quartet (CRI) and of his *Configurations*, for flute and piano (New World Records). Theodore Presser has begun to publish Shapey's music: a score of *Rituals*, for symphony orchestra (1959), is available, and so are the Seven Little Pieces for Piano (1951), six of which are not too difficult for amateur fingers. There are also recordings of the Sixth String Quartet, *Rituals*, *Evocation* (violin, piano, and percussion), *Incantations* (soprano and ten instruments), and the big oratorio *Praise*, all on CRI, and another recording of *Evocation*, on Desto.

Twenty years ago, Shapey was at the height of his fame. Along with Copland, he represented America at the 1958 ISCM Festival; the next year his Violin Concerto, *Evocation*, *Form*, and *Rituals* appeared; in a note that accompanies the *Configurations* recording Harvey Sollberger recalls "the excitement generated by each new work of his." Ten years ago, Shapey declared that he did not want his works to be played anymore, and became a kind of legend, almost an American Kaikhosru Sorabji. He was not unknown, not inactive (at the University of Chicago he continued to compose, teach composition, and conduct the Contemporary Chamber Players), but unpublished, "unpromoted," and, until the recordings started to appear, little heard. The moratorium is now over. *The Covenant* was one of the most important new works to be given here this season. But the performance, which should have sent waves of excitement through musical New York, was poorly attended.

Rituals, done in 1971 by the London Sinfonietta under the composer (they also made the recording), was my introduction to Shapey. It is a vivid and arresting piece—sharp-cut or strongly molded music, energetic and intense. In a better world, it might have found a place in the symphonic repertory across the country. Early on, Shapey expounded his idea of what he called "graven images"—not the things prohibited by the Second Commandment but musical images so definitely and fully formed at their first statement that the composer can, in his own words, "work with the concept of 'it is' instead of the traditional 'it becomes,'" since "at all times the 'it is' remains a pre-fixed, concrete image." So, in *Rituals* as in many other Shapey pieces, there is not progressive dissolution or metamorphosis of the material, not what is called organic growth, but, rather—it is easier to hear these things than to describe them—a sense that the whole piece exists at once and that a listener's (and the performers') progress through it in time is kin to viewing central, unchanging images from different aspects, under different lights, against different backgrounds. Tippett has written works—the Second Piano Sonata, the Fourth Symphony—embodying a similar kind of thought, but the sound of Tippett's music is so different from that of Shapey's that there are no other resemblances. If one seeks to describe by likenesses, then Shapey in his earlier pieces is perhaps most like in sound, in colors, in the way the music moves to Stefan Wolpe. On occasion, the "concrete" quality may bring Varèse to mind. But there is also an emphatic, insistent, sometimes even truculently independent vein that makes Shapey's music personal and distinct. In *The Covenant,* this becomes a blaze of affirmation and fervent moral assertion.

The Covenant, which is for soprano, sixteen players, and two tapes, and which lasted about forty minutes at its première, in Chicago in April 1978, and about fifty in New York, is dedicated to Israel's thirtieth anniversary. (*Praise,* begun in 1961 and completed in 1971, was sent to Israel in honor of its twenty-fifth anniversary.) Of the new cantata, Shapey writes, "Like my oratorio *Praise,* although written and dedicated to the miracle of the Rebirth of Israel, it is meant for all humankind—to walk upright, in dignity, in the image of—as One." The piece opens with a massive, maestoso declamatory chordal statement for the winds, whose melody opens with an emphatic rising fourth. The second image is some elaborate and impassioned string music. The maestoso returns, and now the soprano puts words to it—

> *It was*
> *at the beginning*
> *It was*
> *My beloved*
> *It was—*

from a poem in Nelly Sachs's *O the Chimneys.* This prelude returns as a refrain. To a different maestoso declamation, opening with an emphatic rising sixth and ending on a long, shining high C-sharp, the soprano and the winds start to proclaim the tremendous terms of the Sinai Covenant between God and His chosen people, in words from Isaiah and then from Exodus. At the same time, the strings repeat their impassioned music. The two declamations sound related; the ear catches the likeness of texture and rhythm, and the score reveals that the bass of the first becomes the top line of the second, and vice versa. As the movement continues, the repeated "I AM" is each time thrown into prominence by the rising sixth. In the "It was" refrain, which punctuates it, the pitches of the vocal line remain unaltered, but the voice is heard each time against a different background, provided by, in turn, flute (delicato), clarinet (delicato), oboe (delicato), trumpet and gong (brillante), cello (bravura), strings (maestoso), and tutti (maestoso). At the end, Shapey throws in a line from Whitman ("I sing the body electric") and another from Pierre Louÿs's *Chansons de Bilitis* ("I sing of my flesh and my life"). Reading the text, one starts at an almost Tippett-like prodigality of allusion. Hearing the music, one discovers an ecstatic profession that thoughts of the Covenant are not just a Sabbath-day thing but run through all the composer's life and work.

Part II "tests" God's promise, as it were, in a time of persecution and terror. The texts are Nelly Sachs's "This is the landscape of screams" and Kadia Molodowsky's "O God of Mercy/for the time being/choose another people." Simultaneously, in the background, a baritone, on tape, is chanting the Kaddish. On a second tape, another soprano adds now a despairing, hallucinatory echo of the soloist's complaint, now a repeated invocation, "God of Mercy." (The tape was made by the soloist of the Chicago première, Elsa Charlston.) Through the second poem, the bass drum beats out an inexorable dead march that includes sudden, terrifying sforzando crashes. From time to time, the "Covenant" music rings out with tragic irony. This is a rhetorical, powerful, and passionate stretch of music. The live performers cease; only the Kaddish and the repeated murmur "God of Mercy" continue, until from them arises, as Part III, a Credo: "Out of the Dead Letters welled forth songs of Life," set to the "It was" refrain, followed by lines found on the walls of a Cologne cellar—"I believe in the sun even when it is not shining . . . I believe in God even when He is silent"—set for the soloist, sometimes singing, sometimes speaking, and string quartet. This is succeeded by a duo for the soprano and a solo violin, a quiet song, a setting of Vera Klement's "O give me a stone colossus."

Part IV recounts the promise of peace in Isaiah's second chapter: "And it shall come to pass . . . They shall beat their swords into plowshares. . . . Nation shall not lift up sword against nation." The prophecy is spoken simply, over the simple, thrilling sound of a gong roll, and alternates with bright, archaic-sounding fanfares from horn and trumpet. The other instruments join in, and the work ends with a Cantate Domino: the "I am" melody sung and played over and over again, ritually, gathering in all that has gone before, mounting to a huge affirmation, ringing and dwelling on the high C-sharps, resolving at last on D.

Earnestness, passion, conviction, piety are in themselves no guarantee of musical merit, but since Shapey's fiery invention, vividness of imagery, and toughness of structure have never been in question, a work of his informed by those other qualities makes a great impression. *The Covenant* is not absolute music. Its composer would expect his listeners to be moved to consider their own thoughts and feelings about Israel's history, about Israel today, about its policies and actions. (Other passages of Exodus and Isaiah may come to mind: "For I will cast out the nations before thee, and enlarge thy borders"; "And the land of Judah shall be a terror unto Egypt"; more peaceably, "In that day shall Israel be the third with Egypt and with Assyria, even a blessing in the midst of the land.") During the music, the listeners are moved to share Shapey's own thoughts and feelings as proclaimed, given shape, by his urgent, vital music, and to share his larger vision of life that has some meaning in it. Prejudices die hard: at first, it may come as a shock to hear God's words (and those of the prophet Isaiah) assigned to a very high soprano. But only at first; then it becomes clear that voice and words arise out of and make articulate the deeper, full-voiced imagery. A visionary representation of the Unchanging in different ages and in different contexts is an undertaking to which music is well fitted, and one to which Shapey's music, with its idea of "graven" or unalterable images, is particularly well fitted. *The Covenant* is strenuous, deliberate, and emphatic, and it sounded even more so in the Juilliard performance than (to judge by a tape recording) it did at the Chicago première, for there the composer, conducting his Contemporary Chamber Players, brought more lightness and contrast to the delicato episodes and to the soprano-violin duo. The Juilliard performance was given in the school's splendid Twentieth-Century Music Series, conducted by Richard Dufallo. Gail Dobish rose to the taxing solo role with true, pure tones. Mr. Dufallo drew colorful, committed playing from his admirable young instrumentalists.

The concert began with a première, Eric Ewazen's Concerto for Percussion and Twelve Instruments, introducing a soloist, Clifton J. Hardison, who is not only a virtuoso but also something of a stage performer—a striking mime, and an actor with his instruments in the line of Stomu Yamash'ta, for whom the percussion roles in Henze's *El Cimarrón* and *Natasha Ungeheuer* were written. In Ewazen's concerto, the twelve supporting players provide what he calls "a constantly shifting sonic environment," a background for the star. I remember little about the music now (*The Covenant* drove it from my mind)—only that the work made a bright, lively start to the concert and that Mr. Hardison is someone to watch.

I missed Shapey's Twenty-one Variations. The Thirty-one ended a League-ISCM program consisting of three premières. The point of John Lessard's three Movements for Trumpet (with percussion; vibraphone; and viola, cello, and percussion) eluded me. The delicacy, wit, neatness, and pretty timbres of Lester Trimble's *Panels III*, for harp, harpsichord, percussion, and string trio, delighted me. The Shapey is a rich, thoroughly and almost ruthlessly exhaustive, imposing composition. Its theme is a chromatic chorale, dissonantly harmonized, whose emphatic final cadence—two long, loud chords, marked "majestic"—returns at the end of every variation, unvaried. Brilliantly written for the keyboard, the work was brilliantly played by Robert Black.

July 9, 1979

Unfinished or Unfinishable?

In Boston this season, Deryck Cooke's revised "performing version of the draft for the Tenth Symphony" of Gustav Mahler—Cooke was scrupulous not to call it a "completion" of the symphony—had its East Coast première, from the Boston Symphony under Niklaus Wyss. In Paris, Alban Berg's three-act opera *Lulu,* with its comparatively few missing notes supplied by Friedrich Cerha, had its world première. The Metropolitan Opera began its new production of *Don Carlos* with a Prélude et Introduction that Verdi had discarded. The Welsh National Opera produced *Madama Butterfly* in Puccini's original, emotionally harsher two-act version, not the three-act revision that everyone knows. In St. Louis, Mahler's completion of Weber's three-act opera *Die drei Pintos,* of which Weber had drafted (in musical shorthand) only an act and a bit, had its American première. At Caramoor, Respighi's *Lucrezia,* with some bars orchestrated by his widow, had its American première. Juan Allende-Blin's assemblage and scoring of scattered Debussy fragments for a *Fall of the House of Usher* opera was published by Jobert and is to be staged in Berlin in October. And the Schubert sesquicentennial observances brought "world première" performances of his unfinished Seventh Symphony, of the scherzo of his Eighth Symphony (*the* "Unfinished"), and of the B-minor adagio of his last unfinished symphony (D. 936A in the revised Deutsch catalogue). The Schubert events were "premières" in being new—although not the first—essays in giving life under the fingers and on the breaths of living players to musical ideas that Schubert had conceived and set down in draft but not worked out in full.

Such essays and reconstructions are commonly received in two contradictory ways: with, on the one hand, gratitude on the part of music lovers for the chance of hearing, even if in imperfect form, valuable and beautiful music by a master; with, on the other, a kind of indignation that anyone should have dared to prefer a master's first thoughts to his second, or have dared to speculate on instrumentation, harmony, and further notes that a master might have written, and then to bring those speculations to performance. Often it seems to be treated as a *moral* issue. Cooke considered this in a *Musical Times* article (June 1961), subtitled "Artistic Morality vs. Musical Reality"; and Susan Filler takes up the discussion in her paper entitled "Artistic Morality vs. Musical Reality—The Case for a Performing Version of Mahler's Tenth Symphony," published in the *Journal of Musicological Research* (1981). In the November 1978 issue of *19th Century Music,* there is a curiously unfriendly review, by Richard Swift, of Cooke's performing version, concerned chiefly with pointing out what Cooke had already spelled out in his preface: that "Mahler himself, in bringing [the symphony] to its final form, would have revised the draft ... have expanded, contracted, redisposed, added, or canceled." The controversy about the completion of *Lulu* is fresh. F. X. Süssmayr's completion of Mozart's Requiem and Franco Alfano's of Puccini's *Turandot* are still controversial, and if Busoni's *Doktor Faust* were performed as often as it deserved we should no doubt hear more about the presumption of his pupil Philipp Jarnach in bringing the great opera to completion.

Each work of restoration, reconstruction, or "realization" is a special case. One can try to define a few categories: operas where the composer's original ideas were compromised by singers' demands (or inadequacies), by censorship, by impresarios with one eye on the box office and the other on a stopwatch; music abandoned by its composer, such as Beethoven's opera *Vestas Feuer*, Schubert's Seventh Symphony, and the Scherzo of his Eighth; and compositions cut short by death, such as Mozart's Requiem, Meyerbeer's *L'Africaine*, Mahler's Tenth, *Doktor Faust*, *Turandot*, *Lulu*, Falla's *Atlántida*. But within those categories there is no consistency. In the first: anyone preparing a performance of *Idomeneo, Carmen, Don Carlos, Boris Godunov, War and Peace*, or Kurt Weill's *Mahagonny*—works for which there are no definitive scores—must decide if the bewildering alternatives were forced on the composer by external circumstance against his will, and which, if any, of them he may have embraced as being positive improvements. In the second: Beethoven abandoned *Vestas Feuer* after the first scene, but Schubert wrote out his Seventh Symphony from beginning to end, although only 110 of its 1,340 measures are fully scored. The reasons for the abandonment must in each case be weighed. Even in the last category, an almost mystical distinction between *das Unvollendete* and *das Unvollendbare*—the Unfinished and the Unfinishable—is sometimes made. One can feel sure that if they had lived Mahler would have finished his Tenth Symphony and Berg would have finished *Lulu*, but it seems likely that Debussy found *Usher*, and Elgar found his Third Symphony, and Falla found at any rate Part II of *Atlántida* unfinishable. Any "reconstruction" of those works will to some extent be a record of struggles, false starts, and alternative ideas and possibilities. Yet such a record may be not merely of interest for the light it throws on a composer's last years but also of inherent musical worth. Even in this confused and troubled field, a few simple generalizations are perhaps possible. Let me approach them by considering two Schubert completions so far unreviewed in these pages: the Seventh Symphony scored by Brian Newbould, which was given its first professional performance at the Cheltenham Festival last summer, by the BBC Symphony and David Atherton (a few months earlier, it had been played by the orchestra of Leeds University, where Newbould is a lecturer); and the Scherzo of the "Unfinished" scored and completed by Stephen Casale, which was given its first performance by the orchestra of New York University (where Casale is a graduate student) under Dinu Ghezzo last December.

Schubert's first six symphonies appeared at the rate of roughly one a year, between 1813 and 1818. Then in the canon there is a four-year gap, a missing number, and an astonishing stylistic stride to No. 8, the "Unfinished," of 1822. Another gap and another giant stride precede No. 9, the Great C-Major, of 1825–26. Finally, in 1828 there is the unfinished D-major Symphony, D. 936A—as great an advance on its predecessors as the "Unfinished" had been on the Rossinian No. 6, the Little C-Major; so Peter Gülke, a Dresden scholar and conductor, claimed, speaking at the Detroit Schubert congress last year, and his orchestration of the astonishing, Mahlerian adagio of D. 936A confirmed it. (Breathtaking music! An answer in itself to those who declare that a master's not fully formulated last thoughts should be left in the obscurity of library shelves and facsimile reproductions.) The first gap marks the period during which, in the words of the Schubert biographer Maurice J. E. Brown, "in his instrumental music Schubert was trying to reconcile the thought of his mature genius with the youthful language which was no longer capable of expressing it." Up to the vivacious, confident Sixth Symphony, he brought most of his works to a successful conclusion, but now unfinished and abandoned compositions grow plentiful. There are three unfinished symphonies in the gap before the "Unfinished": sketches for two D-major movements in 1818 (D. 615); sketches for all four movements of a D-major Symphony in 1821 (D. 708A); and the large-scale E-major Symphony of 1821, D. 729, which is designated No. 8 in the autograph (perhaps in one of the D-major drafts Schubert thought he had a potential No. 7) but is usually known as the Seventh Symphony. The autograph passed from Schubert's brother to Mendelssohn, to Mendelssohn's brother Paul, to Sir George Grove, and from him to the Royal College of Music in London, in whose Parry Room it can now be studied. It is not a sketch or a draft but an unfinished full score of the whole symphony. The first 110 bars (a thrilling slow introduction and a spacious exposition of the principal subject) are fully orchestrated; the rest is a "skeleton" full score of the kind Verdi scholars are familiar with: the final autograph pages arrested at a stage when only the salient features (the leading thematic lines, the start of countersubjects, accompaniment figures, and harmonies) have been filled in between the bar lines. The notes are rapidly and fluently written, with very few corrections, as if Schubert were working from a piano draft of the whole symphony. So far as I know, no other Schubert symphonic pages survive in this skeleton form, though pages of opera sketch do.

The invitation to take a copy of the piece and fill in the gaps is so attractive that it is surprising it has not been more often accepted. Mendelssohn and Sullivan contemplated completions, according to Grove. The first to achieve one was John Francis Barnett (Meyerbeer's second cousin once removed); his version was played at the Crystal Palace in 1883—the autograph was on display in the central transept—and published in piano reduction. Felix Weingartner brought out another version, in 1934; it has been both published and recorded. He scored with hindsight provided by the Great C-Major, and he "tightened" (de-Schubertized) the structure by striking out the second occurrence of parallel phrases or paragraphs. Now we have the Newbould version, which seems to me a very happy one. All Schubert's notes are there. The scoring is confident. (Some emphatic brass triplets added to the finale are surprising but convincing.) The harmonies are less richly chromatic than either Barnett's or Weingartner's. For the start of the slow movement, Schubert left only the melody, on first violins and then repeated on first flute. Newbould's very simple presentation strikes me as more Schubertian than those of Barnett and Weingartner; they filled in the pauses with moving inner parts and Franckian passing-notes. Some details may perhaps be questioned. Schubert employed the largest orchestra in any of his symphonies: double woodwinds, three trombones, and *four* horns. He wrote on fourteen-staff paper, began with the two flutes on separate staffs, and then made them share one when he brought all his horns into play at once and needed an extra staff for them. Now—or so it seems to me—when writing in just a first-flute line, Schubert consistently distinguished between implying the later addition of a second-flute part (by turning all the stems of the first flute up) and precluding one (by turning the first-flute stems down, leaving no room for a second part). Sometimes Newbould has added a second-flute line where there is no room for it in the autograph, and sometimes he has omitted one where Schubert seems deliberately to have left room for it. But no doubt he considered this and found less significance in the direction of the stems. For the rest, I wonder only whether the first two notes in measure 7 of the slow movement (which Newbould respects) are a slip of Schubert's pen, a first thought amended at each subsequent occurrence of the melody, or an inspired inconsistency.

The Schubert-Newbould Seventh is a score deserving a place in the repertory that includes Schubert's first six symphonies. (Zubin Mehta could well have included it in his Schubert symphonic survey this season.) The next year, Schubert began the "Unfinished." In the light of that masterpiece, one can understand why he left its predecessor unscored, although a few hours' work could have brought it to completion. The Seventh is an attempt to create on a new, grander, deeper symphonic scale, both structurally and instrumentally, with material that is sometimes insufficient to the purpose. The E-minor introduction is both a magnificent piece of music in its own right and a climax in Schubert's long, well-documented struggle to come to terms—his own terms—with Beethoven's genius. Sometimes it walks in footprints left by the Allegretto of Beethoven's Seventh. The main theme of the Allegro, which is somewhere between Rossini and Mendelssohn in tone (and therefore wholly Schubertian), cannot quite carry the weight it is asked to. The main theme of the finale is Beethoven's "Prometheus" or "Eroica" theme as it might have been composed in extended and buoyant form by Rossini. It was not until the Great C-Major that Schubert came to terms with both Beethoven and Rossini, but here the effortless, horizon-spanning adventures of the melody are already limitlessly exhilarating. The slow movement is beautiful. The weak movement is the scherzo and trio. Schubert experiments with phrases of irregular length, and the result limps, bumps, and stumbles. Barnett provided a crutch in the form of a strong bass counterpoint; Weingartner sustained the more awkward movements on a flow of ingenious inner parts. Newbould, probably with greater honesty, gives us Schubert's theme more or less unsupported. (There is a dissertation to be written on Schubert's slowly acquired mastery of scherzo-and-trio form.) I should add a colleague's contradictory opinion: that "the punchy scherzo . . . was splendid." I concur in the general opinion among those who heard the Cheltenham performance: that in this realization the Seventh Symphony of Schubert is well worth hearing.

Of his Eighth Symphony, Schubert drafted in piano score the first movement (presumably it began at the beginning, but the opening pages have been lost), the slow movement, the scherzo, and—melody line only—the first sixteen measures of a trio; the music peters out in mid-page. This draft (as L. Michael Griffel suggested in a *Musical Quarterly* article in 1977) may represent a *later* stage of one symphony than does the full score. The latter, in a beautifully neat hand, and with important differences from the piano-score draft, contains the first two movements and just twenty measures of the scherzo, breaking off before the last page is quite finished. The last page, detached from the rest, was identified only in 1969; before then, only nine measures of scored scherzo were known. There is no trace of a finale, unless one agrees with the suggestion that it became the B-minor entr'acte of the *Rosamunde* music—a proposition more persuasive on paper than it sounds to the ear in the concert context of an "Unfinished" thus finished. There have been at least three modern attempts to complete the scherzo-and-trio movement, and the three are so different in character as to constitute a warning against accepting *any* orchestration of a Schubert piano draft as more than "one possibility."

The conductor Denis Vaughan recorded his version in 1965 (in an RCA set of Schubert symphonies), before the final page of scored scherzo had turned up. Comparison of his orchestration of measures 10 to 20 with the original reveals both his skill and discernment and Schubert's greater skill. Vaughan's movement is fresh, very attractive, but in places too light, too thin to balance Schubert's grand fortissimo start. Gerald Abraham published another completion, in 1971. (It was recorded, with that *Rosamunde* entr'acte as finale, on an HMV record made by the Royal Liverpool Philharmonic under Charles Groves.) This is a bigger and bolder affair. So is Casale's scherzo. He has audaciously strengthened one of Schubert's cadences and devised some other deft structural changes that make admirable sense. Completing the trio is harder: there is so little to go on. Vaughan and Abraham both found the second limb—E E, C C, E E, C—dull (so do I) and rewrote the melody, without, however, improving it. Casale in a first verion of his score provided it with some interesting harmonies, but on second thought removed them. Abraham opens the trio with loud, full scoring, and ingeniously accompanies Schubert's tune with pizzicato rising scales (as if echoing in inversion the start of the slow movement). Vaughan and Casale favor a slighter, more pastoral approach. The latter's treatment, over a drone bass, recalls the trio of Schubert's Fifth Symphony. (The next person who tries his hand at the piece might like to follow that model even more closely, extending the drone device and adopting the octave-doubling of the melody.) The remainder of the trio has to be composed. Casale's version is melodically dull, harmonically shapely. Abraham's happy solution is to borrow Schubert's song "Der Leidende" (also used in the B-flat entr'acte of *Rosamunde*)—a beautiful melody, and one whose syncopations break for a while the rhythmic monotony that is the movement's main weakness.

It is, Maurice Brown said, "a dubious theory which holds that Schubert abandoned his scherzo because he sensed its inferiority and was dissatisfied with it." In the Norton critical score of the "Unfinished," Martin Chusid proposes a more elegant and precise theory: that Schubert abandoned his movement because its dependence on the trio of Beethoven's Second Symphony was becoming obtrusively apparent. "It is impossible," said Brown, "to assess from these first jottings exactly what Schubert would finally have made of them" (adding, however, that "it is not easy to see how even his alchemical powers could have transmuted" the rhythmic "stodginess"). That is true. But the more one examines these varied and skillful attempts to fashion something sensitively Schubertian from the unpromising material, the less dubious that theory becomes.

Conclusions: That Schubert set down enough of his Seventh Symphony to warrant a reconstruction for public consumption and enjoyment, even though he abandoned it. That the "Unfinished" should probably be left unfinished most of the time, even though it is interesting to hear attempted completions on special occasions. And, generally, that reconstructions are worth attempting whenever a composer has set down but not, for whatever reason, brought to completion ideas that deserve to be heard. The world would be poorer without Cooke's presentation of Mahler's draft for his Tenth Symphony; is there any Mahlerian to whom those last, deep, moving thoughts have not come as a revelation? One may criticize the details of any particular working, propose a different harmony, scoring, accompaniment, even decipherment. One can be severe about immodest or false claims. No one can assemble "Elgar's Third Symphony." But "a performing version of some stretches of music which Elgar drafted for possible use in his Third Symphony" would be worth hearing. Although a restorer's aim is to make his own work indistinguishable from the original, somewhere in his edition he should tell what he has done and what he has used. Cooke's score, published by Associated Music and Faber, is a model in this respect, but the Jobert *La Chute de la maison Usher* nowhere makes it plain that Allende-Blin has brought together two distinct stages of Debussy's elusive opera. Finally—and this is why any moral indignation seems to me misplaced—such restorations and reconstuctions do not do permanent damage to, effect no lasting changes of, the originals. It is not as though a Canova or a Henry Moore were to take a finishing chisel to one of Michelangelo's Slaves. The autographs remain.

July 16, 1979

On the French label Contrepoint there has appeared another recording (VG 409 524012) of the "Unfinished," with the trio completed—none too convincingly—by Florian Hollard and, again, the Rosamunde *entr'acte as finale. A score is published by Éditions Mario Bois. The record, made by the Radio Luxembourg Orchestra, conducted by Mr. Hollard, also contains as much of the Seventh Symphony as Schubert finished scoring.*

Summer Opera

Washington already had, in the Kennedy Center, the best cluster of performing spaces to be found south of the border or east of Adelaide: a grand but not gigantic opera house, a fine concert hall, a busy drama theatre (not one that stands empty for years), all opening onto a lofty foyer, which opens onto a terrace above the Potomac. Above them, there are galleries, three restaurants (one ambitious, one moderate, the third a swift self-service), a Musical Theatre Lab, and a rooftop terrace round the building. The American Film Institute (with its own theatre), the National Symphony, the Washington Opera, the National Opera Institute are among the tenants. And now a visitor to the Kennedy Center finds three things more: a library; a five-hundred-seat house, the Terrace Theatre, apt for plays, operas, and chamber music; and, inside that theatre, for six consecutive weeks of July and August, a resident opera company. Not everyone admires the architecture of this national palace of culture, designed by Edward Durell Stone. From afar, it can look flat and slight; the tall colonnades that case it melt into the building. But I never enter the place without a lifting of the spirits. Unlike Lincoln Center's architects, Stone achieved grandeur without heaviness. There's a playful, scenographic element amid the serious planning. Nobility and lightness combine. The grand foyer is enormous—one of the biggest rooms in the world—but it's welcoming, not pompous or overpowering. One feels happy even before the show has begun. No wonder the Kennedy Center has been a success.

The Performing Arts Library is a joint venture of the Center and the Library of Congress. It's one of the happier Johnson/Burgee designs. One end of the vast upper foyer to the Terrace Theatre and the Musical Theatre Lab has been glazed off to form an airy, inviting hall. The bookshelves are ranged like slanting theatre wings. The "set" they flank is not a possibly daunting battery of desks but something suggesting a comfortable, informal country-house library. Here are the standard encyclopedias, thematic catalogues, biographies, and studies dealing with music, theatre, dance, and film; the performing-arts periodicals; and, on temporary leave from the stacks of the

Library of Congress, scores, librettos, books related to the current Kennedy Center programs. Everything is on open shelf. It's not a lending library but a library for browsing, checking, studying, discovering more about the works one is going to hear, hearing them again (for there are also recordings and tapes). So far, the library is open until concert time only two evenings a week; other days, it's open until six. A pamphlet describes the place as "both a library in itself and a window to the largest library in the world." At a magic console, one can tap out questions to the Library of Congress computer catalogue and read the answers in letters of light. Much of the Kennedy Center's success derives from the wisdom of its executive director, Martin Feinstein, in treating his guests as intelligent, curious, and literate adults. His new library is at once a civilized, enjoyable, and useful thing in itself and, as the Librarian of Congress puts it, "an open invitation to come to the Library of Congress for more extensive scholarly study." A next move might be to put solider, less flibbertigibbety stuff into the Center's shops downstairs; before a performance of *Der Schauspieldirektor* I tried there in vain to buy a pocket score.

The Terrace Theatre, a gift of the government and the people of Japan, opened in January with an evening of Kabuki. The architect is Philip Johnson, and the acoustician is Cyril Harris. It's a valuable and agreeable rather than a visually distinguished performing place. The hall is rectangular, with a steeply raked floor that gives excellent sight lines. The stage is viewed through a set of receding wooden frames, like those of Avery Fisher Hall but trimmed with silver, not gold. The ceiling, with a zigzag profile, is rose pink. The walls, also pink, are punctuated by rows of semicylindrical silver pilasters that get fatter as, climbing the slope, they get shorter. The floor is heavily carpeted in purple tweed; the seats are amply upholstered in mauve. As in much of Johnson's recent work, tradition, decorum, and touches of vulgarity or frivolity are disconcertingly combined. The theatre has already been used, apparently with success, for plays, recitals, talks, and a critics' conference. But at its operatic baptism I wasn't altogether happy about the acoustics. Spoken lines were often unintelligible, and the singing voices lacked sheen and fullness; only the orchestra sounded really good. Although the pit, which can hold a double-wind classical orchestra, is unusually deep, the playing rose from it to fill the house. But the voices didn't fill the house in a way to set it ringing; they didn't flower. My impression was of acoustics somewhat dry, unreverberant, and unresponsive, especially to high frequencies. Perhaps the carpet should be taken up when people sing there. Perhaps theatre seats are best made of wood and wicker.

The new troupe is the Kennedy Center Summer Opera, which is presented by the Center and the Washington Opera. In the first half of its season, it is playing a double bill of Mozart's *Der Schauspieldirektor* and Weber's *Abu Hassan*, and Dominick Argento's *Postcard from Morocco*. In the second half, it will play *Christopher Columbus*, a British Bicentennial confection to Offenbach music, and Donizetti's *Il furioso all'isola di San Domingo*. The musical director of the company is John Mauceri, and its "Dramaturg" (why not "dramaturge," which has been an English term for more than a century?) is Francis Rizzo, the aristic administrator of the Washington Opera. A dramaturge needs to be something of a thaumaturge; and Mr. Rizzo and his colleagues do seem to have worked wonders in creating a fine company at a time when Glyndebourne, Santa Fe, and Aspen were already competing to engage America's brightest young singers. Summer Opera sounds and looks and feels like a real ensemble company, not an ad-hoc assemblage of singers and a pickup orchestra.

Der Schauspieldirektor (The Impresario), words by Gottlieb Stephanie, music by Mozart, is a play, introduced by an overture and closed by a musical finale, in which first two actresses and then two sopranos "audition." (Horrid verb, but apparently here to stay. Does a movie actress "vision" when taking a screen test?) The four sung items—the two display arias, a trio in which the ladies vie for top billing and a tenor tries to calm them, the finale—are clustered at the end of the show, divided by just a few lines of spoken dialogue. Stephanie's play provides both an entertaining account of the difficulties, financial and temperamental, of assembling a new troupe and something like a set of parody illustrations to a chapter of Mozart biography. The author, who had been the librettist of Die Entführung, took the title role himself. The first Constanze played one of the sopranos, and the first Belmonte the tenor. Mozart's sister-in-law Aloysia Lange, née Weber, was the other soprano. (Two years later, the divas were the Elvira and the Anna of Vienna's first Don Giovanni.) The most interesting, amusing, and satisfactory Schauspieldirektor I've seen was a full performance of the whole thing. But usually the libretto is rewritten, and it was for Washington—by Hugh Wheeler. His impresario, Cosmo Maximilian, is about to present Abu Hassan on the stage of Washington's National Theatre during the presidency of Chester A. Arthur. The impresario's assistant, an enterprising young man, fixes things so that neither prima donna is accorded the Weber role; instead, his own pretty young protégée gets her big chance (her audition piece is "Ruhe sanft," from Mozart's Zaide), and the divas must be content with small speaking roles— which they do their outrageous best to build up. All this makes for a pleasant enough morceau d'occasion, but sallies that were once specific, and that keep their savor even when audiences no longer hold the key to the comédie à clef, are replaced by generalized jokes; the jumble of periods (eighteenth-century music, nineteenth-century setting, twentieth-century humor) doesn't help the score; and the mutation of Mme. Herz—a diva whose specialty, as both her name and Mozart's music imply, is the heartfelt and pathetic—into an ice-cold Finnish battle-axe, Päivi-Tuula Paasikivi, is unstylish. (I once saw an Impresario where Mme. Herz gave a naughty, accomplished imitation of Joan Sutherland; it was at once specific, funny, and very well sung.) The dialogue could have been crisper and wittier: there were some leaden exchanges that needed the dramaturge's blue pencil, and a fair amount of undergraduate humor. But it was all well performed and well sung. Claudia Cummings was Mme. Herz. Janice Hall was Mme. Silberklang, alias, in this version, Renata Renati. Faith Esham, the third soprano, sang "Ruhe sanft" beautifully and acted her role perfectly. Jack O'Brien, directing, took things to the pale of caricature, and sometimes his actors went beyond it. But on the whole it was a cheerful and charming show, and I enjoyed it. Mr. Mauceri's conducting was expert, and so was the band.

In *Abu Hassan*, Mr. O'Brien seemed to have lost his head, his taste, and any perception of Weber's music. The plot is a trifle, an Arabian Nights anecdote, but Weber, as in his other operas, showed a miraculous power of transmuting dramatic commonplace into something emotionally penetrating and breathtakingly beautiful. He could do so while working on a spare, tiny scale, by an unusual timbre (a section of Abu Hassan's aria is accompanied by two guitars and a bassoon), a melodic inspiration (several in *Abu Hassan*), or an imaginative juxtaposition, such as Reiza's dream of freedom, "Oh, my wild, exulting soul," soaring from the quaint, stocky strains of the harem guard in the first-act finale of *Oberon*. Reiza's melody is borrowed from an early cantata, the patrol music is lifted from an illustration in an Arabian travel journal—and in combination they are magical. For moments like this, it is well worth trying to save Weber's dramaturgically clumsy late pieces. *Abu Hassan* is early, and neatly fashioned.

It goes well with *The Impresario*. Twenty-five years divide the works— Weber was born in the year, 1786, that his cousin-in-law composed *The Impresario*—but *Abu Hassan* has often, and rightly, been called Mozartian, for its grace, its refinement, its tenderness. Both pieces call for a mixed cast of singers and actors. The idea of setting the *Impresario* company to perform *Abu Hassan* was ingenious, but it was pushed far too hard. In a production of Strauss's *Ariadne auf Naxos* the Ariadne and the Bacchus don't drop out of character to remind us that they are still the ridiculous, conceited prima donna and tenor of the Prologue; but into this *Abu Hassan* the *Impresario* jokes were carried over with such gross insistence that Weber's opera all but disappeared. What should have been delicate occasional extra touches of fun became the whole point. To these larks was added a crust of cliché. The Oxford English Dictionary doesn't yet record *despina* as meaning a feather duster, but anyone who has suffered a flighty, fussy performance of *Così fan tutte* will recognize the etymology. A large despina was much brandished in this production of *Abu Hassan*. That other stale comic-opera frill, playing with a little bird in a birdcage, blotted out the tenderness of the heroine's nightingale aria. If the singers—Miss Esham, Raymond Gibbs, and Harry Dworchak—hadn't been so much occupied with tiresome, unmusical business, they would doubtless have sung better, and with greater musical insight. The main pleasure was listening to Mr. Mauceri's deft, loving treatment of the score and to the well-shaped, colorful playing.

Postcard from Morocco (which was first performed by the Center Opera of Minnesota, in 1971) was something else—a sensitive, poetic, intelligent presentation of a mysterious and beautiful work. John Donahue's libretto is a series of dreams. The action opens with seven characters, seven strangers, in the waiting room of a North African railway station. It might be the start of an Agatha Christie, but what follows is closer to the world of *Last Year at*

Marienbad and Martinů's opera *Julietta*—a drift of dreams, illusions, aspirations, anxieties, memories, sometimes funny but mostly sad. Argento's score is lyrical, various, very skillful in its transitions, its flow, and its formal structure. The work lasts ninety minutes, without intermission. There is an orchestra of eight; the writing for it and for the seven voices, solo and in ensemble, is masterly. The music, like Martinů's for *Julietta*, is eclectic—a touch of Stravinsky here, of Britten there—but the subject calls for shifts in style, and through it all sounds the composer's individual voice, emotional, melodious, and tender. Mr. Mauceri conducted. Lou Galterio directed. Zack Brown (scenery) and William Ivey Long (costumes) designed. The outstanding performers were Barbara Hocher, as the sad, dignified lady who confesses that she keeps her lover in the little box she carries with her; Dennis Bailey, as the man whom the others unkindly force to reveal the emptiness of *his* box (at the end, when the others board the train, he sails away into his dream come true); and Elaine Bonazzi, as the mousy little hatmaker who is transformed for a while into a slinky, sultry cabaret singer. But all were good and all should be mentioned; the others were Claudette Peterson, Michael Best, Wayne Turnage, and William Dansby. This was a performance where the inflection of words, the gauging of gestures, the timing of glances, the composition of the stage groups conspired with the score to hold an audience spellbound.

One hopes that in time the Kennedy Center Summer Opera will be able to drop the "Summer" from its name and play all the year round, not only in Washington. There is an immense repertory of valuable pieces, from the seventeenth to the twentieth century, waiting for it.

July 30, 1979

Conte de Fées

Festival Ottawa, held in the National Arts Center during the month of July, consists of operas and chamber music—twelve opera performances this year, eight chamber recitals, and a concert by the Scottish Chamber Orchestra. It is the formal core of a festival rather than a daylong, nightlong busy round of music, dance, plays, and other events, which so admirable and versatile a building as the Center could readily hold. The opera house, which seats twenty-three hundred, and the theatre, which seats over nine hundred, were in use, but not—at any rate, for festival purposes—the studio theatre, the salon (a dramatic hexagonal space), or the linked terraces and plateaus that roof the building and would be well suited to protest or pop or other fringe activities. My previous visit to the Ottawa Center was in 1971. I thought it a striking, handsome, picturesque, and useful building, excellently sited at the heart of the city, beside the Rideau Canal. It had interesting and beautiful interiors but was perhaps just a shade too grand in feeling. It seemed to expect you to put on a tie before you entered it. But the Center has worn well, and, like Montreal's Place des Arts, it has now relaxed. There was plenty of unembarrassed informal dress to be seen this year at the opening night of Massenet's *Cendrillon*, the major festival event. The canal-side café and the grassy park sloping down from the building to the water make it a friendly place. People arrive by boat. They sun themselves. In winter, they can skate to the shows.

Most people have mixed feelings about Massenet. A defensive note is apt to creep into the plaudits of his champions, and a conciliatory note into the strictures of his detractors. In fact, he was a more various and a more uneven composer than is often allowed. *Manon* and *Werther, Hérodiade* and *Thaïs, Esclarmonde* and *Le Cid* can hardly be lumped together, and the remark in Grove's Massenet entry that "to have heard *Manon* is to have heard the whole of him" is absurd. There are four late Massenet operas—*Cendrillon, Grisélidis, Le Jongleur de Notre-Dame,* and *Don Quichotte*—that it is easy to like without any reservations, and they do have certain things in common. For one, a lack of any conventional, soprano-tenor love interest. (The faithful Grisélidis is tempted through the wiles of a witty, dapper Devil; *Le Jongleur* has an all-male cast; Don Quixote's love for Dulcinea is pure and lofty; and that of Cinderella and her Prince takes on an idealized, innocent quality, since they are both sopranos.) For another, a baritone or basse chantante role of which Lucien Fugère was the first or the first Paris interpreter: Cinderella's father, the Devil, the monastery cook in *Le Jongleur,* Sancho Panza. (I have suggested before that the wise, genial Fugère may have tapped in Massenet a new vein of warmth, tenderness, and sincerity. Fugère made his début in 1874; the mellow des Grieux of *Le Portrait de Manon,* in 1894, was the first role Massenet wrote for him; and he lived on to make fine electrical recordings in his eighties.) Most important, these four operas are decent, mature, unlascivious, free from titillations erotic or religious, unpretentious, exquisitely worked, and high-spirited.

It is surprising that *Cendrillon* should have had to wait so long for a major revival; I suppose it has been waiting for a singer who wanted to do the principal role. Joan Sutherland brought *Esclarmonde* to San Francisco and to the Met, and *Le Roi de Lahore* to Vancouver. Beverly Sills brought *Thaïs* to San Francisco and to the Met. Grace Bumbry and Placido Domingo brought *Le Cid* to Carnegie Hall and to Hamburg. Now we have a Cinderella. Frederica von Stade was the heroine of the recording that Columbia published earlier this year, and of the Ottawa production; next month, this production, with the same cast, opens the Washington Opera season. In Massenet's score, Cinderella is described as a soprano and Prince Charming as a "Falcon ou

Soprano de sentiment." (Cornélie Falcon, a Donna Anna, the first Rachel in *La Juive* and Valentine in *Les Huguenots*, gave her name to the voice type— a dark, powerful dramatic soprano or mezzo-soprano.) In 1911–12, the Chicago Opera performed *Cendrillon* in Philadelphia, in Chicago, and at the Met with two famous Mélisandes, Maggie Teyte and Mary Garden, as Cinderella and her Prince. In Ottawa, there were two mezzo-sopranos—two Octavians, as it were: Miss von Stade and Delia Wallis. They made a beautiful pair. Miss von Stade has the smoother, creamier voice; Miss Wallis's has stronger gleams and colors in it. They were contrasted, but they also blended well. Miss von Stade's strength as an actress lies in the way she listens and responds to others. Louis Quilico, in the Fugère role, was not much of an actor, but Miss von Stade made his aria seem eloquent; and the quizzical glance she gave when her stepmother at the very end bustled forward with aplomb to have the last word—"Ma fille!! Lucette, que j'adore!"—was perfectly achieved. When she was actually singing, Miss von Stade's face and body sometimes became inexpressive; her eyes may have been alert, but poor lighting left them in shadow. Her singing itself was always expressive, clear, delicately shaped in word and in phrase. She who plays Prince Charming, Massenet further specified, should have "le physique du costume"—should look well dressed as a youth—and this Miss Wallis certainly does. She has wonderful stage eyes, cheekbones, and bearing. Teyte's Cinderella was possibly more piquant, and perhaps Garden's Prince was more flamboyant; but Miss von Stade's Cinderella was pure and beautiful and good, and utterly charming. Their mezzo timbres brought extra intensity yet no heaviness to the music.

Cinderella can be a moral tale. Commentators have traced parallels to *King Lear*, Joseph and his brethren, and other stories of sibling rivalry. Perrault, in fact, appended two morals to his telling of it: "Beauty is a treasure rare, but *bonne grâce* [charm?] is worth still more . . . for without it one can achieve nothing; with it, everything." Alternatively: "Wit, daring, birth, and good sense are useful advantages, but they won't get you anywhere unless you also have fairy godfathers or fairy godmothers to provide the chance for you to show them." The underlying moral of Rossini's *La Cenerentola*, a working from which supernatural elements were banished, is less cynical, more humane; in this version the Prince must show himself worthy of Cinderella before the happy ending can be reached. Massenet's *Cendrillon* traces no evident moral; but, on the other hand, my useful French opera guide (bearing the imprimatur of the Bishop of Paris), which assesses operas by their moral worth, assures me that "apart from an allusion to suicide and a slightly sensual dialogue for Cinderella and the Prince beneath the enchanted tree, in Act III, one can impugn no immoral intentions to this agreeable trifle." Not all Massenet's operas escape censure so lightly. *Cendrillon* is not merely decorative. There is something of Louise—a more sensible, more lovable, and, I'd even say, more realistic Louise—about the heroine. The character of her father is drawn with slight but telling strokes. He rings true. So does the aristocratic stepmother. Altogether, the balance of precise human observation, of romance, and of supernatural intervention that is scarcely more than an allegory of the turns real life can take is finely held. Not merely decorative, then; but the work is decorative, too, and as a master of the orchestra Massenet here joins hands with the Tchaikovsky of the ballets, and with Bizet and Berlioz, and he points to Ravel. *Cendrillon* combines the mature honesty of *Don Quichotte*, the tenderness of *Le Jongleur*, and the high-spirited glitter and fun of *Grisélidis*.

The Ottawa staging—scenery by Henry Bardon, costumes by Suzanne Mess—was very pretty, even beautiful, but I didn't feel it was altogether right in style. It wasn't quite elegant or quite "French" enough. It was *comfortable*—Victorian in spirit, an (admittedly exquisite) rendering of high-class British-pantomine décor. Brian Macdonald's direction was fluent but had its odd moments. Cinderella is meant to be a good, industrious, and accomplished little housekeeper—but I'd never let this one near any of my sheets or shirts after seeing what she did with the laundry on the stage. These touches matter: the charm of a fairy tale is that it springs, surprisingly and suddenly, from everyday realistic behavior accurately related. In Act II, for Cinderella's entry to the ball, Massenet takes his cue directly from Perrault:

> The king's son . . . led her into the hall where the company was. And there was a great silence. The dancing stopped, and the violins ceased to play, for everyone was rapt in contemplation of the beauties of the stranger. All that was heard was a confused murmur: "How lovely she is!"

Mr. Macdonald spoiled one of opera's great entries by starting the unaccompanied murmur before Cinderella had appeared. There was a staircase that she could have slowly descended, the cynosure of all eyes; instead, she was dragged round and round the ballroom in a carriage decked with fairy lights. In general, Mr. Macdonald's ideas of court behavior were unconvincing.

Ruth Welting sang the high-lying Fairy Godmother's music, as on the Columbia recording, with sweet, limpid charm. Maureen Forrester played the stepmother with great gusto but she overdid things; Mme. de la Haltière is an aristocrat as well as a shrew. She lost her best number: the catchiest tune in the whole opera, accompanying her Act IV aria, was omitted (except for a brief instrumental reprise in the Marche des Princesses before the final scene), and that was a pity. The stepsisters, Gabrielle Lavigne and Michèle Boucher, were an amusing pair, but they had been encouraged to clown at times. Mr. Quilico, I felt on this as on previous occasions, could be an even better Massenet singer if he would study the recordings of Fugère, Vanni-Marcoux, and Maurice Renaud, and learn from them that a smooth, subtle, telling line, built from the words, is more important than impressive sounds.

The opera house in the Center is a big hall, and the high ceiling makes it seem even bigger. The acoustics are good. One can hear what is happening. But it is not as intimate a place as the Opéra-Comique, where in 1899 *Cendrillon* was one of the earliest—and most spectacular—productions of Albert Carré's regime. Mario Bernardi conducted with a good sense of the tenderness, the romance, and the glitter. The orchestral playing is even better in the Columbia recording, conducted by Julius Rudel; but in that set Prince Charming's music is sung an octave too low, by Nicolai Gedda.

The festival had opened with *Così fan tutte*. The second production was *The Queen of Spades*, a gloss on Tchaikovsky's opera of that title, directed by Václav Kašlík and designed by Josef Svoboda. This was a revival of a 1976 show. The setting throughout was Hermann's cell in the madhouse, where Pushkin ended his tale—but not Tchaikovsky his opera. The walls became transparent, and behind them the scenes of the opera were played as a series of hallucinations. Hermann was allowed out to enter the Countess's bedroom, to join Lisa beside the Petersburg canal, to visit the gaming house. The work became a kind of monodrama for the tenor, with the other performers providing accompaniment, behind a gauze. Hermann, onstage, center stage, and acting all the time, was built into an immense role. It was played with fire and intensity by Jacque Trussel, and was strongly and cleanly sung. His timbre was not the passionate stream of honeyed sweetness that the best Russian tenors produce, but it was admirably, and at times thrillingly, forthright; each vowel (the opera was sung in English translation) was given its distinct color; everything Mr. Trussel did was alive. To this "concept" of the piece were sacrificed the picturesqueness, the charm, the contrasts, the formal structure, and the other characters of Tchaikovsky's opera. Lilian Sukis, a Canadian prima donna of the Munich Opera, made something of Lisa's two arias, even from her subordinate position. Janice Taylor's singing as Pauline was warm and beautiful. Miss Forrester held the house spellbound with the Countess's reminiscences of the old days. Her spectral reappearance to Hermann fell flat, since in this production she had been a specter all along. Allan Monk was an excellent Tomsky. The score had been cut and here and there rearranged. Franz-Paul Decker's reading of it was sensitive and dramatic. As fancy, how-can-I-make-it-other? opera productions go, this was not one of the very worst.

August 6, 1979

Music in the Mountains

This summer, I abandoned Aix for Aspen, Bayreuth for Bandelier, Munich for the Mesa Verde, and Salzburg for Santa Fe and Central City. The curtain of the Tabor Grand Opera House in Denver once depicted a Roman city in ruins and bore an epigraph from Kingsley:

So fleet the works of man, back to the earth again,
Ancient and holy things fade like a dream.

That house, which opened in 1881 with Vincent Wallace's *Maritana*, was razed fifteen years ago. But the Tabor Opera House in Leadville, a century old this year, still stands, and so does the Opera House in Central City, which opened in 1878. Santa Fe has a modern opera house, and Aspen has its modern Music Tent, hospitable to opera. All around, ancient and holy things built by Pueblo Indians and Spanish missionaries are saved from further fading by the discreet care of the National Park Service, while not-so-ancient and unholy things—the mines of the nineteenth century—go back to the earth again. Central City was once larger than Denver; now it is a village of two paved streets, with the Opera House, the splendid Teller House hotel, and three churches as its monuments, set within a hillside tracery of vanished streets and crumbling foundations. The summer visitor to New Mexico and Colorado finds operatic fire in abundance, and also chamber music—in Santa Fe, Telluride, and Aspen—and finds them amid surroundings that stir Ozymandian reflections on transitoriness and human insignificance. The Black Canyon of the Gunnison, a work of nature some two millions years in the making, seemed to me more awesome and more beautiful than any work of man. Among the mountains, it is hard to feel that man and his music are really very important. But that music must now be my concern.

There cannot be many opera companies that have staged three different productions of Alban Berg's *Lulu*, as the Santa Fe Opera has. In 1963, it gave the American première of the opera as it was then available (two acts and fragments of the third), with Joan Carroll and Donald Gramm in the leading roles, Rudolf Heinrich as designer and director, and Robert Craft as conductor. The show was revived the next year. In 1974, there was a new production, with Patricia Brooks and William Dooley, directed by Ragnar Ulfung, designed by John Scheffler and Hugh Sherrer, conducted by John Mauceri. This year at Santa Fe, the complete *Lulu*, available at long last, had its American première, with Nancy Shade and Mr. Dooley, Colin Graham as director, John Conklin as designer, and Michael Tilson Thomas as conductor. It was a performance on a high level: thoughtful, imaginative, and responsible—unlike the world première of the complete *Lulu*, in Paris earlier this year, which was grandiose and affected, musically chilly, and in its settings and actions a willful, perverse distortion of the opera that Berg composed.

The full, three-act *Lulu* is proving to be a startlingly different work from the familiar, truncated version. It is not merely that there are now two more scenes and more music. Since this tightly constructed score is balanced about the—musically palindromic—interlude at the center of the central act, since themes from the first part find their fulfillment in the second, and since Lulu's life now ends on the knife of Jack the Ripper, who is, both musically and in the person of the actor, a reincarnation of Dr. Schön, the only man Lulu has really loved, the emphases of the earlier statements are altered and their intent is differently perceived. *Lulu* is a work of puzzling complexity. I discussed its autobiographical content after the Metropolitan production, in 1977; notably, Alwa Schön, a writer in the Wedekind plays—*Earth Spirit* and *Pandora's Box*—from which Berg drew his libretto, has become a composer, and, specifically, a composer of music that Berg himself composed. It was Berg who identified the three husbands Lulu brings to their deaths with the three clients who visit her, now a syphilitic prostitute, in the London garret of the final scene. The full opera is more painful and more distasteful than the fragment. What a crew! When the ardent love music of Lulu and Dr. Schön returns with Jack the Ripper, one hardly knows who is or has been victim, who destroyer, and what to think, what to feel. The latest edition of the *Lulu* libretto contains a synopsis that begins, "Lulu represents the sexual fascination of Woman." If she is an Earth Spirit, she is also Pandora's Box, source of evils that destroy those who come into contact with her—except (and what significance should be read into this?) her first and last lovers, the mysterious old tramp Schigolch and Jack, the only principals left alive at the end. Should one draw the moral that sexual attraction degrades both those who surrender to and those who exert it? In the two new scenes, one is invited to witness the final stages of that degradation. The Countess Geschwitz, sometimes held up as a paragon of loving self-sacrifice, has been brought very low by her infatuation. Her realization of her state, and her repentance—"This is the last evening I'll spend with these people. I'll go back to Germany. I'll enroll at a university. I must fight for women's rights, study jurisprudence"—come too late. The next moment, Jack is upon her. Wedekind's plays contain comic-strip and French-farce ingredients (in the first scene of Act II, where Lulu's admirers conceal themselves in every cranny of the room; in the first scene of Act III, with its whirl of near-caricature characters) and speeches that are deliberately ridiculous. Berg retained some but not all of them, and he altered Wedekind's tone, making explicit and eloquent the latent pathos, lyricism, and compassion. In Wedekind, Alwa's hymning of Lulu's body, after her escape from prison, reads like a parody:

> Through this dress, I feel your form like a symphony. This slender ankle, this cantabile; this enchanting roundness; and this knee, this capriccio; and then the powerful andante of voluptuousness.

Berg, who changed the lines to bring the musical directions closer to those of his own Lyric Suite, set them to glowing and utterly earnest love music. *Lulu* the opera is as different in tone from its original as Tchaikovsky's *Eugene Onegin* is from Pushkin's. Typically, Berg removed Wedekind's very last words—Geschwitz's "Oh, damn!" when her arms give way while she is crawling toward Lulu—and ended instead with her almost effusive outpouring "Lulu! My angel! Let me see you once again! I am near you, remain near you—for evermore!" But he did keep some of the grim jokes, such as Jack's irritated "These people never have a towel handy" after he's washed his bloodstained hands. Besides imposing new dramatic symmetries on Wedekind, Berg prescribed the speeds of the drama and used the power of music to create contradictions: in the final scene, while events move more and more swiftly, the tempo grows slower and slower. Other tensions are set up between Wedekind's terse, unsentimental text and Berg's generously emotional music, and by his employment of strict forms—sonata, canon, variations— embedded within a score that apparently responds quite freely to the flow of the drama.

The Santa Fe production held all these elements—tragic, farcical, sentimental, rhetorical, laconic—in balance, without distortion or overemphasis of any one of them. In a program note, Mr. Conklin and Mr. Graham disclosed that the late Mr. Heinrich's 1963 designs had been "the imaginative springboard for our approach." The date of the action is neither specified nor easily deducible. Berg omitted Lulu's remark about driving over "the new bridge" at a trot but retained references to revolution's breaking out in Paris (presumably the 1871 Commune) and to the great cholera epidemic in Hamburg (1892), and introduced a telephone. Jack the Ripper was active in 1888–89. The ragtime music and the backstage jazz band of the third scene point to a later date for the opera, and the Santa Fe setting "in Berlin, Paris, and London early in the twentieth century" proved very satisfactory. *Lulu* is an allegory of human behavior (in an extreme form), not a precise period piece, and its chronological contradictions need not be resolved. On the other hand, it does have roots in the fevered, emotionally messy world of Freud's Vienna, and so Mr. Conklin's Jugendstil interiors for the earlier scenes were appropriate. They also looked good. Containing them was a tall outer set built as if from clinker or charcoal, veined with silver. It was of an interesting texture (not the dreary black drapes that have become a designer's cliché for so many contemporary productions), it provided continuity without monotony, and it hinted at the mutually reflecting images and large formal integrity of the drama without heavily underlining them. Some earlier *Lulu* productions—Günther Rennert's in Hamburg and Cologne, Wieland Wagner's in Stuttgart—were set in a circus ring, and that proved unhelpful, apter for Wedekind than for Berg. This décor seemed just right. Mr. Graham's direction was similarly distinguished. Most of the characterizations were firm and consistent, and behavior was credible, but at the same time the inner surrealistic pattern of the drama was subtly revealed. Once again—as in memorable productions of Prokofiev's *War and Peace* and Janáček's *From the House of the Dead*—Mr. Graham showed himself a director who can read a score and perceive what a composer is up to, who can embody in his staging the long line of a music-drama without neglecting or falsifying details on the simple representational level. Bergian purists might object that once or twice, and especially in the final scene, he employed stage directions from Wedekind that the composer had not taken over, but none of these, so far as I could see, did any harm. There was certainly none of the presumptuous, egocentric contradiction of the author's clear intentions which disfigured the Paris *Lulu*. Mr. Thomas's conducting revealed the same happy combination of large-scale understanding with lively incidental action. The emotional tone was warm without being cloying. The orchestral playing was vivid—rich in timbre yet clean of line.

Not everything about the show was right. Berg's protagonist needs the sort of voice that Margarethe Siems must have had (Siems was Strauss's first Chrysothemis, Marschallin, and Zerbinetta, and also a Lucia, Queen of Night, and Aida), together with uncommon looks, allure, and projection. None of the Lulus of my experience—among the best of them Helga Pilarczyk, Evelyn Lear, Anja Silja, Carole Farley—has managed everything. Miss Silja, thirteen years ago, for Wieland Wagner, was probably the most convincing. Her voice was far from ideally limpid and pure (though better than in the recent London recording of the opera), but she had vitality, vigor, sex appeal, and a kind of candid, natural confidence that proved irresistible. Miss Shade, the Santa Fe heroine, was among the least satisfactory. I can't be very severe about her, for there is something very likable, something disarming, about her stage personality, but it must be said that upper notes that should have been sweet and true were strained and harsh, and that dramatically her portrayal was all over the place. For the crucial speech to Dr. Schön in Act I, Scene 2—"If I belong to one man in this world, then I belong to you. Without you I should be—I will not say where," etc.—Miss Shade pulled out a stagy, throbbing, and wholly artificial-sounding speaking voice. Sometimes she pouted and primped, or flounced. Sometimes she was a campus tomboy. Sometimes she seemed to be essaying a Louise Brooks imitation. She missed altogether naturalness, candor, straightforwardness. And while it is true that each of the men, and also the woman, with whom Lulu is involved finds something different in her, that is his or her affair; except when deliberately lying (as she does, odiously, to the Countess Geschwitz in the first scene of Act III), Lulu must be always true to herself, devastatingly direct and honest, not a mass of assorted theatrical affectations.

Dr. Schön is a rewarding role. Mr. Gramm in the Met production was wonderfully human and believable. Franz Mazura in the Paris production was admirably incisive. Mr. Dooley in Santa Fe was most trenchantly the tiger described in the prologue to Berg's opera—"the tiger whose habit it is to strike down whatever might hinder him in his leap." He achieved this partly by musical accuracy and rhythmic verve. The Monoritmica, in which Schön lays waste the fool's paradise inhabited by Lulu's second husband, was rapped out with uncommon precision. Or so it seemed; one will be able to check the impression by listening, score in hand, to the Santa Fe performance, which was recorded by the BBC and will be transmitted this fall throughout Britain and by some American stations. Mr. Dooley also made the words tell. A Berlin-based artist, he is accustomed to communicate with audiences who attend to the detailed sense, and not just to the sounds, of an opera. In Santa Fe, *Lulu* was sung in Arthur Jacobs's skillful English translation. And of course the opera should be done in English when an English-speaking cast performs to an English-speaking audience. But several of the artists used their own language unfeelingly, failed to time and weight the musical phrases in a way to make the words sound natural. Mr. Dooley provided a model of just, eloquent inflection. Everything he sang came to life. And he enacted a Schön so ruthless, so formidable, and, except in his dealings with Lulu, so confident that it was easy to understand why Lulu's life became meaningless without him.

Barry Busse, in the romantic tenor role of Alwa, was disappointing. Although he sang with intelligence and intensity, there was little tone, and his arias—the hymn to Lulu's beauty, the pages that introduce the quartet of the last scene—lacked lyricism. Both he and Leo Goeke, as the Painter, sounded a shade too careful. I heard the first performance; both of them may later, with increasing confidence, have become more expressive. *Lulu* is an opera that singers need to get into. Lenus Carlson, the Acrobat of the Met production, was an even better, subtler Acrobat in Santa Fe, and the Schigolch of Andrew Foldi, whose ninth *Lulu* production this was, was masterly. Katherine Ciesinski's Geschwitz was dignified, vulnerable, beautifully judged, and admirably sung, without gush. Joseph Frank's Procurer, a key figure in the first scene of Act III, was expertly done.

The other opera I saw in Santa Fe was *The Magic Flute*, in a new production, directed by Peter Wood and designed by Sam Kirkpatrick. It was not good. The designs, based on Persian rather than Egyptian motifs, were flimsy and ugly. Two bad ideas marked the staging. One was to turn the band of initiates into a stern Muslim society, Sarastro its ayatollah, where animals and women were badly treated. (Sarastro's lions were cruelly lashed, and Pamina was made to sing "Ach, ich fühl's" before the assembled male chorus, watching her discomfiture.) The other was to introduce a Storyteller, who sometimes described the scenery, sometimes verbalized what was being enacted, and sometimes interjected things like "said Tamino" and "answered Papageno" into the spoken dialogue. Blind members of the audience may have found his contributions helpful. "Bei Männern" became balancing tricks with a trestle; the Queen of Night's second aria became Pamina's dream. Isobel Buchanan's Pamina lacked color and personality. David Kuebler's Tamino was stiffly phrased. Stephen Dickson turned the robust Papageno into a fey, pretty youth. "Unhurried" and "affectionate" are kind words for Raymond Leppard's conducting; "slow" and "soggy" were others that crossed my mind. The English translation, credited to Ruth and Thomas Martin, was a mishmash containing much that the Martins would not recognize. Tinkering with the sequence of numbers in Act II of *The Magic Flute* (Nos. 9 to 21 of the score) is not uncommon, and perhaps Mozart's order need not be held inviolable, but the Santa Fe shuffling—if I remember rightly, Nos. 9, 10, 9 again, 11, 12, 16, 19, 13, 14, 18, 17, 20, 15, 21—went altogether too far.

August 20, 1979

Singtime in the Rockies

It is good to tread with one's own feet scenes where history, art, and the larger imaginative world that makes endurable the real world were created. The *Iliad* becomes more vivid in Troy, and the *Hippolytus* in Troezen. (When I first approached that place, there were women dipping clothes in the swift stream and spreading them on the rocks to dry—as if they knew Euripides' first chorus.) Thucydides comes to life with especial quickness if one reads him in Pylos and in Syracuse, eyes lifting from the page to measure the action. To hear *The Ring* aright, one must know the Rhine. On a humbler level, Adolf Bandelier's slow, heavy novel *The Delight Makers* is lightened by memories of the beautiful Frijoles canyon in which it is set. Willa Cather's *Death Comes for the Archbishop* means more to a reader who has trodden the Santa Fe country so feelingly described. And it is not just a matter of topography and associations, peak and plain, sky and water, and of discovering an original scale with one's own senses. The true sound of *Parsifal* can be heard only in the Bayreuth Festival Theatre (and not even there when Pierre Boulez conducts it). On a simple, practical level, an opera historian needs to discover the sound and size, and feel the feel, of the theatres he is concerned with.

Earlier this month, I was in Colorado, where about a hundred years ago Aspen, Central City, Colorado Springs, Cripple Creek, Denver, Fairplay, Leadville, Pueblo, and other towns all built substantial opera houses, and I visited some of those that still stand. It brought vividness to the accounts of the great American touring companies of the nineteenth century organized by Clara Louise Kellogg, Emma Abbott, Emma Juch. It was exciting to see other settings in which those stars of London and New York once shone. The annals of non-metropolitan American opera in the last decades of the nineteenth century are scanty; from memoirs, biographies, local histories, and a few articles one can pick up some facts and form a general picture. I hope that someone, somewhere, is working on a detailed history of those decades when not just the old favorites but also modern operas were played throughout this country by famous singers. Sadie E. Martin's *The Life and Professional Career of Emma Abbott*, published in Minneapolis in 1891, is one of the more charming of prima donna biographies (a contents page with entries like "A Touching Incident in Washington, Never Before Published" and "Mr. Wetherell [Emma's husband] Pronounces Tights All Right If Modestly Worn" is a collector's item in itself), but it is short on dates and hard facts, and it shuns lists. One learns that during the thirteen years of its existence the Abbott English Grand Opera Company "opened thirty-five beautiful opera houses, and temples devoted to Music and the Drama," but only five are mentioned: houses in Waterloo, Iowa, in Springfield, Ohio, and somewhere in Virginia; the Metropolitan Theatre in Grand Forks, North Dakota; and the New Grand Opera in Ogden City, Utah. The Abbott company also opened the Tabor Grand Opera House in Denver, in 1881, with *Maritana* (followed, it seems, by *La traviata, Faust, Romeo and Juliet,* and *Il trovatore*), and the next year it played the first operas—six of them—heard in Leadville's Tabor Opera House. (Later that year, Oscar Wilde lectured from its stage to the Leadville miners on "The Practical Application of the Aesthetic Theory to Exterior and Interior House Decoration, with Observations on Dress and Personal Ornament.") Emma Abbott, a Marchesi pupil, had made her Covent Garden début in 1876, her New York début the next year. When she took *Anna Bolena* into her company's repertory, she went to Paris to be dressed for the title role by Worth, after historical models, and coached in it by Anne Lagrange (New York's first Violetta) for "dramatical vocalization" and by Sarah Bernhardt for "musical tragedy." Emma Juch, whose Grand Opera Company opened the Denver Broadway in 1890 with *Carmen,* had made her London and New York débuts in 1881.

Today, things are different. There is still opera in the Rocky Mountains, but it is the audiences who travel, to hear the work of troupes who have assembled for summer seasons in Aspen, Central City, Colorado Springs, and Santa Fe. In July and August, Central City becomes an opera town. The Central City Opera House Association not only runs the Opera House, built in 1878, but also owns the Teller House hotel, next door, with its opulent Victorian public rooms; the Assay Office; the Chain O' Mines Hotel; the Williams Stables, now fitted up as two workshop theatres; and clusters of pretty Victorian houses for artists and guests to stay in—most of the town's principal street, in fact, and a gold mine, too. The modern seasons of opera and drama began in 1932, with Lillian Gish in *Camille.* The next year, it was *The Merry Widow,* with Gladys Swarthout and Richard Bonelli. One Saturday and Sunday this year, there were eight operas to be heard—four of them full-scale productions in the Opera House, three of them workshop presentations in the Stables, and one a barroom opera. Many celebrated American singers—Eleanor Steber, Regina Resnik, Sherrill Milnes, Cornell MacNeil—have made youthful appearances in Central City. Beverly Sills sang Aida there in 1960. Some of the young artists I heard there this year are likely to become celebrated. Everything I went to was well attended. Presumably, most of the audience came over from Denver. The Opera House holds about eight hundred people. The Chain O' Mines has only nineteen rooms, and the bedroom floors of the Teller House await restoration. (I hope its elegant architecture won't be spoiled—as many fine Victorian hotels in Britain have been—by the insertion of modern bathrooms. A walk down the corridor is a small price to pay for a bedroom of noble, regular proportions.)

After some years in the dumps, the Central City season, now directed by Robert Darling, is a mixture of consolidation and adventure. Last year, there was Balfe's *The Bohemian Girl*—a nostalgic revival of an opera done by Central City miners in 1877. (The performance, with Leigh Munro and Vinson Cole, was broadcast last week by WNYC.) The two main productions this year were of bread-and-butter operas, *The Merry Widow* and *The Barber of Seville*. Adventure was provided by the apprentice artists, active in the smaller roles of those shows and otherwise engaged in a daylong round of training sessions, rehearsals, public workshop presentations, recitals, and chamber operas—and then in what seemed pretty well nightlong informal recitals in the Teller House opera bar. The most interesting events I heard were three. One was a workshop revival, piano accompanied and in simple settings, of Charles Wakefield Cadman's *Shanewis*. *Shanewis*, first performed by the Metropolitan in 1918, with Sophie Braslau in the title role, was one of the more successful of Gatti-Casazza's American operas. It was revived at the Met, and taken up in Chicago, Denver, San Francisco, Los Angeles, Johnstown, Pennsylvania, and by NBC. Cadman is known to record collectors as the composer of the songs "At Dawning" (sung by John McCormack) and "From the Land of the Sky-Blue Water" (sung by Lillian Nordica and by Alma Gluck). Lately, I've seen him slighted as a slick popularizer of Indian motifs. Ethnomusicologists may flinch from his music, but I find it enjoyable. The heroine of *Shanewis* is "a native forest bird born of our mighty wilderness" who has been discovered and taken up by Mrs. J. Asher Everton, "a prominent California club-woman." At a musicale given by Mrs. Everton, Shanewis sings "a strange primeval song of ancient intervals" and captures the heart of Lionel Rhodes, a wealthy young architect who is engaged to Mrs. Everton's daughter Amy, fresh from Vassar and a European trip. In Act II, set on an Oklahoma reservation, Mrs. Everton and Amy arrive to reclaim Lionel, and Shanewis, who has not hitherto known of his engagement, relinquishes him. But Philip Harjo, Shanewis's fierce foster brother, shoots a poisoned arrow into the heart of the fickle white man. The sketch of the story was given to the librettist, Nelle Richmond Eberhart, by Tsianina Redfeather, of the Creek tribe, and at a Denver performance in 1924 Princess Tsianina sang the title role and Cadman conducted. It's as good a plot as that of *Butterfly*, and occasionally it touches, albeit conventionally, on deeper things, as in Shanewis's principal aria:

> *For half a thousand years*
> *Your race has cheated mine . . .*
> *With one hand you gave—niggardly,*
> *With the other took away—greedily!*
> *The lovely hunting grounds of my fathers*
> *You have made your own;*
> *The bison and the elk have disappeared before you,*
> *The giants of the forest are no more,*
> *Your ships infest our rivers,*
> *Your cities mar our hills.*
> *What gave you in return?*

The music, after some rather awkward recitative has been got out of the way, proves to be tunefully Puccinian, with an occasional hint of Griegian exoticism. It flows, it sounds fresh, and it is affecting. Cadman himself remarked that he "felt that Bizet, Gounod, Verdi, and Puccini were models worth taking." After the Met première, W. J. Henderson (in the *Sun*) praised the composer's command of operatic technique, his good declamation, his fluent and melodious invention, his skillful writing for the voices, and his colorful yet transparent orchestration. The last could not be judged in Central City; the other virtues were apparent. With some discreet retouching of Mrs. Eberhart's libretto (lines like Lionel's "Women never understand" might get a laugh), *Shanewis* could, I think, easily bear a full professional revival. In the title role, Stephanie Friede, a high mezzo with a dark, appealing timbre, a smooth line, and a natural intensity of manner, sounded like a very young Frederica von Stade.

The central act of Conrad Susa's *Black River*, an opera that has already been produced in Minneapolis and in Carmel, is an extended *scena con pertichini* (others who put in remarks) for Pauline L'Allemand, the American diva, another pupil of Mme. Lagrange. She was New York's first Lakmé, in 1886, and later a prima donna of Theodore Thomas's traveling National Opera Company (whose showpiece was Rubinstein's *Nero*, with Emma Juch as Chrysa and Pauline L'Allemand as Lupus). Pauline, it seems, had a colorful career, and in this scena, set in a room of the Wisconsin State Mental Hospital, she relives it in a series of fantasy episodes. The complete opera, subtitled "A Wisconsin Idyll," is based on the plights of three lonely women, the two others being the wife of the judge who committed Pauline, and the judge's young, widowed daughter. The libretto, by Richard Street and the composer, is ambitiously and imaginatively made and reads well. I look forward to hearing the whole opera, for Susa's music in Act II displays the flair, liveliness, neatness, and wit that distinguished his first opera, *Transformations*, and it is also moving. Barbara Brandt, prima donna of the Minnesota Opera, gave a gleaming performance. Susa is still working at details of his opera; the show was part of Central City's excellent scheme for allowing composers—and directors and performers—to try things "live," before an audience, without the expense and paraphernalia of a full-scale production.

Third, there was Henry Mollicone's *The Face on the Barroom Floor*, commissioned by Central City, first performed last year, and revived this year with something like a cult success. It is based freely on the ballad by H. Antoine D'Arcy (" 'Twas a balmy summer evening, and a goodly crowd was there"), and is played in the Teller House bar where that face—a piece of post factum local color, suggested by the ballad, not the source of it—is painted. The opera is a work for three singers—soprano, tenor, and baritone—and an accompaniment of piano, flute, and cello. Two young people drop into the bar, and the barman starts telling them the story of the face on the floor; they pass into playing the characters of the tale, and then back to the present for a sequel with its own tragic climax. The drama is predictable but strangely powerful; the audience is gripped. I found it even more gripping a second time round. (A strong play—*Oedipus Rex*, for example—becomes even stronger when one knows, long before the characters themselves do, exactly what is going to happen to them.) It is a very skillful score, with a very skillful libretto, by John S. Bowman, and Mr. Darling's direction was expert. Two admirable young casts—Shauna Holiman, Tim Campbell, and Scott Neumann; Leanne McGiffin, Gary Jordan, and Kenneth Hamilton—found different emphases in their double roles. *The Face,* which lasts about half an hour, has already been taken up elsewhere. It's a good piece.

Garland Anderson's *Soyazhe,* a new one-act opera on an Indian subject, which was played in the Opera House on a double bill with Menotti's *The Medium,* I thought rather dull; the heroine's main aria was declaimed on a monotone. An act of Richard Cumming's *The Picnic,* given a workshop production, I thought conventional. *The Merry Widow* was much as usual—has there been a stylish, elegant production in our day?—except that, for once, it looked pretty, in Art Nouveau designs by John Conklin. H. Wesley Balk had staged *The Barber* as if he thought it a lame opera needing a good deal of help from the director if it was to get by. "Ecco ridente" was a pantomime septet accompanied by the tenor. "Largo al factotum" was a busy crowd scene. Rosina had to share "Una voce poco fa" with Dr. Bartolo and the two servants. Evelyn Petros, the Rosina, was attractive; here is a mezzo made for Rossini—Rosina, Cenerentola, Isolier, and, in time, Isabella—for her voice is dark yet lustrous, fluent and captivating in the way it moves, a delight to listen to. The way she began her verse of "Fredda ed immobile" sent a thrill of pleasure through me. How she continued it I don't know, for Mr. Balk had prescribed some horseplay for Don Basilio and Dr. Bartolo, and the house rang with guffaws. Rossini and his singers were not well served.

Outstanding among the band of apprentice artists was Thomas Woodman, a twenty-one-year-old baritone, a student at the Hartt College of Music. I heard him in several of the shows and in several exuberant late-night arias. If all goes well—and there seems to be no reason why it shouldn't, for nature has given him an uncommonly powerful and beautiful voice, a frame to support it, energy, and nice musical instincts—he is set to be the next in the great line of big American baritones.

August 27, 1979

Escape

Peter Schat's second opera, *Houdini,* appeared at the Theater Carré in Amsterdam in September of 1977 (a remarkable year for Dutch opera: before *Houdini,* Hans Kox's *Dorian Gray* had been revived, and Jan van Vlijmen's and Reinbert de Leeuw's *Axel* had been brought out at the Holland Festival). The Amsterdam performance reached this country on record, on the Composers' Voice label of Donemus, the publicly funded publishing house and library of Dutch contemporary music. Then the American première of *Houdini* was given at the Aspen Music Festival, early last month. The result was somewhat confused, musically, scenically, and dramatically. With the help of the score (also published by Donemus), the libretto, which is by the English poet and playwright Adrian Mitchell, and the records, I have been trying to discover what sort of piece *Houdini* really is, what its creators' aims were, and whether a strong production could reveal them. The Dutch staging, directed by Donya Feuer, was described in the press as "ineffectual and sometimes decidedly chaotic," and much the same could be said of Aspen's, directed by Ian Strasfogel.

Schat, one of Aspen's two composers-in-residence this year, was born in 1935. His first opera, *Labyrinth* (1966), subtitled "An Opera of Sorts," uses singers, actors, tapes, and film. Three years later, he contributed to *Reconstruction,* a collaborative "morality" about Che Guevara created for the Holland Festival by a group of progressive Dutch composers and writers. Schat's work of the seventies has been characterized by, on the one hand, a growing social conscience, manifested in settings of Mitchell and Pablo Neruda, and, on the other, a rebellion against the music of our day made by processes described in the jargon of engineering: permutation, interpolation, superposition, phase, etc. In a 1976 essay, Schat links the manipulation of people out of city hearts into neatly planned dormitory suburbs and the manipulation of pitches (and of durations, dynamics, timbres) into neatly planned series. He tells how he yelled into the microphone of a "music"-making computer, "Can you sing, can you make a melody?" It couldn't. And writes with scorn of "hundreds and thousands of calculation scores . . . scores full of dead voices—for what each musician was given to play could not by any stretch of the imagination be called pleasant." But their day, he suggests, is coming to an end:

> The 1970s are characterized by a mass apostasy from optimistic faith in the Triumph of Technique. The victory of the Vietnamese farmers over American super-technology, the energy crisis, the destruction of the en-

vironment or of the Nieuwmarkt [an old quarter of Amsterdam razed to make way for a subway] are all events that have shaken this glib faith.

But what now? Must we do without technique, electronic or otherwise, in music? Drop out, back to nature, back to the Tonic, whether attired in the new clothes of the emperors of American minimal mood music or not? Or push on toward that other modish stultification of musical communication, toward the mystical music of Karlheinz Karma Stockhausen?

None of those, Schat replies. "What we must do is employ a homeopathic principle, combat the disease with its own cause, conquer technocracy by technique—a made-to-measure, human, anarchistic technique, a technique that answers instead of astounding." And a first step, he proposes, might be to look again at Schoenberg's "method of composing with twelve notes related only one to another" paying special attention to the "love relationships between the notes" and forgetting the numeration from one to twelve which turned notes into fodder for machinelike processing. And so Schat's latest scores are marked by a careful, loving concern for the effect—the audible and emotional effect—of intervals and of the harmonic tensions they create. The finest of these scores, I think, is his First Symphony, a substantial four-movement work in classical forms. It was commissioned by the city of Amsterdam for the ninetieth anniversary of its Concertgebouw Orchestra. Colin Davis conducted the first performance last year, and it is recorded on the Composers' Voice label.

Schat's musical ideas are most easily followed in straight concert music; in *Houdini* a good deal else must be followed at the same time. The opera is at once a music-theatre biography of the great "escapologist," an unreticent, unabashed paean to a son's love for his mother, a myth or ritual of imprisonment and escape directed toward a final uplifting exhortation, and, not least, a "circus opera" in which turn follows turn with the immediacy, zest, and swift pace of a popular entertainment. Schat was drawn to the subject, he says in a program note, by seeing the BBC television feature "Houdini: The Man Who Made the Impossible Possible":

> Not only did this extraordinary man fascinate me by his art and unique skill, but I also found in his life the myth of Orpheus, his journey into Hades, Orpheus being the mythological Prince of Music, whose art carried him over the River of Death. Did not Houdini try the same, desperately searching for his mother?

Mitchell, invited to write the libretto, accepted enthusiastically. In his note on the piece, he says, "Everyone is on the side of the escapologist. He defies our fears of helplessness, darkness, drowning, strangulation, heights, prison, death, and the unknown. Everybody's heart lifts when Samson or King Kong bursts his chains." The dedication of the opera, "For my mother," he continues, is "a simple thank offering" made by both the composer and the librettist, adding, in his blunt way, that "Houdini doesn't want to go to bed with Cecilia—Freud is up a gum-tree with Jehovah." In several scenes, Houdini puts his head to his mother's breast, saying, "Let me hear your heartbeat." Marimba and pizzicato basses bump out a tritone—until the scene where Cecilia lies on her bier and there is silence. One scene is devoted to Houdini's letter to the safety department of the Bureau of Coal Mines, proposing that miners should be taught his methods of survival when air is limited. Some scenes are devoted to Houdini and spiritualism: his exposure of mediums' frauds, the séances held after his death because of his promise to his wife that he would return if he could. He did not return: the contriver of so many death-defying escapes could not escape death itself. But in the opera he then reappears to lead the full company in a "mass-escape finale," an affirmative hymn:

> Let the people of the world
> Shake off their chains . . .
> There is no heaven but the Earth.
> There is no heaven but the People.

In the production, screens that had been showing manacled hands were reversed, to depict a frieze of hands set free.

Schat began the composition in 1974, and so the Houdini episodes of E. L. Doctorow's *Ragtime*, published the following year, could not have been an influence. But passages in that novel chime with the opera: "He was passionately in love with his ancient mother. . . . In fact Sigmund Freud had just arrived in America to give a series of lectures . . . and so Houdini was destined to be, with Al Jolson, the last of the great shameless mother lovers." And "Every feat enacted Houdini's desire for his dead mother. He was buried and reborn, buried and reborn." And "Houdini never developed what we think of as a political consciousness. He could not reason from his own hurt feelings. To the end he would be almost totally unaware of the design of his career, the great map of revolution laid out by his life." Mitchell and Schat sought to trace at any rate the outline of that revolutionary map. But Houdini's career is an awkward epitome of universal emanicpation, for several reasons. His aim was to be different from and to astound the multitude, not to suggest that everyone could escape from handcuffs, from imprisonment, as easily as he did. Mere illusions of achieving the impossible won't get suffering mankind very far. And, as Houdini says in the opera to the mediums who claim supernatural agency in their feats, "My tricks are simply tricks which call/For skill, strength, and imagination." When anyone learned to duplicate one of his specialties, he went on to devise a new one. So the political statement at the ending of the opera seems abrupt, imposed, a non sequitur. The only part of it that makes connected sense is the negation of an afterlife: "There is no heaven but the People." And that follows not from Houdini's obsession with spiritualism but from his widow's decision to abandon the annual séances.

The Theater Carré is a circus building. (Houdini himself appeared there in 1903—the bill is reproduced in the libretto—as part of a show that included a hundred and fifty equine and two hundred and fifty human performers.) It lends itself to large-scale music productions in which the traditional patterns of opera house presentation are broken and thrown into question. The closest American equivalent to its audience is probably that which packed the Met for the Robert Wilson–Philip Glass *Einstein on the Beach*, in 1976. In America, government, state, and city do not as a rule commission and then underwrite the performance of large-scale works sharply critical of government, state, city, and their social and artistic systems, whereas in West Germany, Italy, Britain, and Holland the practice is common. The Amsterdam audiences could approach *Houdini* as the latest in a line of socially committed works in which hallowed institutions are critically examined. But the Aspen audiences came to *Houdini* cold, unprepared by any such context, and not called upon to take sides in any national debate on what music or opera should be or do. So the work had to stand or fall on its intrinsic merits. That may not be a bad thing. Yet one should always bear in mind that connections, continuity—watching a composer, a concept, an ensemble, or a company grow from year to year—can invest an individual work of art, quite legitimately, with an interest not entered on international or eternal balance sheets. A piece with considerable local currency may still have small credit on its travels. The most important works and the most important performers become international. Radio, records, tapes, scores do something to propagate those less important. But a music critic—for that matter, any music lover of more than narrowly specialist appetite, anyone who feels himself to be living both passionately in the present and as an ephemeral speck on history's stream—tries to balance the local with the universal, the topical with the timeless, the great performers with the mildly meritorious. On the simplest level, it may come to a decision between going to hear Horowitz or Karajan at Carnegie Hall and supporting the local choir at its recital in the church hall down the road.

I'm glad Aspen decided to do *Houdini*. But I think that I, and most of the audience, got less out of it, or found less in it, than European audiences did. We couldn't make all the connections. But it was good to hear what Schat, a leading musician of our day by any standards, has lately been up to, and to attend a kind of music-drama seldom encountered in America. So far as I know, there's been only one American opera—Leon Kirchner's *Lily*, done by the New York City Opera—that deals seriously with America's intervention in Vietnam.

Houdini has five acts, entitled "Birth," "Love," "Fame," "Death," and "Heaven," and seventeen short scenes. There is about a hundred and fifteen minutes of music. The libretto and score specify two intermissions, after "Fame" and after "Death"; Aspen observed only the first, which comes about halfway. Schat wrote for large forces; the Concertgebouw Orchestra, the Netherlands Opera Chorus, the Amsterdam Electric Circus, the Electric Psaltery Quintet, the Studio Silver Strings, and the Circle Ensemble (a steel band) took part in the Amsterdam première. Photographs reproduced in the Donemus magazine *Key Notes* show that the instrumentalists ringed the stage—a large platform made of an inclined square leading into a flat one pouring out into the Carré arena. In the Aspen Music Tent, the same general disposition was followed, and the Dutch designs (set by Floris Guntenaar, costumes by Leonie Polak) were used again. But there is less room in the tent, and Mr. Strasfogel had devised a production so ambitious and complicated that by the young performers and stage crew it was not efficiently executed. One unhappy feature of the Amsterdam show was carried over: a change of floor cloths before almost every scene. The cloths were nice to look at, but any one of them left in position might have served the opera better than all the changing. In Amsterdam, the device was found fidgety; in Aspen, it created awkward silences between episodes planned to proceed without interruption, marked "attacca" in the score. The flow was broken, the opera lamed. In general, the production seemed to me to lack sharp focus. Beneath the confusion, there may have been some good ideas—Mr. Strasfogel's ideas are often better than his execution—but of all the opera's themes the only one to emerge clearly was Houdini's obsessive filial love.

This circus opera opens with Houdini's Straitjacket Escape, performed—during the overture—by an escapologist dangling upside down high above the stage. Various other Houdini stunts are enacted during the work, ranging from simple conjuring tricks to an escape from a locked box and, as a climax, the famous Water Can Escape. (This is specified in the libretto, and at Aspen Houdini's own water can was used for it; in Amsterdam, the more spectacular Water Torture Cell Escape, which Houdini invented when trick water cans became a mail-order item, was chosen.) The role of Houdini is shared by a tenor, who has the principal part; an escapologist; and an athlete or dancer, for the battle with the spiritualists. Schat and Mitchell evidently intended a circuslike flow of activity in which moments sentimental, entertaining, embarrassing, breathtaking, and stirring are close woven. In this presentation, the magic did not enter the fiber of the drama; it was more a matter of "And now we stop for a trick." On the first night, some of the simplest tricks (the handkerchief that changes its color) went wrong, and the climax was tamely presented; so far as the audience was concerned the escapologist, Mark Mazzarella, could simply have taken the lid off the water can and wriggled out of it the moment a curtain was raised around it. According to Elliott Carter, Aspen's other composer-in-residence this year, the real Houdini was so violently and insistently theatrical in manner that he was unpleasant to watch. Mr. Mazzarella was so mild and unassuming in manner that he cast no spell—except in the initial Straitjacket Escape, a feat of physical prowess enacted in public view. There he did have the audience gasping.

The general confusion—"What's it all supposed to be about?"—was compounded by the inaudibility of most of the words. The words of operas, in whatever language, are often inaudible, and therefore ever since the form was invented it has been customary to make a printed libretto available to the audience. The *Houdini* libretto, published by Clowns, an Amsterdam house, was on sale in Aspen. Words are easier to catch when they have been read shortly before a performance. Easier, but not always easy. I still caught little of what was being sung or said. The Aspen acoustics, the singers' enunciation, and the composer's word setting and accompaniments must probably share the blame—in what proportions it would be hard to say. One singer, John-Paul Bogart, as Sir Arthur Conan Doyle, the chief spiritualist, made every word clear. Rose Taylor, as Lady Doyle, made nearly every word clear. The others were variable. Richard Dufallo, who conducted, had presumably taken the ordinary opera-conductor precaution of telling his players to listen to the singers and play more softly if they couldn't hear them. But the singers were often drowned. And even in lightly accompanied passages things were often unintelligible. Schat tends to take his vocal lines above the staff, where words inevitably disappear. His scanning of the English libretto is generally accurate, but some things revealed a less than idiomatic inflection of the language.

The Aspen singers—Jerold Norman as Houdini (he had also done the part in Holland); Rita Shane as his mother; Viviane Thomas as his wife, Bess; John Brandstetter as his manager—were all efficient. Sometimes they were more than that, rising to eloquence; sometimes they seemed limited to finding the right notes at the right time. Questions of balance apart—between stage and instruments, and between groups of instruments—the musical execution was accomplished. Mr. Dufallo handled his huge and far-flung forces with assurance. More rehearsal and more pointed and economical stage direction could have produced a sharper, more precise account of *Houdini*. Nevertheless, this one was a remarkable achievement.

Schat's "homeopathic" remedy for the ills of overschematized contemporary music includes more than a pinch of schematic planning. Each scene, it appears, has its charcterizing theme, in which a particular interval is prominent. There are recurrent motifs—most persistently an animated, jerky figure that seems to represent Houdini's leaping toward the light. Again and again it comes, in various related forms, often on the trumpet. (The largest solo role in the opera, in fact, is the first trumpet's; the vigor and stamina of the Aspen player, John Aley, were extraordinary.) If that computer were to ask Schat, "Can *you* sing, can *you* make a melody?" he could answer yes and point to Cecilia's lyrical aria "I see your future shining," to the love scene of Houdini and Bess, to the expressive Act IV introduction (English horn and cello stealing through a drift of string harmonies). But sometimes one got the feeling that after establishing the basic "music" for a scene Schat had simply sustained it in a way both mechanical and monotonous. There are lively rhythmic episodes: a trio for Houdini, Cecilia, and Bess on the theme "Money makes the heart beat stronger"; chipper choruses for the circus folk and for the police. A good deal of the score is in five-beat measures, and while a rapid 5/4 can sound lilting (as in Tchaikovsky's "Pathétique"), five slow beats begin to limp when the ear loses any sense of the basic pulse. The finale seems to me a failure—clogged and turgid rather than stirring—but the very last idea, an unaccompanied solo for Cecilia, with musical and verbal echoes of the birth scene, soaring out on the words "Towards whatever shines," is beautiful and moving. Schat has an easy command of straightforward theatrical effects: the exhilarating beat of the steel band; in the final scenes, telling "suspense" music. He could claim, quite fairly, that his score is not meant to be listened to just "as music," that it is but one element, if the most important, in an elaborate show. The most nearly self-sufficient musical episodes he has already lifted out to form a *Houdini Symphony; May '75, A Song of Liberation;* and a "ballet to sing," *I Am Houdini,* made of Houdini's challenge to the police forces of the world.

September 3, 1979

Island Operas

The new East Coast company Kennedy Center Summer Opera ended its six-week season last month. It plays in the Center's Terrace Theatre, which I described when reviewing the company's first two productions. When I returned to see the last two, Donizetti's opera semiseria *Il furioso all'isola di San Domingo* and an Offenbach pasticcio, the acoustics had been improved. Cyril Harris, the acoustic consultant for the building, had come to diagnose the dryness many people complained of, and had prescribed a simple remedy—caulking the seams of the orchestra pit. Now that this has been done, the orchestra sounds warmer and the balance between voices and instruments is better. The theatre still seems to me a shade less vibrant and less flattering to young singers than a five-hundred-seater ought to be, but it is a valuable and agreeable place. New Yorkers may well envy Washington both the house and the company.

I have come across four different productions of *Il furioso,* three of them on the East Coast within the last year or so, and all four have been mounted in the same décor: set by Lorenzo Mongiardino and costumes by Claudie Gastine. But Washington's was the first to do something like justice to what is one of Donizetti's more remarkable operas—one that swept the world within a decade of its première, in 1833. The 1967 Spoleto festival and the 1978 Spoleto Festival U.S.A., in Charleston, presented no more than a cut-down and reordered version of the score, with music missing and instruments missing. Earlier this year, the New Opera Theatre at the Brooklyn Academy of Music reinstated some of the missing passages and, sensibly, performed the opera in the language of the artists and the audience; but it still stuck to a reduced orchestration. Washington did the opera almost complete—one cut in Act II was cruel, but the others were negligible—and used a full orchestra, with double woodwinds, two horns, two trumpets, and three trombones. (In the Spoletos and in Brooklyn, flute, oboe, bassoon, trumpet, and trombone were single; in Brooklyn there were only twelve strings, against Washington's eighteen.) Not unexpectedly, the larger orchestra provided a more comfortable and less shrill support for the voices. Donizetti does not score grossly and reserves his full band for moments of power and passion; the emotional force of the opera when heard in the small theatre was considerable. The edition that was used bears the somewhat ominous legend "Revisione di Vito Frazzi" and includes no account of what Mr. Frazzi's revisionary policy has been, but, unlike the vocal score most commonly met with, it does tally with the early librettos. (The New York Public Library has one from the 1833 première, and visitors to Kennedy Center could consult a Naples 1834 libretto in the new Performing Arts Library, outside the Terrace Theatre.) The autograph score, according to Guido Zavadini's big book on Donizetti, is in the Ricordi archives. The Washington troupe has a dramaturge, Francis Rizzo; his program note described the Frazzi score as "authenticated," but mentioned no authority. Did he check Frazzi against the autograph himself? The opera has so many unusual formal features that one would have liked hard assurance that everything one heard was of the composer's own devising.

In all ways, *Il furioso* is unusual. As I suggested after the Brooklyn performance, the twenty-two-year-old baritone Giorgio Ronconi (later Verdi's first Nabucco) seems to have inspired the composer and his librettist, Jacopo Ferretti, to range beyond the formulas of the day and write two psychologically intense dramas with baritone protagonists. (The other work is *Torquato Tasso*, which appeared later in 1833.) The subject matter of *Il furioso* is after—a long way after—the Cardenio episodes of *Don Quixote:* a hero driven mad by his wife's infidelity; her repentance; his fitful return to sanity. The setting was shifted from the Sierra Morena to San Domingo, which provided the chance for picturesque Caribbean décor, a shipwreck, a tropical storm. The black plantation worker Kaidamà supplied a buffo element.

Violence, tenderness, and jokes are deftly and affectingly blended. The more one discovers of Donizetti, the more one admires his warm, generous understanding of human joys and sorrows, the honesty of feeling that marks his music, his delight in what is beautiful and true, and the intensity with which he shares his characters' suffering. (And the more impatient one becomes with productions of *L'elisir d'amore* and *Don Pasquale* which put irrelevant jokiness and farcical business before accurate, amused observation of human character, and productions of the tragedies which treat them as mere prima donna showpieces.) There were discoveries to be made at this latest *Furioso*. One could agree with sentiments that its admirable conductor, John Mauceri, expressed in a program note:

> In respecting Donizetti's own sense of pacing and proportion, we have found that the opera is not only dramaturgically clearer but psychologi-

cally "shorter" than in abridged versions. For *Il Furioso* finally needs no explication or apology to make its mark on the public. Above all, it needs no improvements.

Not everything about the show was right, however. Richard Pearlman's stage direction was a mixture of stale routine not specific to the piece and unwanted activity that simply obscured Donizetti's and Ferretti's drama. But it was a shade cleaner and less insensitive than his direction of the opera in Charleston had been. The title role needed better singing and subtler, less complacent acting than Charles Long brought to it. He pushed a pleasant light baritone until it sounded artificial and ugly. He signaled Cardenio's return to sanity by a grin turned on like an electric light. The tenor—Cardenio's brother, who has come to San Domingo in search of him—is a role that seems to have been written in to satisfy the *convenienze*, because an opera needs a tenor. He has two graceful but almost irrelevant arias. Rockwell Blake sang them with some grace of style and a formidable coloratura technique, but the timbre in the top fifth of his voice—up to high D—was edgy and unpleasant. Mr. Pearlman's fancy direction of the second aria suggested that he either does not understand Italian or presumed on his audience's not understanding it.

But Marianna Christos as Eleonora, Cardenio's peccant wife, was both moving and a great pleasure to listen to. Her accuracy of pitch and exactness of focus are in themselves uncommon. There is just a hint of resin in her timbre—enough to lend it character, not so much as to mar its essential sweetness and purity. She brought to mind Mendelssohn's remark about Fanny Persiani, Donizetti's first Lucia: "Well, I do like Madame Persiani dearly. . . . There is such a pleasant, *bitter* tone in her voice!" When the line rose, Miss Christos's voice seemed to get fuller. Nothing was edgy or strained. She joined notes, molded the phrases, and was passionate in expression but never out of control. James Tyeska, in the buffo role, was a promising but gauche performer in need of direction. The smaller parts—Judith Christin as the seconda donna and William Dansby as the bass—were well taken.

The opera was sung in Italian, and that was a mistake, for it has a good libretto set by Donizetti in such a way that his music can be appreciated to the full only when the words are followed in detail by the audience. And the company had not put a bilingual, or even an Italian-only, libretto on sale. Surely it would not have been difficult to run off facsimiles of the Italian-English libretto printed for a New York performance of *Il furioso* at the Astor Place Theatre in 1848.

Musically, the two-hundredth anniversary of the 1776 colonial rebellion was celebrated almost as prominently in the mother country as in the former colonies. Among other things, a "new" Offenbach operetta, *Christopher Columbus*, was created for the occasion. Offenbach would have recognized the tunes. Some of them he had composed in 1876 aboard the *Canada*, on his way to America to conduct at the Philadelphia Centennial Exposition; they were for *La Boîte au lait*, which appeared later that year. Others—among them a quartet, with castanets clacking, from *Maître Péronilla*, an Atlantic storm from *Vent du soir*—came from various crannies of the treasure house of animated, elegant music represented by his hundred-odd scores. The two directors of Opera Rara, a London organization that has revived unfamiliar operas by Rossini, Mercadante, and Meyerbeer, and last year gave the world première of Donizetti's 1838 *Gabriella di Vergy*, assembled the piece: Patric Schmid, the American operatic scholar, raided the treasure house for music; Don White, a British poet, wrote a witty libretto. Act I plays in Cordova, where Columbus, newly engaged to Beatriz, is embarrassed, Don Giovanni–like, by the arrival of his earlier brides Fleurette, Rosa, and Gretel, and in the Royal Palace, where a susceptible Queen Isabella provides him with the means to escape to a New World. Act II plays aboard the *Santa Maria* and then in "a clearing in the woods, somewhere in downtown Manhattan," where Beatriz, Fleurette, Rosa, and Gretel surprise Christopher with Minnehaha, his newest bride. In 1976, *Christopher Columbus* came out in Belfast and in London. The next year, the Minnesota Opera staged it. Now it has been taken up in Washington.

Of course, I regret that Kennedy Center Summer Opera didn't take up a *real* Offenbach opérette. This piece, a string of hit numbers, doesn't have the feel, doesn't move with the gait, of vintage Offenbach. Why not *Bluebeard?* Why not *Robinson Crusoe?* (It could have been played in the *Furioso* setting.) And, of course, I was captivated by Offenbach's music and had a thoroughly good time. Neil Rosenshein was bonny in the title role. Elaine Bonazzi, Isabella, was a virtuoso comedienne. In a large and accomplished cast, Erie Mills, as Gretel, stood out for her bright tone and the panache with which she delivered her words. Mr. White's libretto made me laugh. Lois Bewley had directed, and if when I saw the show the fun sometimes became rather too broad, that could be forgiven as last-night-of-a-run exuberance. Brian Salesky conducted with spirit.

September 10, 1979

PART III

1979–1980

Bounty

London critics often complain of unadventurous programs, but the city's musical life seemed to me as rich as ever during a ten-day visit I made in late September and early October. The more unusual operas on show were Antonio Cesti's *Orontea*, Charles Dibdin's *The Padlock*, Peter Maxwell Davies's *The Martyrdom of St. Magnus*, and John Tavener's *Thérèse*, Covent Garden's latest commission. The English National Opera repertory included a grandiose new production of *Aida*. Within easy reach, the Welsh National Opera was taking *The Makropulos Affair* and a new production of *Tristan*, conducted by Reginald Goodall, around the country, and Glyndebourne was taking *Fidelio*, *Così*, and Haydn's *La fedeltà premiata*. The principal oratorios to be heard were Handel's *L'allegro, il penseroso, ed il moderato* and his *Athalia*, both with original instruments; Haydn's *Creation*; and, brought by the BBC from Schwetzingen, Josef Mysliveček's *Abramo ed Isacco*. (I just missed the Florence 1589 Intermedi and Monteverdi's Christmas Vespers.) In the Wigmore Hall, a Beethoven cycle by the Orford String Quartet alternated nightly with delectable programs from Anthony Rooley's Consort of Musicke. Orchestral concerts were conducted by Solti, Abbado, Maazel, and Simon Rattle. (Muti and Celibidache had just left.) Concerto pianists included Maurizio Pollini, Murray Perahia, and Krystian Zimerman. Glasgow was finishing its week of Musica Nova, and one of the four big orchestral pieces premièred there, Brian Ferneyhough's *La Terre est un homme*, had its deuxième when Abbado decided to add it to the program of his inaugural concert as principal conductor of the London Symphony.

This feast was not exceptional; Londoners take it for granted. The programs for the previous ten days and those for the next ten showed as bounteous a provision of eminent performers, of contemporary music, and of choice revivals from the music of all ages. (Before October is out, London is to hear *Benvenuto Cellini*, Handel's *Hercules* and *Scipione*, *La finta giardiniera*, and another operatic première, Minoru Miki's *An Actor's Revenge;* Boulez, Tennstedt, Colin Davis, Rozhdestvensky, and Kondrashin join the roster of conductors; and the London Sinfonietta and the London Symphony, under David Atherton, embark on a Stravinsky festival at which every Stravinsky work will be played.) Twenty years ago, London music was not like this. Several mutually sustaining things have conspired to make it so, among them intense music education in schools; the Arts Council's discriminating allotment of the government funds that pay most of the bills; the BBC's Radio 3, which initiates many performances, relays others from all over the world (during my ten days, ears could visit the Vienna, Bath, Tanglewood, Prague, and Malvern festivals, and catch concerts in Manchester, Liverpool, Boston, and Paris, without leaving London), and puts out long, careful series that combine delight with instruction; the existence of five symphony orchestras and several chamber orchestras in regular employment; an abundance of publicly owned halls and theatres, most of them agreeable, attractive, welcoming places; and copious, concerned public discussion of music—in those halls and theatres, in print, and over the air.

Not everything I heard and saw was good. The English National's ostentatious, gold-encrusted *Aida*, directed by John Copley and designed by Stefanos Lazaridis, repeated mistakes of the Met's: a large stage was made small by cramping, cluttered scenery and voluminous, heavy costumes; a nocturnal triumph featured a sadistic, murderous orgy in place of the ballet of maidens with trophies which should grace it. Aiming monotonously at grandeur, the show missed Verdi's alternation of intimacy and pomp. The orchestra, under Charles Groves, lacked color and expression. The singing (Josephine Barstow took the title role) was seldom beautiful, and the acting was dwarfed by the scenery.

Opera was still young in 1649, when *Orontea* had its première, in Venice. The London performance was a delight. At the harpsichord, Jane Glover, directing a small baroque ensemble (five strings, archlute, a second harpsichord), communicated the freshness of the piece, enjoyed Cesti's bright, deft exploration of the varied effects, formal and informal, moving and merry, called for by Giancinto Andrea Cicognini's entertaining libretto. Like *Giasone* (which Cicognini wrote for Cavalli in the same year), *Orontea* is a romantic comedy with poignant, serious episodes. Queen, courtier, and clown, prince and painter, mingle in one flow of dramatic action. Cicognini was once chided for confusing the classes, and for introducing arias that further instead of staying the action; those "faults" of his, which must have helped to insure for the piece its seventeenth-century success, keep it alive today. In the title role, Della Jones was bewitching; she is an English National mezzo who makes every phrase interesting, alive, arresting. The musicianship, lively words, and clear, unforced vocal accomplishment of the young cast, four of them from the National Opera Studio, were remarkable. The production, given in the intimate Riverside Studios, the "arts center" of the London borough of Hammersmith, was in smart modern dress, but was clean and simple, not tiresomely larky. There was an elegant new English translation, by Anne Ridler.

I heard the Welsh National *Tristan* over the air, relayed from Cardiff— and thrilled to the score as if I were hearing it for the first time. Reginald Goodall is now regularly hailed, not only in Britain, as the greatest Wagnerian conductor of our day, sole heir of Furtwängler and Knappertsbusch, last upholder of the great tradition. At a time when most Wagner performances are discussed first for their aberrant scenery and fancy directorial ideas, his are prized for their musical truth, intensity, and grandeur; for once, the music takes precedence of the spectacle. Goodall works only in Britain, and he demands long months of detailed, dedicated rehearsal. He inspires singers and players to new heights of eloquence, to achievements one thought hardly possible. He had coached a new Isolde, the young Scottish soprano Linda Esther Gray, a pupil of Eva Turner, to give a shining, ample, secure, and masterly performance. He had turned John Mitchinson, hitherto a burly, unromantic tenor, into an uncommonly expressive Tristan. Everything Goodall and his interpreters do is charged with meaning. This *Tristan* was long-breathed but urgent, emotional yet firmly controlled, colorful in all its lines, generous, beautiful, and overwhelming.

John Tavener's *Thérèse* is a one-act opera (it lasted ninety-five minutes) about a saint whose life contained little outward incident; it deals with what the librettist, Gerard McLarnon, describes as her "terrible journey . . . to Heaven by way of Hell." Thérèse Martin, the daughter of a Normandy watchmaker, entered a Carmelite cloister in 1888, at the age of fifteen. On Good Friday, 1896, she vomited blood and understood it as a summons from her Bridegroom: "My soul was flooded with joy at the thought that I was going to die." But she lingered on for eighteen months, suffered an obscuration of her faith, lived as if in a dark land, seemed to hear mocking voices ("It's all a dream, this talk of a heavenly country"), yet embraced this spiritual suffering as a new test of love. After her death, her memoirs were published as *The Story of a Soul*. To the high "Way of Perfection" proclaimed by the passionate, patrician, and very active St. Teresa of Avila, Thérèse appended her "little way," which indicated that sanctity could also be attained by obscure, ordinary people going about the trivial round with perfect love. (St. John of the Cross, Teresa's colleague, is a poet Thérèse often quotes.) The autobiography became a best-seller, Thérèse was venerated, miracles were attributed to her, and in 1925 she was canonized as St. Thérèse of Lisieux.

The opera begins with the Good Friday summons. A chanted Alleluia steals through the darkened theatre, and then, from the dome of the auditorium, Christ, a high tenor, calls "Veni speciosa mea," and onstage Thérèse replies. It ends with an ecstatic duet, both voices finally sounding on high, and the return of the Alleluias. Between these scenes, menacing figures of darkness gather round the saint, and she goes on three "journeys." In the first, the poet Rimbaud, who also passed through Hell, taunts her with spiritual arrogance. The second recalls her childhood prayer for the soul of the murderer Pranzini, whose crimes are formally mimed. The third deals with her posthumous career. She once said, "I wish to spend my eternity on earth— doing good on earth." Here she achieves the affirmation "My God, my God, Thou hast not forsaken them" through scenes of Flanders carnage, concentration camp executions, and the vaporization of children—the extinction of all life. Thérèse's version of "Evil, be thou my good"—suffering is blessing, affliction brings joy, Job was a fortunate fellow, and the long agony of her father, who went mad, gave her "les trois années . . . les plus aimables, les plus fructueuses de toute notre vie"—is a difficult creed to embrace, but it does provide one way of coming to terms with the horrors of life. The opera does what it can to make dramatic a heroism that was essentially acceptive, unprotesting, passive.

Thérèse was Tavener's fifth première of the year. (A sixth was due nine days later, at the Little Missenden Festival.) The music is in veins familiar from his large choral pieces (the largest being *Ultimos Ritos*, an immense, cathedral-filling meditation on the Crucifixion, based on poems of St. John of the Cross): sweet strands of mellifluous high melisma; wide-flung, complicated chords long sustained or reiterated as ostinatos; pretty children's songs decked with a tinkle of little bells; Stravinskian, even Orffian, motifs rapped out in the violent passages; chant; rhythmic choral speech; drums crashing and trumpets pealing from the distance. It is impressive, and much of it is beautiful. But at times one feels that Tavener has found all too easy a formula for distilling ecstasy. And the piece requires submission to the repetitions and slow pace of a rite. The Covent Garden performance, conducted by Edward Downes, was very well prepared and was admirably executed. Vivien Townley was secure in the taxing title role, whose range is from D-sharp at the center of the bass staff to high C above the treble staff—nearly three octaves. Keith Lewis was a limpid Christ. (The role is doubled with that of Thérèse's mortal father, but no special point is made of the bold identification.) Robert Tear's Rimbaud was trenchant.

In an uncharacteristically feeble program note, the title of Brian Ferneyhough's *La Terre est un homme* was left unexplained. (London's program books are usually excellent; the BBC's for the Florence Intermedi contained text and translation generously laid out, the Buontalenti designs, and a series of learned essays.) The composer, speaking on Radio 3 on the morning of the London performance, threw no light on it. Abbado said that he had chosen the work because Ferneyhough was a British composer admired by Boulez, Nono, and Berio. His decision to add it to the "safe" program (Brahms's D-minor Concerto and Tchaikovsky's Fourth Symphony) originally billed for his inaugural concert was brave. *La Terre* calls for an act of faith. After hearing Ferneyhough's Sonatas for String Quartet and his *Transit* (both of them now on record), and his Missa Brevis, I am prepared to make it—but only just. The new work, which was commissioned by the BBC, lasts fifteen minutes and is for very large orchestra, with each part individual. The score is the densest and most intricate I have ever seen: some pages contain fifty-five well-filled staves; others (in the copy I had) reach only to Violin 11 by the bottom line, and the thirty-nine remaining string parts "run off the page." Faith is needed because much of the time the ear cannot possibly tell whether the instrumentalists are playing the right notes in the right rhythms. The composer has described his work, perhaps with a touch of teasing, as "twenty-six chamber pieces played simultaneously." At a rehearsal, I enjoyed some of those chamber pieces as they were played by just one or two sections of the orchestra. But when everything came together the result was impenetrable; no more than the general shape and a general sense of energy and passion could be perceived. It is a common experience that scores initially deemed incomprehensibly and self-defeatingly elaborate become limpid with time. (Joseph II told Mozart that *Die Entführung* had too many notes.) Perhaps it will happen with this one.

Athalia, an English Bach Festival performance, conducted by Anthony Lewis, was distinguished by the fiery majesty of Eiddwen Harrhy in the title role and, of course, by Handel's endlessly inventive, ever-exhilarating music. *Abramo ed Isacco*, the Mysliveček oratorio, sounds like Italian-period Mozart—which means that it is well worth hearing. The performance, conducted by Peter Maag, had some dragged, overemphatic recitative, but Werner Hollweg was a fluent and fervent Abraham, and Barbara Hendricks a colorful and lively Isaac.

October 15, 1979

Inventions

The first new production of the Metropolitan season is of Mozart's Singspiel *Die Entführung aus dem Serail*. It is an odd choice for a huge-house company that does not yet have Mozart's grand operas *Idomeneo, La clemenza di Tito,* and *Lucio Silla* in its repertory (*Idomeneo* is due in 1982–83), but the production is cleverly and successfully planned to project the piece as immediately as possible. The expanse of the proscenium opening is reduced by a cutout mask that provides a skyline of Moorish domes and latticework. The raked stage runs out through the proscenium arch and over the back of the orchestra pit. The pit floor is raised (and James Levine, who conducts, is lifted so high that he forms part of the stage picture). Jocelyn Herbert's sets for Acts I and III are simplified, stylized representations of a Moorish palace, outside and then inside, executed in clear colors; there is a pretty and unfussy transformation for the embarkment at the end. But the palace has sliding doors that open automatically, like a supermarket's, when anyone approaches them. In Act II, spanned by a high red fence, the scale is awkward, the effect chic and modern. Gil Wechsler, who lights the show, begins with what looks like a direct tribute to the famous Salzburg *Entführung* directed by Giorgio

Strehler and designed by Luciano Damiani: Belmonte in black silhouette against the background. But then he drops the device, whereas in Salzburg transformations from silhouette to fully rounded figure were recurrent, and delicately matched to the score. In other ways—in lightness, brightness, forwardness, and fearless mixing of realism and mannerism—the Metropolitan production is kin to Salzburg's. But in New York something essential to *Die Entführung* is missing. The performance was dapper and clean but unmoving. Salzburg used artifice more precisely, more musically.

When Weber added *Die Entführung* to his Dresden repertory, in 1818, he told his public that the opera depicted "what every man's joyous, youthful years are to him, years the bloom of which he will never recapture." He continued, "I venture to say that in *Die Entführung* Mozart had attained the peak of his artistic experience, to which only experience of the world had to be added later. . . . With the best will in the world, he could never have written another *Entführung*." In 1781, Mozart was newly engaged to his Constanze (he married her three weeks after the first night of *Die Entführung*), newly settled in the capital, and independent at last both of his archbishop and of his father. Joseph II had established a National Opera in the vernacular, and Mozart had been invited to compose a work for it. He summoned all his abilities: his natural and his acquired dramatic skills; his full range of expressive orchestral writing; his command of forms from simple song to highly developed aria; his instinct for improving a libretto. In *Idomeneo*, his previous opera, he had transformed opera seria. In *Die Entführung*, he broke the bounds of Singspiel; the gap between Ignaz Umlauf's *Die Bergknappen*, which in 1778 had inaugurated the Emperor's German company, and *Die Entführung* is very wide. Mozart's letters to Salzburg during the months of composition tell vividly of his eagerness, his excitement, his inventions and discoveries. And a satisfying performance of *Die Entführung* needs not only to be executed with high accomplishment (the music is as hard to sing as any that Mozart wrote) but also to recapture that sense of youthful excitement and discovery. The audience should rejoice in the freshness and the copiousness of invention.

"Too many notes," maybe. Joseph II thought so. But when the four instrumental soloists—flute, oboe, violin, cello—can be heard to take active delight in what Mozart gave them to play during the long, long introduction to Constanze's "Martern aller Arten," the audience is delighted, too. The four Metropolitan players were polished but reticent, and I thought Mr. Levine held them on too tight a rein. Several of his tempi were too fast to allow full shaping of the music. The vaudeville finale marched to a foursquare beat that inhibited individual rubato on the singers' parts. Damiani framed his light, elegant scenes in colored borders of jeweled brilliance; they reflected the richness of the score in a way that Miss Herbert's trim, elegant décor doesn't. But the main disappointment of the Metropolitan production lay in a heroine and hero, Edda Moser and Nicolai Gedda, who lacked ardor, romance, intensity. She was bleak and careful (and on the opening night the upper fifth of her voice sounded foggy), and he was conscientious and bland.

John Dexter's curiously unemotional direction of the noble pair—some arias were delivered from a single station—did not help them to communicate. Miss Moser's trick of stubbing out repeated notes in place of appoggiaturas also diminished the eloquence of several passages.

The main pleasures of the evening were provided by the servants, and those pleasures were considerable. Norma Burrowes, making her Met début, was an enchanting Blonde. She has always had a voice of quicksilver accuracy, and in recent years it has become both fuller and sweeter. Norbert Orth, another Met débutant, has succeeded Gerhard Unger as the leading international Pedrillo. His timbre is a shade less limpid than Unger's, but its very sturdiness, coupled to his lively manner, is charming. Both Blonde and Pedrillo seemed to be enjoying Mozart's music, to be making much of it— whereas their mistress and master gave the impression of being intimidated and constrained by it. Blonde and Pedrillo were live characters. So was Osmin, played by Kurt Moll with a musical resourcefulness that gave individual life to each phrase. The lowest notes may lie outside Mr. Moll's effective range, but the way he made the audience listen for them was in itself entertaining—and artistic. Werner Klemperer was a lightweight Pasha Selim, and the audience laughed at some of his noblest utterances. In general, Mr. Dexter's production is neat, crisp, and disciplined, but on occasion it misses the style and spirit of the music.

Once the City Opera orchestra and management had composed their differences, the season resumed with the new production of *Falstaff*. The next day, there was *Carmen*, and on the day after that, a Saturday, both *Street Scene* and *Rigoletto* had their first performances of the season. On Sunday, *Falstaff* and *Carmen* were repeated. I attended all the weekend performances—four in two days—and marveled at the prowess of an orchestra that played all four scores not just skillfully but with feeling, with a command of each work's particular dramatic accents and colors.

I praised *Street Scene* last season. It is one of the most important operas in the New York repertory, for reasons both social and musical, and the production remains one of the City Opera's high achievements. John Mauceri conducts the score as lovingly and sensitively as if it were by Mozart (with whom Kurt Weill does have things in common). Eileen Schauler, Catherine Malfitano, Alan Kays, and William Chapman—and, for that matter, just about everyone in a very large cast—give performances that should not be missed. *Rigoletto* and *Carmen* are both of them well-worn repertory productions, *Rigoletto* dating from 1969 and *Carmen* from 1971. Scenically, they are more seemly, picturesque, and effective than the cranky versions on show at the Metropolitan this season. Frank Corsaro's direction of *Rigoletto* (which I had not seen before) suffers in the first scene from his fondness for representing carnal extravagance and suffers throughout from his appetite for embellishment. Rigoletto's frequent tippling is tiresome, and it weakens Verdi's portrayal of a character impelled by strong feelings rather than by strong drink. A trussed Giovanna center stage offers unfair competition to Rigoletto at the first-act curtain. To impose a second, prominent court jester on a drama that has a court jester as its protagonist is foolish. Verdi's stag assembly in Act II is not improved by adding women. (Even the page's music was written for a tenor.) But one of Mr. Corsaro's departures from the book is successful: this is the first *Rigoletto* of my experience in which the action of the second scene is so managed that Rigoletto can plausibly think the courtiers plan to abduct the Countess Ceprano, not his daughter. (It's not a necessary change—the opera got on well for over a century without it—but it works well.) Hans Sondheimer's lighting is often crude: Sparafucile advanced from the shadows in a circus-type spotlight. Cynthia Auerbach, who directed the revival of *Carmen* (the 1971 director was Tito Capobianco), has been infected by the ridiculous fashion for inventing little chorister "cameos" to catch the eye and distract the attention while the principals are singing: the Micaëla-José duet, the séguédille, the quintet, and José's last phrases were spoiled in that way. Nevertheless, both shows moved surely and clearly, in a way to make the dramatic action and the characters' emotions vivid to audiences not fluent in Italian and French.

Rigoletto was played in a text purified by suggestions from Martin Chusid, who is editing the score for the Verdi critical edition. The most striking change appeared before the coda of "Caro nome": Gilda's twice-murmured "Gualtier Maldè" remained on a monotone B instead of rising to E on the last syllable. Verdi altered his autograph to read thus, Mr. Chusid tells me; printed editions from the first onward show the familiar E's. (The assignment of the court usher's command to the posse of guards was, however, a local aberration, not a correct new reading.) Gilda was Mariana Niculescu (who did the role at the Metropolitan last season). She has a strong, well-schooled soprano, ready to ride the storm of Act III, and her reading was carefully studied, along conventional lines. But her timbre lacked charm, her acting was routine, and rhythmically she was a sluggard who kept falling behind the beat. Brian Salesky, conducting his first *Rigoletto,* could not be blamed for losing her at times; whenever he yielded to let her catch up, she dragged still further. But when he lost touch with his tenor and baritone, it was usually because they employed appropriate—indeed, necessary—rubato that took him unawares (when, for example, Rigoletto eloquently broadened the triplets at the start of the final duet). Mr. Salesky's reading needed more weight and breadth at climaxes, but it was shaped with intelligence and feeling. Michele Molese was a bright, ringing, and buoyant Duke. In the murderously high title role, Pablo Elvira sustained both power and exceptional beauty of tone right to the end. Both men gave capable, traditional rather than freshly conceived, performances. Rigoletto's bawling of his daughter's name during a passage that Verdi intended to represent a vain struggle to exclaim ("He wishes to cry out, but he cannot . . . finally [nine measures later] after many efforts he cries ["Ah!"]") is a tradition best forgotten. Ralph Bassett's Sparafucile was also distinguished by beauty of tone. Maddalena in the person of Eunice Hill was for once not a brazen hussy but an attractive young woman worth the Duke's wooing. The score was done almost complete: a verse of "Possente amor" was cut. The stage bands were missing (Verdi prescribed a string band onstage and a fuller band backstage), and were missed.

Carmen brought a new tenor and the return to the New York stage, after eighteen years, of Victoria de los Angeles. She recorded Carmen twenty years ago, with Beecham conducting and Mr. Gedda as José, but sang it onstage for the first time only last season, in Newark. She left it late. Miss los Angeles, who made her début in 1945, and her Met début in 1951, had one of the two or three loveliest voices of our day—lustrous, warm, full, pure. Her Mimì and Cio-Cio-San were captivating; her Elsa was radiant. In recital, some of the old, exquisite quality remains when she sings softly in the middle ranges. But in the State Theater *Carmen* she built up volume at the expense of timbre; notes from E upward were generally attacked flat; the vocal mechanism was no longer supple enough to compass fleet, flickering inflections such as light her recorded performance; and under pressure even some of the lower notes came close to breaking. Her acting was forceful yet unexaggerated. The musical interpretation was achieved with broad strokes, insistently, yet never tastelessly. I have not heard a Carmen more determined to make every single syllable expressive. It was not a moving performance—the vocal uncertainty kept attention on the singer, not on the character she played—but it was oddly compelling, never dull; and as the evening progressed the voice began to flow more easily. International artists are accustomed to being prompted before every phrase—to having the opening words thrown to them and each entry point indicated with a stabbing finger. (For the last act of *Otello*, Verdi prescribed a second prompter, whispering the lines of the "Ave Maria" from behind the altar and then moving to the threshold of the secret door, whence, score in hand, he can prompt sotto voce the complicated moves of Othello's entrance. Tristan in Act III sometimes depends on a prompter lying beneath his couch. In Lisbon, I once heard a virtuoso prompter supply not only the words but also, on a pitch pipe, the first note of each entry.) The Metropolitan, like Covent Garden, London's international house, has a regular prompter's box center stage at the footlights; the State Theater, like the English National Opera, does not. Miss los Angeles bravely essayed the City Opera practice of singing from memory, unaided, unprompted, but must have found that she missed the familiar cues. When these were called in to her from the wings, they were disconcertingly audible in the auditorium. I mention these things only because I heard Miss los Angeles accused—by people evidently unfamiliar with the standard international practice—of "not even knowing the part," and because the company's ability to do without prompting is remarkable and deserves notice.

José was Riccardo Calleo, a young tenor from Binghamton, who won good reviews last year in *Opera* for his performances in *Ballo* and *Elisir* in Innsbruck. Beverly Sills has announced her wish to bring back the best of the American singers now working abroad, and Mr. Calleo is a find. His voice is firm and bright. His phrasing was full. His words were admirably distinct. French when purely sounded is the most expressive and beautiful of all singing languages, and Mr. Calleo clearly knows this. (Anyone who doesn't should listen to records made by Claire Croiza, Plançon, Vanni-Marcoux.) But he must beware of singing sharp under stress. His acting was decent, if a shade too plain. Gwenlynn Little, eschewing a milksop approach to Micaëla, made her almost too vivacious and vigorous, but it was good to hear the air so ardently and fully sung. Robert Hale made a buoyant Toreador, and Charles Wendelken-Wilson was a poised and able conductor.

October 29, 1979

Play

Parnassus, one of New York's best contemporary-music ensembles, directed by Anthony Korf, has moved this season to the concert hall at the Abraham Goodman House (on West Sixty-seventh Street, just north of Lincoln Center), with an attractive series of programs. The first, last month, was well planned and well attended. Its climax was the New York première of Mario Davidovsky's *Pennplay*, composed two years ago for the Penn Contemporary Players, of Philadelphia, and written for eight winds, five strings, two percussions, and piano—a chamber orchestra, in effect. When those forces had been assembled, it made sense to do Stefan Wolpe's Chamber Piece No. 2 on the same bill. This brilliant, difficult score lasts only three and a half minutes but needs thirteen players; eleven of them could be drawn from the Davidovsky ensemble. And when the Wolpe had been learned, it made sense to play it twice, before and after the intermission. Each big-ensemble work was aptly preceded by a smaller chamber work of the same composer: *Pennplay* by Davidovsky's Synchronism No. 3, for cello and tape, and Chamber Piece No. 2 by Wolpe's Quartet No. 1, for saxophone, trumpet, piano, and percussion. The forces were then at hand to provide, as a lighthearted overture, Milhaud's *Scaramouche* suite in its wind-sextet version.

Pennplay is a ten-minute stretch of picturesque music. Shrill and bright at the start, it moves into a scene of mystery and melancholy, punctuated by brass outcrops, and ends serenely. I record an impression, not any clear perception of form and purpose; I have not seen a score. The music has a lively, colorful surface. The incidents hold the attention, and the pace of their presentation is nicely varied. I hope that a full-scale retrospective of Wolpe's music is being planned for 1982, the eightieth anniversary of his birth and the tenth of his death. What is his theatre music like? His big-orchestra pieces (perhaps the Philharmonic should bill some of them)? His cantatas? The handful of chamber pieces that get played and the handful on record tell of a composer learned, witty, vital, and individual, a master (pupil of Busoni, Schreker, and Webern) through whom both serialism and neoclassicism flowed and in whom they mingled and were refined. In the new edition of Joseph Machlis's *Introduction to Contemporary Music*, Wolpe's place is beside Bartók, Schoenberg, and Stravinsky, in the chapter "European Masters in America." The Chamber Piece (1966, revised in 1968) is a spare, terse, charged product of his last years. The Quartet (1950, revised in 1954) is elegant, "Mozartian." The first movement is impassioned, the second witty. The piece has been twice recorded; a note with the earlier recording calls it "as direct as *Beowulf* in its impact, as subtle and powerful as *Guernica.*" That goes too far but does suggest its emotional force. Mr. Korf conducted the Parnassus account of it. The first movement probably gained thereby; it was eloquently molded. In the second, security was won at the expense of playfulness between the four instruments, who no longer seemed to be tossing ideas to one another and exuberantly seizing the lead in turn. A second, unconducted performance would have been interesting to hear, and there was time for it; the program contained only some fifty-five minutes of music, and the Quartet lasts about thirteen. The Parnassus players are dedicated, expert, and earnest. Playfulness is not their strong suit. During the perky *Scaramouche*, dapperly done, they maintained expressions of owlish gravity. But Chris Finckel, the cellist, showed a welcome flash of platform wit when, after his spirited and poised account of Davidovsky's Synchronism, he shared his applause with the loudspeakers.

Three days earlier, the ensemble Musical Elements, directed by Daniel Asia, had also played the Wolpe Quartet, in the opening concert of its series in Carnegie Recital Hall. This performance *was* unconducted, but it was also unbalanced, lumpy. It did not have the precise focus and clear expressiveness of the Parnassus reading. The concert opened with Toru Takemitsu's wispy *Stanza I*, for voice and four instruments, included too plain and assertive an account of Ravel's Introduction and Allegro, and ended with the first performance of Mr. Asia's *Sand II*, a song cycle for mezzo, two flutes, clarinet, two pianos, two percussions. I didn't make much of it and merely wondered—not for the first time—why many contemporary composers write so unfeelingly for the voice and persist in setting words in a way to make them unintelligible.

The opening concert of the Group for Contemporary Music's season, given in the Borden Auditorium of the Manhattan School of Music, was devoted to music from California. Roger Reynolds's *Less Than Two*, receiving its New York première, was enough in itself to make the concert worthwhile: a twenty-one minute stretch of intense, vivid, animated music for two pianos, two percussions, and tape. Much of the time there is a patter of ostinatos and a flickering surface as busy as any in "minimalist" scores, but the effect of *Less Than Two* is stimulating, not mesmeric, and there is nothing simple about its facture. Ideas tumble out in profusion, textures change swiftly; the center of interest shifts suddenly from one player to another, and the listener, enthralled, follows as best he can the discourse of a dazzling and orderly musical mind. Ensemble, rhythms, and the actual notes are exceptionally difficult to get right; so far as I can judge, the work had a masterly performance from Gilbert Kalish and James Freeman, piano, and Raymond DesRoches and Richard Fitz, percussion, for whom it was written.

The concert opened with Paul Chihara's *Willow, Willow,* a dainty essay in timbres. Edwin Dugger's Fantasy for Piano, a long, splashy shower of notes, had its first performance, from the virtuoso Robert Miller. Leonard Rosenman's Chamber Music No. 2, for soprano, ten instruments, and tape—a setting with instrumental or tape-and-instrumental interludes of Lorca's "Your Childhood in Menton"—was new to New York. The composer describes it as "essentially a monodrama conceived in symphonic formal aspects," but there was nothing dramatic about the way Martha Rafferty Page, eyes glued to the score, performed it. It struck me as a sound, well-made, listenable composition.

The Musical Elements program leaflet listed titles, composers, and performers. There was a text sheet for the song cycle, but the lights in the main hall were turned out. (At my insistent request, we had some light in the balcony.) The ventilation system added its bourdon to very soft passages. The Parnassus program leaflet listed just titles, composers, performers, and dates of composition. The concert was exceptionally well lit—a warm glow on the players, and enough light in the hall itself to follow scores by. At the Abraham Goodman House, players have space around them and are in one room with their audience, not tucked away into a box at the end. The place could be a welcoming musical center if the long room beside the little foyer which looks like a buffet became one, open before and after concerts. Informative program notes had been prepared for the Group concert, but they were not available at the hall. They had been mailed in advance to subscribers and critics. An admirable practice, so far as it goes—but there were about four times as many people at the concert as the Group has subscribers. New music still has a hard time of it in New York.

Shura Cherkassky, playing in the music room of the Frick Collection last week, was not the pianist I remembered from twenty-five years before. Then—memory can be checked against the records he made in the early fifties—he was wayward, brilliant, sometimes maddening, always arresting. I once walked away in indignation from a *Carnaval* at which he battered the music out of shape and the piano out of tune, and once stood to cheer a Tchaikovsky First Concerto of superlative elegance, virtuosity, and poetic brio. The Frick recital revealed a pianist whose musical instincts seemed to have coarsened, whose details had become slapdash, who sounded as if he had played the four works on his program (Schumann's Op. 111 Fantasy Pieces, the Rakhmaninov-Corelli variations, Mendelssohn's F-sharp-minor

Fantasy, and the Brahms-Handel variations) so often that he no longer felt concern for them.

November 5, 1979

Critics report on what they hear. But I'm glad I wrote "seemed." I was told later—by someone who had no quarrel with my description of the playing—that there were reasons for Mr. Cherkassky's being below his best. There was a parade that day; he had been unable to get a taxi from his hotel to the Frick and—he is not young—had run most of the way.

Imperial

Mozart's last opera, *La clemenza di Tito*, has joined the City Opera repertory. It is given a serious, noble, and exciting performance, one that should help to reinstate the work, along with the once neglected *Idomeneo*, in the Mozart canon. There was a time—from 1791 to about 1830—when *Titus* (as in English we may as well call it) was Mozart's second-most-popular opera. For a decade, only *The Magic Flute* surpassed it in number of performances and of published scores; then, as the age grew more Romantic, *Don Giovanni* moved into first place while *Titus* remained in second. *Titus* was the first Mozart opera to reach London, in 1806. Paris saw it in 1816, at the Théâtre Italien, and so did Milan, at the Teatro Rè. Two years later, there was an uncommonly handsome Scala production, starrily cast, Alessandro Sanquirico's designs for which are a high point of neoclassical stage architecture. *Titus*, a great and noble opera, has an honored place in the grand line of opera seria which leads on, through Spontini, Rossini, and Bellini, to reach *Aida*. Honored today, that is—but pretty well unrecognized during a century and more when the work was seldom revived, and then as no more than a historical curiosity. I first encountered *Titus* in amateur and student productions, and at the 1949 Salzburg Festival in an edition that was well sung (Julius Patzak took the title role) but had been larded by Bernard Paumgartner with numbers from *Idomeneo*. The first American production, in a version by Boris Goldovsky and Sarah Caldwell, took place at Tanglewood in 1952. (In 1940, NBC had broadcast a studio performance.) It was only in the late sixties that the opera started to crop up with any frequency. It was done at the Piccola Scala in 1966; by the BBC (with Janet Baker as Sextus) and in Dusseldorf in 1967; at the Wexford Festival in 1968. That year, the London recording, conducted by Istvan Kertesz, appeared. (Before that, there had been only an undercast Period album.) In 1969, Colin Davis conducted a concert perform-ance in London, and in Cologne Jean-Pierre Ponnelle directed a production that remained in the repertory there and led to further Ponnelle productions in Munich and in Salzburg (where James Levine conducted it, and Carol Neblett, Tatiana Troyanos, and Catherine Malfitano were in the cast). In 1971, the Juilliard staged *Titus* (Ellen Shade was Sextus), and San Francisco's Spring Opera mounted a fancy version in which the dialogue was spoken by drama students and the musical numbers were professionally sung. (Fre-derica von Stade was Sextus.) None of this, however, did much to disturb the accepted view of the opera: a dull drama scarcely redeemed by some stretches of inspired music. Claudio Sartori's comment in *Opera* after the Piccola Scala version is typical: "The opera is a manifest proof of the general boredom that such a subject must have engendered in audiences, singers, and composers alike." It was the Covent Garden production of *Titus*, in 1974, that caused widespread revaluation.

Covent Garden treated the work as a masterpiece for which no apolo-gies have to be made. The score was not reordered (though some of the long recitatives, which are almost certainly not by Mozart, were abridged). The staging did not pretend to be a quaint reconstruction of a 1791 spectacle; there were no extras sitting in boxes, impersonating Leopold II and the origi-nal audience. Nor was it set in a prison camp, or aboard a spaceship. The scenery was neoclassical in idiom but not a pastiche; it was the strong crea-tion of a modern artist working within an assigned and accepted idiom. (Ponnelle's Cologne décor had been artful monochrome rococo.) When Mo-zart specified a scene change, the scene was changed. The director employed no conceits or données to "bring out contemporary relevance": the opera was played, conducted, and sung straightforwardly, directly, and with pas-sionate intensity. This *Titus* was triumphantly successful, and the moral should have been easy to draw. (The moral was lost, however, on the Covent Garden directors, who for their next Mozart production invited Götz Frie-drich to muck about with *Idomeneo*.)

Here are two tales of *Titus:*

1. In July 1791, Mozart, mortally ill and desperately short of money, accepted an uncongenial commission: to compose an old-fashioned opera seria for the coronation in Prague of Leopold II. In August, he dropped work on *The Magic Flute* and, in the words of his first biographer, Franz X. Nie-metschek, "he began *Titus* on the coach on his way from Vienna, and com-pleted it in Prague in eighteen days." For some reason, this piece of hack-work, this hastily fashioned potboiler, appealed to early-nineteenth-century taste; then, rightly, it was all but forgotten.

2. In the spring of 1789, Mozart was in Prague—the city where *Figaro* had had its greatest success, and for which he had composed *Don Gio-vanni*—and, with the impresario Domenico Guardasoni, laid plans for his next opera, a grand new setting of *La clemenza di Tito*. *Così fan tutte* and *The Magic Flute* intervened; Guardasoni had moved his company to Warsaw for a

while. (Mere chance that Mozart acquired a 1789 guidebook to Poland?) But in 1791 the impresario steered the coronation commission Mozart's way, and all the composer had to do was to set down the splendid piece that had been forming in his mind, and partly on paper, for more than two years. *Titus* is the most carefully planned and pondered of all his operas.

The evidence from which the second tale is built has been turning up in various learned periodicals during the last two decades. Its main points can be gathered together and simply stated. In April 1791—three months before the coronation commission—the Prague soprano Josepha Duschek gave a concert at which she sang "a brand-new gran scena" and "a rondo with obbligato basset-horn," both by Mozart. Neither piece has been identified; in 1959 Tomislav Volek suggested that the second must be Vitellia's rondo with obbligato basset-horn, "Non più di fiori," in Act II of *Titus*. Duschek certainly had "Non più di fiori" in her later repertory. And its allegro section, but not the larghetto, is (as Alan Tyson pointed out in 1975) on different paper from the rest of the *Titus* autograph. If Volek's identification is accepted, two conclusions are possible: that Mozart began to compose a *Titus* opera earlier than was supposed; or that, pressed for time, he dropped an existing concert aria into his score. The second conclusion will be favored by those who think that "Non più di fiori" is all too obviously a concert piece, and that its words would come more aptly from some heroine suddenly balked of a happy marriage to a man she loves. (Vitellia's matrimonial plans are based on imperial ambition, not love.) On the other hand, the words do sound an echo of the preceding Metastasio recitative, and that is generally true of the new verses Caterino Mazzolà wrote expressly for Mozart's setting of *Titus*. Metastasio's *La clemenza di Tito* was made for Vienna and for the composer Antonio Caldara, in 1734; there were some fifty settings of it before Mozart's, and at least four more after it. By Mazzolà, Lorenzo Da Ponte's friend, Saxon court poet, the old Metastasio libretto was—in Mozart's words—"transformed into a real opera." The number of arias was reduced from twenty-five to eleven; three duets, three trios, and two striking finales with solo utterances were added.

Volek also published for the first time the contract that resulted in *Titus*. It is dated July 8, 1791. In its first clause, Guardasoni undertakes to engage a castrato and a prima donna of the first water, and fill in the other roles from his own troupe. The second clause suggests strongly that he already had a "Titus" opera up his sleeve:

> I undertake to arrange for the composition of the poetry of the libretto, to be written on one of two subjects supplied to me by His Excellency the Grand Burggraf, and to have it set to music by a celebrated composer; but if time is too short to allow this, I undertake to procure a new opera composed on the subject of Metastasio's *Titus*.

Two days later, Guardasoni was on his way to Italy. He traveled by way of Vienna, where he could have met both Mozart and (as Helga Lühning pointed out in 1974) Mazzolà, who was serving a three-month spell as Vienna court poet, in succession to Da Ponte. Mozart and Mazzolà could have been talking *Titus* from May onward. In Bologna, Guardasoni engaged his primo musico and prima donna; on the return journey he could have given Mozart some idea of their capacities. Time-and-motion studies of the personages in this tale rule out few possibilities; conjunctions can be found to suit almost any conjecture. And there were always the mails, less laggard in the eighteenth century than they are today. Mozart (as Christopher Raeburn established in 1959) arrived in Prague on August 28, and *Titus* had its première on September 6, so Niemetschek's details must be wrong. Eighteenth-century performances were prepared at amazing speed; even so, and however much Mozart may have thought out during the three-day journey, eight or nine days seems too short a time in which to compose, copy, coach, and rehearse a whole new opera.

The new documents, the analysis of the paper *Titus* is written on, our knowledge of Mozart's working habits—and the music itself—suggest to me a third tale, one that is at least probable, and uncontradicted by any of the new facts:

3. Mozart began work in July 1791, planning the libretto with Mazzolà and then composing the concerted numbers and two arias for the one singer whose voice he knew (Antonio Baglioni, the Titus, who had been the first Don Ottavio). These numbers were sent to Prague in advance. On about August 25, Mozart himself set out, armed with a sheaf of newly bought music paper. Once in Prague, he met the other singers and composed their arias for them. The last few numbers to be written are on Prague-bought paper. Fast work, but not impossible, especially if the singers had already learned their secco recitatives. These are traditionally ascribed (without evidence) to Mozart's pupil Franz Xaver Süssmayr, who accompanied him to Prague. They are scarcely good enough to be by Mozart himself, or even by Süssmayr. I have not seen it suggested that they were prepared in advance by some local hack, or perhaps even lifted from an earlier *Titus* setting. Only cutting would be needed; to Metastasio's recitatives (as William Weichlein noted in 1956), Mazzolà and Mozart added—twice, in two different scenes—just the phrase "il passo affretta" ("Get a move on"), and that may simply be an author's instruction that, like two of Hofmannsthal's to Strauss, got into the music by mistake. The secco recitatives form by far the greater part of the text. Common sense prompts a presumption that the singers would have memorized them in advance, if they had barely a week in which to learn their arias. Some of the cast may even have known their recitative lines already, from other *Titus* performances. Mozart himself intervened in the secco only to achieve an affecting transition from accompagnato to secco in Titus's soliloquy, and to switch a cadence or two into a key that could fitly precede the aria he had composed to follow it.

More generally, I am inclined to believe that, well before the definite commission arrived, Mozart's thoughts had been turning toward the composition of an opera seria—but an opera seria that would also be "a real opera," one that in richness of music and in depth of true emotion would transcend the facile opere serie of his contemporaries as completely as his human comedies had surpassed their lightweight opere buffe. In 1786, he had revised and had composed new music for *Idomeneo*. A sketch sheet of his usually dated 1787 (now in Tokyo) is headed "Idées pour l'opéra sérieux"—ideas for *the*, not *an*, opera seria—and in that year he wrote the great Metastasio scena "Alcandro, lo confesso" and also "Bella mia fiamma." In 1788, there was another Metastasio scena, "Ah, se in ciel." Duschek's 1791 gran scena and her rondo (whether or not the latter was "Non più di fiori") may have been further steps toward *Titus*. The evidence suggests to me that the allegro of "Non più di fiori" *is* an earlier composition, incorporated, and that the decision to use it accounts for the clarinet obbligato in Sextus' first aria. Anton Stadler, the clarinet and basset-horn virtuoso for whom the Clarinet Quintet had been and the Clarinet Concerto was to be written, played the obbligatos.

Finally, however, I believe that the music was indeed composed in haste, after the definite commission for it had arrived. Two months may seem plenty of time for Mozart, but remember that he was also working on the Requiem and *The Magic Flute*. The evidence lies not at all in the autograph, which is uncommonly neat, and not only in the documents, but in the music itself. To a far, far greater extent than in his other operas, Mozart uses—albeit in his inspired way—the small change of eighteenth-century melodic formulae. Long ago, Tovey pointed out a likeness between the music of Sextus' "Could a heart bear such suffering and not die of grief?," in his first aria, and that of Vitellia's "Who could see my sorrow and not feel pity for me?," in "Non più di fiori." The latter melody Tovey described, rightly, as noble, and of the former he said, "It would be difficult to find a more extreme illustration of the efficient perfunctory elasticity of classical convention." I have not seen it noted that of the twenty-seven numbers in *Titus* only two— Sextus' recitative and Servilia's "S'altro che lacrime"—do not start with a figure that sounds the notes of the tonic triad. Or that two consecutive numbers in Act II—Publius' "Tardi s'avvede" and Annius' "Tu fosti tradito"—employ the same tune. (No use listening for this in the City Opera performance; both arias are omitted.) Of course, it could be argued that these are deliberate—or else subconscious but "meaningful"—cross-references: Publius tells Titus that his noble heart makes him slow to perceive treason in others, and Annius tells him that, although Sextus has been guilty of treason, that noble heart gives reason to hope that his life may be spared. Hmm?

Moreover, can one doubt that if Mozart had not been rushed he would have composed his own recitatives? In 1974, R. B. Moberly likened the opera to Michelangelo's *Entombment* in the National Gallery in London:

> The *Entombment* is a complete design, an incomplete picture. In Mozart's autograph mute blank pages precede neatly-written ensembles and arias. But the forlornly separate numbers are excerpts, instalments, fragments of a patterned whole. Bits of the picture are missing. But the abrupt starts suggest a conception of the work as a whole. . . . Time and

again the music makes dramatic sense as soon as we think of it . . . in the context of the preceding and following words.

Moberly suggests that "a competent dramatic composer" should write new recitatives to fill those mute blank pages. In Tanglewood, Goldovsky and Caldwell had in fact already tried new recitatives, fitted to an English translation. The concert performance without secco recitatives at the Mostly Mozart Festival last August was undramatic. The musical numbers are not independent.

Does any of this matter? I'd say it matters very much that the performers of *Titus* should have formed a clear idea what sort of work they are dealing with, and that audiences should know whether they are being offered some cynical hackwork hastily flung together or the score in which "Mozart worked to bring a new and richer kind of vitality to the opera seria," as in *The Magic Flute* he did to the Singspiel. The phrase is quoted from Michael Steinberg's informed and appreciative essay in the City Opera program. (The Mostly Mozart audience was served the old eighteen-day tale, newly garbled by the remark that Mozart "put the finishing touches on the score during the coach journey.") The City Opera billing is ominous. Along with the names of the creators, Mazzolà, Metastasio, and Mozart, and in letters as large, stands that of Federik Mirdita, as author of a "revised scenario." Mr. Mirdita receives even larger billing as director of the presentation, which is a reproduction of one he directed at the Theater an der Wien in 1976; it was then taken up by the Vienna State Opera. In fact, his tinkering is not disastrous, although none of it improves on Mozart's plan. As already noted, two arias are omitted. Servilia's affecting "S'altro che lacrime" is displaced, to become the third number of Act II, and there it loses its dramatic function—which is to make Vitellia examine her conscience and thus to motivate the change of heart given expression in "Non più di fiori." Moreover, the principals' three big parade arias—Sextus', Titus', Vitellia's—now form a strenuous sequence unbroken by Servilia's short, tender minuet. In Act I, Titus' "Del più sublime soglio" replaces the recitative in which the Emperor diverts to the Vesuvius Relief Fund the money that has been raised to erect a temple in his honor; instead of being a private confession to two friends, his aria, sung now before the populace, becomes a smugly self-praising effusion. In general, the recitative is far too severely cut. It may be undistinguished music, but it is noble dramatic verse that lends itself to noble, passionate declamation. Metastasio's lines give life to the characters and create the situations explored in Mozart's music. Voltaire, in the preface to his *Sémiramis*, described Titus' interview with the guilty Sextus and his subsequent soliloquy as "two scenes worthy of the finest that Greece ever produced, if not superior . . . worthy of Corneille when he is not ranting, and of Racine when he is not flimsy . . . two scenes founded not on an operatic brand of love but on the noble sentiments of the human heart."

The influence of French classical tragedy upon Metastasio—and of French heroic opera upon Mozart—has often been noted. The action of *Titus* begins where that of *Bérénice* ends. The actor of Titus must charge his brief reference to his parting from the Jewish queen—

Che terribil momento! Io non credei...
Basta, ho vinto, partì—

with a weight of emotion learned from Racine's tragedy. The opening recitative is long, but most of it is necessary. It tells the audience in quick succession of the insurrection prepared, for which the firing of the Capitol will be the signal, and then of Titus' noble character, Sextus' divided loyalties, and Vitellia's thwarted ambition—the three forces that impel the drama. Thus introduced, Mozart's first musical number becomes more than a pretty piece of music: Sextus' would-be resolute line collapsing in spaniel curves, Vitellia's proud, scornful leaps and incisive rhythms, and the flash of strings which accompanies her take on theatrical meaning. At Covent Garden, this first recitative was too severely abridged; at the State Theater, it is missing altogether.

Of course, there is a difficulty: recitative needs to be understood, line by line, word by word. And so one of the two common eighteenth-century practices—translating the opera into the language of the audience (almost all the early German performances were sung in German) or providing that audience with a bilingual libretto and leaving the house lights up—must be revived. An unsatisfactory Italian-English libretto—the stage directions omitted, the verse run on as if it were prose, and the whole reproduced from typewriting—is on sale at the State Theater. At least, it can give people, before or after the show, some idea of what *Titus* is about. That's not the same as hearing and seeing the drama in action.

Mr. Mirdita's staging contains some inept, and even unmusical, episodes. People shuffle on or off while the music marches. Titus, when filled with shining resolve, makes a hangdog state entrance, and at the end of the opera he walks away from his subjects' plaudits. Comic business with a tiny dagger spoils Sextus' "Parto." Vitellia arouses mirth by *running* in her stately costume. Publius is allowed knowing little reactions. Annius (a transvestite part) suggests stage masculinity with a cheerful-lumpkin rather than a patrician bearing. Most of the faults are gestural equivalents of dropping into a colloquial idiom, even slang; one sees what the director is trying to convey and wishes he had found a stylish way of conveying it. In general, however, the drama is cleanly and accurately laid out, and it moves well. The encounters are effectively achieved. Movement—or stillness—during the long arias looks natural. The cast sings and acts what recitative is left it in a lively fashion. The conductor, Julius Rudel, accompanies it himself and has taught his singers to declaim in the rhythms of dramatic speech; only the Titus retained the old oratorio trick of prolonging the penultimate syllable of each phrase. Mr. Rudel (who also conducted the Vienna performances) is a polished and expert Mozartian. If some of his tempi seemed a shade slow (in particular, the andante of the first-act finale), most of what he did was eloquent. The orchestra pit should be raised, if possible, to allow important instrumental details to tell more strongly.

The cast was good. It included three local débutants. Carol Vaness, who sang Vitellia in a revival of the San Francisco version two years ago, brought to the role a bright and accurate soprano, stage spirit, and musical vitality. I hope we hear a lot more of her. Ann Murray, a British Alceste, Dido, and Cherubino, was a fine Sextus—cogent, fluent, and expressive. Thomas Moser, a Virginian tenor who has sung Titus in Vienna, is a discovery. His tones are fresher than those of today's regular incumbents, Werner Hollweg and Eric Tappy, and he negotiated the coloratura of "Se all'impero" if not with complete success (what tenor can?), at any rate more fluently than they do. In life, Titus was not tall; Mr. Moser is tall, and he made an Emperor both dignified and sympathetic. In this performance, the characters were far from being the puppets Alfred Einstein deemed them. There was life and emotion, too, in Janice Hall's Servilia and Nadia Pelle's Annius. Deprived of Publius' aria, John Seabury had to be content with providing a bass line in ensembles.

Mozart calls for six scenes: Vitellia's apartments; "part of the Forum, magnificently adorned with arches, obelisks, and trophies, a view of the exterior of the Capitol, and a magnificent street leading to it" (Titus makes a processional entry down this street); a "delicious retreat" in the Imperial gardens on the Palatine (used twice); outside the Capitol; a great audience hall; and "a magnificent place before a vast amphitheatre, through whose open arches can be seen the arena, where the conspirators destined for the wild beasts are already assembled." (Titus completed and inaugurated the Colosseum that his father had begun.) Representations of the original settings, three of which were by Pietro Travaglia, Prince Esterházy's house designer, have not survived, but there are many from neoclassical productions of succeeding years. (They were studied to excellent effect by John Stoddart, for the Covent Garden performance.) Mr. Mirdita's production is played on a single set, credited in Vienna to Matthias Kralj but in New York to Lloyd Evans. A segment of heavy barrel vault is uneasily perched atop eight spindly Ionic columns. A bolt of red cloth is run through it and unfurls at the end to reveal on the reverse an allegorical banner representing, I take it, Leopold II as an eighteenth-century heir to Titus. Backcloth and wings are of some plain, pleasing off-white stuff; the backcloth parts at times like a tent flap to permit entrances before a little cutout of a Roman palace. The New York and Vienna sets differ in the cutout and in the iconography of the banner. The costumes are neoclassical. The floor levels—the pillars are set on a raised platform approached by five shallow steps—are skillfully planned to permit effective stage groups. This simple, open set is well matched to Mr. Mirdita's direct, unaffected staging, but it is a pity to lose any definition of Mozart's clearly planned scenes. A cleaner, less fidgety lighting plot would help, and in any case Gilbert Hemsley's needs reworking. In the first-act finale, a bright light catches the right side of Vitellia's face while the other singers are in darkness. The force of Titus' and Vitellia's bravura arias is lessened when they are sung on a dark stage pierced only by a crude, wandering spotlight.

Leopold's Empress, it is said, dismissed *Titus* as "una porcheria tedesca"—"German piggery." The tone of the official Coronation Journal was cool: "The composition is by the famous Mozart and does him honor, though he did not have much time for it." Count Zinzendorf, whose diary is a fruitful source of disagreeable remarks, declared the piece to be "the most tedious spectacle." But others were more appreciative. A certain Professor Meissner, "transported to Heaven," suggested that Mozart rather than Leopold should have been crowned. A critic who attended both the première and Guardasoni's 1794 revival (Raeburn identifies him with Franz Alexander von Kleist, who did take his young nephew Heinrich to the première) had been distressed in 1791 by a prima donna "who sang more with her hands than her throat, and carried on like one demented" and by "a wretched castrato," a mountain of flesh shocking to the eye and ridiculous to the ear. In 1794, when the Italian guest stars had gone and Sextus was played by a woman, he wrote:

There is a certain Greek simplicity, a quiet nobility in the whole music, which gently but thereby the more deeply touches a feeling heart, perfectly suits the character of Titus, the age, and the whole subject, and does honor to Mozart's fine taste and to his genius for observation. The singing line is constant, most excellent in the andantes, heavenly sweet, filled with emotion and expression. The choruses have pomp and are noble. In short, Gluck's nobility is united to Mozart's original art, his outpouring of emotion, and his resistless harmonies. Matchless, perhaps a non plus ultra of music, are the last trio and the finale of Act I. Connoisseurs are unsure whether *Titus* does not even surpass *Don Giovanni.*

The City Opera version can be improved, and I hope it will be. Already, it is one of the few *Titus* productions of our day in which the greatness of the opera is made apparent.

The Vienna State Opera is in Washington, at the Kennedy Center, for a two-week season during which *Figaro, Fidelio, Salome,* and *Ariadne* are being played. The first event was a concert at which Karl Böhm conducted Schubert's Second and Ninth Symphonies. Böhm is eighty-five. He has not proved to be one of those conductors who improve with age. On the contrary, his interpretations both in the opera house and in the concert hall have become increasingly "set," unfelt, even unphrased. Moreover, he seems to pay less and less attention to the quality of the sound. The Vienna Philharmonic could hardly make an ugly noise if it tried, but at this concert it sounded oddly characterless. The clarinets, in particular, were anonymous.

The Vienna concert, starting at seven, was followed at nine thirty by one from the Dresden Staatskapelle, another of Europe's great orchestras. If Vienna specialties are bloom of string tone and charm of individual phrasing, Dresden specialties are breadth and nobility of tone and phrase. The outer works on the program, the *Meistersinger* prelude and Brahms's Fourth Symphony, gave scope for them. Between, there was Beethoven's Eighth. But, even as Böhm had got the Philharmoniker to play in an "uncharacteristic" fashion, so Herbert Blomstedt, the Staatskapelle's music director, led his orchestra through crisp, dapper, and not exactly long-breathed performances.

I went to Washington, I confess, expecting to hear "Vienna sound" and then "Dresden sound," and to be enraptured by both. Expectations—prejudices—were disappointed. It was not a competitive festival: no grades assigned. But, whereas Böhm's Schubert Ninth was efficient and dull, no kind of revelation, Blomstedt's cogently shaped and by the orchestra athletically executed accounts of Wagner, Beethoven, and Brahms held me intent on each move of the music.

November 12, 1979

Heroine

Joanna the Mad, whose life was not uneventful, is a queen strangely neglected on the operatic stage. Her mother, Isabella, figures in various Columbus operas. Her sister, Catherine of Aragon, provided a star part for prima donnas at the Paris Opéra—Gabrielle Krauss, Rose Caron, Lucienne Bréval, Félia Litvinne—in Saint-Saëns's *Henry VIII*. Her son, Charles V, appears in two Verdi operas, *Ernani* and *Don Carlos*. Joanna herself makes a fleeting appearance in Donizetti and Verdi biographies. Scribe wrote a libretto about her, *Jeanne la Folle*, intended for Donizetti. But Donizetti didn't set it. Later, Antoine Louis Clapisson did. It appeared at the Opéra in 1848; Verdi was in Paris, so presumably he heard it. In 1851, Verdi's pupil, Emanuele Muzio, brought out a *Giovanna la Pazza* in Brussels, and then tried in vain to get it staged in Italy. There have been no signs yet of a Clapisson or a Muzio revival, even in London, and Joanna makes only a brief appearance in Krenek's *Karl V*. So Gian Carlo Menotti had an almost clear field when he chose her as the heroine of his tenth, and first grand, opera, *La Loca*.

Scribe set his drama in 1506, in and around Granada. Philip the Handsome is two-timing Joanna with a Moorish girl; Joanna catches them, stabs him, and goes mad. As the curtain falls, his corpse is borne in triumph to its coronation. Plenty of librettist's license there! Menotti's version is closer to history, though not exact. The libretto, his own, traces Joanna's life from her marriage to Philip, in 1496, to her death, in 1555. When the opera opens, she is a brilliant, impetuous seventeen-year-old bride; when it closes, a deranged old woman of seventy-six. The piece was written to provide a virtuoso role for Beverly Sills, who paid her farewell to the New York stage with it, at the State Theater, on November 1. The work, commissioned by the San Diego Opera, was first performed by that company in June, nine days after Miss Sills's fiftieth birthday.

Miss Sills's farewell caught me, as it seems to have caught many people, by surprise, and I am not ready with the long, careful survey and estimate of her art which would be appropriate when America's most famous singer appears on her home stage for the last time. That must wait. But, in any case, it would not be altogether appropriate after this particular performance. There was no big buildup for the evening; it was not any kind of gala farewell but simply an extra *Loca* dropped into the repertory to replace one that was lost during the City Opera labor dispute. Miss Sills has a few dates to keep with other companies, and she will be singing with the City Opera in Los Angeles later this month. Moreover, so far from leaving the company, as its general director she is more closely associated with it than ever. Her curtain speech—the face young again through the gray makeup and beneath the wispy white wig—was brief: "Thank you for the marvelous love affair. The best is yet to come."

Joanna is one of her highest and finest performances. For me, it ranks with the Scala Pamira (in Rossini's *Siège de Corinthe*) in 1969, the first time I heard her, and the Met Violetta in 1976. In recent years, Miss Sills has tended to play her sparkly, bubbly self as Rosina, Norina, the Merry Widow, Fiorilla in Rossini's *Turco in Italia*. She was delightful but predictable in those parts; Pamira, Violetta, Gilda (in Boston's 1977 *Rigoletto*), and now Joanna the Mad have offered more of a challenge to her dramatic abilities as an actress and as a singer. Joanna most of all. Menotti may have planned the role as a composite of all the sparkly ingénues, lovelorn queens, and suffering heroines in the singer's life. What she gave was a gripping portrayal of an individual woman. She was in full, clear voice. Watching and listening to her, one didn't think, This is Sills's New York farewell, or How well Sills does the part; one thought only of the character she created. Within the variety and through the changing appearance there was consistency. It was a remarkable performance.

La Loca is perhaps Menotti's best opera. The dramatic structure is schematic, and history has been adjusted to create symmetries. In successive acts, Joanna confronts her husband, her father, and her son; the three men are played by the same singer. She loves them. From each she hopes, but in vain, for unselfish love; each of them is eager to gain for himself the crown she inherited from her mother. Unselfish love is offered by Don Miguel—a young courtier in the first two acts, in the final scene a priest who opens her heart to God's love. I've heard the piece described as a sung soap opera in Renaissance dress, but it's better than that. The historical setting has saved Menotti's text from the glibness that makes most of his earlier operas, for all their effectiveness, distasteful. His post-Puccinian musical idiom has been strengthened with bright, strong elements derived, it seems, from Prokofiev. He writes a scene for Joanna and her little daughter, Catalina, that is chaste, moving, unsentimental. The opera is not fully worked out, however. The finale, based on a saccharine Puccinian tune for Father Miguel, ends abruptly, as if unfinished. *La Loca* is no masterpiece, and no *Don Carlos*. There is no depth or density in the drama, no sense of the wider world; it is narrowly focused on Joanna's emotions—a monodrama in grand-opera décor. The chorus is merely decorative. But within those limitations *La Loca* is a decent and accomplished piece of work, and I imagine it will bear revival.

Around Miss Sills's incandescent heroine there was an admirable presentation of the piece. John Broecheler was strong as Philip, Ferdinand, and Charles; Joseph Evans was lyrical as Miguel; the smaller parts were well taken. Tito Capobianco's direction was straightforward and capable, and so was Mario Vanarelli's décor—a handsome and practical series of satisfactory, old-fashioned box sets. John Mauceri was a colorful and ardent conductor.

New York's better full-time orchestra is that of the Metropolitan Opera, seldom heard in concert. Its warmth of tone, fullness, and unforced amplitude in climaxes were on show when it was lifted out of the pit for the Sunday-night Wagner-Strauss benefit concert James Levine conducted at the opera house last week. The program was the *Tannhäuser* overture and bacchanale and Elisabeth's greeting, the *Götterdämmerung* funeral march and immolation scene, and the *Salome* dance and finale. The vocalist was Birgit Nilsson; as an encore, she sang Brünnhilde's battle cry. Her voice has lost none of its heroic power, none of its stirring ability to ride a full-orchestra surge effortlessly, triumphantly. Since Flagstad, there has not been a soprano so loud. Although that's a blunt way of putting it, volume is a virtue, a necessary one, in the high-dramatic roles. There have been Brünnhildes and Isoldes more subtle and more intense (Astrid Varnay, Martha Mödl) but none with so directly exciting, secure, and commanding a voice. Where Flagstad shone like the sun, generously, warmly, Nilsson's radiance is on a narrower beam, its luster that of burnished gunmetal. She roused the Metropolitan audience to unconstrained enthusiasm, and justly so, for she is unique. Nevertheless, it could not be ignored that her old failing, inaccuracy of pitch, had become less occasional.

For Wagner, Mr. Levine finds the long breath that often eludes him in Mozart and Verdi—though again I wished that in the *Tannhäuser* overture he would persuade his winds to hold their long notes to the full value. The funeral march had a weight and grandeur, and a vitality, to make one eager for the Metropolitan *Ring* under his baton which must surely be in preparation. The Dance of the Seven Veils was glittering, seductive, delicate. It may be tawdry music, but Mr. Levine and his splendid orchestra made it captivating.

November 19, 1979

Capital Fare

The last four days of the Vienna State Opera season at the Kennedy Center coincided with the 1979 Festival of the Liszt Society of America, presented in co-operation with the Library of Congress. *Ariadne auf Naxos* and *Fidelio* did not show the Vienna company at its best. *Salome* was more exciting. But the keenest moments of pleasure I felt during four busy days of music in Washington were provided suddenly at a modest recital of Liszt songs given in the Coolidge Auditorium of the Library of Congress. Liszt champions tend to choose each a special field in the composer's large and uneven output. Mine is the songs—a hundred-odd of them, collected in three volumes of the Breitkopf Liszt edition. With *Tristan,* published in 1860, Wagner changed the sound of Western music. But the opening measures of Liszt's song "Die Lorelei," composed in 1841, are enough to show that the path to the harmonic world of *Tristan* had already been opened. Liszt's "grand idea," which he described as "a renewal of music through its intimate connection with poetry," informs all his music—the orchestral tone poems, the piano pieces, the oratorios, the liturgical compositions. Nowhere does it find more consistently perfect, shapely, coherent expression than in his songs. Those who hymn the greatness of the oratorio *Christus,* the big organ pieces, the Hungarian Rhapsodies, the tone poems, or the B-minor Sonata usually include a "despite the" reservation somewhere. Several of the songs can be praised as masterpieces without any such reservations. In 1911, Oliver Ditson brought out a collection of thirty Liszt songs. (Reprinted by Dover at four dollars, it is excellent value; but the text needs to be checked against the Breitkopf volumes.) In a foreword, Carl Armbruster remarks on the "overwhelming power of truth" that the music displays, and continues: "His songs are the emanations of his peculiar organization, of his phenomenal technical mastery, and of his Titanlike command of musical expression. . . . It is as if we had entered into a new world, full of well-nigh magic enchantment." Listeners who at a recital have thrilled to "Die Lorelei," "Ihr Glocken von Marling," the Petrarch settings, "Die drei Zigeuner" may well feel that all this hardly needs repeating. But how all too seldom they are sung! How rarely one hears an all-Liszt, or even largely Liszt, recital! How inadequately the songs figure in the current record catalogue!

There were to have been two singers, soprano and tenor, at the Washington recital. The soprano was ill; only half the program was done, and the disappointment was sharp, but what remained was rewarding. Liszt lieder style is not easily mastered. A common charge against the songs is that they are overdramatic, even operatic. But, as Alan Walker observes in the introduction to the Liszt symposium he edited, the composer's music has long been distorted not only by his critics but also by his interpreters. Liszt singers, when they are not too theatrical in approach, tend to be not nearly vivid enough. It is a question not of finding a mean but of understanding just what, and when, the composer borrowed from the theatre, and how he transported and transformed its effects (including the tender graces, swift, brilliant cadenzas, trills, and messa di voce of an elegant, exquisite opera singer). The dramatic exclamations, the picturesque narrative passages, the passionate outbursts, the long, ardent melodies must be not subdued but given their fullest emotional value. The voice of James McDonald, the singer at the Washington recital, is no more as yet than a young, fresh, decently schooled, smallish tenor of agreeable quality. But he used it with an instinctive and unerring sense of Liszt's musical intentions. He brought the songs to life.

The theme of the program—curtailed by the soprano's absence—was earlier and later versions of the same song. Liszt's revisions, we are told, were concerned chiefly with simplification; he himself once described his earlier songs as "for the most part overinflated in sentiment, and often overstuffed in accompaniment." But in rhythm, in harmony, and in subtlety of motivic working the later versions are in fact the more intricate. Mr. McDonald sang the 1844 and 1859 versions of the Victor Hugo setting "Comment, disaientils": fascinating to hear the piano part thinned to the texture of a plucked guitar, and the essence of the rapturous refrain caught in so much shorter space. He sang the 1844 and 1859 versions of the Heine setting "Morgens steh ich auf und frage": here the later working is longer; more richly wrought and *"Tristan*esque" at the start and the close; clarified and more flexible in the central episode. In both cases, and in just about every case of a Liszt revision, earlier and later versions are treasurable. Who could bear to lose either the earlier, expansive version of the Petrarch sonnet "Pace non trovo" (which was glowingly sung by Mr. McDonald and sensitively played by Ruth Ann McDonald) or the late, spare, almost epigrammatically refined transformation?

Liszt's large choral works, as I discovered when *Christus* was done in the Cathedral of St. John the Divine earlier this year, flower in apt acoustics. In Washington, his Missa Solemnis, composed for the consecration of Gran (alias Esztergom) Cathedral, in 1856, was done in St. Matthew's Cathedral, a marbled and mosaicked basilica not very large but lofty and resonant. At the age of twenty-three, Liszt wrote the essay "On the Future of Church Music," in which he proclaimed his vision of a music that would "unite on a colossal scale the theatre and the Church" and be at once "dramatic and religious, splendid and simple, solemn and serious, fiery and unrestrained, stormy and tranquil, clear and heartfelt." In the Gran Mass, he wrote such music. He told Wagner that he had *"prayed* it rather than *composed* it." Critics divide on the merits of the work. Hermann Kretzschmar deplored "passages that are written with an astonishingly great economy of intellectual expenditure"; M. D. Calvocoressi, in his 1906 biography, said that the Mass "besides being an admirable monument of faith . . . stupefies us by its sheer musical beauty, by its structure, by the unity of thought which animates it, and by its logical cohesion, absolutely and perfectly natural in all its parts." Whether one takes the Kretzschmar or the Calvocoressi view—are the sequences and repetitions spun out with uncritical ecstasy, or do they reflect a carefully balanced plan?—may depend on the merits and circumstances of a particular performance. The fervent performance by the University of Maryland Chorus and the Catholic University Orchestra, conducted by Miklós Forrai—one that filled the cathedral with soft entreaties, full-throated paeans, and mystic radiance—left me enthusiastic and exalted. Between the petitions, vocal and orchestral, of the Agnus Dei, soft, solemn reverberations stole through what in a concert hall are holes of silence. The resonance lent wings to the voices of the solo quartet and transmuted the fiery brass into liquid gold that blazed yet hurt not. Do not object that even bad music would sound good with such acoustic enhancement. Not so: it would sound more trumpery, for ear and mind distinguish between adventitious pleasures of ambience and inherent merit fitly revealed. Liszt's invention in the Missa Solemnis is prodigious. I wonder only if he was ever disturbed, as I am, by the likeness of a recurrent "summoning" motif (heard in the Gloria, Et Resurrexit, Hosanna, and Agnus Dei) to the sirens' summons in the Venusberg, "Naht euch dem Strande"— same figure, in the same key. Liszt conducted *Tannhäuser* in Weimar in 1849. For once, an idea found in both his and his son-in-law's music seems to have been the latter's invention.

The Mass was preceded by the tone poem *The Battle with the Huns*, a work that in the concert hall can sound both inflated and naïve, but one that in these surroundings, with the organ breathing and then pealing in triumph the "Crux fidelis" hymn, proved strangely exciting.

The next day, Liszt's Missa Choralis was sung at High Mass, by the cathedral choir. Or, rather, much but not all of it was; the conductor, Paul Traver, explained to the regular worshipers that the musical part of their service would be more extensive than usual, and to the visiting Lisztians that they would hear less of the Missa Choralis than usual, since it did not toe the line of the Church's new liturgical requirements. Liszt's Credo, the longest movement, was omitted altogether, and the other sections were to varying extents abridged—the Benedictus to just a few measures. It is not for a mere music critic to assess the larger pros and cons of the cozy, low-church style now adopted by the Roman Church, but he can fairly regret what she has been doing to her language and her music. The service book used in Washington was not a Missal but a paperback "Missalette" (I'm not making this up), couched in terms of a colloquial chumminess that stopped just short of "Have a good day, God." Is it only by Anglican churches that the rich heritage of Catholic liturgical music can now be preserved? The Church of England's Twenty-fourth Article declares it "a thing plainly repugnant . . . to have publick Prayer in the Church, or to minister the Sacraments in a tongue not understood of the people"—which means that Latin Masses can still be sung in the cathedral and the college chapels of Oxford, on the presumption that Latin is understood there. The only time I have heard Beethoven's

Missa Solemnis in liturgical context was in Westminster Abbey. Last month in New York, Liszt's Missa Choralis was sung—unabridged—at St. Mary the Virgin.

In this Mass, composed in 1865, during Liszt's happy time in the Dominican monastery on Monte Mario, his love of Palestrina, his appreciation of the Cecilian movement for church-music reform, and his belief that a modern poetic spirit should inform all new music are harmoniously combined. Pius IX—a Marcellus II to Liszt's Palestrina—came to visit Liszt on Monte Mario. It must have been music in this vein which prompted his remark "The law, my dear Palestrina"—for thus the Pope would fondly address him—"ought to employ your music . . . to lead hardened criminals to repentance; no one could resist it, I am sure." The festal splendors of the Gran Mass yield to quiet devotion. The Hosanna rises from pianissimo to piano. Plangent *Tristan* harmonies occur only in the repeated "nobis" that ends the first two clauses of the Agnus Dei. The style is studied, not exuberant, but the music flows with quiet intensity. The St. Matthew's choir (which uses women in place of boys) was aptly smooth and gentle, but it was stationed in a side chapel, from which the sound did not really float out to fill the building. The motet was not one by Liszt but, rather unsuitably, a movement of Brahms's German Requiem.

Liszt the young virtuoso was represented at a piano recital given in the Coolidge Auditorium by Idil Biret. She played his transcription of the Fantastic Symphony, made when he was twenty-two. Charles Hallé tells in his memoirs of a concert at which Berlioz conducted the finale and then Liszt played his piano arrangement, producing "an effect even surpassing that of the full orchestra, and creating an indescribable *furore.*" Miss Biret's playing did not have the panchromatic instrumental dazzle for which Liszt's was renowned, but it was dexterous, spirited, and unflagging. Her remarkable feat has been recorded (on the Finnadar label); live, it proved even more impressive. In the first half, she was both efficient and poetic in the two *Legends,* and bright in "Venezia e Napoli" pieces from the second "Years of Wandering" album.

Little new material or new thought turned up in the papers I heard, but "Some Problems in Liszt Research," outlined by Dezsö Legány, of the Hungarian Academy, was a model of quietly elegant, witty discourse. Liszt's letters to Olga von Meyendorff have been published for the first time, in an English translation by William Tyler. (The handsome volume is distributed by the Harvard University Press.) The letters are now in Dumbarton Oaks; twenty Liszt autographs that the Baroness owned are now in the Library of Congress. In the foyer of the Coolidge Auditorium there was a small but enthralling exhibition drawn from the library collection. (A catalogue of the Liszt manuscripts it holds was published to coincide with the festival.) One touching document was Carolyne van Sayn-Wittgenstein's will, dated—presumably predated—October 23, 1861, the day after that set for her wedding. (At the last minute, the Wittgenstein family prevented it.) She leaves her largest turquoise to Cardinal Antonelli, her other jewels and some works of art to her daughter, and everything else to "my husband, M. François Liszt," and signs the testament "Carolyne Liszt."

Vienna's *Ariadne auf Naxos* is a 1976 production directed and designed by Filippo Sanjust; it was conducted then, and again in Washington, by Karl Böhm. The Prologue was distinguished by the Major-Domo of Erich Kunz, who gave a precise, polished, and unexaggerated performance, and by Agnes Baltsa's Composer. Although Miss Baltsa's mezzo was too small to fill the big solos—"Du, Venus' Sohn," "Musik ist eine heilige Kunst"—with the soaring, rapturous sound that her great Vienna predecessors Sena Jurinac and Irmgard Seefried brought to them, and although she moved into the higher and the lower reaches of this soprano role (created by Lotte Lehmann) carefully, not freely, her timbre was so precisely focused and her projection so sure that everything was exquisitely audible, and she gave a delicate, captivating portrayal of the impetuous youth. The rest was so-so. A touch of commonness in Edita Gruberova's Zerbinetta kept her from being charming. Mr. Sanjust's fussy production did not help. While the Composer mused on his heroine ("Sie gibt sich dem Tod hin"), Zerbinetta, who should feel unexpectedly moved by the lad's earnestness and ardor, was offstage; Harlequin claimed our attention with a prominent mime and continued it in competition with Zerbinetta's "Ein Augenblick ist wenig."

The opera-seria company assembled during the Prologue in handsome eighteenth-century costumes, but when the curtain rose on *Ariadne* proper they had changed into draperies suggesting a high-school Greek play. Ariadne went barefoot. Bacchus was wigless. Zerbinetta was dressed as if to play the Governess in *The Turn of the Screw*. Mr. Sanjust evidently shared the Dancing Master's view of the setting: "What could be drearier than a desert island." Ariadne reclined most awkwardly on a steep, bare staircase. Gundula Janowitz sang the role correctly, in clear, secure, and even beautiful tones, but was a cold, blank, unmoving performer. Miss Gruberova's account of "Grossmächtige Prinzessin" was brilliantly exact and was cleverly, fearlessly enacted. The Bacchus was dreadful. Only Murray Dickie, the Brighella, and a veteran of many *Ariadne* productions, brought wit and sharpness to the commedia dell'arte male quartet. Böhm's conducting suggested a late impression of what was originally a fine, crisp engraving; it still had merits, but Bacchus' entrance music can never have blared out more vulgarly.

Fidelio, a 1970 production, suggested a company love-in rather than a serious account of Beethoven's opera. After "Abscheulicher," the Leonore graciously shared her applause with her conductor. Leonore and Rocco's entrance in Act II was delayed, apparently as a sign to the audience that it was expected to applaud Florestan's aria. After *Leonore* No. 3 had been used for *Verwandlungsmusik*, there was a prolonged standing ovation for Leonard Bernstein. (He adopted the trick of turning the last note of the prison duet into the first note of the overture; although there is illustrious precedent for doing so, it seems to me rather slick a device.) Günther Schneider-Siemssen's décor is handsome. When Otto Schenk's staging was new, it presumably treated such episodes as the gravedigging in Act II more convincingly. The outline of a strong, straightforward production, much like the one Mr. Schenk did for the Met, was still perceptible. Leonore does not go barefoot.

I enjoyed Kurt Rydl's realistic, direct, almost casual Rocco. The heroine, Gwyneth Jones, was in poor voice—frequently off pitch, and generally without line. She produced some radiant, powerful individual notes. She spoke the dialogue—what was left of it—urgently, passionately. ("Mir ist so wunderbar" was jammed hard against Marzelline's aria; almost all the conversation from which it should spring was omitted; a few phrases were reinstated *after* the quartet.) When Jess Thomas, the Florestan, began the cry of "Gott!" which opens Act II softly, one's heart lifted to his artistry—and sank as one discovered that the poignant attack was but his method of feeling his way into the note. For he then held it, swelled it, roared it, worried it, pushed it off pitch. The same thing happened at the "le-" of "nichts lebet ausser mir"; here there is at least the small excuse of Beethoven's fermata sign. Mr. Thomas sang with intensity, but his voice sounded worn, and (unlike Julius Patzak in *his* late performances of Florestan) he forced it and exposed its limitations instead of turning them to expressive effect. Theo Adam barked and declaimed Pizarro's music sometimes on and sometimes off the notes. Lucia Popp was an able Marzelline. Jaquino and Don Fernando were undercast. Bernstein's reading was warmhearted but self-indulgent, effusive, and unclassical. In the course of the evening, *Fidelio* and all that it should mean somehow got lost.

In fact, during both these productions one had a sense that the Vienna State Opera was doing its famous thing; that the company and its performance, not the opera, provided the main point of the evening. But *Salome*, a 1972 production, was another matter. Zubin Mehta's reading was poised, colorful, and secure. The score cohered as if it were one long tone poem, and it was superlatively well played. Jürgen Rose's décor is tricked out with some tiresome, fashionable Art Nouveau detail (and Salome's dress has a zipper), but essentially, and effectively, it suggests the courtyard on an ancient Near Eastern palace beneath a warm night sky. Boleslaw Barlog's staging is strikingly spare. Where Joachim Herz, in his production for the English National Opera, employed a cast of sixty, all individualized, Mr. Barlog kept onstage only the characters who actually sing. It was a strong, unaffected, and very musical production, marred only by a prominent and intrusive entrance for the Page during the tense moments while Salome awaits her head. Neither the elderly Herod (Hans Beirer) nor the young Herodias (Gertrude Jahn) overacted. Salome was Leonie Rysanek. Barefoot, she moved like a young woman, alertly, impulsively, and she sounded like one. The upper reaches of the voice still shine. After decades—since the 1951 Bayreuth Sieglinde—of catching Miss Rysanek on vocally untidy evenings, I am at last being luckier and discovering the singer whom so many audiences have admired. Peter Wimberger was a fiery and formidable Baptist.

. . .

The Kennedy Center is a busy place. Before *Salome*, there was *The Dream of Gerontius*, with Richard Lewis and Katherine Ciesinski, in the Concert Hall, and then a concert in the Terrace Theatre given by the Theatre Chamber Players of Kennedy Center, the resident chamber music ensemble. *Gerontius* and *Salome* on the same day—one that had begun with Liszt in St. Matthew's—would be too much for me, I felt, but the chamber music was refreshing. The program opened with Maki Ishii's *Five Elements*, a picturesque piece in which two piccolos seated front-stage, one on each side, shrill or chirrup to one another; percussion adds a soft, pretty chime; violin, viola, and cello join in; and then a guitar enters as protagonist. Next, the première of Charles Wuorinen's *Psalm 39*, a setting for baritone and guitar. It opens as a solemn cantillation. The tension mounts—"My heart was hot within me, and while I was thus musing the fire kindled"—and then, after "And at the last I spake with my tongue," it breaks into free, passionate utterance from both the voice and the instrument. There is a final outburst at the cry of "O spare me a little." An impressive piece. The performers were Richard Frisch, baritone, and David Starobin, guitar; the work was written for them.

There followed Stravinsky's *Three Songs from William Shakespeare*, in a fresh, well-balanced performance; Jeannette Walters was the singer. Then a Hugo Wolf group, in which I thought Mr. Frisch, though intelligent, was a shade heavy. The Chamber Players programs, while devoted largely to twentieth-century music, regularly include one substantial classic. (The audience suggested a happy mingling of those at Lincoln Center who subscribe to the Chamber Music Society and those who prefer the work of Speculum Musicae.) The second half of this concert was Beethoven's "Harp" Quartet—but I went off to prepare my mind for *Salome*. I'd heard good things of the ensemble, which is directed by Leon Fleisher and Dina Koston. They were confirmed. Technical accomplishment, interpretation, program planning, manners, and "presentation" (neat, clean appearance; friendly faces; deft "scene shifting," not long waits, between the items) conspired to make the concert and the music enjoyable.

Agostino Steffani's *La libertà contenta*, composed in Hanover in 1693 and given its American première last month at a Clarion Concert in Alice Tully Hall, deals with adventures in the Peloponnesian War unrecorded by Thucydides. The characters are mostly familiar: Alcibiades, Pericles and his Aspasia, King Agis of Sparta, and his admiral Lysander. It is the time of Alcibiades' Spartan exile, and Decelea has been fortified—about 414 B.C. (Pericles had been dead for fifteen years, but a librettist must be allowed his license.) The action turns on the circumstances that Aspasia is loved by not only Pericles but also Alcibiades, his friend Telamides, and Agis; and that Princess Timaea, betrothed to Agis, is loved by both Alcibiades and Lysander. All ends happily: Agis gives Aspasia and Pericles a safe-conduct to return to Attica, on condition that Athens and Sparta make peace and Alcibiades be allowed to return to Athens. The intrigues are worked out in forty-eight arias, seven duets, and a couple of ensembles, few of whose texts omit the word "love." (The Duke of Mantua is not far away when successive arias include the lines "Woman is . . . unstable and changeable" and "My heart is never happy with but one.") The title refers to Alcibiades' contentment at being freed of all amorous bonds. Ortensio Mauro's libretto is apparently as frivolous as that of *La Belle Hélène*. His Pericles seems to acknowledge as much when he exclaims, "This revered tongue whose thunderbolts made a sensation in Athens, which subdued the fury of Asia's ruler, must now be turned to the seduction of Aspasia!" But just possibly the Hanoverian courtiers may have found "relevance" in the plot: the Elector's son (later George I) was behaving as reprehensibly as any of Mauro's characters; and the year after *La libertà contenta* the Königsmark affair came to its tragic crisis. The opera figures in the Königsmark correspondence. After *Niobe*, the Steffani opera that Clarion did two years ago [see page 47], I remarked that Amphion and Niobe—the ruler versed in science and the arts, preferring study to cares of state, and his brilliant wife so proud of her position, her lineage, her children, and her admirers—suggested German seventeenth-century court portraits taken from the life. Is *La libertà contenta* a daring topical portrait of that court where, as the historian Samuel Rawson Gardiner put it, "it was understood that princes were to arrange their domestic life according to their own pleasure"?

Steffani is a Clarion specialty: *Tassilone* in 1973, *Niobe*, and now *La libertà contenta*. *La libertà* is a simpler, less ambitious score than *Niobe*. It uses a smaller orchestra. The music does not accompany large, picturesque, supernatural scenes or tell of pangs as keen as those Niobe and Amphion suffer. But it does reveal Steffani's splendid resourcefulness. Hugo Riemann, who edited Steffani's *Alarico*, declared him a composer more intimate, more delicate than Alessandro Scarlatti, and one more charming than Lully in tenderness of melodic invention. Scarlatti and Lully are greater composers, but those particular excellences may be allowed to Steffani. Like many another baroque opera, *La libertà contenta* becomes more and more interesting as it proceeds. Handel had a way of displaying familiar merits in a first act and then girding himself in Acts II and III to do things new and arresting. Steffani likewise. Act II reaches its climax in a nocturnal garden scene consisting of five good arias; four of them are magical. Aspasia threads the smooth line of "Foschi crepuscoli" through a soft-pulsing, tenderly woven web of strings and woodwinds. In Agis' "Cara notte," continuo-accompanied, long-sustained notes flower gently into ravishing curves of melody. Recorders and violas accompany Timaea's rhythmically animated "Piante, fiori, ombre, che dite," whose final chord is the first chord of Alcibiades' "Notte, amica," a slow melody, richly accompanied by strings, over a ground bass that teases and pleases the ear with its carefully placed departures from pattern. The sequence ends with a bravura vengeance aria for Timaea. Act III is notable for its rhythmic vivacity—shifting accents, syncopations, irregular phrase lengths in tempos both fast and slow—and for a duet in which Timaea and Alcibiades spin the words "You leave me, you scorn me" into dulcet chains of charming melody. Their *addio senza rancor* is strangely moving.

Once again, Clarion and its music director, Newell Jenkins, earn our gratitude for bringing forward a work of the past well worth hearing. Once again, the gratitude is tempered with regret that the performance was not on a higher level. Mr. Jenkins's loving response to the inventions of Steffani's music was always apparent, but sometimes he laid a heavy hand on the rhythms. Do continuo arias really need a conductor? Would it not be fitter to station harpsichord and string bass where they could see the singer? The best of the cast was John Aler, firm and fluent as Pericles. D'Anna Fortunato (Timaea) and Rodney Hardesty (Agis) had the right style, but her pitch was faulty and the timbre of his high countertenor was unpleasing. It was a mistake to transpose the leading role, Alcibiades, down an octave and allot it to a tenor, Robert White. A bright soprano is called for. Clarion provided generous measure (forty-three arias and six duets), and an English text. The singers sat or stood in a row. The action would have been more clearly defined had only those "onstage" in any particular scene been at center stage.

November 26, 1979

City Lights

The first night of the Metropolitan Opera's latest production, Kurt Weill's *Rise and Fall of the City of Mahagonny*, was a curiously tame affair. The show was thoughtfully prepared and carefully executed. *Aber etwas fehlt*, and that something missing was the vividness that no other *Mahagonny* I've ever come across has missed. The Washington and the Boston productions, in 1972–73, had it in good measure. Vividness may come to the Met's when James Levine conducts the marches with a heavier, stronger tread, when he and his cast feel and sound the lyricism of the music more ardently, when the stage direction gains focus, and when one or two mistaken decisions about the text are reversed. *Mahagonny*, fifty years old now, is one of the most important and exciting operas of our century. I wrote at length about the work after the Washington production and concentrate now on the New York performance. It is sung in English, in a revised version (some lines improved, others not) of the translation that David Drew and Michael Geliot made for Sadler's Wells, in 1963.

Mr. Levine's concern for Mahler (he has now recorded six of the symphonies) might, one felt, have led him surely into *Mahagonny*. In a 1930 essay, T. W. Adorno remarked that "a strange kind of Mahler, stranger than Mahler himself, runs through the whole opera." Early in the score—as the closing section of its first number—Weill placed the Mahlerian finale of the little *Mahagonny* Songspiel he had composed in 1927 "to test the musical style envisioned" for the larger work. Its first four notes are the melodic cell from which much of the *Mahagonny* music grows. (It has already been sounded during Widow Begbick's establishment of the city, at the words "Aber hier gibt es Spass.") At the end of the drama, the thudding, inexorable funeral-march rhythm of the accompaniment recurs, gathers above itself all the principal themes of the work, reveals their relationship, and provides this twentieth-century *Ring* with a shattering finale. Mr. Levine's treatment of the first statement was neat, crisp, light, unemphatic. It didn't lay firm foundations for the finale, the tragic yet exhilarating apotheosis. The Viennese café waltz to whose strains Jakob Schmidt eats himself to death didn't lilt. On the other hand, where a tight, bright, crisp tempo *is* needed, in the band music of the "Fighting" episode, Mr. Levine's handling was oddly relaxed. Weill recommended that for *Mahagonny* the orchestra should be raised to the level of the first row of what in America is, confusingly, also called the orchestra (elsewhere, the *platea, Parkett,* or stalls). The Met pit was raised, but not to stalls level; the sound of the orchestra was not as bright and forward as it should be. The stage, as Weill also recommended, was built out forward, over the orchestra pit (perhaps this roofed in some of the instrumental sound), and much of the action was played in front of the proscenium arch. About nine feet in, the prompter's box poked up through the stage floor, looking awkward. Is it immovable? It popped up likewise in *Die Entführung*. In general, the disadvantages of the Met's immense size were less successfully minimized than in that bright *Entführung*, put on a few weeks ago by the same team: Mr. Levine, John Dexter as director, Jocelyn Herbert as designer.

Mahagonny has a libretto by Bertolt Brecht. Miss Herbert's décor is an expansion of Brecht's textbook recipe for staging his works, but one carried out in an unimaginative and undistinguished fashion, in scenes of unrelenting ugliness. it employs the Brecht *Gardine*—the white half-curtain whisking to and fro on its wire, bearing the projected captions before the scenes and acting as a backdrop to several of them. The device is called for in the stage directions, and I have seen modern *Mahagonnys* (in Hamburg, in Boston) where it has been successfully revived. But enlarged to a Met scale it loses some of its efficacy. Moreover, the open-plan set—like Ming Cho Lee's open sets for the Met *Boris Godunov* and *Lohengrin*—proves acoustically unsatisfactory when the singers are not well forward on it. The sound doesn't get out into the house. Mr. Levine has to keep his orchestra down; the wonderful instrumental inventions can't tell. Backcloth and sides are hangings of funereal black. If they were replaced in white—perhaps the *Entführung* wings could be used—the show might become more vivid. Brighter light would help, too.

This subfusc *Mahagonny* was depressing. Weill and Brecht meant their work to be enjoyable. Usually it is.

Teresa Stratas, the Met's Jenny, is an intelligent and attractive artist. Lotte Lenya sang Jenny in a celebrated Berlin production of *Mahagonny* in 1931, and in 1956 she recorded the role. Her potent and particular artistry has colored the popular idea of the opera and tempted some modern Jennys into essaying a "cabaret" style. (Lenya also recorded some of Jenny's music in 1931, in a clear, fresh "short" soprano very different from the 1956 nightclub voice.) Miss Stratas avoids the temptation. She gives a compelling, direct, honest performance of a direct, honest, straightforward girl who must live in a dishonest world. But her voice is not quite big enough to project the music into so large a house. It is, however, a trained voice, and one that could well manage the original, operatic setting of Jenny's "Ach, bedenken Sie, Herr Jakob Schmidt." For the Berlin production, Weill composed a new setting of the number, apt to Miss Lenya's untrained voice. Miss Stratas, I understand, rehearsed both the operatic and the cabaret version; it was disappointing that in the performance she sang the latter. Weill tried to persuade Marie Gutheil-Schoder (who had made her début in 1891, and from 1900 onward had been one of Mahler's company at the Vienna Opera) to come out of retirement to sing Begbick; she was fifty-six, and she refused. Astrid Varnay, who sings Begbick in the Met production, is sixty-one. She does not command the role. It hurts to be unchivalrous to the most exciting Isolde and Brünnhilde of my life, but a critic's first duty is to the work. Richard Cassilly is Jim Mahoney. He sings with intensity of expression. He plainly knows what the piece is about. But his timbre is often disagreeable. There are other veterans in the cast. Ragnar Ulfung is Fatty, Cornell MacNeil is Trinity Moses, and neither is particularly effective. But Arturo Sergi—my most poetic Lohengrin (seventeen years ago, in Wieland Wagner's Hamburg production)—sings Jakob Schmidt with the bright, forward tones that are needed. Michael Best, a young tenor, had his Met début in the small role of Toby Higgins, and beside his lithe performance several of the others in the cast seemed even more elderly. He, Miss Stratas, and Mr. Sergi alone showed the kind of freshness and gleam that made the City Opera's presentation of Weill's *Street Scene* so attractive, lively, and affecting.

If age, acoustics, and blackness conspire to mute the work, Mr. Dexter's unpointed direction abets them. It, too, could be described as subfusc. There are moments when one has to scan the confused stage pictures to discover who is singing. The shape of the three acts is far from clearly presented. The "Act of Love" scene in the second of them is much weakened by the interpolation of the Cranes Duet, Weill's setting of an early Brecht love sonnet. Weill admitted it to the first edition of the score as a sop to directors too timid to stage the episode as he had composed it, but he stressed that it should be dropped from Act II once theatres had the "courage" to stage the original. At the opera's sixth production, in Berlin in 1931, it *was* dropped— "rightly so," as Mr. Drew remarks in the preface to his critical edition of the score, "for it is completely at odds with the style and structure of the other

Sittenbilder." The duet is good music, however, and Weill had an idea that it might find a place in Act III. His idea wasn't tried in Berlin, since the music lay outside Miss Lenya's range, but other productions have shown that the Cranes Duet can be included and be effective and poignant in that act. In the Met production, it should be moved. *Mahagonny* presents other textual problems than the duet; they arise from Brecht and Weill's decision to work in the six songs from their plotless *Mahagonny* Songspiel. Three of these drop easily into the operatic narrative, and the other three less easily—the "Benares" song most awkwardly of all. In Berlin, and in Brecht's "reading text" of the libretto, "Benares" was simply omitted. In Boston, Sarah Caldwell moved it to Act I, and that didn't really work. Other productions have shown the wisdom of Mr. Drew's suggestion that it should be played as a coda to the trial, without being given—as happens at the Met—the prominence of an independent scene.

The Met *Mahagonny* will surely improve. On the first night, everyone seemed to be inhibited, too respectful. The chorus did not sing out as if it loved the music. When Jim went berserk with a knife, toward the end of Act I, no one seemed to be in any real danger from him. And Mr. Levine's conducting of a new score often takes a performance or two before it kindles into life. The musical roots of *Mahagonny* lie in Mozart, Wagner, and Mahler— three composers Mr. Levine understands. I hope that later in the season I can add a brighter postscript to this review.

Apollo, Cecilia—some musical spirit—must have decided that I shouldn't be allowed to pass a quiet, musicless evening at home the week before last. Before settling down with a good book, I turned on the radio to hear the news; got WNYC; heard an announcer say that a recital by Peter Orth, the winner of this year's Naumburg Piano Competition, was about to be broadcast from Alice Tully Hall and that his program would include Roger Sessions's *Pages from a Diary*. Naturally, I stayed listening. Bach began the program—the Four Duets. Mr. Orth's playing of them was clean, sharply articulated, cogently phrased. The musical discourse was unclouded, unromanticized. Apart from some scurrying in No. 3, this was a model of how to sound Bach on a modern piano. The Sessions then showed that the pianist had wit and temperament, if not quite enough, perhaps, for these endearing pieces. The outer movements of Beethoven's Opus 109, the next work, were played in a large, free, thoughtful way, as if Mr. Orth himself were composing the music as he went along and sometimes wondering what should come next. The Prestissimo whirled out like an improvisation. Sometimes his quasi-extempore approach went too far, till one felt like saying, "Come, now. Everyone does know what happens next in Opus 109, so do stop teasing, and get on with it." But it was an arresting performance. It held my attention and interested me in the player. So when the intermission came I took up an umbrella and sloshed through the night to Tully Hall; the place was well filled, but I managed to find a seat. Part II was Chopin's Op. 25 Studies, played as a set, and they were enjoyably done. Each was sharply characterized, skillfully shaped, and the large, well-founded, and all-embracing technique already heard in the Beethoven was everywhere in evidence. What I missed was some touches of romantic melancholy; the sun seemed to be shining, warm, confident, even on the C-sharp minor. Mr. Orth's command became a shade less precise in the last two studies—a price many pianists pay when they play the twelve studies straight through, as if they formed a suite with three excessively taxing finales.

The live encounter revealed that the piano whose warm, unglassy sound I had liked so much was a Baldwin; that Mr. Orth is a fidgety player to watch (he bounces, tosses his head, shoots his cuffs); that he has a big tone that does not become bangy and an exquisite soft tone that steals out to fill the hall. Yet I still feel somewhat unsure whether—despite the Bach and the Beethoven—he is a profound musician in the making or just a (very accomplished, sensitive, generous) pianist. His first encore was "Handel-Orth," delicately, poetically played. His second was the Schulz-Evler transcription of the *Blue Danube*. One doesn't expect a young pianist to deliver it with the lilting, aristocratic elegance of Joseph Lhevinne, whose famous recording sets the standard, but Mr. Orth didn't seem even to be aiming for it.

December 3, 1979

Tributes

Last month, two new commissioned works were played at concerts of the Chamber Music Society of Lincoln Center, in Alice Tully Hall. Gunther Schuller's Octet, performed on November 2 and 4, and broadcast a week later by WNCN, is composed for the forces of Schubert's Octet—clarinet, bassoon, and horn, string quartet and double-bass. There are four movements, in traditional forms; the work lasted nearly forty minutes at the first performance, a minute or two less at the second. The Octet is an attractive but not, I think, a wholly successful composition; it is hard to feel sure, for the Chamber Music Society performances seemed a sketch of the piece rather than a secure, masterly interpretation. The tone of the violins was thin and keen. The first subject, on strings, was less audible than the winds' tick-tock accompaniment. Passages that look full and rich in the score sounded scrawny and ill-balanced in the hall. The slow movement is a set of variations on a short-winded four-limb theme of regular cut. (The idea for it may have come from the inner parts of the adagio introduction to Schubert's Octet.) The variations give solo opportunities to each instrument in turn; the bassoon's number and the final, exuberant treatment "in a well-known European folk ensemble manner" are especially taking. In the scherzo, Schuller comes closest to open neoclassicism and to the Schubert who rapped out Beethoven's scherzo rhythms. There is a lively fancy at work in this movement, but the composer's daring use of arrests followed by silences needed defter rhythmic handling than it received. The finale, marked "Vivace—with driving energy throughout," sounded neither lively nor energetic: partly the composer's fault, for writing many long notes tied across the bars, but largely the players'. In a program note, Schuller tells of often playing the horn part in the Schubert Octet and of the profound influence that work had on him. He mentions one "subtle, brief bow to Schubert," in the slow introduction to the first movement (both octets begin with a sustained octave F), but also writes of finding "contemporary analogies to those techniques and values we cherish from the past." And several times in this relaxed yet brimming piece the spirit of Schubert seems to haunt a rhythm, a cadence, and the bright, upward-bubbling themes. I would like to hear a warm, witty, ebullient account of the work, in more intimate surroundings. But I think there are passages the composer could tighten.

A fortnight later, George Crumb's *Celestial Mechanics* (*Makrokosmos IV*): *Cosmic Dances for Amplified Piano, Four Hands* had its first performance. This is the fourth in Crumb's *Makrokosmos* series; the first and second are for amplified piano, and the third, entitled *Music for a Summer Evening*, is for the Bartók combination of two pianos (but amplified) and two percussions. The movements of *Celestial Mechanics* are entitled "Alpha Centauri," "Beta Cygni," "Gamma Draconis," and "Delta Orionis," but those names, the composer says in a note, were added after the music had been written. In several earlier works, Crumb's sound imagery has suggested to me the strange, deep emotions that can flood an imaginative watcher of the night skies, but this latest, and disappointing, piece struck me as a dry, uninspired exercise in drawing unusual sounds from a grand piano: rattles, the dull clonk of the hammers on finger-stopped strings, tapping with the hands and various mechanical aids on different parts of the instrument, picking and scratching. A few passages of agitated dance rhythms seem to owe something to Stravinsky's *Rite of Spring*, but they are rhythms pattered out and then dropped; there is little to suggest "the majestic movement of the stars" or "cosmic choreography." When I tried to forget the associations of the title and listen to the dances as "pure music," I still missed the quiet, romantically intense, delicately lyrical charm of timbre of the other *Makrokosmos* pieces. The work was played, with evident efficiency, by Gilbert Kalish and Paul Jacobs. The last number calls in a third pair of hands, those of the page turner. At this performance, he was Richard Goode—so we had three virtuosos at (and sometimes in) one piano.

•   •   •

Zubin Mehta began a Philharmonic concert with Luigi Nono's *Per Bastiana Tai-Yang Cheng,* for orchestra and tape, composed in 1967 for the Toronto Symphony and last heard in New York in 1970, when Hans Werner Henze conducted it with the American Symphony. Mr. Mehta prefaced the Friday matinée performance with a well-judged little introductory talk, warning his listeners that it would be silly to wait for tunes and then complain that they had heard none; the work was constructed of timbres, not melodies. It lasted just fifteen minutes, he continued; owing to the nature of the notation, no two performances were identical; and if the audience liked it he and the orchestra would do it again for them. The applause was not so warm as to justify an encore, but people did listen attentively. In my experience, the Philharmonic's matinée audiences are the most open to unfamiliar music; Thursday seems to bring out the booers and the noisy stompers-out. There *is* a tune, the Chinese song "The East Is Red," deep underneath *Per Bastiana,* but it's not audible in the thick, muddy texture produced by the tape and by three large instrumental groups, two of which do not play from precisely pitched notation and employ microtonally mistuned strings. From the row behind, I caught the comment "Well, that wasn't too bad," and I felt much the same. Nono's mind has fashioned something delicately poised, intricately precise, on paper. In performances—I heard three by the Philharmonic, and the work is recorded on the Wergo label—one becomes aware of shifting balances and occasional arresting incidents, and with a little imagination can even catch the gist of the program hinted at in the composer's note: "The title . . . signifies 'the breaking of the day.' Just so, for Bastiana [Nono's daughter] 'the day breaks'; life begins, tinted with red." *Per Bastiana Tai-Yang Cheng* probably has a place in history as a distinguished composer's essay in the once fashionable manner of composing with clotted masses of timbre. Nono's convictions, political and musical, require him (and his listeners) to "confront each new situation" as it arises; inevitably, some of his compositions are tied to their time. I wonder why Mr. Mehta chose to revive *Per Bastiana* now. *Como una ola de fuerza y luz* (1972), which is recorded on Deutsche Grammophon, is even more elaborate (it is twice as long, and needs a soprano and a pianist as well as orchestra and tape); but it is far more "audible," more beautiful, and more stirring.

The achievements of Josef Marx—oboist, teacher, editor, publisher, and champion of both baroque and contemporary composers—who died last year, were celebrated at a concert given in the Abraham Goodman House by his colleagues and pupils. It began and ended with Stefan Wolpe's Solo Piece for Trumpet (published by the Josef Marx Music Company) and included his *Form for Piano*—two notable examples of his charged, epigrammatic vein. A Suonata da Camera by Johann Gottlieb Janitsch—one of Frederick the Great's musicians, championed by Mr. Marx—made pleasant listening. A sonata by Jan Dismas Zelenka, for two oboes, bassoon, double-bass, and continuo, did something to mark the Zelenka tercentenary, which has otherwise passed almost unobserved in this country, except on WNCN. Charles Wuorinen's fine Second Trio, for flute, cello, and piano, composed in honor of Wolpe's sixtieth birthday, and works by Raoul Pleskow (his Latin songs and a new *Oratio: In Memoriam Josef Marx*), Isaac Nemiroff, and Harvey Sollberger made up a program that, even to someone who had not known Marx and his circle, seemed to draw the portrait of an enthusiastic, lovable, and inspiring musician.

December 10, 1979

Wings of the Soul

Berlioz's last opera, *Béatrice et Bénédict*, composed for Baden-Baden in 1862, is seldom staged. A few German houses took it up in the nineteenth century, but "it is not music for Paris," Berlioz said, and it reached the Opéra-Comique only in 1890. (There was a revival in 1966.) London saw its first stage production in 1960, at University College, and New York its first in 1965, at the Manhattan School of Music. Concert performances turn up from time to time, and there are two recordings, both conducted by Colin Davis. On the American professional stage, two productions of *Béatrice* are chronicled: one by the Washington Opera, in 1964, and the other, earlier this year, at the Indianapolis Romantic Festival, with Delia Wallis as Beatrice. I have seen the opera only at universities: London, Princeton (with Bethany Beardslee as Beatrice), and this month at Stony Brook, as a joint presentation of the Departments of Music and Theatre Arts. None of the three made the work seem what Kobbé calls it, "an operatic masterpiece," but they confirmed two things Berlioz himself said about it: "one of my liveliest and most original achievements" and "difficult to perform well."

The difficulty is not one of size or cost. As the composer said, "unlike *Les Troyens*, it costs nothing to put on." Only three singers have arias—a mezzo and a tenor in the title roles and a soprano as Hero. Only two sets are specified, and in a pinch one set can be made to serve. And only a classical orchestra—plus cornet and touches of color from guitars, harps, and tambourines—is used. *Béatrice* is kept off the modern professional stage, I believe, for another reason: it is a divided work, at once a comedy and something like a romantic cantata, very hard to hold in balance. From one point of view, the piece is like a play with music rather than an opera with spoken dialogue, and calls for a company—and a theatre—that could present *Much Ado*

About Nothing one night and *Béatrice et Bénédict* the next. The three arias, two duets and a duettino, and two trios make up the specifically "operatic" content of the score; the other musical episodes—wedding song, drinking song, etc.—would be musical even in the legitimate theatre. The libretto, Berlioz's own, is *Much Ado* without the ado—without the Hero and Claudio misunderstanding that gives Shakespeare's comedy its substance. When the piece is cut, as it usually is, to the musical numbers linked by a minimum of spoken dialogue, the action is reduced to an anecdote: Beatrice and Benedick tricked, with little difficulty, into an open avowal of their love. It's not quite enough for an evening of theatre, and not enough to balance the score's other "theme," which is treated musically rather than theatrically. That theme, of course, is love. Few people would disagree that Berlioz wrote the most tenderly beautiful of all love music: in Romeo's reverie; in the garden scene of *Les Troyens;* and in Hero's aria, her duet with her handmaid Ursula, and the women's trio of *Béatrice.* Those who know Berlioz's memoirs may also agree that one of the most tenderly beautiful love stories ever told is that of Berlioz's love for Estelle Duboeuf. He lost his heart to her when he was twelve; he saw her for just a moment when he was thirty; he visited her, once, when he was sixty and she was sixty-seven. Thereafter, he sent her letters of ardent devotion, and she answered him wisely, kindly, sensitively, for she seems to have understood him as neither of his wives and very few of his contemporaries did. On the last page of his memoirs, he writes:

> My sky is blank no longer; through tears I look toward my star— distant but bright, soft, seeming to smile on me from afar. True, she does not love me. . . . But . . . now she knows that I adore her.
>
> I must be reconciled to her having known me too late, as I am reconciled to not having known Virgil, whom I should have loved, or Gluck or Beethoven—or Shakespeare, who might perhaps have loved me. (The truth is, I am not reconciled.)
>
> Love or music—which power can uplift man to the sublimest heights? It is a large question, yet it seems to me that one should answer it in this way: Love cannot give an idea of music; music can give an idea of love. But why separate them? They are the two wings of the soul.

Why separate them? Berlioz's own music and life are not separable, and his conjoined imaginative adventures tangle with those of anyone who has once fallen under the spell of his sounds. Although the visit to Estelle came two years after *Béatrice,* Hero's music and much of Beatrice's and Benedick's tell of a passionate yet untempestuous love that through his life Berlioz dreamed of finding. The particular excitement that his music often brings is that of being lifted, with him, to the "sublimest heights" of Michelangelo, of Virgil, Shakespeare, and Goethe, of Gluck and Beethoven. After Berlioz, one responds, exalted, to St. Peter's, to the *Aeneid, Romeo,* and *Faust,* to *Alceste* and the Ninth Symphony through his as well as one's own eyes and ears. As the love of Tristan and Isolde is superhuman, so Dido and Aeneas's "Nuit d'ivresse et d'extase infinie," in *Les Troyens*, sings of a voluptuous rapture more intense and more heroic than common mortals are granted. But the particular rapture that *Béatrice* brings is personal; Hero and Ursula's "Nuit paisible et sereine" is apprehensible as the letter duet of *Le nozze di Figaro* and Susanna's "Deh vieni" are. *Béatrice* is the most intimate of Berlioz's mature compositions; despite the Shakespearean source, we meet him unaccompanied by his giant heroes. His companions in the music of quiet, tender melodies and lapping, enchanted accompaniments are the Mozart of those *Figaro* movements and the trio "Soave sia il vento" and the serenado in *Così fan tutte*, and the Rossini of the trio "À la faveur de cette nuit obscure" in *Le Comte Ory*, an opera Berlioz much admired. After composing *Béatrice*, he said, "Now I have done everything I had to do."

I hope that one day I see a production in which the romance, the flashing wit, and the comedy (represented by the maestro di cappella Somarone, who replaces Shakespeare's Dogberry) are balanced; in which Beatrice is played by an actress born under a dancing star, and the Benedick is dashing and romantic; in which—whatever the language of the show—plenty of Berlioz's dialogue is retained. The décor must combine elegance and glitter with the soft enchantment detailed in the composer's stage directions for park, grove, terrace, roses, and, at the end of the first act, moonlight playing upon fountain and sea. Famous Berlioz conductors—Hamilton Harty, Beecham, Colin Davis—have revealed that what earlier critics, not without reason, deemed awkward, and even amateurish, in the scores can be transformed into eloquence of an individual and thrilling kind. Stage directors and designers have lagged behind; there have been few Berlioz productions (Boston's *Benvenuto Cellini* was one) in which his all too evident theatrical "miscalculations" were made to seem at worst minor flaws in the flow of the whole and at best keen strokes of dramatic genius.

There was some accomplished singing from the women in the mainly professional Stony Brook cast—Doris Manville as Hero, Leah Littlefield as Beatrice, Janice Edwards as Ursula—but none of the singers moved well or acted well. Tom Neumiller, who directed, had not taught them to use their eyes or their words. David Lawton, conducting, drew decent playing from his student orchestra. (After the first Baden rehearsals, Berlioz said, "I have my work cut out in teaching the orchestra, for the thing is a caprice written with the point of a needle, and it needs extremely delicate playing.") Mr. Lawton's reading was on the right lines, but the brilliant music needed more verve, and the love music more intensity and poetry. The chorus was admirable in Somarone's Epithalame Grotesque, which is, as Edward Cone remarked in an essay on *Béatrice*, at once ridiculous, aesthetically gratifying, and oddly moving. Things may well have improved during the run of four performances. At the first of them, *Béatrice* did not cast a spell, but indulgence was called for. A few days before opening night, a fire damaged the lighting system of the theatre. The show went on under makeshift illumination and was played in front of a black hanging; Douglas Kraner's painted backcloth, which looked attractive in sketch, could not be lit.

Cherubini's *Les Deux Journées* (known in English as *The Water Carrier*) is one of the most important and influential operas ever composed. The librettist was J. N. Bouilly, whose *Léonore* was adapted for Beethoven as *Fidelio*. The chief tenor role was first sung by Citizen Gaveaux, the composer of *Léonore*. *Les Deux Journées* appeared in Paris in 1800. It reached Vienna two years later, in two productions that opened on successive days. Beethoven declared that, with Spontini's *La Vestale*, it had the best libretto he knew. Goethe, who produced the piece at Weimar in 1812, held up the text to Eckermann as a model of what an operatic libretto should be. Spohr, Weber, and Mendelssohn are also prominent in the long line of *Deux Journées* admirers. Mendelssohn defined the special qualities of the libretto when, with a London opera in prospect, he asked J. R. Planché to provide him with something similar: "a subject in which some virtuous heroical deed is celebrated, which represents the triumph of some noble feeling known to every listener who has any feeling at all, who could then see his own internal life on the stage, but more concentrated . . . turned into poetry"; and a setting "in a country or time and amid a people that could give a lively background to the whole, one that while reminding us of history could at the same time remind us of the present day (as the dark figure of Cardinal Mazarin forms a background to *Les Deux Journées*)." The City Opera does not have *Fidelio* in its repertory. When it does, then it should turn to *Les Deux Journées*. And any modern librettist wanting to write more than a costumed charade should study Bouilly's work. The heroes of *Fidelio* are aristocrats. Those of *Les Deux Journées* are ordinary people suddenly caught up in, and tested by, the decisions and doings of their rulers. *Les Deux Journées* was a *Street Scene* of its day. (After the première, the water carriers of Paris visited Bouilly in a body and offered him a year's free supply.) And, like Weill's opera, it is very well composed. When Beethoven was asked who, present company excepted, was the greatest living composer, he answered without hesitation Cherubini. In *Les Deux Journées*, the noble sentiments ("Aide ton frère, et sauve l'innocent"; "Le premier charme de la vie, c'est de servir l'humanité") are expressed less strenuously than in Cherubini's grander operas.

Les Deux Journées reached New York in 1827. It was revived this month by Bel Canto Opera—the company's last production in the little midtown church hall where in eleven seasons it has put on an astonishing repertory of some eighty operas, most of them rarities. (Next month, it moves uptown, and does Adolphe Adam's *Le Postillon de Longjumeau*.) Bil Mikulewicz's ambitious décor spanned the stage with a giant effigy of Mazarin trying to contain all France in his embrace. Victor Symonette, translator, conductor, and stage director, rewrote the first stanzas of Antonio's romance "Un pauvre petit Savoyard" as a child's introduction to seventeenth-century France. The added historical touches were too heavy. Bouilly's *Léonore* and *Deux Journées*, both set in the seventeenth century, are based on *faits historiques* that occurred during the Reign of Terror (the originals of his Léonore and Florestan may have attended the opera about them); their subject is valor and virtue in a time—but not one specific time—of oppression. (Is the Spanish king whose name day is celebrated in *Fidelio* Philip III, Philip IV, or Charles II? Does it matter?) The opera was not well sung or acted except by Ron De Fesi, as Mikéli, the water carrier. He played the folk hero with charm, candor, and naturalness, and his singing was warm, unaffected, and lively. The rest was patchy, but something came across.

December 17, 1979

Carol

Christmas, Scrooge's nephew Fred tells his uncle, is "a good time: a kind, forgiving, charitable, pleasant time: the only time I know of, in the long calendar of the year, when men and women seem by one consent . . . to think of people below them as if they really were fellow-passengers to the grave." Dickens said that his chief purpose in writing *A Christmas Carol* was, "in a whimsical kind of masque which the good humour of the season justified, to awaken some loving and forbearing thoughts, never out of season in a Christian land." The story ends happily, but it is a grim and disturbing tale. One of its earliest reviewers praised the author's feeling "not for imaginary and fictitious distresses but for the real grinding sorrows of life." Robert Louis Stevenson "cried [his] eyes out, and had a terrible fight not to sob," when first he read the *Christmas Books:* "But oh, dear God, they are *good*—and I feel so good after them—I shall do good and lose no time—I want to go out and comfort someone—I *shall* give money. Oh, what a jolly thing it is for a man to have written books like these and just filled people's hearts with pity." The scenes of Christmas cheer—Mr. Fezziwig's, Belle's, the Cratchits', Fred's parties—are exuberantly described, but the images that *A Christmas Carol* impresses most powerfully on a reader are the three that close the central "staves," or chapters: Scrooge's vain attempt to extinguish the bright light streaming from the Ghost of Christmas Past, when it has shown him the joys of love which, like Alberich, he had renounced in his quest for gold; the hand of the silent Ghost of Christmas Yet to Come pointing inexorably at the tombstone in the rank city churchyard; and between them, and most shocking, Scrooge's glimpse of a claw beneath the robe of that jolly giant the holly-crowned Ghost of Christmas Present, and the appearance of two children from beneath that robe.

They were a boy and girl. Yellow, meagre, ragged, scowling, wolfish; but prostrate, too, in their humility. Where graceful youth should have filled their features out, and touched them with its freshest tints, a stale and shrivelled hand, like that of age, had pinched, and twisted them, and pulled them into shreds. Where angels might have sat enthroned, devils lurked; and glared out menacing. No change, no degradation, no perversion of humanity, in any grade, through all the mysteries of wonderful creation, has monsters half so horrible and dread.

In its hymning of shared, social joys, Dickens's tale has things in common with *The Mastersingers*, but its moral is not far removed from that of *The Ring*.

Edmund Wilson called Dickens "the greatest dramatic writer the English had had since Shakespeare." The most dramatic presentation of *A Christmas Carol*, I believe, is likely to be that provided by a skillful reader. (Dickens himself, Franklin Roosevelt, and Laurence Olivier are among the famous who have read it aloud.) But there have been countless attempts to give it scenic as well as verbal form: plays (two appeared within weeks of the story's publication), movies (the first appeared in 1908, and the most celebrated in 1951), animated cartoons (Richard Williams's film based on the John Leech drawings of the first edition won an Academy Award in 1973; Scrooge McDuck and Mr. Magoo have starred in other versions), musicals, and operas. The latest *Christmas Carol* opera is, words and music, by Thea Musgrave. It was commissioned by the Virginia Opera Association and was first produced at the Center Theatre in Norfolk earlier this month. In a public lecture, one of a series of six given around the première, Musgrave told how she arranged Dickens for music.

A first draft of the libretto was drawn up using so far as possible Dickens's words for dialogue and stage directions. A one-acter based on the five staves of the original grew to a two-act opera with six scenes in the first act and seven in the second. (Each act lasts about an hour.) At this stage, there seemed to be thirty-eight essential characters. Impracticable! Musgrave decided on some meaningful doubling: the young baritone who played Fred could also play the young Scrooge, and the soprano who played Belle, Scrooge's rejected fiancée, could reappear as Fred's wife. (This works well: as the old Scrooge watches, the spirit pictures of what was, what is, and what might have been are poignantly linked.) Another natural doubling covers Mrs. Fezziwig and Mrs. Cratchit, two mother figures. Quadrupling enables the singer of Scrooge's dear, bright little sister Fan to reappear as three other dear, bright little sisters in the domestic scenes. Other role sharing was dictated by convenience. Some takes on ironic significance; and the recurrent, half-recognized faces and forms aptly suggest the substance of a dream. Eventually, Musgrave arrived at a minimum cast of seven grown-up singers, a dancer (who plays all three Christmas spirits), an actor (for Marley's Ghost), and three children. Not all the doubling is obligatory. More singers can take part if desired. (In Norfolk, six children shared the various juvenile roles; the adult singers, kept at seven, had a fine chance to display versatility.) Supers can be (and were) added to the party scenes. There is an optional children's chorus at the end; Musgrave included it in her scheme when the Virginia Opera decided to form a children's ensemble of some thirty, and four hundred children turned up for auditions. In every way, *A Christmas Carol* displays Musgrave's efficiency and practicality. The orchestra can be as small as fifteen (six winds, five strings, harp, piano, two percussions) and, with extra strings, can be larger. (Twenty-eight players were used in Norfolk.) The company published a model program book, packed with information, to accompany the première. In addition to the libretto, it reproduced libretto and composition sketches, and also the stage plans and charts the composer had made as a guide to insure that her scenario was theatrically workable. The scene changes and costume changes she envisaged would either determine the pacing of the score or need alteration if the music began to make its own demands. Once the text had been drafted, composition and extensive libretto revision proceeded together.

The Virginia Opera, which began life with pilot productions of *La Bohème* and *La traviata* in 1975, is now in its fifth full season. It grew quickly, and in the third season gave the American première of Musgrave's grand opera *Mary, Queen of Scots,* a performance of metropolitan—after the Met's *Entführung* and *Mahagonny* this year, I'm tempted to add of more than Metropolitan—standard. Opera in this country is still extravagantly and discretely organized, largely as a matter of local enterprise and local pride. If all the money that the people of Norfolk, Washington, Baltimore, Wilmington, and Philadelphia spend on their separate, sporadic opera companies were put together, it could surely pay for a stable, year-round company playing a wide repertory in all those cities; and then carefully rehearsed productions would not have to die after a handful of performances. That would be sensible, and one day it may become necessary; but there is also much to be said for individual civic achievements. The people of Norfolk—perhaps one should say of Tidewater, that cluster of contiguous or tunnel-linked cities at the mouth of the James River—are justifiably proud of their opera company, and on my three visits to it, for *La traviata*, for *Mary*, and now for *A Christmas Carol*, I received a strong sense of wide-based community support and enthusiasm. The Virginia Opera guild is one of the largest in the country. Activity does not begin and end with the Center Theatre performances. Around *Mary*, the Central Opera Service held a conference, and Old Dominion University an international convention. Around the *Carol*, opera company and university united to present the lecture series, the National Opera Association held its annual conference, and there were two interesting Dickens exhibitions, one of *Christmas Carol* illustrations through the years and the other of Dickensiana from the Morgan Library. (In one of his letters, Dickens mentions Norfolk.) This year has also seen the founding of the Virginia Opera Theatre, which tours the state (the main company occasionally plays Richmond), and of year-round Opera for Youth programs.

The 1979–80 Norfolk bill is nine performances of the *Carol*, and five performances each of *La Bohème, Don Pasquale,* and *The Tales of Hoffmann.* Each opera is played in a separate run, but continuity is provided by the casting—some singers have become Norfolk favorites over the years—and by the fact that all productions have been directed by David Farrar, and all but the first of them have been conducted by Peter Mark, who is general director of the company and also Thea Musgrave's husband. The continuity played its part in the creation of the *Carol.* All but one of the grown-up singers for whom it was written had appeared in previous Norfolk shows, and all the children were familiar to Musgrave. Not only conductor and director but also set designer, costume designer, lighting designer, and wig and makeup designer were those who had worked on *Mary,* and nearly half the orchestra had played in the earlier opera. In short, *A Christmas Carol* was tailor-made for the Norfolk troupe. This need in no way limit its potential circulation. If anything, the reverse. *Le nozze di Figaro* was tailor-made for the 1786 Vienna troupe, and *Lucia di Lammermoor* for the 1835 Naples troupe; several of Britten's most successful pieces were devised in the first place for specific talents of the English Opera Group. In general, it seems to be a good, even an inspiring, thing for a composer to know exactly what singers, what players, what theatre, and what audience he or she is writing for.

Fifteen years ago, invited to tell American readers about some new British composers, I wrote of Musgrave: "There is a vein of clear common sense in her musical personality. . . . It is as if she has regarded each new discovery of our times with a coolly appraising eye, and then taken possession of such elements of it as can enhance her already considerable skills." At that date, her only opera was the one-actor *The Abbot of Drimock,* a lively, lyrical Scottish version of the Gianni Schicchi story, composed in 1955. In 1967, her full-length opera *The Decision* appeared—an earnest, honest, and ambitious work making no attempt to conceal that in *Boris Godunov, Wozzeck,* and possibly *Mahagonny* Musgrave had heard things she could use as a model. She interrupted a busy, commission-filled career for two years to compose this opera that no one had asked for but that had forced itself upon her. *The Voice of Ariadne* (1974), commissioned for the English Opera Group, included new discoveries that she had made both in Monteverdi and in the expressive possibilities of electronic tape. When *Ariadne* first appeared, I enjoyed but underrated it. The New York City Opera performance, in 1977, revealed to me the poetry and fancy that lie beneath its careful, clearheaded planning. Meanwhile, in a series of orchestral, chamber, and vocal works Musgrave had explored and developed ideas that had been suggested to her by Britten, Boulez, Ives, and many others. She has never been a follower of fashion. She has ever been responsive, in the way that Mozart and Schubert were responsive, to new suggestions, possibilities, procedures, that she can master and make her own. *Mary, Queen of Scots,* a swift, romantic, and dramatic opera, appeared at the Edinburgh Festival in 1977, the next year in Norfolk [see page 164], and this year in San Francisco. Musgrave has lived in this country for nine years now. When I was a London critic, scarcely a month went by, it seemed, without a Musgrave performance. In seven years here, only the Clarinet Concerto (at a Philharmonic women's-music concert), *Space Play* (done by the Chamber Music Society of Lincoln Center), and three operas (two in Norfolk, one in New York) have come my way. This surprises me, for Musgrave's music is at once accessible to conservative ears and satisfying to an adventurous taste. There is plenty of it, and I have never heard a score of hers without being eager to hear it again. Why on earth has the Philharmonic not commissioned a symphony, the Met an opera? I see occasional Musgrave performances turning up in Philadelphia, Los Angeles, Syracuse, Milwaukee, Pasadena; read enthusiastic reviews of them; but hear all too little of one of the ablest composers we have.

Because I at first underrated *Ariadne,* because I would have assessed *Mary, Queen of Scots* rather differently had I heard it only once, and because the confidence and sheer good sense with which Musgrave, in both verbal exegesis and the music itself, expounds her ideas can hide the romance and adventure of her work, I feel reluctant to voice some doubts about *A Christmas Carol.* I saw the piece twice, and the doubts didn't go away. How can I define them? In *A Christmas Carol,* Musgrave has worked within her strengths, and those strengths are many and notable. The challenge she set herself—to turn Dickens's tale into an effective, workable chamber opera, stimulating to perform, enjoyable and affecting to hear—has been ably met. *A Christmas Carol* is on all counts a well-made opera. There is variety and contrast of pace, mood, and texture. Lyricism and declamation, closed forms and straight-line dialogue are deftly balanced. The instrumentation is masterly. The word setting is sensitive, the lines are singable, the roles rewarding. But a greater challenge—to go beyond the narrative, to create a score that might make its listeners feel as Stevenson felt—was perhaps not even considered. There is a sense in which the most intensely interesting character in any of Dickens's books is Dickens himself (and this is particularly true of his *Christmas Carol*). It may be the reason why there have been no lastingly successful Dickens operas, why there perhaps cannot be. Dominick Argento's *Miss Havisham's Fire* comes closest of those I know to being a work at once Dickensian and individual, independent. The tone of Dickens's voice, the movements of his mind—a composer must either catch them or match them by contributions of his own. It is not enough to illustrate the incidents and portray the characters in appropriate music. (In *Wozzeck* and *Lulu,* it is Berg's voice we attend to; without it there would be no call to perform anything but the original spoken plays.) Scrooge is the central figure of *A Christmas Carol,* but he is not the main matter of the tale. He has been made the subject of Musgrave's opera; in her own words, "the opera is . . . primarily about Scrooge and the reasons why he withdrew from his fellow men and later what precipitated his change of heart before it was too late." Nothing in the music replaces the important scenes a chamber opera could not compass: the crisp winter fields of boyhood; the thronged city streets; the mysterious voyage to the Cornish moors, then to the solitary lighthouse, then far out over the black sea. The focus is held close on Scrooge and those immediately around him, and the range and scope of the *Carol* are diminished. The

music does not take wing. I hear neither Dickens's voice nor Musgrave's—
except in tones of lucid, sympathetic explanation of her protagonist's character.

The first of those three chilling images I mentioned is replaced, effectively, by an arietta for Scrooge, "I am the future that he cannot see!" This is
the first-act curtain. For the second image, the Leech illustration was potently re-created by the scenic and costume designers—Miguel Romero and
Alex Reid—and by Martin Ross's lighting. The cruel irony of the third has
been lost: the children emerge not from the festive robe of the jolly, expansive, gift-bearing Ghost of Christmas Present but from the shroudlike gar-
ment of the grim, silent Ghost of Christmas Yet to Come; and they are not
Dickens's wolfish, scowling pair but a clutch of hungry urchins, Tiny Tim and
his youngest sister among them. The practical reasons for the change are evident. From a practical point of view, it is ingeniously made. But it illustrates
the way Musgrave has played safe and sacrificed tragic force to efficiency.

Maybe I'm expecting the impossible. And maybe there is more to the
opera than I have so far heard. Within the limitations suggested above, the
Carol is a first-rate piece of work, of almost impeccable craftsmanship, and
imaginative and subtle in its musical workings. That *almost* slips in because I
feel that the finale should be longer and fuller. Two other weak points were
due not to the score but to the performance. Musgrave has set the fierce, dis-
gusting scene of the haggling over Scrooge's bed curtains and the shirt
stripped from his corpse as a pungent scherzo macabre; it could be strong,
but in Norfolk it was softened, played as caricature, not harsh realism. Most
of the décor is inspired by Leech, but for the costumes of the rag-and-bone
man and his cronies Mr. Reid has adopted the manner of the Ronald Searle
Carol illustrations. And the final party hung fire, because Mr. Farrar had
directed it stiffly and coldly.

The presentation did not have the all-round high accomplishment of the
company's *Mary.* As Scrooge, Frederick Burchinal gave a capital performance, accurate and convincing in every detail. He did not miss the vein of
salty wit that shines in Scrooge even at his scroogiest. Claudette Peterson was
charming and delicate in her series of bright-little-sister roles. Kathryn Mont-
gomery was a pleasing Belle. The other singers were indifferent actors—superficial or, at best, obvious. The children piped. The actor of Marley's Ghost
was feeble (and his final incarnation, as a pantomime dame, was sadly off-
key). The dancer who played the three Christmas Ghosts, to his own choreography, was embarrassing. Scrooge peeked out from the bed curtains, saw a
tall, spangled ballet boy writhing and prancing about his room, and said, "If I
close my eyes and hold my breath/Perhaps it will go away." The sympathetic
laughter that greeted this remark cannot have been quite what the composer
intended. But there was warmly accomplished playing from Mr. Mark's orchestra. The show moved surely. The transformation scenes were smoothly
and skillfully achieved. The lighting was cleverly managed.

.   .   .

The television presentation of the Met *Mahagonny* was expertly directed by Brian Large—the best-managed relay from the house I have seen. In the sound, the voices were favored at the expense of the orchestra. Close up, the intelligence, subtlety, and precision that distinguish Teresa Stratas's Jenny were even more apparent. She is an arresting artist. One began to regret every moment the cameras left her—when, for example, she moved into the refrain of "Benares" and her eyes and mouth caught to perfection the "Wouldn't it be wonderful *if* . . . and yet I know it can't be" expression of Weill's music. The opera took its life from her. Close up, Richard Cassilly's Jimmy was less impressive—robust, forcefully delivered but in a generalized way.

At the eighth performance in the house, there was a new Jenny, Julia Migenes. She has a small, true lyric soprano, a sure sense of phrase, and a good understanding of the role. Jenny is not exactly a Micaëla, but she is closer to Micaëla than to Carmen—fresh, frank, clear-eyed, candid, as Miss Migenes was. Begbick is the dominant woman of the drama, yet even against this sweet, fragile Jenny a new Begbick, Lili Chookasian, did not quite make her that, although she sang strongly. The staging is pallid, and James Levine's conducting remains tight and neat. The weight and force of Weill's score still escape him. The typhoon music became a neoclassical exercise. The eating, loving, and fighting scenes were deadly, but the trial scene is beginning to come to life.

December 24, 1979

The Norfolk production of A Christmas Carol *has been recorded on Moss Music Group 302.*

A Great Composer?

Musicians delight in sharing their discoveries and enthusiasms. Performers champion works they love. And one of the rewards of a music critic's life is being able to share delight with more than an immediate circle of acquaintances. When the work that pleases has been played at a concert, all a critic can do is describe it and urge further performances. But when it has appeared on a record, his readers have a chance of hearing it for themselves. My latest "discovery" is of Alexander Zemlinsky's Second String Quartet, which was recorded in 1978 for Deutsche Grammophon by the LaSalle Quartet. When the disc was issued in England last year, I learned of its excellence from a friend there eager to "share." I've waited to write about it until now, when it receives general American release. The Philharmonic performances, last month, of Zemlinsky's Lyric Symphony have meanwhile brought the composer's name into the news.

Alexander Zemlinsky (he dropped a "von" in 1918) was born in Vienna in 1871—eleven years after Mahler, three before Schoenberg—and died in Larchmont, New York, in 1942. In 1895, he was taken up and taught by Brahms. Two years later, he taught Schoenberg for a few months, and in the 1949 essay "My Evolution" Schoenberg called him "the one to whom I owe most of my knowledge of the technique and the problems of composing." The first of Zemlinsky's seven completed operas, Sarema, appeared in Munich in 1897. Mahler brought out the second, Es war einmal (Once Upon a Time), in Vienna in 1900. The last of them, Der Kreidekreis (The Chalk Circle), had five productions in 1933–34 before the Nazis silenced Zemlinsky's voice in Germany, then in Austria. In New York, Mme. Charles Cahier had sung his Maeterlinck songs in Town Hall, for the Society of Friends of Music, in 1924, and the Society had given his Twenty-third Psalm in 1928. Mitropoulos conducted his Sinfonietta with the Philharmonic in 1940–41, and it received friendly but not exactly enthusiastic reviews. After the war, when the big three of the Second Viennese School were brought to the fore, Zemlinsky's name at least became familiar in footnotes and passing references, for Berg had dedicated the Lyric Suite to him and had quoted a theme from his Lyric Symphony in its fourth movement; he had found Webern a job; Schoenberg had been his brother-in-law and had painted a portrait of him. He had conducted the first performance of Schoenberg's Erwartung, in 1924. In the annals of operatic performance, Zemlinsky also has his niche. At the Vienna Volksoper, he introduced Tosca (with Jeritza), Salome, and Paul Dukas's Ariane. His sixteen years with the German Opera in Prague, 1911–27, have been likened to Mahler's brilliant decade at the Vienna Opera. In 1914, Schoenberg called him "the greatest living conductor." Mahler summoned him to the Vienna Opera, and Klemperer—who had conducted the first performance of his opera Der Zwerg (The Dwarf), at Cologne in 1922—to the Berlin Krolloper. But, above all, it was Schoenberg's dicta about Zemlinsky's music which whetted curiosity. Schoenberg's 1949 essay continues:

I have always thought and still believe that he was a great composer. Maybe his time will come earlier than we think. One thing is beyond doubt, in my opinion: I do not know one composer after Wagner who could satisfy the demands of the theatre with better musical substance than he. His ideas, his forms, his sonorities, and every turn of the music sprang directly from the action, from the scenery, and from the singers' voices with a naturalness and distinction of supreme quality.

I've been playing through the two Zemlinsky operatic vocal scores borrowable from the New York Public Library and looking at two others confined to the research room. *Kleider machen Leute (Clothes Make the Man)*, a comedy that Zemlinsky brought out at the Volksoper in 1910 and revised for Prague in 1922, is a big piece with many roles but not hard to do; one of our large music schools (Bloomington, the Juilliard) should tackle it. *Eine florentinische Tragödie*, after Wilde, first done in Stuttgart in 1917 under Max von Schillings, and later that year in Vienna and Prague, is a one-acter with just three soloists (soprano, tenor, baritone), a large orchestra, and no chorus. It's almost a long baritone scena, rich, romantic, and dramatic—made as if for Sherrill Milnes (failing him, perhaps Brent Ellis or Ryan Edwards). I commend it to enterprising orchestras, for it could be "semistaged" in small space on a concert platform. Then, if it proves as striking as the vocal score promises, it could come to the Met to join the repertory of one-acters there. Like Schillings's own *Mona Lisa* (Stuttgart, 1915), Erich Korngold's *Violanta* (Munich, 1916), and Franz Schreker's *Die Gezeichneten* (Frankfurt, 1918; to a libretto Schreker wrote for Zemlinsky but then decided to set himself), *Eine florentinische Tragödie* represents the taste of the time for passionate Italian costume drama, for *cavalleria* not *rusticana* but *cortigiana*. All four operas were played widely in Germany, and in the Vienna where Klimt painted and Freud practiced. *Der Zwerg*, a one-acter after Wilde's *Birthday of the Infanta*, continues the vein, but with leaner textures and in music of elegant formality. In *Der Kreidekreis*, composed in Berlin in 1930–32, a neoclassical, Weimar Republic astringency enters the music.

Zemlinsky's chamber works can be revived less expensively. At Detroit's Schubert/Vienna festival in 1978, the Bern String Quartet played his Quartet No. 3. The LaSalle bills all four of his quartets in its repertory, and gave the American première of No. 4 in Cincinnati in 1978; it plans to follow its disc of No. 2 with recordings of the three others. That's good news. The Second Quartet is dated on the manuscript 1914–15. (So I discover from Lawrence Oncley's Zemlinsky catalogue in *Notes*, 1977, which is an oasis of facts amid the strangely discrepant accounts of Zemlinsky's career; elsewhere the quartet is dated variously between 1910 and 1915.) It can't, therefore, have influenced Berg's String Quartet, Op. 3, which had its first performance in 1911, but the Berg quartet is among the works one would evoke in any attempt to describe Zemlinsky's by likenesses and apparent influences. Others are Schoenberg's first two quartets and Bartók's first. Max Reger, two years Zemlinsky's junior, may have played a part in suggesting its denser contrapuntal episodes. (In his *Arnold Schoenberg*, Charles Rosen reminds us that Reger and Debussy were the composers most often performed at Schoenberg's Society for the Private Performance of Music.) And Brahms and Mahler are neither of them far away. What this amounts to is that someone coming to Zemlinsky's Second Quartet with an "innocent ear," asked to guess who its composer might be, would, I think, place it correctly in the fertile, adventurous Vienna of the first decades of this century—when Brahms and Wagner were still quarreled over, Mahler and Strauss were close, potent influences, Debussy and Delius sent new kinds of sound from abroad, Puccini drew the large public, Reger challenged orthodoxy, and Schoenberg, Berg, and Webern tried to make sense of it all while remaining true to themselves. The following guesses might pass through our listener's mind: Some early, newly discovered quartet by Berg? No, for the personality is not Berg's and, even in violent, impassioned episodes, the working is gentler, less virile than that of Berg's Opus 3. Schoenberg? No, for there is— how can one put it without being offensive to that mighty genius?—a refinement of feeling, a delicacy, modesty, unassertiveness not found in the composer of *Verklärte Nacht*. An early work of Korngold, before he set his sights on easy success? No, for Korngold was never as aristocratic or as masterly as this; his sweetness was stickier.

And then, perhaps, the listener would stop trying to guess and simply be held, rapt, in the interest and beauty of the discourse. The quartet is an unbroken span of music, lasting nearly forty minutes, within which the four traditional movements are apparent. The key is D, but that is made clear only at the start of the Adagio; the harmonic idiom is a richly and freely extended tonality. Rhythmic and harmonic tensions usually coincide, and there are some strenuous, exciting dialogues, but the most affecting pages are those that breathe an enchanted, tender sweetness. They are not cloying, for they seem to have been "earned": the rapturous Adagio by the vigorous scherzo-coda to the first movement; the long, slow, transfigured close by the taut, mysterious activity of the Scherzo proper and the varied, energetic adventures of the Finale. The LaSalle players are known as masters of Schoenberg's, Berg's, and Webern's quartet music; their Second Vienna School album (also on Deutsche Grammophon) is a treasure on any shelves. To Zemlinsky's quartet they bring the same sweet, pure tone, the same bewitching sense of line and phrase, and—very important here—an alert ensemble control of the highly developed and surprising rhythmic devices. The composer's instruction to the violins in the coda of the first movement to play "without regard to the viola's and the cello's calmer tempo" points to metrical experiments of a much later day. Metres and tempi are ever changing. In lesser hands, the quartet might easily fall apart. In the LaSalle's, it is coherent and beautiful. A pocket score is published in the Philharmonia series.

Zemlinsky's Lyric Symphony was composed in 1922 and orchestrated in 1923, during Prague years when, like Mahler, he conducted winters and composed summers. He described it to his publisher as "something along the lines of *Das Lied von der Erde* . . . seven songs for baritone, soprano, and orchestra, closely related one to the other, to be performed without interruption." It lasts about forty-five minutes. It does recall Mahler's *Das Lied von der Erde* (1908), and also an earlier piece, Schoenberg's *Gurrelieder* (1900–01). The poems are drawn from Rabindranath Tagore's "The Gardener," in German translation. The first of them ("I have no peace, I thirst after far-off things"), set for baritone, is a turbulent, violent outburst. The second ("Mother, the young prince must surely pass by our door"), for soprano, is delicate, virginal yet sensuous. In the third and fourth songs, the tone becomes rapturous, ecstatic. ("Du bist mein Eigen, mein Eigen," in the third, is the phrase quoted in Berg's Lyric Suite.) In the fifth song, the baritone cries "Free me from the bonds of your sweetness." The sixth and seventh are songs of tender, dignified, ardent farewell. A large orchestra is poured out at full strength in the first song. Thereafter, it is often fined down, translucent, Mahlerian; but, Zemlinsky wrote in a note on the Lyric Symphony, these later songs, "no matter how different they are in character, tempo, etc., must be tuned to the atmosphere of the first," with its "tone of profound earnestness, burning intensity." There are recurrent themes. The piece coheres both as an emotional progression and as a large musical structure.

The unmannerly Philharmonic audience—or, rather, unmannerly members of it—did not give it a chance to be heard coherently. For one thing, Cyril Harris has provided the rebuilt Fisher Hall with so resonant a floor that every shuffle, every tap, every fidget is amplified. (The management should consider building racks in the narthex of the auditorium—like those in the porches outside mosques, Buddhist temples, and palaces with fine old floors—and asking its visitors to doff boots and shoes or don felt overslippers before entering.) The fourth song of the Lyric Symphony is one of hushed intimacy: the soprano line is marked *p*, *pp*, and *ppp;* around it, violin solos, soft tendrils of woodwind, and pianissimo plashing from harp and celesta weave an enchanted spell. It is music that should steal out into stillness—music that calls for the utmost concentration. The spell was powerless against the noise of a restless, rustling audience, and there was worse to come: the latter part of the song and all those that followed were accompanied by the stomp-stomp-stomp up the aisles of leavers. (This happened at both the Thursday and the Tuesday performance; are the Philharmonic subscribers losing all taste for late-Romantic works?) One after another, at about ten-bar intervals, perhaps fifty, sixty people upped and went, and wrecked things for those who had come to Fisher Hall to hear the music. This must have disturbed the performers, too; and what should have been a high day in the Philharmonic's history was turned into a mockery. The concert is to be broadcast by WQXR; that will be the time to listen to it. (I hope the station has laid in a stock of text sheets and of the careful Philharmonic program note, by Benjamin Folkman, to supply to interested listeners. Or perhaps it intends to publish both in its new magazine, *Ovation*.) [Vain hope!] Meanwhile, the Lyric Symphony can be discovered and enjoyed in a recorded performance by the BBC Symphony under Gabriele Ferro, on the Italia label, and followed in a study score published by Universal Edition. The recording is not ideal; it lacks depth and detail. But at least the work can be heard uninterrupted except by a side-turn between the fourth and fifth songs.

The solo roles are written as if for Sieglinde and a young Wotan, Elisabeth and Wolfram, or Salome and Jochanaan. (It's a pity the piece was not recorded by Ljuba Welitch and Hans Hotter, or Schwarzkopf and Fischer-Dieskau.) At the Philharmonic performance, Johanna Meier—a Sieglinde and an Isolde—excelled in the fourth and sixth songs. Dale Duesing, a vivid young lyric baritone, was taxed beyond his vocal resources by the heavy role and had to force, but he showed the right feeling for the music. In the recorded performance, it's the soprano, Dorothy Dorow, who is too light. She is almost coy in her first song (in his note Zemlinsky proscribed an approach of "lighthearted playfulness") but delicate and sweet in the others. The baritone, Siegmund Nimsgern, *is* a Wotan, Wolfram, and Jochanaan, and has the power for the role, but to start with he is not lyrical or smooth enough. James Levine drove the passionate pages hard, and urged the Philharmonic to some horridly coarse playing in the first song. His enthusiasm for the work was evident, but so was his tendency to push rather than persuade. Mr. Ferro, whose Gluck and Cherubini have been admired in these columns, shows greater breadth and is more sensuously lyrical.

Schoenberg called Zemlinsky a great composer. Mr. Oncley, who wrote his dissertation (Indiana University, 1975) on Zemlinsky, puts forward a more modest claim:

> Zemlinsky was not a great composer, but he was a good one. Although none of his works qualifies as an undisputed masterpiece, several contain the mix of artistic inspiration and careful construction warranting frequent performance.

"Masterpiece" is a big word, but I'd say that the LaSalle makes Zemlinsky's Second Quartet sound uncommonly like one. And if I headed a rich record company I'd hire Hildegard Behrens, Renato Bruson (if his German is good enough) or Bernd Weikl (if he could be induced to sing legato), Claudio Abbado, and the Philadelphia or La Scala orchestra to record the Lyric Symphony.

In these days of large concert halls and of box-office pressure to bill the proved and popular, listening musicians must resort increasingly to the realm of the phonograph. There a wider repertory invites them; there Adelina Patti and Pol Plançon, the Léner and Busch Quartets, Artur Schnabel and Edwin Fischer, Furtwängler and Beecham are living performers; there chamber music can be heard in a chamber, Mozart's music can be heard on Mozartian instruments, and difficult modern works can be heard many times over. And there—as the Lyric Symphony performances showed—even large-scale works can be heard in conditions that, although not ideal, may be more favorable, more "musical," than those encountered in a large concert hall.

A record label that musicians hold in highest esteem is Nonesuch—the most distinguished part of the Elektra/Asylum/Nonesuch company, itself a division of Warner Communications, Inc. It was founded in 1964, and at first it specialized in music from the fifteenth to the eighteenth centuries, most of it from foreign recordings licensed to the American manufacturer. But for the last fourteen years Nonesuch, under the artistic direction of a wonderful woman called Teresa Sterne, has been a vital force in every area of serious music. Its Explorer series has introduced listeners to the sounds of every continent and culture; thanks to it, my ears have spent enchanted hours in India, Japan, Tibet, Peru, Paraguay, and many parts of Africa. Early music, baroque music, American eighteenth- and nineteenth-century music, Haydn, Busoni, Schoenberg have become Nonesuch specialties; and the records have been published with a "completeness" of presentation—carefully designed covers, program notes that lead to understanding—which reflects Miss Sterne's insistence that everything should be as good and useful and enjoyable as it possibly can be. (It's characteristic that the collected volume of Elliott Carter's major writings contains three essays written for Nonesuch.) Best of all, Nonesuch has been not just an alternative to but an active part of America's musical life. Work after work that I heard in the concert hall and wanted to hear again—Carter's Duo, Crumb's *Makrokosmos III*, William Bolcom's *Open House*, John Harbison's *The Flower-Fed Buffaloes*—soon turned up on the Nonesuch label. When a promising new composition has been billed, when a new ensemble—Renaissance, baroque, or contemporary—has made its début, Teresa Sterne has been there in the hall, eager to insure that the best of what and who deserve recording and dissemination do get recorded. The Boston Camerata, the Composers Quartet, the Contemporary Chamber Ensemble, the Group for Contemporary Music, the Light Fantastic Players, Pomerium Musices, Speculum Musicae are Nonesuch artists. So are Jan De-Gaetani, Joan Morris, Phyllis Bryn-Julson, William Bolcom, Paul Jacobs, Gilbert Kalish. They also appear, I know, on other labels, and I'm not forgetting CRI's important role in recording contemporary American music. But there has been none quite like Nonesuch for making available in this country, and to all the world, the best in American music and American music-making. Last month's announcement of the first six Nonesuch records due this year was characteristic of the company, its vision, and its enterprise: traditional Japanese music, recorded in New York by the Ensemble Nipponia during its tour for the Asia Society; a record of Orlando Gibbons; the début on disc of New York's Concert Royal, in music by Rameau, Clérambault, and Marin Marais; Schubert violin-and-piano music; Miss DeGaetani and Mr. Kalish in a Rakhmaninov-Chausson recital; and a coupling of Milton Babbitt's *Arie da Capo* and Donald Martino's Triple Concerto, played by the Group for Contemporary Music. Four days earlier, I'd picked up the *Times* to read that Miss Sterne had been fired.

Musicians across the country felt shock and dismay. They wrote to Warner Communications to protest, and made their letters public. Ten Pulitzer Prize–winning composers—Carter, Copland, Crumb, Davidovsky, Druckman, Martino, Schuman, Schwantner, Wernick, Wuorinen—joined in a declaration that "the Nonesuch catalogue of music from all periods, as well as ethnic music, is quite beyond compare," that "no other label has attempted to record this range of repertoire, and, certainly, without Miss Sterne's decisive and artistic management, none could have produced it with such taste and imagination." Sixteen leaders of Boston's musical life—from the Symphony, the universities, the performing groups, the ensembles, the radio stations—told Miss Sterne's employers that she is "one of the outstanding creative figures in the musical world" and that "her separation from the recording company she has guided to international prominence" would harm not only musicians but all the community. The music faculty of the University of Pennsylvania ("both composers and musicologists, an indication of the remarkable breadth of interests and concerns nurtured by Nonesuch") pointed out that "no company before Nonesuch has ever contributed more to the cause of contemporary music, through its unfailing insistence upon the highest standards of repertoire, performance, and recording," or "done more to bring exciting performances of early music to the attention of the public."

What should happen next is for Miss Sterne to be reinstated in triumph, with her Nonesuch budget doubled, trebled, quadrupled. Because of what she has done for American musical life, the President should welcome her as the heroine of a White House celebration, heralded by fanfares written for the occasion by Nonesuch composers from Albright, Babbitt, and Carter through the alphabet to Wernick, Wuorinen, and Xenakis. (Zemlinsky's unpublished *Hunting Piece* for horns might round things off.) But Mr. Joe Smith, the chairman of Elektra/Asylum/Nonesuch and the man who fired Miss Sterne, is reported as saying, "For her to keep making the same kind of records with the same repertoire and the same artists would be intolerable for us. . . . Maybe I am making a horrendous error, but the feeling in the company is that this move should have been taken a year ago. And if it offends the press or parts of the creative community, I just have to live with that. . . . If Elektra Records stops being competitive in the marketplace, then Joe Smith is out of a job." Instead, Teresa Sterne is out of a job, and for music in this country the year starts badly.

January 14, 1980

Close and Effectual Don

Joseph Losey's film *Don Giovanni,* like every thoughtful production of a Mozart opera, raises questions. Every *Giovanni* breeds deep feelings. Mr. Losey poses his first question during the overture, which he uses to accompany—or accompanies with—a muster of Don Giovanni and his entourage in the Teatro Olimpico, in Vicenza; shots of sea and sky; a landing at a glass factory on Murano; shots of the scene inside the factory, where the Don and his party watch workers around the furnace; and then closeups of (in the words of a shooting script that comes with a Columbia album corresponding in the main to the soundtrack of the film) "Donna Anna looking at Don Giovanni with desire" and "Don Giovanni aware." As the overture ends, "flames take over the screen," and we are with Leporello, on guard outside the palace within which Don Giovanni is assaulting Donna Anna.

That look of desire on Donna Anna's face revives E. T. A. Hoffmann's Romantic theories about her: that secretly she loves Don Giovanni; that just before the curtain rises he has had his way with her; that her account to Don Ottavio of what happened in her chamber when the muffled man approached her in the darkness is a lie. In some notes that introduce the script, Mr. Losey writes:

> If Donna Anna says that she is expecting someone at two o'clock in the morning and leaves her door open, that's more than a little strange for someone of that period. It must have been a previously arranged assignation. And then she says, "I was expecting you" to Don Ottavio. She couldn't have been expecting him because all through the opera she's been rejecting him.

Mr. Losey adds that "our actors influenced some changes." Kenneth Riegel, who plays Don Ottavio, is smaller than Ruggero Raimondi, who plays Don Giovanni. "They're absolutely totally different—cut of clothes, stature, height and width. So, she was expecting a lover, and that man certainly wasn't Don Ottavio." He continues:

> Then the question of "Was she raped, or did she invite?" What happened? My feeling is that she invited a lover, and the lover was Don Giovanni. So when Donna Anna tells what happened in Act I, I think she lied, at least to herself.

Before going any further, I should add that the shooting script is not always in perfect consonance with Mr. Losey 's notes or with the film itself; for example, the notes say that in this first scene Giovanni "never makes any attempt to conceal his face" from Anna, while the script says "She does not see Don Giovanni's face"—an implied if not a specific contradiction. In the swift action of the film, I got the impression that she didn't recognize him. But if Anna was expecting Giovanni, if she knows all along who he is, the shocking moment later in the act when she claims she has suddenly identified the intruder loses its force, and Anna becomes even more of a hypocrite. There are other objections to Mr. Losey's arguments. For one, Anna says nothing about two o'clock, or leaving her door open, or expecting Ottavio. What she says is:

> The night was already somewhat advanced when into my rooms, where by mischance I found myself alone, I saw enter, wrapped in a mantle, a man whom for a moment I took to be you.

When action or motivation is in doubt, it is often helpful to look at the source from which an opera is taken. Sometimes—often in Mozart—changes, omissions, and alterations may indicate a clear dramatic decision on the part of the new creator. Sometimes—very often in Prokofiev, occasionally in Verdi—an important piece of information may have been inadvertently omitted. The immediate source of Mozart and Da Ponte's *Don Giovanni* is Giovanni Bertati's libretto *Don Giovanni Tenorio, o sia Il convitato di pietra*, set to music by Giuseppe Gazzaniga and performed in Venice eight months before *Don Giovanni*. (A revival was billed in London last month.) Bertati's Donna Anna says:

> I was waiting for you in my apartment for our agreed discussion. My maid had gone out for a few moments; suddenly I saw enter my room, wrapped in his mantle, a man whom for a moment, O Duke, I believed to be you.

It sounds as innocent as could be, on Anna's part. And what if we go back to the source of all the Don Juan dramas, Tirso de Molina's *El burlador de Sevilla y convidado de piedra* (1630)? Here there are two incidents that the later writers combined. Just before curtain-rise, the Duchess Isabel *has* been seduced, and willingly, by a muffled man whom she took to be Ottavio. As Juan says (in Roy Campbell's translation),

> *In this disguise I cheated Isabel*
> *(Who took me for another man) and, well,*
> *Enjoyed her . . .*
> *Pretending I was Duke Octavio.*

In Act II, Doña Ana *is* waiting for her lover; Juan keeps the appointment instead, but Ana discovers his identity and cries out, and her father arrives, sword in hand, before any harm has been done her. Neither of these wronged ladies, then, is *entirely* innocent. But that's no good reason for supposing that Mozart and Da Ponte's Donna Anna is not. This stern, noble woman is their creation—Bertati's Anna disappears after the first scene—and, as Hermann Abert puts it in his wonderful study of *Don Giovanni*, she "owes her dramatic essence not to the poet but to the musician":

> Mozart, by his musical characterization, achieved what at all times has been attainable only by the greatest of dramatic musicians; he has by his music transformed a figure left by the poet in vague, half-finished contours, not only into a living and consistent character, but also into one of the chief personalities in the whole drama.

Mozart the dramatist explored subtleties of human character more profoundly, more intimately, than any other composer. His aim was clarity. The mood may be an elusive dapple of smiles and sorrow. Often it is: the burlesque wooing of Donna Elvira is a "comic" scene heartrending in its poignancy. (In the December 1979 *Musical Times,* Daniel Heartz has sensible things to say about the term *dramma giocoso,* by which *Don Giovanni* is defined.) But Mozart never leaves important dramatic points in doubt. What Abert says about the Romantics' Donna Anna "theories" applies to much else in Mozart over which thousands of words have been poured (who pairs with whom at the end of *Così,* for example): "All those later interpretations show only the almost unlimited potentialities of the subject; they have nothing to do with Mozart's work." When points are in dispute, a plain, sharp reading of the text and the score can cut through the fanciful maybes and "what she's *really* thinking"s of the commentators.

Mr. Losey raises another fancy point in his staging of the final scene, Don Giovanni's supper. In the script we find "Don Giovanni snatches a rose from a beautiful young boy" and "Donna Elvira . . . descends stairs, entering through a group of effeminates." Late at night, when he's at home, not on show, the Don relaxes among an all-male bevy of beauties. Do we have to go through that again? Let me be fair; scholars have suggested that the original of the original Don Juan, Tirso's, was Don Juan de Tassis, Count of Villamediana, reputed to be the lover of Philip IV's queen and discovered after his death (in 1622) to have been the leader of a band of homosexuals. But has that anything to do with Mozart's Don Giovanni? Brigid Brophy, the author of *Mozart the Dramatist,* might answer yes. In a chapter that begins, "In consigning Don Giovanni to hell, Mozart was punishing his infantile and unconscious self for parricidal wishes against Leopold Mozart, and his enlightened self for parricidal wishes against the established order," and continues with an examination of Leopold's and Wolfgang's attitudes toward excrement, she declares, "It is not unexpected, therefore, that Don Giovanni, alone of Mozart's heroes, should be—like Hamlet—an unconscious homosexual." Elsewhere, Miss Brophy has an excursion on Don Giovanni's serenade. A balcony, Freud told us, is in dreams a projection of the bosom. And so the penultimate line of the serenade, "Let yourself at least be seen," should be understood as representing "the dreadful exclusion whereby the child, once weaned, may no longer even look at his mother's breasts." When poor Mr. Mybug looked at the hills and dales around Cold Comfort Farm through Freudian eyes, at least he didn't do any harm to the landscape. The Mozart commentators are less easily ignored when their sillier notions color the performances that are needed to bring his operas to life. We need a Herodias Society for the clear-sighted, accurate representation of operas. That woman, you remember, cut through her husband's blather (in Strauss's opera) with the sensible remark "The moon is like the moon, that is all."

"I read a lot of books on Mozart and found them largely useless," Mr. Losey says. "After a while I threw them away." I think he would have found Abert's study of *Don Giovanni* useful. It was published in English translation in 1976. It combines profound scholarship and knowledge with musical and dramatic perceptiveness, common sense and sound theatrical sense with imaginative analysis.

To Don Giovanni's buffo alter ego, Leporello, Mr. Losey has added a kind of diabolical alter ego in the form of a pretty youth with painted eyes and an enigmatic expression. Like his master, he has a beauty spot on the left temple. He's called the Valet in Black. He accompanies the Don on his amorous adventures, plays the mandolin for his serenade, warms his chair before supper, and on the last chords of the opera quietly closes the doors of the villa from the inside. That final shot looks like an indication to the audience to expect a *Son of Don Giovanni* next year. For the rest—I can't see any sense in it. Giovanni's impelling daemon lives within him; he needs no devil prompter. That—among other things—distinguishes him as a "symbole merveilleux de l'homme sur la terre" (Musset's phrase) from Faust, another typefigure of questing man. In his notes, Mr. Losey says that the Valet in Black "proved useful as a kind of *deus ex machina* in solving some theatrical devices and tricks that otherwise might have been heavy-handed" and credits the invention of the figure to his collaborator on the film, Frantz Salieri. Must Mozart in every age meet a Salieri?

The film can be regarded as the latest contribution to three and a half centuries of Don Juan interpretation. At the latest count—the fifth supplement, in the *West Virginia University Bulletin* for July 1980, to Armand Edwards Singer's "A Bibliography of the Don Juan Theme, Versions and Criticism," in the *Bulletin* for April 1954—there were 7,240 items; to them might be added a few thousand performances of Mozart's opera. At times, Don Juan seems to be almost a self-illustrating theme, its protagonist's unsatisfied quest a parallel to our own long hunt of the protagonist. It is fascinating, and not irrelevant to an understanding of Mozart's opera, to plunge into this sea of Don Juans. A 1669 opera begins:

> *Gran tormento che mi par*
> *Lavorar*
> *La notte e'l dì.*

Which is not far from Leporello's "Notte e giorno faticar," at the start of Mozart's piece. In another opera of the time, we hear the accents and almost the very words of Mozart's Elvira:

> Ma che farò, misera Rosalba, priva d'onore, abbandonata dal mio sposo?
> Ecco, ecco lo spirito mio, che pur ti segue, barbaro traditore.

But behind Mozart's Elvira stands Molière's Elvire (1665), more poignant and beautiful than her counterparts in other versions. Ten years before *Don Giovanni*, Mozart's future father-in-law had presented him with a copy of Molière.

The more one reads other *Don Juans*, other *Stone Guests* and *Libertine*

Punisheds, the more one admires *Don Giovanni*. The essentials of the drama were there from the start; the characters and their actions can all be derived from Tirso's play. There is the same meeting and massing of Juan's foes—the two ladies wronged, the outraged fiancé, the duped, dazzled peasant girl and her stalwart husband—before supernatural intervention anticipates the retribution they plan. Over the centuries, the drama develops. Sometimes it is deepened, sometimes trivialized. Nowhere is it more vivid than in Mozart's opera—not just because of his great music but because music and dramaturgy conspire in textures and forms of such potency. The encounters are carefully managed. Nowhere else is the massing and unmasking of foes as electric as in Mozart's first-act finale; one's hair prickles at the poised menace of their "Tutto, tutto già si sà" entries. Nowhere else is the sequence of divine retribution and a second, now unnecessary gathering of the foes—accompanied by ministers of justice, according to the stage direction, though we seldom see them—handled with such command of tension and release. (It's fair comment, not fancy, to note that Mozart's hero is both times beyond mere human retribution.)

Of course, practical considerations went into the making of the opera. Anna must owe something to the art and temperament of the Prague prima donna Teresa Saporiti. (A pity no one sought her views; she lived until 1869—and was helpful to young Verdi, I'm told, over *Nabucco*.) Mozart followed Gazzaniga in assigning the roles of Masetto and the Commendatore to the same singer, and he retained the doubling in his Vienna production. (Was he simply economizing on basses or is there something here for modern directors to explore?) Nevertheless, after a gripping performance of *Don Giovanni* one is tempted to echo Goethe's exclamations about it to Eckermann:

> How can one say, Mozart has "composed" *Don Giovanni!* Composition! As if it were a piece of cake or biscuit, stirred together out of eggs, flour, and sugar! It is a spiritual creation, in which the details as well as the whole are pervaded by *one* spirit and by the breath of *one* life. The creator did not make experiments, and patch together, and follow his own fancy, but was altogether in the power of the daemonic spirit of his genius and acted according to its orders.

In fact, Mozart did make some experiments. The sketches for Anna's "Or sai chi l'onore" reveal a melody less striking than what it became.

One can object to details of Mr. Losey's production, but as a whole it has the right kind of proud, virile, irresistible surge to it. It's never boring. Nothing Mr. Losey does is. His starting point for getting to know Mozart's opera well was the 1936 Glyndebourne recording, conducted by Fritz Busch—still available, on the Turnabout label—and there could not be a better one. His materials for making the film were a recording of the opera taped in Paris with the Paris Opera orchestra, conducted by Lorin Maazel (who shuttled between Paris and the new production of *Luisa Miller* at Covent Garden), and an international cast; the members of that cast reassembled to mime their roles on location; and the Palladian buildings of Vicenza, Venice, and the Veneto. The musical performance is not particularly distinguished, but it was only when I listened to the records, without the images, that I realized quite how poor much of it is. There is a better performance of the opera on film—better sung, better acted, better played, and far better conducted: Paul Czinner's filmed record of the fifties Salzburg production, with Elisabeth Grümmer, Lisa della Casa, and Erna Berger, Cesare Siepi, Anton Dermota, and Otto Edelmann, director Herbert Graf, conductor Wilhelm Furt-wängler. But that is quite straightforwardly a visual and aural record of an admirable theatre performance, captured as today a good television director might capture it. Mr. Losey's film is something different—what he calls "a real film, told in filmic terms." It is fascinating to watch how he met the challenge of laying out "a real film" along a soundtrack whose timings, tensions, and dynamics had already been twice determined: by Mozart and then by Mr. Maazel. The only freedom of speed he had was in the secco recitatives, which were re-recorded live, on location.

In these recitatives, it is noticeable that the pace grows freer (and generally slower; the dialogue before "Là ci darem la mano" moves at a snail's pace) and that the singing actors come to life. That raises the old question of filmed opera: record in action, or mime to a soundtrack? The answer was predicated in this case: one could hardly afford to cart Mr. Maazel and the Paris Opera Orchestra all over the Veneto to accompany the sequences, or expect to achieve matching sound in different locations; the settings used in the first two numbers alone leap between Vicenza, Venice, and Caldogno. But the locative freedom was obtained at a cost. Operatic acting is a strange, special, and very physical art. The communicative power of a long, loud note is diminished when it is evident that the actor has neither taken the breath nor made the effort that the sound itself implies. The film—quite apart from its out-of-sync moments—does not have the directness that singing actors, whether filmed or live, can impart, and it misses the subtle variations of sound (as Mr. Czinner's filmed *Don Giovanni* does not) when movement on the screen is mirrored in the soundtrack.

The Prague and the Vienna versions are conflated; Elvira's recitative after the catalogue aria and everything between "Il mio tesoro" and "Mi tradì" are cut. The sound at a Tully Hall showing was intolerably loud; people put their fingers in their ears. At a showing in the Plaza Theatre, the volume was acceptable but the sound quality remained crude, with clumsy splices and unsubtle attempts to match the "sonic ambience" to the images. The harpsichord is an amplified, wiry jangle. The two British members of the cast, Kiri Te Kanawa as Elvira and Malcolm King as Masetto, know about Mozartian appoggiaturas. The German Anna, Edda Moser, doesn't, and she also sticks to Teutonic Italian: "Or sai chi l'onor*uh* rapire a me vol*suh*."

On the other hand, we have the settings; and settings matter in a Losey film. (I can hardly remember now what his *Secret Ceremony* was about, and recall only the use he made of that Halsey Ricardo and William de Morgan house on Campden Hill, and how Elizabeth Taylor and Mia Farrow looked in it.) Palladio and Mozart are a good match; Caspar Neher's Palladian settings for *Don Giovanni* served Vienna well for many a year. Mr. Losey's Don Giovanni lives in the Villa Rotonda, though its kitchens and other offices are those of the Villa Poiana. Elvira has taken the Villa Valmarana, nearby, but she goes to the Villa Emo to sing "Mi tradì." The Commendatore and Anna live in the Villa Caldogno, which has acquired the loggia of the Basilica in Vicenza. The Commendatore's tomb is in a churchyard behind the Redentore. We go scooting about the Veneto in the space of bars, and that is distracting to one who recognizes the settings. What must be disturbing to anyone is sudden shifts that make the narrative hard to follow. When Elvira sees Giovanni with Anna, she sings, "Ah, ti ritrovo ancor, perfido mostro! Non ti fidar, o misera, di quel ribaldo cor!," adressing the first clause to Giovanni and the second to Anna. In the film, she cries the first phrase at a departing carriage, and with the second she addresses its occupants at the end of their journey—a long one, from the Villa Valmarana to the Villa Caldogno. She must have run for miles and miles in a matter of seconds, and she's not even panting. But it's not the precise localities and not the lack of realism that matter; it's the violent, unmusical visual break between a recitative cadence and the note that follows, between a dominant-seventh harmony and its full tonic resolution.

Someone making a film of an opera is likely to shift the scenes more often than the composer did. (But even stage directors can do it now; I saw a *Don Giovanni* in the theatre of its first performance where Josef Svoboda provided about six changes during "Vedrai, carino" and destroyed the shape of the aria completely.) Verdi once remarked that the reason he hadn't set Shakespeare more often was the need for continual scene shifting. "When I used to go to the theatre, that was something that distressed me, that gave me the impression of being at a magic-lantern show." He lauded the French fashion of one set per act: "That way, the action flows freely, unhindered, with nothing to distract the public." He liked to compose in long spans. So did Mozart. Mr. Losey tends to break the spans and spoil the musico-dramatic forms. But I enjoyed and was moved by his beautifully composed, carefully framed, carefully lit pictures and his affective use not just of the Palladian architecture but of incidental details—frescoes, trees, shadows. I admired his bold alternations of realism and operatic artifice. The passionate outbursts of the quartet are set in a salon filled with well-conducted persons who pay absolutely no attention. The sextet is played on the stage of the Teatro Olimpico—theatrical décor "tested" against the "realism" of the rest—before an audience in eighteenth-century dress. And I was fascinated by his use of the singers. He did not choose them. Rolf Liebermann, the director of the Paris Opera, and billed as having conceived the film, had already assembled them. By naturalistic cinema standards, only one—Teresa Berganza, the Zerlina—can act (and she gives a warm, impetuous, lovable performance). Miss Te Kanawa pulls extraordinary faces. Mr. King "registers," clumsily but powerfully. Miss Moser, a beautiful woman, maintains a beautiful, tense mask.

Kenneth Riegel, the Ottavio, looks like a plump, puffy clergyman. José van Dam is a visually subdued Leporello, though he sings better than anyone else. Ruggero Raimondi, the Giovanni, moves through the film looking stern and inscrutable—and has been photographed by Mr. Losey in a way that makes him thrice as impressive as I have ever seen him before. The director seems to have looked at all his cast as he looked at the architecture, the frescoes, the trees—as objects to make striking *Don Giovanni* pictures from.

This *Don Giovanni* was in interesting contrast to the "live" televised *Faust*, from Chicago, that Channel 13 put out this month. The *Faust* may have been impressive enough in the theatre. On the screen, it looked ridiculous: a middle-aged unromantic hero in a bright-blue doublet, eyes slewing round to the conductor or the prompter while he tenderly addressed his beloved; a Marguerite coiffed and painted as a modern housemaid, albeit a very pretty one; a prancing principal boy of a Siebel; a burly Méphistophélès uncertain what to do with his hands or his glances. (But a Valentin, Richard Stilwell, convincing and intense, and one who exemplified my point about physical communicativeness in the very act of singing.) Mr. Losey's *Don Giovanni* isn't like that—not at all. (Neither, for that matter, was the film of the Salzburg production.) It's not as Mozartian or as musical a film of the opera as I hoped for. But its images won't leave me.

January 21, 1980

The Theatre of Don Juan: A Collection of Plays and Views, 1630–1963 *edited by Oscar Mandel (University of Nebraska Press, 1963) and* Vita avventure e morte di Don Giovanni *by Giovanni Macchia (Editori Laterza, 1966) are handy collections of Don Juan literature.*

Opera of a Kind

Each day, the Metropolitan Opera announces "a date with genius." When it's a date with Mozart, Beethoven, Wagner, or Verdi, I'll buy the line. So far this season, I have encountered little genius in the performances. There was *some* in this month's revival of *Fidelio*. In the hands, or the voices, of Hildegard Behrens and Jon Vickers, the opera began to mean something. But *Fidelio* as a whole foundered on the prosaic conducting of Erich Leinsdorf. The Met seems to find it hard to attract good conductors for the nights when James Levine, its music director, is not himself in charge. In otherwise comparable houses, Claudio Abbado, Bernard Haitink, Carlos Kleiber, Riccardo Muti, and Georg Solti are among the big names on the bills. Abbado has not been to the Met for eleven seasons (not since he became good), Solti for sixteen. Zubin Mehta has been away for nine seasons; Leonard Bernstein for seven; Lorin Maazel, the American who is to become director of the Vienna State Opera, for seventeen. Haitink, Kleiber, and Muti have never appeared with the company. Nor has Carlo Maria Giulini. Some of those conductors, I confess, I don't miss. Others—notably Abbado and Haitink—I do. I've never heard Kleiber in the theatre, and want to. When I ask the management about a particular conductor, I'm told sometimes that he was invited but couldn't make it, sometimes that the rehearsal time he considered essential was more than the Met could afford. (But other companies manage to meet conductors' requirements—perhaps by doing fewer operas at a time, so as to do them better.) In sum, the long list of absentees from the rostrum inevitably suggests a house content to parade the world's famous singers across its boards without bothering too much how they're "accompanied." Well, that provides opera of a kind—and it can be a very enjoyable kind. It doesn't happen to be Mr. Levine's kind, any more than it was Mahler's. Levine's own performances, like them or hate them, burn with conviction that opera means more than a glorious sing.

Mr. Leinsdorf had given thought to *Fidelio*. He had made two unusual textual decisions—one of them potentially interesting, the other horrid. To the familiar music of the "Gold" aria, Rocco sang the unfamiliar words of the 1805 libretto, which are a close translation, by Joseph Sonnleithner, of the verses in J. N. Bouilly's *Léonore*, that stirring libretto penned during the Reign of Terror. In 1806, for Beethoven's first revision of his opera, Stephan von Breuning replaced Rocco's pointed remarks about wealth and corruption with sentiments more innocuous, but that year the "Gold" aria was omitted altogether. Beethoven restored it in 1814, to words partly Sonnleithner's but mainly Breuning's. (He also snipped out a few measures, and canceled the trumpets and drums that underline Rocco's refrain.) In this bowdlerized form, the second verse runs:

> *When nothing is added to nothing*
> *The sum remains small;*
> *He who finds only love on the table*
> *Rises from the table hungry.*
> *So may fate smile graciously on you*
> *And bless and guide your efforts;*
> *Your sweetheart in your arms, and gold in your purse,*
> *So may you live many years.*

But in 1805 Rocco said:

> *Provided gold smiles in your purse,*
> *Every earthly happiness is yours:*

Pride and arrogance and vengeance
Will soon be satisfied.
And that's why Fortune smiles on the rich;
They do exactly as they please;
Craftily with gold conceal the dealings
Of which they should be ashamed.

That portrays a different Rocco from the easygoing, mercenary jailer who sings the 1814 verses. It turns the sense of the aria inside out, and throws a new light on the later scene where Pizarro bribes Rocco at least to connive at and assist in, since he draws the line at committing, a murder. Paul Plishka, the Met Rocco, made nothing of it, however, and gave the usual plain, easygoing performance. Rather that than an obtrusive, elaborately overinflected interpretation; but it hardly seems worth changing to the 1805 text if the character is to remain unaltered.

Mr. Leinsdorf included the *Leonore* No. 3 overture as scene-change music in the second act—a deplorable but common practice. But if *Leonore* No. 3 is to be played, then let it be played in its own right, to stand as a great and glorious symphonic summary of the drama. In these pages, I have protested at the trick of lapping its first bar with the last bar of the Leonore-Florestan duet; that diminishes it, thrusts the role of *Verwandlungsmusik* upon it. (John Mauceri did that at the Met, in 1976; Leonard Bernstein did it in Washington last year, with the Vienna company.) Mr. Leinsdorf started the overture correctly, but—this was his horrid decision—he spliced at the other end. From Beethoven's score he cut the thirty-three excited measures that open the finale—that masterpiece of tonic and dominant harmony, with touches of subdominant, set out with the control of rhythm and texture which makes Beethoven the most stirring of all composers: to the last chord of the overture the chorus added the "Heil!" of measure 34, and went on from there. In Vienna, I am told, Richard Strauss used to perpetuate this slick trick.

A few smaller textual points. First: It has become customary, particularly when *Leonore* No. 3 is played, to rewrite the trumpet calls—signals of deliverance which cut across the dungeon quartet—to accord with the form they take in the overture. (Bruno Walter, for example, does so in the 1941 Met performance, enshrined on record by the Metropolitan Opera Guild.) Mr. Leinsdorf left them as Beethoven wrote them. The difference is most easily described as, after the first long note, a "*dum*-diddle-dum-dum" pattern in the quartet but a "diddle-dum-dum-*dum*" pattern in the overture. Second: Miss Behrens changed the last word of the first line of her aria from "Stern" to "Strahl"—which doesn't rhyme with "fern," two lines later. A memory slip or a vowel preference? Third, and more important: The spoken dialogue was grievously abridged. In particular, the conversation that prepares and "places" the Act I quartet—filling a double-column page in the Eulenburg score—was reduced to just nineteen words. *Fidelio*, like *The Magic Flute* and like *Carmen*, is a drama enacted sometimes in spoken dialogue, sometimes in music. The music matters more, but to proceed as if the music were *all* that mattered is another way of reducing a great opera to a sing.

Miss Behrens spoke the words that were left her keenly, tellingly, without exaggeration. Mr. Vickers made a meal of his. Her singing combined vividness, passion, intensity with a perfect control of phrase; the voice shone and rang; the acting was noble. His singing was vivid, passionate, and intense, but he overdid the expressiveness. His first word was a shout; his first paragraph closed "steht [pause] bei [pause] dir." His voice cut through the finale with a powerful, hideous snarl. The force, the conviction he brings to the role are thrilling; the execution was exaggerated to the point of self-indulgence, impressive but terrible. Franz Ferdinand Nentwig made his Met début, as Pizarro. His voice seemed a shade light for the house; he pushed its resonance, and sometimes pushed notes out of tune. Catherine Malfitano was a delightful Marzelline—no blond German minx but a full-blooded, full-voiced Latin, and one with a voice that sailed out to match Leonore's in the double ascent to B-flat in the quintet of the second finale. Jon Garrison was a good Jaquino. Mr. Plishka sang well. Julien Robbins, deputizing for James Morris, was too slight a Don Fernando. The bass of the Ninth Symphony is needed; Mr. Robbins was an ill-at-ease school prefect.

The stage direction is now credited to David Alden; beneath it are the bones of Otto Schenk's clear, if occasionally stagy, original. Some inept business in the crowd scenes looked childish. There was little evidence of hard thought about the opera or about how these particular singers might work together to inspire one another and inspire the audience. The lighting would shame a provincial circus. But what I minded most was the lack of depth, weight, expression, meaning in Mr. Leinsdorf's conducting.

Four days earlier, the Met revived *Lohengrin,* and in the title role Siegfried Jerusalem, Bayreuth's Parsifal last year (and Florestano in the London recording of Paer's *Leonora*), made his local début. He has a beautiful voice, full toned, lyrical, and pure; just occasionally it was disturbed by a slow vibrato. His words were clearly and truly formed. But he had no stage presence and, it seemed, not much idea what the opera is about. Where René Kollo in the long white coat of the Met production had suggested, at the least, a high-minded young doctor, able to take charge in an emergency, Mr. Jerusalem played a junior nurse, embarrassed and diffident when called on to make a statement. He lacked command, as an actor and as a musician. Teresa Zylis-Gara sang her first Elsa here. The Dream was tenderly vocalized. The Song to the Breezes fell to the ground; the unfortunate cuckoo-clock setting—Met Elsas are confined on a tiny window ledge, just big enough to hold them— seemed to cramp the musical interpretation, to inhibit Miss Zylis-Gara from sending long phrases soaring out into the night. She gave an attentive performance, but her voice does not have the limpid, uncomplicated sound Elsa needs. Moreover, she was playing in a void: to a cipher of a Lohengrin; to an Ortrud and Telramund, Mignon Dunn and Donald McIntyre, giving their standard performances, unresponsive to the nuances of this particular Elsa; to an Emperor without stature, Bonaldo Giaiotti.

Mr. Levine conducted the première of this production, in 1976. For the revival, he ceded the baton to Giuseppe Patanè, whose reading was conventionally "lyrical"—the orchestra sounded good—but rhythmically inert. The music slid forward, often beautifully. Under Mr. Levine, it had moved, no less beautifully, toward a goal. The production is credited to August Everding, the stage direction to Phebe Berkowitz. Miss Berkowitz, it seems, has retained the moves but not the motivation, such as it was, of Mr. Everding's 1976 staging. There are silly things: flag waving at the first finale; drunken boys hustled out of the women's quarters, as if from a women's college, in the first scene of Act II. Ming Cho Lee's scenery is drab, unhelpful to the drama, confused in Act II, and acoustically unfortunate. The night scenes were lit by spotlights more or less following the principals.

As a whole, this *Lohengrin* meant nothing. One went away thinking what a deal of recitative there is between the numbers. A decent cast had been assembled, and nothing had been made of it. Late that night, puzzled and distressed, I took from the shelf the EMI album "Sänger auf dem grünn Hügel" and listened to a long sequence of *Lohengrin* excerpts, most of them recorded in the first decade of this century. The artists are no longer famous; only two of them, Edyth Walker and Charles Dalmorès, are mentioned in J. B. Steane's *The Grand Tradition*, and they are not the two best. But from Katharina Senger-Bettaque's Elsa and from Lilly Hafgren-Waag's I heard clear, steady shining sound and soft, pure, floating high notes. From Fritz Vogelstrom's Lohengrin and from Wilhelm Grüning's I heard phrases tenderly molded and words caressed. Grüning's turn in "Höchstes Vertrau'n," on the word "sanft," is wonderfully gentle and unhurried. Vogelstrom's tone warms into radiance as he sings "Du süsse, reine Braut!"; the way he utters "Monsalvat" conjures up an image of that place; at his "Graal" a flood of steady radiance pours out. Rudolf Berger's Telramund, Carl Nebe's Emperor, and Hermann Horner's, don't sing mere recitative; they make music of Wagner's declamatory phrases. It was like "hearing in color" what at the Met had been an inadequate, monochrome representation of a beautiful score. The moral to be drawn is not simply the old lament—people today don't sing as well as they used to—but something more specific. There are today a few remarkably eloquent Wagner interpreters. But in general the understanding of how to express Wagner's music is imperfect, and the lessons contained in recordings made by artists who were closer to him and his style remain unlearned. Conducting, orchestral playing, acting, staging, décor, lighting are all very important. We do right to pay attention to them, and when they are good they can do much to compensate for merely competent singing. But what matters most of all—what should be the chief carrier of what Wagner has to say—is detailed, eloquent musical interpretation of the vocal lines.

Bel Canto Opera has moved uptown, to the auditorium of the Robert Wagner Junior High School, on East Seventy-sixth Street. It's a good home for the company: a cleanly designed 1955 building; an auditorium, holding about four hundred and fifty, apt for small-scale opera; a cafeteria where free coffee and cookies were served in the intermission. The first production there was of Adolphe Adam's *Le Postillon de Longjumeau* (1836), an ingenious opéra comique with a tuneful, elegant, and prettily wrought score. There was a tenor, Robert Van Valkenburg, with an easy high D for the celebrated postillion song; a resourceful soprano, Patrice Burgstahler; a little orchestra of sixteen (ten strings, five winds, glockenspiel), conducted by John McCauley; simple, clever scenery by Robert McBroom, which with different trimmings could house just about any work the company chooses to do. Acts II and III were thrown into one, with some cutting. The performance, directed by Nelson Sheeley, was not polished but was good enough to show why *Le Postillon* held the world's stages for so long. The City Opera could have a hit with it.

January 28, 1980

An Opera That Matters

The four operas that Verdi composed after *Les Vêpres siciliennes*—*Simon Boccanegra, Un ballo in maschera, La forza del destino*, and *Don Carlos*—are dramas about duty and responsibility. Three of them—*Forza* is the exception—have as protagonist a ruler who must weigh conflicting claims of public duty and personal inclination. This is a nobler, subtler, more earnest development of the old, familiar operatic plight represented at its simplest by the prince who loves the daughter of his father's or his country's implacable foe. In Verdi, it is a tragic theme. A recurrent, austere moral of his works is that duty often compels an upright man to decisions that destroy his hopes of personal happiness.

The theme of a ruler's responsibility is stated at the start of *Ballo*. The men of Colonial Massachusetts sing of their loyalty to their governor, Richard, Count of Warwick (while a few conspirators who do not admire him sing of their hate). The governor enters and in ringing tones declares that "power is not beautiful unless it dries subjects' tears and aims at uncorrupted glory." A few measures later—with a sudden leap of harmony, and a switch from clear, bright keys into troubled chromatics—the counter-theme is introduced, as the name Amelia leaps from an official guest list that Warwick is scanning. Amelia is the wife of his secretary, closest friend, and loyalest supporter, and Warwick loves her. The secretary enters. In Italian, his name is Renato; old translations Anglicized him as Reinhard, but that sounds too Teutonic; since he's described as a Creole, one might settle for René. In a famous aria, René at once restates the theme of a ruler's responsibility: "To your life . . . the destiny of thousands and thousands of other lives is linked." The Lord Chief Justice joins them, presenting for Warwick's signature a sentence of exile on an undesirable black fortune-teller, and we see the governor in action: listening to both sides of the case (the sparky young ensign Oscar defends the woman and her ways), deciding to examine the evidence for himself. Verdi designated this first stretch of music, comprising a chorus, three arias (Warwick's "sortita," René's "cantabile," and Oscar's "ballata"), and an ensemble finale, as a single number, "Introduzione." In the scenic synopsis of the program for the Metropolitan Opera's new production of *Ballo*, which opened last week, it is rightly entitled "The Governor." It presents a vivid, individualized portrait of the Count, a ruler well aware of his public duties but also volatile and various: passionately in love with Amelia, high-spirited, eager to combine entertainment with office, suddenly moody. Othello may be more powerful, but "Riccardo, Conte di Warwich" has always been recognized as the fullest and most detailed character study in Verdi's tenor gallery. Moreover, in this introduction the tragedy is already implicit, given Warwick's character, René's single-hearted devotion to his best qualities, Oscar's encouragement of his frivolous side, and the gathering conspiracy.

In Warwick, duty triumphs at last. (In the inner struggle, Warwick, one might say, conquers Richard.) He decides to renounce his love, to send René and Amelia to England. Signing the order for their departure, he cries, "Ah! I have signed my sacrifice." But it is too late to set right the harm he has done. Duty has already triumphed in Amelia: when first we meet her, she has resolved at whatever cost to tear Richard from her heart and be a faithful wife. The ostensible "villain" of the piece is René, who allows passion to master him, joins the conspirators, and murders his friend. But it is easy to understand his impetuous criminal rage; since his life has been built on blind trust, love, and admiration, when he believes that the wife he loves and the friend for whom he has risked that life have together betrayed him, and when he has been publicly ridiculed, his fury is equally blind. His is the greatest betrayal in an opera that shows many kinds of trust and betrayal. Emotionally, if not in deed, Amelia has betrayed her husband, and Richard his friend. (In the Act II trio, Richard reflects that he would boldly confront the traitors gathering around him were he not a traitor himself.) Even Oscar, in the last act, is tricked into a betrayal of his master. Frivolity and vanity lead him to it, and it is innocently, even benevolently, committed, but its consequences are fatal. A similar irony inflects every turn of the plot. The action by which Amelia strives to conquer her illicit love provides René with the "evidence" that she is unfaithful to him. Julian Budden, in the second volume of *The Operas of*

Verdi, supplies a convincing demonstration that common sense and sharp observation were all that Ulrica, the fortune-teller, needed to achieve her uncannily accurate predictions.

If I begin a review by telling the story of a well-known opera, it is because before the new Met production (my tenth) I had never seen the story of *Ballo* told on the stage in quite that way, never before seen *Ballo* treated quite so seriously as a drama of real and recognizable human behavior. The director is Elijah Moshinsky, an Australian, who has the post of principal guest producer at Covent Garden. He made his Covent Garden début with a tough, vivid, intense staging of *Peter Grimes* five years ago. After that *Grimes,* I asked him where he had got his training. "By writing a thesis on Alexander Herzen, for Isaiah Berlin," he said. Herzen, like Verdi, was Paris-based in 1848, the year in which Europe's history took a new turn. I've not found any direct contact between the two men, and can't remember whether there are any of Herzen's books on the well-stocked shelves of Sant' Agata, Verdi's villa. But both were close observers of human character. Both were concerned with the way individual temperament could affect the fate of nations. (The passages in Herzen's memoirs about his encounters with Mazzini and Garibaldi are useful reading for any Verdian.) And both of them in their fictions—Herzen's stories, Verdi's operas—pressed the theme of individual responsibility. So Herzen can open a way to *Ballo,* and the new Met production, for all its evident imperfections, is something that shows Verdi's opera to be (in Shaw's words for *The Ring*) a work "frightfully real, frightfully present, frightfully modern." The Met directorate may not have deliberately intended, at a moment in America's history when potential rulers' actions in a time of personal stress must color the voters' decision whether or not they are fit to rule, to throw its voice into the public debate, but willy-nilly it has done so. Serious opera has always been a political art, and it was not for nothing that Bourbon censorship forbade the performance of *Ballo.* Of course, in 1857 Verdi intended no narrowly specific allegory. But the composer when rejecting the idea of a medieval setting for his drama insisted that it embodied modern kinds of thinking, and in ways unacceptable to Naples's rulers its action came close to modern life. A few years earlier, Verdi's own sovereign, Charles III of Parma, had been assassinated while stopping to admire a ballerina on a balcony. On the day Verdi arrived in Naples to put *Ballo* into rehearsal, Felice Orsini tried to assassinate Napoleon III on his way to the theatre; when the news reached Naples, a production of *Ballo* in any form that the composer might recognize was doomed. More generally, the character of the protagonist may have set Italians thinking about the character of the man soon to become their king—Victor Emmanuel, the many-mistressed *re galantuomo.*

Some other points may be relevant. In 1859, the year *Ballo* reached the stage, in Rome, Verdi did two unexpected things. He sought the acquaintance of Cavour, the great statesman who, in Giuseppina Verdi's words, "had conserved (unique privilege!) a heart in the midst of diplomacy and politics"; and he made an honest woman of Giuseppina, with whom he had been living in what the world deemed sin for some fourteen years. In 1861, at Cavour's persuasion, he became a member of the newly formed Italian parliament, and he embarked on an opera, *Forza,* concerned with the vanity of trying to achieve personal peace by disengaging oneself from the world. In the final speech of his next opera, *Don Carlos,* where his librettists had made the Emperor say that the sorrows of the world come to an end in the cloister Verdi himself changed "viennent expirer" to "nous suivent encore." It can hardly be denied, I think, that, just as the subject matter of *Stiffelio* and *La traviata* reflects Verdi's personal preoccupations at the time of their writing, so *Ballo* marks the start of a new, thoughtful concern for the public responsibilities of an individual, whether he be statesman or opera maker. (Gustavus III of Sweden, the protagonist of *Ballo* in its original form, happened to be both.)

Yet it *has* been denied. The Italian critic Massimo Mila has written, "Even more than *La traviata, Un ballo in maschera* is a pure, exclusive poem of love. In *La traviata,* the love song is mixed with a strong vein of social protest. . . . None of this exists in *Un ballo in maschera,* which is truly the swirling, tragic poem of an impossible and desperate love. . . . *Un ballo in maschera* is Verdi's *Tristan und Isolde.*" Mr. Budden has suggested another parallel: "Throughout, danger appears not only when least expected but in an utterly unexpected form. . . . In a word, *Un ballo in maschera* is Verdi's *Don Giovanni.*" The leading Italian critic of Verdi's day, Filippo Filippi, ended his celebrated account of *Ballo* with the declaration that opera lovers of every kind could find what they wanted in this work—tunes, formal shapeliness, "pure music," drama, well-defined characters, unusual forms, interplay of orchestra and stage: "Help yourselves; there is plenty for all your needs."

In the new Met production, I don't find everything I want. The opera is treated seriously, and that is good. The individual characterizations are clearly studied and sharply defined; the situations are effectively executed. It is evident that Mr. Moshinsky has profitably consulted the "official production book" published in 1859, not in order to stage a move-by-move recreation but to know the kinds of action that Verdi had in mind when he composed his score, and the dispositions in real space of the various voices. The plot makes sense, and this is a *Ballo* about things that matter. But it is a director's and designers' *Ballo;* the musical interpretation, led by Giuseppe Patanè, is commonplace, not marked by any similar thoughtfulness. The show is not the *Gesamtkunstwerk* of Verdi's intention. Onstage, the main thing wrong is the scenery—which will be the constant element, alas, when casts and conductor change. The decision to set the action in eighteenth-century Boston seems to me a brilliantly right solution to the recurrent problem of where and when. Verdi began his opera in the royal Swedish setting of the Scribe libretto *Gustave III,* on which his own is based. Knowing that regicide could not be represented on the Naples stage, he completed it in a setting of seventeenth-century Stettin, with an imaginary Duke of Pomerania, not the historical Gustavus III of Sweden, as its protagonist. For Rome, he changed the scene to seventeenth-century Boston. In Paris in 1861, *Ballo* was set in Florence; in London that year, it was set in Naples. In our day, it has often been set in Stockholm. It would be wrong to conclude that it could happen *anywhere*. The composer laid down certain conditions for its migration. The nature of the drama and the distinct "color" of his score predicated a Northern, not a Latin, court. The protagonist had to be someone in a position of political importance, at a time when much depended on his conduct and decisions. (In *Gustave III*, one of the conspirators' grievances is that their ruler frivols with masked balls when a war with Russia is impending.) The society had to be one of a certain elegance; the Dark Ages were out, and the Middle Ages would not match the music. Eighteenth-century Boston on the eve of the Revolution fits Verdi's bill at all points. Great issues were stirring. The Bostonians, as the traveler Daniel Neal recorded, were "as polite as in most of the cities and towns in England," and "their houses, their furniture, their tables, their dress and conversation . . . as splendid and showy." Hawthorne, in "Legends of the Province House," described a spectacular masked ball in the governor's mansion: "It was the policy of Sir William Howe to hide the distress and danger of the period . . . under an ostentation of festivity." The Boston painter John Singleton Copley could—and at the Met did—provide the inspiration for the scenes, the costumes, and the lighting. As E. P. Richardson says in his *Painting in America*, Copley "created the most brilliant and convincing expression of the aristocratic ideal that American eighteenth-century painting was to produce," and—the words apply equally well to Verdi—taking up the forms of his predecessors, he "poured into them an imaginative power to observe and to experience reality that filled them with the glow, vitality, and mystery of life."

So far, so good. The Met costumes, designed by Peter J. Hall, are fine. It is in the realization of the Boston setting, designed by Peter Wexler, that things go wrong. Mr. Moshinsky has a "method." He stages operas in a plain, severe box, endeavoring to throw all emphasis into the actors. For *Grimes*, the box was the shifting grays of North Sea skies. For Covent Garden's *Lohengrin*, it was white, enclosing jeweled costumes. For *Ballo*, it is brown. It is meant to suggest wood but looks like nasty imitation wood. The sides and back don't meet the floor; they are suspended above a black-curtained gap, high enough to permit entrances. When Renzo Mongiardino designed a basic wooden box for the Scala *Ballo* of 1972–73, he put doors and windows in it and arranged for it to vary in size from scene to scene; a spectacular transformation introduced the last scene as the plain panels swung round to reveal elaborate carving. The Met box, huge, stark, and ugly, hangs unchanging over every scene. In Act II, some steel scaffolding is added, which houses the action rather well but looks unsuitable. In the first scene of Act III, Amelia and René are dwarfed by an enormous family portrait, in the style of Copley but blown up on a monster scale. Larger-than-life representations, whether paintings or sculpture, always diminish living actors; the device can be potently used, but I don't see its purpose here. Act II apart, each scene by itself is striking and effective. But the cumulative result of this assertively "minimalist" scenery is that it draws attention to itself more insistently, more obtrusively, than even the most elaborately realistic décor does. Moreover—the complaint must be made of all the Met's recent Verdi productions—the unit set does away with the contrast between shallow scenes and deep which is built into the very structure, musical and dramatic, of most nineteenth-century operas. (When Claudio Abbado conducted the Scala *Ballo*, in 1977, he wrote in the program book that the stage plans of the 1859 production book had clarified for him the successive "sound pictures" that Verdi had in mind.) The sets are stark but the costumes are lavish; and, with his profusion of redcoats, red ensigns, and Union Jacks, Mr. Moshinsky may even have pinned down *Ballo* too tightly to one particular place and time.

Paradoxically, then, the décor does the opposite of what its creators must have intended. It claims too much attention. In time, however, one may stop noticing it and look only at the actors. With them, Mr. Moshinsky has had his success. For many years, I had not seen and heard Luciano Pavarotti give a performance that could be taken seriously. The nearest he came was in that Scala *Ballo* of 1977. Franco Zeffirelli, the director, had minimized the tenor's physical awkwardness (at Covent Garden in the same role he had been ridiculous), and Mr. Abbado had persuaded him to phrase and express Verdi's music. Mr. Pavarotti's Met Richard last week was not musically on the same level, but for one act, at least, he played not merely a plausible governor but a serious, interesting, and complicated character. His alert, nervous treatment of "È scherzo od è follia" was thrilling. (Verdi expressly forbade the interpolation of naturalistic laughter, and Mr. Pavarotti added none.) After that, he tended to relapse into being the Luciano everyone loves, but there were still some touches of interest in what he did. He has built up his voice into a firm and sure instrument, admirable so far as it goes but monochrome; the contrasting tones of tenderness, sweetness, lyricism were missing, and there was little feeling for sense in the phrasing of the love duet and the final aria.

Katia Ricciarelli's singing was not monochrome, but what colors came out often seemed to be the result of chance; she displayed neither the voice nor the technique for the uncommonly difficult role of Amelia. Still, she has nice feelings, a touching personality, and a pleasing appearance, and some of her notes were good. For those qualities one could be grateful. But of neither aria was her performance anywhere near adequate. When Verdi described René as a Creole, he may have been intending a "shorthand" indication of the streak of passion the secretary suddenly displays. (In Romantic convention, there is an equation of looks and temperament: blonds are steady and good and noble; fiery men like Edgar of Ravenswood and Heathcliff are raven-haired, Byronic.) Louis Quilico, who took the part of René, is not a passionate performer, and, like all plump men, he must work hard—harder than he did—to suggest vengeful fury. He voiced the role quite well, but in the Act II finale one heard him pattering out "Thus he repays me, who saved his life" in an equable, almost jolly way, without a flash in either his eyes or his timbre. Bianca Berini, the Ulrica, carried no big guns, but she was more acceptable than star mezzos who, intent on making their mark with the fortune-teller's single scene, exaggerate. Judith Blegen's Oscar was neat but small and a shade dull. In both arias, she conveyed the impression that she was thinking about where she had to move to next. Her numbers are rather trickily staged. In general, Mr. Moshinsky's work is a strange mixture of, on the one hand, unobtrusive yet wonderfully exact, revealing movement and, on the other, arrant, obvious staginess. The first two scenes are splendidly accomplished. Act II moves very well, amid the unhappy scenery. But in the first scene of Act III props—a rocking horse, a portable portrait of the governor—are prominent and are prominently used. For the F-major section of "Eri tu," René moves to sit on an upstage chair, and his purpose in doing so—so that as the climax of the aria approaches he can rise and advance to the footlights, waving his arms—is all too clear in advance. Sometimes the solos are isolated by choral "freezes." (This happens even in Richard's aria, to which the "frozen" chorus must add a sung commentary.) But to isolate the intimate dialogues of the last scene, René's with Oscar and Richard's with Amelia, Mr. Moshinsky provides a realistic distraction for the rest of the company: a large lady who swoons and receives much attention. She succeeds in diverting the attention of the party away from the soloists—at the cost of diverting the audience's attention, too.

In sum, I'm puzzled. And a little worried by what seems to be a very "special" kind of production, which could be refined and strengthened if Mr. Moshinsky were to stay on and work at it through a run of performances, but which won't lend itself to housing a series of changing casts put through the "moves" by a house director. Perhaps one could describe it as an arresting, imaginative, highly intelligent, and then in patches suddenly incompetent production. On the conducting side, there's little to note except that Mr. Patanè gave a routine, superficial performance, insensitive to the strange colors, the contrasts of light and blackness, laughter and anguish in this marvelous score. He made several passages sound vulgar. There was no string band in the wings to play the mazurka; it came from the pit. I thought that happened only in small provincial houses.

February 18, 1980

Heart and Mind

Mozart's C-minor Fantasy (strictly, Maximilian Stadler's completion for solo piano of a magnificent movement Mozart began for piano and violin) was billed to open Radu Lupu's recital in Avery Fisher Hall last week. In the event, Mr. Lupu played Mozart's B-minor Adagio, a long, serious stretch of music and perhaps Mozart's greatest solo composition for the instrument. He played it thoughtfully, beautifully, amply, and without exaggeration, sounding the strong dynamic contrasts yet never breaking the scale of the music. Then he played Schubert's A-minor Sonata, D. 845. A modern Steinway, with its thick, "rich" tone, is no fit instrument for Schubert, but then the immense Fisher Hall is equally no fit place for it—or for a fortepiano. Last time I heard Mr. Lupu, playing Schubert's A-major Sonata, D. 959, in Carnegie Hall, I felt that the big modern instrument got in the way of the music, and in the way of a wonderful performance. And in the A-minor last week there were passages—where the thick-clumped chords of the opening Moderato move low, where the A-flat variation of the second movement needs unstinted fortissimo on an early-nineteenth-century but not a twentieth-century scale—to make a listener regret the sweetness and clarity of a piano that Schubert would have recognized. But regrets were fleeting, no more than evanescent flecks on the rapture that Mr. Lupu's playing inspired. In fact, I would hesitate to bring up once again the question of the instrument (except to praise this one as a fine specimen of its kind) had not the program announced that Mr. Lupu is to record a complete cycle of Schubert's sonatas. Already he has put four of them on disc. One can understand his using a Steinway when he plays to an assembled multitude. But records are heard at home, and through them he could reach more people still, without having to sacrifice the kinds of sound the composer had in mind—to hold back, to "transcribe," in effect, for a different instrument. The superior merits of a Schubert piano, for Schubert, will never be widely recognized until a great Schubert pianist of our day—and that Mr. Lupu now is—joins his musical understanding and his technical command to its tones and action.

Since he won the Leeds Piano Competition, in 1969, Mr. Lupu has grown steadily, shed mannerisms, matured into a master of the most satisfying kind. None of the three works on his program was in any sense a display piece, even though the third was Brahms's formidable, fiery Third Sonata. Played for show, the sonata can sound extravagant and extreme. Mr. Lupu played it as poetry, rather as Edwin Fischer used to (though Mr. Lupu played its finale more accurately), and it was stirring. For encores, he returned to

Schubert: the Andante of the A-major Sonata, D. 664, lifted out as a gentle romance, and well able to stand on its own; and the F-minor Moment Musical, exquisitely light and enchantingly poised.

Mozart's C-minor Fantasy did begin Russell Sherman's recital the week before, at Washington Irving High School. For several years, Bostonians (and others) have been recommending Mr. Sherman to me as if he were America's answer to Alfred Brendel. On records, I have admired arresting Beethoven and masterly Liszt. This was my first "live" encounter with his playing, and I was disappointed. The Mozart promised well. Two pieces by Stefan Wolpe, *Form for Piano* and *Form IV: Broken Sequences,* were finely and strongly done. But then his account of the Brahms-Paganini Variations suggested an interpretation thought out, worked over, worried at, pondered in intellectual and technical details to a point where the music lost any natural flow. There was none of the improvisatory quality that can make the work so exciting, so exhilarating to hear. In the second half, Mr. Sherman's Chopin was similarly personal and "cultivated" to the point of preciousness.

A few days later, Alfred Brendel came to Carnegie with an unexpected repertory: three Schumann cycles—*Kinderscenen, Carnaval,* and *Kreisleriana.* He is a pianist who holds one's attention on everything he does. The *Kinderscenen* pieces were shapely, sharply characterized, nervously alive. So were the *Carnaval* pieces, and yet—how can I put it without sounding philistine?—there seemed to be too much brain and not enough simple feeling in their performance. *Kreisleriana* was wonderful in its way, but one was aware of points that were being made, of problems that had been solved. In his collection of essays *Musical Thoughts and Afterthoughts,* Mr. Brendel wrote, "*Feeling* must remain the Alpha and Omega of a musician," and "The moment an audience feels that a performer wants to teach them, his case is lost." I quoted those sentences when praising Youri Egorov's first Carnegie recital, last season; and after Mr. Brendel's recital I returned to the Egorov recording of *Kreisleriana* for reassurance that I hadn't been wrong to miss something—spontaneity, simplicity—in Mr. Brendel's brilliantly disciplined, formidably polished performance. I don't think he was consciously trying to teach, but perhaps he is still rather too close to the results of lessons he himself must have learned while restudying this Schumann repertory. He provides pleasures for the mind. He can play Beethoven in a way that seems to convey Beethoven's very thought. But there are pleasures of the senses— rapture in warm, beautiful, romantic piano sound—which escape him. I'm trying to avoid the easy label "intellectual," so often attached to him. He *is* communicative, exciting, and direct. But this Schumann lacked natural impulsiveness.

Mr. Egorov's Carnegie recital this season was not quite the sensation that his earlier one had been. I enjoyed his Bach E-minor Partita—not as stylish Bach playing but as the fresh response of an exuberant, instinctive pianist-musician to the music. Bartók's Sonata was potently done. Then Mr. Egorov attempted the well-nigh impossible: to sustain not merely one complete set of Chopin's Studies but both sets in a single recital. There were many, many pleasing and beautiful things along the way. Mr. Egorov seems to be a born, not a made, pianist.

Early this month, the Juilliard American Opera Center gave the first performances of a new two-act opera, *Feathertop*, by Edward Barnes, a twenty-two-year-old Juilliard student. The subject is from Hawthorne's story of the same title, in *Mosses from an Old Manse*. In eighteenth-century New England, a witch sends her scarecrow out into the world dressed as a fine young lord, and the world accepts him as one. But in a mirror he and the girl he plans to marry see "not the glittering mockery of his outside show, but a picture of the sordid patchwork of his real composition, stripped of all witchcraft," and he chooses not to live. Maurice Valency adapted the story for television in 1963, and later for the stage, and has now fashioned his play as a libretto. In a program note, he says that any debt to Gogol's *The Government Inspector* is accidental. A similar idea provided the plot of Hans Werner Henze's opera *The Young Lord* (1965), but there it is an ape, not a scarecrow, whose outré deportment is enthusiastically copied. Hawthorne could have known the Wilhelm Hauff story (1827) on which Henze's opera is based, but he need not have: the donnée has a folk-tale, fabular quality. Its moral is stated by Hawthorne's witch:

> My poor, dear, pretty Feathertop! There are thousands upon thousands of coxcombs and charlatans in the world, made up of just such a jumble of wornout, forgotten, and good-for-nothing trash as he was! Yet they live in fair repute, and never see themselves for what they are.

And the sentiment is provided by her further reflection "He seems to have too much heart to bustle for his own advantage in such an empty and heartless world." Dramatists and composers can make much or little of the subject. Henze expanded it into a big opera, packed with character studies, caricatures, thoughts about individual and social human behavior, and almost too much music. Barnes's treatment is light. Both the moral and the emotions are touched on without emphasis. It was hard to tell whether the composer's heart was engaged, whether he was drawn to the familiar matter by more than its evident stage effectiveness. But his skill was not for a moment in doubt. The opera moves confidently, sings well, and sounds good. A small orchestra—strings, woodwind quartet, horn, trumpet, plentiful but delicate percussion, piano, and an offstage women's chorus used instrumentally—is handled in a masterly way. Points of reference for the music are Britten (the witch's familiar is a new version of Britten's Puck), Boulez, and Maxwell Davies. *Feathertop* is a slight piece, but one of the most efficient first operas I have ever heard.

The only voice of much note in the cast was J. Patrick Raftery's baritone, in a small role; but the production, directed by H. Wesley Balk, designed by Peter Perina, and staged in the school's Drama Theatre, was one of the most accomplished that New York has seen, up on a level with the Met's *Lulu*. Mr. Perina, a Czech who lives and works in Canada, is a discovery. The designing style was "school of Svoboda" at its most poetic, and apt for this adventurous, imaginative presentation of a contemporary opera. The Juilliard Philharmonia, conducted by Richard Dufallo, played admirably.

Earlier this season, in the Juilliard Theatre, the Opera Center put on four performances of Puccini's operetta *La rondine* in elaborate stock scenery acquired from the Opera Company of Philadelphia. That décor, too, matched the work it housed. The singers weren't particularly good; Laszlo Halasz's conducting was sometimes ungainly; Ian Strasfogel, the director, handled the crowd scenes very well but had devised some awkward bits of business for the principals. The first night was sticky; at a later performance I surrendered happily to the charm of Puccini's tuneful score.

Massenet's *Hérodiade* (1881), which succeeds the oratorio *La Vierge* in his catalogue, is a surprisingly decorous work, despite the scene in Act II of Herod's repose attended by the masseuses of the day. (Even there, the proprieties are saved when the love philter Herod drinks proves sporific.) As H. E. Krehbiel remarked when the piece reached New York, in 1909, "the names of the principal characters were those which for a few years had been filling the lyric theatres of Germany with a moral stench; but their bearers in Massenet's opera did little or nothing that was especially shocking to good taste or proper morals." Salome proves to be a chaste and devout cousin of the frivolous Manon Lescaut. Herodias is a tender mother and jealous wife. (It is late in the piece before she discovers that her rival is also her long-lost daughter.) John the Baptist is "a voice—but not one crying in the wilderness." In the last act, he allows himself a love duet with Salome, regarding it as a sign of divine favor that she has come to visit him in his prison. The scene includes a saxophone obbligato.

Hérodiade is a grand opera with multiple choruses, processions, ceremonies, dances in each of the four acts. As the first event of its season, the Opera Orchestra of New York gave it a large-scale concert performance, in Carnegie Hall. There was a strong, confident chorus, formed of the New York University Choral Arts Society and the C. W. Post College Chorus of Long Island University. Eve Queler had assembled an orchestra of expert players. Her conducting was broad, spirited, and sensitive in the intimate scenes. The only large cut was of the Act IV ballet. At the Wexford Festival production of *Hérodiade*, in 1977, the role of Salome was sung by a Pamina, Eilene Hannan. In New York, Montserrat Caballé was billed for it, but she became ill. Awilda Verdejo, a pretty Pamina at the Juilliard three years ago (and later a touching Jenůfa), brought charm, piquancy, and clear, fresh tones to the part, and also the ability to spin a long, soaring line. Nicolai Gedda had withdrawn from the role of the Baptist. A young tenor from North Carolina, Richard Estes, made a brave and stylish shot at a role calling (like Berlioz's Aeneas, Rossini's Arnold, Don José) for that combination of elegance and heroic ring of which Jean de Reszke was a famous and Georges Thill perhaps the last exemplar. Bernadette Greevy, Wexford's Herodias, repeated her role; she was potent and passionate. Juan Pons produced fine, smooth tone as Herod. Paul Plishka was an imposing Phanuel, the Chaldean astrologer. Miss Queler had engaged a real and magisterial cantor, Herman Malamood, to sing the off-stage "Hear, O Israel" of the Act III temple rite.

The director of the Paris Opera, Auguste Vaucorbeil, turned down *Hérodiade*, according to Massenet's memoirs, as needing the attentions of a *carcassier*—someone who could articulate an operatic skeleton firmly. One sees what he meant. The matter of *Hérodiade is* rather a muddle of loves, faiths, and the Judeo-Roman power struggle; the opera is an accumulation of striking scenes rather than a dramatic progress. Plainly, it's not a piece deserving a full-scale stage revival, but it does show Massenet's merits: his rhythmic flexibility in word setting, which opened the way to *Manon* (and was perhaps not without influence on *Pelléas*); his delicate handling of voices and instruments; and—as also in *Le Cid,* which Miss Queler did four years ago—his easy command of very large operatic forces. Like most of Miss Queler's revivals, this *Hérodiade* was at once enjoyable and instructive.

February 25, 1980

Impressions

Milton Babbitt has brought out three brilliant and substantial solo pieces this season. The first of them, *Images,* is not strictly solo; it is for saxophone and synthesized tape. Harvey Pittel, who commissioned it, gave the first performance at his Tully Hall recital in December. Babbitt likes to pack a program note into a single sentence, and his sentence about *Images* is a corker. It took twenty-five lines of the program book. "The multiple mutualities of music issuing from the loudspeakers and the instrument of the 'human' performer, and ... definitive properties of the composition, particularly the complementary parallelisms of transformation between temporally proximate events projected by the different media, and between and among temporally distant, dimensionally distinct, events occurring in corresponding locations in the large design" is a scrap of it. If Babbitt wrote music the way he writes English, one wouldn't be able to keep one's mind on his scores. But he doesn't, and one can. Finding words afterward to describe his music isn't easy. What I see jotted on the margin of my program is simply "very beautiful"—a straightforward if imprecise piece of criticism. I can amplify the two words with two facts—*Images* lasts ten minutes and forty-three seconds; the outer sections are for alto saxophone, while the central section is for soprano and sopranino saxophones—and with the assertion that the play of timbres and rhythms between the loudspeakers and the live player gave delight. One listened eagerly for what was going to happen next, liked it when it happened, and decided—intuitively, at least—that the work held together and made sense. The balance seemed to me slightly awry; the tape machine should surely have been turned up.

The two other Babbitt pieces appeared at a League-ISCM concert last month in Carnegie Recital Hall. The first was *Tableaux*, for solo piano, composed back in 1973, for Robert Helps, but given its first performance at this concert, by Matthias Kriesberg. Mr. Kriesberg is a gifted and forceful young composer, whose Short Symphony was done by the Juilliard Orchestra in Tully Hall last year; at the Juilliard he was a pupil of Babbitt. As a pianist, he played Babbitt's *Tableaux* with brio and brilliance. The piece lasts about ten minutes, ranges the keyboard vigorously, is bright, sharp, and exciting. The second Babbitt première was of *My Ends Are My Beginnings*, for solo clarinet, composed in 1978 for Anand Devendra, who played it at this concert. The composer's program note says, "The appropriation and pluralization of Machaut's title [the rondeau "Ma fin est mon commencement"] should intimate the, I hope, appropriate, and the—I know—plural relations of, and multiple paths to, fro, and between initiations and terminations, so as to require, for their coherent realizations, this exceptionally extended one-movement, instrumentally tripartite composition." The work lasted for some fifteen minutes; in the central section the player moved to a bass clarinet. Mr. Devendra, beckoning with his musical pipe, shooting out keen, piercing glances, seeming to search for inspiration as much in the air as in the score set out before him, is rather like a snake charmer to watch. He draws soft, smoky, seductive notes from his instrument in a way that does suggest the casting of a spell: instead of a drowsy cobra, strange melodies uncoiled, or single notes were molded and given form until they seemed to rise and float before him, almost palpable. Then, with a sudden, sharp signal, they were dismissed. The effect was musically picturesque. At first acquaintance, *My Ends* seems to be a charming piece, mysterious and gravely lyrical where *Tableaux* is tough, glittering, and fervent. Of course, I'm reporting only on what Babbitt has elsewhere called "local coherences and immediate modes of progression and association which are instantly apparent." After a single hearing, without scores, I can only guess at the constructive thought in the making of the works. But *Images, Tableaux,* and *My Ends* are all pieces I'd like to hear again, and I hope they will be recorded soon.

Between the Babbitt works at the League concert, there was a serious, beautifully fashioned suite, Seven Trios for String Quartet, by Mark Brunswick, who died in 1971. And then John Graziano's *In Memoriam Mark Brunswick,* five well-fashioned tributary movements, for string quintet. Good playing, with Rolf Schulte as first violin. As the second half of the concert, the veteran pianist Beveridge Webster gave a "retrospective" recital of music by composers associated with the League, the ISCM, or both. Artur Schnabel's Piece in Seven Movements, dated 1947 in the program (is it a different work from the Piano Piece in Seven Parts played at the 1941 ISCM Festival in New York?), is earnest and thoughtful. There is a moving passage toward the close which suggests the Andante of Beethoven's Opus 28, the D-major Sonata, pared down, epigrammatic, and tragic. But the work as a whole is prolix. So is Erich Itor Kahn's *Ciaccona dei tempi di guerra*" (1943). Marc Blitzstein's Piano Sonata (1927), on the other hand, is terse and punchy. I'm glad to have heard some music by Schnabel, and the memory of certain episodes stays with me. It was instructive to hear some early Blitzstein. But—to apply once more that simplest of critical tests—I don't really care whether or not I hear any of the three pieces again.

On Sunday last week, at the Great Performers concert in Avery Fisher Hall, there was veteran pianism of another kind. Claudio Arrau gave a recital, eleven days after his seventy-seventh birthday, playing Beethoven, Debussy, Liszt, and Chopin. His technique was as fluent as ever, his platform presence as spry and dapper. He seems not to change at all. If he had given this recital ten, twenty, thirty years ago, I feel I might have reviewed it in much the same terms—with the same admiration and yet with the same, difficult-to-define reservations.

Admiration first. Mr. Arrau gave an exquisite account of Debussy's first book of *Images*. The timbres in "Reflections in the water" were delicate and beautiful; the control of rubato was masterly. In "Homage to Rameau," he seemed to stroke the theme from the keyboard; again, the play of timbres and the flexible shaping of the phrases within a clearly perceived pulse were wonderful. And "Movement" was breathtaking. "With fantastic lightness but precise" is Debussy's indication; Mr. Arrau's two hands sounded a quicksilver moto perpetuo of shifting colors and shifting rhythmic phrases to suggest the kaleidoscopic intricacies of a full Steve Reich ensemble. The Liszt works, the B-minor Ballade and "The Fountains at the Villa d'Este," were equally fine: virtuosity and lyricism were combined; pianistic impressionism at its most captivating was put at the service of poetic thought. Liszt set as an epigraph to the "Fountains" a text from St. John ("But the water that I shall give him shall be in him a well of water springing up into everlasting life"), and in all the *Years of Wandering* pieces the seductively picturesque instrumental writing enshrines deep feeling. In the works of nature and of man and in famous places of history, he discovered not "fruitless images" but, in the words of his preface to the *Wandering* volumes, "a vague yet direct relationship, unidentified yet real bonds, a sure yet inexplicable communication," which he sought to render in "a poetic language perhaps even better able than poetry itself to express everything in us that . . . is linked to inaccessible profundities, imperishable desires." In performances like Mr. Arrau's of the Ballade and the "Fountains," Liszt's greatness as a composer, as poet and visionary, is made apparent.

Mr. Arrau was using a Hamburg Steinway, a warm, full instrument without harshness or glare, aptly protean in most of its range but a shade constricted—more bassoon than cello—in the octave below middle C, where the main melody of the Liszt Ballade lies. For Chopin, one is accustomed to a fresher, more buoyant timbre, but the instrument matched the pianist's grave, even slightly somber approach to the A-flat Ballade and the B-minor Scherzo. The performances were thoughtful, large, and beautifully "voiced"—satisfying, if not exactly exhilarating.

Why the reservations, which I find many people share? Some may be the result of prejudice: a feeling that a pianist whose "specialties" encompass those of Schnabel, Cortot, Kempff, Rubinstein, and Serkin must be something of a chameleon; that someone who plays so much, day after day, in country after country—here Brahms or Beethoven, there Debussy, next Schumann or Chopin—cannot be fully committed to everything he does. The evidence of one's ears suggests otherwise—there was nothing uncommitted about any part of his Fisher Hall recital—but such thoughts can cloud the way people listen. "Arrau never has anything to tell me about the pieces he plays" is a comment I've heard. It's true that he doesn't "make statements," decisively set out personal perceptions or points of view, in the way that younger pianists such as Alfred Brendel, Charles Rosen, and Paul Jacobs do. He himself has declared, "I believe that in interpretion the pianist is transformed and plunged into a world which is not normally his own. Like an actor he must be capable of transformation, for just as one becomes Hamlet one must also live Beethoven's sonatas." His recital began with Beethoven's Opus 109, followed by the "Waldstein." Something was missing, I felt. Perhaps it was just the assertiveness, the individuality, that, paradoxically, always seems to stamp the most convincingly "Beethovenian" performances of the sonatas. There was nothing wrong, and there was much that was marvelous. Not since Gieseking have I heard the "Waldstein" finale flow so bewitchingly—and Mr. Arrau, without being any less fleet or fluent, avoided the hint of daintiness that Gieseking used to bring to the movement. When Gieseking proved less than inspiring, it was, one felt, because he turned argument into melody. Mr. Arrau turns argument into timbre. Was it grit, a keener clash of harmonic incidents, a touch of roughness that I missed? I don't know. But I do know that Mr. Arrau, who (after child-prodigy years in Chile) made his formal début in 1914, aged eleven, is still one of the world's great pianists.

March 3, 1980

King and Count

Radamisto, Handel's first opera for the Royal Academy, performed in April 1720, has a high reputation. The plot concerns two royal couples linked by marriage but divided by conflict. Radamistus' sister Polyxena is married to Tiridates, King of Armenia, who lusts afer Radamistus' wife, Zenobia. The other characters are Tigranes, a Pontic prince, who loves Polyxena; Phraates, Tiridates' brother, who loves Zenobia; and Pharasmenes, King of Thrace, father of Radamistus and Polyxena. A Radamistus (son of a Pharasmenes), a Tiridates, and a Tigranes were successive kings of Armenia in the mid-first century; Phraates is a Parthian royal name; and some of the plot is taken from the twelfth book of Tacitus' *Annals.* But *Radamisto* is a heroic, not a historical, drama, and renowned as being the first Handel opera whose libretto permitted—in Winton Dean's words—a "sustained response" on the composer's part, when he "outsoars the convention and presents us across the centuries with a great work of art"; as being a work in which "the central conflicts ring true, the different strands are skillfully woven together, and the motives of the characters . . . are reasonably clear and consistent, so that the music can develop a high emotional pressure."

All the same, in the performances I've encountered—two in the theatre, and a concert version last month in Carnegie Hall—*Radamisto* hasn't lived up to its reputation. It seems to me not as exciting as the great trio of the mid-1720s—*Giulio Cesare, Tamerlano,* and *Rodelinda*—although there are many great things in it. Radamistus' "Ombra cara," his lament when he believes Zenobia has killed herself, deserves the praise that has been heaped on it. (Dean calls it "one of the profoundest expressions of grief in the history of opera.") Zenobia's "Quando mai spietata sorte," with its oboe obbligato over full string accompaniment, is a lovely movement. And there are many other passages in which devotion, defiance, hope, despair, ardor, rage, or resolve is memorably expressed. The characters are consistent. Their plights are credible. Nevertheless, *Radamisto*—carefully made, impressive, strong—hardly has the cumulative dramatic power of Handel's greatest operas or the exuberance of breathtaking inventions which makes so many of his operas a musical feast.

The Carnegie performance, billed as the New York première of *Radamisto,* didn't help. It was conducted by Stephen Simon, who, as music director of the Handel Society of New York, for four years did much to allay the city's Handel starvation. (The last fully professional staging here of a Handel opera was the City Opera's *Giulio Cesare* in 1972.) Then he moved his activities to Washington; and this *Radamisto* reached us from the Kennedy Center.

Mr. Simon has done Handel great service, but, it must be said, he could do him greater service still if he forwent the baton and engaged an expert Handelian conductor as well as singers and players. On number after number of *Radamisto* he laid a leaden hand. At earlier Simon performances, I had sometimes heard the singers and the music break free and move and flow. At this performance, the Zenobia, Hilda Harris, and her oboist, Kathleen Golding, took charge, or so it seemed, of "Quando mai spietata sorte." But the rest was held to a plod: heavy rhythms, whether fast or slow; unnatural tempi; square-toed phrasing.

The chief pleasures of the evening were provided by the vividness of Miss Harris, a mezzo with emotional sparks in her singing, and by the fluent divisions of Nancy Shade, as Tigranes—though Miss Shade was occasionally wild. In the title role, Beverly Wolff sounded sometimes brassy, sometimes blowsy, and sometimes beautiful. The Benita Valente I heard as Polyxena was a singer whose voice lost purity of focus when it rose, whose phrasing was dull, who made nothing of the words. There must be another singer of the same name—the one I see enthusiastic reviews of and have heard on record. I hope to hear her in the flesh one day. Richard Lewis, the Tiridates, tended to shout. In the cadet roles, Linda Mabbs, the Phraates, and Kenneth Bell, the Pharasmenes, were passable. It was interesting to hear Handel's original score. He composed it for a soprano Radamistus, Margherita Durastanti (Miss Wolff, a mezzo, was taxed by the tessitura, and lowered one of the arias), and a tenor Tiridates, a Mr. Gordon. There were three Britons in his cast, and two of the male roles were taken by women. In December 1720, Handel recomposed the opera, writing much of the music afresh, for an all-Italian cast in which the great alto castrato Senesino took the title role, Durastanti moved to Zenobia, and the wide-ranging bass Giuseppe Maria Boschi was Tiridates. This second *Radamisto* is what we usually hear today. As a rule, the second—and any subsequent—versions of Handel operas, rejigged for a new cast, are less strong than the originals. His dramas took shape in the medium of the singers he had available; later, it was a question of adjustments, of fitting in the newcomers. But *Radamisto* may be an exception: Senesino and Boschi, as the magnificent new arias composed for them make clear, were a potent source of inspiration.

Eight of the twenty-nine arias were omitted and three were abridged. That's generous measure for a modern Handel revival. (In London's latest production of *Giulio Cesare*, at the English National Opera, with Janet Baker as Caesar, eleven arias were omitted and three were abridged.) But it was not a good idea to redivide the three acts as two, dropping in a single interval after "Ombra cara." Handel's sense of act structure, musically and emotionally, was sure, and he knew what kind of number made a good finale. I hope that when the City Opera revives *Giulio Cesare* it uses a strong and sound edition.

. . .

The City Opera's spring season opened with *Le Comte Ory*, a production new last fall. *Ory*, Rossini's penultimate opera and only French comedy, is a bewitching work when it is properly done and an attractive work even when, as here, the performance lacks grace and wit. The City Opera production is derived from one given three years ago by Opera Theatre of St. Louis; the New York version is bigger but not better. Christopher Alden's coarse direction is based on stale, stock devices of the comic stage, not on high-spirited and subtle observation of these characters or this particular score. The overture is treated as accompaniment to a pantomime. The level of taste and sensitivity may be judged from the parody of the Eucharist in Act II. The "pious sisters"—lusty young men who have gained entrance to the Countess's castle diguised as nuns—are caught with a bottle of wine. Ory, in his garb as Soeur Colette, quickly consecrates it and elevates it before his companions. A little later, the "joke" is resumed as the "nuns" kneel in line to receive a mock host. On the nineteenth-century Italian stage, sacraments could not be represented: hence all those marriages performed by notaries, not priests; the stage directions for Verdi's *I lombardi* carefully avoid specific mention of the baptism clearly implied by the action and the score. We are less nice today, but even those whose faith is not offended by Mr. Alden's lark may find that their sense of fitness is.

St. Louis has a thrust stage; on it Paul Steinberg, the designer, placed a colorful, cuddly castle, a pleasant piece of soft art. He has framed and draped the State Theater stage in deepest black and palled the comedy. Within this funereal box is a two-dimensional arcade that must serve for both the countryside of Act I and the bedroom of Act II. A toy castle is there again, but within the arcade it loses its point and it seems to be a less embraceable model. Gilbert Hemsley's lighting is low through the merry opening assemblies. When it brightens at the Countess's entry, well into the act, and when a night sky is revealed in the last scene of all, one's spirits lift.

The Countess was Gianna Rolandi, and in the cabaletta of her aria she produced two flights of coloratura whose rapidity recalled that of Rosalia Chalia and Maria Galvany, singers who made records early in this century. Rapidity is not all, but it is good to be astonished—in an apt place, as the Countess's cabaletta is—by virtuosity. Elsewhere, she was uneven, sometimes sweet and shapely, sometimes peaky. She hasn't got the role quite right yet and needs direction. The Ory was Rockwell Blake, fluent as ever in divisions but disappointing in timbre until he reached the trio, whose long opening strophe he sang exquisitely. He proved no kind of actor. Isolier (Faith Esham), Raimbaud (David Holloway), and the Tutor (Samuel Ramey) all had good voices, but again misdirection or lack of direction kept them from making much of their roles. The conductor, Imre Pallo, seemed content to let the recitatives be sung in 4/4, not as pointed dialogue. For example, Miss Esham gave to each syllable of the phrase "the proud disdain that flames in your bright eyes" the same length and the same stress. (Try saying it that way.) Tom Hammond's English translation got in the way of the music as it didn't seem to in London, where the opera has been in the repertory for seventeen years. Mr. Pallo's handling of the miraculous instrumental writing was workaday. The City Opera is usually careful about details, but in this show Dame Ragonde, the castle portress, wore elaborate eye makeup, Isolier's cheeks were painted with brown streaks, and the men's wigs were sorry things.

March 10, 1980

Eleleleleu!

John Eaton's latest opera, *The Cry of Clytaemnestra*, a powerful one-act drama, was given its first performance this month by the Indiana University Opera Theatre, in Bloomington's Musical Arts Center. His previous opera, *Danton and Robespierre*, also created at Bloomington [see page 174], employed very large orchestral and choral forces. *The Cry of Clytaemnestra* has a small orchestra: five winds (flute, oboe, clarinet, bassoon, horn), two pianos, a well-stocked battery commanded by three players, and nine strings; also, onstage or in the wings, stierhorn fanfares, crumhorns, and drum; and electronic music that can roll around the theatre. There is no chorus. The principal characters are Clytemnestra and Agamemnon; Iphigenia, Electra, and Orestes; Aegisthus; Cassandra. Calchas has a brief, telling role in a scene at Aulis, where six Greek princes provide a semichorus. But *The Cry of Clytaemnestra*, which lasts seventy-five minutes, is hardly a "chamber" opera. It makes a big sound. Its gestures are large. It has grandeur and force.

Rash the composer who endeavors to match the *Agamemnon* itself by his music. Demetre Cuclin, G. F. Linstead, Felix Weingartner, and Norman Demuth are among those who have tried; S. I. Taneyev's earnest *Oresteia* trilogy (1895) had some success, and a recording of it has recently been published. Eaton and his librettist, Patrick Creagh, have been bold but not temerarious; their opera, inspired by Aeschylus, drawn from his drama, is not a new *Agamemnon* but, in effect, a long dramatic scena for Clytemnestra. The scene is the royal bedchamber of the Argive palace and the garden below it, the time a few days before Agamemnon's return. In visions, Clytemnestra's mind travels thence back to Aulis and the sacrifice of her daughter, and across to Troy, where Cassandra prophesies to Agamemnon. As if in a dream, the queen imagines her husband's homecoming, and the scene of her murderous welcome to him is enacted *coram populo*. The visions alternate with a "real" present. Waking from the last of them, Clytemnestra discovers that her resolution is formed. As the beacons of Agamemnon's victory blaze out across the backcloth, she prepares to meet him.

The *Oresteia* is a moral and political drama whose large theme is justice and the reconciliation of fate with individual responsibility; as in *The Ring* (which has Aeschylean roots), the workings of a primitive curse yield at last to the workings of human enlightenment. And then—as Philip Vellacott puts it in the introduction to his translation—"there is a second great question which Aeschylus considers in the *Oresteia;* and it concerns the central figure of Clytemnestra. . . . Clearly the relation of man and woman in marriage must be named, after the 'quest for justice,' as the second great theme of the trilogy." Clytemnestra embodies it. The Choephori restate it: "Our whole sex is cursed, by men disfranchised, scorned, and portionless." Apollo and Athene return to it in the trial scene of *The Eumenides.* Omitting the Chorus of Elders and Clytemnestra's and Aegisthus' speeches of self-defense, Eaton and Creagh leave the first theme unstated. The second is implicit in their drama, but the particular character of their heroine, not the "great question," is their first concern. In a preface to the libretto (which is published by the Shawnee Press), the opera is described as "an intense, personal drama showing the agony and sufferings which lead Clytaemnestra to decide to kill her husband," and it is claimed that her decision is "almost unique in ancient Greek theatre" in being reached independently of gods, oracles, or fate. Something has been lost: the mythic, terrible grandeur of the daughter of Zeus hatched with her sister Helen as twin instruments of the curse on the house of Atreus. Clytemnestra is presented as a grieving, indignant mother, a betrayed, angry wife, and a sensual woman; and it may be that in the libretto too full an attempt has been made to explain and "motivate" her. In the Western imagination, Clytemnestra *is.* But it was a deliberate decision, and the libretto, despite a few uncertainties of tone, has enabled Eaton to compose a full-scale and imposing musical portrait. Dramatic mezzo-sopranos should be eager to get their voices and presences into the role, and *The Cry of Clytaemnestra* is, I believe, a modern opera that should find a place on the international stage.

In line 592 of the *Agamemnon,* Clytemnestra tells of the triumph cry she gave when the fiery beacon first announced the destruction of Troy. More than one translator has added specific cries of Clytemnestra to Aeschylus' text. In Walter Headlam's version, when the news has been taken to her "her jubilant cry is presently heard within." Likewise in Vellacott's version: "A cry of triumph is heard from Clytemnestra within." Later, when Agamemnon sets his blasphemous foot on the purple carpet, Vellacott's Clytemnestra greets the moment with "a prolonged triumphant cry; which the Chorus accept as a formal celebration of the victor's return, while only Cassandra understands its true meaning." In Gilbert Murray's version, Clytemnestra's women raise a triumphant "Ololûgê" at both those places. Eaton's opera opens with a prolonged and terrible cry from Clytemnestra, an outburst and ululation of anguish. She is recalling Iphigenia, and her cry is answered by high, clear arpeggios from an Iphigenia beheld in vision. They are written in

C-major just intonation, kept on pitch by a precisely tuned electronic accompaniment, and this seems to invest them with an unearthly purity and radiance. Clytemnestra's cry punctuates the opera, developing and altering with each step of the action, until at the last it has become "a pure and terrifying cry" at once the expression of a fulfilled woman now certain of her path and, as it were, the vocal embodiment of a bright, destructive flame in which grief and fury alike have been consumed.

In *Danton and Robespierre*, Eaton showed the mastery of vocal gesture which is the mark of a born opera composer, and in *The Cry of Clytaemnestra* his command of it is even more confident. His whole armory of expressive devices is large. It includes different kinds of tuning, which can provide not only consonances truer than those achievable by the twelve fixed notes of equal temperament but also telling inflections of melodic lines, curiously colored harmonies, and tonal oppositions between notes close yet different. Microtones (or "off pitch" notes), voluntary or involuntary, are familiar enough in the opera house. Eaton's fine ear and soaring musical imagination have been able to catch and give precision to that emotional "bending" of pitch which all accomplished singers employ at times, almost instinctively. He has carried the expressive possibilities into his orchestra and has woven them into his harmonic textures. But his controlled enrichment of the traditional melodic and harmonic palettes sounds spontaneous and natural, not calculated. His handling of the electronic devices has the same merit. Practically, as I have suggested, synthesized sounds can accurately indicate and sustain the unfamiliar pitches for humanly fallible voices and instruments. Other electronic arts can, for example, invest Iphigenia's voice with a radiant aureole of resonance. Electronic music of various kinds steals into or surges up through the score. It sounds natural, necessary, not like applied sound effects. The nineteen instrumentalists are treated as virtuosos, and the range of colors and dynamics that Eaton draws from them is large. The vocal writing looks fiendishly difficult: his four women need each a range of about two and a half octaves. One would have said that the composer had been recklessly extravagant in his demands had not those demands been so ably met—not only by the cast of the first performance but also by a second cast that I heard at a rehearsal. They sang the music as if it were good to sing, and convinced their listeners that it was.

I have not visited the Indiana University Opera Theatre often, but at my visits—for Busoni's *Doktor Faust*, Rimsky-Korsakov's *Christmas Eve* [see page 60], *Danton and Robespierre*, and now *The Cry of Clytaemnestra*, Busoni's *Arlecchino*, and *Porgy and Bess*—it has struck me as just about the most serious and consistently satisfying of all American opera companies. The Musical Arts Center helps—a fifteen-hundred-seater, well designed and very well equipped, a match for the best German house and so far as I know unrivaled in this country. It may seem perverse to prefer these student performances to the international productions of the big houses; and I'll readily admit that on occasion roles calling for seasoned voices have been underplayed. But the high level that Bloomington reaches can be heard on the recording of *Danton and Robespierre* now available on CRI. A campus company can devote to such a work the long rehearsals difficult to schedule—and the enthusiasm difficult to inspire—in the commercial hurly-burly of the ordinary operatic round. *The Cry of Clytaemnestra*, like *Danton*, was conducted by Thomas Baldner. The performance was confident and—as I discovered afterward when listening to a tape recording of it—astonishingly accurate. The playing was sure. The singing was dramatic, and several of the voices were beautiful. As Clytemnestra, Nelda Nelson was warm, eloquent, strong. Sally Wolf's singing as Iphigenia was pure and radiant. Tim Noble was a powerful Agamemnon. Rebecca Field was an incisive Electra, and Edith Diggory an affecting Cassandra. Joseph Levitt's Calchas was cleverly done. All these parts were played with presence. Larry Paxton's Aegisthus and Randall Black's Orestes were sung with assurance but were less convincingly portrayed. Not altogether their fault: the men's roles are less firmly limned, less roundly conceived than the women's.

Agamemnon is simplified to a monarch blunt, brutal, arrogant, and inwardly weak. He is presented as if through Clytemnestra's eyes—fairly enough, as his only appearances are in her visions. But Orestes and Aegisthus are there in "real time." Young Orestes takes no active part in the drama, and most of his utterances are jejune ("Electra, O Electra, a little charity! Ten years without her man . . . have driven her to this"). Aegisthus' role, which should be important, remains shadowy. In Aeschylus, as brother of the two children Agamemnon's father served in a stew to their own father, he claims responsibility for the murder of his cousin: "I planned his killing, as was just." In the opera, the revenge motif is unstated; Aegisthus seems to be little more than what Electra calls "my own mother's stud." Creagh's libretto, as I said, does slip in tone. Most of it is direct, but sometimes it becomes fancy ("Sad evening jades the day"), stilted ("This last impertinence I cannot stomach"), or unseemly. Sometimes the wordplay ("The army is at Aulis. All is well") is strained and ineffective. Some ambiguities seem more careless than deliberate: the ear asked whether a singer meant "no" or "know," whether an emphatic "lies" was a noun or a verb. An invented scene in which Aegisthus makes lubricious advances to Electra is an awkward and unnecessary diversion from the main line of the action. The "family row" that follows—a quartet for Clytemnestra, Electra, Aegisthus, and Orestes—is musically trenchant but verbally clumsy. Otherwise, the dramaturgy is strong. The sequence of scenes is at once practical (Clytemnestra cannot be singing all the time) and theatrically potent.The lyrical episodes for the royal children in the garden are well placed. Electra and Orestes first appear as tots; the infant roles were very poorly taken in Bloomington, but the fault lay with the performers, not the piece.

Max Röthlisberger designed and directed. His use of gestures was less precise, less communicative than the composer's. One could have wished for a nobler, sharper, more imaginative kind of staging, hard-edged settings, more revealing light. The singers handled the classical names as things unfamiliar. I offer them this imperfect but possibly instructive limerick:

> *The chief of the gods would turn puce,*
> *And exclaim, with an oath, "What the deuce*
> *Are these accents barbaric!*
> *I'm monosyllabic;*
> *My name isn't Zay-oos, it's Zeus."*

Musically, all was well. Eaton is an opera composer who is doing something new not for the sake of novelty but because his imagination has reached out to encompass the new techniques of our day. His works—let the *Danton* recording provide evidence for the assertion—are at once challenging to perform, adventurous, and accessible.

The Cry of Clytaemnestra was done on a double bill with an enchanting performance of the enchanting *Arlecchino*, an opera with a distinct, elusive flavor unlike that of anything else in the repertory. In Busoni's words, the piece "has a tendency to ambiguity and hyperbole in order to place the listener, momentarily, in a position of slight doubt; it adheres consciously to the constant play of color between grim jest and playful seriousness." The composer wrote that in a little essay to which he prefixed a remark of Bernard Shaw's: "From Mozart I learned to say important things in a conversational way." *Arlecchino* is aristocratic, learned, witty, and melodious. Mr. Baldner conducted, Mr. Röthlisberger designed and directed, and they got the tone exactly right. Cast and orchestra were elegant, poised, accomplished. Praise to Jon Farris (Arlecchino), Sulie Girardi (Colombina), Thomas Faracco (Leandro), William Parcher (Ser Matteo), and Lewis Schlanbusch and James Ramlet (Abbot and Doctor). To *The Cry of Clytaemnestra* this *Arlecchino* made an ideal companion piece, refreshing, exquisite, and subtly disturbing.

The Indiana company boasts of the most extended opera season in the Western Hemisphere. In 1980–81, *Prince Igor*, *The Love of Three Oranges*, and the American première of Martinů's *Greek Passion* are due. A week before the première of *The Cry of Clytaemnestra*, *Porgy and Bess* could be seen—and I thought it the most enjoyable and persuasive presentation of Gershwin's opera I've ever come across. There was, as the composer required, an all-black cast. In fact, the campus had been able to provide double casting, through a run of six performances, of which I caught the last. The full operatic score—not the abridged version of a "musical," with numbers, spoken dialogue, and a pit band—was used. The singers were without exception full and forward. There was a wonderful series of rich, warm voices in the women: Diane J. Johnson (Bess), Paula Redd (Maria), Denise Myers (Serena), Luvenia Garner (Clara). Michael Smartt was a striking and poignant Porgy. Ben Barnes was a neat Sportin' Life, dapper, lively, and unexaggerated. There was bright, clear singing from Albert Neal's Peter, the honey man, and from Colenton Freeman's crab seller, and in the threnody one chorister's voice after another poured out movingly. Mr. Röthlisberger, taking advantage of the theatre's movable side stages and retrostage, had created large, elaborately realistic settings that changed swiftly. Ross Allen's direction was both detailed and unfailingly natural. So was Charles Webb's conducting; he inspired cast and orchestra to feel and to fill their phrases, smoothly, freshly. Everything told. Performed thus, *Porgy* revealed its kinship with *Carmen* and with *Peter Grimes*. The genre scenes built into a coherent whole; the threads of personal tragedy ran through them unbroken; the sense of a linked community and of the individual sufferings and solaces of those within it was vividly conveyed. The Houston *Porgy* that came to Broadway was less coherent, though it gave some idea of what the opera might be. The Cleveland complete recording, though very much a concert performance, showed that the more of the score that is done the better. This Bloomington *Porgy* is the first to make me add my voice to the chorus of those asking why neither New York house has Gershwin's opera in its regular repertory.

March 31, 1980

CalSounds

The California Institute of the Arts, known as CalArts, a school founded (in the words of its president) "with a focus on the contemporary and a commitment to the avant-garde," is housed in two large modern buildings boldly and beautifully set on a hill in the Santa Clarita Valley, north of Los Angeles. The main building contains a variety of theatres, halls, and performance spaces, formal and informal. Here in 1978 there was held a three-day spring festival of contemporary music, directed by Morton Subotnick, at which the CalArts Twentieth-Century Players and the Sonor ensemble of the University of California at San Diego played. Last spring, there was a nine-day festival: three days at CalArts, three in San Diego, and then three more at the University of Nevada in Las Vegas; the Las Vegas Chamber Players provided a third performing ensemble. But the peripatetic scheme proved unwieldy. This spring, the composers and players of CalArts, of UCSD, and of the University of Nevada settled at CalArts for a busy six-day festival, with Virko Baley, Bernard Rands, Roger Reynolds, and Subotnick as artistic directors. The programs were adventurous. There were several first or West Coast–first performances. During a two-day visit, I heard five concerts.

The excellent Sequoia String Quartet, quartet-in-residence at CalArts, played Schoenberg's Second Quartet, with Bethany Beardslee as soprano soloist, and continued with Mel Powell's *Little Companion Pieces* (1979), a cycle of six songs for soprano and string quartet, composed for Miss Beardslee and the Sequoia, and planned to "go along with" the Schoenberg. The songs are lyrical, gentle, varied, and attractive. Miss Beardslee is an even more captivating performer in English than in German, and the Sequoia lived up to the golden reputation it has recently been winning. [The Schoenberg quartet and its Powell companion are now recorded by the Sequoia on Nonesuch D-79005.] The program ended with Charles Wuorinen's lively Second String Quartet, written last year. This was a mid-afternoon recital. There followed at once a slightly trying concert, demanding patience, as concerts at contemporary-music festivals often do. Jo Kondo's *Standing*, for double-bass, tuba, and xylophone, was a relentlessly thorough study in sustained rhythms. Stephen Mosko's *Cosmology of Easy Listening* (1979), for percussion trio, offered clonks, bonks, scrapes, and small, exquisite sounds. Nils Vigeland's *Vara* (1979) was an interminable string of clichés for flute and piano. The chief interest was provided by the dexterity and electric skill of the Antenna Repairmen, a CalArts percussion trio.

More flute and piano at the evening concert: Ernst Krenek's Flute Piece in Nine Phases (1959), a work at once elegant and passionate, played with consummate art by the Swiss flutist Bernard Batschelet, who is spending two years with Sonor at San Diego. This Sonor concert began with William Kraft's *The Sublime and the Beautiful* (1979), a romantic piece for tenor and six players, composed with the expert ear that marks all Kraft's work. Later, there was Jacob Druckman's bright, appealing *Animus IV*, for tenor, small ensemble, and tape, written, as was the Kraft, for Paul Sperry and sung by him here with intelligence and art. Robert Erickson's *Night Music* for solo trumpet and ensemble (1978) is a piece in which advanced instrumental techniques, the special skills developed by Sonor, serve a romantic imagination. It brought forward a virtuoso trumpeter in Edwin Harkins. The concert reached its climax in a shattering performance of Bernard Rands's powerful cantata *Metalepsis 2*, commissioned for the 1971 English Bach Festival, "a nondenominational Requiem Mass for all who suffer at the hands of tyrants." Rands is director and conductor of Sonor; Ann Chase was a striking soprano soloist.

The next day, there was play: Earle Brown's *Calder Piece* (1963–66), written to be beaten out, by a percussion quartet, on and around the large Alexander Calder mobile called *Chef d'Orchestre*. The piece has often been done in Europe; this was the first time the mobile had been set up and played on in America. Calder himself, Brown's program note said, was slightly disappointed after the very first performance: "I thought you were going to hit it much harder, with hammers." I, too, was slightly disappointed with the small sound of Calder's plates as here attacked. After a while, the entertainment of watching four players—the Antenna Repairmen joined by John Bergamo, head of percussion at CalArts—striking out at or pursuing the revolving arms of the mobile, beating whatever parts of it fell to hand, began to pall. The static episodes when the players retired to well-stocked batteries to be "conducted" by the mobile produced something more like music. A piece difficult to take seriously but easy to watch and enjoy.

At the last concert of the festival, the Las Vegas Chamber Players, conducted by Virko Baley, played Ralph Shapey's early Concerto for Clarinet and Chamber Group (1954), an arresting and masterly work, with a masterly soloist here in Felix Viscuglia; Baley's own *Lamentation of Adrian Leverkuehn* (1980), for tenor and nine players, an effects piece; and Leonard Rosenman's Chamber Music V (1979), which the composer described in a note as "monolithic in character" but which sounded incoherent at a first hearing. Finally, the CalArts Twentieth-Century Players, conducted by Mr. Mosko, gave an alluring account of Subotnick's *After the Butterfly*, a delicate, dainty study in sonorities natural, electronic, and mixed.

Two big works brought out earlier in the festival were *Fwyynghn* (1979), a "stage piece with music and a ballet dance," created collectively by Gordon Mumma, Pauline Oliveros, Christian Sinding, Louise Frazer, Beatrice Manley, and others; and *Eclipse* (1980), for videotapes, film, seven-channel sound system, computer-synthesized materials, and computer- and analog-processed voices, for which Ed Emshwiller created the images and Roger Reynolds the score. Later, in San Diego, I had a chance to hear the score of *Eclipse* and found it an enthralling composition, very strongly built, engrossing in its own right. Reynolds is a composer doing new things that are beautiful, exciting, shapely, eloquent.

Most of the composers were present in person. Young composers from across the country had been invited to share in the events, the rehearsals, the related seminars and discussions. CalArts is isolated. Most visitors have to stay several miles away, well beyond walking distance. Going there is not like going to contemporary-music festivals in Warsaw, Palermo, Budapest, Glasgow, or Cheltenham. And, except for Rands's *Metalepsis 2*, the music I heard seemed to be somewhat isolated, too, from social and political concerns. But there is a sense in which the CalArts Festival may well become America's Donaueschingen or Dartington: a focus for new musical ideas and techniques, a stimulus for creators, performers, and listeners. The concerts were recorded for local broadcasting. Next year, the whole festival should be broadcast nationally, day by day, as European festivals often are, so that all the country can hear, enjoy, and discuss the new music that is being made and played in the West.

May 19, 1980

Heroic-Romantic

The production of Schubert's *Fierrabras* given this month by the Academy of Vocal Arts, of Philadelphia, in the Walnut Street Theatre was billed as the American première of the piece. It may even have been the first-ever production of *Fierrabras* with the music more or less as Schubert wrote it. Although in recent years the opera has received a handful of concert and radio presentations, only two earlier stagings are recorded: the first of them, in Carlsruhe in 1897, had a musical text revised by Felix Mottl, and at the second, in Brussels in 1926, the Mottl version seems to have been used again. Maybe there were other productions, which slipped past the chroniclers; as Julian Budden writes in the April 1980 *Musical Times*, "there are few more dangerous statements in music history than those beginning 'X was the first. . . .' " (I think I have seen a "first performance" of Mahler's early piano-quartet movement announced on the bills of at least four New York recitals.) And *Fierrabras* has been in print for nearly a hundred years. The odd fact is that one of Schubert's most important scores should have been played so seldom.

Fierrabras, composed in 1823, at the same time as *Die schöne Müllerin*, is the more dramatic of his two big "heroic-romantic" operas. The other, *Alfonso and Estrella*, completed the year before, is concerned as much with "ideas"—reconciliation and forgiveness—as with characters in conflict. It is large, leisurely, and rather schematic in its dramaturgical planning. *Fierrabras*, which has the Calderón play *La puente de mantible* (translated by A. W. Schlegel) in its literary ancestry, contains far more incident—exploits, excursions, and alarums. The action is set during Charlemagne's Spanish campaign: on the one side, there are Charlemagne and his knights Roland, Eginhard, and Ogier; on the other, the Moorish ruler Boland and his son Fierrabras. Fierrabras and Eginhard both love Emma, Charlemagne's daughter; Roland loves Florinda, Boland's daughter. The libretto, by Josef Kupelwieser, Schubert's friend and Court Theatre secretary, suggests a Cherubinian rescue opera with added romantic complications. The music suggests the rescue operas *Faniska* and *Fidelio* with added romantic influence from *Der Freischütz* and from Rossini's *La donna del lago*.

It should be stressed that *Alfonso* and *Fierrabras* were conceived at an exciting point in musical history: in a Vienna where Gluck and Mozart were still performed; where *Fidelio* had at last had a success; where Rossini captivated the crowds (and not only the crowds, since Schubert's admiration for his genius is documented in the Great C-major Symphony) while Weber opened the way toward German romantic opera; where the great singers for whom Rossini and Beethoven and later Donizetti, Bellini, and Wagner wrote

were active. Schubert's operas reflect all this. In 1822, there occurred the famous revival of *Fidelio* with Wilhelmine Schröder-Devrient as its heroine—
the singer admired by Beethoven, by Weber (the Vienna Agathe), and by
Wagner (his first Adriano, Senta, and Venus). That year, the Kärntnertortheater and the Theater an der Wien were managed by the great impresario
Domenico Barbaia, whose empire extended from Naples, through La Scala,
to Vienna, who employed Rossini and Donizetti as house composers and
launched the careers of Mercadante, the Riccis, and Bellini. Barbaia brought
Rossini in person to Vienna—his works were already very popular there—
and commissioned new operas from Beethoven, Schubert, and Weber.
(Beethoven couldn't find a suitable subject; Schubert submitted *Alfonso*, but
it was turned down; Weber wrote *Euryanthe*, which went on in 1823, with
Henriette Sontag—the famous Rossini singer, and the soprano of the Ninth
Symphony and the Missa Solemnis—as its heroine.) In October 1823, *Fierrabras* was announced for performance at the Kärntnertortheater, but a month
later the production was canceled.

Schubert's operas were, and perhaps still are, too ambitious for general
use. Like Haydn, another great composer who wrote a great deal for the
stage but is remembered principally for his concert-hall and chamber music,
Schubert poured unstinting into theatre music his "symphonic" ideas, structural and instrumental. (*Alfonso* and *Fierrabras* do much to close the famous
gap between the Sixth Symphony and the highly developed mastery of the
late works.) As in Haydn's operas, the numbers tend to be long—often un-
theatrically long. Schubert's most successful "opera" is the monodrama for
voice and piano *Die schöne Müllerin*, where scenic description, narrative,
emotions, and dramatic progress are held in perfect balance; *Alfonso* and
Fierrabras employ means more elaborate. *Alfonso* is sung all through. (Mr.
Budden's letter cited above was provoked by a claim that Spohr's *Jessonda*,
of July 1823, was the first German opera without spoken dialogue.) *Fierrabras*
has some spoken dialogue, some striking melodrama (words spoken over instrumental accompaniment), and very fine accompanied recitatives; there is
more variety, a larger musical sweep in the forms, and less repetition. Eginhard's serenade in Act I, "Der Abend sinkt," is like a Schubert song scored
(clarinet over pizzicato strings, minor turning to major as his beloved appears), and so is the "Lied mit Chor" that opens Act II—though what modern orchestrator could imagine Schubert figuration scored in quite this magical way? The unaccompanied chorus "O theures Vaterland" is one of his best
part-songs—sweet, strong, and moving, as Verdi's exiles' choruses are. There
are straightforwardly dramatic episodes: the protagonist's passionate "Was
quälst du mich, o Missgeschick," in Act I; a colloquy for Florinda and her
confidante near the start of Act II, which is like Weber with a touch of Rossini; and, later in the act, Florinda's powerful B-minor aria, of Weberian cut.
Eginhard's serenade and Fierrabras's aria are in fact solo movements in larger
numbers; there are surprisingly few isolated solo set pieces in the score, and
long stretches of beautifully complicated, closely woven ensembles, three of
them in several movements. The instrumental elaboration of a movement for

Emma and her maidens suggests some Hans Werner Henze of the day, pouring out lovely music in greater profusion than the dramatic situation requires; then a few sentences of tense dialogue spoken over its coda effectively return us to the plot. And, so far as I know, there is nothing in German opera on the scale of the extended ensemble numbers in *Fierrabras*—not even the finale of *Fidelio*—before *Die Feen*, *Das Liebesverbot*, and *Rienzi*. The formal extensions match those of Schubert's late piano and chamber music and his last symphony; the forces used are far larger.

Not only in scale does Schubert anticipate early Wagner. *Fierrabras* opens with a spinning chorus, during which Emma is "sunk in gloomy reflections"; then she rises, to continue the song with a verse (in G minor, after the C major of the chorus) that chimes with her own thoughts. Some of Charlemagne's accompanied recitatives would not sound out of place in *Lohengrin*. But the chief link between Schubert and Wagner is one of tone, temper, and intention. There is the same eschewal of easy "effects without causes" and the same high ambition. One of Schubert's aims, it seems clear, was to bring together the high seriousness of Gluck, the energy and grandeur of Cherubini and Spontini, the directness of Beethoven, the picturesqueness of Weber, and the ready charm of Rossini. But, beyond that, *Alfonso* and *Fierrabras* suggest that he had his own, individual vision of what a serious opera should be. It has been plausibly proposed that the "Essay on the Aesthetics of Dramatic Composition," by Ignaz von Mosel—to whom Opus 3, a group of Goethe settings, was dedicated—influenced Schubert's operatic thinking. Mosel rehearsed Gluck's ideals and prescribed an uncomplicated plot, slow-moving action, a historical or mythological setting, and music concerned with "ideas." The standard view of *Alfonso* and *Fierrabras* is that they contain much fine music wasted on worthless librettos; that they could not stand up in the theatre; that sporadic concert performances, recordings, and perhaps an occasional campus revival are all they deserve. (In 1977, *Alfonso* was staged at Reading University, its British première; in 1978, there was a concert performance in Detroit [see page 261]; and last year an Angel recording appeared.) I believe that in ignoring them we ignore two noble, elevated, and attractive works, two important scores by a great composer; that the librettos, for all their ungainliness, were carefully chosen and planned to bear the kinds of music that Schubert wanted to write; and that one day some manager, conductor, and director who know and love the pieces for what they *are* will, by presenting them as such (instead of chopping and revising them to accord with conventional operatic expectations), make audiences love them, too. It will call for courage, imagination, and historical insight coupled with passionate belief—and large resources. Sarah Caldwell might be the person to bring it off. And perhaps a campus able to afford professional soloists would be the place for it, where a large chorus could be lovingly rehearsed, scholarly thought could be applied to the unconventional requirements, and running time would not be subject to commercial clipping. Operas once deemed, for one reason or another, no less intractable and unstageable than Schubert's—*Giulio Cesare*, *Idomeneo*, *La clemenza di Tito*,

Les Troyens—have, from campus revivals, gone on to enter the international repertory.

The Academy of Vocal Arts must be praised for its adventure in choosing *Fierrabras*, but in the event the Philadelphia production, sung in an acceptable English translation by Marcie Stapp, offered no more than a rude sketch of what the opera might be. For one thing, the piece was abridged. Last time I heard *Fierrabras*—the BBC production of 1971—it was given with just three small cuts and lasted a little over three hours. In Philadelphia, some two and a quarter hours was done. (One sad loss was Schubert's bold stroke in ending Act II with a long melodrama.) More important, the piece was ineptly and inadequately staged, in a manner suggesting an amateur production of *Princess Ida* rather than a grand heroic-romantic opera. Robert Yodice's set consisted of two flanking towers, one of them with a (much used) practicable second-floor opening. Projections on the backcloth simply and not ineffectively indicated the nine scenes, three in each act, that are called for, but "projected" scenery on a shallow stage precludes bright light on the singers. The costumes, designed by Val Read and supplied by the Brooks–Van Horn Costume Company, were a mixed bag—stock medieval, with some visible zippers—and were uneasily worn. Charlemagne's great cape rakishly wrapped around him ninety degrees off center, suspended from a shoulder, provided the comic high point, but the heroines' troubles with their trains ran it close. What *Fierrabras* needs is a twentieth-century scenic designer's re-creation of Carolingian splendors as a nineteenth-century artist—perhaps Moritz von Schwind—would have seen them. The staging was credited to Dino Yannopoulos, the artistic director of the Academy; all that was apparent was some rudimentary "blocking" of a coarse, obvious, and occasionally risible kind; little could be dignified by the word *acting.* I rather like old-fashioned operatic gestures of the Delsarte school—back of the hand raised gracefully to brow to convey distress, hands tighty clasped out front to signal intensity, and so on—but only when they flow from and within a consistent, convinced, and convincing style of presentation. In this *Fierrabras*, the stock gestures jumped out in a way perilously close to parody of the philistine notion of "operatic acting." The Academy of Vocal Arts should pay attention to the dramatic arts when opera is in question. On the purely vocal side, things were happier. All the voices were clear, well formed, easily produced, and in tune. But one wanted more: some confident feeling for the way Schubert intended his musical inventions to be given shape on the stage, not village-hall theatricals. The purely musical worth of *Fierrabras* has never been in question.

Am I being unkind? One must make allowances. The stage of the Walnut Street Theatre is too small for *Fierrabras*, and the choral forces—eight women and sixteen men—were too small for the piece. But even within that space and with those forces more could have been done. I am not severe when with scenic and vocal means less than those a composer intended a serious and imaginative attempt is made to convey his intentions; the Academy's presentation of Rossini's *Otello*, last year, delighted me. But in this *Fierrabras* there was much silliness; for example, four dancing girls tripping around in the confined space during choruses. Alessandro Siciliani, who made his American début with that *Otello* and seemed to me then just about the best living Rossini conductor, was less impressive in Schubert. His reading lacked weight, grandeur, dramatic impact. It was neat, nicely shaped, even sensitive, not exciting or forceful. The instrumental playing, by members of the Concerto Soloists of Philadelphia, was deft, but the curious split-level formation of the pit—strings raised, winds deep under the stage—took more toll of Schubert's intricate, often densely doubled scoring than it had, last year, of Rossini's clear, bright textures. After *Otello,* this *Fierrabras* was a disappointment. The challenge, admittedly, was greater. But so was the gap between what might have been and what was.

May 26, 1980

Isaac and David

June began well, with a substantial recital of rich, noble, and beautiful music nobly and beautifully sung by Cappella Nova, in St. Joseph's Church in the Village. "Heinrich Isaac: Versatile Flemish Master" was the title of the concert. Only Isaac's church music was performed—none of the secular songs and dances that have become hit numbers of the Renaissance revival. His versatility was still in evidence, and his towering genius more apparent than ever. Richard Taruskin, the director and conductor of Cappella Nova, has a flair for devising shapely, nourishing, and illuminating programs. For this concert, he brought together radiant, magisterial liturgical music that Isaac composed for the Emperor Maximilian's chapel and earlier, exuberant compositions that he wrote when he was in Lorenzo the Magnificent's service. Mr. Taruskin had compiled a Missa de Confessoribus—Ordinary from Maximilian choirbooks, Propers from the great *Choralis Constantinus* collection—and within this grand structure set five large motets, four of them Marian, of the Italian years. In a program note, he made high claims: "For floridity and grandeur, 'O decus ecclesiae' has scarcely a peer in the music of any era." And:

> There is scarcely another composer among the Renaissance masters whose works could have provided a comparable gamut of styles, colors, and moods. But all Isaac's works, of no matter what manner, display the

same superlative craftsmanship and wealth of invention, along with the very human warmth of expression that makes him for us, no less than for his contemporaries, one of the most endearing of his school.

Impassioned, intense, precisely molded, and colorful performances reflected those beliefs and persuaded listeners to share them. The work of Cappella Nova—some twenty singers, male and female—has regularly been praised in these pages; I have never heard them sound more impressive than in this Isaac recital. The thrilling sequence "Ad laudes salvatoris," a high point of the "L'Homme Armé"-plus-*Choralis Constantinus* composite Mass that Mr. Taruskin presented at Corpus Christi last year, was even more grandly, more brilliantly done. The Cappella has many virtues. One is its range of timbres. When Isaac's writing, as in a "Salve Regina" that ended the program, became almost more instrumental than vocal, the voices "spoke" with instrumental accuracy and precision; at the words "Nobis post hoc exsilium ostende" one seemed to hear virtuoso viols. St. Joseph's is not reverberant, though it has firm, clear, fresh acoustics, but in sustained music the Cappella produced a full and resonant sound, and the austere building, a Greek Revival temple of 1834, Roman in rite but Protestant plain in its décor, took on a glow. The singers were equally adept at joyful pealing, at spreading a tender, soft-shining radiance, at laying strong cantus-firmus foundations to support flamboyant tracery, and at high-spirited patter (in a fleet, brisk Credo). Not all aspects of Mr. Taruskin's approach were uncontroversial. He closed the first section of the motet "Illumina oculos meos" with a cadence whose melting sweetness and softness of timbre were almost indecorously sensuous; likewise a cadence in the Sanctus, before the Hosanna. (Yet the result was so beautiful that no one could really complain.) The sixteenth-century musical historian Glareanus remarked that Isaac "embellished the ecclesiastical chants in which he found any majesty or force with such harmony as made them superior to any new subjects of modern times"; in several of his pieces chant alternates with composition founded upon it. There was nothing plain about the Cappella's handling of plainsong; it tackled the chants with a vividness and a rhythmical boldness that turned them into fascinating, arresting "subjects." They sounded newly composed. Another Cappella Nova virtue is its skill at rendering the special, individual qualities, emotional and structural, of a piece. In stoutly formal compositions, the ground plan was stressed—those works displaying what Glareanus described as Isaac's particular fondness for "making one part sustain a note while the rest were moving about like the waves of the sea against a rock, during a storm." Elsewhere, when it was apt, the Gregorian underpinning disappeared into the structure. Throughout the evening, Isaac's quick response to words was relished. Mr. Taruskin made the most—but not too much—of what he discerned in each work. His sense of flow and balance saved the vivid, revelatory performances from becoming exaggerated. I had never come upon so much Isaac brought together before—perhaps no one since Maximilian has—and count the concert a landmark in the adventure of hearing large-scale Renaissance music brought to life. It closed the Cappella's first series in St. Joseph's; a second series begins in November. For the Musical Heritage Society, the choir has made two fine records, of Ockeghem's Missa Prolationum and of his motets.

Ezra Laderman's one-act chamber opera *And David Wept* was given its first stage production at the 92nd Street Y last month. The piece was commissioned by CBS and broadcast in 1971, with Sherrill Milnes, Rosalind Elias, and Ara Berberian in its three roles—David, Bathsheba, and Uriah the Hittite—and with choreography by José Limon. David and Bathsheba are stricken in years and Uriah is dead when the work begins; in a series of speeches, songs, duos, and trios they recall David's adultery, his murder of Uriah, and the doleful consequences—but not the bright result of the affair, Bathsheba's second son, the splendid Solomon. The librettist, Joe Darion, has simplified the vivid, intricate character of the King and has invented characters for Uriah and Bathsheba: he cares more for his martial profession than for his wife; she, bored with him, deliberately exposes herself beneath David's roof in the hope that the King's eyes will fall on her. The tone of the libretto varies from the fancy ("The cry of the mournful owl and the bark of the desert fox made tender music in the night"), through the colloquial ("Bathsheba . . . did not turn a hair"), to the coarse ("Oh wife! wife! you slut! you bitch in heat!"). The characters become stock figures. "It is a story," the authors write, "that happened long ago, and could happen today, and no doubt will happen tomorrow." Their story could. The story told in II Samuel 11 is particular, stronger, and stranger. By being generalized, the Biblical narrative is lessened. Still, both libretto and score are competent as far as they go. The idiom of the music is mildly lyrical, enlivened with moments that suggest sentimental pop song and others that suggest commercial jingles. The piece contains almost as much speech as song—but speech over instrumental accompaniment, speech to whose phrases are assigned "reciting notes" harmonically related to the music. The composer describes the suggested pitches as "approximate" but surely intended them to be taken a little more seriously than they were by the Y singers—Howard Bender as David, Annie Lynn Bornstein as Bathsheba, and Kenneth Bell as Uriah. The staging—in which five dancers as well as three singers moved, for the most part gauchely, about the tiny space—was not competent.

And David Wept was the second opera in the series "Jewish Opera at the Y." In March, there was David Schiff's opera in Yiddish *Gimpel the Fool*, an expanded version of a work first performed at the Y last year. I missed the production but can report on a tape recording of the March performance, which shows *Gimpel* to be a colorful, entertaining, inventive, and original opera. The libretto is from Isaac Bashevis Singer's story of the same title: Gimpel, a credulous baker's apprentice, is married off to Elka, the town whore; on her deathbed, she confesses to him that her six children are not his; the Evil One tempts him to take revenge on the people who made a fool of him, but Elka, in a dream, dissuades him. Schiff uses a small orchestra (fourteen players) suggested by a traditional *klezmer* ensemble, tangy with trumpet and clarinet solos, busy fiddle, tuba bass, and harpsichord in place of cimbalon. Sometimes the timbres of Stravinsky's *Soldier's Tale* and *Reynard* are evoked, sometimes those of a Moroccan, Tunisian, or Near Eastern popular ensemble. Kurt Weill's *Dreigroschenoper* band is another influence, acknowledged by the composer. "All the music," Schiff writes, "is quite consistently based on the four Jewish modal scales," and its eclecticism "reflects the basic eclecticism of the Jewish musical inheritance." There are Mahlerian melodic moments, allusions to cantoral *nusach*, or traditional chant (the town rabbi has an important role), a catchy Jewish cabaret song, a traditional lullaby, and, at the very end, an authentic Torah cantillation. It is all held together by Schiff's lively musical imagination, his wit, his sharp, clean sense of form (the opera is written in distinct numbers), and a command of dramatic gestures—vocal and instrumental; melodic, harmonic, and of timbre—which seems to proclaim him a natural theatre composer. *Gimpel*, in two acts, lasts about ninety minutes. Slightly pared perhaps—one or two passages go on a bit—it might easily become a popular success, something to do on one-acter bills instead of *Gianni Schicchi*. The composer is working on an English translation, which should help to give his work wider circulation.

Rameau's acte de ballet *Pygmalion* is a small jewel. The action is slight: Pygmalion admires his newly completed statue; his girl friend sings a jealous air and leaves him; the statue, brought to life by Cupid's flame, is taught by the Graces to dance; and dances—broken only by two joyful airs for Pygmalion, "L'Amour triomphe" (with chorus) and "Règne, Amour"—continue the entertainment. The music is exquisitely fashioned. The chain of little dances— air, gavotte gracieuse, menuet, gavotte gaie, chaconne, loure, passepied, rigaudon, sarabande, tambourin—in which the statue is instructed form a pattern book of Rameau's skill. *Pygmalion* is quite often revived. What was billed as its New York première was given last month in the Schimmel Center of Pace University by Concert Royal, directed by James Richman, and the New York Baroque Dance Company, directed by his wife, Catherine Turocy. It was good to hear Rameau's music played on the right instruments, and good to see his dances danced in choreography (by Miss Turocy) and in costumes (by Marilyn Skow) based on those of the mid-eighteenth century. The show had gentleness and grace but lacked other Ramellian qualities—incisiveness, force, aristocratic accuracy of accent. The Pace theatre, in which audience and stage are separated by a wide empty space, was unhelpful. (The orchestra was off to one side.) The singer of the title role, Stephen Oosting, was poor. Ann Monoyios, the statue, sang sweetly and truly, but her timbre was soft in grain and her words were weakly shaped. Both from singers and from players, Rameau's music needed more decisive etching. *Pygmalion* was preceded by Couperin's eighth Concert Royal and by an entrée from Campra's opéra-ballet *Les Fêtes vénitiennes*, for which contemporary choreography, notated at the time, was re-created by Ann Jacoby.

The first of three concerts that Klaus Tennstedt conducted with the Philharmonic last month, in its spring Beethoven cycle, added nothing to his or to the orchestra's reputation. The *Coriolan* overture began raggedly and continued at a tempo of unwonted staidness. Beethoven's marking is "Allegro con brio." The opening of the First Piano Concerto bears the same marking, and again Mr. Tennstedt set a speed more comfortable than energetic. The pianist was Malcolm Frager; his playing, on a solid, equable Bösendorfer that advertised its manufacturer's name to the audience in large letters of gold, was neat, shapely, and thoughtful. The second half of the concert was the Seventh Symphony. Three movements were plain, uneventful, with dynamic contrasts understated. The finale, another Allegro con brio (but this time in 2/4, not 4/4), went so fast that the strings' sixteenths became mere smudges. The orchestra's playing was not a pleasure; the brass brayed, the first flute was wispy, and the woodwinds' chording was often far from purely tuned.

June 16, 1980

Summer Miscellany

The April 1980 issue of *Early Music* contains an arresting article by that fine player of pianos new and old Malcolm Bilson. It is called "The Viennese Fortepiano of the Late Eighteenth Century" and deals in detail with four passages, by Mozart, Beethoven, and Haydn, that "cannot be played adequately on a modern piano." It also contains some striking general observations. "The harpsichord and the modern piano share one thing in common that is contrary to the aesthetic of the fortepiano: continued resonance." (An implicit conclusion is that *in some ways* a modern Steinway does less harm to harpischord music than it does to piano music of the late eighteenth and early nineteenth centuries.) Then:

> The later the music, the more crucial is the choice of instrument. I rather think that for Beethoven it is more crucial than for Mozart, and even more so for Schumann because as pianos developed, and as pianistic style developed, they became ever more interrelated.

And, most controversial:

> I have often heard it stated by scholars and others interested in perform-
> ance on early instruments that they would rather hear a great artist on
> the wrong instrument than a mediocre player on the right one. I am no
> longer willing to accept that statement. Perhaps it is wrong to put the
> instrument before the artist, but I have begun to feel that it must be
> done.

In conclusion, Mr. Bilson looks forward to a time when "all instruments
will find their proper place in concert halls and on recordings." His remarks
recurred to me as I listened to a recital last week by the Canadian pianist
Jane Coop, in Carnegie Recital Hall. Miss Coop came with high recommen-
dation. At this, her first New York public recital, she played a standard kind
of introductory program: music of the early eighteenth century, of the early,
middle, and late nineteenth century, and of the twentieth century—Handel,
Beethoven, Chopin, Brahms, and Bartók. She played it all on the same piano,
which I would describe as a slightly drab, all-purpose kind of Steinway: not
too thick, not too thin; not too rich, not too brittle; essentially characterless.
Or so it seemed to me, after an attempt to distinguish between the sound of
the instrument itself and the sounds its player sought to produce—but one
shouldn't blame only the instrument without having heard Miss Coop play
another, and another pianist play this one. Perhaps it was the best kind of
piano to "cover" all this program with reasonable efficiency. Yet there was
no performance that its timbre did not diminish. It was not fiery or fierce
enough for Bartók's Sonata (1926); it was too thick and resonant for Beethoven's "Eroica" variations (1803), and pretty colorless in Chopin's Polonaise-
Fantaisie (1846) and Brahms's Op. 119 Piano Pieces (1893). Handel's G-minor
Harpsichord Suite (published in 1720) came off best, even though one had to
regard it as a "transcription" into a new sound medium. This old-fashioned
kind of piano recital—ranging through the centuries on a modern grand—
will probably be with us for a while yet, as will the symphony concert at
which an orchestra plays a miscellany of, say, Handel, Mozart, Beethoven,
and Stravinsky on the same instruments. Indeed, for practical reasons, such
recitals and concerts will be difficult to replace. But as more and more of the
public grows to learn and love the right sounds it will become increasingly
exigent. The right sounds can already be enjoyed on many recordings—
among them Mr. Bilson's of Haydn, Mozart, and Beethoven played on forte-
pianos.

Miss Coop was doing only what most pianists do, what they are taught
to do. She showed herself to be a cultivated and intelligent musician with
clearly formed ideas about the details, the progress, and the general shape of
each work she played. She was decisive, diligent, and sometimes unconventional, but always in a persuasive, not a quirky, way. What I missed was a
sense of spontaneous warmth. Beethoven's more exuberant variations lacked
not energy but verve. The waltz episode of Brahms's B-minor Intermezzo

didn't dance; the E-flat Rhapsody was scarcely rhapsodic. The recital gave pleasure but touched no heights; the playing was strong, but it lacked strong emotions.

The quarterly *Early Music* is a magazine relevant to living music in New York. Another article in the April issue, "The Role of the Keyboard Continuo in French Opera 1673–1776," chimes with the Rameau performance I wrote about last week; its illustrations remind us that Rameau's players sat where they could see the dancers and the singers they accompanied, and that he used a substantial bass contingent, not clumped but balanced left and right. Yet another article, "The Golden Age Regained," the second part of a survey of English cathedral and college choirs, reaches the heartening conclusion that "the standard of performance in [England's] cathedrals has never been as high as it is now." Girls have been admitted to one cathedral choir, that of Bury St. Edmund's, apparently with happy results. The account of the diversity of favored boys' timbres—a spectrum from "Continental" power and passion to King's College gentleness and refinement—is fascinating. So is the relation of prevailing timbres to the acoustics of different buildings.

Cappella Nova, the New York choir I was writing about last week, is happy in St. Joseph's, in the Village; the church seems to enhance and amplify the sound of the twenty-one-voice choir (which has women sopranos but altos of both sexes). The Musica Sacra Chorus, thirty-six strong (nineteen women and seventeen men), did not sound good in Avery Fisher Hall when, earlier this month, it opened a Basically Bach Festival with the B-minor Mass. Fisher Hall, admittedly, is no apt place for Bach, in performances "authentic" or otherwise. All the same, I wondered whether Richard Westenburg, the conductor, had sufficiently considered its acoustics—whether if he had gone down from the podium to listen in the body of the hall, he would have admired the sound his chorus was making. I found it clear but weak, insubstantial. (I decided to listen to the second half over the air—the performance was broadcast by WNYC—but even then no knob twiddling could bring strength and body to the choral tone.) Aspirated staccato articulation—the Gloria became "Glo-ho-ho-ho-ho-ho-ho-ho-horia in ek-she-he-he-he-helsis" (the Italianized, or "eggshell-sis," pronunciation of Latin was favored)—suggested an excessive striving for clarity such as the richly resonant St. John the Divine acoustics might provoke. In Fisher Hall, the effect was ridiculous. The St. John space could also have smoothed the painfully raw trumpet playing. The orchestra was top-heavy—fourteen violins over two double-basses clumped to one side and ersatz pedal tone from an electronic organ.

Mr. Westenburg's reading was odd and largely unconvincing—sometimes stodgy, sometimes jaunty. Movements—the "Et resurrexit," for one—that rattled along like a sewing machine, unmolded in their phrases, suddenly pulled to a broad rallentando close. Four distinguished soloists had been engaged, but their singing was for the most part undistinguished. Carol Vaness sounded ill at ease in Bach. Lorna Myers was hooty and heavy in the first half, rather good in the Agnus Dei. John Aler shaped the phrases of the Benedictus sensitively. The bass music took Thomas Paul both above and below his effective range. All in all, the kind of performance to make a listener think that he could have spent his time better with a recording.

The May 1980 Newsletter of the Institute for Studies in American Music, at Brooklyn College, contains an arresting short article by the composer Conrad Cummings. It is called "American vs. French Avant-Gardism" and summarizes its conclusions thus:

> (1) American avant-garde music tends to be *presentational* while French tends to be *rhetorical;* and (2) American tends toward a concern with *harmonic language* while French tends toward a concern with *texture and sound-masses.*

Mr. Cummings bases his observations mainly on last year's Festival d'Automne, in Paris, which presented twenty-four *"performances,"* twenty-one of them by American musicians. (*Une performance,* it seems, is the new French term for a one-composer recital some or all of which is executed by the composer. An equivalent series of twenty-one recitals in New York devoted to avant-garde French composers would be an unlikely event.) Tom Johnson, Paul Dresher, John Adams, and Ingram Marshall are composers mentioned. All but the first, I suspect, are names unfamiliar to the man on the plaza, although Dresher's *This Same Temple* and Adams's *Phrygian Gates,* both played in Paris, were two of the most impressive works heard at the three concerts the Reich Music Foundation put on at the Guggenheim Museum last year. By "presentational," Mr. Cummings describes, first, what I have criticized as a lack of "presentation" affected by so many American executants. He contrasts Johnson's plain, intent performance of his *Nine Bells* with Joëlle Léandre's vividly mimed performance of Johnson's *Failing;* Dresher's "cool presentational style" in his own music with the "theatrical and virtuosic style" of the French two-piano team that played *This Same Temple;* Marshall's quiet listening at the tape deck with the dramatic activity of the Groupe de Recherche Musicale de Bourges around its mixing console. Mr. Cummings is on to something. The manner of public execution he deems French is not, I think, exclusively so—European, rather—but the "presentational" (or "nonpresentational") manner is indeed American. In these pages, I once speculated whether the Juilliard and other American schools teach their students that it is bad form ever to let an audience perceive that players can enjoy playing and take delight in their music. In Europe, faces light up, eyes sparkle, applause is acknowledged with a friendly smile, and a communication beyond the bare presentation of the notes is established with the audience. In America, everything tends to be deadly serious; even when the playing shows wit, the players remain stern, owlish, remote. Compare the demeanor of the Fires of London with that of Speculum Musicae! And this manner seems all of a piece with the spartan, cheerless conditions of much American concertgoing—the indifference to everything except the actual music played. (Carnegie Recital Hall has poor lighting, no buffet, no bar; at Miss Coop's recital her softest passages sank below the noise made by the ventilating system.) Mr. Cummings makes the point—I am still pondering it—that American music is at one with, and best served by, the American performance style; that the French players of American music tended to distort it.

His other observation, about harmony, is perhaps drawn from too narrow and partial a sample of what American and European composers are doing. (In his last paragraph, France is extended to become Europe.) "One suspects that the hypnotic quality of Philip Glass's music is more appreciated by European ears than its elegantly controlled harmonic evolution." Glass and Mario Davidovsky both speak of a concern for harmonic language, and "one sees a connection that might not be obvious." It's certainly not obvious to me. "It is exactly that common element which falls in the center of a big European blind spot."

Philip Glass gave an organ recital of his music this month in the Plymouth Church of the Pilgrims, in Brooklyn Heights, to benefit Barge-music, that attractive new home for chamber music which floats in the East River at the Brooklyn end of Brooklyn Bridge. (Each weekend this month, there are two concerts of chamber music from a resident ensemble; the setting is simple but not spartan.) The recital ended with the American première of *Fourth Series, Part 4,* a work commissioned by Bremen Radio and first played last month in Germany. Now, I suspect that by most Americans, not only by Europeans, the "hypnotic quality" of Glass's music is more appreciated than its "elegantly controlled harmonic evolution." Basically, his works of the seventies suggest toccata or moto perpetuo figuration imposed on or providing episodes between the statements of a simple passacaglia theme—a theme as simple, on occasion, as a straightforward three-chord cadence. The result is fascinating. After *Einstein on the Beach,* I wrote of rhythmic patterns and short melodic motifs endlessly repeated but slowly altering; of bright, insistent timbres whose colors gradually shift as one instrument, then another cuts into or drops from the texture; of simple harmonic progressions underpinning the moto perpetuo activity. In *Einstein,* the large forms are also apprehensible, and impressive. I had not heard Glass in solo recital before. Given out thick and loud on a big church organ with no changes of registration in the long sections, stripped of its glittering, sensuous surface—the play of saxophones and other winds and of voices upon the crisp sparkle of electric keyboards—his music loses some of its instant appeal. *Evolution* seems to be the wrong word to describe its harmonic progress; *repetition*—however "elegantly" controlled—is apter. Eastern music at its most apparently repetitious retains the charm of the individual performers' timbre and technique. Glass's ensemble music, even through the fierce amplification he habitually uses, has something of that quality. But by the church organ his ideas seemed to be coarsened. (How would the program have sounded if played on the lightest, clearest registers of the Tully Hall organ?) All the same, the result was not a bore. Two numbers from *Dance* remained buoyant, and the new piece, constructed in short contrasting sections, pointed to what may be a new Glass development.

Speculum Musicae's only New York concert of the season, apart from an appearance at the Bottom Line, was given this month in the Symphony Space, that shabby yet friendly and agreeable auditorium on Broadway at Ninety-fifth Street. The concert ended with Tobias Picker's *Nova*, composed last year. *Nova* was planned as a companion piece, in forces, to Schubert's "Trout" Quintet—for the unusual ensemble of violin, viola, cello, double-bass, and piano. That's why it's named for a form of fish. (When—if—*Nova* is played in Paris, the joke will need a footnote.) The piece, in three movements, and lasting ten minutes, is thoroughly enjoyable—rich, exuberant, unschematic. I don't understand what makes this young composer tick but do know that I like his music. It flows forth—uninhibited, unconventional, accessible, yet not undisciplined. It's not exactly "like" anything else. *Nova* lived along every instrumental line, and held the attention.

By adding flute and clarinet to the *Nova* forces, Speculum had an ensemble that compassed five pieces, each for a different combination. The program began with Charles Wuorinen's youthful, cunning *Bearbeitungen über das Glogauer Liederbuch* (flute, clarinet, violin, and double-bass). Then Joe Hudson's *Fantasy/Refrain*, for string trio, a refined but rather bitty piece. Martinů's Three Madrigals, for violin-viola duo, were done with wit—if without what I call "presentation." George Crumb's slender, exquisite *Eleven Echoes of Autumn*, for flute, clarinet, violin, and piano, was delicately sounded. A delightful summer concert, with no "heavy" music in it but filled with skill and distinction. Benjamin Hudson, the violinist, an artist who combines musical insight and cogency with a full, beautiful tone, played in every piece and was the star of the evening.

June 23, 1980

Ceremony of Innocence

There is an opinion that *The Turn of the Screw* (1954) is the greatest of Benjamin Britten's fifteen operas. Hans Keller proposes it in the keen, crackling introduction he wrote for *The Operas of Benjamin Britten*, a handsome volume of essays and librettos edited by David Herbert (Columbia). In January, the editor of the magazine *Opera* stated it. And it could be heard voiced after the beautiful and moving account of the opera presented this month by the Opera Theatre of St. Louis. But "greatest" is a superlative hard to assign among the works of a great composer who has been prolific. (Which is Mozart's "greatest" opera? Which Verdi's?) Some one-epithet characterization is perhaps possible. *Peter Grimes* (1945) has undoubtedly been Britten's most successful opera. *The Rape of Lucretia* (1946) is perhaps his most beautiful; *Gloriana* (1953), for all its intimate scenes, his grandest; *Death in Venice* (1973) his most delicate and, one might add, most personal. Among the rest, the comedy of *Albert Herring* (1947), with its serious inner theme, has proved unfading. *A Midsummer Night's Dream* (1960) is an enchanted and enchanting piece. How should one rank *Billy Budd* (1951), so potent and arresting, or the puzzling *Owen Wingrave* (1971), with merits, some claim, that have still to be discovered, or *The Turn of the Screw*, which in performance can seem to be as beautiful, delicate, personal, potent, enchanting, and arresting as any of its companions, and which is fast becoming another popular favorite? It was a long while before any of Britten's operas except *Peter Grimes* found wide acceptance in his native land, but now *The Turn of the Screw* as well as *Grimes* is in the repertory of four full-time companies—those doing *The Turn of the Screw* being the English National Opera, the Welsh National Opera, Scottish Opera, and Kent Opera, each of which from a home base plays up and down the country. In New York, the City Opera continues to show from time to time its strong production, first seen in 1962. Western Opera Theatre did the piece in 1972–74. A sensitive and accomplished Juilliard production in 1975 remains unforgotten, and that year there were also productions in Texas (by the touring Texas Opera Theatre) and in Chicago. Scanning *Opera* back to 1977, I find reports, too, of productions in Wexford, Paris, Vienna, Genoa, and at the Herrenhausen festival. The Scots took their production to Łodz, Warsaw, and Zurich. This month, the Welsh played theirs in Leipzig and Dresden. Whenever *The Turn of the Screw* is done now, it is admired. The superlative that Peter Evans uses of it in his austere, thorough, penetrating study *The Music of Benjamin Britten* (University of Minnesota Press) is "Britten's most intricately organized opera." After a masterly analysis of its thematic and harmonic marvels, he concludes his chapter on the piece by noting that a conscious appreciation of all these marvels is not needed for a listener to be emotionally overwhelmed, "drained," by the opera in performance.

In that introduction mentioned above, Mr. Keller suggests that Britten's *Death in Venice* transcended the Thomas Mann novella on which it is based, because while Mann's work was "packed with personal complications without universal significance," in Britten's "universal significance and uncompromising personal statement . . . coalesced without the slightest friction," as never before in the history of opera. For similar—not quite the same—reasons, Britten's *Turn of the Screw* transcends, I believe, its Henry James original. James's novella, which appeared in *Collier's Weekly* in 1898, is a chilling ghost story (I remember my prickling spine when first I read it), a brilliantly controlled narrative, and an imaginative psychological study of a twenty-year-old Victorian governess confronted for the first time in her life with, at once, erotic infatuation, great responsibilities, the aftermath of human evil, and, she believes, the continued, haunting presence of that evil. Britten's opera seems to be more: both a vivid drama in which nothing essential in James is lost and a stretch of music so eloquent that it can stir and shake its listeners to emotions of terror, pity, and love—to "identifications" and understanding far beyond those felt by the reader of the tale. The allurements by which the ghosts of Peter Quint and Miss Jessel seek to gain possession of the two children in the Governess's charge steal into our own minds. Through Britten's music, we feel their attractiveness and respond as the children do. We share Quint's arrogant confidence in his own seductive powers; throb with the anguish and despair of Miss Jessel, whom he seduced and then spurned; know the ghosts' yearning to be reunited to the children whom when alive they had corrupted. Not only through the Governess's eyes (as in James) do we behold these things; they become as real to us as they were to her. And so the opera ignites strange, fierce feelings in those who watch and hear it.

The librettist of *The Turn of the Screw*, Myfanwy Piper, contributes an essay, "Writing for Britten," to *The Operas of Benjamin Britten* and tells of her difficulty in devising words for the ghosts to sing; in James they are silent. For the refrain of their colloquy, which opens Act II, she borrowed a line from Yeats's apocalyptic poem "The Second Coming" (1921)—"The ceremony of innocence is drowned"—which, she says, "seemed to epitomize the story." How much of the line's context did she intend to evoke in listeners' minds? It is a well-known poem:

> *Things fall apart; the centre cannot hold;*
> *Mere anarchy is loosed upon the world,*
> *The blood-dimmed tide is loosed, and everywhere*
> *The ceremony of innocence is drowned;*
> *The best lack all conviction, while the worst*
> *Are full of passionate intensity.*

On a trivial level, listeners who know Yeats may be disturbed by the ability of the mid-nineteenth-century ghosts to quote him. More important, the line moves from the Governess's particular plight to suggest the horror of a world where the fixed and familiar are lost. "Innocence" ("the murderous innocence of the sea") and "ceremony" are important words in "A Prayer for My Daughter"—the poem that follows "The Second Coming" in the collection *Michael Robartes and the Dancer*—in which Yeats, like the Governess, meditates on a sleeping child.

Colin Graham, the director of the St. Louis production, presented this spectral colloquy as a nightmare of the Governess, and by doing so he raised a question to which different productions of *The Turn of the Screw* have given different answers: Did the Governess imagine it all? James sets her story within a double frame: a first-person narrator introduces a friend who then reads aloud a tale the Governess penned and on her death entrusted to him. As evidence of the ghosts' independent existence, the Governess cites her ability to describe persons she had never seen in life. But the "facts" are of her presentation; it is still left open to the reader to reinterpret them. In the theatre, however, Britten's music gives "reality" to the evil haunting; as Mr. Evans says of the work, "the view that all its shadows of evil darken only the Governess's mind cannot be sustained in the opera." I saw, in 1966 at Morley College, a powerful production of *The Turn of the Screw* whose director, Geoffrey Connor, took a different view. Of the Governess, he wrote, "She conjures up two ghostly adversaries, endowing them with seductive, sensuous qualities absent in herself, and Bly [the country house where the action takes place] gradually becomes a neurotic world of watching eyes. . . . So many revealing phrases of pride, sexuality, and frustration fall from her lips that, in the end, sides cannot but be taken in deciding where the evil lay." The opera is so rich and strong that it can bear that interpretation, but I do not now believe it to be a right approach. In her essay Mrs. Piper says, "Neither Britten nor I ever intended to interpret the work, only to re-create it for a different medium," and: *"The Turn of the Screw* . . . is vague only in one thing: in what, if anything, actually happened between the children and the haunting pair. This vagueness does not affect the drama in any way, it only affects what people think of it. In every other particular Henry James is precise." And:

> What is absorbing and fascinating about *The Turn of the Screw* is not the sin that lies beneath the fine mist of evil, nor yet the Governess's unfulfilled love, which it was at one time the Freudian fashion to make responsible for the whole affair, but the vulnerability of innocence at all ages. The children's inquiring innocence is assailed from outside, the young woman's is attacked from within by her own fears and imagination and from without by the evidence of her bemused senses, which she constantly mistrusts.

In James, for an "instant confounding and bottomless" the Governess wonders whether she is mistaken in believing Miles, the boy in her charge, to be possessed: "If he *were* innocent what then on earth was I?" Mr. Graham's treatment of the colloquy—which is followed at once by the Governess's monologue "Lost in my labyrinth"—reflects that instant. The Governess's own fevered imaginings have here led her beyond the "evidence." For the rest, he has, rightly, presented the ghosts with the clarity, the sharp physical presence, insisted upon in the story. James's ambiguity, his "frame," *is* retained in the opera, which begins with a narrator: "It is a curious story. I have it written in faded ink." But when that story begins it is up to the director to follow Britten and present it as reality, something that happened, not gloss it as a self-induced hallucination of the protagonist. That possibility can be left to the spectators.

Mr. Graham was stage manager at the première of *The Turn of the Screw*, given by the English Opera Group. He directed the second EOG production of it, and directed the work again for the English Music Theatre Company. He directed the premières of six of Britten's later operas (*Noye's Fludde*, the three church parables, *Owen Wingrave*, and *Death in Venice*) and was, in effect, a collaborator in their creation (for, as he notes in a contribution to *The Operas of Benjamin Britten*, the composer "usually wanted to involve the director and the designer at the libretto stage of conception . . . *before* he started composing"). He directed the British stage première of *Paul Bunyan*. Over the years, he has directed all but one (*Billy Budd*) of Britten's operas. In short, he has a thorough command of Britten's style and a thorough understanding of Britten's intentions, and he inspired the St. Louis cast to wonderfully vivid and sensitive performances, fine in details, strong in impact. Sheri Greenawald was the Governess. A flame of emotion burns in everything this singer does. To hear and watch her in Pamina's "Ach, ich fühl's" (*The Magic Flute* was another St. Louis production this year) or as the Governess is an experience almost alarming in its intensity. It is as if part of her substance were consumed by each performance she gives. One fears for her, yet is reassured by the professional discipline and the sure vocal technique that accompany her passion. Her voice is purely projected, exact in its focus. Sometimes under stress its timbre can become too narrow, when emotional and physical tensions seem to pinch the tone. But usually the sound flows freely and beautifully, alike in pianissimi that can be clearly heard and in full-throated outbursts—such as the Governess's climactic song at Miles's death—that soar out to fill the theatre. Her phrasing has uncommon distinction. She uses words tellingly. She is a beautiful woman and a subtle actress. I should dearly like to hear her as Mozart's Countess, Ilia, and Donna Elvira.

Miss Jessel was cast at strength in the person of Marianna Christos, lustrous in appearance and lustrous of voice; I have never heard and seen a better account of the role. Nor since Joan Cross's in 1954 have I heard and seen a better account than Judith Christin's of Mrs. Grose, the "stout simple plain clean wholesome woman" who is housekeeper at Bly. In recent years, it has become common to assign the parts of the Prologue and Peter Quint, both created by Peter Pears, to different singers. I regret it not for dramatic reasons (such as make a division between the Two Priests and the Two Men-in-Armor of *The Magic Flute* regrettable) but because the very economy of *The Turn of the Screw*—so much achieved with a cast of six and an orchestra of thirteen—constitutes one of its beauties. (When Sir Peter himself, still a matchless Prologue but no longer easy in Quint's coloratura flights, is at hand, it's a special case.) In St. Louis, Neil Rosenshein did both roles and did them well, for he is an elegant tenor with a gleaming presence. Miles was Peter McDowell, a treble pleasantly audible and an able little actor. Beverly Hoch, a skillful young soprano, played his sister with tact and resource.

William Harwood, who seems to me the most stylish and sensitive of America's young opera conductors, led a first-rate performance, in which emotion and musical structure, passing dramatic incident and the long formal line of the acts were excellently balanced. The orchestra—all thirteen players must be soloists—drawn from the St. Louis Symphony, was eloquent. About the look of the show I had reservations. Maxine Willi Klein's set was a stand of tall Mylar screens ranged to form a projecting V, with behind them a labyrinth of tall mirrors. It looked rather like store decoration. Onto the screens projections vaguely suggestive of locality were thrown. It was ill devised for a theatre with a thrust stage, for only from center seats could all the projections be seen. *The Turn of the Screw* can hardly be played in solid realistic scenery, since in each of its two acts there are eight scenes. Britten plainly expected suggestive, evocative décor. But the more closely the sets suggest the reality of a nineteenth-century country house and the park around it the stronger the effect of the piece. Ghosts are unsurprising when they materialize in a vague, ghostly setting. Practically, too, there were awkward things. Essential pieces of furniture drifted in and out on pontoons. When the ghosts sailed out on them, advancing for the colloquy as if in two punts, they looked silly. But Mr. Graham kept most of the action forward of the screens, and the singers held our eyes on their vivid acting.

June 30, 1980

Popular Elements

As half of its double bill this year, the Opera Theatre of St. Louis had planned to give the first stage production of Prokofiev's early one-act opera *Maddalena*. It was composed in 1911, when Prokofiev was just twenty; only the first of its four scenes was fully scored. There was some revision in 1913, and more in the late twenties or early thirties. Then the score was left behind in Paris, in the famous trunk whose top layer held the composer's brown-striped pajamas, when Prokofiev returned to Russia in 1936. He died in 1953, and the rights to *Maddalena* were in dispute. On March 25 last year, the opera had its first performances, given by the BBC, in Russian and then a few hours later in English translation. Edward Downes had completed the orchestration (he also made the translation and conducted the piece). Critics were enthusiastic: "It will demand a stage performance." "The work should now join the regular canon of Prokofiev operas." "By any standards *Maddalena* is a substantial and stageworthy piece." One looked forward to the St. Louis production, even while wondering how its "vast orchestra" would fit into the little Loretto-Hilton pit.

But performing rights to *Maddalena* were then withdrawn from the St. Louis company, which had to cast around for something else that singers already engaged could fit into. It came up with Emil von Reznicek's *Spiel oder Ernst?* *Maddalena* is a—well, *tragedy* is perhaps not the just word, for at the end its heroine rejoices that, since her husband and her lover have both died in a duel, she is now free. At any rate, it is a heated drama of high emotions. *Spiel oder Ernst?* mocks high emotions; it is a backstage anecdote—a *Pagliacci* without the passions. A tenor, a fine singer but hitherto indifferent actor, learns the way to play a convincing Otello (Rossini's, not Verdi's) when he discovers that his soprano wife, who sings Desdemona, is unfaithful to him with the bass of the company. But then soprano and bass persuade him that their affair was simulated, a ruse to rouse his emotional temperature. The tone is light.

Spiel oder Ernst? appeared in Dresden in 1930, the year of Weill's *Mahagonny*, Krenek's *Leben des Orest*, Janáček's *From the House of the Dead*, Milhaud's *Christophe Colomb*, Antheil's *Transatlantic*, and Gurlitt's *Soldaten*. During the Weimar Republic, opera was generally more than light entertainment. Reznicek himself had composed serious operas, from *Die Jungfrau von Orleans* (1886), after Schiller, to *Holofernes* (1923), after Hebbel, and had spent many years in the hurly-burly of opera-house life. When *Spiel oder Ernst?* appeared, he was seventy. The cast of five includes a composer of serious operas that no one any longer wants to hear; and he joins the tenor in a duo outburst against cruel critics. It is possible—just—to find in the score some keen comments on the composition and execution of opera and on the conduct, personal and professional, of opera singers. But it was hardly possible to do so in St. Louis, where the piece was directed and played as rank farce, without historical sense. On the simplest level, Henry Pleasants's English translation (*Fact or Fiction*), first heard in Philadelphia in 1941, kept referring to Caruso's famous performance as Rossini's Otello—a role that every musical schoolboy knows Caruso never played. (The first twentieth-century revival of *Otello* was in London in 1961.) It mattered more that there was no wit or elegance, and much philistine obviousness, in the presentation. Reznicek uses passages of *Otello* in his score, and Rossini needs better singing than the St. Louis cast provided. All in all, what might have been an amusing trifle was coarsened.

But on the bill there was also an admirable performance of one of the greatest, most moving—and most charming—tragedies of the twentieth-century lyric stage: Kurt Weill's *The Seven Deadly Sins* (to which title Bertolt Brecht, Weill's librettist, later added *of the Petit-Bourgeoisie*). This *ballet chanté* is a suite of seven songs, with prologue and epilogue, for soprano, male-voice quartet, and small orchestra. The protagonist, Anna, a divided role, is played by a singer who expresses the heroine's hard sense and by a dancer who expresses her natural feelings—two aspects of a girl who must learn by painful experience that sin does not pay. For if you are Slothful in the rat race you'll never get on. Don't take Pride in putting forward the best work you do; give the public the low-grade stuff it wants. Feeling Anger at social injustices merely makes you unpopular. Gluttony costs you your figure and your clients. Avarice—or stripping customers to their last cent—earns you a bad name and is bad for business. No use feeling Envy for those who have leisure, who protest at evils, who love as love directs them; such foolish folk never get rich. But Anna, with the voice of the singing Anna to check every decent, generous impulse in her does get rich; and back in Louisiana the little house where her family lives, chanting from time to time a pious prayer to God the Dollar, becomes as splendid as a presidential ranch. Her journey takes her from city to city—to Memphis, Los Angeles, Philadelphia, Boston, Baltimore, and San Francisco—as burlesque dancer, starlet, star, and expensive mistress.

Weill and Brecht had not been to America when they wrote this work, in 1933, but Europe had already given them ample opportunity to observe the corrupting effects of capitalism and to write this fierce morality play in which conventional moral precepts are with chilling realism turned inside out. *The Seven Deadly Sins* is a salutary work, and those who, nearly half a century later, have an easy time within a system that still prevails need reminding of the cost. Yet beside the fierceness there is fun, and the work is also a high-spirited celebration of those "sins"—enjoyment of life, of good food (the Gluttony episode contains some of the most deliciously greedy music ever written), of young love—from which Anna must be "saved." Moreover, the music is irresistible. In his *Music Ho!* (1934), Constant Lambert wrote, "I feel that this work has considerable strength in the way that it manages to deal with a modern and emotional subject without chichi, false sentiment, or mechanical romanticism." It is indeed a strong work, and very subtly composed. Brecht and Weill gave new life to classical procedures by introducing elements of a popular idiom (to the Mozartian orchestra Weill adds banjo and guitar), but, as the Weill scholar David Drew has written, "however popular the forms may have seemed, they were rooted in the best classical traditions and they were capable of considerable complexity."

Most productions of *The Seven Deadly Sins* distort the piece—by bringing chichi, camp, false sentiment, and "nostalgia" for thirties Berlin to the staging and, musically, by employing an edition in which the music is transposed down by a fourth, with disastrous effect on the vocal line and on Weill's marvelous orchestration. The singing Anna was composed for a light, clear soprano with a range from the B below the staff to the F-sharp on its top line. Its first interpreter was Lotte Lenya, whose records of the thirties reveal such a voice, not strong but true. Her manner was frank and forthright, and she had a great sense of how to shape a melody and utter a phrase. The work's affecting power lies partly in the paradoxical counterpoint of words against music and the similar contrast between the shocking sentiments and the limpid, innocent tones in which they are uttered. Jenny in *Mahagonny* has a similar role. All too often, for Anna and Jenny tough, raucous diseuses are cast.

But in St. Louis everything, or nearly everything, was right. The piece was sung at the proper pitch. The direction and choreography, by James

Cunningham, were sensitive, apt, effective, and unpresuming. So were the designs—scenery by Timothy Jozwick, costumes by John Carver Sullivan. Jennifer Donohue, the dancing Anna, was delicate, natural, touching. Elaine Bonazzi, the singing Anna, displayed an admirable sense of phrase, accent, and emphasis. There were some moments that call for fuller, bigger singing than she seemed to think was proper, but otherwise her feeling for the role was secure, and she and Miss Donohue played together movingly. Randall Behr, quite rightly, conducted most of the music as if it were by Mozart, but in the final episode, which needs to be conducted as if it were by Mahler, he reduced the weight of the funeral march; its tread was too light and its climaxes were too gentle.

Victor Herbert, Irish-born, Stuttgart-trained, was a good composer. Bel Canto Opera has been proving it since 1976 with its productions of *Babette, Sweethearts, The Red Mill,* and now, last month, *The Debutante,* unheard in New York since a short run at the Knickerbocker Theatre in 1914. These Bel Canto shows are labors of commitment and love on the part of the Herbert scholar Frederick S. Roffman, who for *The Debutante,* as for the previous works, edited the score, revised the book, wrote learned program notes, directed, and conducted. Mr. Roffman is not equally skillful in all his parts. I approve his insistence as an editor on going back to the autograph and discovering the composer's first and later intentions, rather than meekly accepting printed scores. Sometimes this means acts of Wagnerian dimensions (the first act of *The Debutante* lasted for nearly ninety minutes; during it, alternative versions of the heroine's entrance aria were both done), but if one is going to revive an unknown piece one might as well revive all of it. Of his work as dramatist and lyricist I cannot speak, not having scanned the original books. As a director, he has found a style—a simple, unpretentious style not ill suited to the fairly modest acting ability of the Bel Canto regulars and chorus. As a conductor, he seems to me inefficient, lackluster, and readier to follow the music than to form it. Nevertheless, the music is animated enough to lead him to entertaining performances, and *The Debutante* was enjoyable.

The plot is a Jamesian soufflé: no-nonsense American heiress somewhat adrift in England but resourceful in Paris; reunion at the end with a Princeton boy who has got over his dazzle with French society. The plot finds place for a brief "Cubist" opera—rather a pretty one, kin to both Satie's *Parade* and Ligeti's *Aventures* (while sharing a solfeggio text with Philip Glass's *Einstein on the Beach*), but ending in a turkey trot. The score is light, tuneful, accomplished, thoroughly agreeable. Sullivan, Richard Strauss, and Ravel play upon its popular idiom. It is cunningly orchestrated. As the heroine, Melanie Helton displayed an offbeat, unstereotyped charm, a freshness that won all hearts, and some bright high notes to shine out as descant to a catchy ensemble rag. Lauren Scott, with some polish and wit, played an American suffragist. The words of the hero, sung by Robert Urbanowicz, were excellently clear.

. . .

Despite its name, the group Polyhymnia, which styles itself "a women's chamber-music collective," is not dedicated to the performance of sacred music. Last month, in the little Theatre Opera Music Institute (or TOMI) theatre, atop the Park Royal Hotel, on West Seventy-third Street, it revived two rarities, Albert Roussel's *Elpénor* and Louis Gruenberg's *The Daniel Jazz*. In 1937, as his death was approaching, Roussel entrusted to his friend Joseph Weterings, the librettist of his ballet *Aeneas*, some music he had composed for an unspecified dramatic action and invited Weterings to write a play to go with it. In 1946, Weterings told Roussel's biographer Norman Demuth about the elaborate scenario he had devised; Demuth writes of an overture, an interlude, a prelude to Act II, and overtures to Acts III and IV. But the "poème radiophonique" *Elpénor* that was published in 1947 has a much simpler plot, and the score consists of only a four-minute prelude and two brief interludes; the coda of the prelude is repeated at the end. Basil Deane, a later Roussel biographer, calls the piece "unremarkable," and I think he is too hard. *Elpénor* is no *Naissance de la lyre*, no *Bacchus et Ariane*, no *Aeneas*, and there is very little of it; but what there is is exquisite. Roussel was a stern self-critic. He destroyed several of his compositions. He would not have entrusted to posterity the pieces that became *Elpénor* had he been unsure of their merit.

The music is for flute and string quartet. (Demuth talks of timpani, but there are none in the score as published.) The prelude serves aptly to introduce Circe's enchanted island; a little bustle at the end of it suggests that Ulysses and his crew are preparing to depart. In Homer, Elpenor, a weak-headed young fellow who has gone up to the roof to sleep off a hangover, loses his step, tumbles down, breaks his neck, and misses the boat. But Weterings's Elpenor is a romantic who misses the boat from choice; he cannot bring himself to part from Clymene, one of Circe's nymphs. The poetic playlet starts with merry, saucy conversation between another of Ulysses' followers and another nymph. The interludes set the tone for the gentle romance, passionate yet chaste, of the serious pair. Roussel had a rare gift for "atmosphere"; his antique world is closer to Fauré's than to Ravel's, and the *Elpénor* music, on its tiny scale, suggests a distillation from his big classical ballets. It is at once modest, vivid, intense, and refined, and it was attractively played. The performance was "semistaged," and Weterings's play, in an English translation by Robin Kronstadt, was nicely spoken.

The Daniel Jazz—spirituals by Vachel Lindsay set for voice, string quartet, clarinet and trumpet, percussion and piano—is a lively piece. It was first heard at a League of Composers concert in 1925, along with *Pierrot Lunaire*. It caused quite a stir when it was done a few months later at the ISCM Festival, in Venice (along with Carl Ruggles's *Angels* and Stravinsky's Piano Sonata). It swept Europe. It may well have given Weill some ideas. But at the Polyhymnia performance the mezzo-soprano Laurie Carley, who had played Elpenor with charm and discretion, was a self-conscious and unstylish soloist, uncertain of her approach; Joshua Greene overconducted the little ensemble; and the suite stayed earthbound. Leontyne Price, an explorer whose latest recital record ranges from Handel's Jupiter, by way of Norma and Isolde, to Britten's Gloriana, might be the person to bring *The Daniel Jazz* back to life. When it was new, Egon Wellesz described it (in the influential *Anbruch,* the Vienna magazine devoted to new music) as "a landmark in the history of American music."

July 7, 1980

Albertus Magnus

The aim of the Aston Magna Foundation for Music, as set out on its latest broadsheet, is "to bring together artists, scholars, instrument makers, and serious students to contemplate the meaning of the glorious music of the seventeenth and eighteenth centuries—considering not only the instruments, techniques of playing and of improvisation, and pitch and tunings proper to the music but also the broader social and cultural context in which the music was created and originally functioned." For three summers now, the foundation has held a three-week Academy on the campus of Simon's Rock of Bard College, outside Great Barrington, in the Berkshires. The theme of the first Academy was music in the Rome of Queen Christina and Cardinal Ottoboni; of the second, music in the age of Louis XV. This year's theme is "Confluences and Contradictions in German Culture" for the half century 1725 to 1775. It was the age, as the broadsheet reminds us, of Frederick the Great and Joseph II, of Winckelmann, Lessing, and Schlegel, of Balthasar Neumann and the Bibienas, of Bach's sons, Gluck, and the young Haydn. The contradictions are between the revived classical ideal and the new "Storm and Stress," or early Romanticism. The confluences bring currents from France and Italy into the German streams.

The artists of the Academy also give public concerts at St. James's Church in Great Barrington—a mid-nineteenth-century, aisleless, Gothic building of no particular distinction but apt enough in sound and size. (It holds about four hundred people.) At the second of this year's concerts, Gluck's cool, poised Flute Concerto in G major, which began the program, and John Christian Bach's celebrated Symphony in G minor, Op. 6, No. 6, which ended the first half, illustrated contradictions—by way of both the big, evident contrast between them and, more subtly, their own inner complexities of emotion. Gluck's mature operas draw life from tensions between their classical clarity—Winckelmann's ideal of "noble simplicity and calm greatness" rendered in forms, melody, harmony, and orchestration—and their passion and intensity of utterance. Passion is not prominent in the concerto, but I enjoyed its boldness (there is brave writing for the two horns that join the string band), its grace, and the poised playing of John Solum, the soloist. The Bach symphony, on the other hand, sets its listeners atingle from the start and ends with a chilling, almost spectral recession into silence. The goblins that Helen (of E. M. Forster's *Howards End*) heard in Beethoven's Fifth are stalking here, too; but in the central movement, andante più tosto adagio, there is a foretaste of Schubert in his most poetic and charming orchestral vein. *Galant* is the textbooks' regular epithet for the London Bach. A fair amount of his instrumental music is available on records, most of it played on modern instruments and in a conventionally *galant* way. What I have heard of his operas (a pasticcio entitled *Temistocle*, assembled by Edward Downes and H. C. Robbins Landon, including some noble stretches of the *Temistocle* Bach composed for Carl Theodor together with numbers from his *Amadis de Gaule, Artaserse, Orione, Catone*, a prentice fugue, a symphony, and a concert scena; and his last London opera, *La clemenza di Scipione*) suggests a more vigorous and potently temperamental composer. So did the Aston Magna performance of the symphony.

Confluences were represented by a virtuoso Vivaldi trio for recorder, bassoon, and continuo, two sacred arias by Joseph de Mondonville for soprano, violin, and harpsichord, and two operatic arias by Niccolò Jommelli. The violinist was the poetic Stanley Ritchie, playing a 1679 Stainer. The singer was Judith Nelson, a Californian who has been winning golden reviews in Europe for her skill as a baroque interpreter. The voice is small but beautiful, and finely audible, because it is pure, true in pitch, and firm in timbre. It is also steady; Miss Nelson uses vibrato—a touch of slow, gentle vibrato—as an expressive device to be added at will only when the music seems to call for it. Her command of phrasing and articulation, of attack and release, of linking or dividing notes seems to be complete. Tones so exactly struck and lines so stylishly drawn delight mind and ear. But she had a failing, a serious one: her words lacked color and force. The text of the second Mondonville aria was not the text printed in the program; what it was, one could not tell. The second Jommelli piece was a grandly dramatic scene from *Ifigenia in Tauride*—a violent recitative and a broad yet brilliant aria of lament sung by the heroine on learning of her mother's slaughter. I am glad Miss Nelson chose it, and was thrilled to hear it; we hear all too little Jommelli nowadays. She sang it with understanding. The long-sustained notes at the start of the aria, "Ombra cara," were exquisitely shaped and moving. But the fierce outbursts were less vivid than the composer plainly intended.

Aston Magna overrates the erudition or underrates the curiosity of its audiences. Program notes were confined to a few lines about Jommelli and a spoken introduction—admirable but very brief—by Albert Fuller, the founder, artistic director, and daily inspiration of Aston Magna. There was no "placing"; connections were not made. Of the *Ifigenia* aria, the program said simply "originally sung by Anna de Amicis." Was that enough to remind any but academicians that John Christian Bach discovered and developed de Amicis's merits as a tragedian; that she was later Jommelli's leading lady in Naples; that Mozart heard her in both London and Naples (writing home that she "cantò à meraviglio") and later composed the great prima donna role of his own *Lucio Silla* for her? Giunia's wonderful "Dalla sponda tenebrosa," in that opera, seems to be recognizably for the voice and the art that inspired "Ombra cara."

Mozart ended the program: his Violin Concerto in D major, K. 211, composed in 1775, tenderly, lyrically, and buoyantly played by Jaap Schröder, on a Stainer of 1665. It was a freer, more flowing, more graceful performance of the concerto than the one Mr. Schröder recorded some years ago with the Amsterdam Mozart Ensemble (ABC Records on its SEON label). It filled the spirit with joy. But then all these performances were of a kind in which the instruments "sang" and "danced."

A few years ago, I had reservations about the Aston Magna performances I heard. Now intentions have become achievement. The string band is probably as good as any in the world. The winds are in tune. The old self-consciousness has been replaced by confidence, by character, and beyond that, by something one might almost describe as a philosophy intelligently and joyfully embraced. For there is more to Aston Magna than authentic instruments, stylistic insights, and technical ability. What it is is hard to describe but was very easy to feel on even a brief visit to the Academy, during which I talked to its members, discovered what they had been learning about, heard them rehearse and play informally as well as at the public concert. (The setting helps—a wooded hillside away from the never-ceasing mechanical rumble that is continuo to life in New York. On ears attuned to the fine sound of a clavichord, the call of a bird outside struck with trumpet tones.) Is it "escapist," this retreat into the eighteenth century? Mr. Fuller began his opening address to the Academy by quoting Wallace Stevens:

> *Just as my fingers on these keys*
> *Make music, so the selfsame sounds*
> *On my spirit make a music, too.*
>
> *Music is feeling, then, not sound.*

He put the question "What are we all doing here?" In part, he suggested, it was to rediscover with *all* the senses what the great composers sought to communicate by their music—to hear the sounds they heard, to move hands as their hands must have moved to excite a particular instrument to speak. But he went on to talk, earnestly and without embarrassment, of the idea "Noblesse oblige" as it was understood by Louis XIV and as it should be understood now by anyone with special knowledge or a special vision. That phrase in the foundation's statement of aim "to contemplate the meaning of the glorious music" is important. At Aston Magna, much time is spent considering what the music meant to the men who wrote it and those who first heard it; that is preparation for learning and revealing what it can mean now.

Music's realm is large. A few miles away, at Tanglewood, hundreds of students were massing for the courses of the Berkshire Music Center. At the Tanglewood concerts, the Boston Symphony will play Vivaldi, Haydn, and Mozart to audiences of thousands. Lessing's theory of limitations—that each art achieves its greatest results within the borders of its special functions—can perhaps be extended to the various fields of music making. Some eighteenth-century music was written for large-scale performance; most of it must be distorted if it is to be played before an audience of more than hundreds. But thousands can hear it on its true scale and in intimacy when it is recorded or broadcast. In time, one hopes, this country will have a coherent national broadcasting system to carry such concerts as Aston Magna's from coast to coast. There was, in fact, a television crew all too evidently present at the concert I attended, taping the event for PBS. Its methods were crude: bright lights were shone into the faces of the audience, a camera moved back and forth, a stream of audible chatter poured from the cameraman's earphone, and between pieces there were long, long waits while the players' placing was adjusted for the sake of the picture. At public concerts, good television teams are seen as little as possible and heard not at all. But the distractions can be forgiven if there was no other practicable way in Great Barrington to capture for the small screen and the big public a glimpse of Aston Magna and its director at work. In troubled times, they provide a model of dedication, discipline, idealism, beauty, ferment made fertile, and tumult ordered. As the company sings in one of Britten's operas, "Albert the Good! Long may he reign!"

July 14, 1980

Hero

Jon Vickers is not a subtle interpreter. That sentence is enough to bring down a flight of angry letters upon me, so let me add quickly that I retract none of the epithets I have been using of him regularly since his British début, early in 1957, singing Gustavus (alias Riccardo) in *Un ballo in maschera* with the Covent Garden company in Cardiff. In everything he does onstage, Vickers has been and remains powerful, poetic, noble, intense, exciting. During his first season at Covent Garden, he sang Gustavus, Don José, and Aeneas in *Les Troyens.* The next two seasons, he appeared in new productions of *Aida, Don Carlos,* Handel's *Samson, Parsifal,* and *Médée* (with Callas) and sang his first Siegmund. With new productions of *Pagliacci* (1959) and *Fidelio* (1961) and with Saint-Saëns's Samson, a role he sang in America, the tenor's basic repertory for the next twenty years took shape. Peter Grimes, Othello, and Tristan have been the three great additions to it. His has been an operatic career. But now, at the Florence Maggio Musicale and then last month at Tanglewood, he has come before the public as a lieder singer, in Schubert's *Winterreise.*

No tenor of our day has hurled at Carmen a fiercer, more desperate howl of "Eh bien, damnée." Mario Del Monaco's trumpet tones were more brilliant, more ringing, at "Sacerdote, io resto a te," at the end of the *Aida* Nile scene, but it was Vickers who invested the phrase, overwhelmingly, with noble desperation. Despair that found an outlet in wild, heroic resolve filled his account of "En un dernier naufrage," Aeneas' great scena. The most stirring phrases I have ever heard him utter were Samson's

> *Total eclipse! no sun, no moon,*
> *All dark amidst the blaze of noon!*

Each syllable was charged with, his own darkness was ablaze with, the despair of a powerful man rendered powerless, his career in God's and his nation's service blasted. Vickers has been most eloquent of all when singing in his native tongue to an audience that hangs on each of his words. To have heard his Aeneas at Covent Garden both in English and in French gave the clear proof of that.

His art, vocally and emotionally, has been ever a matter of extremes. In interviews, he talks of a lay-minister father who brought him up reiterating "You will do with your might what your hands find to do." Whatever he undertakes bears the full force of his character, and sometimes he loads phrases too heavily. The voice has always been an unwieldy instrument. (Well, since I have known it it has been, though in early days in Canada Vickers sang Don Ottavio, the Duke of Mantua, and Alfredo in *La traviata.*) The fluency he displayed in the divisions of the *Messiah* he recorded with Beecham is rare. There is seldom any conventional beauty in his full tones. His loud singing is often effortful; the effect can be tremendous, because it is an expressive effort. His soft singing—Siegmund's "Nun weisst du, fragende Frau, warum ich Friedmund nicht heisse," the cadences of "Celeste Aida" and Don José's Flower Song—can be potently affecting. In *The Grand Tradition,* J. B. Steane remarks that "perhaps it is only the very strong who can be quite so quiet and gentle as Vickers often is." But this soft singing has often, and fairly, been described as "crooning" or "marking." The alternation of blunderbuss and feather stroke can be thrilling; the unremitting intensity can be tiring—exaggerated rather than subtle.

Vickers's approach to the interpretation of the parts he plays is suggested by his regretful letter, made public, to the head of Covent Garden in

1977 when he pulled out of a forthcoming *Tannhäuser*: "As you know, it has always been essential for me to have a point of personal contact with the personality of each role I portray so that by my identification with the role I can bring the character to life on stage. I have failed completely to find any point from which to begin. I am therefore convinced of the impossibility for me to interpret Tannhäuser." (The company revived *Otello* for him instead.) Bernard Shaw pointed to the limitations of an "identification" approach in his review of an 1891 *Dutchman* with the young Scottish soprano Margaret Macintyre as a vivid but incomplete Senta: "Her notion of dramatic singing at present hardly goes beyond intensely imagining herself to be the person in the drama, and then using the music to relieve her pent-up excitement." Vickers goes beyond that, but there have been moments when I've wondered whether I was watching and hearing Jon Vickers as Peter Grimes or Peter Grimes as Jon Vickers. In the *Tristan* chapter of *Opera on Record*, Robin Holloway has this to say of the 1972 Angel recording:

> Vickers . . . is the outstanding feature of this set and (for all except Karajan-freaks) its *raison d'être*. For urgency and intensity his third act is without rival. It is absolutely authentic and extremely painful—the ravings of a stricken beast. . . . There is no doubt whatsoever about the stature of this *tour de force*, but it remains an extreme—something unique as if the story were, just this once, literally true. I can pay no higher tribute; but I never want to hear it again.

From such a singer, a *Winterreise* might be tremendous, inspired, catastrophic. . . .

There was a Siegmund-like setting for the Tanglewood *Winterreise*. Storm had broken over the Berkshire hills. The rain poured down. From time to time, thunder rolled. The recital was given in the Theatre Concert Hall, a kind of large shed, seating eleven hundred people, open at the back to the storm. Mr. Vickers came on with his pianist, Gilbert Kalish, smiled at us, declared us heroes to be there, meditated for a moment, and then began. Some features of his performance were deducible in advance, others not. The scale of the setting proved awkward: it is not an intimate place (*Peter Grimes* had its American première there), and I wondered whether Vickers's extreme pianissimi carried to the farther rows, but it is not so large as to call for a "heroic" performance. And Vickers did not give one. He began gravely, soberly, singing the first two verses of "Gute Nacht" without any emphases, in a tone that was little more than "marking." In the third verse, he became louder and faster. At the turn to the major, he slowed down again, uttering "Will dich im Traum nicht stören" in a rapt pianissimo. This more or less set the pattern of his interpretation. The poignancy of Schubert's moves to the major—in the second verse of "Der Lindenbaum," the second verse of "Der Wegweiser"—was regularly underlined by a slower tempo and a dulcet timbre. "Frühlingstraum" was *very* slow.

Between full voice and a thread of voice there were seldom any gradations. Lines that should be smoothly traced with varying pressures became bumpy. Sometimes the tenor seemed to lurch through the songs. Some small notes were merely sketched, or missing altogether. About two-thirds of the way through the cycle, his voice did become more ductile. He sang "Der greise Kopf," "Die Krähe," and "In Dorfe" on a larger scale, which enabled him to make some of the nonextreme contrasts that lieder singing calls for: from *f* to *ff* is a smaller step than from *ppp* to *f*. In "Der greise Kopf," the line "Und hab' mich sehr gefreuet" was very big but now not unbalanced with what had gone before. For the start of "Die Krähe," he found a full yet gentle tone. In the second verse of "Der Wegweiser," at "Welch' ein törichtes Verlangen," there was a passionate crescendo that proved thrilling. But for "Das Wirtshaus" he returned to "crooning," and each note was so carefully placed that line was lost. At the very end, a thin, bleak, yet oddly prosaic account of "Der Leiermann" suddenly rose in a huge crescendo on "deine Leier drehn," as if the hurdy-gurdy had become a mighty organ with a fierce Swell pedal.

That for this music Vickers would seek to restrain his natural violence of expression was predictable. That he restrained it to a point where much of the singing proved—well, dull is too hard a word, so let us say ordinary—was disappointing. I didn't think Vickers could be ordinary. I am not sure that the narrator of *Winterreise* does have a dramatic personality with which a singer can "identify"; it is easier to think oneself into the skin of the miller lad in *Die schöne Müllerin*. One does not put features to the winter wanderer: at the most, I think while listening of Schubert himself, not "wandering" but responding to these sad poems so intently, so deeply. Much of what Vickers did was understated; what was overstated seemed, as a result, the more so. He sang in German, and there is something to be said for that (the program book supplied text and translation), but he would probably have been more communicative in English. Mr. Kalish played a modern Baldwin grand, an instrument on which Schubert's piano writing cannot properly be rendered, but one matched to the un-Schubertian scale of the singer and the setting. His handling of the music was sensitive.

July 21, 1980

Flute

I hadn't planned to go to Lincoln Center's Mostly Mozart Festival. Avery Fisher Hall is no apt home for eighteenth-century music; and although some eminent artists were billed to appear, the thought of even the ablest pickup orchestra playing four concerts (two programs) a week six weeks in a row did not suggest loving and carefully rehearsed performances. (Tuesdays and Thursdays are given to chamber music—but also in the huge spaces of Fisher Hall.) The music is played on modern instruments. And, in any case, the vulgarity of the festival's radio advertisement—in which the G-minor Symphony bursts, after a few measures, into the allegro of *Eine kleine Nachtmusik*—was enough to keep serious Mozartians away. But on the day the festival was due to open I was crossing Lincoln Plaza—on my way to the Library of the Performing Arts to consult, as it happens, a facsimile of the original *Magic Flute* libretto. And I heard magical flute music. In the open air, clustered in the shade beneath the north wall of the Met, the flutist James Galway and the festival orchestra, conducted by Gerard Schwarz, were rehearsing Mozart's D-major Concerto, K. 314. It was more of a run-through than a rehearsal. The sound was coming from loudspeakers. But it was the heavenly andante, with those stretches of simple, enchanted three-part writing for the soloist and the first and second violins which are among Mozart's miracles. And Mr. Galway was playing purely, steadily, without wobbly vibrato. I felt rather as those wild beasts in Act I, Scene 15, of *The Magic Flute* must feel, stayed to listen, wanted more, and was lucky enough to get tickets for that night's concert.

The program book of the festival contains a good essay, "Mozart and Friends," by David Hamilton, which is about, mainly, the wind players who inspired the composer. Among them, Anton Stadler, for whom the Clarinet Quintet, the Clarinet Concerto, and a major "role" in *La clemenza di Tito* were written, has pride of place. (The quintet appears on the Mostly Mozart bill; also the clarinet trio, whose minuet Eric Blom chose to exemplify "a kind of Emily Brontë–like quality of smouldering passion in Mozart.") The clarinet and its dark, gentle brother the basset-horn color the last year of Mozart's life, until in his final opera the clear flute proclaims music's power to lead us surely through spiritual peril. The first flowering of music with woodwind soloists starts during Mozart's stay in Mannheim, from the end of October 1777 to mid-March 1778. There he became friendly with the members of an orchestra celebrated for its wind playing—and, to judge from numerous references in the Mannheim letters, particularly friendly with the flutist Johann Baptist Wendling. With Wendling, the Mannheim oboist Friedrich Ramm, and the Mannheim bassoonist Georg Wenzel Ritter, he planned to visit Paris. Once in Paris, for them and the horn player Giovanni Punto he composed a symphonie concertante. For Wendling's wife, Dorothea, and for the same four concertante instruments he wrote Ilia's great aria "Se il padre perdei," in *Idomeneo*. That was in Munich; the Mannheim company had moved there when their employer, Carl Theodor, became Elector of Bavaria. In Munich, Mozart composed his oboe quartet, for Ramm. (This piece also figures on the Mostly Mozart bill.) The flute quartets and flute concertos date from Mannheim—the result of a commission (passed on to Mozart by Wendling) from a Dutch amateur, one De Jean, for a clutch of such pieces. The D-major Concerto, the one Mr. Galway played, is in fact a reworking of an earlier oboe concerto, in C, which Ramm had taken up with great success. All this Mannheim and Munich wind music is written in an eager, youthful vein, bright with a sense of new worlds waiting to be mastered.

Commentators on the flute quartets and flute concertos regularly observe, first, that Mozart disliked the flute and, second, that this dislike did not stop him from composing admirable music for it. (The Mostly Mozart program note, for example, began, "Mozart's professed distaste for the flute is not evident in the music he wrote for it.") The evidence for the distaste is a parenthesis in a letter Mozart wrote home from Mannheim on February 14, 1778, while he was busy with the De Jean commissions (which he never completed). Emily Anderson translates it thus: "Moreover, you know that I become quite powerless whenever I am obliged to write for an instrument which I cannot bear." But the translation in the Eulenburg miniature score of K. 314 suggests something different: "And then, as you know, I am always 'stuck' if I have to write all the time for one and the same instrument (which I dislike)." Does the relative relate to the flute itself or to the tedium of constantly composing for the same—for any—instrument? It would be pleasant to assert that the composer of *The Magic Flute* did not dislike the flute. The original German, alas, does not quite permit that assertion; the placing of Mozart's parenthesis does seem to point to the flute: "dan bin ich auch, wie sie wissen, gleich stuff wenn ich immer für ein instrument /das ich nicht leiden kann:/ schreiben soll." But *maybe*—presuming some loose syntax—one could render the sense as "Moreover, as you know, I always get fed up when—something I can't bear—I have to go on and on writing for the same instrument." The letter continues, "So, for an occasional change, I've done something else, such as piano-violin duets, and some work on the Mass."

The instrument that Mozart composed for—whether he disliked it or not—was not the instrument that Mr. Galway played. Eighteenth-century flutes were made of wood, usually of boxwood, and, according to C. Max Champion, in Grove, "the tone of a boxwood flute is unsurpassed for sweetness." My own experience of them confirms it. They had a conical bore, wider at the blowing end. And they were hard to keep in tune. (Mozart praised Wendling as one of the rare flutists who inspired confidence, not apprehension whether the next note would be sharp or flat.) The modern, more easily pitched cylindrical flute—a descendant of which Mr. Galway uses—with the big air holes, and keyed caps to cover them, was a nineteenth-century invention, and it makes quite a different sound. Theobald Boehm designed it in about 1846, and with his invention (again I quote Mr. Champion) "the flute gained enormously in freedom of speech and richness and volume of tone." Boehm built his first specimens of metal, usually silver. (Mr. Galway's flute was made of gold.) In the right place—in the right works—freedom of speech and richness and volume of tone are virtues, but the sound of a modern flute in eighteenth-century music can be, and often is, offensive: when it produces a fat, thick, overnourished tone, and when it throbs and wobbles. (There are flutists who seem to cultivate, and even revel in, a heavy vibrato.) Mr. Galway, however, played lightly, cleanly, neatly. I had not heard him since his orchestral days—in the Stratford, Sadler's Wells, and Covent Garden pit bands, then with the BBC Symphony, the Royal Philharmonic, and the Berlin Philharmonic—but had read quite a lot about him, for he has become a celebrated and popular flutist: Ireland's answer to Jean-Pierre Rampal, as it were. RCA has sent me curious records of Mr. Galway playing (on the flute) Japanese melodies, the Mozart Clarinet Concerto, the César Franck Violin Sonata, Bach harpsichord concertos, Vivaldi's *Four Seasons*, and rather awful duet arrangements, with Cleo Laine as vocalist, of things like "the" Pachelbel canon and Sir Henry Bishop's "Lo, Here the Gentle Lark." But after hearing him as soloist in K. 314 and, on the same program, in the Mozart Concerto for Flute and Harp I am happy to report that musicians can, after all, still take him seriously. Both concertos were attractively and even sensitively played, though just occasionally Mr. Galway plunged into the flute's equivalent of an empurpled chest voice, and both finales were perhaps indecently fast.

The sound of an eighteenth-century flute in the D-major Concerto can be enjoyed from a two-disc record album (MCA SEON 67040) in which Frans Vester plays all Mozart's flute-and-orchestra music, with the Amsterdam Mozart Ensemble, conducted by Frans Brüggen. I recommend it, but not without reservations. The timbre of the flute Mr. Vester uses for K. 314, a Dresden instrument of 1796, is beautiful—fuller, more intense, far sweeter than that of a twentieth-century metal flute. It has neither the "hollowness" nor the "silvery" quality of modern flute tone. This sounds like a *wood*wind instrument and—how can one put it?—also like something alive and breathing beneath the player's breath and fingers. The music is not hurried but taken at paces that allow careful molding of Mozart's phrases. Baroque style is as much a matter of articulation as of timbre. (The two are not separable, of course: melodic articulation is bound up with the way the fingers must move on a particular instrument, and modern mechanical "improvements" can destroy the essential character of a melody.) On the other hand, Mr. Vester, unlike Wendling, is not always perfectly in tune, and while the easy tempi and the balanced, unforced timbres of the baroque ensemble enable one to "hear" the instrumental textures far more exquisitely than usual, Mr. Brüggen's handling of the music is possibly *too* loving and careful.

Mozart's Concerto for Flute and Harp, composed in Paris in 1778, is a work often underrated—not by the public, to judge from the number of recordings it receives, but by commentators who deem it no more than a piece of skillful, pretty salon music composed for a duke and his daughter to play. It seems to me a work whose beauties of invention can make the heart stand still, and three of its recordings are especially dear to me. One, made by Beecham in 1947, with René Le Roy and Lily Laskine as the soloists, is perhaps the most graceful and aristocratic of all in its gait. Another, a Vox record of the mid-fifties, has as its flutist Camillo Wanausek; and Mr. Wanausek, who has also recorded the solo concertos and the flute quartets, is a marvelous Mozartian. The third appears in the MCA album. The duke who commissioned the concerto had been French ambassador in London, and he evidently returned to Paris with one of the new English six-keyed flutes, reaching down to the low C, for Mozart thrice uses the note. For the MCA recording, Mr. Vester plays a London flute of about 1800, and keeps it in tune. Edward Witsenburg, the harpist, plays a "simple pedal harp" made in London, by Erard, in 1802. The sound is beautiful—not just of the solo instruments but also of the baroque strings, oboes, and horns, for which Mozart writes so deftly. I enjoyed the Fisher Hall performance, in which Marisa Robles, a polished harpist, made her New York début. I returned home to enjoy the Dutch performance even more—because here the scale of the execution, the phrasing, and, above all, the marvelous timbre of the flute match Mozart's music precisely.

And for another reason: at the live performance, Mozart and his conductor, Mr. Schwarz, had to suffer competition, in the part of the hall where I sat, from one of the Miss Jenkynses of this world. Another essay in the festival program book, by Speight Jenkins, deals wisely and firmly with audience behavior—and stresses the clarity with which the new acoustics of Fisher Hall throw the noisier audience manifestations into prominence. But Mr. Jenkins does not mention the time-beater who with hand, program, or foot sets up counter-rhythms to the composer's. A mild sentence from the first chapter of Mrs. Gaskell's *Cranford,* if printed somewhere in the program, might help to deter those whose bodily reactions to music get out of control: "We were none of us musical, though Miss Jenkyns beat time, out of time, by way of appearing to be so."

The titular flute of Mozart's last opera is meant to be an exceptional instrument. At its first appearance, a stage direction describes it as "golden." Much later, Pamina announces that her father "cut it in an enchanted hour from deep within the thousand-year-old oak tree." Leslie Kopp, who has worked with the vast Dayton C. Miller collection of flutes in the Library of Congress, tells me she has come across walnut and mahogany instruments but none made of oak. I've seen it suggested that "golden" refers to the color of the wood (but oak normally darkens with age), or that the flute had golden fittings (the writer must have had a post-Boehm model in mind; the sort of flute the first Tamino played had just one little metal key). Some writers instance the apparent contradiction as one of the loose ends the authors of the *Flute* left when they decided to convert a fairy tale into a Masonic allegory. My suggestion is that the flute is a wooden one gilded to look good—and magical—on the stage. One *could,* I suppose, declare that Pamina's father had cut a golden metal flute out of an oak tree where, like Excalibur in the stone or Nothung in the ash tree, it had been resting. People are ready to say almost anything about *The Magic Flute:* consider some of the other things that have been claimed for the instrument itself.

There are at least three good reasons why the instrument is a flute, and not, say, a magic oboe or a magic clarinet. First, the plot of the opera had its starting point—and more—in a story called *Lulu, or The Magic Flute.* Second, the first Tamino, Benedict Schack, actually played the flute. (Or so we are always told, but I've not found prime evidence of the fact.) And, third, like the lyre and the lute, the flute is an aptly mythic and "timeless" instrument. The timbres of the oboe and the clarinet are too intricate and their actual manufacture, even in eighteenth-century versions, is too complicated to provide a clear, effective symbol of music's power; a listener might start wondering whether Tamino knew how to cut new reeds if the one supplied by the Queen got damaged. While the *Flute* was being prepared, a rival theatre brought out *Caspar the Bassoon-Player,* another opera based freely on *Lulu;* and the timbre of *that* instrument gave rise, we are told by Jahn, to "some very questionable pleasantry."

By simpleminded Freudians, the flute has, of course, been dubbed a phallic symbol. When one pursues the implications of that suggestion, some of them are too obvious—for Tamino is again and again exhorted to "be a man"—to add anything to our understanding of the work, while at others the mind boggles. For the commentator Alfons Rosenberg, however, the flute is an androgynous symbol, because of its "phallic form with a feminine high voice." To Jacques Chailley, in his book about the opera's Masonic aspects, the flute represents the four elements, since Father cut it on a stormy night amid rain, thunder, and lightning (which Chailley glosses as water, earth, and fire), while it is sounded by air: "It unites the four Elements, whence its perfection." Dorothy Koenigsberger, in an essay in *European Studies Review,* finds in the flute a symbol of completeness (because it can play all the notes of the scale), of purity (because it has a pure tone), and of alchemical transmutation (because, although once oaken, it has become golden). What the flute primarily—and, I would say, sufficiently—symbolizes is proclaimed in so many words by Pamina before the trials by fire and water: the power of music to "protect us on our way" and, again, to "lead us on our fearsome way." When the Three Ladies hand Tamino the flute, they tell him that with it he can "transform human passions," since when he plays it "the sad will become happy, and the stony-hearted affectionate." (Papageno's bells—described by Schikaneder in his libretto by an old term for a xylophone, a "wooden laughter," and by Mozart in his score by an old term for a glockenspiel, a "steel laughter"—represent, on the other hand, the disarming power of music to turn hostility into merriment.) The Ladies' statement is true as far as it goes but incomplete. New and deeper truths await us at every turn of *The Magic Flute,* and in this profound and inspiring work not only music's affective power but, eventually, music's spiritual power is celebrated. After Pamina's declaration, four voices—those of Pamina, Tamino, and the Men in Armor—join to sing "Through music's power, we/you pass, joyful, through death's gloomy night."

> When . . . the four voices combine in an exalted quartet, we experience a feeling of concord and perfect fulfillment of which there are few parallels in music. After that there is a pause; and then, as Pamina and Tamino pass through the fire and the water, comes the strangest thing in the score, a climax of mysterious stillness. Without raising his voice, and

by means of a quiet march played by a handful of instruments—a slow but florid melody for solo flute, punctuated at the end of each phrase by brass chords followed by soft drumbeats (always on the offbeat)—Mozart creates an overwhelming sense of tension, the ordeals of a lifetime compressed into a few bars.

That is from David Cairns's "A Vision of Reconciliation," the latest—and one of the most eloquent—of the hundreds of essays that have been written about *The Magic Flute.* It appears in a guide to the opera—libretto and translation, documentation, and essays—just issued by the English National Opera (published in this country by the Riverrun Press).

I have often wondered why ambitious tenors do not acquire enough flute technique to be able to play at least the brief, C-major solos of *The Magic Flute* expressively. So far as I know, no Tamino since Schack has played his own flute. At Sadler's Wells or Covent Garden, I suppose I have heard Mr. Galway play the solos. (Does he also sing? If so, Tamino's Act I scena might be a stunt worth trying for his next record.) And lately I have been longing to hear a *Magic Flute* in which the title role is played by the right kind of flute. The tone of that instrument, I find, touches the heart more nearly, more keenly than any modern flute can do. *The Magic Flute* was the first opera I heard, and sometimes I feel that ever since then my life has been lived in, with, against its music; that by its precepts I should judge my own failings, failures, and occasional achievements. The feeling has been particularly strong with me this year, during which I made a new translation of the opera, and the sound of it was with me day and night. Great creators—Bach, Mozart, Beethoven; Shakespeare, Goethe, George Eliot—teach one how to live, and modern creators (for me they have been Roger Sessions, Michael Tippett, and Peter Maxwell Davies) reinterpret lessons of the past for our own day. Adam and Eve may be type figures of our human condition, but beside Adam and Eve—as the father in Goethe's *Hermann und Dorothea* observes—we can set Tamino and Pamina. Since music comes to life in performance, I find it sustaining that a true performance of *The Magic Flute*, executed with something like the sounds Mozart expected, remains a bliss to look forward to, and find it encouraging that there are players, singers, and conductors who feel as I do and are likely to bring it about.

August 4, 1980

This piece produced a big correspondence. German scholars were almost equally divided between those who believed that Mozart's sentence could and those who believed it could not be "twisted" to yield the meaning I—tentatively—suggested. Reading das as was would help, and one of my correspondents pointed out that Mozart's d and w are readily confused. I have not yet seen the original letter.

There is another point to make. I often have to remind students that what a man says in a letter is not "hard" evidence. (Many misdatings have resulted from composers' assurances to publishers or creative managers that a work is "all but finished.") Mozart was writing an exculpatory letter to his father, who had chided him for not completing the De Jean commissions. What he may have put forward as a handy "excuse" should not be upheld as his considered lifelong opinion of the flute.

Index

Compositions reviewed are indexed under their composers. Boldface figures indicate extended discussion or, in long entries, distinguish reviews of the work or the performer in question from passing references. Musical organizations outside New York based in a particular city are generally listed under that city (*e.g.,* "Philadelphia: Academy of Vocal Arts").

575

Index

Index

Index

Index

585

Index

Index

Index

Index

Index

Index

Index

Index

A NOTE ON THE TYPE

This book was set via computer-driven cathode ray tube in Caledonia, a face originally designed by W. A. Dwiggins. It belongs to
the family of printing types called "modern face" by printers—a
term used to mark the change in style of type letters that occurred
about 1800. Caledonia borders on the general design of Scotch
Modern but is more freely drawn than that letter.

Composed by American–Stratford Graphic Services, Inc.,
Brattleboro, Vermont.
Printed and bound by R. R. Donnelley & Sons Company,
Harrisonburg, Virginia.

Typography and binding design by Virginia Tan.